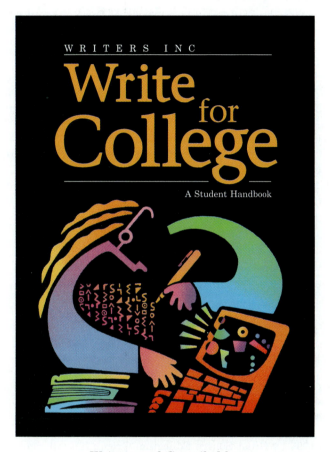

WRITERS INC

Write for College

A Student Handbook

Written and Compiled by
Patrick Sebranek, Verne Meyer, and Dave Kemper

WRITE SOURCE

GREAT SOURCE EDUCATION GROUP
a Houghton Mifflin Company
Wilmington, Massachusetts

Acknowledgements

Write for College is a reality because of the help and advice of a number of people, among them, Laura Apol, Ellen Leitheusser, John Van Rys, Connie Stephens, Ken Taylor, Randy VanderMey, Sandy Wagner, and Dawn Weis. We also want to thank those who reviewed the handbook: Scott Weber, Lexington (MA) High School; Carol Jago, Santa Monica (CA) High School; Bruce Sonner, Corning (NY) Community College; Philip Coleman-Hull, Luther College (IA); John Boe, University of California - Davis; Jennifer Workman, University of Kentucky; Johnny Bennett, Fort Scott (KS) Community College; Deidre Hughes, Fullerton (CA) College; John Mascaro, University of California - Los Angeles; Barbara S. Gross, Rutgers University (NJ). Finally, several of our students allowed us to use their papers as samples in the handbook. We thank them all.

Editorial: Laura Bachman, Diane Barnhart, Lois Krenzke

Illustration: Chris Krenzke

Art/Production: Colleen Belmont, Sherry Gordon

Using the Handbook

Write for College emphasizes the kinds of writing most often asked for in college courses. But the handbook covers much more than writing. It also provides information and guidelines for speaking, thinking, test taking, studying, researching, and nearly every other topic essential to success in college.

In addition, the **Almanac** at the back of the book provides many useful extras like maps, tables, lists—even a copy of the Constitution.

The **Table of Contents** gives you a list of the major sections in the handbook and the chapters found in each.

The **Index** includes every topic discussed in the handbook. The numbers found there are topic numbers, not page numbers. Since there are often many topics on one page, this method of organization will help you find information more quickly.

As you page through the **Body** of your handbook, notice the wide variety of material. Pay special attention to "Mastering the College Essay" (110-127) and the "Forms of Writing" (145-283). Within these two parts, you should find almost everything you need to handle your assigned writing tasks. Continue to search for other helpful material—then use it.

> *"Knowledge is of two kinds. We know a subject ourselves, or we know where we can find information upon it."* —Samuel Johnson

Table of
Contents

THE BASIC ELEMENTS OF WRITING

THE FORMS OF WRITING

THE RESEARCH CENTER

THE TOOLS OF LEARNING

PROOFREADER'S GUIDE

ALMANAC

Why Write?

Writing is important (1) because it helps you make meaning out of your experiences, (2) because it helps you think more clearly, which in turn helps you learn more effectively, and (3) because it helps you form new understandings or make new connections.

All three of these points are important reasons to write, and will, most assuredly, be seconded by your writing instructors. But rather than have us (or your instructors) tell you why writing is so valuable, read what the following distinguished writers have to say about the power of putting pen to paper or fingers to the keyboard. Their thoughts eloquently echo these same three reasons.

Making Meaning Out of Your Experiences

*"Writing is not apart from living.
Writing is a kind of double living."* —Catherine Drinker Bowen

"Writing, like life itself, is a voyage of discovery." —Henry Miller

Thinking More Clearly

*"Writing is not a preplanned recitation
of what you know; writing is thinking."* —Donald Murray

*"Writing and rewriting is a constant search
for what one is trying to say."* —John Updike

Forming New Understandings

*"The two most engaging powers of an author are
to make new things familiar and familiar things new."* —Dr. Samuel Johnson

*"When you write, you lay out a line of words. . . .
You wield it, and it digs a path you follow.
Soon you find yourself deep in new territory."* —Annie Dillard

Experience the Power of Writing

Write for College is designed to help you with your academic writing. The handbook contains guidelines and models for essays, reports, research papers, and so on. Page through the text, and you will begin to appreciate how extensively we cover academic writing.

In addition to your assigned writing tasks, however, we urge you to practice journal writing and writing to learn. To experience the true power of the pen (to help you make meaning, think clearly, etc.), you must write for yourself as well as for your instructors and your peers.

PERSONAL JOURNAL WRITING ● What makes personal journal writing so attractive is the freedom that it offers you. You write when you want, where you want, and about what you want. (Any thought, feeling, or experience can be a starting point.) Naturally, it is most helpful when you journal on a regular basis. Don't worry about how your writing sounds or looks; you are writing for no one except yourself. New insights and meaning will emerge if you make an honest effort; and, in time, journal writing will make you feel a little sharper, as if your senses have been fine-tuned.

"The journal is a record of experience and growth, not a preserve of things well done or said." —H. D. Thoreau

WRITING TO LEARN ● You should also write in a learning log (notebook, journal, etc.) about new concepts covered in your classes. Again, this type of writing is completely under your control. You can react to lectures or readings, describe processes, analyze new concepts, and make thoughtful connections. The linearity of writing—recording one word after another—leads to coherent and sustained thought. It personalizes learning so you understand new ideas more effectively. Writing in this way serves as the ultimate learning tool. (See 494-495 in your handbook for more information.)

"It's good to rub and polish our brain against that of others." —Montaigne

bottom LINE

Your ability to write well is your key to success in college. In most of your classes, you will have to show your mastery and understanding of new concepts in assigned writings. But also remember that writing for yourself—free from the gravitational pull of grades and expectations—is important, too. Not only will it help you deal more thoughtfully with your experiences and your course work, but it will also help you gain confidence in your ability to write in general. (Real improvement in writing comes through regular practice.) Approach all writing, then, as a special opportunity to learn and to grow, and you will soon appreciate its value in the classroom—and beyond.

The Writing Process

One Writer's Process

How does a writer get from the start—"My psych professor gave me this writing assignment"—to the finish—"Hey, I like this piece!"? You may know the answer already: He or she uses the writing process. This important process can help you

- collect and focus your thoughts *(prewriting),*
- generate an initial version of your writing *(drafting),*
- improve upon your writing *(revising),* and
- prepare it for submission *(editing / proofreading).*

You should also know that (1) the writing process is personal—different writers follow different routes; (2) it's reciprocal—you may go from revising back to prewriting, and then to revising again, and (3) it's adaptable to any writing task—from research papers to essay tests.

WHAT'S AHEAD

In this chapter, you will see firsthand how a writer uses the writing process to shape an initial writing idea into an effective personal essay.

- Prewriting and Planning
- Writing the First Draft
- Revising and Refining
- Editing and Proofreading

Prewriting and Planning

Student writer Mark Klompien received the following assignment in his composition class:

> **Write a two- or three-page essay relating a personal experience to a current cultural, social, or political issue.**

As you follow his work on the next four pages, you'll see how he collected and focused his thoughts for writing. During this initial step in the process, he carried out a number of effective prewriting strategies, including clustering and free writing.

Selecting a Subject

Choosing a subject was no problem. Mark decided to write about the time he led a group of high-school students to Valle Verde, Mexico. The people he met, and their living conditions, made him think about many issues, including the current debate about illegal immigration.

Collecting Ideas

As part of his initial thinking on his subject, Mark listed these three questions: *What was at the core of this experience? What should be the specific focus of my writing? What details should be included?* To explore possible answers, Mark began his prewriting with a cluster.

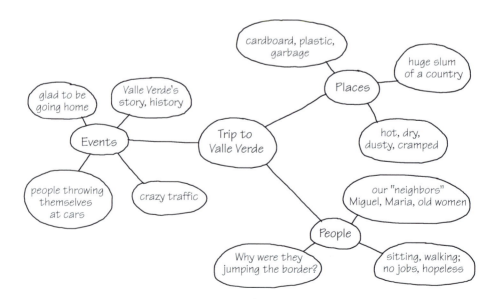

Free-Writing for Ideas

To continue gathering and focusing his thoughts, Mark wrote freely about three dominant ideas in his cluster.

Huge, slumlike country . . .

Everything around seemed hopeless. Mothers were often single as their husbands left for jobs elsewhere because they couldn't support the family. But what about the mothers?

Visions of hot, dusty plains, dust devils, dry wind constantly chopping and beating down whatever is around. Many buildings are empty outside of Tijuana. Most concrete is covered with graffiti. Many men walk around the city when it seems they should be at work. Many kids aren't in school. Remember cars on blocks, half-finished buildings, stacks of bricks saved/salvaged from past buildings, shacks made of tin and plywood, packed together like sardines.

People there are just like you and me. What do they think about the situation? They must be hopeless to be jumping across the river like we see on the news.

Glad to be going home . . .

We jumped back in the station wagon and headed back home. We could just leave and retreat back to our prosperity. I thought about a good dinner and clean water that didn't need to be delivered by the water truck. I wished I could take the friends we met home.

So did anything change? Did this experience make any difference on my return home? Should you become involved in fixing these problems? What's important to do with your life?

How about those young people . . . will they remember this as they deal with their friends and when they decide what clothes to buy and when they vote in the next election and when they choose a major in college? We must work together to remember this trip and encourage each other.

Why are these people jumping the border?

Never mind facts, figures, and rational arguments, remember REAL LIVES! Remember the lady whose husband took off under pressures of the family . . . lost his job and fled because of the debt he's run up.

Remember the guy we met who had fled north because of the violence and civil wars in the South of the country. His brother was shot and he feared for his own life . . . This wasn't the only reason the refugees fled to "Valle Verde" (the green valley??).

The city was established because of a large flood . . . these hopeless folks needed some hope and a place to live.

The immigration issue is often about facts and figures and how much it costs Americans. We always look at immigrants as objects that cost us money but don't give us any benefits. But what about the real issue. Miguel and Maria living hopelessly in Mexico. They seem to be trapped—lost brother, lost husband. You see it in their homes, their faces, and especially their EYES.

Carrying Out Additional Research

Mark knew that he had to connect his personal experience with an important issue currently in the news. His issue—illegal immigration—was hotly debated in his home state of California. But he needed to know more about the immigration problem, so he headed to the library to consult current periodicals addressing this issue. (His notes from two magazine articles are listed below.)

Farley, Christopher J. "Dangerous Tides." Time 145 (April 10, 1995) 56-57.
- article explores new route for illegals trying to get to U.S. since crackdown on Mexico—shows people desperate to get in
- route: people from all over world → Dominican Republic > small boats to Puerto Rico > plane to U.S.
- perilous and expensive journey: $4,000-$35,000, corruption and scams, physical danger of journey—in search of work, a decent life
  - woman assaulted but still determined to complete her "three-month quest to reach America" (57)
  - 10-20% of boats capsize

Leland, John, and John McCormick. "The Quiet Race War." Newsweek 127 (April 8, 1996) 38.
- Moreno Valley, California: citizen complaints, e.g., Theresa Canady's concern for her daughter (with mild learning disability): "She's supposed to get one-on-one help. But she's in a class with too many kids because of illegal immigrants."
- complexity of opinions on imm. issue—people strongly support immigration, but angry about illegal immigration
- Dave Briggs: "Washington makes the rules, and we have to pay for illegals' education, health care, and welfare."

Establishing a Focus

Mark next considered a focus for his writing. After reviewing all of his prewriting and collecting notes, he decided to concentrate on the living conditions of the people he met in Mexico rather than on the facts or politics concerning illegal immigration. He then wrote this working thesis statement to serve as a general guide for his planning and drafting:

WORKING THESIS STATEMENT: **People are immigrating illegally into our country for a reason, but what exactly is this reason?**

NOTE: A thesis statement usually contains two main elements: a manageable or limited subject (*illegal immigration*) plus a specific feeling or idea about it (*what is the reason for it*).

Designing a Writing Plan

Mark's thesis statement establishes a general question-and-answer pattern for his writing. (His thesis asks a question, which he will attempt to answer in the main part of his writing.) At this point, Mark was ready to sketch out a basic writing plan. He decided to share significant aspects of his trip before making a connection to the reality of illegal immigration.

Basic Plan
- Entry into Mexico
- Description of Tijuana
- Description of Valle Verde
- People in Valle Verde
- Reality of Immigration Problem

Getting Ready to Write

Mark read through his free writing one last time for ideas to help him get started on his first draft. As you can see below, he noted important points or feelings to include in his writing:

→ Remember Maria!

Everything around seemed hopeless. Mothers were often single as their husbands left for jobs elsewhere because they couldn't support the family. But what about the mothers? broken windows

Visions of hot, dusty plains, dust devils, dry wind constantly chopping and beating down whatever is around. Many buildings are empty outside of Tijuana. Most concrete is covered with grafitti. Many men walk around the city when it seems they should be at work. Many kids aren't in school. Remember cars on blocks, half-finished buildings, stacks of bricks saved/salvaged from past buildings, shacks made of tin and plywood, packed together like sardines. ← How old was Miguel—16? 17?

People there are just like you and me. What do they think about the situation? They must be hopeless to be jumping across the river like we see on the news.

Writing the First Draft

In his first draft, Mark pulls together ideas, images, and questions that address his thesis. He completed this draft in one sitting, using his basic plan as a general guide for his writing. He also referred to his collecting ideas and notes as needed during his drafting.

The writer identifies the thesis of his writing.

Though the illegal immigration problem is often about facts and figures, the issue is much bigger. People are immigrating illegally into our country for a reason, but what exactly is this reason?

Last year I took our youth group down to Mexico on a service trip. We didn't know what to expect. What would the city look like and how would we be accepted?

As we drove we saw hopelessness. Old buildings with broken windows towered on either side of the car. Graffiti covered the walls.

He uses details from his free writing to help readers visualize the setting and the people.

The dusty road that stretches to the suburban city is lined with cars on blocks. Men who should be at work stare down at the car. Children aren't in schools.

On daily trips around the city I meet a few of the inhabitants of the city. Maria was a single mother who, speaking in broken English, told about her husband. While a child was hanging in a diaper from her side, she told us that her husband had left under the pressures of fatherhood. After losing his job, the household bills kept rising so he left.

The writer focuses on developing ideas rather than on producing correct copy.

Miguel scowled at us from his seat—a 5-gallon bucket. He recalled the story of his brother's murder in the civil wars of the South and how he fled from his own life to "Valle Verde."

I'm still haunted by Miguel's and maria's eyes. Nobody's eyes should have that look in it.

Why did they (and so many others) come here? The city was built as a refugee camp by citizens washed out of Tijuana by a flood. With the rains, the hope the city had for its future was washed away as well.

A small town started on a dry dusty plain outside of Tijuana. The people took cardboard, plastic, tin, and plywood to build homes close together like sardines. When the wind blows through them, they make a depressing moan. Though they squatted on land owned by the government there was little the government could do but let them stay.

In closing, he makes a connection with the issue of immigration.

Mostly the front yards are bare except for ornamental plastic wrappers. Latrines are dug into the tough dirt by the women. Every household has at least one bone-skinny dog guarding the homes filled with nothing.

Whatever one thinks about the immigration situation, this place and these people can't be forgotten. Can we neglect real people and their situations when we deal with the immigration problem?

Revising and Refining

Mark took a break before he reviewed his first draft. When he was ready to review his work, he made a printed copy of his draft and looked carefully at the developing ideas. He wrote brief notes in the margin, indicating parts that needed to be reworked, expanded, or cut. In the copy below, you can see some of the changes he made.

First Revision

Mark's Comments:

Focus more on the trip.

Two years ago I led a group of excited young people on a ~~Though the illegal immigration problem is often about~~ service project to Valle Verde, Mexico. The city was only 15 ~~facts and figures, the issue is much bigger. People are~~ miles over the border, so we weren't too apprehensive. How ~~immigrating illegallly into our country for a reason, but what~~ much different could it be? What insights would it give us ~~exactly is this reason?~~ into the immigration problem? We soon found out.

~~Last year I took our youth group down to Mexico on a~~

Tell about guards and street vendors.

~~service trip. We didn't know what to expect. What would the~~

~~city look like and how would we be accepted?~~

After a couple of perfunctory checks, the border ~~As we drove we saw hopelessness. Old buildings with~~ guard . . . ~~broken windows towered on either side of the car. Graffiti~~

~~covered the walls.~~

The dusty road that stretches to the suburban city is lined with cars on blocks. Men who should be at work stare down at the car. Children aren't in schools.

On daily trips around the city I meet a few of the

Tell about Maria and Miguel— remember how he cried!

inhabitants of the city. Maria was a single mother who, speaking in broken English, told about her husband. While a child was hanging in a diaper from her side, she told us that her husband had left under the pressures of fatherhood. After losing his job, **and house,** the household bills kept rising so he left.

One of the boys, ∧ Miguel scowled at us from his seat—a 5-gallon bucket. He recalled the story of his brother's murder in the civil wars of the South and how he fled from his own life to "Valle Verde."

He clenched a fist to hold back tears . . .

∧I'm still haunted by Miguel's and maria's eyes. Nobody's

eyes should have that look in it.

Why did they (and so many others) come here? The city

was built as a refugee camp by citizens washed out of Tijuana

by a flood. With the rains, the hope the city had for its future

was washed away as well.

Use this idea
earlier and
add details
about cars,
junk, and
"green valley."

A small town started on a dry dusty plain outside of

Tijuana. The people took cardboard, plastic, tin, and plywood

to build homes ~~close~~ together ~~like sardines~~. When the wind

blows through them, they make a depressing moan. Though

they squatted on land owned by the government there was

Rewrite

little the government could do but let them stay.

Mostly the front yards are bare except for ornamental

plastic wrappers. Latrines are dug into the tough dirt by the

women. Every household has at least one bone-skinny dog

guarding the homes filled with nothing.

Change
conclusion.

~~Whatever one thinks about the immigration situation, this~~

~~place and these people can't be forgotten. Can we neglect real~~

~~people and their situations when we deal with the immigration~~

~~problem?~~

Today, as I remember the looks in Miguel's and Maria's

eyes, it's hard for me to listen to American complaints.

Can we hate immigrants because they want decent

lives . . .?

Second Revision

After revising his first draft, Mark asked a writing peer to review his work. Her comments are in the margin. Mark noted her concerns, and made additional changes in his essay. (In the copy below, you can see some of the additional changes Mark made.)

NOTE: Even though the original thesis is no longer stated in one sentence, the focus of Mark's essay is still clear.

Reviewer's Comments:

The Immigration Problem

Connect your experience to a news item.

During the past few years, TV and other media have ~~Two years ago I led a group of excited young people on a~~ carried two kinds of stories about Mexicans entering the ~~service project to Valle Verde, Mexico. The city was only 15~~ U.S.— Mexicans sneaking in and Americans mad about it. ~~miles over the border, so we weren't too apprehensive. How~~ But what's the cause? Two years ago I led 11 high school ~~much different could it be? What insights would it give us into~~ students on a . . . ~~the immigration problem?~~

~~We soon found out.~~
These students, another adult, and I drove . . .
~~After a couple of perfunctory checks, the border guard~~

Strong—I can see these people!

~~sent us through.~~ But less than 50 feet from the check point, a bunch of street vendors began throwing themselves at our cars. I couldn't figure out what was wrong with them, young boys and old men, risking getting hurt for the few American cents they made selling fake roses, gum, and candy bars.

With each mile, an unending slum unfolded beside us. Steel bars guarded window panes, and graffiti covered every wall. Buildings looked outdated and lifeless except for taverns

"Green Valley" sounds like a sick joke.

marked by glaring neon beer signs.　　— *Develop irony?*

Valle Verde, the "Green Valley," is located outside of Tijuana on a dusty, sun-beaten plain. It started about five years ago, after a freak storm swept away most of Tijuana. Along with kitchen tables and family pictures, the water flooded any hope

History is interesting, but is it important?

that the struggling town had for the future.　　*Cut paragraph?*

One evening under cover of darkness, hundreds of disillusioned refugees came to the government-owned plain that became Valle Verde. After marking out their territories with ropes and chicken wire, they utilized cardboard, tin, and plywood to put homes together. Ripped up carpets had to do for doors; windows were made of plastic. By morning, there was a city stretching as far as the eye could see and the government could do little but let them stay.

Sounds desolate—painful.

Along the dusty road through Valle Verde a long lines of cars sit on blocks. Bone-skinny dogs and dozens of chickens guard front-yard latrines that wives burrow out of the dry-packed dirt. Rusting soup cans and plastic tortilla wrappers ~~ornament~~ *litter* yards. Vaporizing breezes swirl in and around rickety dwellings, playing them ~~ike~~ *like* wind chimes.

Strong simile!

Refugees fill Valle Verde. Nobody wants to be there. Even though flood victims constitute the majority of the population, political and economic refugees have become an increasing percentage.

Your details help me see Miguel and Maria. Are they the focus? Why?

One of them, Miguel, sat on a five gallon bucket ~~stoicly~~ *and asked* ~~searching the horizon. Sensing that I was an American, he talked to me~~ about my home in broken English. When ~~I felt that the right moment had come,~~ I asked him about himself/\. Miguel's head sank and he ~~clinched a first~~ *clenched a fist* to hold back tears, apparently he'd fled from the civil-war stricken south after his only brother was killed by a stray bullet.

Another English-speaking refugee was Maria. With a . . .

How does the conclusion connect with what you say in the opening?

~~Today, as I remember the looks in Miguel's and Maria's~~ *But what about the other question? What causes average people to get angry when discussing immigration?* ~~eyes, I wonder how we can hate immigrants because they want decent lives?~~ Do we send illegals back because we are unwilling to let them share in our prosperity? Don't we have room for Miguel and Maria? Immigration raises many difficult questions, but hopefully before we seek answers to them, we look beyond our own interests.

Editing and Proofreading

After one more revision, Mark edited his writing for style and accuracy. He read each sentence aloud to help check for clarity and smoothness. He used the computer spell checker, his dictionary, and his writing handbook to help check for errors. Mark also asked one of his peers to edit his text. After making the necessary corrections (see below), he printed out a final copy of the essay. Before submitting his text, he carefully proofread it for errors.

In the Heart of Green Valley

During the past few years, TV news and other media have commonly carried two types of stories about Mexicans entering the U.S. illegally. In the first type, news cameras catch illegals sneaking cross the Mexican-U.S. border. In the second type, reporters show Americans angry about ~~illegal's~~ *illegals'* access to jobs, education, and health care. These typical stories bring two critical questions to mind: What causes illegal immigration? And what causes people to get so angry? *about it* An extended visit to Mexico helped me better understand, and answer, both questions.

Words are added for clarity.

Two years ago, I led eleven high-school students on a ten day service project in Mexico. These students, another adult, and I drove a van and station wagon ~~toward~~ *to* a mission in Valle Verde where we planned to help residents improve their housing and promote the work of the mission. As we approached the border, three armed guards stopped us and asked where we were going and how long we would stay. *We expected the questions* ~~which we expected to be asked~~, but didn't expect what happened next. ~~Less~~ *Fewer* than 50 feet from the checkpoint, dozens of street vendors mobbed our accelerating vehicles—risking broken limbs for a few U.S. dollars.

A long, clumsy sentence is separated and revised to read smoothly.

From there, we followed a riddled road through the grim sites of Tijuana, beyond its outskirts and into Valle Verde, a

town whose name means "Green Valley." In this valley, junk
cars sat on blocks beside shacks. Bone-skinny dogs and spindly
chickens guarded front-yard latrines. Rusting soup cans and
plastic tortilla wrappers littered yards. Gusty breezes swirled
in and around rickety buildings, playing them like wind
chimes.

People fill Valle Verde, but ~~didn't~~ *none of them* want to be there. One
individual, Miguel, sitting on a five-gallon bucket, asked me
about my home. After telling him what I could, I returned the
question. Miguel's head sank, and he clenched a fist to hold
back tears. He had fled from the civil-war-stricken ~~south~~ *South* after
his only brother was shot.

Another English-speaking refugee ~~was Maria~~ *named Maria offered her story.* With a dirty
~~kid in a diaper~~ *infant* hanging ~~from~~ *on* her hip, and three more running
around, she told me about the time she lived in a three-
bedroom house with a once-faithful husband who brought
home a check every week. But later, he lost his job, ~~couldn't~~
~~find another one,~~ ran up the bills, and then just left. Now
Maria and the kids barely ~~surivived~~ *survive in a* makeshift shack.

The answer to the first question—what causes the flood of
illegal immigrants?—seems obvious: thousands of people like
Miguel and Maria have lost hope where they live. They see no
future in their country.

But what about the other question? What causes average
~~people~~ *Americans* to respond so angrily to *illegal* immigration: "Illegals are
breaking the law!" "~~Their~~ *"They're* taking our jobs!" "They're raising
our taxes!" "If they want to live here, *fine, but* let them apply legally,
and walk in the front door rather than sneak in the back!"

Is it possible that the answer to the second question is
that those who speak with anger haven't crossed the border
themselves? Would their anger turn into compassion if they
met the Marias and Miguels and heard their stories?

The active verb (offered) strengthens the idea.

The present tense lends immediacy to the style of the piece.

The Writing Process

QUICK GUIDE

Think of the writing process as an approach to writing based on the following premise: an effective paper is almost always the result of a great deal of planning, writing, and rewriting (as demonstrated in Mark's essay). For the sake of discussion and analysis, the writing process is divided into the five steps listed below. (Remember, however, that writers seldom follow a straight path from one step to the next.)

PREWRITING

1. **Find a worthwhile idea to write about**.
2. **Learn as much as you can about the subject.** (See 021.)
3. **Form a thesis and plan your writing.**

WRITING THE FIRST DRAFT

1. **Write the first draft while your prewriting is fresh in your mind.**
2. **Write as freely as you can, using your planning as a guide.**
3. **Keep writing until you come to a natural stopping point.**

REVISING

1. **Review your first draft, keeping in mind the purpose of the assignment, your thesis, and your audience.**
2. **Also have your instructor or a writing peer review your work**.
3. **Add, cut, rework, or rearrange ideas as necessary.**

EDITING AND PROOFREADING

1. **Read your final draft aloud to test it for sense and sound.**
2. **Check for errors in usage, punctuation, capitalization, spelling, and grammar.** (Have a peer editor check your work as well.)
3. **Prepare a neat final copy of your writing**.
4. **Then proofread the final draft for errors before submitting it.**

PUBLISHING

1. **Submit your work in class or for publication.**
2. **Collect your best writing in a portfolio.**

A Guide to Prewriting

Writer Joyce Carol Oates made the following observation in reference to the writing process: ". . . as soon as you connect with your true subject you will write." Her comment refers to fiction writing, but it really holds true for all writing, including your academic essays. Writing, in the early stages, is the process of "connecting with your true subject."

How you make this connection depends on the writing task. If you are developing a personal reminiscence, it may be quite easy to identify your true subject since you're drawing ideas from your own experience. On the other hand, if you are writing a research paper or an essay of argumentation, it may take a great deal of careful prewriting (researching, reflecting, etc.) to connect with a worthy writing idea.

WHAT'S AHEAD

Prewriting refers to various strategies that help you select and shape a subject for writing. This chapter explains a number of these strategies. Experiment with them to determine which ones can best help you plan your papers.

- Selecting a Subject
- Free-Writing Guidelines
- Shaping a Subject
- Taking Inventory
- Focusing Your Efforts

Selecting a Subject

The following strategies will help you find a worthy subject for your writing, or an interesting angle for a subject already assigned to you. Read through the entire list before you choose a strategy to begin your search.

1 **Journal Writing**

Write in a journal on a regular basis. Explore your personal feelings, develop your innermost thoughts, and record the happenings of each day. Periodically go back and underline ideas that you would like to explore in writing assignments.

2 **Free Writing**

Write nonstop for 10 minutes or more to discover possible writing ideas or angles. Begin writing with or without a particular focus in mind; either way, you'll soon be discovering and exploring ideas that might otherwise never have entered your mind. (See 020 for more.)

3 **Clustering**

Begin a cluster with a nucleus word or phrase (like *weight lifting*) that is related to your writing topic or assignment. Then record or cluster ideas around it. Circle each idea as you write it, and draw a line connecting it to the closest related idea.

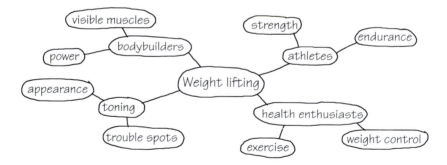

NOTE: After a few minutes of clustering, scan your cluster for a word or an idea to explore in a free writing. A specific subject may begin to emerge during this writing.

4 **Listing**

Freely list ideas as they come to mind. Begin with a concept or a key word related to your assignment and simply start listing additional words or ideas. (Brainstorming, listing ideas with members of a group, is an effective way to search for writing subjects.)

5

Creating a Dialogue

Create a dialogue between yourself and an intended reader of your piece. The topic of this conversation should be related to your writing assignment. Continue the conversation as long as you can, or until a possible writing idea begins to unfold.

6

Reflecting, Participating, Listening

Think about possible writing ideas as you read, as you ride or drive to school, as you take a break in the Union, and so on. Watch for unusual events, persons, objects, or conversations. Participate in group activities related to your writing assignment. Interview some-one who is knowledgeable or experienced about a writing idea. Also talk with friends and family members about possible subjects.

7

Using the "Essentials of Life Checklist"

Below you will find a checklist of the major categories into which most essential things in our lives are divided. The checklist provides an endless variety of subject possibilities. Consider the fifth category, education. It could lead to the following writing ideas:

● on-line education
● funding higher education (student loans)
● a new approach in education
● an influential educator

ESSENTIALS OF LIFE CHECKLIST

clothing	communication	exercise	health/medicine
housing	purpose/goals	community	entertainment
food	measurement	arts/music	literature/books
exercise	machines	faith/religion	recreation/hobby
education	intelligence	trade/money	personality/identity
family	agriculture	heat/fuel	natural resources
friends	environment	rules/laws	tools/utensils
love	science	freedom/rights	plants/vegetation
senses	energy	land/property	work/occupation

bottom LINE

Before beginning any prewriting strategy, be sure you thoroughly under-stand the assignment you've been given. Some assignments allow a lot of freedom in topic and approach; others are more directed and specific. A good writer takes these differences into account and uses prewriting strategies accordingly.

Free-Writing Guidelines

Free writing is the writing you do without having a specific outcome in mind. You simply write down whatever comes to mind as you explore your topic. Free writing can be used as a starting point for your writing, or it can be used in combination with any of the other prewriting strategies to help you select, explore, focus, or organize your writing. If you get stuck at any point during the composing process, you can return to free writing as a way of generating new ideas.

REMINDERS

- **Free writing helps you get your thoughts down on paper.** (Thoughts are constantly passing through your mind.)
- **Free writing helps you develop and organize these thoughts.**
- **Free writing helps you make sense out of things you may be studying or researching.**
- **Free writing may seem awkward at times, but just stick with it.**

THE PROCESS

- **Write nonstop and record whatever comes into your mind.** Follow your thoughts instead of trying to direct them.
- **If you have a particular topic or assignment in mind, use it as a starting point.** Otherwise, begin with anything that comes to mind.
- **Don't stop to judge, edit, or correct your writing;** that will come later.
- **Keep writing even when you think you have exhausted all of your ideas.** Switch to another mode of thought (sensory, memory, reflective) if necessary, but keep writing.
- **Watch for a promising writing idea to emerge.** Learn to recognize the beginnings of a good idea, and then expand that idea by recording as many specific details as possible.

INSIDE info

Always have a notebook or journal on hand, and write freely in it whenever you have an interesting idea to explore, an important point to remember, or a few random thoughts to reflect upon. Over time, these free writings will help you become a better writer.

THE RESULT

- **Review your writings and underline the ideas you like.** These ideas will often serve as the basis for more formal writings.
- **Determine exactly what you plan (or are required) to write about;** add specific details as necessary. (This may require a second free writing.)
- **Listen to and read the free writings of others;** learn from your peers.

Shaping a Subject

The following strategies will help you develop your subjects for writing. If you already have a good "feel" for a particular writing idea, you may attempt only one of these. If you need to explore your idea in some detail, and time permits, you may attempt two or more of the strategies.

Free Writing ● At this point, you can approach free writing in two different ways. You can do a focused free writing to see how many ideas come to mind about your subject as you write, or you can approach your free writing as if it were an instant version of the finished product. An instant version will give you a good feel for your subject and will also tell you how much you know or need to find out about it.

Clustering ● Try clustering again, this time with your subject as the nucleus word. This clustering will naturally be more focused or structured than your earlier prewriting cluster since you now have a specific subject in mind. (See 018 for a model cluster.)

5 W's of Writing ● Answer the 5 W's—Who? What? Where? When? Why? (and How?)—to identify basic information about your subject.

Directed Writing ● Do a variation of free writing by selecting one of the six thinking modes below and writing whatever comes to mind. (Repeat the process as often as you need to, selecting a different mode each time.)

> **Describe it.** What do you see, hear, feel, smell, taste . . . ?
>
> **Compare it.** What is it like? What is it different from?
>
> **Associate it.** What connections between this and something else come to mind?
>
> **Analyze it.** What parts does it have? How do they work (or not work) together?
>
> **Apply it.** What can you do with it? How can you use it?
>
> **Argue for or against it.** What do you like about it? Not like about it? What are its good points? Its bad points?

Creating a Dialogue ● Create a dialogue between two people (one of whom may be you) in which your specific subject is the focus of the conversation. The two speakers should build on each other's comments, reinforce them, or give them a new spin.

Researching and Reflecting ● For almost all of your academic writing, you will need to research your subject. (See 444-461 for different sources of information.) Reserve a special part of a notebook to question, evaluate, and reflect upon your research as it develops. A record of your thoughts and actions during this process will often mean as much or more to you than the actual information you uncover. It helps you make sense of new ideas, refocus your thinking, and evaluate your progress.

Asking Questions

To gain a thorough understanding of a writing idea, it helps to ask questions about it. The basic questions to ask are the 5 W's and H: *Who? What? When?* and so on. The chart below provides a far more comprehensive set of questions to use. These questions are based on the type of analysis practiced by ancient scholars. The chart addresses problems, policies, and concepts, but it can be used for other types of subjects as well.

	Description	Function	History	Value
P R O B L E M S	What is the problem? What type of problem is it? What are its parts? What are the signs of the problem?	Who or what is affected by it? What new problems may it cause in the future?	What is the current status of the problem? What or who caused it? What or who contributed to it?	What is its significance? Why? Why is it more (or less) important than other problems? What does it symbolize or illustrate?
P O L I C I E S	What is the policy? How broad is it? What are its parts? What are its most important features?	What is the policy designed to do? What is needed to make it work? What will be its effects?	What brought this policy about? What are the alternatives to this policy?	Is the policy workable? What are its advantages and disadvantages? Is it practical? Is it a good policy? Why or why not?
C O N C E P T S	What is the concept? What are its parts? What is its main feature? Who or what is it related to?	Who has been influenced by this concept? Why is it important? How does it work?	When did it originate? How has it changed over the years? How may it change in the future?	What practical value does it have? Why is it superior (or inferior) to similar concepts? What is its social worth?

Taking Inventory

Let's say you still don't feel comfortable with your subject. That is, you've done some searching, and you've discovered some interesting things about your writing idea, but you still don't feel ready to write a first draft. Now may be a good time to see how well *you* match up with your subject. After considering the following questions, you should be able to decide whether to move ahead with your writing or reexamine your subject. (See 050 for a discussion of these questions related to writing and style.)

WRITING TASK:

- What are the specific requirements of this assignment?
- Do I have enough time to do a good job with this subject?
- Am I writing to inform, to analyze, to persuade, or to entertain?

SUBJECT:

- How much do I already know about this subject?
- Is additional information available?
- Have I tried any of the shaping activities? (See 021-022.)

READERS:

- How much do my readers care or already know about this subject?
- How can I get my audience interested in my ideas?

SELF:

- How committed am I to my writing subject?
- What can I learn or gain by continuing to write on this topic?

LANGUAGE AND FORM:

- How will I present my ideas: reminiscence, essay?
- Can I think of an interesting way to lead into my paper?

Continuing the Process

Research ● If you feel that you need to know more about your subject, continue collecting your own thoughts and/or investigating other sources of information. Remember that it is important (or at least helpful) to investigate a few secondary sources of information. Reading helps stimulate or clarify your thinking about a writing idea.

Review ● If you feel ready to move ahead, consider reviewing your initial prewriting notes and collecting. As you read through this material, circle or underline ideas that seem important enough to include in your writing. Then look for ways in which these ideas connect or relate. This activity will help you focus your thoughts for writing. (See the next page.)

Focusing Your Efforts

All types of writing—research papers, lab reports, essay exams, business letters, etc.—have a central thought holding them together. Your early prewriting will probably produce an abundance of information and ideas. Then, as you continue exploring and gathering, you should develop a more focused interest in your subject. If all goes well, this emerging interest will eventually become the thesis, or focus, of your writing.

Forming a Thesis Statement

The central thought, or thesis, in a piece of writing usually takes a stand, expresses a feeling, or highlights a feature of a subject. Sometimes a thesis statement develops early and easily; sometimes it takes several stages of prewriting. At other times, the true center of your writing emerges only after you finish your first draft.

Try to state your thesis in a sentence that expresses what you believe and want to explore. Use the following formula:

A manageable or limited subject (multicultural education)

+ **a specific stand, feeling, or feature**
(is vital to a society made up of many different peoples)

= **an effective thesis statement.**

THESIS STATEMENT: **Multicultural education is vital to a society made up of many different peoples.**

NOTE: The stronger your thesis statement, the easier it is to bring the rest of your paper into focus. (See 113 for more examples.)

Designing a Writing Plan

With a clear focus in mind, you may be ready to start your first draft. If, however, your subject is quite complex, you will need to design a writing plan before you start to write. Your plan can be anything from a brief list of ideas to a detailed sentence outline. The following guidelines may help:

1. Study your thesis statement. It may suggest a logical method of organization for your writing.

2. Review the facts and details that support your thesis. See if an overall pattern of organization begins to emerge.

3. Consider the patterns of organization listed in the handbook. (See 114.)

4. Organize your ideas into a list, a cluster, or an outline. Feel free to insert, delete, or draw arrows as you work with your plan.

5. If nothing seems to work, consider gathering more information, or simply writing your first draft to see what unfolds.

A Guide to Drafting

After the rehearsals, there's a performance. After the drills, there's the first match. After the conditioning, the race begins. And after the prewriting, there's the first draft. If you've done a careful job of prewriting, your first draft should go well. You should have more than enough raw material to shape and expand into an effective piece of writing.

It's important to remember that a first draft is a first look at a developing writing idea. For now, you'll want to concentrate on getting all of your ideas on paper. Use your writing plan (if you have one) as a basic guide for drafting, but also be open to new ideas or directions as they emerge in the heat of composing. (Remember that you may have to write more than one draft before your writing really begins to take form.)

WHAT'S AHEAD

This chapter offers guidelines and suggestions that will help you develop your initial draft (or drafts). You will find important information related to getting started, continuing, and completing your initial writing. Also included is information related to diction and the pitch or "speed" of your writing.

- Developing Your Text
- Bringing Your Writing to a Close
- Staying in Pitch

Developing Your Text

The information below addresses three important questions: What is the best way to begin a first draft? What types of information should you include in the opening paragraph? How should you develop or advance your thesis in the body of your essay?

Writing the Opening

Some writers pay special attention to the opening, its wording and general impact, before they concern themselves with developing a complete draft. Once their opening is set (at least tentatively), they are ready to tackle the larger task at hand. Remember that an opening paragraph should (1) introduce the general subject and spark the reader's interest, (2) establish a tone, direction, and level of language for your writing, and (3) identify or suggest your thesis. (Listed below are several possible starting points.)

- **Open with a fitting quotation.**
- **Challenge your readers with a thought-provoking question.**
- **Offer a little "sip" of what is to follow.**
- **Provide important background information.**
- **Begin with a dramatic anecdote or scenario.**

NOTE: You may decide to work out the exact wording of your opening later, after you have roughed out a draft or two. That's fine. Many writers work in that way. (See 118 for sample openings.)

"The writer writes with information, and if there is no information, there will be no effective writing." —Donald Murray

Advancing Your Thesis

When you write a first draft, you're really testing your initial thinking on your subject. You're determining whether or not your thesis is valid, and whether or not you have enough compelling information to develop it. At the core of a text are the main points and supporting details that advance your thesis. Generally speaking, you should develop each main point in a separate paragraph or two.

Remember that specific details add substance and depth to your writing and make it worth reading. Writing that lacks effective detail only gives a partial picture—a vague image—of a writing idea. Types of details that you can use include facts, examples, anecdotes, definitions, analysis, and so on.

 INSIDE info
In some cases, supporting a main point with examples, facts, or definitions may not be enough. You may also need to add analysis or commentary to complete the picture. (See 119 for examples.)

Bringing Your Writing to a Close

Sometimes your writing will come to an effective stopping point after the last main point is made. Whenever that is the case, don't tack on a closing paragraph. Leave well enough alone. If, however, you need to add a closing, and you're not sure what to say, check below for help. (Also included on this page is information about the appropriate levels of diction for academic essays.)

If Endings Could Talk

Closing paragraphs are important when you feel it is necessary to tie up any loose ends or clarify certain points in your essay. But successful closings say much more than "In summary . . . ." They help readers appreciate the importance of the essay or, perhaps, help readers relate the writing to their own experience. Here's the closing paragraph in an essay about the eccentric billionaire Howard Hughes.

> **Though he died more than 15 years ago, the legend of Howard Hughes lives on. He represented the American Dream turned on itself, a victim of the multibillion-dollar empire that he almost single-handedly created. We will always be fascinated by celebrities, heroes, the wealthy, and the sick. Howard Hughes was all of these. And more.**

This closing puts the story of Howard Hughes in perspective by saying, in effect, "Weird, isn't it?" It tells us that our interest in celebrities is natural—they'll always get under our skin. (See 120 for more examples.)

USING THE APPROPRIATE LEVEL OF DICTION

Most academic writing (especially research papers, literary analyses, and most analytical and argumentative essays) should meet the standards of **formal English**. This level of language is characterized by a serious tone, a careful attention to word choice, longer sentences, a strict adherence to traditional conventions, and so on.

> **Formal English, such as you are reading in this sentence, is worded correctly and cautiously so that it can withstand repeated readings without seeming tiresome, sloppy, or cute.**

You may write other papers (especially reminiscences, personal essays, commentaries, and reviews) in which informal English is appropriate. **Informal English** is characterized by a personal tone, the occasional use of popular expressions, shorter sentences, the use of contractions and personal references *(I, he, you)*, an adherence to basic conventions, and so on.

> **Informal English sounds like one person talking to another person (in a somewhat relaxed setting). It's the type of language you are reading now. It sounds comfortable and real, not too jazzy or breezy.**

Staying in Pitch

Writer James K. Kilpatrick says that writers need to "stay in pitch" when they develop a particular piece. To illustrate what he means, let's suppose you are writing an editorial to voice your opinion against a new housing policy. Your first few sentences suggest that you are extremely upset by this decision. To stay in pitch, you would maintain that same level of intensity throughout your writing. The whole idea of staying in pitch is directly related to your style of writing, to the words and sentences you use.

Writing Fast

When you want to be assertive and direct (as in an editorial), you should write "fast." That is, you should write strong declarative sentences that move readers along at a steady clip: no hemming or hawing; no interesting little asides or digressions; no long, airy thoughts. Just hit hard, one point after another.

Here is an example of writing that hits hard and fast. The writer, Linda Chavez, makes it sound as if multiculturalism is ready for an attack.

> **Multiculturalism is on the advance. . . . If you believe the multiculturalists' propaganda, whites are on the verge of becoming a minority in the United States. The multiculturalists predict that this demographic shift will fundamentally change American culture—indeed destroy the very idea that America has a single, unified culture. They aren't taking any chances, however. . . .**

Slowing Down

When you want to be more reflective and thoughtful, you should "slow" things down. Express yourself with sentences that are more loosely constructed, and with words that are soft in tone and slow in pace (*propose* rather than *assert; collect* rather than *take*).

Here is an example of writing that slowly wends its way from one point to the next. The writer, Annie Dillard, is reminiscing about the study where she once wrote.

> **I walk up here from the house every morning. The study and its pines, and the old summer cottages nearby, and the new farm just north of me, rise from an old sand dune high over a creeky salt marsh. From the bright lip of the dune I can see oyster farmers working their beds on the tide flats and sailboats under way in the saltwater bay. . . .**

INSIDE info

Write fast for certain persuasive pieces, especially when the writing stems from strongly felt beliefs. And slow things down for more reflective pieces—reminiscences, analytical essays, and so on. Always try to maintain the appropriate pitch, or tone, in each piece you develop.

A Guide to Revising

Writer Kurt Vonnegut once told a class of writing students that there are two categories of writers: swoopers and bashers. Swoopers write 17 drafts at high speed and finally say, "I quit. Here, publish this." Bashers, on the other hand, won't move on to the next sentence until they have chiseled and polished the one before it.

Fortunately, there is a third type, halfway between swoopers and bashers. Writers in this group let their thoughts flow freely in the early drafts and then have enough courage and discipline to revise later on.

Courage? Yes, revision takes courage. It's easy to edit and proofread your writing and then turn it in. It's not so easy to improve the content of your writing—the thoughts, feelings, and details that carry your message—before submitting it. **Revising** is the important process of making changes in your writing until it says exactly what you want it to say.

WHAT'S AHEAD

This chapter will introduce you to some valuable revising guidelines and strategies. It also presents examples of "classic" revising problems as well as guidelines for conducting peer reviewing sessions.

- Using Basic Revising Guidelines
- A Revising Strategy That Works
- "Classic" Revising Problems
- Peer Reviewing

Using Basic Revising Guidelines

No writer gets it right the first time. Few writers get it right the second time. In fact, professional writers often have to write a number of revisions before they are satisfied with their work. Don't be surprised if you have to do the same. The guidelines that follow will help you work your first draft into shape.

- **First look at the big picture.** Take it all in. Decide if there is a thesis (or focus) either stated or suggested in your writing. If you can't find the thesis, write one. Or, if your original thinking on your subject has changed, write a new thesis statement.

- **Then look at specific chunks of information.** Examine your organization and reorder your ideas if you feel they could be arranged more effectively. (See 114.)

- **Also cut information** that doesn't support your focus; **add information** if you feel additional points need to be made. Make sure that each part of your writing supports the main idea you're trying to get across; **rewrite parts** that aren't as clear as you would like them to be.

- **Review your opening and closing paragraphs** to make sure they introduce and wrap up the thesis effectively.

- **Finally, refine your writing** so the ideas flow smoothly and hold the readers' interest.

 INSIDE info The paragraph is the basic unit of information in almost all academic writing. Each of your paragraphs should develop an important point related to your subject. In addition, each paragraph should serve as an effective link to the information that comes before it and after it.

Revising on the Run

Writer Peter Elbow recommends "cut-and-paste revising" when you have very little time to make changes in your writing. For example, let's say you are working on an in-class writing assignment, and you have only a short time to revise your writing. The five steps that follow describe this quick revising technique:

1. Don't add any new information to your writing.

2. Remove unnecessary facts and details.

3. Find the best possible information and go with it.

4. Put the pieces in the best possible order.

5. Do what little rewriting is necessary.

A Revising Strategy That Works

The revising strategy discussed below covers everything from reading the first draft to refining specific ideas. Use this strategy when you have time for in-depth revising.

READ: Sometimes it's hard to keep an open mind when you read your first draft. You need to put some distance between yourself and your writing.

- Whenever possible, put your writing aside for a day or two.
- When you return to it, read your piece out loud.
- Ask others (peers, family members) to read it out loud to you.
- Listen to your writing: What does it say? How does it sound?

REACT: Here are some questions that will help you react to your own writing on the second or third read-through:

- What parts of my writing work for me?
- Do all of these parts work together?
- Have I arranged the parts in the best possible order?
- Where do I need to go from here?

REWORK: Reworking your writing means making changes until all of the parts work equally well. There is usually plenty of reworking to do in the early stages of revising.

REFLECT: Write comments in the margins of your paper (or in a notebook) as you revise. Here are some guidelines for reflecting:

- Explore your reactions freely. Be honest about your writing.
- Note what you plan to cut, move, explain further, and so on.
- Reflect upon the changes you make. (How do they work?)
- If you are unsure of what to do, write down a question to answer later.

REFINE: Refining is checking specific ideas for logic, readability, and balance. Use these questions to help you refine your ideas:

- Will readers be able to follow my train of thought from idea to idea?
- Did I use transitional words or phrases to link ideas? (See 108.)
- Have I "overdeveloped" (or "underdeveloped") certain points compared to others?

"Classic" Revising Problems

Revisers often have to wade through misspellings, twisted sentences, and misused words to get to the content problems that deserve the most attention. Here are some samples of student writing that require major revision, not just tinkering. Compare your own revision suggestions with the comments that follow each sample.

Lack of Content

Brad, the author of the following paragraph, didn't really have much to say about his subject:

> **Two possible ways of analyzing literary works is to be discerning regarding the quality of the piece and its author, or to be judgmental of a piece and in turn its author. Essentially what I mean by discernment regarding literary analysis is the process of giving critical insight into the true significance and meaning of a literary piece and, in turn, its author. On the other hand, judgment in relation to the analysis of literature has a much more definitive and consequential nature to it. . . .**

DISCUSSION: Notice that if you remove empty abstractions and needless repetitions, this paragraph says only the following:

> **Discernment and judgment are two different ways of analyzing the relationship between a literary work and its author.**

Rather than trying to "fix" the paragraph, the reviser should start with this one substantial idea and go on from there.

Lack of Focus

In the following passage, Gregory, in a dry tone, classifies the three main types of government-supported health care:

> **There are three types of federal-controlled health care programs: Medicaid, Medicare, and socialized medicine. Medicaid is a program that assists the poor in paying for their health care. Medicare is a type of social security that helps people over sixty-five in paying their health costs. Socialized medicine, which is the third type of federal program, is when the federal government pays for everyone's health care by higher taxation. This program pays the doctors a flat salary and the individuals have no choice of doctor to see. They are told who they will see and when they will be seen. . . . These government programs may sound effective, but they have many problems.**

DISCUSSION: Notice the lack of overall focus in the writing. The first half defines three programs. The second half focuses on socialized medicine. And the last sentence introduces the subject of "problems." Nothing has prepared us for that. The paragraph should probably be broken into two parts, and the issue of problems may not even belong in this part of the essay.

Passive Expressions

Danny included the following paragraph in an essay complaining about roommates and drinking:

> **Sliding the movie in, Dale turns and says, "You can go to bed if you want." Does alcohol really impede the processes of the brain that much? Instead of a place for sleep, the top bunk becomes my cell, which is visited on a far too frequent basis. The movie itself can be enjoyable for me; that is, if blinders, like those used by racehorses to focus on only what is directly in front of them, can be put on long enough to ignore the atmosphere and focus solely on the 18x20-inch screen.**

DISCUSSION: Perhaps you noticed the length and wordiness of the fourth sentence. However, the bigger problem here is that Danny has taken himself almost completely out of the picture. Notice how often he uses the passive voice: *is visited, can be enjoyable, can be put,* etc. Objects such as the bunk, the cell, the movie, and the blinders seem to perform all the "action." The writer needs to become an active agent in his own narrative.

Overworked Expressions

Her college composition teacher showed Merry how to write longer, more complex sentences using a variety of modifying phrases and clauses. Putting her new knowledge to work, she wrote this opening in an essay:

> **Stephen Cruz is a näive young man slowly realizing his ethnicity, his elaborate economic and social support system giving way, discrimination finally rearing its ugly head everywhere. Poor boy, he's tried so hard, believed in himself so much, he's attributed his successes to his native intelligence, his judgment sacrificing itself to social constructs, his ethnic identity being sorely tested.**

DISCUSSION: Merry's writing is filled with ideas. The problem? No brakes! Phrases like "his ethnic identity being sorely tested" (technically called a nominative absolute phrase) roll on like cars on a long train. Each of her long sentences would read more clearly if broken into two or three parts.

What to Revise

These are just a few of the most serious revising problems: lack of content, lack of focus, and passive and overworked expressions. There are others to watch for—poor logic, inaccuracy, inconsistent voice, disorganization, and incoherent ideas.

A RULE OF THUMB: Deal with revising problems in the following order:

1. Problems with **content.**
2. Problems with **focus.**
3. Problems with **organization.**
4. Problems with **manner of expression.**

Peer Reviewing

All writers can benefit from an interested audience, especially one that offers constructive and honest advice during a writing project. And who could make a better audience than your writing peers? Some of you might already be part of a writing group, so you know the value of writers sharing their work. Others of you might want to start a writing group so you, too, can experience the benefits. The information on the next three pages will help you get started.

The Value of Feedback

Your fellow writers can tell you what does and doesn't work for them in your writing. This feedback is valuable throughout the writing process (prewriting through editing and proofreading), but it is especially helpful early in the revising process. At this point, you need to find out if your writing is making sense, if it holds the readers' interest, and so on.

Some experts go so far as to say that talking about writing is the most important step in the writing process. By sharing ideas and concerns, a community spirit develops, a spirit that will help make writing a meaningful process of learning rather than just another assignment. This enthusiasm is bound to have a positive effect on your final products.

"Comment on what you like in the writing. What you say must be honest, but you don't have to say everything you feel."

—Ken Macrorie

Maintaining Good Relations

To maintain good relations among group members, focus your comments or questions on specific things you see and hear in the writing. For example, an observation such as "I'm not sure the closing connects with the thesis of your essay" will mean much more to a writer than a general (negative) comment such as "Your closing is boring" or "Make your closing more relevant." The specific observation helps the writer better understand how to deal with a potential problem in his or her work.

Always base praise on something you observe or feel in the writing. Here is a meaningful, positive compliment based on a specific observation: "The series of questions and answers is an effective way to organize your essay." And here is an example of an honest, helpful reaction to a piece of writing: "There is an energy in this writing that I really like."

INSIDE info

At first, you may only be able to comment on a surprising detail, the length or brevity of the writing, or a point you don't understand. Fine. Just keep trying—and listening. Your ability to make observations will naturally improve with practice.

"Keep away from people who try to belittle your ambitions. Small people always do that, but the really great make you feel that you too can become great." —Mark Twain

Reviewing Guidelines

The guidelines that follow will help you conduct effective group revising sessions.

THE AUTHOR/WRITER

- **Come prepared with a substantial piece of writing.** Prepare a copy for each group member if this is part of normal group procedure. (Work with a group of three to five fellow writers.)

- **Introduce your writing.** However, don't say too much; let your writing do the talking.

- **Read your copy out loud.** Speak confidently and clearly.

- **As the group reacts to your writing, listen carefully and take brief notes.** Don't be defensive about your writing, since this will stop some members from commenting honestly about your work. Answer all of their questions.

- **If you have some specific concerns or problems, share these with your fellow writers.** But wait until they've had a chance to give you their responses.

THE GROUP MEMBERS

- **Listen carefully as the writer reads.** Take notes, but make them brief so you don't miss the reading. (See 036 for reviewing strategies.)

- **Imagine yourself to be the audience the writer intended.** If the piece was meant for an admissions office, a civic organization, or a newspaper, react to the text as if you were that audience.

- **Keep your comments positive, constructive, and concrete.** Instead of "Great job," make more meaningful (and helpful) responses: "Countering the opposition early in the argument establishes a believable tone of authority in your essay."

- **Focus your comments on specific things you observe.** An observation such as "I noticed many 'There are' statements in the body of your essay" is much more helpful than "Add some style to your writing."

- **Ask questions of the author.** "What do you mean when you say . . . ?" "Where did you get your facts about . . . ?"

- **Listen to other comments and add to them.** Listening to everyone's reactions and suggestions can help you and your peers become better writers.

Peer Reviewing Strategies

CRITIQUING A PAPER

Use the checklist that follows to help you evaluate compositions during peer reviewing sessions.

Purpose: Is the writer's purpose evident? In other words, is it clear that the writer is trying to analyze, to inform, to persuade, etc.?

Audience: Does the writing address a specific audience? Will the readers understand and appreciate this subject?

Form: Is the subject presented in an effective or appropriate form?

Content: Is the thesis, or focus, of the writing clear? Does the writer consider the subject from a number of angles?

Conventions: Does the writing adhere to the basic conventions of formal or informal English? (Consider style, sentence structure, usage, and mechanics.)

Voice: Does the writing sound sincere and honest? That is, do you "hear" the writer when you read his or her paper?

Personal Thoughts and Comments: Does the writer include any personal thoughts or comments in the writing? Are they needed or desirable?

Purpose Again: Does the writing succeed in enlightening, persuading, or informing readers? What is especially good about the writing?

"An editor should tell the author his writing is better than it is. Not a lot better, a little better."

—T. S. Eliot

REACTING TO WRITING

Peter Elbow, in *Writing Without Teachers,* offers four types of reactions to consider as you participate in a peer reviewing session: *pointing, summarizing, telling,* and *showing.* **Pointing** refers to a reaction in which a group member "points out" words, phrases, or ideas in the writing that make a positive or negative impression on him or her. **Summarizing** refers to a reader's general reaction or understanding of the writing. It may be a list of main ideas, a sentence, or a word that gets at the heart of the writing.

Telling refers to readers expressing what happens as they read a piece: first this happens, then this happens, later this happens, and so on. **Showing** refers to feelings expressed about the piece. Elbow suggests that readers express these feelings metaphorically. A reader might, for example, refer to something in the writing as if it were a voice quality, a color, a shape, a type of clothing, etc. ("Why do I feel like I've been lectured to in this essay?" or "Your writing has a neat, tailored quality to it.")

A Guide to Editing and Proofreading

It is sometimes hard to let go of your writing, but there comes a point in any project (like an impending deadline) when you must prepare it for publication. At this point, you must edit and proofread your revised writing so that it speaks clearly and accurately. When you edit, look first for words, phrases, and sentences that are unclear or awkward. Then turn your attention to spelling, mechanics, usage, and grammar errors.

Before you begin, make sure that you have the proper editing tools on hand: handbook, dictionary, thesaurus, computer spell checker, etc. Also ask one of your writing peers to help you edit your work. Then prepare your final draft, following any guidelines established by your instructor and proofreading this copy for errors.

WHAT'S AHEAD

This chapter contains two checklists that will help you edit and proof-read your writing. There is also a list of the most common errors in college writing. This list can serve as a quick reference for editing and proof-reading.

- ● **Editing Checklist**
- ● **Proofreading Checklist**
- ● **Common Writing Errors**

Editing Checklist

All of the reviewing, reworking, and refining that you do will naturally bear the stamp of your personal style. But you must also look closely at your revised writing to make sure that all of your ideas speak clearly and correctly. The following list of basic reminders will help you check your writing for style and correctness.

OVERALL STYLE

1. Read your revised writing aloud to test it for style. Better yet, have a writing peer read it aloud to you. Your writing should read smoothly and naturally from start to finish.

2. Check for these stylistic reminders:

Be Purposeful ● Does your writing sound like you genuinely care about your subject?

Be Clear ● Are the ideas expressed concisely and directly?

Be Sincere ● Does the writing sound authentic and honest?

 INSIDE info The best stylists write in an invisible style. That is, their thoughts and ideas always come first, and their language, though it may be engaging or colorful, never draws attention to itself. (See 046-067 for more information on style.)

SENTENCE STRUCTURE

3. Carefully check your sentences for correctness. Does each one express a complete thought? Have you used the most appropriate subordinate conjunction (*although, because,* etc.) or relative pronoun (*that, who,* etc.) in your complex sentences?

4. Watch for sentences that all sound the same and ones that limp along. Rely on your writer's sixth sense to sort out the good from the bad.

5. Examine your sentences for variety:

Vary the Length ● Are any sentences too long and rambling? Are there too many short, choppy sentences?

Vary the Beginnings ● Do too many sentences begin with the same pronoun or article (*There, It, The, I,* etc.)?

WORD CHOICE

6. Replace any words or phrases that may be awkward or confusing. Substitute overused words and phrases (cliches) with words and expressions that are specific, vivid, and colorful. (See 053-054.)

7. Check your writing for the appropriate level of diction. In most cases, academic writing should meet the standards of formal diction. (See 027.)

NOTE: To edit your writing for usage, mechanics, and grammar, use the checklist on the next page.

Proofreading Checklist

The following guidelines will help you check your revised writing for spelling, mechanics, usage and grammar, and form. Also refer to the "Proofreader's Guide" for additional help. (See 552-851.)

SPELLING

1. Check your writing for spelling errors using these tips as a guide:
- Use the spell checker on your computer. (It won't, however, catch all of the spelling errors.)
- Read your writing backward to help you focus on each word.
- Circle each spelling you are unsure of.
- For help, consult the list of commonly misspelled words in the handbook (663-667) as well as an up-to-date dictionary.

MECHANICS

2. Review each sentence for end punctuation marks.

3. Also check each sentence for proper use of commas: before coordinating conjunctions (*and, but, or,* etc.) in compound sentences, after introductory clauses and long introductory phrases, between items in a series, and so on.

4. Look for apostrophes in possessive expressions and in contractions.

5. Examine quoted information or dialogue for proper use of quotation marks.

6. Review the text for proper use of capital letters: for first words in sentences and in written conversation, and for proper names of people, places, and things.

USAGE AND GRAMMAR

7. Look for misuse of any commonly mixed pairs of words: *there/their/they're; accept/except.* (See 669-757.)

8. Check for subject/verb agreement problems. Subjects and verbs should agree in number: singular subjects go with singular verbs; plural subjects go with plural verbs.

9. Review for pronoun/antecedent agreement problems. A pronoun and its antecedent must agree in number.

FORM

10. Check the title. Does it effectively lead into the writing? Is it appropriate for the writing task?

11. Examine any quoted or cited material. Are all sources of information properly presented and documented? (See 300-361 and 372-429.)

12. Look over the finished copy of your writing. Does it meet the requirements for a final manuscript?

Common Writing Errors

Here is a guide to 12 of the most common errors (other than spelling) to watch for when editing and proofreading your writing. (The corrections are in red.)

SENTENCE FRAGMENT (See 070.)

Because she studied at a conservatory, *, she had a thorough understanding of classical music.*

COMMA SPLICE (See 071.)

Fighting looks like play*;* it teaches cubs important survival skills.

RUN-ON SENTENCE (See 073.)

Weather is one cause of famine*. P* political strife is another cause.

COMMA OMISSION AFTER LONG INTRODUCTORY PHRASE (See 562.)

Considering all of the incredible hype*,* the show was a disappointment.

COMMA OMISSION IN A COMPOUND SENTENCE (See 556.)

The first customer came before dawn*,* and the last one left after midnight.

COMMAS OMITTED AROUND A NONESSENTIAL ELEMENT (See 563.)

Dr. Paulus*,* who currently teaches in the school of business*,* has asked for a leave of absence.

PRONOUN/ANTECEDENT AGREEMENT ERROR (See 849.)

Each candidate should report all of ~~their~~ *his or her* income.

SHIFT IN PERSON (See 091.)

When people have heart attacks, ~~you~~ *they* experience pain in the left arm.

SUBJECT/VERB AGREEMENT ERROR (See 837.)

The problem with the new facilities ~~are~~ *is* the ventilation.

SHIFT IN VERB TENSE (See 091.)

After the trustees met, we ~~are~~ *were* allowed to ask questions.

DANGLING MODIFIER (See 076.)

After studying so long, *I found* the exam was a snap.

FAULTY PARALLELISM (See 092.)

Juma wants to graduate from college, become a volunteer medic, and *serve humankind in the African sub-Sahara.* ~~in the African sub-Sahara perform services for humankind.~~

Writer's Resource

To be a complete student of the writing and communication process, you need to have a command of the field's vocabulary. Especially in college, instructors have come to expect students to have a working knowledge of the terms and concepts relevant to the business of writing. With your handbook, you should be able to handle whatever challenge is tossed your way.

WHAT'S AHEAD

The following pages contain a glossary of writing terms you should find useful in your course work. The list of foreign words and phrases will serve as a compact reference to the Latin, French, Spanish, Yiddish, and other unfamiliar words or phrases you may encounter. Both glossaries should prove helpful as you work to improve your writing skills and vocabulary.

- ● **Writing Terms**
- ● **Foreign Words and Phrases**

Writing Terms

Analysis: Writing that carefully examines and explores a subject with the objective of gaining understanding.

Argumentation: Writing or speaking in which reasons or arguments are presented in a logical way.

Arrangement: The order in which details are placed or arranged in a piece of writing.

Audience: Those people who read or hear what you have written.

Balance: The arranging of words or phrases so that two ideas are given equal emphasis in a sentence or paragraph; a rhythm created by repeating a pattern.

Brainstorming: Collecting ideas by thinking and talking freely and openly about all the possibilities; used most often with groups.

Case study: The story of one individual whose experiences speak for the experiences of a larger group of people.

Central idea: The main point or purpose of a piece of writing, often stated in a thesis statement or topic sentence.

Claim: An assertion or proposition (thesis) in argumentation, occurring as a claim of fact, value, or policy.

Classification: Writing that breaks a subject down into its most meaningful parts and carefully examines each part.

Coherence: The arrangement of ideas in such a way that the reader can easily follow from one point to the next.

Commentary: Writing that presents a thoughtful reaction to some aspect of life.

Concession: Giving credit to a claim on the opposing side of an argument.

Data: Information that is accepted as being true—facts, figures, examples—and from which conclusions can be drawn.

Deductive reasoning: The act of beginning with a general idea and reasoning one's way to a specific point or conclusion.

Definition: Writing that explains, describes, and clarifies a complex concept, an abstract idea, or a complicated idea.

Description: Writing that paints a colorful picture of a person, a place, a thing, or an idea using concrete, vivid details.

Details: The words used to describe a person, convince an audience, explain a process, or in some way support the central idea; to be effective, details should be vivid, colorful, and appeal to the senses.

Emphasis: Placing greater stress on the most important idea in a piece of writing by giving it special treatment; emphasis can be achieved by placing the important idea in a special position, by repeating a key word or phrase, or by simply writing more about this idea than the others.

Essay: A piece of prose writing in which ideas on a single topic are presented, explained, argued, or described in an interesting way.

Evaluation: Writing that explores a subject's value, impact, or significance; its strengths and weaknesses; its place in the scheme of things.

Explication: Writing that presents a detailed analysis or thoughtful interpretation of a subject.

Exposition: Writing that explains.

Extended definition: Writing that goes beyond a simple definition of a term in order to increase understanding; it can cover several paragraphs and include personal definitions and experiences, similes and metaphors, quotations, and even verse.

Figurative language: Language that goes beyond the immediate meaning of the words used; writing in which a figure of speech is used to heighten the meaning.

Focus: Concentrating on a specific subject to give it emphasis or clarity.

Form: The arrangement of details into a pattern or style; the way in which the content of writing is organized.

Free writing: Writing openly and freely on any topic; focused free writing is writing openly on a specific topic or angle.

Generalization: An idea or statement that emphasizes the general characteristics rather than the specific details of a subject.

Grammar: The study of the structure and features of a language; it usually consists of rules and standards that are to be followed to produce acceptable writing and speaking.

Idiom: A phrase or expression that means something different from what the words actually say. An idiom is usually understandable to a particular group of people (using *over his head* for *didn't understand*).

Illustration: Writing that uses an experience to make a point or clarify an idea.

Inductive reasoning: The act of beginning with specific examples or facts and reasoning one's way to a generalization or conclusion.

Inverted sentence: A sentence in which the normal word order is inverted or switched, as when the verb comes before the subject.

Journal: A daily record of thoughts, impressions, and autobiographical information; a journal can be a source of ideas for writing.

Juxtaposition: Placing two ideas (words or pictures) side by side so that their closeness creates a new, often ironic meaning.

Limiting the subject: Narrowing the subject to a specific topic that is suitable for the writing or speaking task.

Literal: The actual or dictionary meaning of a word; language that means exactly what it appears to mean.

Logic: The science of correct reasoning; correctly using facts, examples, and reasons to support your point.

Narration: Writing that tells a story or recounts an event.

Objective: Relating information in an impersonal manner; without feelings or opinions.

Personal narrative: Personal writing that covers an event in the writer's life; it often contains personal comments and observations as well as a description of the event.

Persuasion: Writing that is meant to change a reader's thinking or actions.

Point of view: The position or angle from which a story is told.

Position paper: Writing that takes a particular stance on a noteworthy issue (based on extensive analysis), aiming to inform and explain rather than persuade.

Premise: A statement or point that serves as the basis of a discussion or debate.

Process: A method of doing something that involves several steps or stages; the writing process involves prewriting, composing, revising, and proofreading.

Profile: Writing that reveals an individual or re-creates a time period, using interviews and research.

Proposition: The main idea to be discussed in an argument.

Prose: Writing or speaking in the usual or ordinary form; prose becomes poetry when it takes on rhyme and rhythm.

Purpose: The specific reason a person has for writing; the goal of writing.

Reminiscence: Writing that focuses on a memorable past experience.

Report: A writing that results from gathering, investigating, and organizing facts and thoughts on a topic.

Review: Writing that presents a critical evaluation of a literary work or an artistic endeavor.

Revision: Changing a piece of writing to improve it in style or content.

Subjective: Thinking or writing that includes personal feelings, attitudes, and opinions.

Summary: Writing that presents the main points of a larger work in condensed form.

Syntax: The order and relationship of words in a sentence.

Theme: The central idea in a piece of writing (lengthy writings may have several themes); a term used to describe a short essay.

Thesis statement: A statement of the purpose, intent, or main idea of an essay.

Tone: The writer's attitude toward the subject; a writer's tone can be serious, sarcastic, tongue-in-cheek, solemn, objective, etc.

Topic: The specific subject covered in a piece of writing.

Transitions: Words or phrases that help tie ideas together.

Unity: Writing in which each sentence helps to develop the main idea.

Universal: A topic or idea that applies to everyone.

Usage: The way in which people use language; language is generally considered to be standard (formal and informal) or nonstandard. Only standard usage is acceptable in writing.

Vivid details: Details that appeal to the senses and help the reader see, feel, smell, taste, and hear the subject being written about.

Foreign Words and Phrases

a cappella (It) without instrumental accompaniment

ad hoc (L) "for this purpose"; for the present matter or situation; temporary

ad infinitum (L) endlessly; forever

ad nauseam (L) to a sickening degree

aficionado (Sp) enthusiast; fan

alfresco (It) in the open air

alma mater (L) "fostering mother"; old school

alpha (Gk) first; the beginning

alter ego (L) another side of oneself

antebellum (L) before the war, especially before the Civil War

a posteriori (L) "from what comes after"; inductive

a priori (L) "from what comes before"; deductive

au contraire (Fr) on the contrary

au courant (Fr) up-to-date; contemporary

avant-garde (Fr) "vanguard"; forward; advanced

beau geste (Fr) noble gesture

bête noire (Fr) "black beast"; pet peeve

blitzkrieg (Gr) a swift, sudden effort, usually in war

bona fide (L) "in good faith"; sincere; genuine

bon appetit (Fr) "good appetite"; enjoy your meal

bon mot (Fr) clever turn of phrase

bon vivant (Fr) a person who has refined tastes

campesino (Sp) peasant farmer

carpe diem (L) "seize the day"; live for today

carte blanche (Fr) "blank document"; unlimited authority or power

cause cèlébre (Fr) "celebrated case"; scandal; notorious incident, person, or thing

caveat emptor (L) "let the buyer beware"; buyer takes the risk; no warranty

c'est la vie (Fr) "that's life"

chef d'œuvre (Fr) masterpiece

chutzpah (Y) gall; daring

circa (L) about; approximately

cogito, ergo sum (L) "I think, therefore I am."

coup de grâce (Fr) a decisive finishing blow, act, or event to end suffering

coup d'etat (Fr) a sudden, decisive exercise of force in politics; overthrow of government

crème de la crème (Fr) "cream of the cream"; the very best

cum laude (L) "with praise"; with honor

déclassé (Fr) fallen in social standing

de facto (L) functioning or existing in fact, or in reality, but not in accordance with the usual or legal process

de jure (L) legally, according to the law

détente (Fr) easing of strained relations

dramatis personae (L) "persons of the drama"; cast of characters

en masse (Fr) in a large group

e pluribus unum (L) "one out of many"

errata (L) a list of errors

ersatz (Gr) fake; imitation

esprit de corps (Fr) common spirit within a group

eureka (Gk) "I have found"; expression of triumph or discovery

ex cathedra (L) "from the chair"; with high authority

exemplum (L) example; model; anecdote

ex officio (L) by virtue of, or because of, one's office or position

ex post facto (L) after the fact or event; retroactive

fait accompli (Fr) accomplished fact

faux pas (Fr) "false step"; a social blunder

fiat (L) "let it be done"; a command; a decree

glasnost (R) "publicity"; openness

KEY:	Fr	French	L	Latin
	Gk	Greek	R	Russian
	Gr	German	Sp	Spanish
	It	Italian	Y	Yiddish
	J	Japanese		

habeas corpus (L) "you should have the body"; writ summoning one to court

haute couture (Fr) high fashion

haute cuisine (Fr) elaborate cooking

hoi polloi (Gk) common people, masses

hubris (Gk) exaggerated pride; arrogance

in extremis (L) "in extreme circumstances"

in loco parentis (L) "in place of a parent"; acting as a guardian

in medias res (L) "in the middle of things"

in memoriam (L) "in memory of"; as a memorial to

ipso facto (L) "by the fact (act) itself"; by the nature of the thing; automatically

joie de vivre (Fr) "joy of living"; good spirits; exuberance

kamikaze (J) "divine wind"; suicide pilot

klutz (Y) clumsy person

kudos (Gk) "glory, renown"; fame; honor; accolade

kvetch (Y) complain; carp; gripe

laissez-faire (Fr) "let [people] do [as they wish]"; noninterference

lingua franca (It) "Frankish language"; a common language among people of different tongues

magna cum laude (L) with great honor

magnum opus (L) a masterpiece

mea culpa (L) "my fault"; expressing personal fault or guilt

modus operandi (L) "manner of operating"; a working method or arrangement; a procedure

noblesse oblige (Fr) honorable behavior that is considered to be the obligation of people of noble birth or rank

nom de plume (Fr) pen name

nonpareil (Fr) having no equal

non sequitur (L) "it does not follow"; a response that doesn't follow logically from a previous statement; fallacy

nouveau riche (Fr) the newly rich

par excellence (Fr) above all; superior

per capita (L) "by heads"; for each one

per diem (L) "by the day"

per se (L) "by, of, or in itself, oneself, or themselves"; of its own accord

persona non grata (L) an unacceptable person

pièce de résistance (Fr) the main dish of a meal; the main thing or event

prima facie (L) "on first appearance"; at first glance; self-evident; sufficient to establish a fact

pro forma (L) "for form"; carried out as a formality; for the record

pro rata (L) proportionately

quid pro quo (L) "something for something"; something given for something received

raison d'être (Fr) reason for being

reductio ad absurdum (L) "reduction to absurdity"; disproving an argument by showing its absurd direction

savoir faire (Fr) "knowing how to do"; ability to say and do the right thing

schlemiel (Y) unlucky person; loser

schmaltz (Y) excessive sentimentality

schtick (Y) gimmick; a performer's idiosyncracy

sine qua non (L) "without which not"; like no other; something essential

status quo (L) "the condition in which"; present condition; the state of affairs up to now

summa cum laude (L) with highest honor

tabula rasa (L) "erased tablet"; clean slate

terra firma (L) "solid land"; dry land; solid ground

tête-à-tête (Fr) "head to head"; together without intrusion by another

tour de force (Fr) a feat of great strength

veni, vidi, vici (L) "I came, I saw, I conquered."

verbatim (L) "word for word"; exactly as said or written

verboten (Gr) forbidden

vis-à-vis (Fr) "face-to-face"; opposite; in relation to

vox populi (L) "voice of the people"

wanderlust (Gr) desire to travel

Weltschmerz (Gr) "world pain"; world weariness

wunderkind (Gr) prodigy

The Basic Elements of Writing

Writing with Style

Making Sentences Work

Developing Strong Paragraphs

Mastering the College Essay

Taking Care of Business

Writing with Style

Fashion is a cultural thing. If you're in fashion, you dress right, eat right, and play right. And it's obviously a big economic thing. Our major suppliers of chicness have created a dynamic industry. Wherever fashion goes, most people are sure to follow—no matter what the cost.

Not so with style. Style is more inner directed. It's based on personal taste and comfort. It always seems to fit. You may love denim. The next person may feel comfortable in something more colorful. That's okay; that's style.

WHAT'S AHEAD

So what does all of this have to do with writing? Well, there is nothing trendy about good writing. It looks and feels like the genuine article. It has a long shelf life. It is definitely a matter of style. This section provides you with all kinds of information about writing style, including a "short list" of key stylistic reminders, tips for developing a sense of style, plus much more.

- Key Stylistic Reminders
- Developing a Sense of Style
- Special Features of Style
- Using an Alternative Style
- Checking for Common Ailments
- Using Clear, Fair Language

Key Stylistic Reminders

If you remember only three things about style, let them be the following three points: *(1) Be purposeful. (2) Be clear. (3) Be sincere.* Almost nothing else really matters. Writing with purpose, with clarity, and with sincerity is the key to an effective style. Our best writers have almost always been plain talkers, speaking directly and honestly to their readers. Writers like Mark Twain, Rachel Carson, Kurt Vonnegut, and E. B. White are our role models. Follow their lead, and you are sure to write with style.

 Be purposeful.

Writing without genuine concern for your subject is like trying to bake bread without yeast. One of the most important ingredients is missing. Good writing begins (and ends) with purpose and commitment. As Vonnegut states, "It is the genuine caring [about a subject], and not your games with language, which will be the most compelling and seductive element in your style." The bottom line is this: If you expect to produce effective writing, select subjects that interest you.

Let's say that your sociology instructor asks you to write a paper about recreation. But you're not sure which part of recreation interests you most. Use one of the selecting strategies listed in your handbook (018-019) to help you explore possible subjects.

 Be clear.

You might think that style is something you add to your writing— a slick phrase here, a clever aside there. But that is not how style works. In fact, trying to add style usually just clutters things up. It's much more important to be clear and orderly, to keep things simple and direct. Your writing will always be in style if it's easy for your readers to understand and to follow.

> *"Have something to say, and say it as clearly as you can. This is the only secret of style."* —Mathew Arnold

 Be sincere.

Writing works best when it sounds like one person (you) sincerely communicating with another person. It doesn't sound tentative, breezy, or pushy. Nor does it try to impress readers with a lot of ten-dollar words. It simply rings true. In order to write well—in essays, reports, and reminiscences—you must be able to use an honest, sincere, and natural voice.

Writing That's in Style

Here are two examples of writing that is in style. The first one comes from *The Paradise of Bombs* by Scott Russell Sanders. In this excerpt, Sanders discusses one difference between city life and country life. This piece exhibits all of the basic elements of writing with style. It stems from a subject that the author feels strongly about—country life. The ideas are presented simply and clearly. The voice is honest and sincere.

> It is easy to pretend, in a city, that humans have made the world and dwell there alone. In the country, you know better. It's the difference between living in *a* creation and living in *the* creation. Life in the boondocks discourages you from claiming with a straight face that humans are omnipotent. If you think our works are mighty and permanent, drive down any back road and study the caved-in barns, the cellar holes grown up in thickets. If you begin to doubt we have companions on spaceship earth, try clearing a patch of ground beside a woods and gardening for a summer. Insects and worms and rabbits and raccoons and possums and beasts you never identify will gobble your plants; weeds and forest seedlings will sprout between your neat rows. Go away for a month and when you come back the woods will be occupying your garden plot.

This next piece comes from a *National Geographic* article about Sir Joseph Banks, an eighteenth-century adventurer and natural scientist. It is clear in this excerpt that writer T. H. Watkins is captivated by his subject and takes special care to share this enthusiasm with his readers. Watkins' description is clear, orderly, and engaging.

> In his 20s he was full of the juices of life, standing six feet tall and weighing in at about 13 stone (182 pounds), with dark liquid eyes and a mouth that romance novelists of today probably would describe as sensuous. His voice boomed with good fellowship, and he displayed a talent for the social arts and a passionate interest in the world around him. Once, when asked by a friend where in Europe he would go for the traditional grand tour expected of any young man of means, Banks is said to have replied, "Every blockhead does that. My grand tour shall be one round the whole world."

"I've been called a stylist until I really could tear my hair out. . . . The style is you."

—Katherine Anne Porter

Developing a Sense of Style

How can your writing style—your special way of saying something—best develop? You can begin to answer this question by reading the information below. "Becoming a Student of Writing" explains how accomplished writers learn about and practice stylistic writing. Then, on the following two pages, you can learn about specific traits of effective style as well as a special matrix (or graphic organizer) that will help you write with style.

Becoming a Student of Writing

Read widely. William Faulkner was once asked what advice he would give to young writers. He said, "Read everything—trash, classics, good and bad, and see how they do it. . . . Read! You'll absorb it. Then write." Follow Faulkner's advice, and gain an appreciation for the written word in all of its different forms.

Keep your eyes open, and be on the lookout for those unique slices of life that can add so much to your writing. You may enjoy this "slice" recorded in Ken Macrorie's book *Uptaught:*

> An elderly, sparse man who makes a career out of auditing classes is sitting next to me taking notes on both sides of a paper. Now he turns it upside down and writes over his own notes.

Keep track of your reading and observing. Get into the habit of recording and reflecting upon your experiences. Some of these ideas may later serve as inspiration or models for your own writing.

Experiment with a variety of writing forms. In the process, sharpen your writing abilities: Journaling promotes writing fluency. Corresponding helps you develop your writing voice. Writing articles gives you a sense of form and structure. Crafting poems helps you gain an appreciation for word choice.

Write to learn. Writing helps you examine ideas and feelings more thoughtfully. As Ray Bradbury once said, writing "lets the world burn through you." The more experiences you have as a writer (exploring your personal thoughts), the better able you will be to express yourself intelligently, meaningfully, and stylistically.

Understand the basics. Gain an understanding of the core principles governing sentence structure, grammar, and mechanics. (Your handbook will help you in all of these areas.) Also begin to build your writing vocabulary. Learn, for example, what it means *to narrate* or *to analyze.* Know the difference between terms like *active* and *passive, abstract* and *concrete.*

Writing with a Plan in Mind

Wise writers think about style *before* they begin to write. You can do the same by asking key questions in five key areas related to a particular writing task. These five areas form a matrix out of which your style will be born.

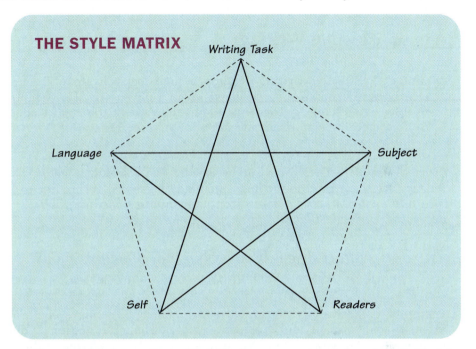

THE STYLE MATRIX

Writing Task

Language

Subject

Self

Readers

NOTE: The matrix shows that all of the key areas are interrelated. That is, your understanding of your writing task, and your feelings about your subject, will affect the way in which you communicate your ideas to your readers.

Asking the Key Questions

These are the types of questions you want to ask yourself as you plan your writing:

Writing Task: What is the nature of my assignment? Do I understand all of the requirements? Am I writing to inform, to analyze, to persuade, or to entertain?

Subject: What will I write about? Does my subject meet the requirements of my assignment? What will be the specific focus or main point of my writing?

Readers: Who are my readers? Why will they be interested in my subject? What do they need to know?

Self: What compels me to write about this subject? What do I hope to gain from this experience?

Language (and Form): How will I present my subject? How will I gain and maintain my readers' interest? What will I say first, second, and third?

Evaluating Your Style

A few pages back (047) you were reminded to be purposeful, clear, and sincere in your writing. Those three points will serve you very well as a basic guide to style. However, if you want to reach for something a bit higher, you may want to evaluate your style using the following traits as a guide.

Traits of Effective Writing

Design ● Effective writing displays a clear focus. It stems from a clearly established feeling you have about your subject. It attempts to inform, persuade, surprise, or entertain. And in the end, it adds up to something significant for you and for your readers.

Concreteness ● Effective writing is specific and colorful. It helps readers see, hear, and feel things. Instead of general terms like *race, administrator,* or *emotion,* it contains specific ones like *1500-meter run, Dean of Student Affairs,* or *pent-up anger.*

> *"An abstract style is always bad. Your sentences should be full of stones, chairs, tables, etc."* —Rudolf Flesch

Energy ● Effective writing crackles with energy. It shows signs of intensity and emotion, and it engages readers from start to finish. You build energy into your writing by speaking honestly about your subject and by providing plenty of stimulating, thought-provoking information.

Freshness ● Effective writing may contain surprises. For example, you may decide to use a sentence fragment (or two) or a long, rambling sentence for dramatic effect. (See 057 for examples.) Then again, you may develop an idea using a negative definition (what something is not) or a poetic expression.

Coherence ● Effective writing contains no unnecessary bumps or rough spots. It links important ideas from sentence to sentence and from paragraph to paragraph. It moves smoothly and clearly from the opening paragraph to the closing remarks. Coherence is achieved by working and reworking your ideas many times.

Correctness ● Effective writing is exact and correct. It is writing that attends to every detail, from the accuracy of the facts and details to the proper placement of punctuation marks.

Special Features of Style

There are a number of special features that can add style to your writing. One of these features, using metaphors, is discussed below. Other features, including the use of colorful words and repetition, are discussed on the following four pages. Whenever you feel that your writing needs a jump start, turn here for help. *But a word of caution:* Your writing will sound forced or artificial if you overuse any of these features.

Writing Metaphorically

A **metaphor** connects an idea in your writing to something new and creates a powerful picture for your readers. (Remember that a metaphor compares two ideas without using *like* or *as*.) In the following examples, notice how the basic ideas come to life when they are stated metaphorically:

BASIC IDEA: Environmentalists are trying to preserve natural resources.

Stated Metaphorically:
Environmentalists are the design engineers for spaceship earth.

BASIC IDEA: There is a lot of activity under the grass.

Stated Metaphorically:
The world is a wild wrestle under the grass. —Annie Dillard

Extending a Metaphor

Sometimes a metaphor can serve as the unifying element throughout a series of sentences. Extending a metaphor in this way helps you expand or clarify an idea in your writing. Notice how a metaphor is effectively extended in the following passage:

A writer is a kind of **forest ranger, leading** his readers **like a troop of tenderfoots along an unfamiliar trail.** If the **guide** does a good job, his **charges** will not **stumble** over strange words or awkward clauses; they will not **lose their way** in an **underbrush** of ambiguity. —James J. Kilpatrick

Making Metaphors Work

- **Create original comparisons:** The student who wrote "Demi Moore's last movie sent me to the moon" has spent too much time gazing into space and not enough time creating fresh comparisons. (See 059 for more information about overused comparisons.)
- **Be clear in your thinking:** The student who wrote "Homelessness is a thorn in the city's image" has created a confusing figure of speech. Homelessness may be a thorn in the city's side, but not in its image.
- **Be consistent:** The reporter who wrote "In the final debate, Senator Jones dodged each of his opponent's accusations and eventually scored the winning shot" has created a *mixed metaphor*. He shifts from one comparison (boxing) to another (basketball).

Using Strong, Colorful Words

Suppose, in your mind, you see a soaring power forward, with the ball held high in his right hand, slam home a dunk shot. Now, suppose you write "The forward scored a basket." How clearly do you think you have communicated this thought? Obviously, not very clearly. By using specific words, you can create clear and colorful word pictures for your reader.

CHOOSE SPECIFIC NOUNS: Some nouns are general *(boots, movement, fruit)* and give the reader a vague, uninteresting picture. Other nouns are specific *(desert boots, Civil Rights, mango)* and give the reader a clear, detailed picture. In the chart that follows, the first word in each category is a general noun. The second word is more specific. Finally, each word at the bottom of the chart is definitely a specific noun. These last nouns are the type that can make your writing clear and colorful.

General to Specific Nouns

person	*place*	*thing*	*idea*
woman	school	book	theory
actress	university	novel	scientific theory
Meryl Streep	**Notre Dame**	***Pride and Prejudice***	**relativity**

USE VIVID VERBS: Like nouns, verbs can be too general to create a vivid word picture. For example, the verb *looked* does not say the same thing as *stared, glared, glanced, peeked,* or *inspected.* The statement "Ms. Shaw *glared* at the two goof-offs" is much more vivid and interesting than "Ms. Shaw *looked* at the two goof-offs."

◉ Whenever possible, use a verb that is strong enough to stand alone without the help of an adverb.

Verb and adverb:	John fell down in the Union.
Vivid verb:	**John collapsed in the Union.**

◉ Avoid overusing the "be" verbs *(is, are, was, were, . . .).* Also avoid overusing *would, could,* or *should.* Often a better verb can be made from another word in the same sentence.

A be verb:	Cole is someone who follows national news.
A stronger verb:	**Cole follows national news.**

◉ Use active rather than passive verbs. (Use passive verbs only if you want to downplay who is performing the action in a sentence. See 058.)

Passive verb:	Another piercing essay was submitted by Kim.
Active verb:	**Kim submitted another piercing essay.**

◉ Use verbs that show rather than tell.

A verb that tells:	Dr. Lewis is very thorough.
A verb that shows:	**Dr. Lewis prepares detailed lectures.**

SELECT SPECIFIC ADJECTIVES: Use precise, colorful adjectives to describe the nouns in your writing. Strong adjectives make the nouns even more interesting and clear to the reader. For example, the adjectives used in the phrase "*sleek, red* convertible" give the reader a clear picture of the car.

◉ Avoid using adjectives that carry little meaning: *neat, big, pretty, small, old, cute, fun, bad, nice, good, dumb, great, funny,* etc.

Overused adjective:	His **old** Thunderbird is in storage.
Specific adjective:	His **classic** Thunderbird is in storage.

◉ Use adjectives selectively. If your writing contains too many adjectives, they will simply get in the way and lose their effectiveness.

Too many adjectives:	A tall, shocking column of thick, yellow smoke marked the exact spot where the unexpected explosion had occurred.
Revised:	A column of thick, yellow smoke marked the spot where the unexpected explosion had occurred.

INCLUDE SPECIFIC ADVERBS: Use adverbs when you think they are needed to describe the action in a sentence. For example, the statement "Mayor Meyer *reluctantly* agreed to meet the protesters" tells much more than "Mayor Meyer agreed to meet the protesters." Don't, however, use a verb and an adverb when a single vivid verb would be better.

USE THE "RIGHT" WORDS: The words in your writing should not only be specific and colorful, but should also have the right feeling, or *connotation*. The connotation of a word is the sense suggested or implied beyond its literal meaning. Notice how the boldfaced words in the following passage connote the distaste that the writer feels for newspaper photographs depicting personal tragedies.

> Too many times I have picked up the evening newspaper to see a photograph of some **tortured-looking** person **splashed** all over the front page. Usually, this person has just gone through a **trauma**—a car accident, a fire, or a shooting. You would think newspapers could use a little **discretion** and not choose such pictures to **emblazon** the front page of their papers. It's bad enough that these people have had to **suffer misfortune** to begin with; to have their **grief broadcast** in this vivid way seems very wrong. It **inflates their tragedy** and unnecessarily delays their forgetting and their healing. They will be reminded over and over again by neighbors, friends, coworkers, and well-wishers just how **"terrible"** and **"awful"** and **"frightening"** all of this must have been. They will be **forced to relive** an event weeks and months and perhaps years after it would otherwise have been forgotten. This is the power of the press—**at its worst.**

"The common thread in all of my work is people—and what they're up to, as it's expressed through their work." —John McPhee

Using Anecdotes

Writer Donald Murray suggests that you put people in your writing whose actions communicate important ideas for you. Brief slices of life add spark to your writing. They allow you to show readers something in a lively and interesting manner, rather than tell them matter-of-factly.

 INSIDE info "Anecdote" is the more technical term for "brief slices of life." *The American Heritage College Dictionary* (3rd edition) defines an anecdote as "a short account of an interesting or humorous incident."

Example I

In the following example, student writer Amy Douma opens her research paper with an anecdote about a homeless man:

> **On a chilly February afternoon, an old man sits sleeping on the sidewalk outside a New York hotel while the lunchtime crowd shuffles by. At the man's feet is a sign which reads: "Won't you help me? I'm cold and homeless and lonely. God bless you." He probably spends his days alone on the street begging for handouts, and his nights searching for shelter from the cold. He has no job, no friends, and nowhere to turn.**

DISCUSSION: This anecdote helps the writer establish an effective tone for her research paper. In her writing, she attempts to answer two questions: Who are the homeless people? What are the reasons for their predicament?

Example II

In this passage, writer Mary Anne Hoff shares the story of a visitor to her childhood home in North Dakota:

> **His "bee-yoo-tee-ful" stopped me short. This lanky Mr. Sophisticate from just outside Paris was describing the North Dakota prairie. The wild grasses and big sky, the black-eyed Susan and sagebrush, the hum of dog days were new to him. Now all he could say as he lay exhausted in Mother's recliner was "bee-yoo-tee-ful."**
>
> **Two days later we all huddled around a book about Paris. Our guest pointed to a photo and repeated "bee-yoo-tee-ful." It was the Champs Elysee at night. The Champs Elysee and the North Dakota prairie described with the same word? That was when I knew I would like him.**

DISCUSSION: Notice how much more effective this story is than a telling statement like "A visitor helped me see my North Dakota home in a new way." All of the wonderful details help readers share in the experience.

Using Repetition

Another important stylistic technique is to repeat similar grammatical structures (words, phrases, or ideas) for the purpose of rhythm, emphasis, and unity. When used effectively, **repetition** can do more to improve your style of writing than just about any other technique.

TAKE note

The key point to remember when using repetition is to keep the words or ideas *parallel,* or stated in the same way. (As you read the examples below, you will see parallelism in action.)

FOR RHYTHM AND BALANCE: Notice in each of the sentences below how smoothly the repeated words or phrases flow from one to the next. They are in perfect balance.

> **Baseball, football,** and **boxing** are the most popular spectator sports.

> The floor was littered with **discarded soda cans, crumpled newspapers,** and **wrinkled clothes.**

> Olivia wants to **write a Broadway play, make a lot of money,** and **retire to the country.**

FOR EMPHASIS AND EFFECT: Notice in the passages below how the repetition of a basic sentence structure adds intensity to the writing.

> The two singers changed styles to match the songs. **They crooned love ballads. They moaned the blues. They scat sang to jazz.** Their artistry was in perfect harmony with their material.

> **We shall fight on the beaches, we shall fight on the landing grounds, we shall fight in the fields and in the streets, we shall fight in the hills; we shall never surrender.**
> —Winston Churchill

FOR UNITY AND ORGANIZATION: Notice in the passage below how repetition is used to unify and organize all of the ideas. (This passage is from *The Land Remembers* by Ben Logan. Copyright © 1975 by Ben T. Logan. Reprinted by permission of Northwood Press/Heartland Press.)

> **Let the smell of mint touch me.** I am kneeling along a little stream, the water numbing my hands as I reach for a trout. I feel the fish arch and struggle. I let go, pulling watercress from the water instead.

> **Let me see a certain color** and I am standing beside the threshing machine, grain cascading through my hands. The seeds we planted when snow was spitting down have multiplied a hundred times, returning in a stream of bright gold, still warm with the sunlight of the fields.

> **Let me hear an odd whirring.** I am deep in the woods, following an elusive sound, looking in vain for a last passenger pigeon, a feathered lightning I have never seen, unwilling to believe no person will ever see one again.

Using an Alternative Style

When you write an essay, you are expected to follow some well-established principles: Form a thesis. Develop main ideas in paragraphs. Use complete sentences, and so on. These principles obviously serve you well. But from a stylistic standpoint, it's important to know that there are alternative ways to express yourself effectively. We have listed a few of these alternative techniques below. Experiment with them in your own essays (but only when circumstances are appropriate).

SENTENCE FRAGMENTS: Single words or phrases set off as sentences can have a dramatic effect. Notice below how writer Anna Quindlen uses a series of fragments (in bold) to dramatize the problems facing urban youths.

> The problem is that when we look into this abyss, it goes so deep that we get dizzy and pull back from the edge. **Teenage mothers. Child abuse. Crowded schools. . . . And always the smell of urine in the elevator.** I have never been in a project that hasn't had that odor.
>
> —from "To Defray Expenses"

MEANDERING SENTENCES: Long, rambling sentences provide a powerful sensory experience, immersing readers in a description, in an action, or in a particular train of thought. Writer Tom Wolfe is a master of the meandering sentence, as you will see in the following description of suburban life.

> The incredible postwar American electro-pastel surge into the suburbs!—it was sweeping the Valley, with superhighways, dreamboat cars, shopping centers, soaring thirty-foot Federal Signs & Signal Company electric supersculptures—Eight New Plexiglas Display Features!—a surge of freedom and mobility, of cars and the money to pay for them and the time to enjoy them and a home where you can laze in the rich pool of pale wall-to-wall or roar through the technological wonderworld in motor launches . . .
>
> —from *The Electric Kool-Aid Acid Test*

LISTS: Presenting a list of related ideas gives readers a general, holistic look at a subject. Here is the start of a whimsical list that writer Peter Stillman developed in a personal correspondence. (The actual list includes 19 cars in all.)

> A '38 Buick convertible with a rumble seat and a Fireball eight
> A '32 Packard Victoria with cut-glass bud vases and a 7-foot hood
> A '38 Packard sedan whose clutch my girlfriend blew out
> A '40 Plymouth 2-door with the shift right up there on the wheel
>
> —from *Families Writing*

MULTIGENRE WRITING: A paper consisting of a series, or collage, of "mini compositions" challenges readers to determine the unifying principle or theme. A number of different genres may be employed: poetry, lists, brief reminiscences, reports, dialogues, etc. Multigenre writing allows you to develop your thoughts about a subject from a number of different angles.

Checking for Common Ailments

To write with style, you must know what to look for when a piece doesn't sound smooth and natural. Always check for the three ailments listed below as well as the one on the following page ("Avoiding Cliches"). You should also refer to the information on sentences in the next chapter.

PRIMER STYLE: If your writing contains many short sentences, one right after another, it may sound like a primary-grade textbook, or "primer."

> A special faculty committee announced a new policy for makeup exams. It seems unreasonable. Students must complete makeup exams within a week. Extensions will be granted only in emergency situations. Emergencies include serious health problems. They also include family crises.

The Cure: The main cure is to combine some of your ideas into longer, smoother-reading sentences. Here's the same passage revised.

> A special faculty committee announced a new policy for makeup exams that seems unreasonable. Students must complete makeup exams within a week. Extensions will be granted only in emergency situations, including serious health problems and family crises.

PASSIVE VOICE: If your writing seems slow moving and impersonal, you may have used too many passive verbs. With passive verbs, the subject of the sentence receives the action: *The tree was struck by lightning.* Here's an example passage written in the passive voice.

> The latest poetry jam was enjoyed by everyone. Every reading was greeted with hoots, hollers, and foot stomping. The final performance was the object of the most vocal outpouring by the audience. This poem about "macho men" was performed by Larry Smith.

The Cure: Unless you need a passive verb, change it to the active voice: *Lightning struck the tree.* Here is the passage written in the active voice.

> Everyone enjoyed the latest poetry jam. Hoots, hollers, and foot stomping greeted each reading. The final performance garnered the audience's most vocal outpouring when Larry Smith shared his poem about "macho men."

INSECURITY: Does your writing contain many qualifiers (*to be perfectly honest, to tell the truth,* etc.) or intensifiers (*really, truly,* etc.)? Ironically these words and phrases may suggest that you lack confidence in your ideas.

> I totally and completely agree with Dr. Stark about expanding the course offerings, but that's only my opinion.

The Cure: Never hesitate to say exactly what you mean. Here is the revised example.

> I agree with Dr. Stark about expanding the course offerings.

Avoiding Cliches

Cliches are comparisons we use so much that we don't see them as comparisons anymore. We speak of the "face" of a clock, a chubby man's "spare tire," or the class "clown" without even thinking about the effectiveness of the language.

Sensitive writers try never to use cliches unthinkingly. But sometimes they twist them, stretch them, or turn them upside down to raise the metaphor from the dead. The face of the clock might become the face of time; a chubby man's spare tire might become the B. F. Goodrich around his waist.

 INSIDE info The word "cliche" is itself a metaphor. Literally, a cliche was a metal plate used in a printing process called "stereotyping." Figuratively, we use the words "cliche" and "stereotype" to refer to words and ideas that are cranked out again and again.

Worn-out Expressions

Here are a few tired words and phrases you may want to avoid:

like a house on fire	beat around the bush
kick the bucket	piece of cake
between a rock and a hard place	stick your neck out
easy as pie	green with envy
as good as dead	burning bridges
up a creek	working like a dog
throwing your weight around	waging a lonely battle
wet blanket	planting the seed
rearing its ugly head	an axe to grind

Other Types of Cliches

There are other aspects of your writing that may also be tired and overworked. Be alert to these types of cliches as well.

CLICHES OF PURPOSE

- Essays to please the instructor
- Sentimental papers mourning over lost loves, gushing about an ideal friend or family member, or droning on about moving experiences
- Short stories with simple lessons at the end

CLICHES OF VOICE

- **The junior analyst:** "I have determined that there are three basic types of newspapers. My preference is for the third."
- **The faceless reporter:** "Overall, homecoming weekend went beautifully. A good time was had by all."
- **The gum-cracking enthusiast:** "I flipped when I saw *Romeo and Juliet*."

Using Clear, Fair Language

When it comes to depicting individuals or groups according to inherent differences, use language that implies equal value and respect for all people. To guide your thinking and help you produce bias-free writing, read through the main points listed below. Also refer to the following three pages when you have a specific question about identifying an individual or a group in your writing. Listed on these pages are preferred references arranged according to ethnicity, age, disabilities, gender, and occupations.

Treating Others Fairly in Writing

Know what's recommended or acceptable. ● United States citizens of African descent have been called, at various times over the years, colored, Negro, black, Afro-American, people of color, and African-American. The latter reference is widely used and accepted today, but may or may not be in the future. It's up to you to remain sensitive to the recommended or acceptable ways in which to refer to individuals and groups.

Put people first. ● When writing about people with disabilities, remember to put the person first and the disability second. Using terms like "disabled," "neurotics," "paraplegics," and "wheelchair users" emphasizes the disability, not the person. Always focus your attention on the individual and refer to his or her disability only if it is essential information. For example, use the phrase *patient with neurosis* rather than calling someone a *neurotic.* (See 063 for more information about referring to individuals with disabilities or impairments.)

Avoid unnecessary references or labels. ● Unless it is absolutely necessary, avoid identifying a person's sex, age, ethnicity, or disability. A paper about the religious differences in a specific community would certainly require references to religious affiliations and, perhaps, references to the ethnicity of various individuals. However, if you are simply describing an incident in a college lab, it is unnecessary to state whether the students were Chinese, Latino, or African-American.

Don't lump people together. ● Spanish-speaking citizens of the United States may object to the term *Hispanic* because it brings to mind the colonial history of Spain in the New World. They may prefer more specific terms such as *Mexican Americans, Cuban Americans,* etc. Others may feel that another term such as *Latino* is best. Native Americans may prefer being called by the name of their specific nation, or tribe.

Be understanding and empathetic. ● Put yourself in the place of whomever you are writing about, and refer to this person or group in a fair and thoughtful way. Using the term "juvenile" to refer to someone ages 13-19 might be unacceptable because of its association with juvenile delinquency. Individuals over 65 may prefer being called "older adults" rather than "the elderly."

A Fair Writing Style

Be aware that nonsexist terms, cultural and age references, and disability descriptions change over time. Make every effort to know individual and group preferences in these matters. The information that follows will help you write in a bias-free manner.

061 ADDRESSING ETHNICITY

Acceptable General Terms	Acceptable Specific Terms
American Indians, Native Americans	**Cherokee people, Inuit people,** *etc.*
Asian Americans (not *Orientals*)	**Chinese Americans, Japanese Americans,** *etc.*
Hispanic Americans or **Hispanics**	**Mexican Americans, Cuban Americans,** *etc.*

African-Americans, blacks

"African-American" has come into wide acceptance, though the term "black" is preferred by some individuals.

Anglo-Americans (English ancestry), European Americans

Use these terms to avoid the notion that "American," used alone, means "white."

Additional References

Not Recommended	Preferred
Eurasian, mulatto	**person of mixed ancestry**
nonwhite	**people of color**
Caucasian	**white**
Americans (to mean U.S. citizens)	**U.S. citizens**

062 ADDRESSING AGE

General Age Group	Acceptable Terms
Up to age 13 or 14	**boys, girls**
Between 13 and 19	**youth, young people, young men, young women**
Late teens and 20's	**young adults, young women, young men**
30's to age 60	**adults, men, women**
60 and older	**older adults, older people** (not *elderly*)
65 and older	**seniors** (*senior citizens* also acceptable)

063 ADDRESSING DISABILITIES OR IMPAIRMENTS

In the recent past, some writers were choosing alternatives to the term *disabled,* including *physically challenged, exceptional,* or *special.* It is now generally held that these new terms are not precise enough to serve those who do live with disabilities. Of course, degrading labels like *crippled, invalid,* and *maimed,* as well as overly negative terminology, must still be avoided.

Not Recommended	*Preferred*
(too negative)	
handicapped	**disabled**
birth defect	**congenital disability**
stutter, stammer, lisp.	**speech impairment**
an AIDS victim	**person with AIDS**
suffering from cancer.	**person who has cancer**

064 PUTTING PEOPLE FIRST

People with various disabilities and conditions have sometimes been referred to as though they *were* their condition *(quadriplegics, depressives, epileptics)* instead of simply people who happen to have a particular disability. As much as possible, remember to refer to the person first, the disability second.

Not Recommended	*Preferred*
(emphasis on disability)	
the disabled.	**people with disabilities**
the retarded	**people with mental retardation**
dyslexics	**students with dyslexia**
neurotics.	**patients with neuroses**
subjects, cases	**participants, patients**
quadriplegics.	**people who are quadriplegic**
a wheelchair user	**people who use wheelchairs**

065 ADDITIONAL TERMS

Make sure you understand the following terms that address specific impairments:

hearing impairment	= partial hearing loss (not deaf, which is total loss of hearing)
visual impairment	= partially sighted (not blind, which is total loss of vision)
communicative disorder	= speech, hearing, and learning disabilities affecting communication

066 ## ADDRESSING GENDER

- Use parallel language for both sexes:

   The **men** and the **women** rebuilt the school together.

   Hank and **Marie**

   Mr. Robert Gumble, Mrs. Joy Gumble

   NOTE: The courtesy titles *Mr., Ms., Mrs.,* and *Miss* ought to be used according to the person's preference.

- Use nonsexist alternatives to words with masculine connotations:

   humanity (not *mankind*)   **synthetic** (not *man-made*)
   artisan (not *craftsman*)

- Do not use masculine-only pronouns *(he, his, him)* when you want to refer to a human being in general:

   A politician can kiss privacy good-bye when he runs for office.
   (not recommended)

   Instead, use *he or she,* or change the sentence to the plural:

   Politicians can kiss privacy good-bye when they run for office.

- Do not use gender-specific references in the salutation of a business letter when you don't know the person's name:

   Dear Sir: **Dear Gentlemen:**

   Instead, address a position:

   Dear Personnel Officer:

   Dear Members of the Economic Committee:

067 ## OCCUPATIONAL ISSUES

Not Recommended	Preferred
chairman	chair, presiding officer, moderator
salesman	sales representative, salesperson
mailman	mail carrier, postal worker, letter carrier
insurance man	insurance agent
fireman	firefighter
businessman	executive, manager, businessperson
congressman	member of Congress, representative, senator

Do use gender-inclusive terms.

What NOT to Use	What to Use
steward, stewardess	flight attendant
policeman, policewoman	police officer

Making Sentences Work

Editor Roscoe Born describes a good sentence as a "rifle shot—one missile, precisely aimed—rather than a buckshot load sprayed in the general direction of the target." This metaphor calls attention to a few key points related to sentence structure: Sentences work when they are clear, direct, and to the point. They work when they have the right sound, balance, and substance. And they work when they move smoothly from one point to the next. When the sentences in a piece of writing consistently hit the mark, the end result is an effective finished product.

WHAT'S AHEAD

This chapter will help you write "precisely aimed rifle shots." You'll find sets of guidelines to help you write clear, complete, and natural sentences, as well as guidelines to help you write sentences modeled after your favorite authors. Turn here whenever you have a question about your sentences.

- **Writing Complete Sentences**
- **Writing Clear Sentences**
- **Writing Natural Sentences**
- **Writing Acceptable Sentences**
- **Combining Sentences**
- **Modeling Sentences**
- **Expanding Sentences**

Writing Complete Sentences

Except in a few special situations, you should use complete sentences when you write. By definition, a complete sentence expresses a complete thought. However, a sentence may actually contain several ideas, not just one. The trick is getting those ideas to work together to form a clear, interesting sentence that expresses your exact meaning.

Among the most common sentence errors that writers make are **fragments, comma splices, rambling sentences,** and **run-ons.**

"A sentence should read as if its author, had he held a plough instead of a pen, could have drawn a furrow deep and straight to the end." —Henry David Thoreau

070   A **fragment** is a group of words used as a sentence. It is not a sentence, however, because it lacks a subject, a verb, or some other essential part. That missing part creates an incomplete thought.

Fragment: **The mountainous coastline with grand, fjord-like waterways.** (This phrase lacks a verb.)

Sentence: **The mountainous coastline greets you with grand, fjord-like waterways.**

Fragment: **If you approach New Zealand's South Island from the southwest.** (This clause is an incomplete thought. We need to know what happens "if you approach New Zealand's South Island from the southwest.")

Sentence: **If you approach New Zealand's South Island from the southwest, the mountainous coastline greets you with grand, fjord-like waterways.**

Fragment: **We plan to visit the strangely beautiful Lake Taupo area of North Island. Boiling springs, hot geysers, pools of steaming mud, and waterfalls cascading from volcanic peaks.** (This is a sentence followed by a fragment. You can correct this error by combining the fragment with the sentence.)

Sentence: **We plan to visit the strangely beautiful Lake Taupo area of North Island with its boiling springs, hot geysers, pools of steaming mud, and waterfalls cascading from volcanic peaks.**

071 A **comma splice** is a mistake made when two independent clauses are connected ("spliced") with only a comma. The comma is not enough: a period, semicolon, or conjunction is needed.

Splice: **The commuters had been bottlenecked on the freeway for two hours, the type A's had a crazed look in their eyes, the type B's were napping.**

Corrected: **The commuters had been bottlenecked on the freeway for two hours; the type A's had a crazed look in their eyes, but the type B's were napping.**
(A semicolon and the coordinating conjunction *but* have been added to correct the two splices.)

Corrected: **The commuters had been bottlenecked on the freeway for two hours. The type A's had a crazed look in their eyes, but the type B's were napping.**
(A period corrects the first splice in this instance.)

072 A **rambling sentence** is one that seems to go on and on. It is often the result of the overuse of the word "and."

Rambling: **The intruder entered through the window and moved sideways down the hall and under a stairwell and she stood waiting in the shadows.**

Corrected: **The intruder entered through the window. She moved sideways down the hall and under a stairwell where she stood, waiting in the shadows.**

073 A **run-on sentence** is actually two sentences joined without adequate punctuation or a connecting word.

Run-on: **I thought the test would never end I had a classic case of finger cramps with brain-drain complications.**

Corrected: **I thought the test would never end. I had a classic case of finger cramps with brain-drain complications.**
(A period corrects the run-on sentence.)

SOUND
advice When you write dialogue, fragments are not mistakes. In fact, they are often preferable to complete sentences because that's how people talk:

"Hey, Vin. B'ball at Towner Court?"
"Yeah, 'bout 2:30."
"Ciao, till then."

074 Writing Clear Sentences

Writing is thinking. Before you can write clearly, you must think clearly. Nothing is more frustrating for the reader than writing that has to be reread just to understand its basic meaning.

Look carefully at the common errors that follow. Do you recognize any of them as errors you sometimes make in your own writing? If so, use this section as a checklist when you revise. Conquering these errors will help to make your writing clear and readable.

"If any man wishes to write in a clear style let him first be clear in his thoughts." —Johann Wolfgang von Goethe

075 **Misplaced modifiers** are modifiers that have been placed incorrectly; therefore, the meaning of the sentence is not clear.

Misplaced: **The pool staff offers large beach towels to the students marked with chlorine-resistant ID numbers.** (Students marked with chlorine-resistant ID numbers?)

Corrected: **The pool staff offers students large beach towels marked with chlorine-resistant ID numbers.**

076 **Dangling modifiers** are modifiers that appear to modify the wrong word or a word that isn't in the sentence.

Dangling: **Positioning himself to make the winning goal in the water polo match, Jacque's father yelled from the sideline.** (The phrase "positioning himself to make the winning goal in the water polo match" appears to modify Jacque's father.)

Corrected: **Positioning himself to make the winning goal in the water polo match, Jacque heard his father yelling from the sideline.**

Dangling: **Still failing to understand the concept, the biophysics prof gave the students a list of extra reading assignments.** (In this sentence, it appears as though the professor is "still failing to understand the concept.")

Corrected: **Still failing to understand the concept, the students received a list of extra reading assignments from the biophysics professor.** (Now the phrase clearly modifies those who are "failing to understand"—the students.)

077 An **incomplete comparison** is the result of leaving out a word or words that are necessary to show exactly what is being compared to what.

Incomplete: **Helium is a lighter gas.**

Clear: **Helium is a lighter gas than oxygen.**

Incomplete: **I get along better with Rhoda than my roommate.** (Do you mean that you get along better with Rhoda than you get along with your roommate, or that you get along better with Rhoda than your roommate does?)

Clear: **I get along better with Rhoda than my roommate does.**

078 **Ambiguous wording** is wording that is unclear because it has two or more possible meanings. It often occurs when sentences are combined.

Ambiguous: **Todd decided to have pizza delivered to the lab where he was doing his experiment, which ended in disaster.** (What ended in disaster—Todd's ordering pizza in, or the experiment?)

Clear: **Todd decided to have pizza delivered to the lab where he was doing his experiment, a decision that ended in disaster.**

079 An **indefinite reference** is a problem caused by careless use of pronouns. As a result, the reader is not sure what the pronoun or pronouns are referring to.

Indefinite: **When the pizza man arrived, *she* came wheeling around the corner with an enlarged copy of the "No Food in the Lab" rule sheet.** (Who is *she*?)

Clear: **When the pizza man arrived, Ms. Fenton, the TA, came wheeling around the corner with an enlarged copy of the "No Food in the Lab" rule sheet.**

Indefinite: **As a startled Mr. Pizza Man attempted to slide the pizza next to the test-tube rack, it fell to the floor.** (What fell, the pizza or the rack?)

Clear: **As a startled Mr. Pizza Man attempted to slide the pizza next to the test-tube rack, the rack fell to the floor.**

080 Writing Natural Sentences

Samuel Johnson, the noted eighteenth-century writer, had this to say about the great temptation to overwrite, using big words, clever words, fancy words: "Read over your compositions and, when you meet a passage which you think is particularly fine, strike it out." For some reason, many people think that writing simply, is not writing effectively. Nothing can be further from the truth.

The very best writing is ordinary and natural, not fancy and artificial. That's why it is so important to master the art of free writing. It is your best chance at a personal style. A personal voice will produce natural, honest passages you will not have to strike out. Learn from the following samples, which are wordy and artificial.

"Read over your compositions and, when you meet a passage which you think is particularly fine, strike it out." —Samuel Johnson

081 **Deadwood** is wording that fills up lots of space but does not add anything important or new to the overall meaning.

Deadwood: I must tell you that, according to a lot of research out there, excessive partying, plus the chronic sleeping in that goes with it, will almost assuredly result in dismally poor grades.

Concise: Excessive partying and chronic sleeping in will probably result in poor grades.

082 **Flowery language** is writing that uses more or bigger words than needed. This writing often contains too many adjectives or adverbs.

Flowery: The gorgeous beauty of the Great Barrier Reef is fantastically displayed in coral formations of all the colors of the rainbow and in its wonderful, wide variety of tropical fish.

Concise: The beauty of the Great Barrier Reef is displayed in rainbow-colored coral formations and in a wide variety of tropical fish.

083 A **trite expression** is one that is overused and stale; as a result, it sounds neither sincere nor natural.

> *Trite:* **In view of the fact that the class is filled, we regret to inform you that we cannot admit you to Microbiology 202.**
>
> *Natural:* **Unfortunately, because the class is filled, we cannot admit you to Microbiology 202.**

084 **Jargon** is language used in a certain profession or by a particular group of people. It is usually very technical and not at all natural.

> *Jargon:* **I'm having conceptual difficulty with these academic queries.**
>
> *Natural:* **I don't understand these review questions.**

085 A **euphemism** is a word or phrase that is substituted for another because it is considered a less offensive way of saying something. (Avoid overusing euphemisms.)

> *Euphemism:* **This environmentally challenged room has the distinct odor of a sanitary landfill.**
>
> *Natural:* **This filthy room smells like a garbage dump.**

086 **Redundancy** occurs when words (or synonyms for words) are repeated unnecessarily to add emphasis or to fill up space.

> *Redundant:* **Don't drive through the construction site, and be sure to pick a different route if you want to avoid riding over nails and risking a flat tire.**
>
> *Concise:* **Don't drive through the construction site if you want to avoid a flat tire.**

NOTE: Here are some common redundancies to avoid: *refer back, close proximity, during the time when, enter into, red in color, repeat again.*

087 A **cliche** is an overused word or phrase that springs quickly to mind but just as quickly bores the user and the audience. A cliche gives the reader nothing new or original to think about and may even be confusing. (See 059 for more information.)

> *Cliche:* **Advice for freshmen: Put your best foot forward!**
>
> *Natural:* **Advice for freshmen: Have confidence that you can succeed!**

088 Writing Acceptable Sentences

What Robert Frost says below is very true. Much of the color and charm of literature comes from the everyday habits, the customs, and especially the speech of its characters. It's important to keep that in mind when you write fiction of any kind. However, when you write essays, reports, and most other assignments, remember that it's just as important to use language that is correct and appropriate.

> *"You can be a little ungrammatical if you come from the right part of the country."* —Robert Frost

089

Substandard (nonstandard) **language** is language that is often acceptable in everyday conversation and in fictional writing, but seldom in other forms of writing.

Colloquial:	Avoid the use of colloquial language, such as *go with* or *wait up*. **Hey, wait up! Cal wants to go with.** (Substandard) **Hey, wait! Cal wants to go with us.** (Standard)
Double preposition:	Avoid the use of certain double prepositions: *off of, off to, from off*. **Pick up the sandwich scraps and dirty clothes from off the floor.** (Substandard) **Pick up the sandwich scraps and dirty clothes from the floor.** (Standard)
Substitution:	Avoid substituting *and* for *to*. **Try and get to class on time.** (Substandard) **Try to get to class on time.** (Standard) Avoid substituting *of* for *have* when combining with *could, would, should,* or *might*. **I should of studied for that exam.** (Substandard) **I should have studied for that exam.** (Standard)
Slang:	Avoid the use of slang or any "in" words. **Darrell is *livin' phat!*** **This *herb* thinks he's *bad.***

090 A **double negative** is a sentence that contains two negative words used to express a single negative idea. Double negatives are unacceptable in academic writing.

Awkward: **After paying for food and other essentials, I haven't got no money left.**

Corrected: **I haven't got any money left. / I have no money left.**

NOTE: Do not use *hardly, barely,* or *scarcely* with a negative; the result is a double negative.

091 A **shift in construction** is a change in the structure or style midway through a sentence.

Shift in number: **When a person first goes apartment hunting, *they* ought to look for one that is both comfortable and affordable.**

Corrected: **When a person first goes apartment hunting, *he or she* ought to look for one that is both comfortable and affordable.**

Shift in tense: **Sheila looked over nine apartments in one weekend before she *had chosen* one.**

Corrected: **Sheila looked over nine apartments in one weekend before she *chose* one.**

Shift in person: **You really should check the cupboards, too, or *one* may be surprised later by mice and other critters.**

Corrected: **You really should check the cupboards, too, or *you* may be surprised later by mice and other critters.**

Shift in voice: **As you continue** (active voice) **to look for just the right place to live, many dirty, dumpy apartments will probably be toured** (passive voice).

Corrected: **As you continue to look for just the right place to live, you will probably tour many dirty, dumpy apartments.**
(The verbs *continue* and *will tour* are both active voice.)

092 **Inconsistent** (unparallel) **construction** occurs when the kind of words or phrases being used changes in the middle of a sentence.

Inconsistent: **In my hometown, students use free time to shoot hoops, play video games, and eating fast food.**
(The sentence switched from the base verbs *shoot* and *play* to the participle *eating.*)

Corrected: **In my hometown, students use free time to shoot hoops, play video games, and eat fast food.**
(Now all three activities are expressed in a consistent or parallel fashion.)

Combining Sentences

Most mature sentences contain several basic ideas that work together to form a complete thought. For example, if you were to write a sentence about the construction of the Great Wall of China, you would probably be working with several different ideas:

1. The longest and largest construction project in history was the Great Wall of China.

2. The project took 1,700 years to complete.

3. The Great Wall of China is 1,400 miles long.

4. It is between 18 and 30 feet high.

5. It is up to 32 feet thick.

The Process in Action

Of course, you wouldn't express each idea separately like this. Instead, you would combine these ideas (some or all of them) into longer, more mature sentences. Sentence combining is generally carried out in the following ways:

● Use a **series** to combine three or more similar ideas.

The Great Wall of China is **1,400 miles long**, between **18 and 30 feet high**, and up to **32 feet thick**.

● Use a **relative pronoun** *(who, whose, that, which)* to introduce subordinate (less important) ideas.

The Great Wall of China, **which is 1,400 miles long and between 18 and 30 feet high**, took 1,700 years to complete.

● Use an **introductory phrase** or **clause**.

Having taken 1,700 years to complete, the Great Wall of China was the longest construction project in history.

● Use a **semicolon** (and a conjunctive adverb if appropriate).

The Great Wall took 1,700 years to complete; it is 1,400 miles long and up to 30 feet high and 32 feet thick.

● Repeat a **key word** or phrase to emphasize an idea.

The Great Wall of China was the longest construction **project** in history, a **project** that took 1,700 years to complete.

● Use **correlative conjunctions** *(either, or; not only, but also)* to compare or contrast two ideas in a sentence.

The Great Wall of China is **not only** up to 30 feet high and 32 feet thick, **but also** 1,400 miles long.

● Use an **appositive** (a word or phrase that renames) to emphasize an idea.

The Great Wall of China—**the largest construction project in history**—is 1,400 miles long, 32 feet thick, and up to 30 feet high.

Modeling Sentences

What you find when you study the sentences of your favorite authors may surprise you—sentences that seem to flow on forever, sentences that hit you right between the eyes, sentences that sneak up on you, and "sentences" that are not, by definition, sentences at all. Writers do occasionally break the rules.

 INSIDE info   Generally speaking, contemporary authors write in a relaxed, somewhat informal style. This style is characterized by sentences with a lot of personality, rhythm, and varied structures.

The Modeling Process

You will want to imitate certain sentences in your own writing simply because they sound good or make a point so well. This process is sometimes called **modeling.** Like sentence combining, sentence modeling can help you improve your writing style. Here's how you can get started:

- ⊚ **RESERVE** a special section in a notebook or journal to list effective sentences you come across in your reading.

- ⊚ **LIST** well-made sentences that flow smoothly, that use effective descriptive words, or that contain original figures of speech (metaphor, simile, personification, etc.).

- ⊚ **STUDY** each sentence so you know how it is put together. Read it out loud. Look for phrases and clauses set off by commas. Also focus on word endings (-*ing*, -*ed*, etc.) and on the location of articles (*a, an, the*) and prepositions (*to, by, of,* etc.).

- ⊚ **WRITE** your own version of a sentence by imitating it part by part. Try to use the same word endings, articles, and prepositions, but work in your own nouns, verbs, and modifiers. (Your imitation does not have to be exact.) Practice writing a number of different versions.

- ⊚ **CONTINUE** imitating good sentences. The more you practice, the more you will find professional-sounding sentences in your own essays and stories.

The Process in Action

Study the following interesting sentence:

> **He has a thin face with sharp features and a couple of eyes burning with truth oil.**   —Tom Wolfe

Now look carefully at the modeled version: (Compare it part by part to the original sentence. Can you see how the imitation was carried out?)

> **He has an athletic body with a sinewy contour and a couple of arms bulging with weight-room dedication.**

Expanding Sentences

All the right elements seem to spill out of accomplished writers' minds naturally. Readers marvel at how effectively these authors can **expand** a basic idea with engaging details. We envy good writers for this special ability, and we wish we could write in the same way.

Cumulative Sentences

The specific type of sentence that marks an accomplished and stylistic writer is the *cumulative sentence*. What you normally find in a cumulative sentence is a main idea that is expanded by modifying words, phrases, or clauses. In such a sentence, the details usually build after the main clause, creating a stylistic, image-rich thought. Here's an example: (The main idea is in italics.)

Julie was studying at the kitchen table, memorizing a list of vocabulary words, completely focused, intent on acing her Spanish quiz.

DISCUSSION: Notice how each new modifier adds another level of meaning to the sentence. Also notice that each of these modifying phrases is set off by a comma. (When you write cumulative sentences, plan on using a lot of commas.) Here's another sample sentence:

Tony is laughing, halfheartedly, with his hands on his face, looking puzzled.

DISCUSSION: Notice in this example that one of the modifiers is a single word *(halfheartedly)*. Also note how each modifier changes the flow, or rhythm, of the sentence.

Expanding with Details

Here are seven basic ways to expand a main idea:

1. with **individual words:** *halfheartedly*
2. with **prepositional phrases:** *with his hands on his face*
3. with **absolute phrases:** *his head tilted to one side*
4. with **participial (-ing or -ed) phrases:** *looking puzzled*
5. with **infinitive phrases:** *to hide his embarrassment*
6. with **subordinate clauses:** *while his friend talks*
7. with **relative clauses:** *who isn't laughing at all*

bottom LINE

It will take time and effort on your part to write stylistic sentences. First, start modeling sentences (see the previous page). Second, practice sentence expanding, following our advice above. And third, become a regular reader and writer. This last step is probably the most important. You must immerse yourself in the language in order to use it well.

Developing Strong Paragraphs

When it comes to writing well in college, you must remember these two words: support and organization. You need to select details that support your main point, and you need to organize those details effectively. That's where the simple, time-honored tradition of paragraphing comes into play. Paragraphs help you organize your thoughts and make it easier for readers to follow your line of thinking.

During the sometimes messy revising process, it is the paragraph that makes it possible for you to rearrange your details into logical units that deliver a strong, clear message from start to finish. You'll know your writing is finished when each paragraph works by itself and with the others that come before and after it.

WHAT'S AHEAD

Using guidelines and models, this chapter offers good advice for managing topic sentences. Then it shows how to arrange details so that your paragraphs will "flow." At the end, you'll find a "Quick Guide" to help you revise for stronger paragraphs.

- **Writing Focused Paragraphs**
- **Selecting Supporting Details**
- **Arranging Your Details**
- **Connecting Your Details**

Writing Focused Paragraphs

In order for a paragraph to be an effective unit of thought, it must

1. **address a topic,**
2. **communicate a specific idea about the topic, and**
3. **develop that idea with supporting details.**

The specific idea, often stated explicitly in a topic sentence, establishes the focus for readers and suggests where the paragraph will lead. The rest of the paragraph expands the idea through analysis, definition, examples, and support in the form of facts, statistics, details, and quotations. As a paragraph writer, you want readers to understand the idea, accept it, and care about it.

The Topic Sentence

The topic sentence tells readers what your subject is and what you plan to say about it. Because it forecasts what the paragraph will say, the topic sentence helps you, the writer, decide what to include and exclude from the paragraph. If any words or sentences do not expand on the idea in the topic sentence, they do not belong in the paragraph. To write an effective topic sentence, use the formula below:

Formula: A topic sentence = a limited topic + a specific idea

Example: The economic mind-set of the baby-boomer generation [limited topic] is an enigma to survivors of the Great Depression [specific idea].

Positioning the Topic Sentence

As you develop paragraphs, you may naturally place your topic sentence first, but that isn't always necessary. You can position your topic sentence anywhere in the paragraph, as long as you have a good reason and can logically lead up to and away from it. When deciding where to put the topic sentence, consider the following:

THE WRITING OCCASION ● What type of writing are you doing, and what does that form dictate about paragraph development? Is the piece informal or strictly academic?

THE READER ● What would the curious reader find to be clear, interesting, and effective?

THE CONTEXT ● How does the entire paragraph fit with those that precede and follow it?

Placing the Topic Sentence First

Put the topic sentence first when you want to be absolutely direct—stating the main idea and then developing it. With this placement, readers understand the direction of your thinking right from the start, and can see how that thinking relates to the previous paragraph. (The excerpt below, taken from student writer Heather Hamilton's essay on Scotland, begins with the last sentence of the paragraph that precedes the model.)

. . . If what you seek is quiet, peace, and a time to reflect, I can think of no better hideaway than Scotland.

However, the paradox of Scotland is that violence had long been the norm in this now-peaceful land. In fact, the country was born, bred, and came of age in war. The Picts were the first inhabitants, fierce men so named by the Romans because tattoos covered their bodies like paint. The mighty Romans could not conquer them, so the Empire had to erect two huge walls to keep them out. Eventually, both walls fell, and the Romans left. By 844, Picts were united with the Scots, invaders from Ireland, under Kenneth MacAlpin, the first king of Scotland. The loosely knit nation of clans then spent nearly the next millennium fighting against the English and each other. But unlike the Irish nationalists, the Scots fell silent after the last uprising was crushed in the eighteenth century.

Placing the Topic Sentence at the End

Put the paragraph's key idea at the end when you want to give details or arguments that build up to it, a strategy particularly useful in persuasive writing. The paragraph below, from student writer Jeff Krosschell's paper on changes in affirmative action, uses a question to introduce the main idea, but saves the topic sentence for the end.

How, exactly, has the definition of "affirmative action" changed since the concept became an issue in the 1960's? William Bradford Reynolds, former assistant attorney general in the Civil Rights Division, describes this process in "Affirmative Action and Its Negative Repercussions." When affirmative action started in the sixties, it was meant to help everybody, not just certain ethnic groups. As Reynolds says, it was "originally defined in terms of active recruitment and outreach measures aimed at enhancing employment for all Americans" (38). But in the '70s this broad definition narrowed. Reynolds argues that during that decade, affirmative action turned into a tool for creating racial balance in the workplace. It became more selective about which groups it enhanced employment opportunities for. After several court battles in the '80s and the Civil Rights Act of 1991, the definition of affirmative action changed again: it came to be seen as a tool of last resort in cases of persistent discrimination. **Thus, through four decades of struggle and social change, affirmative action has shifted from its original meaning and purpose.**

Placing the Topic Sentence in the Middle

Put the topic sentence in the middle of the paragraph when you want to build up to the main idea, and then lead away from it. Such an approach can let you show two sides of an issue, hinged on a central topic sentence. In the paragraph below, student writer Jacqueline Williams compares events portrayed in a film with events that were part of the filmmaking process.

During the making of *Apocalypse Now,* Eleanor Coppola, wife of the film's director, gathered documentary footage of how the movie was being made. This footage became a separate film called *Hearts of Darkness: A Filmmaker's Apocalypse.* In the first film, the renegade Kurtz has disappeared with his men and native followers into the Cambodian jungle. Having gone insane, he carries on his own war using his own brutal methods. The film's main character, Captain Willard, is to "find and terminate" Kurtz. As Willard's search for Kurtz lengthens, the screen fills with horror—flames, smoke, exploding bodies, burning bodies, and blood. **However, as *Hearts of Darkness* . . . relates, the horror and insanity portrayed in the fictional *Apocalypse Now* was, in fact, being lived out in the real lives of the production company.** In the second film, director Francis Ford Coppola says about the first one, "too much money, too much equipment, and little by little we went insane" *(Hearts).* In the same film, Larry Fishburn, who played one of Willard's men, says, "War is fun. You can do anything you want to. That's why Vietnam must have been so much fun for the guys out there" *(Hearts).* Toward the end of the filming of *Apocalypse Now,* Martin Sheen, who played Willard, suffered a life-threatening heart attack. When one of Coppola's assistants sent the news back to the investors in the United States, the director exploded: "Even if Marty dies, he's not dead unless I say he's dead" *(Hearts).*

Creating Coherence

In addition to writing a clear topic sentence, you can do several other things to keep your paragraphs coherent and focused.

- **Monitor the use of tense throughout a paragraph to avoid confusion.** The above paragraph opens and closes in the past tense; references to the screenplays, however, are all in the present tense, as they should be.

- **Use parallel constructions to increase readability and clarity.** Phrases such as "In the first film," "In the second film," and "In the same film" help readers keep the two films straight.

- **Repeat key words or phrases for added meaning and emphasis.** "Having gone insane" and later "little by little we went insane" emphasize the focus of the paragraph.

- **Use transitions to improve the flow of ideas.** Words like "during," "however," and "toward the end" serve to keep readers on track throughout the paragraph.

Selecting Supporting Details

Whatever the writing occasion—research paper, informal essay, or business letter—your paragraphs need interesting, specific details to lend support and substance to your ideas. It is, after all, the details that make a paragraph worth reading. The information below will help you look for and find appropriate support for your writing.

TYPES OF DETAILS

When writing any paragraph, ask, "What types of details will best support and develop my key idea?"

facts	anecdotes	analyses	paraphrases
statistics	quotations	explanations	comparisons
examples	definitions	summaries	analogies

SELECTING SPECIFIC DETAILS

From the types listed above, choose specific details based on your writing situation:

- If you're **describing** something, ask . . .

  What details would help readers see, smell, taste, touch, or hear what I'm describing?

- If you're **explaining** something or giving instructions, ask . . .

  What details would help readers understand what this term or concept means, or what details would help the reader follow this procedure?

- If you're **persuading**, ask . . .

  What details would help readers understand why my argument is reasonable, logical, and true?

- If you're **narrating**, ask . . .

  What details would help readers understand the progression and significance of my story from beginning to end?

FINDING DETAILS

How do you find the details to support your topic sentence? Broadly speaking, you do four things:

1. **REFLECT:** By brainstorming, mapping, and free-writing, you can generate memories, explanations, descriptions, and analogies.
2. **OBSERVE:** By looking and listening attentively, you can discover important details and facts.
3. **TALK:** By talking with experienced, knowledgeable people, you can gather material from their firsthand knowledge of a subject.
4. **READ:** By reading newspapers, journals, books, or articles on the Internet, you can find facts, statistics, analyses, and quotations.

Arranging Your Details

Depending upon the type of writing you are doing, you may find it helpful to follow one of the many time-honored methods of arranging details in a paragraph. On the next several pages, you will find explanations and models of each of these methods.

CLASSIFICATION

If you are classifying a subject, begin by placing the subject in the appropriate class, and then provide details that show how the subject is different from others in its class. In the following paragraph from a research paper on medical practices during medieval times, a student writer uses classification to talk about the theory of temperament.

> Medieval doctors believed that "four temperaments rule mankind wholly." According to this theory, each person has a distinctive temperament or personality (sanguine, phlegmatic, melancholy, or choleric) based on the balance of four elements in the body, a balance peculiar to the individual. The theory was built on Galen and Hippocrates' notion of "humors," that the body contains blood, phlegm, black bile, and yellow bile—four fluids that maintain the balance within the body. First, the sanguine person was thought to be dominated by blood, associated with fire: blood was hot and moist, and the person was fat and prone to laughter. Second, the person thought to be dominated by phlegm (associated with earth) was squarish and slothful—a sleepy type. Third, the melancholy person was dominated by cold, black bile (connected with the element of water), and as a result was pensive, peevish, and solitary. Finally, the choleric person was thought to be dominated by hot, yellow bile (air) and thus was inclined to anger.
>
> —Jessica Radsma

Classification is commonly used by science and nature writers to divide subjects into categories. In the following excerpt from a book that has become an environmentalist classic, the author classifies outdoorsmen who do not fit his previously mentioned "deer hunters, duckhunters, bird hunters, and non-hunters."

> There are good outdoorsmen who do not conform to these categories. There is the ornithologist who hunts by ear, and uses the eye only to follow up on what his ear has detected. There is the botanist who hunts by eye, but at much closer range; he is a marvel at finding plants, but seldom sees birds or mammals. There is the forester who sees only trees, and the insects and fungi that prey upon trees; he is oblivious to all else. And finally there is the sportsman who sees only game, and regards all else as of little interest or value.
>
> —Aldo Leopold, *A Sand County Almanac*

CHRONOLOGICAL ORDER

Chronological (time) order is effective for reporting an event, telling a story, or presenting steps in a process. Information is organized according to what happens first, second, third, etc. In the following paragraph, a student writer describes the process of making cement. Notice how he explains every step, carefully using transitional words to lead readers through the process.

> The production of cement is a complicated process in itself. The raw materials that go into cement consist of about 60 percent lime, 25 percent silica, and 5 percent alumina. The remaining 10 percent is a varying combination of gypsum and iron oxide, because the amount of gypsum determines the drying time of the cement. First, this mixture is ground up into very fine particles and fed into a kiln. Cement kilns, the largest pieces of moving machinery used by any industry, are colossal steel cylinders lined with firebricks. They can be 25 feet in diameter and up to 750 feet long. The kiln is built at a slant and turns slowly as the cement mix makes its way down from the top end. A flame at the bottom heats the kiln to temperatures of up to 3,000 degrees Fahrenheit. When the melted cement compound emerges from the kiln, it cools into little marble-like balls called clinker. Finally, the clinker is ground to a consistency finer than flour and packaged as cement.
>
> —Kevin Maas

On many occasions you may include a narrative or an anecdote in your writing. Telling your story in chronological order will help your readers understand and experience the event, as shown in this excerpt from Annie Dillard's writings.

> When I was six or seven years old, growing up in Pittsburgh, I used to take a precious penny of my own and hide it for someone else to find. It was a curious compulsion; sadly, I've never been seized by it since. For some reason I always "hid" the penny along the same stretch of sidewalk up the street. I would cradle it at the roots of a sycamore, say, or in a hole left by a chipped-off piece of sidewalk. Then I would take a piece of chalk, and, starting at either end of the block, draw huge arrows leading up to the penny from both directions. After I learned to write I labeled the arrows: surprise ahead or money this way. I was greatly excited, during all this arrow-drawing, at the thought of the first lucky passer-by who would receive in this way, regardless of merit, a free gift from the universe. But I never lurked about. I would go straight home and not give the matter another thought, until, some months later, I would be gripped again by the impulse to hide another penny.
>
> —Annie Dillard, *Pilgrim at Tinker Creek*

ILLUSTRATION

Illustration (general to specific) is an organization method in which you first state a general idea (like a topic sentence) and follow with specific reasons, examples, facts, and details to support the general idea. In the paragraph that follows a female student talks about her obsession with thinness. The first sentence states this fact, and the sentences that follow supply a variety of details and anecdotes from the writer's agonizing struggle to be thinner than thin.

As the years passed, my obsession grew. Every fiber and cell of my body was obsessed with the number on the scale and how much fat I could pinch on my thigh. No matter how thin I was, I thought I could never be thin enough. I fought my sisters for control of the TV and VCR to do my exercise programs and videos. The cupboards were stacked with cans of diet mixes, the refrigerator full of diet drinks. Hidden in my underwear drawer were stacks of diet pills that I popped along with my vitamins. At my worst, I would quietly excuse myself from family activities to turn on the bathroom faucet full blast and vomit into the toilet. Every day I stood in front of the mirror, a ritual not unlike brushing my teeth, and scrutinized my body. My face, arms, stomach, buttocks, hips, and thighs could never be small enough.

—Paula Treick

In the following paragraph, journalist Pete Hamill offers his definition of courage. He begins with a general definition and then goes on to illustrate this definition with a specific example, an example that clearly shows readers what he means by courage.

Ernest Hemingway once defined courage as grace under pressure, and that's always struck me as an eminently useful definition. The best professional athletes not only possess that kind of courage but, more important, are willing to display it to strangers. Baseball's Reggie Jackson or Richard ("Goose") Gossage, for instance, function most completely as athletes and as men when appearing before gigantic crowds under pressure: bases loaded, late innings, a big game. They come to their tasks with gladness and absolute focus, neither whimpering, complaining nor shirking when doing their job: they just try their best to get that job done. And, of course, sometimes they fail. Gossage gives up a single and his team loses. Jackson strikes out. No matter. The important thing is that such men keep their appointments with confidence and grace. Courage has become so deep a part of their character that they don't even think about it. (They certainly want to win. Sometimes they absolutely lust for victory. But they know that winning isn't everything. All a man can do is his best.)

—Pete Hamill, *Winning Isn't Everything*

CLIMAX

Climax (specific to general) is a method in which you present details followed by a general statement or conclusion drawn from the specific information provided. In this type of paragraph, the details build toward a climactic sentence, as shown in the example below.

> **The cockroach is unhonored and unsung. It walks about with downcast eyes. Its head hangs dejectedly between its knees. It lives on modest fare and in humble circumstances. It is drab-colored and inconspicuous. But don't let that Uriah Heep exterior fool you. For there you have Superbug, himself!**
>
> —Edwin Way Teale, *The Lost Woods*

The next paragraph presents various details and examples of the writer's failure as a fashion maven and builds to a conclusion that he has reached by reflecting on this subject.

> **I'm also hopeless at buying clothes. My twelve-year-old daughter says I dress like somebody out of a time-capsule. It is true my wardrobe hasn't changed much except in the size of collars and pant legs since I turned eight. (I have heard rumors that men these days sometimes go without collars altogether, but I started with collars and am sticking by them.) In my defensive moods—which come over me occasionally, like the flu— I repeat Thoreau's dictim: "Beware of all enterprises that require new clothes, and not rather a new wearer of clothes." Like many folks whose tastes were formed in the boondocks, I'm not so much hostile to fashion as oblivious to it. The breezes of fashion blow hardest where people have time and money on their hands—two items in short supply in the country.**
>
> —Scott Russell Sanders, *The Paradise of Bombs*

In the final paragraph a student writer explains how discussions during carpooling led to her "addiction" to ballet. Notice how the paragraph builds to its climactic three-word finale.

> **While other people entertain friends in their living rooms, I have had some of my most memorable discussions in the car. I have carpooled with several dancers, but Kirsten has been the most influential of the group. She showed me the degree of sacrifice, determination, and devotion needed to succeed, not just in ballet, but in life. I began to study video-tapes of ballets to see what made dancers like Gelsey Kirkland and Makarova truly outstanding. I read books, magazines, and anything remotely related to ballet. I was addicted.**
>
> —Tristan Ching

CAUSE AND EFFECT

Cause-and-effect organization helps you show the relationship between events and their results. If you start with a general statement giving the effect, follow with specific causes; if you begin with a general statement giving the cause, follow with specific effects. In the example below, Lucy More catalogs a list of apparent causes for the dramatic increase in the number of American children on behavior-altering drugs.

> More than 1 million American children are currently on drugs—legally. The drug is Ritalin, a prescription drug considered a Schedule II controlled substance in the same category as cocaine and methadone. So why are these children on such a potent drug? Because they supposedly suffer from Attention Deficit/Hyperactivity Disorder, or ADHD for short. Children who have been labelled ADHD have difficulty focusing their minds and attention. Parents, eager to deal with children who are acting out in school and creating problems at home, ask doctors to prescribe Ritalin. Teachers, seeing dramatic calming effects and academic success for students on medication, are often tempted to recommend the treatment to parents. And doctors, yielding to parental pressure, seem willing to treat children suspected of suffering from ADHD, but who may actually suffer from learning disabilities, anxieties, depression, or other ailments. Where will this lead? What message is it sending to the next generation of parents and children? The use of Ritalin for controlling children's behavior could have far-reaching effects, as young people learn to turn to medication to face life's challenges, rather than working through their problems.
>
> —Lucy More

In the following paragraph, Laura Black discusses the effects of hypothermia on the human body. It shows you another way to arrange details utilizing the cause-and-effect method of development.

> Even a slight drop in the normal human body temperature of 98.6° F causes hypothermia. Often produced by accidental or prolonged exposure to cold, the condition forces all bodily functions to slow down. The heart rate and blood pressure decrease. Breathing becomes slower and shallower. As the body temperature drops, these effects become even more dramatic until somewhere between 86° and 82° F the person lapses into unconsciousness. When the temperature reaches between 65° and 59° F, heart action, blood flow, and electrical brain activity stop. Normally such a condition would be fatal. However, as the body cools down, the need for oxygen also slows down. A person can survive in a deep hypothermic state for an hour or longer and be revived without serious complications.
>
> —Laura Black

COMPARISON AND CONTRAST

In the paragraphs that follow, student writer Kevin Jones both compares and contrasts the literary characters Ulysses and Arthur. More particularly, he is comparing Lord Tennyson's version of these characters, as they appear in two of Tennyson's poems. The writer covers similarities in the first paragraph, and moves on to differences in the next.

In Alfred, Lord Tennyson's *Ulysses* and *Idylls of the King,* the title heroes, Ulysses and Arthur, are alike in many ways, yet significant differences are apparent. Indeed, both Ulysses and Arthur deal with problems that all men face. Both heroes are disappointed in people. In Ithaca, the Greek hero of the Trojan War rules a "savage race" of people who do not know him and do not appreciate him; while in Britain, Arthur must engage in battle with knights who once loved him. Furthermore, both Ulysses and Arthur must recognize that their sons do not share their ideals. Telemachus is not a hero; he is "centered in the sphere of common duties." Arthur's illegitimate son, Modred, lacks morals and leads a rebellion against him. Finally, both Ulysses and Arthur face death. The aged Ulysses recognizes that his life is almost over, and in winter, King Arthur is mortally wounded in battle. Clearly, both legendary heroes struggle with universal problems.

Nevertheless, these legendary heroes have distinctly different personalities. Tennyson portrays Ulysses as a self-centered man, while Arthur is a model ruler. Ulysses leaves his subjects in Ithaca before order is fully restored because he finds life too dull there and wants to do some "work of noble note"—possibly to increase his fame. Arthur, on the other hand, loves his people, struggles against evil, and dies trying to restore the glory of the past. In addition, Ulysses draws no emotional response, while Arthur is both hated and loved. Although Ulysses was absent for ten years after the Trojan War, his wife and son are lukewarm toward him and do not beg him to stay at home. Modred, on the other hand, wickedly plots against the virtuous English king. Sir Bedivere weeps as he carries Arthur out of the church, and the three queens receive the dying king with tears. Finally, the gods seem unimportant to Tennyson's Ulysses, while Arthur is religious. Although Ulysses briefly mentions striving with gods in the past, they do not appear to play a role in his daily life. Arthur, however, is a devout Christian who tries to do the will of God and believes in the power of prayer. It seems fair to conclude that, even though Tennyson's Ulysses and Arthur are similar on the surface, a closer look reveals significant differences.

—Kevin Jones

DEFINITION

A definition offers the meaning of a subject. In an essay, a definition usually goes beyond the simple dictionary meaning. Such a definition compares or contrasts a subject to other subjects, gives examples, tells what something is not, etc. In the following model, a student writer gives a variety of definitions for the word "hope," and then analyzes the theme in some of Eudora Welty's short stories.

"Hope is a dangerous thing," Morgan Freeman tells his fellow inmate in the recent movie *Shawshank Redemption.* "It can drive a man insane." In this negative view, the prisoner sees hope only as wishful thinking, not determination. Freeman believes that hope cannot coexist with what he calls being institutionalized—accepting fate and living it; and Freeman prefers his world safe, without the disappointments hope brings. When serving a life sentence in jail, this is logical, but not entirely human. In contrast, others have taken a more romantic, optimistic view of hope. An early Christian named Pliny the Elder said, "Hope is the pillar that holds up the world. Hope is the dream of the walking man." This is a grand view, but questionable as well. Finally, Webster defines hope as "a feeling that what is wanted will happen." So who is right? Is hope good, bad, or neutral? Does hope run contrary to cultural norms and institutions, or is it intrinsic to humanity? Eudora Welty might answer that hope is all of these things. She portrays hope as a paradox that is both part of being human and a defiance of everyday normal behavior. In her short fiction, Welty shows hope to be the reason her heroines break from the expectations of their surrounding culture.

—Nathaniel Gaede

A common way to organize a definition is to begin with a single-sentence definition and follow with examples, analogies, and quotations that elaborate upon and illustrate the definition. In the paragraph below, the writer defines "grotesque" by beginning with a question.

First of all, what is the grotesque—in visual art and in literature? A term originally applied to Roman cave art that distorted the normal, the grotesque presents the body and mind so that they appear abnormal— different from the bodies and minds that we think belong in our world. Both spiritual and physical, bizarre and familiar, ugly and alluring, the grotesque shocks us, and we respond with laughter and fear. We laugh because the grotesque seems bizarre enough to belong only outside our world; we fear because it feels familiar enough to be part of it. Seeing the grotesque version of life as it is portrayed in art stretches our vision of reality. As Bernard McElroy argues, "The grotesque transforms the world from what we 'know' it to be to what we fear it might be. It distorts and exaggerates the surface of reality in order to tell a qualitative truth about it."

—Joan Van Rys

Connecting Your Details

Once you've gathered and arranged all your details, you need to tie them together into a smooth, easy-to-read paragraph or essay. Transitional words do this by showing your readers how pieces of information are linked in terms of location, time, or logic.

TRANSITION AND LINKING WORDS

● **Words that can be used to SHOW LOCATION:**

above	behind	down	on top of
across	below	in back of	onto
against	beneath	in front of	outside
along	beside	inside	over
among	between	into	throughout
around	beyond	near	to the right
away from	by	off	under

● **Words that can be used to SHOW TIME:**

about	during	next	till
after	finally	next week	today
afterward	first	second	tomorrow
as soon as	immediately	soon	until
at	later	then	when
before	meanwhile	third	yesterday

● **Words that can be used to COMPARE THINGS (show similarities):**

also	in the same way	likewise
as	like	similarly

● **Words that can be used to CONTRAST THINGS (show differences):**

although	even though	on the other hand	still
but	however	otherwise	yet

● **Words that can be used to EMPHASIZE A POINT:**

again	in fact	to repeat
for this reason	to emphasize	truly

● **Words that can be used to CONCLUDE or SUMMARIZE:**

all in all	finally	in summary	therefore
as a result	in conclusion	last	to sum up

● **Words that can be used to ADD INFORMATION:**

additionally	and	equally important	in addition
again	another	finally	likewise
along with	as well	for example	moreover
also	besides	for instance	next

● **Words that can be used to CLARIFY:**

for instance	in other words	put another way	that is

Paragraphs

QUICK GUIDE

CHARACTERISTICS: Basically, a paragraph is a unit of thought—a group of related sentences. The paragraph . . .

- is organized around one controlling idea that is usually stated in a topic sentence.
- is made up of supporting sentences that develop this main idea.
- rarely stands by itself—usually it is used with other paragraphs to build a longer piece of writing.
- can be designed for specific functions like opening a piece of writing, closing it, telling a story, describing something, building an argument, and so on.

EVALUATING: To decide whether your paragraph is a viable unit of thought, ask these questions . . .

- What is the topic or controlling idea?
- Is the topic clearly stated?
- Do all phrases and sentences relate to the topic, or do some go off in a different direction?
- Is the paragraph coherent—do linking and transitional words show how various elements are related?
- Is the organization clear—the line of thought reasonable and understandable?
- Is the organization effective—utilizing the best method of arranging the details?
- Is the paragraph complete—having enough of the best details to support the topic sentence?

RELATIONSHIP BETWEEN PARAGRAPHS: To decide whether your paragraphs work together, ask these questions . . .

- Does the opening paragraph introduce the topic?
- Do the opening paragraphs establish the thesis or primary argument of the paper?
- Does each paragraph logically follow the one that precedes it and lead into the one that follows it?
- Does the overall organization of paragraphs build toward the conclusion of the paper in a way that's clear and logical?

Mastering the College Essay

According to award-winning essayist Lee Gutkind, essay writing is essentially the process of researching, reading, reflecting, and, of course, writing. Essayists immerse themselves in their work, researching a subject from every conceivable angle. Their research usually begins with reading, not only to learn about their subject, but also to see what has already been written about it. They reflect upon their work as it develops—asking questions, forming new understandings, and so on. And they carefully craft their writing through as many drafts and revisions as needed.

You may not have time to immerse yourself so completely in all of your college writing. But you can approach each new writing task with as much curiosity and diligence as time permits. If you keep time on your side, you'll write effective essays.

WHAT'S AHEAD

The first part of this chapter discusses the basic steps in the essay-writing process. The second part provides two sample essays, each one representing a different approach and writing style.

- ● **Focusing Your Efforts**
- ● **Forming a Thesis Statement**
- ● **Planning and Organizing Your Essay**
- ● **Writing the Initial Drafts**
- ● **Improving Your Writing**
- ● **Two Sample Essays**

College Essays

QUICK GUIDE

As you know, the essay is the primary form of writing in all academic areas. Anytime you are asked to inform, explain, analyze, evaluate, or write persuasively about a subject, you are developing an essay. Refer to the guidelines in this chapter whenever you have a question about the basic essay-writing process. Refer to the index whenever you have a question about a specific type of essay (literary analysis, essay of argumentation, etc.).

1 **Focusing Your Efforts** (112) Before you begin your essay, gain a clear understanding of your assignment. Then explore and research possible writing ideas. Continue your search until you identify a specific writing idea that you can successfully develop in an essay.

2 **Forming a Thesis Statement** (113) Express in a sentence (or two) the specific subject of your writing. A thesis statement establishes the tone and direction for your writing. (Carry out additional research as needed to support your thesis.)

3 **Planning and Organizing Your Essay** (114-116) Either sketch out or carefully plan the basic shape of your essay. Your first job is to establish a pattern of development (*comparison, cause/effect, classification,* etc.) for your writing.

4 **Writing the Initial Drafts** (117-120) Write as much of your first draft as possible in one sitting, while your thinking and research are still fresh in your mind. This draft is your first complete look at a developing writing idea.

5 **Improving Your Writing** (121) Change or revise the content of your essay until you have effectively developed all of your main points. Then turn your full attention to editing your revised writing for style and mechanics.

Insights into Writing

The golden rule of college essay writing—one that cannot be overemphasized—is to seek guidance and clarification when you need it. If you ask for help from your instructor and writing peers, you're more likely to produce an essay that you feel good about and that satisfies—or exceeds—the requirements of the assignment.

Focusing Your Efforts

In most cases, you'll be writing an essay in response to a specific assignment. Your instructor will provide some basic guidelines, including the purpose of the assignment, a due date, a minimum page length, and so on. On the surface, everything will seem clear enough. But once you actually sit down to write, you may not feel so sure of yourself, and just getting started may become a real struggle. Sound familiar? If so, you need to put your writing tasks in better focus right from the start.

Understanding the Assignment

In order to write with confidence, be certain that you clearly understand the assignment.

- **Analyze** your writing task word for word. Locate the key terms *(define, compare, evaluate,* etc.), and make sure you know what they mean. (See 505-506 for help.)
- **Rephrase** the assignment or question into your own words to make sure you understand it.
- **Find out** what criteria will be used to evaluate your essay.
- **Discuss** the assignment and your plan of action with the instructor.

Selecting a Specific Writing Idea

In most cases, your assignment will address a general topic (or topics) related to your course work. Your job is to investigate this topic in search of a writing idea for your essay. Continue your research until you discover a manageable or limited subject that interests you and meets the requirements of the assignment. Finally, find your focus by deciding which specific aspect of the subject you want to explore.

THE SELECTING PROCESS

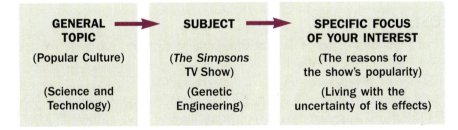

GENERAL TOPIC	SUBJECT	SPECIFIC FOCUS OF YOUR INTEREST
(Popular Culture)	(*The Simpsons* TV Show)	(The reasons for the show's popularity)
(Science and Technology)	(Genetic Engineering)	(Living with the uncertainty of its effects)

INSIDE info

Carry out as much research as necessary to expand your knowledge of your writing idea. Skilled essayists always collect many more facts and details than they actually use in their writing. (See 021 for shaping and collecting strategies.)

Forming a Thesis Statement

A **thesis statement** identifies the specific part of a subject that you will write about. Stated in another way, a thesis statement declares your unique perspective, your spin, on the subject. It gives you the necessary focus and direction to develop your essay. At this point, you're dealing with a working thesis statement—a statement in progress, so to speak. You may find it necessary to revise it once or twice as your thinking evolves. The following information will help you write clear, effective thesis statements.

Stating Your Case

A thesis statement is usually a single sentence that contains two main elements: a manageable subject plus a specific feeling about (or a particular feature of) that subject.

> **A manageable subject** (genetic engineering)
> + **a specific feeling** (living with uncertainty about its effects)
> = **an effective thesis statement.**

THESIS STATEMENT: **The present generation has to live with uncertainty about the effects of genetic engineering.**

Example Thesis Statements

- **Lewis Carroll's *Alice's Adventures in Wonderland* (subject) is a charming reminder of the imaginary world of children (specific feeling).**
- **Barbed hooks (subject) should be banned from lure fishing to protect undersized fish (specific feeling).**
- **The main categories of weight lifters (subject) are health enthusiasts, toning devotees, athletes, and bodybuilders (particular feature).**
- **Who are these people we call "the homeless" (subject), and what are the reasons for their predicament (particular feature)?**

Thesis Checklist

If you can answer *yes* to each of these questions, then you have written an effective thesis statement:

1. Does your thesis focus on a specific writing idea?
2. Is the thesis stated in a clear, direct sentence (or sentences)?
3. Is the thesis supported by the information you have gathered?
4. Does the thesis suggest a pattern of development for your essay? (*Comparison, cause/effect,* and *classification* are example patterns. See 114-115.)

NOTE: In the final form of an essay, the thesis does not have to be stated directly (although it usually is).

Planning and Organizing Your Essay

Think of your working thesis statement as the active ingredient that initiates the whole planning and organizing process. Without this statement, you're still in the selecting and searching stage, still trying to identify a specific writing idea. But once you've written your thesis statement, you're ready to tackle a bigger issue—the development, or shape, of your essay. The information on the next three pages will help you plan and organize your work.

Organizing Patterns

Almost all academic essays follow a basic pattern of development. As you will see in the charts below, some of these patterns are specific and others are more general. Knowing how these patterns work will help you plan and organize your essays. (The topic numbers refer to sample essays in the handbook that are organized according to the different patterns.)

SPECIFIC PATTERNS

Types	Organizing Principles
Process (How something works)	Chronological Order (190-192)
Narrative (How something happened)	Chronological Order (158-161)
Description (How something/someone appears)	Spatial Order—Location (177-180)
Comparison (How two things are alike/different)	Whole vs. Whole Comparison Point-by-Point Comparison (194-197)
Cause/Effect (How one thing affects something else)	Identify Cause/Explore Effects Identify Effect/Explore Causes (208-210)
Problem/Solution (How a problem can be solved)	Study the Problem/Solution(s) (212-215)
Classification (How something can be categorized)	Name Categories/Examine Each One (199-202)
Argumentation (How a position or an opinion can be asserted and supported)	Assert and Support/Counter the Opposition/Reassert Position (233-237)

GENERAL PATTERNS

Types	Organizing Principles
Logical Order	
Working Deductively	Follow an opening thesis with supporting details in the most compelling order (206, 230-231).
Working Inductively	Provide examples and details leading up to the main idea (thesis).
Question and Answer	Ask a question (thesis) and answer it in the body of the essay.
Explanation and Analysis	Move back and forth between explanation (or examples) and analysis (264-266, 268-271).

"An effective piece of writing has focus. There is a controlling vision which orders what is being said." —Donald Murray

Establishing a Pattern of Development

An organizing pattern for your essay may be built into your assignment. For example, you may be asked specifically to develop an argument or to write a process paper. When a pattern is not assigned, one may still evolve quite naturally during your initial thinking and planning. If this doesn't happen, take a careful look at your thesis statement (and supporting information). An effective thesis will almost always suggest an organizing pattern. However, if your thesis doesn't provide this "controlling vision," consider changing it. Notice how the thesis statements below provide direction and shape for the writing that would follow each.

Example Thesis

Bigger in *Native Son* and Alan in *Equus* are both entering adulthood and have come to realize that they are tragically controlled by work, religion, and the media.

DISCUSSION: The writer of this thesis is preparing to compare two literary characters. Comparisons are patterned in two different ways: Either you discuss one of the subjects completely and then turn to the other subject (whole vs. whole), or you discuss both subjects according to specific criteria (point by point). Since the example thesis establishes three criteria for comparison—work, religion, and the media—the writer will naturally follow the point-by-point pattern of development. (See 194-195 for this essay.)

Example Thesis

The present generation has to live with uncertainty about the effects of genetic engineering.

DISCUSSION: This thesis suggests that the writer is developing a cause/effect essay. Essays following this pattern usually begin with a cause (development, condition, etc.) followed by an explanation of the effects, or they begin with an effect followed by an explanation of the causes. To develop the example thesis, the writer will obviously follow the first route, identifying a cause (or condition) before carefully examining the effects. (See 123-124 for this essay.)

bottom LINE

Remember that you're looking for a basic frame or structure for your essay. Within that general frame, other patterns may come into play. For example, you may be developing a comparison essay, but within that structure, you may do some describing or classifying. Or you may be developing an argumentative essay, and within that structure, you may decide to place some of your supporting points in an imagined narrative (scenario).

Outlining Your Ideas

Once you've established a general pattern of development, you're ready to organize the information (main points, supporting details, etc.) that you expect to cover in your essay. It may suffice simply to jot down a brief list of ideas to follow. Then again, you may find it helpful to organize your ideas in a topic or a sentence outline.

Topic Outline

An outline is an orderly listing of related ideas. In a topic outline, each new idea is stated as a word or phrase rather than as a complete sentence. Before you start, write your working thesis statement at the top of your paper to keep you focused on the subject of your essay. Do not attempt to outline your opening and closing paragraphs unless specifically asked to do so. (Also see 363.)

Introduction
  I. The technology of genetic engineering
     A. Gene manipulation
     B. Gene copying and transferring
     C. Gene recombining and cloning
 II. The uses of genetic engineering
     A. Unpredictable in past
     B. More predictable now
     C. More potential in future
III. The fears about genetic engineering
     A. Release of dangerous organisms
     B. Lack of trust in scientists
Conclusion

Sentence Outline

A sentence outline naturally contains more detail than a topic outline because each new idea is expressed as a complete sentence. It is usually required for longer, more formal writing assignments.

Introduction
  I. Genetic engineering is a new biotechnology.
     A. Scientists can manipulate genes.
     B. Genes can be copied and moved to cells in other species.
     C. Scientists can recombine genes and clone entire organisms.
 II. Genetic engineering affects animal and plant breeding.
     A. Past species improvement efforts took decades and proved unpredictable.
     B. Now development time is cut dramatically with better results.
     C. Animals are potential chemical factories, and new animals can be created and patented.
III. Genetic engineering is feared by some.
     A. Dangerous organisms could be released.
     B. Public confidence in scientists has been undermined.
Conclusion

Writing the Initial Drafts

Write your first draft as freely as you can, using your outline (or listing) as a general guide. Your goal is not to produce a winning essay the first time through. It can't be done. A first draft is clearly a work in progress, or, as writer Donald Murray states, "a vision of what might be." At this point, you simply want to get all of your ideas on paper. In most cases, you will then need to develop another early draft (or two) before your essay really begins to take shape.

Remember that most academic essays develop in predictable fashion: The opening paragraph introduces the thesis, the body of the essay supports it, and the closing paragraph reaffirms it. (Check below and on the following three pages if you have questions about developing your essay.)

Shaping the Opening Paragraph

Opening paragraphs usually start general and end specific. That is, the first part draws readers into the essay with important ideas related to the subject. The second part states or suggests the thesis and leads readers into the main part of the text. (See the examples on the next page.)

Introduce the subject with . . .
- **interesting background information,**
- **a telling quotation,**
- **an illustrative story,**
- **a series of questions, etc.**

Introductions to Avoid
- **Using obvious or worn-out expressions:**
   "I would like to tell you about . . . "
   "According to the dictionary . . . "
- **Using say-nothing sentences:**
   "Subject A and B are alike/different in many ways."
   "World War II was a colossal war . . . "
   "Uncontrollable forest fires devastate the landscape."

INSIDE **info**

Some writers pay special attention to the exact wording of their opening paragraph *before* they draft the rest of their text. It gets their juices flowing for the larger task at hand. Other writers would rather get everything on paper before they pay careful attention to any specific part.

Sample Openings

Review these examples of essay openings. For additional ideas, see the essays in "Forms of Writing" section.

> **In many ways, our grandparents had a harder life than we have today. Typing letters on clunky manual typewriters, canning their own vegetables, and sharing the telephone with neighbors on "party lines" were a few of the inconveniences they faced that we don't. However, in one area, at least, we have it harder than our grandparents did. *The present generation has to live with uncertainty about the effects of genetic engineering.***

DISCUSSION: In this opening, Steven Jones makes an interesting historical reference to introduce his thesis. He begins with a description of "hardships" experienced by his grandparents' generation and then turns to a more pressing hardship facing the present age.

> **A new breed of hunter dwells among North America's hidden waterways. Armed with a $50.00 rod and reel, $60.00 hip waders, and a wide array of lures from glowing gadgets to old-fashioned worms, today's fisherman has improved his arsenal well beyond the bent nail and old twine Huck Finn used to go jigging. However, most modern fishermen do still carry one piece of equipment that is outdated: the barbed hook, still added to almost every lure produced commercially. This obsolete mechanism plagues the sport of fishing with the damage that it can cause to young fish stocks. *Barbed hooks should be banned from lure fishing to protect undersized fish.***

DISCUSSION: This writer, David DeHaan, first creates a clear image of the well-equipped modern angler. At a midway point in the paragraph, the transitional word "however" effectively turns the opening toward the specific thesis: that one piece of the angler's equipment—the barbed hook—is outdated and should be banned.

> **The Simpsons, stars of the TV show by the same name, are a typical American family, or at least a parody of one. Homer, Marge, Bart, Lisa, and Maggie Simpson live in Springfield, U.S.A. Homer, the father, is a boorish, obese oaf who works in a nuclear power plant. Marge is an overprotective, nagging mother with an outrageous blue hairdo. Ten-year-old Bart is an obnoxious, "spiky-haired demon." Lisa is eight and a prodigy on the tenor saxophone and in class. The infant Maggie never speaks but only sucks on her pacifier.**
>
> **What is the attraction of this yellow-skinned family who star on a show in which all the characters have pronounced overbites and only four fingers on each hand? *I contend that we see a little bit of ourselves in everything they do. The world of Springfield is a parody of our own world, and Americans can't get enough of it.***

DISCUSSION: The writer of this opening, Nathaniel Zylstra, describes his subject—the Simpson family—in the first paragraph. It isn't until the second paragraph that the focus, or thesis, of the essay is addressed. The writer intends to analyze the popularity of *The Simpsons*.

Developing Your Main Points

How do you add dimension and depth to your writing? How do you develop complete and insightful essays? You make sure that you have carefully explored and reflected upon your writing idea. You also make sure that you have gathered plenty of compelling evidence to support your thesis.

It's in the main part of your essay—in the body—that you develop your thesis. The process usually works in this way: You present each main point (as indicated in your outline), expand upon it with supporting facts or examples, and offer additional analysis or commentary as needed.

Adding Support

The examples that follow show different ways to develop main points:

> **With so much to be said for genetic engineering, why would anyone be leery of it? Some people naturally fear the unknown, and there is much that we still don't know about how genes work. The greatest fear is that some dangerous organism could escape from a scientist's laboratory—an airborne AIDS virus, for example—spreading uncontrollably through the human population. People also point to the unplanned spread of pests such as starlings, fire ants, killer bees, or the kudzu vine in the southeastern United States as examples of how genetic experiments, too, could get out of hand. . . . It seems clear that not everyone who possesses knowledge uses it for the good of humanity.**

DISCUSSION: Steven Jones's main point is stated as a question. His *examples* and *closing comment* provide answers.

> **The Red Guard played an important role in the Cultural Revolution, serving as Mao's frontline troops in the struggle against "class enemies." They "raided people's houses, smashed their antiques, tore up their paintings and works of calligraphy and burned their books" (Chang 284). What is a puzzle to me is how these otherwise nice, normal young people could bring themselves to participate in such a horrible campaign.**

DISCUSSION: To develop her main point, Qian Zhang cites a *specific reference* in a text and follows with *personal commentary*.

> **Waistlines have continued to grow, even in an intense era of fat watching. A 1994 study published in the *Journal of the American Medical Association* showed that one-third of adults were overweight between 1988 and 1991. In previous years, those figures held steady at one-quarter of the population. Despite America's current fixation on fat, Maureen Pestine, Northwestern campus nutritionist, said sugar may return as the focus of people's health in the future.**

DISCUSSION: In this example, Jenni Engebretsen offers *authoritative facts* and *professional analysis* to support her main point.

Writing the Closing

Generally speaking, an effective closing adds to the readers' understanding of an essay. The first part of the closing usually reviews (or ties together) important points in an essay, reinforces or stresses one particular point, and/or reasserts the thesis. The closing's final lines may expand the scope of the text by making a connection between the essay and the readers' experience, or between the essay and life in general.

Sample Closings

> **Still, genetic engineering is here, and we must deal with it. It's a good news/bad news situation. The good news is that the genie of genetic engineering is out of the bottle. It may be able to grant us some of our best wishes. The bad news is that we're not sure the genie is completely friendly, and we're quite sure we will never get it back into the bottle. Our grandparents would be and are amazed at what scientists have been able to accomplish. In their day, though, if they had been asked to choose between hardships they could see and understand, and using new-fangled conveniences that promised unknown side effects, I wonder which they would have chosen.**

DISCUSSION: In this closing, Steven Jones first reviews the main points discussed in the essay. The second part brings the essay full circle by calling attention to the opening comments in the text (the hardships experienced by his grandparents' generation). Also notice the final reflective comment, which will keep the essay on readers' minds for some time.

> **Ultimately, both Alan and Bigger fail to gain real control over the outside forces in their lives. Alan forfeits his interest in life, and Bigger forfeits life itself. They, like so many people, become victims of the world in which they live.**

DISCUSSION: In this closing, writer Janae Sebranek summarizes the main points of comparison she made in the body of her text. Her final point ("They, like so many people, . . . ") extends the scope of the essay.

> **Still, it is hard to pin down the exact reason that Simpsons fans love the show so much. I have over 70 of the more than 150 episodes on tape. Yet I cannot say exactly why I watch. I enjoy the social parody, the mocking of popular culture. But I also am attracted to the simpleness of the concept. I don't have to worry about the show attempting to teach me deep moral lessons, or insulting my intellect. When I watch *The Simpsons,* I feel that I am being treated like a thoughtful viewer. These reasons keep me and the rest of America laughing.**

DISCUSSION: The first sentence in this closing reinforces a central point made in the essay. The writer, Nathaniel Zylstra, then relates his personal experience with the subject to summarize and reinforce his thesis.

Improving Your Writing

After you have written one or two early drafts, developing an essay is really the process of working out the kinks in the sense and flow of your ideas. The best way, really the only way, to work things out is to proceed very carefully through a series of revisions—adding, cutting, and rearranging information as needed.

". . . there are days when the result is so bad that no fewer than five revisions are required. In contrast, when I'm greatly inspired, only four revisions are needed." —John Kenneth Galbraith

Revising and Editing Checklist

Use the following checklist as a general guide when you revise and edit your essays:

1. **Pace yourself.** If possible, set your draft aside for a day or two before you review it. Everything looks much clearer with a fresh set of eyes. Also make sure that other sets of eyes—including your instructor's—see your work throughout the revising and editing process. (Conferencing is an essential part of the revising process.)

2. **Think globally at first.** Look for gaps in the overall development of your work. Is your explanation, argument, or analysis complete? Do you need to carry out additional research? Do the basic parts work together and point to one main idea? Finally, does your essay follow one of the basic patterns of development?

3. **Then carefully examine each part.** Does the opening paragraph draw readers into the essay and state (or suggest) your thesis? Have you supported each main point with effective examples and analysis? Does the closing tie up any loose ends and help readers appreciate the significance of your essay?

4. **Check the style of your writing.** Edit your revised writing using one of the lists of stylistic traits in the handbook as your basic guide (047 or 051). To check the flow and rhythm of your sentences, read your essay out loud.

5. **Lastly, carry out a close editing.** Check your writing for accuracy (mechanics, usage, etc.) before preparing a final copy of your essay.

 INSIDE info
On one level, writing an essay is the process of clarifying and fine-tuning your thinking on a subject. On another level, it is the process of informing or persuading your readers. You'll know that you've made enough changes when your essay clearly and accurately reflects your thinking on the subject, and when it answers any questions your readers may have. (For more revising and editing guidelines, see 029-040.)

Two Sample Essays

The two sample essays included here are about the same subject, genetic engineering. As you will see, however, the second essay illustrates a higher level of writing proficiency, a level that few student writers can achieve without a great deal of time, effort, and guidance. Depending upon your writing background and experience, one or the other of these pieces will serve well as a model for your own writing. Comprehensive notes precede each model.

Essay I: Notes

OVERVIEW: "The Uncertainty of Genetic Engineering," starting on the next page, represents a traditional academic essay in terms of approach and structure. This essay follows the thesis/support/summary format:

Paragraph 1: The opening paragraph draws attention to the subject and states the thesis.

Paragraphs 2-4: The paragraphs in the body of the essay define the subject and speculate upon its effects.

Paragraph 5: The closing paragraph reaffirms the thesis and ends with a thought-provoking idea.

ASSESSMENT: This essay is consistently focused on a single interesting and timely topic. It sticks to one main pattern of development throughout the essay (the *effects* of genetic engineering). The body of the essay raises some valid points in terms of the potential effects of the subject. Clearly, the writing stems from a fair degree of reading and reflecting on the subject. The overall text is coherent and unified, the sentence structure is clear and accurate, and in places, the voice is engaging. The result is an effective piece of college writing.

SUGGESTIONS: How might the essay be improved?

- **Create a more intriguing title.**
- **Polish the opening, making it a bit more formal.**
- **Include more specific examples.**
- **Delve further into the subject.**
- **Cite more references to respected sources.**

TAKE note Some of your instructors may find this essay too tied to the traditional essay format. They may encourage you to follow more freely and naturally your critical thinking on a subject. (At the end of this chapter, the sample essay— "Jangling the Keys of Life"—is approached in this way.)

Essay I: Traditional Approach

This essay by Steven Jones considers the potential effects of genetic engineering. As indicated in the notes on the previous page, it follows the traditional thesis/support/summary format. Notice how tightly organized the essay is and how it moves smoothly and clearly from one point to the next.

The opening paragraph draws readers into the essay and introduces the thesis (boldfaced).

Background information concerning the development of the subject is identified.

Potential positive effects are explored.

The Uncertainty of Genetic Engineering

In many ways, our grandparents had a harder life than we have today. Typing letters on clunky manual typewriters, canning their own vegetables, and sharing the telephone with neighbors on "party lines" were a few of the inconveniences they faced that we don't. However, in one area, at least, we have it harder than our grandparents did. **The present generation has to live with uncertainty about the effects of genetic engineering.**

What is genetic engineering? According to an educational leaflet by the Australian Biotechnology Association distributed on the World Wide Web, genetic engineering is a revolutionary new form of biotechnology. Scientists have learned how to manipulate genes—the chemical information inside living cells that tells the cells how to reproduce. They can copy a gene in one cell and transfer it to a cell in a different species, such as a mouse. Then the receiver cells start producing the desirable trait in the new species. Scientists can also take genes out of a cell and put them back in in different combinations. Using genes, they have discovered how to clone cells, making exact duplicates of an original organism. Twenty years ago, such scientific achievements were only a dream.

If this sounds exciting, it is—up to a point. Animal and plant breeders used to take decades to develop improved species by mating subjects, trying to match up desirable traits. Even then, they couldn't guarantee that a cross between a dwarf, sweet tomato and a tall, bitter tomato would produce a tall, sweet tomato. It could produce a dwarf, bitter tomato. But now, using genetic engineering techniques, scientists can cut the development process down to two or three years, and better guarantee their results. For the first time in history, it is possible to talk seriously about designer vegetables. It is also possible to use the body of one animal as a "factory" to manufacture a chemical that another species needs. New animals created in labs can be patented, bringing substantial profits to the creators. It is not even hard to imagine that soon scientists will be able to clone human beings.

With so much to be said for genetic engineering, why would anyone be leery of it? Some people naturally fear the unknown, and there is much that we still don't know about how genes work. The greatest fear is that some dangerous organism could escape from a scientist's laboratory—an airborne AIDS virus, for example—spreading uncontrollably through the human population. People also point to the unplanned spread of pests such as starlings, fire ants, killer bees, or the kudzu vine in the southeastern United States as examples of how genetic experiments, too, could get out of hand. Scientists tell us there are safeguards; and that even if a mutant life-form does escape, it is not likely to survive in the evolutionary scheme of things. But many people have seen movies that depict scientists as distracted, one-track minded, or even evil. They do not trust scientists' reassurances. It seems clear that not everyone who possesses knowledge uses it for the good of humanity. After all, computer hackers have been known to plant destructive viruses.

Still, genetic engineering is here, and we must deal with it. It's a good news/bad news situation. The good news is that the genie of genetic engineering is out of the bottle. It may be able to grant us some of our best wishes. The bad news is that we're not sure the genie is completely friendly, and we're quite sure we will never get it back into the bottle. Our grandparents would be and are amazed at what scientists have been able to accomplish. In their day, though, if they had been asked to choose between hardships they could see and understand, and using new-fangled conveniences that promised unknown side effects, I wonder which they would have chosen. ▪

Here potential negative effects are considered.

The closing summarizes the main points and calls attention to the opening comments in the text.

Essay II: Notes

OVERVIEW: "Jangling the Keys of Life," starting on the next page, follows the unique organization of the writer's critical thinking. An outline of the essay might look something like this:

I. We are at a crucial juncture in history as we begin to map human genes.
 A. Gene mapping is already producing medical miracles.
 B. Thus, the keys of human biological development are in our hands.

II. Now we must begin asking questions about positive vs. negative potential.
 A. Many books are already asking those questions.
  1. Currently many popular books explore biogenetics.
  2. A number of writings on this subject have been circulating for more than 20 years.
 B. These books show that genetic engineering is a mixed blessing.
  1. Biotechnology has had many successes.
  2. Biotechnology has commercial clout.
  3. There are concerns over unintended consequences.
   a. Some of the fears are fanciful.
   b. Some of the fears are based on facts.

III. We live in "the future" that was only predicted in the '70s.
 A. Public discussion lags behind scientific advances.
 B. Biomedical ethics must become part of our everyday lives.

ASSESSMENT: This essay succeeds in a number of significant ways: (1) It has an intriguing title, which is given a surprising twist at the end of the essay. (2) It does not rely on any prefabricated structure (thesis/support/summary). (3) It makes solid use of research. The evidence of this is seen not only in the helpful references, but also in the many concrete examples and illustrations. (4) This essay uses both language and ideas in a fresh, vigorous way. (5) The sentence structure is fairly demanding as well as clear, fluid, and grammatically correct.

In short, this second essay offers readers an interesting and engaging analysis. The result is an excellent piece of college writing, originating from a great deal of planning, drafting, and revising.

SUGGESTIONS: How might the essay be improved?

- Address more critically the ethical issues of the subject.
- Maintain a more interesting voice throughout the essay.
- Incorporate an effective unifying motif through the text.
- Provide a more thoughtful historical perspective on the subject.
- Provide better balance between the positive and negative effects.

Essay II: Original Approach

This essay by Randall VanderMey also explores the potential of biogenetic engineering. Its less traditional structure closely reflects the writer's unique, well-reasoned perspective on the subject. Notice the careful attention to detail and authoritative information throughout the essay.

Jangling the Keys of Life

The opening line immediately engages the readers' attention.

Interesting details about gene research lead up to the general subject of this essay.

The main focus of the essay— questions about handling this new science—is identified.

Imagine how nuclear scientists must have felt the first time they split an atom, knowing how much good, but also how much destruction, might eventually be unleashed. We are at an equally important point in human history as scientists at the National Institutes of Health have embarked on a 15-year, $3 billion effort to map the chemical codes hidden in human genes, which are the keys to our heredity.

So far, the Human Genome Project, as the worldwide effort is called, has successfully identified only about 6 percent of the roughly 100,000 genes found on each chromosome in each of the body's more than 10 trillion cells. And yet, medical miracles are already occurring, thanks to genetic engineering, or biotechnology, as it is often called. In 1990 doctors healed two girls with unhealthy immune systems by using gene therapy. They inserted healthy genes into the girls' bloodstreams to induce the manufacture of important enzymes that their defective genes had failed to produce. Many other diseases, such as schizophrenia, severe alcoholism, Alzheimer's disease, Huntington's disease, and hemophilia are known to be genetically influenced. Someday soon, these and other human traits, such as intelligence, sex, body size, or even speed of aging, may be ours to design as we choose. The keys to human biological development are in our hands.

Clearly, then, it is not too early to begin asking hard questions about how our society should handle this powerful new science. We should not wait until we have the genetic equivalent of a Hiroshima or Chernobyl disaster to properly weigh the positive against the negative potential.

In the last 10 years, in fact, dozens of influential books have been written on the subject, bearing provocative titles such as *Wonderwoman and Superman: The Ethics of Human Biotechnology* (John Harris, 1992), *The Human Body Shop: The Engineering and Marketing of Life* (Andrew Kimbrell, 1993), or *Superpigs and Wondercorn: The Brave New World of Biotechnology . . . and Where It All May Lead* (Michael W. Fox, 1992). However, books such as *Genetics and the Future of Man* (John D. Roslansky, ed., 1966) and *Genetic Fix* (Amitai Etzioni, 1973) or articles such as "Genetic Engineering in Man: Ethical Considerations" (*Journal of the American Medical Association,* May 1, 1972) were circulating more than 20 years ago.

Jangling the Keys of Life
(continued)

Each main point is supported with extensive, compelling detail.

Such writings and many more have already alerted the general public to the fact that genetic engineering may be a mixed blessing. On one hand, they have demonstrated the magic of biotechnology and its commercial promise. An "antifreeze" gene has been taken out of the Arctic flounder and inserted in strawberries, making the strawberry frost resistant. The Calgene Corporation has reversed a gene in a tomato to invent a "FLAVR SAVR" variety that can be ripened on the vine without rotting in the supermarket. Cows have been treated with a genetically engineered growth hormone (bovine somatotropin, or BST) so that they produce more milk. Genetically engineered laboratory mice have been used to test vaccines that may be successful in treating human diseases.

By the year 2000, according to reliable estimates, genetic engineering is likely to have become a $50 billion-a-year industry, with strong backing from major commercial powers such as the United States and Japan. The whole enterprise has already given and will continue to give a huge boost to basic biomedical research in colleges and universities.

At almost every point, the essay reflects a careful and knowledgeable writer at work.

On the other hand, the literature on biotechnology points to many real concerns. Some are hypothetical and almost hysterical, such as the fear that a careless scientist will accidentally release a mutant form of virus, starting a biological chain reaction that will make AIDS look like a flu epidemic. Other concerns are based on fact or probability. For example, when pigs were genetically altered to carry a human growth gene, they didn't become healthy superhogs, as hoped. Instead, according to Michael W. Fox, they suffered unnecessarily with bad eyes, painful arthritis, and a weakness for pneumonia. For another example, if corn were genetically "fixed" to be resistant to herbicides, the use of environmentally polluting chemicals might actually increase. For these and many other reasons, we may discover, as a popular TV commercial used to say, "It's not nice to fool Mother Nature."

After a thoughtful closing analysis, the final lines offer an effective reference to the essay's title.

Two decades ago it was easy to see genetic engineering within a futuristic glow. As long as people viewed it as a kind of science fiction, they could postpone answering some of the ethical questions that responsible scientists were already raising. But we live in that future now, and many problems that were envisioned are now ours to deal with as facts. Unfortunately, public discussion of the ethical issues lags far behind the dazzling advances of science. Conversation about biomedical ethics must become more and more a part of everyday life.

Are those the keys to a glorious future we hear jangling? Or are those our nerves? ■

Taking Care of Business

The one thing you already know about writing in college is that you have to do a lot of it—and it has to be good. Nothing does more to help you make a good impression (and a good grade) than writing well. You also know that college is very much like real life—you have to take care of business in and out of class. There are bills to pay, letters to write, memos to fax, messages to e-mail. And it's your personal responsibility to get the job done clearly, concisely, and on time.

WHAT'S AHEAD

This chapter should help prepare you to take care of the business at hand. Sample letters and memos will help you communicate effectively with everyone from the registrar to scholarship committees. The sample applications and résumé will help you make a favorable impression when you apply for that part-time or summer job. There's even a special set of guidelines to help you master e-mail messages so that you can "take care of business," no matter where in the world it may be.

- Writing the Business Letter
- Preparing a Résumé
- Applying for a Job
- Writing Memos and E-Mail

Business Writing

All business writing—whether it is a letter, a résumé, or a memo—shares the following characteristics:

STARTING POINT: Business writing begins with your need to communicate an important idea to another person. ("I would like to apply for, request, inform you, . . . ")

PURPOSE: The purpose is to discuss, announce, clarify, or confirm a specific business-related matter. (On another level, the purpose is to begin or continue some action pertaining to the matter.)

FORM: When you are taking care of business, it's important to follow the basic standards of form and style (as outlined in this chapter). People in the workplace don't have time for surprises. They want letters, memos, and résumés to be presented in recognizable formats that are easy to follow. Business writing is a highly structured and practical form of communication.

AUDIENCE: In most cases, you are speaking to one specific individual (or group) about one particular business matter. Always provide your audience with the necessary information to act upon your request, concern, or announcement.

VOICE: Speak clearly, concisely, and courteously in business writing. Think of your writing as one part of a direct and sincere conversation with your readers.

POINT OF VIEW: Use the first-person (*I*) point of view in person-to-person communication and the third-person (*she, he, they*) in most general messages and memos.

The Big Picture

Business writing is the process of sharing information in a standardized format (letter, résumé, memo, etc.). The writer must know why he or she is writing (the specific message), how the writing should be presented (the correct form), and how it should be sent (mail, fax, e-mail). One final thought—always make a copy of your writing and file it for future reference.

Writing the Business Letter

Business letters are written for "business" reasons: to make a request, to order materials, to file a complaint, to apply for a job, and so on. A business letter is usually concise and to the point. Preferably, it should fit on one page. Business letters also have a very businesslike appearance and follow a specific pattern of form, style, and spacing, as you'll see in the guidelines below.

Semi-Block

Full Block

BC Box 143
Balliole College
Eugene, OR 97440-5125
August 29, 1996

Ms. Ada Overlie
Ogg Hall, Room 222
Balliole College
Eugene, OR 97440-0222

Dear Ms. Overlie:

As the president of Balliole's Earth Care Club, I'd like to welcome you to college. I hope that your freshman year is a great learning experience both inside and outside the classroom.

That learning experience is the reason I'm writing—to encourage you to join the Earth Care Club. As a member, you could participate in the educational and action-oriented mission of the club. The club has most recently been involved in the following:
• organizing a reduce, reuse, recycle program on campus
• promoting cloth rather than plastic bag use among students
• giving input to the college administration on landscaping, renovating, and building for energy efficiency
• putting together the annual Earth Day celebration

What environmental concerns and activities would you like to focus on? Bring them to the Earth Care Club. Simply complete the enclosed form and return it by September 4. Then watch the campus news for details on our first meeting.

Yours sincerely,

Dave Wetland

Dave Wetland
President

DW:kr
Encl. membership form
cc: Esther du Toit, membership committee

BC Box 143
Balliole College
Eugene, OR 97440-5125
August 29, 1996

Ms. Ada Overlie
Ogg Hall, Room 222
Balliole College
Eugene, OR 97440-0222

Dear Ms. Overlie:

As the president of Balliole's Earth Care Club, I'd like to welcome you to college. I hope that your freshman year is a great learning experience both inside and outside the classroom.

That learning experience is the reason I'm writing—to encourage you to join the Earth Care Club. As a member, you could participate in the educational and action-oriented mission of the club. The club has most recently been involved in the following:
• organizing a reduce, reuse, recycle program on campus
• promoting cloth rather than plastic bag use among students
• giving input to the college administration on landscaping, renovating, and building for energy efficiency
• putting together the annual Earth Day celebration

What environmental concerns and activities would you like to focus on? Bring them to the Earth Care Club. Simply complete the enclosed form and return it by September 4. Then watch the campus news for details on our first meeting.

Yours sincerely,

Dave Wetland

Dave Wetland
President

DW:kr
Encl. membership form
cc: Esther du Toit, membership committee

FORMAT GUIDELINES

● Use a consistent style: semi-block or full block.
● Use a print size and typestyle that make reading easy.
● Use left and right margins of 1 to 1.5 inches.
● Center the letter vertically (top to bottom) on the page, leaving margins of 1 to 1.5 inches.
● If you use computer software to develop your own personal letterhead, keep the design simple.

Parts of the Letter

HEADING

The **heading** gives the writer's complete address, either in the letterhead (company stationery) or typed out, followed by the date.

INSIDE ADDRESS

The **inside address** gives the reader's name and address.

- If you're not sure which person to address or how to spell someone's name, you could call the company for the information.
- If the person's title is a single word, place it after the name and a comma. A longer title goes on a separate line.

SALUTATION

The **salutation** begins with *Dear* and ends with a colon, not a comma.

- Use *Mr.* or *Ms.* plus the person's last name, unless you are well acquainted. Do not guess at *Miss* or *Mrs.*
- If you can't get the person's name, replace the salutation with *Dear* or *Attention* followed by the title of an appropriate reader. (Examples: Dear Dean of Students: or Attention: Personnel Manager)

BODY

The **body** should consist of single-spaced paragraphs with double spacing between paragraphs. (Do not indent the paragraphs.)

- If the body goes to a second page, put the reader's name at the top left, the number 2 in the center, and the date at the right margin.

COMPLIMENTARY CLOSING

For the **complimentary closing,** use *Sincerely, Yours sincerely,* or *Yours truly* followed by a comma; use *Best wishes* if you know the person well.

SIGNATURE

The **signature** includes both the writer's handwritten and typed name.

INITIALS

When someone types the letter for the writer, that person's **initials** appear (in lowercase) after the writer's initials (in capitals) and a colon.

ENCLOSURE

If a document (brochure, form, copy, etc.) is **enclosed** with the letter, the word *Enclosure* or *Encl.* appears below the initials.

COPIES

If a **copy** of the letter is sent elsewhere, type the letters *cc:* followed by the person's or department's name beneath the enclosure line.

Model Letter

Heading
BC Box 143
Balliole College
Eugene, OR 97440-5125
August 29, 1996

Four to Seven Spaces

Inside
Address
Ms. Ada Overlie
Ogg Hall, Room 222
Balliole College
Eugene, OR 97440-0222
Double Space

Salutation
Dear Ms. Overlie:
Double Space

As the president of Balliole's Earth Care Club, I welcome you
to college. I hope your freshman year is a great learning
experience both inside and outside the classroom.
Double Space

That learning experience is the reason I'm writing—to
encourage you to join the Earth Care Club. As a member,
you could participate in the educational and action-oriented
mission of the club. The club has most recently been
involved in the following:

Body
• organizing a reduce, reuse, recycle program on campus
• promoting cloth rather than plastic bag use among students
• giving input to the college administration on landscaping,
  renovating, and building for energy efficiency
• putting together the annual Earth Day celebration
Double Space

What environmental concerns and activities would you like
to focus on? Bring them to the Earth Care Club. Simply
complete the enclosed form and return it by September 4.
Then watch the campus news for details on our first meeting.
Double Space

Complimentary
Closing
Yours sincerely,

Dave Wetland **Four Spaces**

Signature
Dave Wetland
President
Double Space

Initials
Enclosure
Copies
DW:kr
Encl. membership form
cc: Esther du Toit, membership committee

The Letter of Complaint

One of the most common letters you'll write now and in the future is the complaint letter. When a mistake happens that affects you—a defective product, poor service, a negative housing condition—you often need to write a letter to get satisfaction.

1. **Describe the problem.** When, where, and how did you purchase the product or receive the service? Provide copies of receipts, canceled checks, warranties; use the model or serial number; be specific about what went wrong and how the problem inconvenienced you.

2. **Describe attempted solutions.** If you've already tried to solve the problem, explain what you did and whom you talked to.

3. **Explain what solution you would like.** Do you want a refund, an apology, a replacement, a credit, or a review of policy or procedure? Be specific.

2112 Jefferson Park Ave. #10
Charlottesville, VA 22903-5790
April 11, 1996

The Shoe Company
123 West Adams
Beaverton, OR 97005-9870

Dear Customer Service Department:

Describe the problem.

On February 22, I bought size 10 Jump Max running shoes for $64.95 at the Runner's Roost in Walker, Virginia. The store was going out of business, but the salesperson told me that your guarantee would still apply.

I wore the shoes for six weeks with no problem. But on April 7 I noticed a loss of cushioning in my left shoe.

Describe attempted solutions.

I spoke to John in your customer service department yesterday, and he told me to send the shoes and related details to his attention.

Explain desired solution.

I am enclosing my Jump Max running shoes along with a copy of the canceled check. Please send me a new pair of shoes in the same model and size. I've enjoyed using your products over the years, and I expect to use them in the future.

Sincerely,

Mark Hammons

Mark Hammons

Encl. shoes, check copy

Folding the Letter

An 8½″ by 11″ letter should be mailed in a standard businesssized 4⅛″ by 9½″ envelope.

- Fold the bottom third of the letter up, and crease.
- Fold the top third of the letter down, and crease.
- Insert the letter (with the open end at the top) into the envelope.

Addressing the Business Envelope

Address the letter correctly so it can be delivered promptly. Make sure that the destination and return addresses match the inside address and the heading on the letter. Use the model below as a guide for placement of these addresses.

```
MR DAVE WETLAND
BC BOX 143
BALLIOLE COLLEGE
EUGENE OR 97440-5125


            MS ADA OVERLIE
            OGG HALL ROOM 222
            BALLIOLE COLLEGE
            EUGENE OR 97440-0222
```

Sample addresses:

ATN MANAGER TRAINING
MCDONALDS CORP
1 MCDONALDS PLZ
OAKBROOK IL 60521-1900

MS TERESA CHANG
GOODWILL INDUSTRIES
9200 WISCONSIN AVE
BETHESDA MD 20814-3896

Official USPS Envelope Guidelines

1. **Capitalize everything in the address and leave out ALL punctuation.**

2. **Use the list of common abbreviations found in the National ZIP Code Directory.** (See 657.) Use numerals rather than words for numbered streets and avenues (9TH AVE NE, 3RD ST SW).

3. **If you know the ZIP + 4 code, use it.** You can get ZIP + 4 information by phoning the Postal Service's ZIP Code information unit.

Preparing a Résumé

A strong résumé isn't generic—a ho-hum-fill-in-the-blanker. Rather, it's a vivid word picture of your skills, knowledge, and past responsibilities. It says exactly who you are by providing the kind of information listed below.

PERSONAL DATA: name, address, phone, e-mail address (enough for the reader to know you and reach you easily)

JOB OBJECTIVE: the type of position you want and the type of organization you want to work for

SKILLS SUMMARY: the key qualities and skills you bring to a position, listed with supporting details
Here are some skill areas that you might consider for your own résumé:
- communication
- organization
- computer (languages, systems)
- sales, marketing, public relations
- management (people, money, other resources)
- problem solving
- working with people, counseling, training

EXPERIENCE: positions you've held (where and when), specific duties and accomplishments

EDUCATION: degrees, courses, special projects

OTHER EXPERIENCES: volunteer work, awards, achievements, teaching assistantships, dormitory resident assistantships, off-campus programs, hobbies, extracurricular activities (related to your job objective)

tips FOR RÉSUMÉ WRITING

- Design each résumé to fit the particular job.
- Be specific—use numbers, dates, names.
- First present information that is the most impressive and/or important to the job for which you are applying. This guideline will help you determine whether to put experience or education first.
- Use everyday language and short, concise phrases.
- Use boldface type, underlining, white space, and indentations to make your résumé more readable.
- Get someone else's reaction before typing the final copy.
- Proofread for spelling, punctuation, and typographical errors.

Sample Résumé

Ada Overlie

Home
451 Wiser Lake Rd.
Ferndale, WA 98248-8941
(360) 354-5916

School
Ogg Hall, Room 222
Balliole College
Eugene, OR 97440-0222
Phone: (503) 341-3611
E-Mail: dvrl@balliole.edu

Job Objective: Part-time assistant in nursery or greenhouse.

Skills Summary:

Horticultural Skills: Familiar with garden planting, care, and
   harvesting practices--planning, timing, companion planting, fertilizing.

Lab Skills: Familiar with procedures for taking fruit
   samples, pureeing them, checking for foreign objects, and
   testing sugar content.

Work Experience:

Summer 1995 and 1996: Lab Technician.
   Mayberry Farms and Processing Plant, Ferndale, WA.
   Worked in Quality Control testing raspberries to make sure
   they met company standards.

Summer 1993 and 1994: Camp Counselor.
   Emerald Lake Summer Camp, Hillsboro, WA.
   Supervised 12-year-olds in many camp activities, including
   nature hikes in which we identified plants and trees.

Education:

August 1996 to present: Balliole College, Eugene, OR.
   Environmental Studies and Communication major.
   Courses completed and in progress include environmental
   studies and general botany. First semester gpa 3.7.

August 1992-June 1996: Ferndale High School, Ferndale, WA.
   Graduated with honors. Courses included biology,
   chemistry, agriculture, U.S. government, economics.

   Special Projects: Completed research papers on
   clean-water legislation and organic farming practices.

References available upon request.

Applying for a Job

When you apply for some jobs, you have to do nothing more than fill out an application form. With other jobs, it's a different story. You may find yourself writing a letter of application, gathering letters of recommendation, and putting together a résumé. Each job is different in what will be required. The following pages provide models to fit nearly every occasion.

The Letter of Application

Your letter of application (or cover letter) introduces you to an employer and often highlights information on an accompanying résumé. Your goal in writing this letter is to convince the employer to invite you for an interview.

Ogg Hall, Room 222
Balliole College
Eugene, OR 97440-0222
April 17, 1997

Address a specific person, if possible.

Professor Edward Mahaffy
Greenhouse Coordinator
Balliole College
Eugene, OR 97440-0316

Dear Professor Mahaffy:

State the position, how you heard about it, and your chief qualification.

I recently talked with Ms. Sierra Arbor in the Financial Aid Office about work-study jobs for 1997-98. She told me about the Greenhouse Assistant position and gave me a job description. As a student completing my freshman year, I'm writing to apply for this position. I believe that my experience qualifies me.

Focus on how your skills meet the reader's needs.

As you can see from my résumé, I spent two summers working in a raspberry operation, doing basic plant care and carrying out quality-control lab tests on the fruit. Also, as I was growing up, I learned a great deal by helping with a large farm garden. In high school and college I studied botany. Because of my interest in this field, I'm planning a double major in Environmental Studies and Communication.

Request an interview and thank the reader.

I would be available for an interview. You may phone me at 341-3611 (and leave a message on my machine) or e-mail me at dvrl@balliole.edu. Thank you for considering my application.

Yours sincerely,

Ada Overlie

Ada Overlie

Encl. résumé

The Recommendation Request Letter

When you apply for a job or program, it helps to have references or recommendations. To get the backup support you need from people familiar with your work (professors and employers), you need to ask for it. You can do this in person or by phone, but a courteous and clear letter or e-mail message makes your request official and helps the person complete the recommendation effectively. Here is a suggested outline:

SITUATION: Remind the reader of your relationship to him or her; then ask the person to write a recommendation or to serve as a reference for you.

EXPLANATION: Describe the work you did for the reader and the type of job, position, or program you are applying for.

ACTION: Explain what form the recommendation should take, whom to send it to, and where and when it needs to be sent.

2456 Charles St.
Lexington, KY 40588-8321
March 23, 1996

Dr. Denise Blueblood
Biology Department
University of Kentucky
Lexington, KY 40506-1440

Dear Dr. Blueblood:

The Situation

As we discussed on the phone, I would appreciate your writing a recommendation letter for me. You know the quality of my academic work, as well as my qualities as a person, and my potential for working in the medical field.

The Explanation

As my professor for Biology 201 and 302, you are familiar with my grades and work habits. As my premed advisor, you know my career plans and have a good sense of whether I have the qualities needed to succeed in the medical profession. I am asking you for your recommendation because I am applying for summer employment with the Lexington Ambulance Service. I recently received my Emergency Medical Technician (Basic) license to prepare for such work.

The Action

Please send your letter to Rick Femur at the University Placement Office by April 1. Thank you for your help. Let me know if you need any other information (phone 231-6700; e-mail jnwllms@ukentucky.edu).

Yours sincerely,

Jon Williams

Jon Williams

The Application Essay

For some applications, you may be asked to submit an essay, a personal statement, or a response paper. For example, you might be applying for admission to a program (social work, engineering, optometry school), or for an internship, a scholarship, or a research grant. Whatever the situation, what you write and how well you write it will be important factors in the success of your application.

On the facing page is a model application essay. Jessy Jezowski wrote this essay during her freshman year as part of her application to a college social work program. She wrote in response to this request: "Please enclose with your application a one-page typewritten statement explaining why you have chosen the social work major as a course of study and social work as a vocation."

tips FOR AN APPLICATION ESSAY

● **Understand what you are being asked to write and why.** How does the essay fit into the entire application? Who will be reading your essay? What will they be looking for?

● **Focus on the instructions for writing the essay.** What type of question is it? What topics are you being asked to write about? What hints do the directions give about possible organization, emphasis, style, length, and method of submitting the essay?

● **Be honest with yourself and your readers.** Don't try to write only what you think readers want to hear.

● **Develop your essay using the following organization** (if the instructions allow for it):

  • an introduction with a fresh, interesting opening statement and a clear focus or theme
  • a body that develops the focus or theme clearly and concisely—with some details and examples—in a way appropriate to the instructions
  • a conclusion that stresses a positive point and looks forward to participating in the program, internship, organization, etc.

● **Write in a style that is personal but professional.** Use words that fit the subject and the readers. Avoid cliches, and balance generalizations with concrete examples and details.

● **Refine your first draft into a polished piece.** First, get feedback from another student or, if appropriate, a professor, and revise the essay. Second, edit the final version thoroughly: you don't want typos and grammar errors to derail your application.

NOTE: For more guidelines on writing essays, see 110-127.

Model Application Essay

February 28, 1997
Professor David Helmstetter
Jessy Jezowski

Personal Statement

The opening provides a clear focus for the essay.

While growing up in Chicago, I would see people hanging out on street corners, by grocery stores, and in parks—with no home and barely any belongings. Poverty and its related problems are all around us, and yet most people walk by them with blinders on. I have found myself quick to assume that someone else will help the poor man on the corner, the woman trapped in an abusive relationship, or the teenager suffering from an eating disorder. But I know in my heart that all members of society are responsible to and for each other. Social welfare issues affect every member of society— including me.

Because these issues are serious and difficult to solve, I wish to major in social work and eventually become a social worker. In the major, I want to gain the knowledge, skills, and attitudes that will make me part of the solution, not part of the problem. By studying social work institutions, the practices of social work, and the theory and history behind social work, I hope to learn how to help people help themselves. When that pregnant teenager comes to me, I want to have strong, practical advice—and be part of an effective social work agency that can help implement that advice.

The writer demonstrates knowledge of the field and explains what she hopes to learn.

Two concrete examples help back up her general statements.

I am especially interested at this point in working with families and teenagers, in either a community counseling or school setting. Two experiences have created this interest. First, a woman in my church who works for an adoption agency, Ms. Lesage, has modeled for me what it means to care for individuals and families within a community and around the world. Second, I was involved in a peer counseling program in high school. As counselors, we received training in interpersonal relationships and the nature of helping. In a concrete way, I experienced the complex challenges of helping others.

The conclusion summarizes her goals for the future.

I believe strongly in the value of all people and am interested in the well-being of others. As a social worker, I would strive to make society better (for individuals, families, and communities) by serving those in need, whatever their problems.

Interviewing for the Job

Your letter of application and résumé represent you. If the employer likes the overall picture and wants a closer look at the real thing, he or she will ask you to come for an interview. Here are some tips to help you get ready:

BEFORE THE INTERVIEW

Think about yourself.

What are your goals? Strengths? Weaknesses?

Think about the employer.

Why is the organization interested in you?

What are the business's goals? Products? Services? Plans?

Think about the interview.

What questions can you expect: Strengths? Weaknesses? Reason for seeking the job?

What materials may the employer want to see: Work samples? Portfolio?

Think about the job.

What does the job involve? What are the hours? Wages? Opportunities for advancement?

DURING THE INTERVIEW

Be attentive.

Introduce yourself to the office staff and say why you're there.

Complete forms neatly and quietly.

Shake hands and look the interviewer in the eye.

Listen carefully.

Be clear.

Answer questions clearly and briefly.

Restate questions in your own words if you are unsure about what the interviewer means.

State your strengths and how you use them.

Ask about the job.

What is the job description? Salary? Benefits? Work schedule? Opportunities for advancement?

AFTER THE INTERVIEW

Tell when and where you can be reached.

Shake hands and thank each person involved in the interview.

Write a follow-up letter.

Writing the Follow-Up Letter

Your application materials have gotten you an interview, and that interview went well. Now what? Pace the floor and chew your nails? You'd be better off putting your hands to work doing another piece of writing that helps an employer or program director make a final decision in your favor. As soon as possible after the interview, send a follow-up letter containing the following:

- **a thank-you comment**
- **a statement confirming your interest in the position or program, and your potential value as an employee, intern, etc., with specific reference to the interview**
- **a statement about your willingness to answer further questions**
- **details about how and when the interviewer can contact you**

2456 Charles St.
Lexington, KY 40588-8321
April 22, 1996

Ms. Ricky Bukowski
Lexington Ambulance Service
245 Resuscitation Row
Lexington, KY 40525-9111

Dear Ms. Bukowski:

Thank you for the interview yesterday. I enjoyed meeting you and some of the other emergency response team members, as well as touring your facilities and seeing LAS's equipment.

I would also enjoy contributing to the important work that your service carries out in the community. I'm convinced that my volunteer work with Hinton's Ambulance Service and my Emergency Medical Technician license (with training in defibrillator monitoring, IV maintenance, and endotracheal intubation) would make me an asset to your team. This experience and training would lessen the amount of on-site training I would need.

I appreciate your considering me for this summer position at Lexington Ambulance. If you have any further questions, please contact me or leave a message on my machine at 231-6700, or e-mail me at jnwllms@ukentucky.edu.

Yours sincerely,

Jon Williams

Jon Williams

Personal Writing

Personal Reminiscence

Personal Essay

Essay of Experience

Writing Memos and E-Mail

A memorandum is a written message sent from one person to other people, usually in the same organization. As such, it is less formal than a letter. A memo can vary in length from a sentence or two to a four- or five-page report. It can be delivered in person, dropped in a mailbox, or sent via e-mail.

Memos are written to create a *flow of information* within an organization—asking and answering questions, describing procedures and policies, reminding people about appointments and meetings. Here are some guidelines:

● **Write memos only when necessary, and only to those who need them.**

● **Distribute them via appropriate media—mail, fax, bulletin boards, kiosk, e-mail.**

● **Make your subject line precise so that the topic is clear and the memo is easy to file.**

● **Get to the point: (1) state the subject, (2) give necessary details, (3) state the response you want.**

The subject line clarifies the memo's purpose.

Date: September 27, 1997

To: All Users of the Bascom Hill Writing Lab

From: Kerri Kelley, Coordinator

Subject: New Hours/New Equipment

Additional details are added as necessary.

Beginning October 15, the Bascom Hill Writing Lab will expand its weekend hours as follows: Fridays, 7:00 A.M.-11:00 P.M.; Saturdays, 8:00 A.M.-11:00 P.M.

Also, six additional computers will be installed next week, making it easier to get computer time. We hope these changes will help meet the increased demand for time and assistance we've experienced this fall. Remember, it's still a good idea to sign up in advance. To reserve time, call the lab at 462-7722 or leave your request via e-mail at bhill@madwis.edu.

The desired response is indicated.

Finally, long-range planners, mark your calendars. The lab will be closed on Thanksgiving Day morning and open from 1:00 P.M.-11:00 P.M. We will also be closed all day on Christmas and New Year's. We will post our semester-break hours sometime next month.

Sending E-Mail

With e-mail, people can correspond through computer networks around the globe. If you have access to e-mail, you can . . .

- ◉ send, forward, and receive many messages quickly and efficiently, making it ideal for group projects and other forms of collaboration;
- ◉ set up mailing lists (specific groups of e-mail addresses) so that you can easily send the same message to several people at the same time;
- ◉ organize messages in "folders" for later reference, and reply to messages;
- ◉ communicate with "home base" while on the road if you have a laptop computer with a modem.

E-MAIL tips

- ● **Revise and edit messages for clarity and correctness before sending them.** Confusing sentences, grammatical errors, and typos limit your ability to communicate on a computer screen just as they do on paper.

- ● **Use e-mail maturely.** Sooner or later you will send e-mail to the wrong person. Keep this in mind at all times and never write anything that would embarrass you if it were sent to the wrong party.

- ● **Make messages easy to read and understand:** (1) provide a clear subject line since readers will scan it and decide whether to read or delete the message; (2) type short paragraphs, with line lengths of no more than 65 characters.

```
From:        "Sherry West" <SWEST@stgeorge.edu>
To:          outreach@stgeorge.edu
Date sent:   Mon, 23 Sept 1996 14:13:06 CST
Subject:     Agenda for Student Outreach Committee Meeting
Priority:    Normal

Just a reminder that our next meeting is this Wednesday, Sept.
25 at 8:00 p.m. in SUB Room 201.  We'll discuss the following
agenda items:

1.  the minutes of our Sept. 11 meeting
2.  a proposal from SADD about Alcohol Awareness Week
3.  a progress report on the Habitat for Humanity project

Before the meeting, review the minutes and the SADD proposal
linked to this message.
```

Personal
Writing

Personal Reminiscence

Personal Essay

Essay of Experience

Personal Writing

We are told that our world is rapidly becoming a global village, and that we can thank all of our technological know-how for this new community. Silicon chips, fiber optics, satellite dishes—there is all manner of sophisticated gadgetry that makes it possible for us to network worldwide.

This new notion of village may lead to some interesting interplay between peoples that, until now, have had little if any contact. You, for example, may be able to link up with students in places as far-flung as Costa Rica and Kenya and the Ukraine.

To think that you can exchange ideas and stories with individuals from just about anywhere in the world sounds truly exciting. Sharing life experiences is powerful stuff. It is how you build true relationships and a meaningful community life. So get ready to link up!

WHAT'S AHEAD

Sharing life experiences defines *personal writing*. It is the type of writing that has you, the writer, at the center. This section in your handbook will help you tell your own story in reminiscences and personal essays. As you write, expect to gain some interesting insights into your life—past, present, and future.

> *"The primal story from which all others come, is your own story—your own personal history."* —**John Rouse**

Personal Writing

QUICK GUIDE

Every time you put fingers to the keyboard (or pen to paper) you disclose something about yourself. It can't be helped. Personal writing, of course, is the most telling type of writing because it is based on your own experiences. As writer John Mayher states, "Our stories point like dreams to certain themes or concerns in our lives, containing either explicitly or implicitly some moral tag, which sums up where we've been."

All personal writing shares the following characteristics:

STARTING POINT: Personal writing begins with a memorable event that you would like to explore and share.

PURPOSE: This type of writing helps you make sense out of your experiences. On another level, personal writing is designed to inform and/or entertain your readers.

FORM: A reminiscence moves in a linear direction, with the details unfolding one after another until the story is told. A personal essay may develop in much the same way, but it will also include explanation and analysis.

AUDIENCE: In most cases, you will be addressing your immediate audience—your writing peers and your instructor.

VOICE: Use your best storytelling voice in a reminiscence. Help readers relive the experience right along with you. And speak openly and honestly in a personal essay. Your writing should sincerely reflect your thoughts and feelings.

POINT OF VIEW: In almost all cases, use the first person (*I*) point of view in personal writing. You are, after all, writing about yourself.

Insights into Writing

Try to picture your subject, a personal experience, as if you were seeing it through the lens of a camera. First pan the camera back and forth. What picture or image appears? Is everything clear? How does this picture make you feel? Then zoom in to get some closer shots. What are people saying? What are they wearing? What expressions do they have on their faces? Once you can see a personal experience from different angles, you're ready to write about it.

Writing a Personal Reminiscence

In developing an autobiography, one question a writer must ask is this: What have been the defining experiences in my life? Or stated in another way, what specific events have made a difference to me? As you plan a reminiscence, you, too, should think of "defining experiences," those events that help to communicate who you really are, and where you have been. Your goal is to re-create a specific time and place so it comes alive for your readers. Refer to the steps below and the models that follow to help you with your writing.

SEARCHING AND SELECTING

Selecting ● You should have little trouble thinking of something to write about. Focus on experiences that appeal to you personally and that will have some appeal to your readers.

Reviewing ● If necessary, freely list ideas until you hit upon incidents or events that seem like defining experiences. You may also want to brain-storm for ideas with your writing peers.

GENERATING THE TEXT

Collecting ● Gather your thoughts about your subject through free writing or clustering. Then collect additional details as needed—by talking to someone about the experience, by referring to old photographs, or by continuing your memory search.

Focusing ● Plan your work as needed. Focus your attention on ideas and details that help readers see, hear, and feel the experience as you recall it.

WRITING AND REVISING

Writing ● Write your first draft freely, working in details according to any planning you may have done. (A reminiscence is a form of narrative writing, so make use of basic storytelling devices—description, dialogue, suspense, etc.—to develop your work.)

Revising ● Carefully review, revise, and refine your writing before publishing it. Remember that your goal is to re-create an incident or event for your readers.

EVALUATING

Is the writing focused around a specific incident or event?

Does the writing contain effective details, descriptions, and/or dialogue?

Does the writing sound sincere and honest?

Will readers appreciate the treatment of the subject?

Personal Reminiscence

The writer of this reminiscence, Kristen Cnossen, shares an experience that has become something of a family tradition—a rite of passage, if you will. The portrayal of the brother/sister relationship is a particularly strong feature in this piece.

The Pond in Ralph's Swamp

The opening paragraph sets the scene for the story to follow.

Every one of us has a story about the pond in Ralph's swamp, and it is always the same story—to get across it on some contraption. My dad and Aunt Carol built a log raft that never made it farther than the middle of the pond before it sank. Both of them still laugh and blame the other person when they talk about it. When my two oldest brothers, Bill and Bob, were around 10, they tried to float across in a cow tank. They were successful only a couple of times before the tank tipped and forced them to abandon ship in the center of the pond and slosh through the water to the shore.

My own pond story happened when I was about seven years old. My brother Darwin, the closest one to my age even though he was seven years my elder, had built a raft that he floated on that pond for the

"The world seemed so much different when I was away from land and floating in the middle of the pond."

whole summer. It was getting to be fall when I joined Darwin on the raft that day. The oaks had turned a burnt orange color that always reminded me of the pumpkins in our garden, and the maples were McIntosh-apple red. The air smelled like fall, and there was enough of a chill that Mom insisted I start wearing my stocking cap—John Deere colors, bright yellow with two narrow green stripes and no yarn ball on top.

The writer captures the sights and smells of this particular time and place.

I walked back to the pond and found Darwin already out there in the middle, poking at something in the water with a branch.

"Can I come out there?" I called to him.

"Sure, walk on out." Smart aleck.

"No, I mean, will you come and get me?"

Without another word, he turned the raft and began to push with the pole so that he was coming my way. When he got to the shore, he slapped down a two-by-four for me to walk up to keep from getting wet. He reached out a hand covered with a dirty gold barn glove to pull me up beside him. After pulling the board back onto the raft, we pushed off again to the middle.

The world seemed so much different when I was away from land and floating in the middle of the pond. I remember that time out there with Darwin as a quiet moment when I just stared at the woods and the circle of open sky over the pond and started to realize that maybe this brother of mine was my friend, too.

Then, suddenly, Darwin ripped my beloved stocking cap off my head. He held it away from me over his head.

"Give it back!" I shouted, furious.

"Nope." He just grinned.

"I know what I can do with this," he said with the fake brilliance that was supposed to make me think that he hadn't been planning this all along. He stuck the hat on the end of the pole and held it out over the water. I screamed for my dear cap, trying to reach it without falling. I stretched my hand toward the end of the pole, and the farther I reached, the farther he held it away from me.

"Give it back!" I gave another fierce scream.

Just then I reached a little too far, and slipped. Darwin grabbed my arm and pulled me back before I had a chance to fall into the water.

He pulled the pole back in. My stocking cap was safe and sound, not a drop of water on it. He flipped it off the end of the pole and into his hands, then put it not so gently on the top of my head, pulling the front flap down over my eyes in his own brotherly show of affection. The war was over. I cooled from furious to just perturbed. The truce was signed as he flipped the edge of my cap back up again so I could see.

That day is only an image in my memory now. Five years ago Darwin died in a farm accident on a sunny day in June. I haven't visited the pond in years, my childhood time there with my brother has passed. But I am reminded today by my two nephews that the pond in Ralph's swamp still has a power over us. They tried to cross it on an old raft, but didn't get very far before they were knee deep in water and had to slosh back to shore. ■

Specific details help readers see the action in progress.

The closing reflects upon the significance of the experience.

Personal Reminiscence

In this reminiscence, Nelson Mandela, president of South Africa, shares a memorable experience that made him intensely proud to be a Xhosa. (The Xhosa are part of the Nguni people in the southeastern region of South Africa.) Mandela re-creates this particular time and place in great detail. (From *Long Walk to Freedom* by Nelson Mandela. Copyright © 1994 by Nelson Rolihlahla Mandela. By permission of Little, Brown and Company.)

from *Long Walk to Freedom*

The opening sentence immediately grabs the readers' attention.

In my final year at Healdtown, an event occurred that for me was like a comet streaking across the night sky. Towards the end of the year, we were informed that the great Xhosa poet, Krune Mqhayi, was going to visit the school. Mqhayi was actually an *imbongi,* a praise singer, a kind of oral historian who marks contemporary events and history with poetry that is of special meaning to his people.

The day of his visit was declared a holiday by the school authorities. On the appointed morning, the entire school, including staff members both black and white, gathered in the dining hall, which was where we held school assemblies. There was a stage at one end of the hall and from it a door led to Dr. Wellington's house. The door itself was nothing special, but we thought of it as Dr. Wellington's door, for no one ever walked through it except Dr. Wellington himself.

Suddenly, the door opened and out walked not Dr. Wellington, but a black man dressed in a leopard-skin kaross and matching hat, who was carrying a spear in either hand. Dr. Wellington followed a moment later, but the sight of a black man in tribal dress coming through that door was electrifying. It is hard to explain the impact it had on us. It seemed to turn the universe upside down. As Mqhayi sat on the stage next to Dr. Wellington, we were barely able to contain our excitement.

The writer stresses the importance of the experience.

But when Mqhayi rose to speak, I confess to being disappointed. I had formed a picture of him in my mind, and in my youthful imagination I expected a Xhosa hero like Mqhayi to be tall, fierce and intelligent-looking. But he was not terribly distinguished and, except for his clothing, seemed entirely ordinary. When he spoke in Xhosa, he did so slowly and haltingly, frequently pausing to search for the right word and then stumbling over it when he found it.

At one point, he raised his assegai into the air for emphasis, and accidentally hit the curtain wire above him. Which made a sharp noise and caused the curtain to sway. The poet looked at the point of his spear and then the curtain wire and, deep in thought, walked back and forth across the stage. After a minute, he stopped walking, faced us, and newly energized, exclaimed that this incident—the assegai striking the wire—symbolized the clash between the culture of Africa and that of Europe. . . .

'What I am talking about,' he continued, 'is not a piece of bone touching a piece of metal, or even the overlapping of one culture and another, what I am talking to you about is the brutal clash between what is ingenious and good, and what is foreign and bad. We cannot allow these foreigners who do not care for our culture to take over our nation. I predict that, one day, the forces of African society will achieve a momentous victory over the interloper. For too long we have succumbed to the false gods of the white man. But we shall emerge and cast off these foreign notions. . . .'

Mqhayi then began to recite his well-known poem in which he apportions the stars in the heavens to the various nations of the world. I had never before heard it. Roving the stage and gesturing with his assegai towards the sky, he said that to the people of Europe—the French, the Germans, the English—'I give you the Milky Way, the largest constellation, for you are a strange people, full of greed and envy, who quarrel over plenty.' He allocated certain stars to the Asian nations, and to North and South America. He then discussed Africa and separated the continent into different nations, giving specific constellations to different tribes. He had been dancing about the stage, waving his spear, modulating his voice, and now, suddenly, he became still, and lowered his voice.

'Now, come you, O House of Xhosa,' he said and slowly began to lower himself so that he was on one knee. 'I give unto you the most important and transcendent star, the Morning Star, for you are a proud and powerful people. It is the star for counting the years—the years of manhood.' When he spoke this last word, he dropped his head to his chest. We rose to our feet, clapping and cheering. I did not want ever to stop applauding. I felt such intense pride at that point, not as an African, but as a Xhosa; I felt like one of the chosen people. ■

Re-creating parts of the guest's speech adds drama and energy to the writing.

The writer captures the climactic conclusion to the speech—and the response it elicited.

Writing a Personal Essay

According to writer Phillip Lopate, writing the personal essay is the process of exploring the "stomach growls," the strong feelings you have about some aspect of your life. You may want to explore an earlier time in your life—perhaps a time of change, or a time of joy or pain. Then again, you may want to write about some part of your present life—perhaps your relationship (or lack thereof) with an individual or a group. Your goal should be to develop an essay that informs and/or entertains, and that impels readers to think about their own lives. Refer to the guidelines below and the models that follow for help with your writing.

SEARCHING AND SELECTING

Reviewing ● Review your journal entries for ideas, or list subjects that come to mind after you read the model essays. Just about anything in your life that interests you, amuses you, angers you, or makes you think is a possible subject for a personal essay.

Searching ● If you're still stuck, think about different people in your life, review photo albums, talk to people, check your purse or wallet for membership cards or ticket stubs. (You shouldn't have to look far for ideas.)

GENERATING THE TEXT

Collecting ● Write freely about your subject, letting your ideas take you where they will. Dig as deep as you can into your experience.

Assessing ● Examine your free writing carefully to help you get a feel for your subject. Look for parts that you like and want to explore further. Also look for any emerging main idea or viewpoint that could serve as the focus of your essay. Continue searching and shaping as needed.

NOTE: A personal essay is a blend of narrative (sharing some aspect of your life) and analysis (commenting upon this time).

WRITING AND REVISING

Writing ● As you write your first draft, allow your own personality and feelings to come through in your writing.

Revising ● Review, revise, and refine your writing. As you work with your essay, try to maintain its original freshness of thought.

EVALUATING

Is the voice sincere, indicating a personal attachment between the writer and the work?

Has the writer established a viewpoint about the subject, and is the essay built around this point of view?

Will readers appreciate the treatment of the subject?

Personal Essay

In this essay, Kevin Hoogendoorn explores a time and place in his life that is lost forever—working cattle on the family farm. Notice how the passage of time has changed the writer's attitude about his subject.

Working Cattle—We'd Hate to Love It

The opening paragraph sets the scene and identifies the subject of the essay.

I grew up on a 400-acre farm five miles southwest of Inwood, Iowa. Our entire crop, and more, was fed to the 1,000 head of finishing cattle we kept on the place. One thousand cattle means a lot of work, especially when they need to be "worked." Working cattle consists of running them through a process of vaccination, deworming, and implantation. We worked two bunches of cattle twice a year. Four separate days out of the year were set aside for this. Usually it was a Saturday during one of our school vacations. It was a long, hard day.

We worked the cattle into our barn, and then from the small holding pen to another room where there was a self-catching headgate. First, all the boys went outside to chase cattle from the yard into the holding pen. We had a row of feed bunks that formed a wide alley through which we would chase the cattle. As soon as we rounded the corner of the alley, we had a straight shot to the holding pen in the barn. At the corner we would raise a ruckus by hollering, running, and siccing Smokey on the cattle. Smokey was a real cattle dog.

The writer clearly has a working knowledge of his subject.

Once we got enough cattle (approximately 30 at a time) in the pen, we would all head to our prospective jobs. The jobs were divided according to age, responsibility, and danger. The oldest boy would chase the cattle, four at a time, toward the holding chute leading to the headgate. The next eldest injected wormers, the next moved along the alley to keep the cattle up and moving, and the youngest pulled the gate rope.

Since I was the youngest, I usually ran the gate. I would hold the gate open and let one steer into the chute. The steer, thinking it was free, would move through the chute and be trapped by the automatic headgate. Kent would slip a holding bar behind the other three cattle while work began on the first. Mom poured Dursban, a delicing agent, on the steer's back. Dave reached through the side and shot Levasole, a wormer, under the skin of the animal's neck. Mom would then hit the steer in the rump with a Rednose/Virus Diarrhea vaccination. At the same time, Dad would be trying to catch the tossing head to put Ralgro, a steroid implant, in the ear.

As soon as everything was finished, Dad opened the headgate to let the steer out. I then opened the back chute

Working Cattle—We'd Hate to Love It
(continued)

gate to let another one in. Then the process began again.

This digression
effectively
captures the
difficulty
of working
cattle.

It seems easy writing about it on paper; however, at the time, it seemed like a million things could go wrong, and they usually did. I would let two steers in, Dad would let one out before Mom was done. Needles broke, syringes had to be held in armpits to keep them from freezing, cattle would turn around in the alley, and so on. It was a long, hard day, and when things went wrong, we were further aggravated. Tempers grew short, words were exchanged, and verbal abuse was doled out equally to humans and cattle.

At noon we would all troop into the house and eat a huge plate of Mom's hotdish, which would have been cooking in the oven since morning. What a welcome break! After dinner we would try to sneak to the other room to read the paper only to be rousted back out of the house by Dad.

Working cattle changed as I grew older. I did different jobs, and more jobs, since fewer people were left to work. My last summer before college was really hard on my Dad. He asked me to work for him, but I decided to work for my uncle at Hoogendoorn Construction to establish my own reputation as a worker in the community. That left only my dad to do almost everything by himself. Eventually, he had to sell all of his cattle and retire into "crop only" farming.

In closing,
the writer
reflects upon
this lost time
in his life.

It's been three years since I've worked cattle, and I feel an empty spot inside when I think of it. Never again will our entire family get together to do a job the way we did back then. It amazes me how quirky life is. The things we think we hate, if taken away, we begin to love again. I'm sure my father went through this feeling when he left Grandpa's home, I went through it, and my kids will go through it when they leave my home. As time moves on, we must move also. ■

Personal Essay

In this essay, journalist Cheryl A. Davis expresses strong feelings about one important aspect of her life—her use of a wheelchair. As you will see, Davis establishes a definite point of view about her subject. (Reprinted by permission from *The Progressive,* 409 East Main Street, Madison, WI 53703.)

A Day on Wheels

The writer begins with a "telling" experience to grab the readers' attention.

"Man, if I was you, I'd shoot myself," said the man on the subway platform. No one else was standing near him. I realized he was talking to me.

"Luckily, you're not," I said, gliding gracefully away.

For me, this was not an unusual encounter; indeed, it was a typical episode in my continuing true-life sitcom, "Day on Wheels." . . .

I use a wheelchair; I am not "confined" to one. Actually, I get around well. I drive a van equipped with a wheelchair-lift to the train station. I use a powered wheelchair with high-amperage batteries to get to work. A manual chair, light enough to carry, enables me to visit the "walkies" who live upstairs and to ride in their Volkswagens.

My life has been rich and varied, but my fellow passengers assume that, as a disabled person, I must be horribly deprived and so lonely that I will appreciate any unsolicited overture.

"Do you work?" a woman on the train asked me recently.

I said I did.

"It's nice that you have something to keep you busy, isn't it?"

She also provides commentary or analysis throughout the essay.

Since we are thought of as poor invalids in need of chatting up, people are not apt to think too hard about what they are saying to us. It seems odd, since they also worry about the "right" way to talk to disabled people.

"How do you take a bath?" another woman asked me, apropos of nothing.

One day, an elderly man was staring at me as I read the newspaper.

"Would you like to read the sports section?" I asked him.

"How many miles can that thing go before you need new batteries?" he responded. . . .

For those whose disablement is still recent, the gratuitous remarks and unsolicited contributions can be exceptionally hurtful. It takes time to learn how to protect yourself. To learn how to do it gracefully can take a lifetime.

Many of us take the position that the people who bother us are to be pitied for their ignorance. We take it upon ourselves to "educate" them. We forgive them their trespasses and answer their questions patiently and try to straighten them out.

A Day on Wheels
(continued)

A "defining experience" is given special attention.

Others prefer to ignore the rude remarks and questions altogether. I tried that, but it didn't work. There was one woman on the train who tipped the scales for me.

"You're much too pretty to be in a wheelchair," she said.

I stared straight ahead, utterly frozen in unanticipated rage. Undaunted, she grabbed my left arm below the elbow to get my attention.

"I said, 'You're too pretty to be in a wheelchair.' "

In my fury, I lost control. Between my brain and my mouth, the mediating force of acquired tact had vanished.

"What do you think?" I snapped. "That God holds a beauty contest and if you come in first, you don't have to be in one?"

She turned away, and a moment later, was chatting with an old woman beside her as if nothing had been said at all. But I was mortified, and I moved to the other end of the train car. For that one lapse, I flagellated myself all afternoon. When I got home, I telephoned one of my more socially adroit disabled friends for advice.

Nick is a therapist, a Ph.D. from Stanford, and paraplegic. "How do you deal with the other bozos on the bus?" I asked him.

"I just say, 'Grow up,' " Nick answered.

That was a bit haughtier than I could pull off, I told him.

"Well, look," he said. "If those words don't do it, find something else. The main thing is to get them to stop bothering you, right?"

Dialogue gives the essay a sense of immediacy.

"Nick, if I'm *too* rude, they won't learn a thing. They'll just tell themselves I'm maladjusted."

"Then tell them their behavior is inappropriate."

"Inappropriate. That's marvelous!" I decided to try it next time.

"Next time" arrived last week. I didn't see the man coming. I was on the train platform, and he approached me from behind and tapped me on the shoulder.

"What's your disability?" he asked, discarding civilities.

I turned and looked at him. "That is not an appropriate question to ask a stranger," I said quietly.

"Well, *I* have schizophrenia," he said proudly.

"I didn't ask you."

"I feel rejected," he said.

"Well, then don't say things like that to people you don't know."

The train came and we got on together. I offered him a conciliatory remark, and he quieted down. Clearly he was not the best person for my new approach, but I think I'm headed in the right direction. ■

Writing an Essay of Experience

Henry David Thoreau found great satisfaction in "pursuing, keeping up with, and circling round and round his life." He was at the center of his writing universe. You, too, must "circle round and round" your life in order to write perceptively about it. Your perceptions are especially important in an essay of experience, in which you reflect upon a pivotal time and place in your life. The focal point of your writing is the change the experience has brought about. Refer to the guidelines below and the models that follow for help with your writing.

SEARCHING AND SELECTING

Searching ● Explore your past for events that changed your attitude about people, places, and long-held beliefs. Remember that you're looking for life-changing experiences.

Selecting ● Make sure your subject can pass the before-and-after test: "*Before* a particular experience, I was . . . , but *after* this time, I . . ." (This structure provides an effective frame for this form of writing.)

GENERATING THE TEXT

Free Writing ● Once you select a subject, cluster or write freely about it to recapture some of the details related to this time.

Focusing ● You will probably make some interesting discoveries about your subject during your free writing. Don't, however, think you must understand everything about the experience before you start your first draft.

WRITING AND REVISING

Writing ● Experiment with different starting points for your essay: establishing background, describing the setting, jumping into the action, and so on. Also consider how you will discuss the significance of this experience in your life.

Reviewing ● If you're concerned about the freshness or immediacy of your writing, go back to your free writing. Scan your initial writing for interesting phrases and ideas to incorporate into your essay. Also review the model essays for inspiration.

Refining ● Proofread and edit your essay, using the style section and Proofreader's Guide in your handbook.

EVALUATING

Is the experience re-created with specific detail?

Is the significance of the subject—the change it has brought about—effectively presented?

Will readers appreciate the treatment of the subject?

Essay of Experience

Tamecka L. Crawford's essay explores a turning point in her recent past—when she stopped feeling sorry for herself, and started to take control of her life. As you read, notice that the essay follows the "before and after" structure—the basic frame for an essay of experience. (Copyright © 1995 by Youth Communication. Reprinted from *Foster Care Youth United,* Sept./Oct. 1995.)

From "Group Home Child" to College Success

The writer establishes her special situation— a foster child entering college.

Going off to college for the first time can be a scary experience for anyone, but especially for a foster child. We don't have the support of a parent, and a lot of times we feel as if we're alone in the world. When I left for Sullivan County Community College back in January of 1994, I wondered what college life would be like for me.

When I first started classes, things seemed fine. I had six classes, and the workload was about right. But after a little while, I met a guy and started spending lots of time with him, skipping classes and not studying. I felt I had all the time in the world to pull my grades up. So I slowed down, and started missing classes that I didn't like. As the semester progressed, I started having trouble, and my grades dropped tremendously in history and math.

The "before" part of the essay explores her early college experience.

I found myself using the excuse of being in foster care every time I missed a class or failed an exam. A lot of times I would say to myself, "Oh, I'm in a group home. Who cares if I go to class or not, or if I fail an exam, or even if I pass one?" My self-esteem was very low during my first semester. I sometimes just gave up and didn't care. As a result, I completed my first semester with a 1.0 grade point average, and ended up on academic probation.

I felt nobody cared for me. And it showed. I kept making the mistake of comparing my life to that of students who had parents calling often and coming to visit them. I wanted so badly to have someone care about me like that. I felt neglected, not to mention jealous.

This self-analysis serves as the turning point in the essay.

Just before the end of the first semester, I realized that I had wasted time feeling sorry for myself and had to do something about it. I realized that time was passing me by, and nobody was going to care for me until I cared for myself. I was so wrapped up in worrying about having people do things for me and care for me, that I wasn't taking the time to care for myself.

Tired of Excuses

I got tired of using my foster-care experience as an excuse. I was tired of failing my exams. I was tired of crying. At the same time, I also noticed that some of the people that I was envying weren't doing so well in their classes, either.

I finally realized that I wasn't failing my classes because I was in foster care. I was failing because I had been paying too much attention to what people thought of me and how they treated me, and too little attention to my schoolwork. I had to accept the fact that I was in foster care and move on. It wasn't being in a group home that was holding me back; it was me holding myself back.

The "after" part explores the writer's later success.

In my second semester my grade point average shot up to 3.25. I was studying night and day, especially in subjects like history, which I always had problems with. I went to a tutor who worked with me, and I also found peer tutors (fellow college students who were good in a particular subject) to help me. In exchange, I'd type for them or make them dinner.

Help from Counselor

My next step was to get counseling. I had a nice female counselor who talked to me about school, my group home, and other things on my mind. At the end of the sessions, she would give me suggestions on how to deal with my problems. It helped me realize that while I couldn't have the family relationships that I wanted so badly, I could thank God for the people who were taking time to help me in any way they could.

I also got a part-time job to make some extra money to pay for whatever the group home couldn't help me with. I was even able to put some money in the bank. Basically, I started trying not to depend on the system so much.

Strength from Foster Care

The closing focuses on the real learning that has taken place.

Through counseling, I realized that in some ways being a foster child had its advantages for me. For example, living in a group home was a big help in adjusting to college life; I had already learned how to live with people's different personalities and attitudes. Also, I had already learned a sense of independence. Just like in a group home, when you're in college, you have to do things for yourself and make sure things get done on time.

Most importantly, I learned that in order for anything to change, I first had to care about myself. Then I'd be able to care about the situation and do what I needed to do. Now my overall grade point average is 3.0, which is great compared to how things were looking during my first semester. And I'm looking forward to finishing my last semester. ■

Essay of Experience

In this model, author Amy Tan reflects upon an experience that taught her an important lesson about being an American—and being Chinese. Notice how effectively Tan uses specific details to make the experience come alive. (From *Fish Cheeks* by Amy Tan, © 1989 by Amy Tan. Reprinted by permission of the author and the Sandra Dijkstra Literary Agency.)

Fish Cheeks

I fell in love with the minister's son the winter I turned fourteen. He was not Chinese, but as white as Mary in the manger. For Christmas I prayed for this blond-haired boy, Robert, and a slim new American nose.

When I found out that my parents had invited the minister's family over for Christmas Eve dinner, I cried. What would Robert think of our shabby *Chinese* Christmas? What would he think of our noisy *Chinese* relatives, who lacked proper American manners? What terrible disappointment would he feel upon seeing not a roasted turkey and sweet potatoes but *Chinese* food?

The questions help build suspense in the writing.

On Christmas Eve I saw that my mother had outdone herself in creating a strange menu. She was pulling black veins out of the backs of fleshy prawns. The kitchen was littered with appalling mounds of raw food: A slimy rock cod with bulging fish eyes that pleaded not to be thrown into a pan of hot oil. Tofu, which looked like stacked wedges of rubbery white sponges. A bowl soaking dried fungus back to life. A plate of squid, their backs crisscrossed with knife markings so they resembled bicycle tires.

"On Christmas Eve I saw that my mother had outdone herself in creating a strange menu . . ."

Specific verbs like "licked" and "murmured" make the experience come alive.

And then they arrived—the minister's family and all my relatives in a clamor of doorbells and rumpled Christmas packages. Robert grunted hello, and I pretended he was not worthy of existence.

Dinner threw me deeper into despair. My relatives licked the ends of their chopsticks and reached across the table, dipping them into the dozen or so plates of food. Robert and his family waited patiently for platters to be passed to them. My relatives murmured with pleasure when my mother brought out the whole steamed fish. Robert grimaced. Then my father poked his chopsticks just below the fish eyes and plucked out the soft meat. "Amy, your favorite," he said, offering me the tender fish cheek. I wanted to disappear.

At the end of the meal, my father leaned back and belched loudly, thanking my mother for her fine cooking. "It's a polite Chinese custom to show you are satisfied," explained my father to our astonished guests. Robert was looking down at his plate with a reddened face. The minister managed to muster up a quiet burp. I was stunned into silence for the rest of the night.

After everyone had gone, my mother said to me, "You want to be the same as American girls on the outside." She handed me an early gift. It was a miniskirt in beige tweed. "But inside you must always be Chinese. You must be proud you are different. Your only shame is to have shame."

The writer concludes with an analysis of the experience.

And even though I didn't agree with her then, I knew that she understood how much I had suffered during the evening's dinner. It wasn't until many years later—long after I had gotten over my crush on Robert—that I was able to fully appreciate her lessons and the true purpose behind our particular menu. For Christmas Eve that year, she had chosen all my favorite foods. ■

Report
Writing

Summary Report

Compiled Report

Interview Report

Observation Report

Personal Research Report

Report Writing

In some ways personal writing is easy. After all, you alone possess the information your readers need to appreciate your subject. But in report writing, you engage in a search that goes beyond your personal reservoir. You learn as much as you can about a subject other than yourself and shape your findings in a way that makes sense and holds your readers' attention. You're interested in sharing information, not in sharing memories.

Reports function in a number of different ways. An interview report, for example, cites the views of a person you have interviewed. A summary report distills the most important elements of a chapter or an article, and a personal research report explains what you have learned about a subject that interests you. What makes any report work is your clear understanding of the information you have gathered.

WHAT'S AHEAD

This section provides guidelines and models for a variety of reports—summary reports, compiled reports, interview reports, observation reports, and personal research reports. Each type gets you thoughtfully involved in the whole investigating and reporting process.

"There's something in life that's a curtain, and I keep trying to raise it."

—Maxine Hong Kingston

Report Writing

QUICK GUIDE

Reports explore timely subjects—people, places, and events. It is the type of writing you find in all current magazines, addressing the needs and interests of various audiences. The best report writing contains interesting ideas plus personality; it is informative and pleasing to read. At the heart of an effective report are a writer's genuine curiosity about a subject and a sincere commitment to present his or her findings in a professional manner.

All report writing shares the following characteristics:

STARTING POINT: Report writing begins with your interest in a particular person, place, or event.

PURPOSE: The purpose is to learn about a subject of current interest. On another level, the purpose is to educate or enlighten your readers.

FORM: Report writing follows a variety of formats. For example, an interview report may be set up in a basic question-and-answer format. An observation report may simply present sensory details as they were observed. A personal research report may be essentially narrative in structure.

AUDIENCE: In most cases, you will be speaking to your writing peers and your instructor, unless, of course, your report is intended for a campus or community publication.

VOICE: Speak to your readers sincerely and honestly about your subject; keep them engaged in your story.

POINT OF VIEW: Use third-person point of view *(he, she, they)* in reports, unless you have a strong personal attachment to your subject (as in a personal research report). Then use first-person point of view *(I)*.

Insights into Writing

Remember that report writing is the process of looking outward—the process of observing, listening to, experiencing, and learning about the world around you. Your ability to write effective reports depends upon your willingness to gather a lot of information. As writer Donald Murray states, "Readers hunger for specific information. The more concrete and detailed the information, the more it will interest readers."

Writing a Summary Report

A summary report highlights the main points in a longer text (usually an article or a chapter). To prepare a summary report, you need to ask three questions: What is the main point in the text? What information (facts, statistics, examples, etc.) does the writer use to support this point? What are the most compelling or important features in the selection? Use the guidelines below and the model that follows to help you write your report.

SEARCHING AND SELECTING

Searching ● In most cases, your instructor will either assign a text for you to summarize or ask you to find an article related to a particular topic.

Selecting ● To find your own article, check indexes in your library (like the *Readers' Guide to Periodical Literature*), the on-line catalog, the Internet, and so on. Skim a number of articles that seem interesting and fit the assignment before you make your choice.

GENERATING THE TEXT

Noting ● Carefully read through the article, paying special attention to the key ideas and important supporting details. Take notes on this information.

Assessing ● Review your article and your notes. Did you identify the important information? And do you fully understand the main point of the text?

Focusing ● If necessary, skim the article once more. Then plan your summary. Decide what you want to say first, second, third, etc. Organize your ideas in a brief outline.

WRITING AND REVISING

Writing ● Write your first draft, using your planning and organizing as your guide. Your opening sentence or paragraph should clearly state the main idea of the selection.

Revising ● Ask yourself these questions when you review your first draft: Does the summary stick to the author's main points? Is my summary complete? Are the ideas clearly stated? Revise and refine accordingly.

EVALUATING

Does the summary report display a clear understanding of the text?

Has the text been effectively reduced to "summary" size?

Does the summary move smoothly from point to point?

Summary

In this report, student writer Julie Ewers presents a summary of a chapter called "Superkids" in the book *Growing Up Poor.* Notice how Ewers focuses on the author's main point and briefly summarizes the stories of two young people who manage to succeed against great odds.

Give Me a Chance

The first paragraph summarizes the chapter's main point.

Many students take education for granted. For students in inner-city schools, however, getting through high school can be incredibly challenging. Yet some teens, supported by their parents, their teachers, and their religious faith, overcome almost insurmountable odds.

An example from the chapter is cited.

Inner-city schools lack resources needed to educate students. The chapter mentions one school that "had no laboratory sciences, no band, no college-bound classes, and no football team." Imagine trying to motivate students in such an environment! Alain was encouraged by his dad, who made sure his kids made it through school. Alain began to work at a young age, and all too soon, he witnessed gambling and terrible acts of violence. He "learned that you trust no one at all, under no circumstances." He knew that he had to work hard to achieve anything. That work ethic, combined with motivating words from his father and with special guidance from some adult mentors, helped him work his way to graduation.

Bits of dialogue capture the essence of the original text.

Other students avoided traps, such as drugs and gangs, by getting involved in school and religious groups. Sticking with similarly minded peers, these teens focused on doing well in school. Tammy credits God and friends for her success. A journal entry reflects her dedication: "I thanked God for another day, and I went to school and to all my classes. I worked in the office at school." Tammy's teachers recognized her positive attitude and gave her leadership roles and the kind of encouragement she needed.

The final paragraph ties the piece together and gives a clear summary statement.

Tammy and Alain are two of the teens mentioned in "Superkids." They are lucky, but many others slip through the cracks. Some kids are blessed with "talent, determination, and positive adult influences," while others who desperately need attention find little support. Parents, schools, and religious groups must join together to help these kids, all of whom deserve the chance to reach their full potential. Then maybe successful students won't be newsworthy exceptions among their inner-city peers. They will all be superkids. ■

Writing a Compiled Report

In developing this type of report, you consult a variety of sources about a timely, interesting subject. Your sources may include reading material, interviews, questionnaires, the Internet, and so on. Your goal is to bring together (compile) this information into a unified report that informs and/or entertains your readers. Compiled reports are often found in newspapers and magazines. Use the guidelines below and the models that follow to help you develop your writing.

SEARCHING AND SELECTING

Reviewing ● Your instructor may provide a list of subjects for you to choose from. Otherwise, review news headlines, library indexes, or computer resources for possible writing ideas.

Selecting ● You may also want to brainstorm for ideas with a small group of your peers. Consider new products or procedures, interesting careers and pastimes, and intriguing individuals or groups. (Make sure that you have access to information about a potential subject.)

GENERATING THE TEXT

Collecting ● Consult multiple sources to learn about your subject. (Try to carry out at least one interview or discussion.) Make sure to take careful notes on important facts, figures, and quotations.

Assessing ● Come to some conclusion about the significance of the information you have collected. Let that conclusion be the focus of your report. Then plan your report, selecting and arranging facts to support this focus.

WRITING AND REVISING

Writing ● Write your first draft, working in details according to your planning. However, before you get into the meat of your report, experiment with a few opening paragraphs. Try to come up with something that grabs your readers' attention.

Revising ● Carefully review, revise, and refine your report. Make sure each fact, figure, and quotation is accurate and that the source of the information is clearly cited.

EVALUATING

Is the report clearly focused around a timely, interesting subject?
Does the report include specific information from multiple sources?
Will readers appreciate the information provided?

Compiled Report

The United States is in the middle of a "fat-free frenzy," even as waistlines continue to grow. Jenni Engebretsen explores this phenomenon in the following report compiled for a college newspaper. Notice how she weaves information from the American Medical Association, the American Dietetic Association, and several interviews into this provocative report. (© 1996 *The Daily Northwestern,* Student Publishing Co.)

Fat Substitutes Are Deceptive Cure-All for American Waistlines

We're all familiar with slogans such as "low-calorie" and "sugar-free." But those are phrases of the past. These days it's hard to walk down a supermarket aisle and not notice America's fixation, perhaps even obsession, with fat. It is a game of how little fat one can ingest while still enjoying all those snack-time favorites. In today's market of "nonfat" and "zero fat," it is even questionable whether products offering modest "low-fat" slogans can remain contenders. But how long can this fat-free frenzy hold its grip on the American population?

> **A question identifies the focus of this commentary.**

Waistlines have continued to grow even in an intense era of fat watching. A 1994 study published in the *Journal of American Medical Association* showed that one-third of adults were overweight between 1988 and 1991. In previous years, those figures held steady at one-quarter of the population. Despite America's current fixation on fat, Maureen Pestine, Northwestern campus nutritionist, said sugar may return as the focus of people's health in the future.

> **Quotations from a professional add authority to the report.**

"My big concern is that people are eating all these fat-free products thinking this is a way to lose weight," Pestine said. "Generally, the fat-free products have more sugar."

Unfortunately, these empty calories are a culprit of weight gain.

"I don't think the companies see it as a problem," Pestine said. "They think, 'Let's get rid of all the fat and give them all the sugar.' "

Fat leads to satiety, a feeling of satisfaction. Without it, people tend to feel less full and often eat more as a result. This leads to trouble for some people.

"They think they can eat a whole box of fat-free something," Pestine said.

> **National dietary guidelines are cited.**

Current dietary guidelines issued by the American Dietetic Association call for a diet moderate in sugar that includes plenty of grain products, vegetables, and fruits. Making broader food choices, focusing on proportionality and balancing food with physical activity are additional suggestions. But such guidelines lack the magical, cure-all appeal Americans desire.

Dan Henroid, a dietitian for Evanston Hospital, sees a future trend in the increasing popularity of meal-replacement shakes. Boost, a shake made by Mead Johnson, is specifically marketed for people under 30. The availability of replacement shakes has risen, but consumers should be cautious, Henroid said.

"I don't necessarily view that as a good trend," he said. "Taking time to prepare a balanced meal is a preferred option."

Olestra, Proctor and Gamble's brand of the fat replacer olean, was recently approved by the Food and Drug Administration. Though not available in products currently on the market and only appearing in test markets this fall, Olestra may be the trend of the future. Without sacrificing taste, Olestra allows consumers to cut back on fat and calories and satisfy their urge to crunch at the same time. Its additional fatty acids make Olestra too large to be digested or absorbed, so instead, it passes directly through the body. For example, a regular 1-ounce bag of chips containing 10 grams of fat and 150 calories would contain 0 grams of fat and only 70 calories with Olestra. Same taste. No guilt. Certainly there must be a catch.

More than 100 tests have been performed on Olestra over the past 25 years. In high quantities, consumers may experience abdominal cramps or loose stools. A decrease in the absorption of karotenoids and the fat soluble vitamins A, D, E, and K from other foods can also occur.

While Olestra may appear to be a quick solution, some might use it as another excuse to jump on the fat-free band-wagon. Olestra may eliminate fat grams, but consumers must remain on the lookout for lingering calories.

Henroid sees bio-engineered foods as prominent in the nutrition world of the future. Among the pioneers of these foods is Monsanto, a national company based in St. Louis, that currently offers a slow-ripening, cross-bred tomato. Such advancements might encourage consumers to increase their fruit and vegetable intake, Henroid said.

"They might make (fruits and vegetables) more available," he said. "Personally, I think the flavor is much better."

And where does this leave the health-conscious shopper? Scrutinizing popular trends, decreasing overall fat consumption, and eating a reasonable amount of food are solid suggestions. But the maze of food and nutrition fetishes won't become any clearer in the future. "We're all going to need to be better consumers," said Patti Lucin, NU co-director of health education. ∎

Another professional adds a word of caution.

Information from clinical tests is summarized and presented.

The ending includes the writer's summary and a final authoritative quotation.

Compiled Report

The Vietnam War may have been the "most unpopular war in U.S. history," but it was a war in which Hispanics served and died in large numbers. Laura Figueroa details the contributions of those soldiers in the following report that she compiled for *Hispanic Magazine*. Note that she saves her most dramatic statistic for her conclusion. (This article is copyrighted © 1994 by *Hispanic Magazine*. It is reprinted by permission.)

Not Without Honor

The opening provides necessary background information.

World War II has been celebrated all year, but this year also marked the twentieth anniversary of the end of the Vietnam War, a fact that passed without comment. While the aims of World War II seemed clear, the Vietnam War (1959-1975) divided the nation. Further separating the two conflicts is a belief that World War II was a war with a clear victory, whereas Vietnam was a murky conflict, the first foreign war the U.S. "lost."

Three million men and women served in the most unpopular war in U.S. history, and more Hispanics served and died in Vietnam than in any other U.S. war. Many Americans protested the number of young people dying in Vietnam, while others believed it was America's duty to fight Communism. But no one felt the war's impact more than those actually serving there. In the beginning, Hispanics were eager to fight, but this eagerness turned to concern as the body count rose.

Telling one soldier's story adds human interest to the report.

Sergeant Jerry Soto of Austin, Texas, was anxious when he was drafted, but he remembers landing in Pleiku, Vietnam, and thinking it was beautiful. "It was so green. It was hard to believe it was a war zone." Then five-feet-seven and 118 pounds, Soto soon discovered the danger lurking beneath that thick foliage. As a medic in charge of sick call, he prepped wounded soldiers for surgery and made sure they were tagged properly. He also dispensed morphine to those beyond help to ease their pain as they died.

"It was like being in hell. But I would do it again."

Another first-person account is cited.

The memory of seeing his buddies die violently still disturbs him. Although Soto believes that the Vietnam War made him a different person, his allegiance to his country remains apparent. "It was like being in hell. But I would do it again. It's my job. Even if you don't believe in it, a good soldier does as he's told."

Master Sergeant Roy Benavidez did just that—he went

back again. After being wounded during his first tour of duty and told he would never walk again, he not only proved his doctors wrong but also made it into the elite Army Special Forces. Upon his return to Vietnam in 1968, he volunteered for Unit 56, a unit that had very high casualties. Benavidez volunteered to help rescue twelve men from his unit. In his [1995] book, *Medal of Honor,* he says, "I couldn't leave them down there. We had to do something." He led the wounded soldiers back to the rescue helicopter, recovered the bodies of the dead, and went back to destroy classified documents so they would not fall into the hands of the enemy. For these actions, he earned the Congressional Medal of Honor.

The writer shares information from an authoritative source.

According to Robert Jay Lifton in his book *Home from the War,* many Vietnam vets suffer from post traumatic stress disorder. Being viewed negatively by stateside Americans only served to intensify this illness. While many vets today maintain a healthy respect for the war and its aftermath, others struggle to put the past behind them. Many refuse to speak of their experiences in Indochina, possibly in an attempt to forget them. But no one should ever forget the horrors of one of the bloodiest wars of this century, which left almost 58,000 Americans dead. An often-cited figure indicates that Hispanics made up 19 percent of Vietnam casualties at a time when they comprised only 5 percent of the U.S. population. But Tony Morales of the American G.I. Forum says this figure is larger—more than 27 percent of the names on the Vietnam War Memorial are Hispanic. ■

The article ends with a powerful set of statistics.

Writing an Interview Report

Writer William Zinsser states, "Nothing so animates writing as someone telling what he thinks or what he does—in his own words." Zinsser is referring here to one of his favorite forms of writing, the interview report. This form of writing, of course, is based on the information you gather while interviewing a particular individual. You are, in effect, sharing another person's story. The success of an interview report depends upon your ability to make your subject's story come alive for readers. Use the guidelines below and the models that follow to help you develop your writing.

SEARCHING AND SELECTING

Reviewing ● Your instructor may ask you to interview someone who is knowledgeable in a particular field, or who is (or was) involved in a specific event or experience. Otherwise, simply think of individuals you would like to interview. Consider campus officials, community leaders, local personalities, professionals, skilled workers, neighbors, and so on.

GENERATING THE TEXT

Preparing ● Gather background information about your subject, and generate a list of questions you would like to ask. (Avoid questions that call for "yes" and "no" answers.) Also make arrangements to meet with your subject.

Recording ● Take abbreviated notes during the interview. If your subject agrees, also consider recording the interview. As soon as possible after the interview, write out (or keyboard in) your notes, filling in any gaps as you go along.

Assessing ● Review your notes (and recording) to determine how you want to shape your report. Present your findings in a basic report, introducing your subject and highlighting important points shared by him or her, or write an as-it-happened question-and-answer script. Plan accordingly.

WRITING AND REVISING

Writing ● Develop your report according to your planning and organizing. Make sure to experiment with different openings.

Revising ● As you review your first draft, pay special attention to the quotations: Are they clear and complete? Also have your subject review the draft to make sure that all quotations are accurate.

EVALUATING

Does the report read clearly and smoothly from the opening idea to the closing thought?

Are quotations carefully integrated?

Does the report contain interesting information?

Interview Report

Have you ever wondered what it would be like to be famous? What would you gain and what would you have to give up? In the spring of 1996, for *YO!* newspaper, student writer Stanley Joseph talked to members of the R & B group H-Town about their climb to fame. (Stanley Joseph is on the staff of *YO! [Youth Outlook],* a youth newspaper produced by Pacific News Service. The report is reprinted by permission.)

Learning the Lessons of Fame

The introduction draws in the readers with a series of questions.

You come home from your voice lessons and head right up to your room. Standing in front of the mirror, you sing along to your favorite CD until even the dog begs you to keep it down. You bow down to your reflection and give a tearful thank-you speech to your imaginary fans. Next you take out your notebook and start planning for your future. How many bedrooms will your house have? Which celeb should you date for the sake of the tabloids? . . .

What happens when dreams of fame become a reality? Searching for an answer to this question, I had a talk with G.I. and Shazam of the Houston R & B group H-Town. H-Town first hit the scene in 1993 with "Knocking Boots." In 1994 they followed with the smooth slow jam "Part Time Lover" on the *Above the Rim* sound track, and in 1995 they came out with the soulful single "Emotions" from their album *Begging After Dark.* Now they're back with a remake of "It's a Thin Line Between Love and Hate," from the sound track of Martin Lawrence's new movie of the same name.

"Did you expect this to happen?"

The writer provides background information.

H-Town worked for years before their big break came— six years, to be exact. Dino and Shazam, who are brothers, grew up in a family of singers and musicians. They and G.I. went through an endless series of pageants, talent shows, and plays until they hooked up with a local producer. He sent their tape to Luke Campbell of Luke records, who wasn't overly impressed. But then, as the story goes, the producer intentionally made Campbell miss a flight out of town and dragged him to the studio, where he heard H-Town sing live. "He liked our voices and was ready to sign us," testifies Shazam.

It was 1993, the year of the "freak me" ballad, and raunchy music was in. H-Town got in the mix with "Knocking Boots," which took America by storm. I asked G.I. if he'd expected to have such a big hit. "Nah," he replied. "Maybe I didn't have faith in my record. I knew it'd do it, but not so fast."

Learning the Lessons of Fame
(continued)

"It really took us by surprise," agrees Shazam. "I didn't think it'd blow up that big. When we did this album we didn't go into it as big stars."

"What's the downside?"

With fame, say the members of H-Town, came new responsibilities. "There's certain things I can't do anymore," confides Shazam, "like going out to clubs all the time, and kicking it with girls. You have to watch who you talk to."

"I still do the things I like to do," adds G.I., "but people I grew up with look at me differently. They watch me, expecting me to be stuck up." . . .

The group also had to learn how to take care of business. "There's always people trying to take money from you," explains G.I. "There's more crooked people than nice people. The crooked ones are full of promises but never come through with them."

Then there are the "playa haters"—the ones who are jealous of anyone who's in a better position than they are. "It got to a point in Houston where we couldn't go anywhere," complains Shazam. "You got brothers who are jealous and want to hurt you because you came up. They talk about you, want to destroy you and your career. It's shocking to me. They should be happy to see a brother raise up."

"But aren't there any good times?"

Two years ago, H-Town won the Best New Artist award from *Soul Train*—an honor the group members say took them by surprise. "We weren't even dressed for the occasion," recalls G.I. "We came there in our street clothes."

So the next time you're up in your room belting out those tunes and dreaming those dreams, think of H-Town, and remember that stardom has a price along with its rewards. Be ready for changes in your friends, and be aware of playa haters, bothersome fans, and industry crooks. Because who knows—your dream may come true. ■

Quotations are woven naturally into the text.

The conclusion wraps up the subject and gives the interviewer's assessment.

Interview Report

Newsmagazines often feature interviews with news makers of the day. Carlos Salinas de Gortari, one of the prime movers of the North American Free Trade Agreement (NAFTA), was the subject of a *Newsweek* article summarizing important events of the year. Note the structure of this simple interview: a brief summary of the subject's vital statistics followed by four questions and answers. (From *Newsweek,* 12/18/95 and © 1995, Newsweek, Inc. All rights reserved. Reprinted by permission.)

A Conversation with Carlos Salinas de Gortari

Born: April 3, 1948, Mexico City

Significant background information is given.

Educated: National Autonomous University of Mexico, and Harvard

Profile: Supertechnocratic child of the Mexican elite; nicknamed "the atomic ant," but despite unmacho looks became his country's president in 1988; modernized Mexico's economy and (under pressure and less radically) its politics; prime mover of the North American Free Trade Agreement; left office in December; now lobbying to be the first head of the World Trade Organization. We caught him in Washington, D.C., on his way to schmooze governments in India, Pakistan, and South Africa.

Questions are carefully worded to enable the subject to clarify important issues for the readers.

Newsweek: What are the most important challenges facing the world as we approach the year 2000?

Salinas: Trade wars. The expectations brought by the end of the cold war can only be fulfilled by high economic growth. And in today's world of globalization, the only way we can have economic growth is through freer trade. That's why it was so important that the U.S. ratified the Uruguay Round of the GATT. We hope other countries will follow suit.

You're fascinated by the links between migration and economic policy. Is that issue growing in importance?

Inevitably: look at the migration trends in Europe, Africa, Asia, and Latin America. In today's world, migration is a fact of life. The only way to introduce order and reduce it [migration] substantially is to increase economic opportunity at home. With globalization, this can only happen with freer trade.

A Conversation with Carlos Salinas de Gortari
(continued)

Which countries do you think are best suited to take advantage of the new international economy?

A few years ago the answer would have been those in South and East Asia. But the U.S. has shown a tremendous ability to upgrade its industrial capacity. So have Mexico and other places in Latin America. This is a very dynamic situation in which some countries are going to be left behind.

You think it's important for people to have both an international perspective and a sense of where they come from. What's the link between the local and the global?

It's like the link between tradition and modernization. If you lose your traditions and values, you lose your guiding light. But if you don't change and modernize, you also lose your guiding light. The United States is a country made up mainly of migrants who never forgot their roots. I'm very proud of being Mexican, but either we belong to the rest of the world, or the winds of change will become storms of transformation. The term "global village" is a very proper one. We are all villagers who also want to be part of the world. ■

The subject's response to the question brings the interview to a thoughtful conclusion.

Writing an Observation Report

An observation report is sometimes called a saturation report because it is based on your ability to take in all of the sights, sounds, and smells related to a specific location. You present these sensory impressions in such a manner that readers can get a real sense of the location themselves. You may choose to present your writing as a continuous flow of sensory impressions or as a more traditional report, incorporating a focus statement and supporting details.

SEARCHING AND SELECTING

Searching ● Select a location that genuinely appeals to you and that meets any requirements established by your instructor. Also make sure you have ready access to the location.

Brainstorming ● If you have trouble selecting a location, enlist the help of one or more of your writing peers. A small group of you could generate ideas together.

GENERATING THE TEXT

Noting ● Record as many sensory observations as you can for as long as you can (at least 15-30 minutes) at the location of your choice. Don't forget to record snippets of any conversations you happen to hear. (Focus all of your attention on recording sensory details. Don't spend time thinking about your observations.)

Assessing ● Remember that in its most natural form, an observation report presents the sensory details as they were recorded. However, depending on the nature of your observations, you may decide that it is better to establish a focus for your writing and then organize the necessary supporting details. Plan accordingly.

WRITING AND REVISING

Writing ● Write your first draft freely, working in sensory details as they were recorded or according to your planning and organizing. (Keep personal comments and analysis to a minimum.)

Refining ● Review, revise, and refine your writing before sharing it with your readers. Make sure that your report flows smoothly from beginning to end.

EVALUATING

Is the report based on a location of interest to readers?

Does the writing contain the specific details necessary for readers to clearly see (hear, smell, etc.) this location?

Does the writing reflect a sincere effort to record a variety of sensory impressions?

Observation Report

All of the senses come alive in this observation report of a skating rink by student writer Shea Stutler. Notice how she not only describes the scene but also provides interesting bits of insight and analysis.

Young Lions, Young Ladies

After some general remarks, the writer describes the sights, sounds, and smells as she enters the building.

Adolescents like to have a place they can call their own. In the fifties, teenagers hung out at the malt shop, sipping cherry cokes and rockin' with Elvis. Today, in a small town in Tennessee, they're jam skating to Montell Jordan. I was amazed to find a microcosm of life blooming on a 70- by 160-foot cement slab known as a roller-skating rink.

As I entered the building which housed the rink, the warm, nostalgic scent of popcorn hit that part of my brain where dusty, cobwebbed memories live, memories of my own adolescence. I made my way past a group of exuberant teenagers at the snack bar until I reached the skating rink. Skinny, hard benches, made for small butts, lined one wall. I took a seat and scanned the rink. My eyes paused to read a sign; white block letters on a black background warned, "Skate at Your Own Risk."

Two young men swaggered past me: confident, heads held high, eyes focused on their destination. I leaned over, looking down the long row of benches, curious to find out where they were going. Their confidence lagged a bit as they approached a large group of their peers, including several young ladies. All of them exhibited signs of discomfort as the girls crossed their arms over their nubile bodies, and the boys tried hard not to stare.

Abruptly, a silent signal sent the entire assembly to the benches. Pairs of dexterous hands laced up skates as quickly as possible, while other hands aided in conversation that only the listener was allowed to hear. I was struck by the intimacy of this scene. They all knew each other well. They had come

The writer shares her feelings as an outside observer.

together in the freedom of this one place to share and explore without the encumbrance of parents, teachers, or any other meddlesome adult. I sat bolt upright, feeling very much like someone who had accidentally stumbled into a room full of naked people.

Attempting to recover from my embarrassment, I was suddenly startled by a cacophony . . . music, perhaps? It must have been music, because I glanced down to find my foot tapping away to a beat long forgotten. As if on cue, young people from every corner of the room flocked to the rink. The awkwardness their bodies had expressed off the rink had been replaced by grace. Like the albatross, they were clumsy in their approach to flight, but, once airborne, they were a soaring sight to behold.

I was mesmerized by the effortlessness of their movements, weaving in and out, endlessly circling. Skates became a blur of color: green, purple, blue, pink, red—speeding by fast and furious. I felt the rush of wind on my face as I caught the musky scent of cologne mixed with sweat. A swirl of communication was taking place, none of it involving speech. The tactile sense had kicked in: punching and shoving of young lions trying to impress their ladies of choice, bodies brushing by each other, and the gentle touch of hand on arm. A statuesque blonde, six inches taller than her partner, slipped. "Catch me, I'm falling on purpose," her body language seemed to say. Eye contact was prevalent. Most skaters continually scanned the rink, found the one they were looking for, and BAM! eyes quickly darted away. This testing of emotional water went on for several hours; boys and girls trying on relationships of men and women like kids playing dress up in their parents' clothes.

I remembered the sign, "Skate at Your Own Risk." At the time, I had worried about broken arms and legs, but as I watched the dance unfold on that skating rink, I realized that these young people risk so much more. The pain of rejection, the fear of making fools of themselves, and the devastation they feel when they believe that they have, makes life for these adolescents a risky business. Perhaps that sign should have read, "LIVE at Your Own Risk." ■

Observation Report

Professional writer Randall VanderMey bases this report on the observations he recorded while waiting for a bus in a Greyhound station. As you will see, this report is much more than an as-it-happened record of what the writer saw and heard. It is also a brief documentary of a particular slice of American life.

"Scab!"

The tense tone established in the opening paragraph is maintained throughout the report.

The driver of the airport shuttle bus had to drop me off on the street so as not to cross the line of Greyhound drivers marching with their picket signs in the dusk. The picketers were angry. Had he turned in at the driveway to the terminal, they would have spat on him and yelled "Scab!" or "Strikebreaker!" Newspapers and TV had carried stories of rocks and bottles being thrown at passenger-filled buses by disgruntled Greyhound drivers whose demands for decent wages had not been heard. Most of the drivers in other unions were honoring the picket lines. Someday, they knew, they might be in the same fix.

Inside the terminal I sat with my feet on my suitcase. I didn't want to pay four quarters for a storage box and didn't want to turn my back on my belongings. In the strange, tense atmosphere of the bus depot, I wondered if I was better off there or on a bus. Writing notes became my shield:

The detailed sensory account of this experience begins here.

A Hispanic couple behind me plays Spanish music for everyone in the terminal to hear. Men go in the men's room and stay there for a strangely long time, punching the button on the electric blow dryer over and over as if to cover up their talk. Near me an old man in a blue baseball cap and blue nylon jacket mumbles to himself as he paces the floor slowly. I hear him say, "My children is all grown up." Another man in a white yachting cap strides around the terminal making a sliding, streaking sound with a metal heel protector that's working its way loose. He seems to like the sound because he keeps walking around on the hard tile floors, over to the video game room, over to the cafeteria, over to the bathroom, over to the ticket window, around and around in the open spaces in front of the nuns, college kids, young black girls with children, and Texas farmers waiting for their bus to Dallas. I know where the man in the yachting cap is without even looking up.

A tiny boy, curiosity in a red sweater, is twirling around. Everybody who sees him smiles. A while ago I saw an older man teasing him, saying "Hey, I'm gonna get you" and trying to slip a 10-gallon straw cowboy hat over his ears.

A policeman with his hair shaved off all over his round, bumpy head, takes his drawn nightstick into the men's room and brings out, by the elbow, a young black man who doesn't seem to know where he is. He cradles a radio in his arm that blasts its music to everyone's discomfort. The cop says, "Didn't I throw you out of here last night? Come on with me." The guy looks dazed and says, "Where we going?" The cop says, "We're just going to have a little talk." Turning off the blaring radio, he walks the young man toward the entrance.

Something weird is in the air, as if drugs are being dealt in the bathrooms, though the place remains calm and well lit. The odor of french fries and cleaning solutions fills the air.

The Hispanic music plays much more softly now, and I hear the dyed-blond lady break out of her Spanish to say to her husband or boyfriend, "Thang you very mush."

The iron screen benches are starting to lay a print in my back and rear end, so I shift and squirm. When I bought my ticket at the front counter, I asked the lady who took my money what I'd have to do for two hours and a half. She had laughed and said, "Look at the walls," and she had been right.

The man in the blue baseball cap is mumbling again. But now I see that he's reading the newspaper and seems not to be able to read unless he pronounces the words aloud. I hear him say, "That's a liquidation sale."

The man with the metal heel protector is back again, clicking and shrieking across the tile floor, carrying a blue nylon satchel. Out of the video-game room come noises like echoes in a long hollow pipe. A kid behind the cash register in the cafeteria has neatly combed hair and glasses. He keeps smiling all the time, looking comfortingly sane. Overhead in there, the ceiling-fan blades turn hardly faster than the second hand on a clock.

It has taken me some time to realize fully how I felt on that hard metal bench for two and a half hours among so many different kinds of people harboring so many different purposes. I said not a word to anyone. Only wrote and wrote. With my eyes and ears I broke into their lives while giving nothing of myself. I got in and got away without any real contact.

I hope the drivers get their money. But I'm not sure my being there helped. I felt like a scab. ■

In addition to carefully describing the people and the terminal, the writer includes snippets of actual conversations.

A brief personal reflection is provided here.

To conclude, the writer attempts to put this experience into perspective.

Writing a Personal Research Report

A personal research report presents the story of a writer's investigation into a subject of personal interest. A research report may discuss a writer's experience with a certain new technology, describe a writer's attempt to learn about a particular place, share the story of a writer's investigation into a current fad, and so on. It's important to remember that this type of reporting is based, for the most part, on firsthand methods of research. Use the guidelines below and the models that follow to help you develop your writing.

SEARCHING AND SELECTING

Searching ● To begin your subject search, think of the different categories listed in the opening discussion (new technologies, interesting places, current fads) plus any others that come to mind (professions, lifestyles).

Reviewing ● If that doesn't work, review the local newspaper, the Internet, or perhaps the yellow pages for ideas. You could also brainstorm for subjects with your writing peers. (Make sure to select a subject that stems from a genuine interest and is within your abilities to research.)

GENERATING THE TEXT

Planning ● Determine what you already know about your subject, what you hope to find out, and how you plan on conducting your research. (Start by thinking of people to meet and places to go.)

Exploring ● Make contacts. Conduct interviews and record observations. Also refer to magazines and books that have been recommended to you.

Assessing ● Decide how you are going to compile the results of your research. A personalized account of your work should address four basic areas: *what I already knew, what I hoped to find out, what happened as I conducted my investigation,* and *what I learned.* (If you are going to compile a more traditional report, decide on a focus and plan accordingly.)

WRITING AND REVISING

Writing ● Develop your first draft, using your planning as a guide.

Revising ● Carefully review, revise, and refine your writing. Make sure that it accurately reflects the results of your investigation, and double-check to make sure that you quote your sources correctly.

EVALUATING

Is the report informative, interesting, and based on sincere investigative efforts?

Has proper attention been given to accuracy and detail?

Will readers appreciate the treatment of this subject?

Personal Research Report

Cancer is the second leading cause of death in the United States. To student writer Kim DeRonde, however, cancer is more than a scary statistic. In this personal research paper, DeRonde investigates the disease that killed three of her grandparents before she had a chance to get to know them.

Three Family Cancers

DeRonde opens by describing the assignment that got her thinking about cancer.

One day back in fourth grade, my teacher said, "Use your imagination and make an invention—something new and useful." I grumped all the way home from school. An invention? For what, I thought. What could I invent that we could use? "What about a cure for cancer?" Mom asked.

A few weeks earlier my family had learned that Grandpa DeRonde had cancer, so I went to work imagining my very own miracle cure. I drew a picture of a medicine bottle, similar to a bottle of cough syrup, with a drop of liquid coming out of it. I called my masterpiece, "The Cure for Cancer."

I can remember those school days pretty well, but I can't say the same for three of my grandparents—Grandma and Grandpa DeRonde and Grandpa Vernooy. Before I could grow up and get to know them, their lives were invaded, taken over, and destroyed by different forms of cancer—multiple myeloma, prostate cancer, and lung cancer. Now, years later, here I am a college freshman, faced with another assignment that gives me a chance to think about cancer: What is it and what causes it? And what were these cancers like for my grandparents? To get some answers, I checked out some recent research on cancer and talked with my mother.

Important background information is given.

Cancer, as my family learned firsthand, is a serious killer. In fact, it's the second leading cause of death in the United States. Each year, the disease kills about 50,000 Americans, and doctors discover more than one million new cases. Cancer is so powerful because it's not *one*, but *many* diseases attacking many parts of the body. All cancers are basically body cells gone crazy—cells that develop abnormally. These cells then clone themselves using an enzyme called telomerase. As they multiply like creatures in a sci-fi horror movie, the cells build into tumors, which are tissues that can "invade and destroy other tissues."

Researchers aren't exactly sure what triggers these cancerous growths, but they think that 80 percent of cancers happen because people come into regular contact with carcinogens—cancer-causing agents. Carcinogens fall into three groups: chemicals, radiation, and viruses. People can be exposed to these carcinogens in many ways and situations.

Three Family Cancers

(continued)

A 1990 study showed that 5 percent of cancers could be traced to environmental pollution, including carcinogens in the workplace. Radiation, for example, devastated the population of Chernobyl, Russia, after the nuclear power plant meltdown. But carcinogens don't cause cancer overnight—even from exposure in a terrible accident. The cancer may take 30 to 40 years to develop.

I don't know what carcinogens attacked my Grandma DeRonde, but I do know the result: she developed multiple myeloma. For a multiple myeloma patient, the average period of survival is 20 months to 10 years. When I talked with my mother, she said that my family doesn't really know when Grandma came down with multiple myeloma, but she lived for two years after learning she had it. For two years, she suffered through radiation and chemotherapy treatments, and life seemed measured by the spaces between appointments to check her white blood cell count.

What causes multiple myeloma remains a mystery, though its effects are well known. This cancer is a malignant growth of cells in the bone marrow that makes holes in the skeleton. The holes develop mostly in the ribs, vertebrae, and pelvis. Because the holes make the bones brittle, the victim cannot do simple things like drive and cook. In the end, patients fracture bones and die from infection and pneumonia. It was this weakening of the bones, along with the chemotherapy treatments, that made my grandmother suffer.

My Grandpa DeRonde was diagnosed with prostate cancer several years after my grandma died. The doctors began radiation therapy right away, and my family was hopeful because the cancer was caught in its early stages. At first, the cancer seemed to go into remission, but actually cancer cells were invading other sites in his body. Because the cancer spread, the doctors couldn't treat all of it through radiation or surgery. Grandpa lived for only two years after learning he was ill; and during that time he had many chemotherapy treatments and spent a lot of time in the hospital. On his death certificate, the doctor wrote that Grandpa died of cardiac arrest and carcinoma of the lung, with metastasis.

Like multiple myeloma, prostate cancer is a powerful killer. Even though many technological changes help doctors catch this cancer at an early stage, the number of deaths per year is still going up. Prostate cancer is the second most common cancer in the United States, and experts believe that it can be found in about 25 million men over the age of 50.

Prostate cancer is a tumor (called a carcinoma) lining the

Note how smoothly the writer incorporates the interview with her mother.

The writer describes and summarizes each of the three types of cancer.

inside of the organ—in this case the prostate gland. Many factors trigger this form of cancer: age, diet, environmental conditions, or maybe just having a cancer-prone family. A survey of more than 51,000 American men showed that eating a lot of fat, found mostly in red meat, can lead to advanced prostate cancer. On the other hand, researchers concluded that fats from vegetables, fish, and many dairy products are probably not linked to the growth of a carcinoma.

My second grandfather died from a different carcinoma— lung cancer. Doctors found a tumor in the lower lobe of Grandpa Vernooy's right lung, recommended surgery, and removed the lung. The next winter, he weakened, got pneumonia, and died. His doctors believed that his smoking habit caused the cancer. Smoking, in fact, remains the most important factor in lung cancer's development. The truth is that cigarette smoking causes almost half of all cancer cases, even though only one out of ten smokers actually comes down with this disease.

Some studies have concluded that genetics may play a role in whether a person develops lung cancer or not. A 1988 study suggested that if a person is missing positive genes called tumor suppressor genes, it's bad news. If these genes weren't inherited, or if smoking destroyed them, then cancer-related genes are free to do their damage. Another 1990 study identified a special gene that is inherited from one or both parents and that metabolizes chemicals from cigarette smoke. In this case, if the gene is there, the cancer risk goes up, especially for smokers.

I still wish I could cure cancer with a magic miracle liquid in a medicine bottle. But today I understand that cancer is a complicated disease. My grandparents died from three types of the disease—multiple myeloma, prostate cancer, and lung cancer. If it hadn't been for cancerous tumors taking over their bodies, my grandparents might still be alive, and I'd have many more memories of them. Maybe I'd even be sharing with them stories about my first year at college. On the other hand, maybe this paper is a cure of a different type—while it can't change what happened, it can help me understand it. ■

One grandfather's cancer is linked to smoking—a nonhereditary factor important to the writer.

The writer concludes on a wistful but realistic note.

Personal Research Report

In *PrairyErth* author William Least Heat-Moon explores the landscape, history, and people of Chase County in central Kansas. This excerpt focuses on the 1931 plane crash in the county that killed legendary Notre Dame football coach Knute Rockne. (Excerpts from *PrairyErth: A Deep Map.* Copyright © 1991 by William Least Heat-Moon. Reprinted by permission of Houghton Mifflin Co. All rights reserved.)

from *PrairyErth*

The opening draws readers into the report, helping them visualize the crash site.

The crash site lies a little more than a mile west of Highway 177. The first time I visited it I had to be shown the way because you can't see the marker until you climb the first ridge; a sign pointing the direction is long gone, the closest fence gate is now locked, and the present owner, an out-countian, discourages visits. At the spot stands a thick marble tablet atop a limestone base, all of it about ten feet high, inscribed ROCKNE MEMORIAL and below that the names of the eight men, with the coach, alphabetically last, listed first, and the pilot's name at the bottom. The monument, fenced to protect it from scratching cattle, has been chipped at by souvenir vandals and shot here and there by gunners. The area is flatish but uneven upland, a piece of Chase County as faceless as you can find, a place visually ordinary except for its extreme austerity, and it is quiet and unmomentous, although it does have an apprehensible aura: the mystery of what actually happened on 3-31-31.

The writer describes his research process.

I went to the historical society in Cottonwood and looked at the relics: a large piece of the red fabric, a chunk of propeller, the pilot's Indian-head insignia pin, the cockpit nameplate, a piece of seat belt. I read the newspaper accounts; columnist "Peggy of the Flint Hills" wrote a week after the crash: *If Knute Rockne's pockets contained all the articles which local souvenir fans claim to have removed from them, it must have been that extra weight which brought down the plane.* An article four years later carried this headline: GOLD TOOTH IS FOUND ON SITE OF ROCKNE CRASH—VALUE $7. I read a 1942 story: MISSING ROCKNE PLANE TIRE TURNS UP AS SCRAP RUBBER. I talked with a half-dozen people who had been at the scene right after the accident and others who had visited it only years later; I saw in one home a wastebasket made from a piece of the Fokker rudder, and everywhere I heard as many tales as truths: *So-and-so carried off the coach's head in a basket,* and *They tied a rope around Rockne's waist to pull him from the ground with a team of horses,* and *What's-his-name years later found a human jawbone with two teeth out there.*

The layers of information in this paragraph immerse readers in the research.

I noticed in the citizens a repugnance about the callous and cavalier keepsake hunting, about the distortions of celebrity and the proposals to capitalize on the horror: only days after the accident the local chamber of commerce, recognizing the most sensational thing ever to occur in the county, recommended constructing a big landing field so commercial aircraft could bring in sightseers; Emporia businessmen wanted a park on the site with picnic tables, a swimming pool, tennis courts; the *Wichita Beacon* suggested a colossal football stadium in the Bakers' isolated pasture, where each year the Fighting Irish would play *for the championship of the United States.* Slim Pinkston, whose brother-in-law was one of the four to see the plane fall, said to me, *I'm disgusted with it—it's always "Knute Rockne and Seven Others." Them other lives was worth just as much.* And Edward "Tink" Baker, who was eighty-nine when I talked with him and recently retired from digging graves in the Matfield Cemetery (his only souvenir of the crash was a pair of pliers from 99E that a trucker later stole when he learned their history), told me how his father set out the first monument, a small fieldstone. Tink said, *The Catholics put up that marker out there now. They wanted to just forget everybody but Rockne. My dad owned the land then, and he told them he wouldn't stand for that—if they wanted to include all the names, he'd let them put one up.* The much newer monument in the Matfield service area on the turnpike, however, commemorates only Rockne and his football success and doesn't even suggest that seven other men also died. But neither the monuments nor accounts of the accident say how aircraft history changed in the Baker pasture.

The writer reflects on his research efforts.

In all my looking, I couldn't find what actually happened to Fokker 99E while it was struggling above old Route 13, what had caused the wing to break off. Then one day I came across something called "Report on the Crash of Fokker F-10A Transport Near Bazaar, Kansas." It contained excerpts from records held at Wright-Patterson Field near Dayton, Ohio. At the top of page one in parentheses this: "Formerly Classified Secret." Within, hidden among all the official words, were things I hadn't heard or read anywhere else, bits and pieces scattered about like debris from the crash itself.

[*The author learned, among other things, that there was a rapid drop of atmospheric pressure in the area of the crash, that the wings on an F-10 were known to flutter in bumpy air, that some of the glue on the wing joints had deteriorated. But the actual cause of the crash still remained a mystery.*] ■

Analytical Writing

Analysis of a Process

Essay of Comparison

Essay of Classification

Essay of Definition

Cause/Effect Essay

Problem/Solution Essay

Essay of Evaluation

Analytical Writing

It's 10 p.m., and you finally force yourself to look at the assignment sheet for Sociology 101. *Analyze one aspect of computer technology in terms of its effect on modern society,* it says. You flash back to those happy times in high school when you cranked out creative essays on the life of a shoelace and what you would do if you won the lottery. Now, you're not sure you can analyze your lunch, much less anything to do with computers.

Actually, there's nothing mysterious about analytical writing. It's simply a type of writing that requires some high-octane thinking. In analysis, you interpret information rather than report on it; you form new understandings rather than simply give the facts. You might, for example, evaluate the impact of computers on education. Or you might examine a problem related to computers in the workplace.

WHAT'S AHEAD

Analytical writing covers a lot of territory, as you will see in this section. Included are guidelines and models for essays that explain, compare, classify, define, evaluate, and so on. Remember to approach your analytical writing with the proper mind-set, with a genuine interest in your subject, and with the patience to explore it carefully and thoroughly.

"Writing is how we think our way into a subject and make it our own." —William Zinsser in *Writing to Learn*

Analytical Writing

QUICK GUIDE

In analytical writing, you break a subject down to understand it better. You get inside of your subject until it becomes part of your own thinking. Try to work scientifically—gathering information, testing it, gathering some more, forming conclusions, and so on. Then, when you're ready, share your analysis in a clearly developed essay.

All analytical writing shares the following characteristics:

STARTING POINT: The starting point for analytical writing is usually a specific assignment in which you are asked to examine or investigate a subject related to your course work.

PURPOSE: The general purpose of your writing is to demonstrate a clear understanding of your subject and its relationship to other similar subjects. The specific purpose will depend on the nature of your assignment. You may be analyzing a process, making a comparison, proposing solutions, and so on.

FORM: Share the results of your work in traditional essay form, identifying your thesis in your opening paragraph, developing the thesis in the middle paragraphs, and summing things up in the closing.

AUDIENCE: Analytical writing is generally intended for your instructor and writing peers in a specific course of study.

VOICE: In most cases, use semiformal English in this type of writing. Semiformal English is worded cautiously so that it can be reread many times without sounding tiresome or cute. Obviously, you want to avoid slang and colloquialisms.

POINT OF VIEW: Use third-person point of view *(he, she, they)* unless your writing is clearly experience based.

Insights into Writing

How can you really get to know your subject for an analysis? You could try one or both of these prewriting techniques: Carry out a *directed free writing,* in which you describe your subject, compare it, apply it, and so on. (See 021 for more information.) Answer *structured questions* about it. These questions (listed on 022) will help you understand what is important or unique about your subject.

Writing an Analysis of a Process

A process analysis shows the reader how to do something (register for class, obtain a passport) or explains how a process works (immigration, respiration, the NBA draft pick). Whenever you explain a process to a reader, you must be clear, accurate, and organized. Use the guidelines below and models that follow to help you write a process analysis.

SEARCHING AND SELECTING

Selecting ● Keep in mind that your subject should be of genuine interest to you and your readers. And it should conform to any requirements established by your instructor. (How the Gullah language evolved might be an interesting subject from both a historical and a contemporary point of view. How a bill becomes a law sounds too elementary. How to stare into space might work, if it is approached in the right way.)

Reviewing ● Review your class notes or texts for ideas. Try free-writing or clustering about your course work, noting potential subjects as they come to mind. Or brainstorm for ideas with your writing peers.

GENERATING THE TEXT

Recording ● List related facts and details about your subject as they come to mind, or write an instant version of the finished product to see how much you already know and what you need to learn about your subject.

Collecting ● Collect additional information and details accordingly.

Organizing ● If necessary, organize your ideas before you write your first draft. (See 220 for a graphic organizer.) Also think about the feeling or impression you want to express in your writing. (Depending on your subject, it is okay, even desirable, to entertain as well as inform your readers.)

WRITING AND REVISING

Writing ● Write your first draft freely, working in details and ideas according to your planning—or according to the steps in the process you are analyzing. (Remember that process papers are organized according to time—*first, second, third, then, finally,* etc.)

Revising ● Review, revise, and refine your writing before sharing it.

EVALUATING

Does the essay form a meaningful whole? Does each step lead readers clearly and logically to the next?

Are main points supported by specific details and examples?

Will readers appreciate the treatment of this subject?

Analysis of a Process

"How-to's" are written on many subjects. In this essay, California student writer Luke Sunukjian singles out one aspect of surfing and leads us through it step-by-step. Though he is obviously familiar with the process himself, notice how Sunukjian carefully brings his readers along, defining the jargon and giving detailed instructions for an audience who may know nothing about getting "tubed."

How to Enter the "Green Room"

The opening defines the subject and explains its importance.

It is important to learn how to get "tubed" (to place yourself under the curl of the wave) before going surfing. Major consequences await those who try to get tubed improperly: You may get caught too far behind the wave's lip or get sucked to the top of the wave. Or you may be thrown down the wave's face, knocked unconscious, or worse. Do not let this dangerous situation stop you from learning how to get tubed. There is nothing to fear if you follow my instructions on how to enter the "green room," or the curling part of the wave.

Transitional phrases like "before you enter the green room" guide readers through the process.

Before you enter the green room, you must first learn how to stand up on your board. To get to your feet, put your hands on the rails (sides) of the board and push your body up as though you are doing a push-up. Then swing your feet underneath your body. You are now ready to place yourself on the correct part of the wave.

"There is nothing to fear if you follow my instructions . . ."

As you get to your feet, you will be dropping down the wave's face (the front of the water rolling toward shore) and will need to prepare for the bottom turn. Your feet should be spread apart near the tail (back) of the board facing perpendicular to the direction in which you are moving. Put your weight on your back foot to avoid sinking the nose into the water. After dropping past the bottom of the wave, lean toward the face of the wave while continuing to put pressure on the tail of the board. This action will turn the board toward the face of the wave and accelerate you alongside the wave.

Terms like "stall" and "wrap-a-round" add authority to the essay.

At this point you are slightly ahead of the barreling part of the wave, and you need to "stall," or slow yourself, to get into the tube. There are three methods of stalling used in different situations. If you are slightly ahead of the tube, you can drag your inside hand along the water to stall. If you are a couple of feet in front of the barrel, apply all your weight to your back foot and sink the tail into the water. This is known as a "tail stall" for obvious reasons, and its purpose is to decrease your board speed. If you are moving faster than the wave is breaking, you need to do what is called a "wrap-a-round." To accomplish this maneuver, lean back away from the wave while applying pressure on the tail. This shifts your forward momentum away from the wave and slows you down. When the wave comes, turn toward the wave and place your-self in the barrel.

While surfing in the barrel, your body position is key. Duck your head (unless the wave is over ten feet) and lean toward the face of the wave so the lip does not crash on your body. You want the breaking part of the wave to completely cover you without the water touching your body. Be careful not to get too close to the face of it because the wave will pull the board upward, causing you to be hurled off. To avoid this scenario, position your board a foot's distance away from the wave's face.

The writer describes two ways of completing the final step.

The final step in completing a tube ride is coming out of the tube, and there are two ways to do this. You can increase your board speed to move faster than the wave is breaking. Or you can have the wave "spit" you out. The latter option refers to the barreling wave creating so much air pressure inside the tube that some of the air is forced out. The air being spit out of the barrel hits your back, forcing you out of the wave.

The writer concludes by sharing his love of the sport.

Once you complete your first tube ride you will be hooked, and come back again and again, always in search of the perfect table, always looking for that twenty-foot wave with a curl that looks like a giant hollow cylinder. Nothing you ever do in life will match the thrill of entering and exiting the perfect "green room." ■

Analysis of a Process

A process analysis is often mixed with other types of writing. John McPhee, in the following excerpt from *Oranges,* describes the first part of the process that turns oranges into concentrated juice, but he also explains the origins of the orangeade flavor of Florida milk and describes two types of juicing machines. (Excerpt from *Oranges* by John McPhee. Copyright © 1967 and copyright renewed © 1995 by John McPhee. Reprinted by permission of Farrar, Straus & Giroux, Inc.)

from *Oranges*

The first sentence creates a sense of movement.

As the fruit starts to move along a concentrate plant's assembly line, it is first culled. In what some citrus people remember as "the old fresh-fruit days," before the Second World War, about forty percent of all oranges grown in Florida were eliminated at packinghouses and dumped in fields. Florida milk tasted like orangeade. Now, with the exception of the split and rotten fruit, all of Florida's orange crop is used. Moving up a conveyor belt, oranges are scrubbed with detergent before they roll on into juicing machines. There are several kinds of juicing machines, and they are something to see. One is called the Brown Seven Hundred. Seven hundred oranges a minute go into it and are split and reamed on the same kind of rosettes that are in the centers of ordinary kitchen reamers. The rinds that come pelting out the bottom are integral halves, just like the rinds of oranges squeezed in a kitchen. Another machine is the Food Machinery Corporation's FMC In-line Extractor. It has a shining row of aluminum jaws, upper and lower, with shining aluminum teeth.

Note the transitions: when an orange, while at the same time, etc.

When an orange tumbles in, the upper jaw comes crunching down on it while at the same time the orange is penetrated from below by a perforated steel tube. As the jaws crush the outside, the juice goes through the perforations in the tube and down into the plumbing of the concentrate plant. All in a second, the juice has been removed and the rind has been crushed and shredded beyond recognition. ■

Writing an Essay of Comparison

When you compare two subjects (ideas, events, objects, experiments, etc.), you help your reader understand their similarities and their differences. The ultimate challenge when writing a comparison is to "make the familiar seem new and the new seem familiar." Use the guidelines below and the models that follow to help you write balanced and logical comparisons.

SEARCHING AND SELECTING

Selecting ● The subjects for your writing will depend upon the course in which these guidelines are being used. Keep in mind that the subjects must be related in some *important* way and be of some interest to you and your readers.

Searching ● If no subjects come readily to mind, review your course notes or your text for ideas. Brainstorm for ideas among a small group of your peers. Also try writing freely about your course work, noting potential subjects—ideas, objects, characters, or events—as they come to mind.

GENERATING THE TEXT

Collecting ● Gather ideas and details related to your subjects using a Venn diagram (see 220) or some other organizing device.

Assessing ● Review your collecting to determine how much you already know about your subjects and how much you need to find out. Continue collecting if necessary.

Focusing ● State a possible focus for your work; then plan or organize your writing accordingly. (You might, for example, do a point-by-point comparison of the subjects, or you might address each separately, allowing the comparison to evolve more naturally.)

WRITING AND REVISING

Writing ● Write your first draft, working in details and ideas according to your planning and organizing.

Revising ● Review, revise, and refine your writing before you share it with your readers. (Make sure your comparison has the proper balance.)

EVALUATING

Is the writing effectively organized so readers can follow and understand the similarities and differences between the two subjects?

Are main points supported by specific details and examples?

Does the writing form a meaningful whole, moving clearly and smoothly from the opening section to the closing thoughts?

Will readers appreciate the treatment of the subjects in this essay?

Essay of Comparison

In this essay, student writer Janae Sebranek compares the fate of two tragic characters, Bigger in *Native Son* and Alan in *Equus*. Notice that the writer makes a point-by-point comparison, exploring the effects of work, religion, and the media on the characters' lives.

Beyond Control

The opening remarks lead up to the focus, or thesis, of the essay.

Most children, no matter what their personal or family situation, lead more or less controlled lives. As they grow, they begin to sense the pressure of controlling factors in their lives, and start struggling to take control themselves. This can be a difficult process. In the works *Native Son* and *Equus,* Richard Wright and Peter Shaffer respectively create two characters who must deal with this struggle. Bigger in *Native Son* and Alan in *Equus* are both entering adulthood and have come to realize that they are controlled by work, religion, and the media. In the midst of these characters' efforts to gain control, each character falls into a tragic situation.

We find Alan experiencing the pressure of working as a clerk at Bryson's appliance store. The customers are demanding, and the many products and brand names are confusing. He finds that he cannot function in this work environment. Later, under hypnosis, he admits to Dr. Dysart that his "foes" are the myriad of brand names he is challenged to locate and explain to the customers—"The Hosts of Hoover. The Hosts of Philco. Those Hosts of Pifco. The House of Remington and all its tribe!" (73). However, by recognizing the demands of this job, Alan attempts to take some control over his life.

The writer presents a thoughtful analysis of each character's actions.

Alan exercises further control when he decides to look for another job. He likes being around horses, so he pursues and lands a job with Mr. Dalton, a stable owner. He enjoys his job and begins to deal more effectively with the whole concept of work.

Bigger must also struggle with the pressure and anxiety of his first job. Because of his family's desperate financial situation, he is forced to take the one job he is offered, coincidentally, by a Mr. Dalton. He works as a chauffeur for Mr. Dalton's wealthy suburban family. Bigger cannot relate to them. He sees himself as a foreigner, forced to live and work among the privileged. The Daltons tell him where, when, and even how to drive. Bigger struggles; but, like Alan, he cannot deal with the extreme discomfort he is feeling. He quits after only two days on the job. Unlike Alan, however, he does not have the option of getting a job that interests him.

Specific
references
to the texts
are made.

Alan and Bigger also find religion to be a controlling factor in their lives. Alan's mother, Dora, "doses [religion] down the boy's throat" as she whispers "that Bible to him hour after hour, up there in his room (33)." Obviously, Alan's mother believes that he needs the controlling force of religion in his life, so she preaches to him every night. For a time, he is fascinated by the Bible's imagery and ideas. Eventually, though, this fascination begins to fade.

Bigger's mother does not push the issue of religion to the extreme that Alan's mother does. Instead, she tries to make her son see its value with daily comments such as "You'll regret how you living someday" (13). She offers her advice by singing religious songs from behind a curtain in their one-room apartment. She tries to show Bigger that religion is a valid way of dealing with a world out of control. But Bigger refuses to accept her religion, and he is left with no spiritual footing or direction.

Finally, we find the media playing a tormenting, controlling role in both Alan's and Bigger's lives. Alan's father calls television a "dangerous drug" (27) that can control the mind. Alan still manages to watch television, but only because his mother "used to let him slip off in the afternoons to a friend next door" (31) to watch. Later, while he is under psychiatric care, he watches television every night and eventually finds himself becoming controlled by the medium.

Bigger, in a more tragic way, is also controlled by the media. He reads about himself in the newspapers and begins to believe certain things that have no valid basis. He is referred to as a "Negro killer" who looks "as if about to spring upon you at any moment" (260). The papers remark that Bigger "seems a beast utterly untouched" (260) by and out of place in the white man's world. Unfortunately, he has no control over what is printed or over what other people believe about him.

The closing
remarks
focus on the
tragic fates
of the two
characters.

Bigger's ultimate fate is clearly beyond his control. He is falsely accused of raping and killing a woman, and he cannot convince anyone of the truth. Bigger's identity is too closely linked with the descriptions given in the newspapers. And this identity tragically leads to his death. Alan's fate is different, although tragic in its own right. While in the psychiatric ward, he gains a certain control with the help of therapy and medication. However, he loses his passion for life: "Passion, you see, can be destroyed by a doctor. It cannot be created" (108). This is Alan's personal tragedy.

Ultimately, both Alan and Bigger fail to gain real control over the outside forces in their lives. Alan forfeits his interest in life, and Bigger forfeits life itself. They, like so many people, become victims of the world in which they live. ■

Essay of Comparison

People who are fortunate enough to observe two cultures at length often discern fascinating contrasts. In the following model, Professor Yi-Fu Tuan, writing for *Harper's Magazine,* takes one aspect of culture—the sense of space or place—and contrasts the Chinese view with the American. (This article first appeared in *Harper's Magazine.* Copyright © 1974 by *Harper's Magazine.* All rights reserved. Reproduced from the July issue by special permission.)

American Space, Chinese Place

The writer introduces one of his subjects in the first paragraph.

Americans have a sense of space, not of place. Go to an American home in exurbia, and almost the first thing you do is drift toward the picture window. How curious that the first thing you do is drift toward the picture window. How curious that the first compliment you pay your host inside his house is to say how lovely it is outside his house! He is pleased that you should admire his vistas. The distant horizon is not merely a line separating earth from sky, it is a symbol of the future. The American is not rooted in his place, however lovely: his eyes are drawn by the expanding space to a point on the horizon, which is his future.

The transitional words "by contrast" lead readers into the second subject.

By contrast, consider the traditional Chinese home. Blank walls enclose it. Step behind the spirit wall and you are in a courtyard with perhaps a miniature garden around a corner. Once inside his private compound you are wrapped in an ambiance of calm beauty, an ordered world of buildings, pavement, rock, and decorative vegetation. But you have no distant view: nowhere does space open out before you. Raw nature in such a home is experienced only as weather, and the only open space is the sky above. The Chinese is rooted in his place. When he has to leave, it is not for the promised land on the terrestrial horizon, but for another world altogether along the vertical, religious axis of his imagination.

The author explains why the Chinese tie to place is so strong.

The Chinese tie to place is deeply felt. Wanderlust is an alien sentiment. The Taoist classic *Tao Te Ching* captures the ideal of rootedness in place with these words: "Though there may be another country in the neighborhood so close

"The Chinese tie to place is deeply felt."

that they are within sight of each other and the crowing of cocks and barking of dogs in one place can be heard in the other, yet there is no traffic between them; and throughout their lives the two peoples have nothing to do with each other." In theory if not in practice, farmers have ranked high in Chinese society. The reason is not only that they are engaged in a "root" industry of producing food but that, unlike pecuniary merchants, they are tied to the land and do not abandon their country when it is in danger.

Nostalgia is a recurrent theme in Chinese poetry. An American reader of translated Chinese poems may well be taken aback—even put off—by the frequency, as well as the sentimentality, of the lament for home. To understand the strength of this sentiment, we need to know that the Chinese desire for stability and rootedness in place is prompted by the constant threat of war, exile, and the natural disasters of flood and drought. Forcible removal makes the Chinese keenly aware of their loss. By contrast, Americans move, for the most part, voluntarily. Their nostalgia for hometown is really longing for a childhood to which they cannot return: in the meantime the future beckons and the future is "out there," in open space. When we criticize American rootlessness, we tend to forget that it is a result of ideals we admire, namely, social mobility and optimism about the future. When we admire Chinese rootedness, we forget that the word "place" means both a location in space and position in society: to be tied to place is also to be bound to one's station in life, with little hope of betterment. Space symbolizes hope; place, achievement and stability. ■

Again, the words "by contrast" signal a shift.

The conclusion sheds light on both subjects.

Writing an Essay of Classification

When you classify, you generally break a subject down into its most meaningful parts. *(Weight lifters come in four basic varieties.)* You may also classify a subject by explaining how it fits into a larger category or grouping. *(Slang is a localized, jazzy level of diction.)* When writing an essay of classification, your goal is to help readers better understand the whole (your subject) by presenting the parts. Your goal may also be to show how your subject fits into the larger scheme of things. Use the guidelines below and the models that follow to help you develop your work.

SEARCHING AND SELECTING

Selecting ● Focus your subject search on general areas of interest that lend themselves to classification (perhaps music, sports, etc.). Also make sure that you follow any guidelines established by your instructor. Then think of a suitable subject to classify. For example, maybe you're interested in popular music. If that subject is too broad, narrow it to something more manageable, like Latin music.

Reviewing ● Think about the different ways a possible subject could be classified. Latin music could be analyzed according to the different types popular in the United States (salsa, merengue, tango, etc.).

GENERATING THE TEXT

Organizing ● Decide on a classifying focus (such as the example above) that you will use to analyze your subject. Then plot out your essay by dividing or categorizing your subject according to this focus. (See 220 for a graphic organizer.)

Collecting ● Gather as much information as you need to develop your essay. Adjust your focus as necessary after conducting your research.

WRITING AND REVISING

Writing ● In your opening remarks, establish your focus—how and why you are classifying this subject. Then continue your draft by discussing the different categories or groupings that you have plotted out.

Revising ● Review your essay for clarity and coherence. Make sure that all of your categories are clearly related and of equal importance. Revise and refine your work accordingly.

EVALUATING

Is the focus of the essay meaningful and manageable?

Is each category effectively explained or developed?

Does the essay move smoothly from one category to the next?

Essay of Classification

How many kinds of weight lifters are there? In this essay student writer Caitlin Eisenhart describes the four types she has observed working out in the university gym. Notice how the ending echoes the opening, providing "bookends" for the essay.

Weight Lifting 101

The opening explains the writer's personal interest in the subject.

I'd heard rumors about it before I ever left for college, and once I moved into the dorm, I realized it was not just a rumor. I needed a way to combat the "Freshman Fifteen," that dreaded poundage resulting from a combination of late-night pizzas, care-package cookies, and cafeteria cheesecakes. So, my roommate and I headed to the university gym where the weight-training rooms are filled with student "chain gangs" sweating and clanging their way through a series of mechanical monsters. As I looked around, it became obvious that people work out for quite different reasons. Health enthusiasts, toning or defining devotees, athletes, and body builders seem to be the main categories of those lifting weights.

She describes the first of her four categories.

Some students lift weights as part of an exercise program aimed at maintaining or improving health. They've heard about strong abdominals reducing lower-back problems. They've learned that improved flexibility can help to reduce tension buildup and prevent the headaches and other problems related to prolonged periods of sitting or studying. They know that combining weights with aerobic exercise is an efficient way to lose weight. A person can eat the same amount of food and still lose weight, since increased muscle mass burns more calories. Typical weight-lifting routines for students eager to stay healthy amid the strain of college life are around 20 minutes a day, three times a week.

Each paragraph describes one type of weight lifter.

The "toners" hope to produce smoothly defined muscles. Not surprisingly, this category includes many young women. Lifting weights can target problem spots and help shape up the body. To develop solid arms, these people use dumbbells and a bench press. Other equipment focuses on achieving toned legs, abdominals, and buttocks. Toning workouts must be done more often than three times a week. I talked to a few young women who lift weights (after aerobic activity of some kind) for about 30 minutes, five times a week.

Athletes must lift weights. Volleyball, rowing, basketball, football—all of these sports require weight training. It may seem obvious that a football player needs to be muscular and strong, but how do other athletes benefit from weight lifting? Muscles are a lot like brains; the more they

Weight Lifting 101
(continued)

Various
strength
needs of
different
athletes are
discussed.

are used, the more they can do. Strong muscles can increase a person's speed, flexibility, endurance, and coordination. Consider the competition required in various sports; different muscle groups matter more to different athletes. Runners, especially sprinters, need bulging thighs for incredible speed. Basketball players need powerful arms and shoulders for endless shots and passes. Gymnasts need all-over muscle development for demanding balance and coordination. Football brings all these areas into play in a contest that requires great strength, speed, and agility. Weight lifting is a vital part of athletes' intensive training programs.

Eisenhart
saves the
heavy lifters
for last—
a logical
organization.

One last group can't be ignored. Some people lift weights to become as big and as strong as possible. I worked out with a guy who is about six foot two and weighs more than 200 pounds. He bench-presses more than I weigh. In a room devoted to dumbbells and barbells (also known as free weights), body builders moan as they struggle to lift super-heavy bars. After only a short time in this grunt room, it's clear the goal is not simply to be healthy, toned, or strong. These lifters want their strength to show. They want their muscles to bulge. Many participants do little if any aerobic activity. They spend most of their time lifting very heavy weights that build bulk and strength. My partner works out for an hour or more, five days a week.

The writer
concludes
with her
personal
preferences.

Not everyone fits neatly into these four categories. Personally, I work out to be healthy *and* toned, and find that I can benefit from lifting only three times a week. Weight lifting has become more and more popular among college students who appreciate exercise as a great stress reliever. And for me, the gym proved to be the best place to combat that dreaded "freshman fifteen." ■

Essay of Classification

In this essay John Van Rys classifies four basic approaches to literary criticism. His essay is intended to help college freshmen interpret literature. (Reprinted by permission of the author.)

Four Ways to Talk About Literature

The opening paragraph effectively draws readers into the essay.

Have you ever been in a conversation where you suddenly felt lost—out of the loop? Perhaps you feel that way in your literature class. You may think a poem or short story means one thing, and then your instructor suddenly pulls out the "hidden meaning." Joining the conversation about literature—in class or in an essay—may indeed seem daunting, but you can do it if you know what to look for, and what to talk about. There are four main perspectives, or approaches, that you can use to converse about literature.

Each new category, or approach, is clearly identified.

Text-centered approaches focus on the literary piece itself. Often called formalist criticism, this approach claims that the structure of a work and the rules of its genre are crucial to its meaning. The formalist critic determines how various elements (plot, character, language, etc.) reinforce the meaning and unify the work. For example, the formalist may ask the following questions concerning Robert Browning's poem "My Last Duchess": How do the main elements in the poem—irony, symbolism, and verse form—help develop the main theme (deception)? How does Browning use the dramatic monologue genre in this poem?

Audience-centered approaches focus on the "transaction" between text and reader—the dynamic way the reader interacts with the text. Often called rhetorical or reader-response criticism, these approaches see the text not as an object to be analyzed, but as an activity that is different for each reader. A reader-response critic might ask these questions of "My Last Duchess": How does the reader become aware of the duke's true nature, if it's never actually stated? Do men and women read the poem differently? Who were Browning's original readers?

How each approach functions (to interpret a poem) is a primary feature in the essay.

Author-centered approaches focus on the origins of a text (the writer and the historical background). For example, an author-centered study examines the writer's life—showing connections, contrasts, and conflicts between his or her life and the writing. Broader historical studies explore social and intellectual currents, showing links between an author's work and the ideas, events, and institutions of that period. Finally, the literary historian may make connections between the text in question and earlier and later literary works. The author-centered critic might ask these questions of "My Last Duchess": What were Browning's views of marriage, men and

Four Ways to Talk About Literature
(continued)

women, art, class and wealth? As an institution, what was marriage like in Victorian England (Browning's era) or Renaissance Italy (the duke's era)? Who was the historical Duke of Ferrara?

The fourth approach to criticism applies ideas outside of literature to literary works. Because literature mirrors life, argue these critics, disciplines that explore human life can help us understand literature. Some critics, for example, apply psychological theories to literary works by exploring dreams, symbolic meanings, and motivation. Myth or archetype criticism uses insights from psychology, cultural anthropology, and classical studies to explore a text's universal appeal. Moral criticism, rooted in religious studies and ethics, explores the moral dilemmas literary works raise. Marxist, feminist, and minority criticism are, broadly speaking, sociological approaches to interpretation. While the Marxist examines the themes of class struggle, economic power, and social justice in texts, the feminist critic explores the just and unjust treatment of women as well as the effect of gender on language, reading, and the literary canon. The critic interested in race and ethnic identity explores similar issues, with the focus shifted to a specific cultural group.

Such ideological criticism might ask a wide variety of questions about "My Last Duchess": What does the poem reveal about the duke's psychological state and his personality? How does the reference to Neptune deepen the poem? What does the poem suggest about the nature of evil and injustice? In what ways are the Duke's motives class based and economic? How does the poem present the duke's power and the duchess's weakness? What is the status of women in this society?

If you look at the variety of questions critics might ask about "My Last Duchess," you see both the diversity of critical approaches and the common ground between them. In fact, interpretive methods actually share important characteristics: (1) a close attention to literary elements such as character, plot, symbolism, and metaphor; (2) a desire not to distort the work; and (3) a sincere concern for increasing interest and understanding in a text. In actual practice, critics may develop a hybrid approach to criticism, one that matches their individual questions and concerns about a text. Now that you're familiar with some of the questions defining literary criticism, exercise your own curiosity (and join the ongoing literary dialogue) by discussing a text that genuinely interests you. ■

Subcategories are identified and analyzed to give the complete picture.

The closing paragraph explores the "common ground" between the critical approaches.

Writing an Essay of Definition

In an essay of definition, you clarify a complex concept (inflation), an abstract idea (hope), or a complicated ideal (democracy). To develop (and extend) a definition, you can give a dictionary definition, make a comparison, provide a fitting quotation, offer a negative definition (tell what it is not), and so on. The effectiveness of your essay depends upon your ability to understand your subject, to know what really sets it apart from all other members (related ideas) in its class. Use the guidelines below and the models that follow to help you develop your work.

SEARCHING AND SELECTING

Selecting ● Choose a term or concept that meets the requirements of your assignment. Your subject must be complex enough to require some careful thinking on your part; likewise, it should get your readers thoughtfully involved.

Reviewing ● If no subject comes readily to mind, think about topics in the news, concepts in your course work, and ideas you explore in your journal. (Also consider terms people misuse or use too freely.)

GENERATING THE TEXT

Collecting ● Explore your own thoughts and feelings about your subject. Then gather information—dictionary definitions, interviews, personal anecdotes, etc.—to include in your essay. (See 221 for a graphic organizer.)

Organizing ● Determine how you want to present your definition. You may want to begin with a dictionary definition or a personal anecdote and end with a negative definition or the thoughts and feelings of other people. Work with a number of different approaches.

WRITING AND REVISING

Writing ● Keep these points in mind when you write your first draft: In your opening remarks, identify your subject and help readers appreciate its significance—why it's important to know more about the subject. As you continue, include enough information (comparisons, examples, etc.) to bring your subject to life.

Revising ● Review your first draft, paying special attention to the logical flow of ideas in your essay. Revise and refine your work accordingly.

EVALUATING

Is the definition clearly presented and effectively developed?

Is the content organized and easy to follow?

Will readers appreciate the treatment of the subject?

Essay of Definition

Words mean different things to different people. In this essay student writer Kirsten Zinser takes a whimsical approach to defining the word *eclectic.* The personal approach she uses ends up telling us as much about her as it does about the word she defines.

A Few of My Favorite Things

The introduction piques the readers' interest.

Purple cows, purple bruises, jet fuel, boxes on skate-boards, dresses with bells, a dog named Tootsie, a neighbor named Scott, a song about meatballs, a certain good-night kiss, a broken swing. What have all these to do with each other? Nothing.

Go-carting, Handel's *Messiah,* a blue bike, pump organs, box cities, tenth grade . . . "But what do these have to do with each other?" you wonder. Like I said, nothing. My memories, like the things I enjoy, can only be described as one thing: *eclectic.* But this paper is not about my life. It's about my fascination with a word.

Before defining the word, the writer asks her readers to say it and feel it.

E-clec-tic. Say it out loud, savoring each syllable—*e . . . clec . . . tic.* Notice the different positions of your tongue. Odd how a word made of nothing more than clicking noises conveys meaning. I love to say the word. The lips do absolutely no work.

Now try to say it with your lips separated as little as possible. It still works. All the work is done on the inside, a dance of the muscular tongue on the teeth. If I were a ventriloquist, I would use the word as often as possible. Notice how the sound emerges as you form the letters. *E*—here it comes right down the center, *cl*—out from either side, *e*—an open corridor, *c*—the sound cut off, *ti*—the sound explodes past the tongue and over the teeth until pinched off with the last—*c.*

A dictionary definition is given.

Webster defines *eclectic* as selecting or choosing elements from different sources or systems. *Eclectic* implies variety. But what a grand way of saying variety. Variety sounds so generic; so discount. But *eclectic* is rich with imaginative sound.

The writer describes a highly imaginative experience.

I think if I could get inside the word I would find air so pure it would sting my lungs. I imagine the space inside the walls of the word to be like a long hallway that differs in shape every few feet. At one point, the distance between the walls would offer so much space, you could run and jump with little caution. In the next few feet, the walls would be so close together, that you would need to crawl on your belly to pass through. A few feet later, open space again, and so on. You would need to be limber to move through the many different-shaped spaces within the word.

Zinser describes her earliest history with the word.

For me, *eclectic* is one of those words that isn't simply used to describe something. It is a word that fits my soul. When I was young and first heard the word, I said it all the time, though I did not really understand its meaning. Then, as I began to internalize its definition, something inside me vowed allegiance. I knew this word would become not only a part of my vocabulary, but a part of my life.

The writer's "loyalty" to the word is described.

And so I pledge my loyalty to the variety of life. To enjoy theater, music, science, the outdoors, sports, philosophy, everything—this is my strategy. I want to be mature enough to carry on a conversation at elite restaurants, and young enough to squish my toes in thick mud. I want to be wild enough to walk on top of tall fences, and wise enough to be afraid of falling.

When I have a house of my own, I want an eclectic house—an old lamp here, a new dresser there, a vintage couch with a knitted afghan. The walls crowded with paintings, pictures, and stencils. Wild plants filling a yard of fragrant, clipped grass and popping up in unexpected places in the gravel driveway. Or perhaps I'll ditch the possession thing and root myself in the poetry of life, soaking in everything by osmosis, but being owned by nothing. I'll adopt a policy of "no policy." I won't be eclectic based on the things I possess, but on the experiences that I have.

The conclusion echoes the beginning and rounds out the discussion.

Purple cows, purple bruises, jet fuel, boxes on skateboards, dresses with bells, a dog named Tootsie, a neighbor named Scott, a song about meatballs, a certain good-night kiss, a broken swing. "But these have nothing to do with each other," you say. Precisely. ■

Essay of Definition

In this solemn essay, nineteenth-century abolitionist Frederick Douglass defines the word *slavery.* As you will see, he also builds a powerful argument against this oppressive institution. (This excerpt was taken from *Frederick Douglass, Selections from His Writing,* edited by Philip S. Foner, Ph.D., International Publishers Co., Inc., copyright 1945. It is reprinted by permission.)

What Is Slavery?

Douglass begins with a definition of slavery.

Slavery in the United States is the granting of that power by which one man exercises and enforces a right of property in the body and soul of another. The condition of a slave is simply that of the brute beast. He is a piece of property—a marketable commodity, in the language of the law, to be bought and sold at the will and caprice of the master who claims him to be his property; he is spoken of, thought of, and treated as property. His own good, his conscience, his intellect, his affections, are all set aside by the master. The will and the wishes of the master are the law of the slave.

Examples of the circumstances of the slave are listed.

He is as much a piece of property as a horse. If he is fed, he is fed because he is property. If he is clothed, it is with a view to the increase of his value as property. Whatever of comport is necessary to him for his body or soul that is inconsistent with his being property is carefully wrested from him, not only by public opinion, but by the law of the country.

He is carefully deprived of everything that tends in the slightest degree to detract from his value as property. He is deprived of education. God has given him intellect; the slaveholder declares it shall not be cultivated. If his moral perception leads him in a course contrary to his value as property, the slaveholder declares he shall not exercise it.

The author ends with a rhetorical question designed to stir consciences.

The marriage institution cannot exist among slaves, and one-sixth of the population of democratic America is denied its privileges by the law of the land. What is to be thought of a nation boasting of its liberty, boasting of its humanity, boasting of its Christianity, boasting of its love of justice and purity, and yet having within its own borders three millions of persons denied by law the right of marriage?—what must be the condition of that people? ■

Writing a Cause/Effect Essay

A cause/effect essay is based on a writer's careful examination of a timely issue. When you develop this type of essay, your first task is to identify the most important points related to your subject. Your second task is to make clear cause/effect connections between these points. The effectiveness of your essay depends upon your ability to establish sound, logical relationships between all of your main points. Use the guidelines below and the models that follow to help you develop your work.

SEARCHING AND SELECTING

Reviewing ● Think about recent experiences, conversations, newscasts, and headlines for possible ideas. A cause/effect essay could focus on an improved or deteriorating situation on your campus or in your community. It could focus on a recent development in medicine or in science, an exciting discovery, a milestone in history or in politics.

Searching ● If a subject does not readily come to mind, review copies of your college, local, and state newspapers or periodicals such as *Discover, The New Republic, Time,* and *Newsweek* for ideas. You might also think of recent events that have changed your life: moving from a dorm to an apartment, learning to play the banjo, starting a part-time job in the physics lab.

GENERATING THE TEXT

Collecting ● Once you have a subject in mind, determine what you already know about it and what you need to find out. Collect additional information by reading and talking with classmates about your subject. (Consider using a graphic organizer for your collecting. See topic number 221.)

Focusing ● Establish a specific focus or purpose for your writing as well as an effective order for presenting your ideas (either the cause stated first, supported by specific effects, or the effect stated first, supported by specific causes). Write a number of focus or purpose statements and then choose the one that is most effective and clear.

WRITING AND REVISING

Writing ● Develop your first draft according to your planning. Don't, however, be afraid to follow a new line of thinking if one begins to emerge.

Revising ● Review, revise, and refine your writing before sharing it with others. (Make sure each paragraph or main point supports your focus.)

EVALUATING

Has the cause/effect relationship been effectively addressed?
Does the writing contain an effective opening and closing?
Has sufficient supporting detail been included?

Cause and Effect Essay

In the following essay, student writer Jessica Radsma explains the cause behind some strange medical practices of the past. She argues that doctors' belief in "humors" caused two effects in the practice of medicine. Notice the antiquated cause-effect thinking that she describes in the second paragraph.

The Effects of Humors Theory on Past Medical Practices

A personal reference connects the writer's historical subject with modern readers.

Recently, while viewing the film *Sense and Sensibility*, I watched an early nineteenth-century English doctor treat his feverish patient, Marianne, by making an incision in her arm and draining some of her blood. I knew that the practice was called bloodletting, but what would motivate any doctor to take from his patient a resource she actually needed to get well? The cause, I learned, was the humors theory—a theory that strongly affected medical practice from ancient Greek times to the nineteenth century. My essay will examine the humors theory and then show how it dictated diagnoses and treatment.

Radsma summarizes the cause-effect thinking that once governed medical practice.

First, what was the humors theory? Doctors thought that the body held four liquids, or "humors," namely blood, phlegm, black bile, and yellow bile. The unique balance or mix of these four fluids created a person's temperament and affected his or her appearance (Lindberg 332). For example, doctors thought that the domination of blood made someone sanguine—fat and jolly. The domination of phlegm made a person phlegmatic—lazy and sleepy. A lot of black bile created a cold fish, a melancholy person—pensive and solitary. Finally, a lot of yellow bile made a person choleric—quick to get angry (Bettman 72). People became ill when their normal combination of humors was upset in some way.

Belief in the humors theory leads to the use of three diagnostic tools.

The humors theory strongly affected how doctors diagnosed illness. When someone got sick, doctors tried to figure out why the patient's humors were out of whack, and to what degree. To help them decide, doctors used three diagnostic tools: pulse reading, urinalysis, and astrology. Doctors read the pulse to check out the heart and blood. In fact, they came up with a complex classification scheme to measure pulse types and figure out whether such things as the strength, duration, regularity, and breadth were normal for the type (Lindberg 335-337). Examining urine, too, was a way of checking how the humors were working. Urine was checked for color, consistency, odor, and clarity (Lindberg 335). In fact, doctors were trained to detect as many as 18 colors in this precious liquid. The instrument used, the urine glass, was divided into four even parts, each standing for a part of the body. For example, if the urine at the top was cloudy, then the patient had head trouble (Bettman 73). Finally, because the doctor believed that the heavens influenced the human body, he had to connect the unbalanced humors to planetary influences (Lindberg 339).

Humors theory (the cause) leads to both helpful and foolish practices (the effects).

Humors theory also affected how doctors treated illness. Having figured out why and how far the humors were out of balance, the doctor would try to restore order using a variety of treatments—some surprisingly helpful, and others out-right quackery. Some helpful prescriptions included changes in diet or daily activities, as well as medicines (age-old remedies tested by experience). But the doctor's faith in the humors also caused foolish practices, like bloodletting, or phlebotomy, to restore the balance of the humors. Since doctors believed that the four humors were linked by tubes, bloodletting would release excess bodily fluids. As a medieval medical guidebook put it, "Bleeding soothes rage, brings joy unto the sad, / And saves all lovesick swains from going mad" (Rapport and Wright 84). Bloodletting was a tune-up when the humors were out of sync, a procedure often done in spring and fall (with the help of astrology) to "attune the humors to new climactic conditions" (Bettman 74-75).

A quotation from an old medical text adds a note of authority.

Such medical practice may sound bizarre to us. The humors theory (the cause) surely led to strange diagnoses and treatments (the effects). But this practice made good sense to doctors in the past.

Works Cited

Bettman, Otto L. *A Pictorial History of Medicine.*
 Springfield, IL: Charles C. Thomas, 1962.

Lindberg, David C. *The Beginnings of Western Science:*
 The European Scientific Tradition in Philosophical,
 Religious, and Institutional Context, 600 B.C. to A.D.
 1450. Chicago: University of Chicago Press, 1992.

Rapport, Samuel, and Helen Wright. *Great Adventures in*
 Medicine. New York: Dial Press, 1956. ■

Cause and Effect Essay

Zora Neale Hurston's essay explores her feelings about racial pride. According to Hurston, racial pride has one major effect: to make an individual "continually conscious of what race [he or she] belongs to." In Hurston's mind, this condition has been one of the major causes of world suffering. (Excerpt from appendix to *Dust Tracks on the Road* by Zora Neale Hurston. Copyright 1942 by Zora Neale Hurston. Copyright © renewed 1970 by John C. Hurston. Reprinted by permission of HarperCollins Publishers, Inc.)

Seeing the World As It Is

In the first two paragraphs, the writer explores her personal feelings about her subject.

There could be something wrong with me because I see Negroes neither better nor worse than any other race. Race pride is a luxury I cannot afford. There are too many implications behind the term. Now, suppose a Negro does something really magnificent, and I glory, not in the benefit to mankind, but in the fact that the doer is a Negro. Must I not also go hang my head in shame when a member of my race does something execrable? If a Negro does something fine, I gloat because he or she has done a fine thing, but not because he is a Negro. That is incidental and accidental. It is the human achievement which I honor. I execrate a foul act of a Negro but again not on the grounds that the doer was a Negro, but because it was foul. A member of my race just happened to be the fouler of humanity. In other words, I know that I cannot accept responsibility for thirteen million people. Every tub must sit on its own bottom regardless.

So "Race Pride" in me had to go. And, anyway, why should I be proud to be a Negro? Why should anybody be proud to be white? Or yellow? Or red? After all, the word "race" is a loose classification of physical characteristics.

The serious consequences of racial pride are explored in the second part of this writing.

It tells nothing about the insides of people. Pointing at achievements tells nothing either. Races have never done anything. What seems race achievement is the work of individuals. The white race did not go into a laboratory and invent incandescent light. That was Edison. The Jews did not work out Relativity. That was Einstein. The Negroes did not find out the inner secrets of peanuts and sweet potatoes, nor the secret of the development of the egg. That was Carver and Just. . . .

No, instead of Race Pride being a virtue, it is a sapping vice. It has caused more suffering in the world than religious opinion, and that is saying a lot. ■

Writing a Problem/Solution Essay

In a problem/solution essay, the writer examines all aspects of a problem (personal, social, political, etc.) and then suggests a reasonable solution, often after explaining why other solutions will not work. The effectiveness of a problem/solution essay depends upon your ability to understand a subject in all of its complexity, and to share that insight with your readers. Use the guidelines below and the models that follow to help you develop your work.

SEARCHING AND SELECTING

Searching ● Think about issues your peers complain about: required courses, campus safety, the cost of living, etc. Or conduct a brainstorming session, listing 10 problems or concerns of college students. Can you discover a reasonable solution for any of these problems?

Selecting ● Also consider problems that concern the local, national, or world community. Can you analyze and propose a solution for one of these problems? Do you know of anyone who solved a difficult problem in a unique way? Have you resolved a significant problem in your own life or helped to solve someone else's problem?

GENERATING THE TEXT

Forming ● After you've selected a problem, write it out in a clear statement. Then analyze it thoroughly, exploring the problem's parts, history, and causes. Weigh possible solutions. (See 221 for a graphic organizer.)

Assessing ● Carefully review your notes. Are you dealing with a manageable problem? Have you collected enough background material to present the problem and propose a solution? Gather additional support as needed.

WRITING AND REVISING

Writing ● Write your first draft after analyzing and assessing your subject. Pay special attention to your opening remarks. Think of an anecdote, a statistic, or a detail that you could develop into a provocative or compelling introduction. You want to begin by convincing readers that your subject is significant.

Refining ● Carefully review your first draft for clarity and logic. Also have one of your peers review your work. Revise and refine accordingly.

EVALUATING

Has a reasonable solution to a real problem been established?
Is the writing perceptive, the opening engaging, the conclusion logical?
Will readers appreciate the treatment of the subject?

Problem/Solution Essay

Overpopulation is not just a problem among humans. Student writer Gilbert Angelino focuses on the problem of a growing deer population that is encroaching on urban areas and upsetting the natural ecosystem. Notice how he describes the magnitude of the problem and discusses several possible solutions before he gives what he thinks is the most effective solution.

Practical Wildlife Management

The author states the problem clearly and gives statistics to back up his assertions.

One of the most pressing wildlife management issues is that of growing deer populations in many parts of the country. Deer populations have risen nationally from 500,000 at the turn of the century to more than 20 million today. According to Cathy Blumig in an article in the September 1995 issue of *Deer and Deer Hunting*, Pennsylvania spends $30 million annually in deer-related costs. Wisconsin has an estimated annual cost of $37 million for crop damage alone. Conservative estimates place auto/deer collisions at 500,000 yearly in the United States. Furthermore, Lyme's disease, an infectious human disease that is carried by the deer tick, now trails only AIDS as the fastest growing infectious disease in the United States.

The historical origins of the problem are laid out.

Much of the conflict between humans and deer has been caused by humans moving into the deer's forest habitat and developing it for housing. Modern suburbs sometimes divide the woods into five-acre plots, and after the houses are built, the plots have an area of woods bordering an open meadow like a feeding area. This is perfect whitetail habitat. The food is at the deer's front door for nocturnal feeding; they simply step back into the woods for cover when daylight comes.

Due to the close proximity of houses in suburbs, most of these areas banned hunting in the mid 1970's. In the ensuing 20 years there was a deer population boom, and now the deer are eating forests and private shrubbery alike. People who moved to these suburbs for the beauty of nature are experiencing the drawbacks of living too close to nature. Some even call the deer "rats with hooves."

Possible solutions are introduced and dismissed.

One attempt at controlling deer population has been an intensive study of birth control for deer, but there are several problems with this method. One major problem is cost—from $500 to $1,000 per deer sterilized per year. In order to maintain or reduce deer population, 50 percent or more of the does must not give birth. If this program were implemented in place of hunting in Iowa, for example, it would cost from $22.5 to $45 million to keep the deer from overpopulating.

Another question is whether it is safe for humans to consume deer that have been vaccinated with an immuno-contraceptive (ICC). Since millions of Americans eat venison, the drug would have to be tested and approved by the Food and Drug Administration.

Deer transitory movements could also nullify the effects of ICC's. Deer do not stay in one area long enough to be certain that 50 percent of the does have been sterilized. Even in urban areas, deer move up to 25 miles in their eight-year life span.

Another concern about ICC's is the chance of other animals ingesting the contraceptives by eating the bait or by preying or scavenging on deer. This is an obvious danger to the ecosystem. Considering those negative facts, deer contraceptives may be safely used in zoos, but not with wild animals.

Some suburbs have tried to trap deer and release them in other areas of the country. However, according to Bill Gordon in the November issue of *North American Hunter,* this method results in a 25 percent mortality rate. Additionally, there are scarcely any areas that want more deer. This method, therefore, has proved to be inviable.

The best and most effective solution to controlling deer populations is to stay as close to nature's ways as possible. Game management by hunting meets this criteria. Since we have eliminated the natural predators, we must provide others—hunters. The strongest animals have the best chance of escaping hunters, so natural selection is implemented.

Hunting with guns in the suburbs is impractical and dangerous. However, bow hunting is a viable alternative. In Fox Chapel Borough, Pennsylvania, a town of 5,600 residents, 45 deer were being killed each year by autos, and deer were destroying greenery. The town implemented a deer management program that matched an experienced bow hunter with a private landowner. Rules were implemented to provide safety for humans and humane treatment of the deer. During the 1993 season, there were no shooting accidents, no wounded deer escaped, and 128 deer were harvested with a bow. In the 1994 hunt, 185 deer were taken by bow. Since the deer herd numbers around 4,300, Fox Chapel Borough still has some deer to cull, but they are well on their way to an effective deer management program.

Of all the methods tried or considered to rid urban and suburban areas of unwanted deer, this last one holds the most promise. It is practical, efficient, safe, and humane; and while the sentimentalist may not want to see deer dispatched in any way, it is actually in the long-term interest of the deer population that they be managed. In this way we can keep a heritage alive for many generations and minimize the damage to humans and the ecosystem. ■

After dismissing the alternatives, the writer introduces his solution.

The writer explains why his solution is the best.

Problem/Solution Essay

Jonathan Kozol explores the problem of illiteracy in the United States in his book *Illiterate America,* from which this excerpt was taken. Though Kozol feels passionate about his subject, he also brings in a supply of facts to prove that his all-out "war" on illiteracy is the only solution. (From *Illiterate America* by Jonathan Kozol. Copyright © 1985 by Jonathan Kozol. Used by permission of Doubleday, a division of Bantam Doubleday Dell Publishing Group, Inc.)

from *Illiterate America*

Illiteracy in any land as well-informed and wealthy as the U.S.A. in 1985 is not an error. It is not an accident. There is no way that it could be an accident or error. Illiteracy among the poorest people in our population is a logical consequence of the kind of schools we run, the cities that starve them, the demagogues who segregate them, and the wealthy people who escape them altogether to enroll their kids in better funded, up-to-date, and more proficient institutions. It is a consequence, too, of pedagogic class selection which for many decades has regarded certain sectors of the population as the proper persons to perform those unattractive labors which no man or woman would elect to do if he or she received the preparation for more lucrative and challenging employment. Finally, it is a consequence of the illiterate condition of the parents of poor children—parents, in turn, who have been denied all recourse for self-liberation by the absence of a conscientious government initiative on their behalf.

> **The opening paragraph uses repetition ("... is a consequence") for emphasis.**

Politicians tell us that they want Americans to read, even the invisible American, even black, Hispanic, and poor white Americans. But is this protestation honest and sincere? We read in the Bible: "By their fruits ye shall know them." We might update these words to fit the present decade: "By their fiscal allocations you shall know them. By their cutbacks you shall spy them out. By their commissions, press releases, and reports, you shall ascertain that they are not your friends." . . .

What should be done?

We need an all-out literacy war in the United States.

> **The solution is dramatically stated in one sentence.**

The war must be launched by the millions of people who will never read this book, who cannot wait to get their invitations from their benefactors, who need to start the process on their own but cannot know what they must do unless their allies or exceptional convictions can draw, out of such words as they *can* read and understand, some hint of where the origins of freedom may reside. We need, above all else, to do away with the idea of literacy as training for domestication, contrived to fill existent or imagined lower-level job slots and consumer roles, and search instead for instruments of moral leverage strong enough to scrutinize those roles and to examine the political determinants of subjugation: examine, study, stand back, and reflect upon their purpose and, by virtue of reflection and examination, first to denounce and finally to transform.

Literacy, so conceived, is civil disobedience in pedagogic clothes: a cognitive denunciation of dynastic power, an ethical affront to an imperial injustice. Critical and analytic competence on such a scale is more than "functional." It is a literacy for human liberation. It is cultural action: an event, not an idea. It is political; it is endowed with anger; it is not neutral.

Those who speak as I have spoken in these pages can expect to be accused of advocating agitation, of aspiring to awaken discontent, to muddy the water, to confuse the pedagogic goal with a political intention. The waters are already muddy; the discontent exists already; politics is present in the heart of this injustice.

Kozol uses alarming statistics to underscore the seriousness of the problem.

When nearly half of all the adult black citizens in the United States are coming out of public schools without the competence to understand the antidote instructions of a chemical container, instructions on a medicine bottle, or the books and journalistic pieces which might render them both potent and judicious in a voting booth, who can pretend that literacy is not political?

When over one third of the adult population is unable to read editorial opinions, when millions cannot understand the warning on a pack of cigarettes or comprehend the documents they sign to rent a home, to buy a car, to purchase health insurance, who can persist in the belief that literacy is not political?

The author builds his case with a series of carefully selected facts.

When the government itself has been elected by exclusion of one third of the electorate, when the third which is excluded is the third which also gets the most deficient nutriment, least adequate health care, poorest housing, and which has an infant death rate twice that of the middle class, and when that government—having arrived in power—has actively engaged in the reduction of all services and funds which might at least alleviate the pain if not the cause of so much needless subjugation, who can still adhere to the belief that this is not political?

The answer is that no one can believe this. The most that we can do is to *pretend* that we believe it. It is a fragile pretense, and it will not hold. ■

Writing an Essay of Evaluation

In an essay of evaluation, a writer acts like a roving critic, exploring the significance of a particular event, a current trend, an extended project, a recent decision, a new product, and so on. To develop an essay of this type, think in terms of a subject's value, impact, and significance; its strengths and weaknesses; its place in the scheme of things. Use the guidelines below and the models that follow to help with your writing.

SEARCHING AND SELECTING

Searching ● If you have trouble thinking of a subject, write *people, places, events,* and *trends* on a piece of paper turned lengthwise. Then list ideas under each heading. Along the way, you may discover a suitable subject.

Reviewing ● You may also focus your attention on more consumer-oriented subjects. Think of purchases you have made (or are considering). Consider entertainment you enjoy (or dislike).

GENERATING THE TEXT

Recording ● Once you select a subject, list all the points that you want to evaluate. For example, if your subject is a product, you might evaluate its appearance, durability, manageability, affordability, usefulness, etc. (See 221 for a graphic organizer.) Also explore your own thoughts and feelings about the subject. What does it mean to you? How does it fit into your life?

Assessing ● Review your notes to see how much you know about your subject, and how much you need to find out. (Remember that you are trying to put your subject into perspective, to rate it, to measure it.) Consult primary and secondary sources of information as needed.

Focusing ● Write a focus statement—a sentence (or two) identifying the main idea or feeling you want to address in your evaluation. Then plan and organize your essay accordingly.

WRITING AND REVISING

Writing ● Write your first draft, working in main points and supporting details according to your planning and organizing.

Revising ● Review your first draft, paying special attention to the arrangement and flow of your ideas. Have one of your writing peers react to your work as well. Then revise and refine your work accordingly.

EVALUATING

Does the essay indeed evaluate or assess the subject?
Does the writing have a clear sense of order and purpose?
Will readers appreciate the treatment of the subject?

Essay of Evaluation

Student writer Nathaniel Zylstra evaluates *The Simpsons,* the popular TV show, in the following model. Zylstra explains why he tunes in and what makes the show unique and worthwhile.

The Rise of the House of Homer

The Simpsons, stars of the TV show by the same name, are a typical American family, or at least a parody of one. Homer, Marge, Bart, Lisa, and Maggie Simpson live in Springfield, U.S.A. Homer, the father, is a boorish, obese oaf who works in a nuclear power plant. Marge is an over-protective, nagging mother with an outrageous blue hairdo. Ten-year-old Bart is an obnoxious, "spiky-haired demon." Lisa is eight and a prodigy on the tenor saxophone and in class. The infant Maggie never speaks but only sucks on her pacifier.

What is the attraction of this yellow-skinned family who star on a show in which all the characters have pronounced overbites and only four fingers on each hand? I contend that we see a little bit of ourselves in everything they do. The world of Springfield is a parody of our own world, and Americans can't get enough of it.

However, *The Simpsons* was much maligned during its early years. Several school administrators banned Simpsons merchandise from their schools, claiming that the show promoted underachieving and misbehavior.

These criticisms threatened the show's popularity. Even more dangerous, however, was the possibility that the Simpsons would lose their novelty. Even the writers of the show expressed this idea: In one episode the Simpson family achieves fame and fortune, and a bystander remarks, ". . . they used to be cute and funny, but now they're just annoying." *The Simpsons* withstood the barrage of criticism, and the popularity of the show has remained high.

David Thigpen in *Time* magazine gives several reasons for *The Simpsons'* popularity. First, the show has diversified. In the first few years, the show focused primarily on Bart and his rebellious activities. Now it has expanded to include dozens of characters from Springfield, and episodes focus on all members of the Simpson family. Characters like the convenience-store owner, Apu Nahasapeematpetilan, the incompetent police chief, Wiggum, and the Simpsons' super-sincere Christian neighbor, Ned Flanders, give the show added variety.

The show also diversified by broadening its themes and toning down the crude joking. In the early seasons, jokes that involved a character sneezing on the sneeze guard at a salad

The opening paragraph describes the main characters in the TV show being evaluated.

The writer explains the reasons for the show's continued popularity.

The Rise of the House of Homer *(continued)*

bar were typical. In contrast, recent episodes have focused on issues in politics and pop psychology.

Second, despite all the criticism of the Simpsons' poor family values, the family sticks together through thick and thin, in distinct contrast to today's quick-divorce, single-parent society. Both Homer and Marge have resisted affairs with more attractive and successful people. They have endless money problems, and Marge has kicked Homer out of the house on several occasions; but their love always overcomes their problems. Even bratty Bart has been beaten up by the school bully in order to protect his sister Lisa.

Third, while the Simpsons are perceived as underachievers, they all have accomplished some pretty amazing things. Homer has saved two nuclear plants from meltdown, won a Grammy award, been an astronaut, and driven the city's monorail. Even baby Maggie has helped Bart and Lisa capture a robber in their house.

Fourth, the jokes on *The Simpsons* often require intelligence or significant education to understand. The show's creator, Matt Groening, says, "There are jokes you won't get unless you've actually attended a few classes in college." For instance, the prison number worn by several Simpsons characters, 24601, is the same as Jean Valjean's in *Les Miserables*. Also, the show makes regular allusions to both classic and recent movies, from *Citizen Kane* and *King Kong* to *Cape Fear*. There are usually allusions to more than 10 movies or TV shows in each episode. Even experienced Simpsons viewers need to watch each episode a few times in order to catch all the subtle jokes.

Finally, *The Simpsons* has been able to remain fresh throughout its seven seasons on the air. Some of the most talented writers and producers in Hollywood are on its staff. The executive producer, James L. Brooks, has received three Oscars for *Terms of Endearment* and nine Emmy awards. The show's writers have included talented people such as current late night talk-show host Conan O'Brien. These talented people have kept the show from becoming tired and repetitive.

Still, it is hard to pin down the exact reason that Simpsons fans love the show so much. I have over 70 of the more than 150 episodes on tape. Yet I cannot say exactly why I watch. I enjoy the social parody, the mocking of popular culture. But I also am attracted to the simpleness of the concept. I don't have to worry about the show attempting to teach me deep moral lessons, or insulting my intellect. When I watch *The Simpsons,* I feel that I am being treated like a thoughtful viewer. These reasons keep me and the rest of America laughing. ▪

Specific examples are given to prove the writer's point.

In closing, the writer sums up his evaluation of the show and gives some personal reasons for liking the show.

Essay of Evaluation

John F. Kennedy was president for less than three years before he was assassinated. Arthur Schlesinger, a member of Kennedy's administration and a Pulitzer-prize-winning author, evaluates the effects of Kennedy's short stay in office in a personal, touching way. This excerpt from *A Thousand Days: John F. Kennedy in the White House* is as much a tribute to Kennedy as it is an evaluation of his effect on the nation. (From *A Thousand Days.* Copyright © 1965 by Arthur M. Schlesinger, Jr. Reprinted by permission of Houghton Mifflin Co. All rights reserved.)

from *A Thousand Days*

Schlesinger begins with a list of Kennedy's accomplishments.

Yet he had accomplished so much: the hope for peace on earth, the elimination of nuclear testing in the atmosphere and the abolition of nuclear diplomacy, the new policies toward Latin America and the third world, the reordering of American defense, the emancipation of the American Negro, the revolution in national economic policy, the concern for poverty, the stimulus to the arts, the fight for reason against extremism and mythology. Lifting us beyond our capacities, he gave his country back to its best self, wiping away the world's impression of an old nation of old men, weary, played out, fearful of ideas, change and the future; he taught mankind that the process of rediscovering America was not over.

The author continues by evaluating the intangible effects of Kennedy's presidency.

He re-established the republic as the first generation of our leaders saw it—young, brave, civilized, rational, gay, tough, questing, exultant in the excitement and potentiality of history. He transformed the American spirit—and the response of his people to his murder, the absence of intolerance and hatred, was a monument to his memory. The energies he released, the standards he set, the purposes he inspired, the goals he established would guide the land he loved for years to come. Above all he gave the world for an imperishable moment the vision of a leader who greatly understood the terror and the hope, the diversity and the possibility, of life on this planet and who made people look beyond nation and race to the future of humanity. So the people of the world grieved as if they had terribly lost their own leader, friend, brother.

Schlesinger returns to the narrative to end this chapter of the book.

On December 22, a month after his death, fire from the flame burning at his grave in Arlington was carried at dusk to the Lincoln Memorial. It was fiercely cold. Thousands stood, candles in their hands; then, as the flame spread among us, one candle lighting the next, the crowd gently moved away, the torches flaring and flickering, into the darkness. The next day it snowed—almost as deep a snow as the inaugural blizzard. I went to the White House. It was lovely, ghostly and strange.

It all ended, as it began, in the cold. ■

Using Graphic Organizers

Graphic organizers can help you think through your analytical writing. At a glance, you will know what to do when you are asked to compare, classify, define, evaluate, and so on.

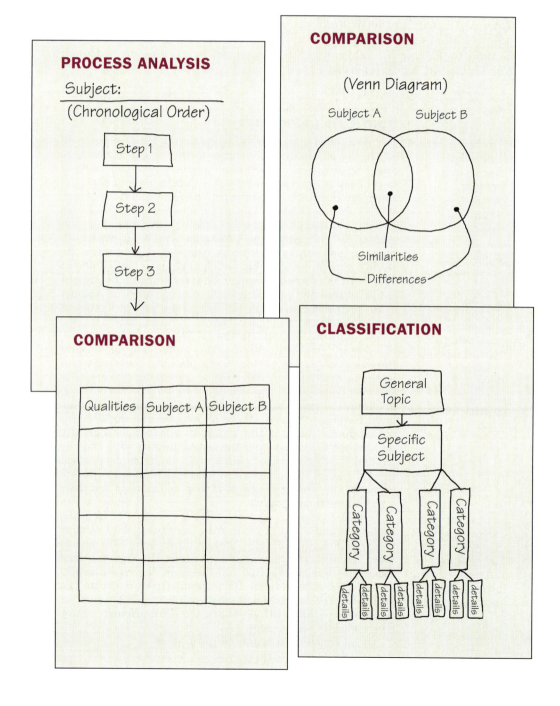

PROCESS ANALYSIS

Subject: _____

(Chronological Order)

Step 1

Step 2

Step 3

COMPARISON

(Venn Diagram)

Subject A   Subject B

Similarities

Differences

COMPARISON

Qualities	Subject A	Subject B

CLASSIFICATION

General Topic

Specific Subject

Category   Category   Category   Category

details details details details details details

DEFINITION

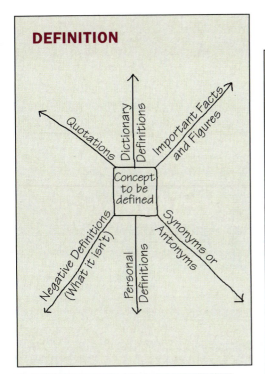

CAUSE/EFFECT

Subject: _____

Causes	Effects
(Because of...)	(... these conditions resulted)

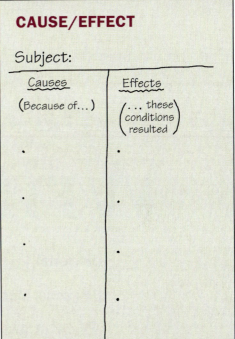

PROBLEM/SOLUTION

Causes of
the Problem

Parts
of the
Problem

Problem

Future
Implications

Possible
Solutions

EVALUATION

Subject: _____

Points to Evaluate	Supporting Details
1.	
2.	
3.	
4.	
5.	

Persuasive Writing

Editorial

Personal Commentary

Essay of Argumentation

Position Paper

Thinking Through an Argument

Persuasive Writing

You may have heard universities and colleges called institutions of higher learning. "Higher learning" is one of those odd phrases that seems to define itself: What is higher learning? It is learning at a higher level. What the phrase suggests, obviously, is that learning at the university level is more challenging than the schooling that came beforehand.

In truth, the notion of higher learning has a long history, back to the primary mission of our first universities. These schools were, for the most part, think tanks where students sought answers to big questions about life. While engaging in these lofty thoughts (higher learning), individuals were supposed to develop into independent thinkers. Our universities today are much more specialized, tied to specific career training; but helping students become independent thinkers is still part of the grand design.

WHAT'S AHEAD

If there is one section in your handbook that focuses on the original intent of higher learning, this is it. *Persuasive writing* promotes critical thinking. It forces you to take a stand and defend it. Included here are guidelines and models for writing editorials, personal commentaries, essays of argumentation, and position papers.

> *"Education means developing the mind, not stuffing the memory."* —**Anonymous**

Persuasive Writing

QUICK GUIDE

Preparing a persuasive essay is much like preparing for a debate. You study an issue from different perspectives. You then establish your main argument and gather your support. You also plan a strategy to counter the opposition, and so on. When you write your essay, always keep your silent debating opponent in mind; never let this person gain an advantage.

All persuasive writing shares the following characteristics:

STARTING POINT: Persuasive writing begins with a strong feeling you have about an important issue, one about which there are differing opinions.

PURPOSE: Your goal is to convince readers to agree with your argument (or to accept its validity).

FORM: Most persuasive writing follows a predictable pattern: An opinion is expressed and fully supported. Opposing arguments are addressed. Then, in closing, the opinion is reasserted.

AUDIENCE: Always have a clear sense of your readers, whether you are addressing your writing peers or a more general audience. What do they already know about the subject? What objections may they have to your opinion?

VOICE: Speak with confidence and assurance, but also be reasonable and fair in your comments. This will help you gain the confidence of your readers.

POINT OF VIEW: Use the third person *(he, she, they)* in most of your persuasive writing. However, in personal commentaries and persuasive essays stemming from direct experience, the first person *(I)* may be appropriate.

Insights into Writing

Try one of these prewriting activities to help with your planning: Create a *dialogue* between two people (one of whom may be you) who disagree about your subject. Play the dialogue out to a logical stopping point. Or simply *list* arguments for your opinion in one column, and arguments against it in another column. Both activities will help you gain control of your subject.

Writing an Editorial

An editorial is a brief persuasive essay expressing an opinion about a timely issue. When writing an editorial, come quickly to your main point, speak with confidence, and present a clear argument. (Editorials are usually fast paced, written in brief paragraphs.) It's common to conclude with a call to action or with a suggestion for a new course of action. Since editorials are written for news publications, they are usually intended for a general audience. Refer to the steps below and the models that follow for help with your writing.

SEARCHING AND SELECTING

Selecting ● Choose a subject that you have definite, strong feelings about. Make sure it is a timely topic, relevant for your readers.

Reviewing ● Editorials are usually tied to people, places, and issues in the news. If you keep up with current events (on campus and beyond), you should have a number of worthy subjects at pen point.

GENERATING THE TEXT

Collecting ● Write freely about your subject, recording everything you know about it. Consider additional collecting as well—reading, asking questions, making visits, etc.

Assessing ● Review your material to make sure that you have enough information to develop your argument.

NOTE: See "Thinking Through an Argument" (244-246) for insights into developing your writing.

Focusing ● State your opinion, identify your support, and consider opposing points of view.

WRITING AND REVISING

Writing ● Develop your first draft using your planning as a guide. Spend a little extra time on the opening lines. The first few sentences must draw readers into your text and clearly state the subject of your writing.

Refining ● As you review your first draft, note any loose ends in your ideas. Then make the necessary changes to tighten your argument.

EVALUATING

Does the editorial present a single, focused point of view?
Is the argument organized and logical?
Are main points effectively developed and supported?
Does the editorial progress smoothly from one point to the next?

Editorial

No matter how you feel about the issue of illegal aliens, it would be hard not to sympathize with the plight of the young woman described in this editorial by student writer Mitzi Mitchell. Editorials are particularly effective when they put a "face" on an issue that is in the public debate.

Immigration, Take a Number

The opening sentences narrow and personalize the subject.

Jasmin Salehi. More than likely it is a name you do not recognize, unless you happened to page through the Metro section of Thursday's *Los Angeles Times*. Though her name may not be important, her situation is.

You see, Jasmin is facing deportation to her native country of South Korea because she is not a legal citizen of the U.S. "Why should I be concerned?" you may ask. "After all, this country is struggling to support its legal citizens as it is. Shouldn't they take precedence over illegal residents?"

Facts from the case are cited.

While that issue is debatable, it is not the case with Jasmin. She was well on her way to achieving legal U.S. citizenship. But all that, and much more, was yanked from her grasp when her husband fell victim to a fatal robbery. Now, without the assistance of her late husband's citizenship, the United States Immigration and Naturalization Service (INS) considers Jasmin an illegal alien who should be deported.

How can this be? According to the INS, Jasmin's marriage to her husband did not meet the two-year minimum that is required for immigrants to acquire permanent residency. Here is a woman still mourning the loss of her beloved husband being told that she is no longer fit for U.S. citizenship. There is something wrong with this situation.

The editorial clearly states the author's outrage.

Jasmin's marriage was not one of mere convenience. According to the *Times,* it was "an American love story." Jasmin's marriage, like many of our own ancestors, embodied the American dream. She and her husband came to the "Land of Opportunity" to live and raise a family in a country that accepts all races, creeds, and nationalities. Jasmin is not one of the many illegal residents in the U.S. relying on government aid. She immigrated not for financial assistance, but to pursue her dreams.

A call for action is made to reverse the injustice.

It is time to step back and ponder the intentions of our government when it will not allow a widow to gain the citizenship she was on her way to achieving, yet will sanction the dispersion of myriad benefits to hundreds of illegal aliens. Perhaps we ought to establish an ad campaign directed toward those who are considering potential citizenship in the U.S.—"Welcome to America, land of the free, if you fit our profile." ■

Editorial

This editorial, appearing in a large urban newspaper, discusses the economic inequality between blacks and whites. The purpose of this editorial is to open (or continue) the debate on an important national issue. (*Milwaukee Journal Sentinel,* September 7, 1996. Reprinted with permission of the Milwaukee Journal Sentinel.)

Narrowing the Education Gap

An opening question leads readers into the text.

Why are blacks and whites unequal, according to the gauges of economic well-being? An oft-stated answer historically has been that whites have more education than do blacks. Stay in school, get your high school diplomas and things will work out, African-Americans were told.

Well, apparently they heeded that advice. The U.S. Census Bureau reports that the gap in high school graduation rates between whites and blacks has all but vanished.

Last year, young black adults boasted a high school graduation rate of 86.5%; young white adults boasted a rate of 87.4%. Once blacks had half the graduation rate whites had.

Statistics support the writer's ideas.

Still, the economic gap persists between blacks and whites. In 1974, blacks on average earned 70 cents for every dollar whites earned. By 1994, the black part of the ratio had risen only to 74 cents.

One argument has been that, while the racial gap in *quantity* of education has closed, a gap still remains in *quality* of education. However, other evidence—namely, the results of standardized tests—suggests that African-Americans have been narrowing the gap there, too.

Possible answers to the opening question are discussed.

Yet another explanation has some weight. As Christopher Jencks, a Harvard sociology professor, puts it, "This may be a case of running fast to stand still."

Though young African-Americans are better qualified now than formerly, the jobs for which they are qualified are shrinking. Post-secondary education is increasingly more important now, and blacks have not closed the college graduation gap as fast as they have the high school graduation gap.

The obvious solution is to increase the number of college campuses—which will take some societal intervention—to help remove financial and other nonacademic barriers to college.

At the same time, though, total education equality won't completely solve the economic gap. White high school dropouts still have an easier time getting jobs than do black high school graduates. Similarly, white college dropouts can get jobs faster than can black college grads. Society must continue to fight racism in the labor market through affirmative action and other tools. ■

Writing a Personal Commentary

A commentary is essentially a thoughtful reaction to some aspect of life. Think of this form as one step removed from an editorial. An editorial usually attacks or applauds a specific event in the news. A commentary speaks more evenhandedly and reflectively about some aspect of popular culture (like body piercing) or about something more fundamental (like human dignity). News publications often include commentaries. Refer to the steps below and the models that follow for help with your writing.

SEARCHING AND SELECTING

Reviewing ● Think about recent experiences or conversations you have had. In addition, review campus newspapers as well as national periodicals and other media for possible ideas.

Brainstorming ● If you have trouble thinking of potential subjects, enlist the help of your peers. A small group of you could brainstorm for ideas. Consider current affairs, trends, and developments that elicit strong feelings among members of your group.

GENERATING THE TEXT

Exploring ● Free-write about your subject to see what you already know about it, and how much you need to find out. Continue searching for more information as needed.

Focusing ● State a possible focus for your commentary—a sentence (or two) expressing the main point you want to convey. Then, if necessary, develop a basic writing plan, listing the main ideas you would like to cover.

WRITING AND REVISING

Writing ● Develop your first draft, working in observations and details as they come to mind, or according to any planning you may have done.

Refining ● As you review your draft, make note of parts that either need more explanation or need to read more smoothly. Also ask one of your peers to react to your work. Then revise and refine accordingly.

EVALUATING

Does the commentary explore an issue that will be of interest to the intended readers?

Is a statement or feeling about this issue conveyed?

Is the writing sufficiently supported by details, examples, and personal reflections?

Does the writing form a meaningful whole, moving smoothly from one point to the next?

Personal Commentary

In this commentary, student writer Stanley Joseph comes to the defense of "the projects" where he lives. He counters the bleak stereotype of inner-city housing with comments that paint quite a different picture. Notice the specific detail Joseph weaves into the piece to make his point. (Stanley Joseph is on the staff of *YO! [Youth Outlook],* a youth newspaper produced by Pacific News Service. It is reprinted by permission.)

Why I Like the Projects

The writer begins with a statement that reflects his experience— appropriate for a personal commentary.

Bernal Dwellings is where I live, and it's cool.

Usually when people talk about "the projects" they talk about what's wrong with them. That's easy. I'm going to do something different and harder. I'm going to tell you about what's good in my neighborhood.

My hood is diverse. You've got your Latinos, African-Americans, whites, Asians, and Samoans. Hang around long enough, and you might read a Spanish billboard, step over a Chinese newspaper, hear rap music blasting from a bucket at the stoplight, or see a pair of rosy, pink lips smiling at you in the local store. One store in my neighborhood has taught me that it's not true that all Asians hate blacks. When I get my change back it's counted out in English and Spanish. Thanks for the Spanish lesson.

Specific references to the neighborhood illustrate his point.

A lot of times projects are built in remote areas, an afternoon's bus ride from the nearest supermarket, in deserted neighborhoods where people look too scared to be out in the sunlight. But my neighborhood—the Mission—has it all, from fresh fruits and vegetables, to hard-to-find herbs and roots for old country remedies, to drinks I've grown to love, such as Malta and Coco-Rico.

"My hood is diverse. You've got your Latinos, African-Americans, whites, Asians, and Samoans."

You think that parks are only for drug dealing? Check out Garfield Park, where they play soccer round the clock. If anybody says that soccer is for punks, I'd like to see that person spend the whole day running up and down the field trying to keep up with these guys.

My favorite place in the neighborhood is the library on 24th Street. The smell of books, the perfume of rusty finger prints off the tan pages, charges me like nothing else. I always stop in the children's section just to catch up on all the books I didn't get to finish in "kid" school. Nobody seems

Why I Like the Projects
(continued)

to understand my love for the library. To go to a place and get your curiosity satisfied—it's such a treasure to me.

I'll admit that before I moved into Bernal Dwellings, my expectations were generic: drug dealers, hookers, never-smiling folks. The image of the sun never shining down on Bernal Dwellings was stuck in my mind. And I figured the brothers would start tripping on me as soon as I moved in because I was a stranger and nobody knew me.

Some of these visions did become reality. There are a couple of pharmaceutical engineers who hang around in the darkest night selling nickel bags. The police are up on Folsom Street every night, and the fire truck comes nearly every Friday night. Then there's the guy blasting his car speakers from 2 a.m. until sunrise, the winos in the parking lot drinking their blues away, an occasional boxing match (fight) on weekends.

But that's not the whole story. When people discover where I live, I always prepare myself for "those questions." You know, is it really like "Boyz 'N the Hood"? Are there gangs and turf fights? Have you ever been shot at? Are you scared? I just remind my interrogators that people are people, and you can't always judge them by their home turf and how they're dressed. What you call "the projects," I might call home. What you call "a dude" because of his mean mug and braids might be a rocket scientist in the making. ■

Personal Commentary

In this commentary, Neil Postman reflects upon the information explosion. As you will note in the introduction, his comments are framed by two questions: "Where is the darkness?" and "Where is the light?" (This article first appeared in *Utne Reader,* July-Aug., 1995, Vol. 70. It is reprinted by permission of the author.)

Where is the darkness?

Utne Reader held a public salon at The Town Hall in New York City earlier this year. Twenty-seven of the thinkers, writers, artists, activists, and businesspeople we selected as the UTNE 100, featured in our January-February 1995 issue, "100 Visionaries Who Could Change Your Life," gathered onstage to respond to the questions "Where is the darkness? Where is the light?" Here are a few of the most provocative answers.

The main part of the commentary addresses the first question: "Where is the darkness?"

The darkness of which I am most acutely aware was spoken of in a prophetic poem by Edna St. Vincent Millay. The poem is from her book *Huntsman, What Quarry?* and in this fragment of it Ms. Millay describes precisely the problem that darkens our horizon:

> Upon this gifted age, in its dark hour,
> Rains from the sky a meteoric shower
> Of facts. . . . They lie unquestioned, uncombined.
> Wisdom enough to leech us of our ill
> Is daily spun, but there exists no loom
> To weave it into fabric . . .

A historical analysis of the information glut is provided.

What the poet speaks of here is a great paradox. Beginning in the 19th century, humanity creatively addressed the problem of how to eliminate information scarcity, how to overcome the limitations of space, time, and form. And we did so in spectacular fashion, especially in the 19th century.

For those of you unfamiliar with the 19th century, here are some of the inventions that contributed to the solution: telegraphy, photography, the rotary press, the transatlantic cable, the electric light, radio, movies, the computer, the X ray, the penny press, the modern magazine, and the advertising agency.

". . . we have transformed information into a form of garbage, and ourselves into garbage collectors."

Where is the darkness?
(continued)

Of course, in the first half of the 20th century, we added some important inventions so that the burdens of information scarcity were removed once and for all. But in doing so, we created a new problem never experienced before: information glut, information incoherence, information meaninglessness. To put it far less eloquently than Ms. Millay did, we have transformed information into a form of garbage, and ourselves into garbage collectors.

Like the sorcerer's apprentice, we are awash in information without even a broom to help us get rid of it. Information comes indiscriminately, directed at no one in particular, in enormous volume, at high speeds, severed from import and meaning. And there is no loom to weave it all into fabric. No transcendent narratives to provide us with moral guidance, social purpose, intellectual economy. No stories to tell us what we need to know, and what we do not need to know.

The closing paragraph addresses the second question: "Where is the light?"

This, then, is the problem we have to confront with as much intelligence and imagination as we can muster. How to begin? We will have to stop consulting our engineers, our computer gurus, and our corporate visionaries, who, though they claim to speak for the future, are strangely occupied in solving a 19th-century problem that has already been solved. Instead, we will need to consult our poets, playwrights, artists, humorists, theologians, and philosophers, who alone are capable of creating or restoring those metaphors and stories that give point to our labors, give meaning to our history, elucidate the present, and give direction to our future. They are our weavers, and I have no doubt that there are men and women among us who have the looms to weave us a pattern for our lives. The prospect of their doing so is, for me, the gleam of light on the horizon. ■

Writing an Essay of Argumentation

An essay of argumentation presents a sensible discussion of a subject based on thorough research and logical thinking. You build this type of essay around a proposition or main idea that you argue for. Your argument should include convincing evidence to support your proposition as well as reasonable counters to opposing points of view. An effective essay of argumentation enlightens as much as it persuades. It helps readers make informed decisions about the subject. Refer to the steps below and the models that follow for help with your writing. (For additional help, see "Thinking Through an Argument," topic numbers 244-246.)

SEARCHING AND SELECTING

Searching ● Review your texts or class notes for possible subjects. Also consider issues you hear debated locally or nationally. Focus on subjects that are serious, specific, timely, and debatable.

Selecting ● Test a possible subject in the following way: (a) identify a reasonable proposition to argue for, (b) list at least one argument supporting this proposition, and (c) list at least one argument opposing it.

GENERATING THE TEXT

Collecting ● Gather your own thoughts by writing freely about your subject, or by discussing it in an imaginary dialogue. Then collect as much additional information as necessary through reading, interviewing, observing, and so on. Take notes, especially on strong arguments forwarded by authorities. Label arguments "pro" (for your proposition) or "con" (against).

Assessing ● As you review your research, assess the strength and credibility of your proposition. You may have to adjust it in order to defend it more effectively. Then decide on the best arrangement of your ideas. (Consider saving your best pro argument for last.)

WRITING AND REVISNG

Writing ● Develop your argument using your planning as a guide. If you become stuck, talk through your argument with one of your writing peers.

Revising ● Review, revise, and refine your argument before presenting it to your readers. Ask one or more of your peers to review your work as well.

EVALUATING

Is the proposition reasonable and clearly stated?
Are supporting arguments logical and convincing?
Are opposing arguments addressed?

Essay of Argumentation

This essay provides a convincing argument for banning the barbed hook from sport fishing. Notice that student writer David DeHaan takes a reasonable and sensible approach throughout the essay.

Evening the Odds

A new breed of hunter dwells among North America's hidden waterways. Armed with a $50.00 rod and reel, $60.00 hip waders, and a wide array of lures ranging from glowing gadgets to old-fashioned worms, today's fisherman has improved his arsenal well beyond the bent nail and old twine that Huck Finn used for jigging. But most modern fishermen still carry one piece of equipment that is outdated: the barbed hook, which is still added to almost every lure produced commercially. This mechanism continues to plague the sport of fishing by damaging young fish stocks. Barbed hooks should be banned from lure fishing to protect fish that are not yet ready for anglers to keep.

A smooth (barbless) fishing hook is much easier to remove from a fish's mouth than a barbed hook. A smooth hook comes out cleanly, leaving only a small puncture, and giving fishermen the opportunity to release undamaged fish. A properly set barbed hook, on the other hand, often inflicts serious injury to the jaw of the fish. While this is not a problem for the larger keepers, it does have serious consequences for smaller fish that should be released back into the waterway. Many of these small fish are kept because the anglers know that releasing them would be inhumane, while others are released with portions of their jaws missing, unable to feed properly. By improving the angler's chances of safely releasing unwanted fish, barbless hooks help to preserve our limited fish stocks.

Supporters of barbed fishing hooks say that banning the hooks would decrease the number of fish they are able to land. They claim that enjoyment of the sport would be limited by the increased difficulty of keeping fish on the line. They are at least partially correct; playing a fish is difficult without a barb. However, this does not have to limit the enjoyment of the sport.

When sportsmen stop to reflect on why they find fishing so enjoyable, most realize that what they love is the feel of a fish on the end of the line, not necessarily the weight of the fillets in their coolers. Fishing has undergone a slow evolution over the last century. While fishing used to be a way of putting food on the table, most of today's lure fishermen do so only for the relaxation that it provides. The barbed hook was invented to increase the quantity of fish a man could

The opening comments draw readers into the main point of the argument.

An objection is effectively addressed.

land in order to better feed his family. This need no longer exists, and so barbed hooks are no longer necessary.

According to some anglers who do use smooth hooks, their lures perform better than barbed lures as long as they maintain a constant tension on the line. Smooth hooks can bite deeper than barbed hooks, actually providing a stronger hold on the fish. These anglers testify that switching from barbed hooks has not noticeably reduced the number of fish that they are able to land. In their experience, and in my own, enjoyment of the sport is actually heightened by adding another challenge to playing the fish (maintaining line tension).

Some people have argued that replacing all of the barbed hooks in their tackle would be a costly operation. While this is certainly a concern, barbed hooks do not necessarily require replacement. With a simple set of pliers, the barbs on most conventional hooks can be bent down, providing a cost-free method of modifying one's existing tackle. These modified hooks are also much safer to use. Young children who are just learning to fish often pose a certain danger using fishhooks. While the possibility of snagging someone still remains with a smooth hook, the hook is much easier to remove from skin, clothing, and branches.

The gradual evolution of fishing for food into fishing for sport has outdated the need for barbed hooks. Just as in any other sport, enjoyment comes from being able to achieve a goal despite considerable difficulty. If anglers chose their equipment solely on the quantity of fish they were able to land, we would all be fishing with dragnets. While everyone agrees that nets take the sport out of fishing, they must realize that barbed hooks do the same thing. Fishing with smooth hooks is a way of caring for and conserving our fish stocks while still maintaining the enjoyment of sport fishing for the angler. ■

Each new claim is thoroughly explored.

In closing, the writer emphasizes a key point.

Essay of Argumentation

Writer Linda Chavez's essay argues against the "advance of multiculturalism" in the United States. Chavez speaks confidently and assertively throughout the essay—conceding little to the opposition. (© 1994 by *National Review,* Inc., 150 East 35th Street, New York, NY 10016. Reprinted by permission.)

Demystifying Multiculturalism

A strong opening statement grabs the readers' attention.

Multiculturalism is on the advance, everywhere from President Clinton's cabinet to corporate boardrooms to public-school classrooms. If you believe the multiculturalists' propaganda, whites are on the verge of becoming a minority in the United States. The multiculturalists predict that this demographic shift will fundamentally change American culture—indeed destroy the very idea that America *has* a single, unified culture. They aren't taking any chances, however. They have enlisted the help of government, corporate leaders, the media, and the education establishment in waging a cultural revolution. But has America truly become a multicultural nation? And if not, will those who capitulate to these demands create a self-fulfilling prophecy?

At the heart of the argument is the assumption that the white population is rapidly declining in relation to the nonwhite population. A 1987 Hudson Institute report helped catapult this claim to national prominence. The study, *Workforce 2000,* estimated that by the turn of the century only 15 percent of new workers would be white males. The figure was widely interpreted to mean that whites were about to become a minority in the workplace—and in the country.

The writer provides statistics to back up one of her claims.

In fact, white males will still constitute about 45 percent —a plurality—of the workforce in the year 2000. The proportion of white men in the workforce *is* declining—it was nearly 51 percent in 1980—but primarily because the proportion of white women is growing. They will make up 39 percent of the workforce within 10 years, according to government projections, up from 36 percent in 1980. Together, white men and women will account for 84 percent of all workers by 2000— hardly a minority share. . . .

Multiculturalists insist on treating race and ethnicity as if they were synonymous with culture. They presume that skin color and national origin, which are immutable traits, determine values, mores, language, and other cultural attributes, which, of course, are learned. In the multiculturalists' world view, African-Americans, Puerto Ricans, or Chinese Americans living in New York City have more in common with persons of their ancestral group living in Lagos or San Juan or Hong Kong than they do with other New Yorkers who are white. Culture becomes a fixed entity, transmitted, as it were, in the genes, rather than through experience. . . .

Such convictions lead multiculturalists to conclude that "[T]here is no common American culture." The logic is simple, but wrongheaded: Since Americans (or more often, their forebears) hail from many different places, each of which has its own specific culture, the argument goes, America must be multicultural. And it is becoming more so every day as new immigrants bring their cultures with them.

Indeed, multiculturalists hope to ride the immigrant wave to greater power and influence. They have certainly done so in education. Some 2.3 million children who cannot speak English well now attend public school, an increase of 1 million in the last seven years. Multicultural advocates cite the presence of such children to demand bilingual education and other multicultural services. The Los Angeles Unified School District alone currently offers instruction in Spanish, Armenian, Korean, Cantonese, Tagalog, Japanese, and Russian. Federal and state governments now spend literally billions of dollars on these programs.

An argument from the "other side" is countered.

Ironically, the multiculturalists' emphasis on education undercuts their argument that culture is inextricable from race or national origin. They are acutely aware just how fragile cultural identification is; why else are they so adamant about reinforcing it? Multiculturalists insist on teaching immigrant children in their native language, instructing them in the history and customs of their native land, and imbuing them with reverence for their ancestral heroes, lest these youngsters be seduced by American culture.

The writer analyzes multicultural proponents.

The impetus for multiculturalism is not coming from immigrants, but from their more affluent and assimilated native-born counterparts. The proponents are most often the elite—the best educated and most successful members of their respective racial and ethnic groups. College campuses, where the most radical displays of multiculturalism take place, are fertile recruiting grounds. Last May, for example, a group of Mexican-American students at UCLA, frustrated that the university would not elevate the school's 23-year-old Chicano studies program to full department status, stormed the faculty center, breaking windows and furniture and causing half a million dollars in damage. The same month, a group of Asian-American students at UC-Irvine went on a hunger strike to pressure administrators into hiring more professors of Asian-American studies. These were not immigrants, or even, by and large, disadvantaged students, but middle-class beneficiaries of their parents' or grand-parents' successful assimilation to the American mainstream.

Demystifying Multiculturalism
(continued)

Whatever their new-found victim status, these students look amazingly like other Americans on most indices. For example, the median family income of Mexican-American students at Berkeley in 1989 was $32,500, slightly above the national median for all Americans that year, $32,191; and 17 percent of those students came from families that earned more than $75,000 a year, even though they were admitted to the university under affirmative-action programs (presumably because they suffered some educational disadvantage attributed to their ethnicity).

Multiculturalism is not a grassroots movement. It was created, nurtured, and expanded through government policy. Without the expenditure of vast sums of public money, it would wither away and die. That is not to say that ethnic communities would disappear from the American scene or that groups would not retain some attachment to their ancestral roots. American assimilation has always entailed some give and take, and American culture has been enriched by what individual groups brought to it. The distinguishing characteristic of American culture is its ability to incorporate so many disparate groups, creating a new whole from the many parts. Lately, we have nearly reversed course, treating each group, new and old, as if what is most important is to preserve its separate identity and space.

It is easy to blame the ideologues and radicals who are pushing the "disuniting of America," to use Arthur Schlesinger's phrase, but the real culprits are those who provide multiculturalists the money and the access to press their cause. Without the acquiescence of policy makers and ordinary citizens, multiculturalism would be no threat. Unfortunately, most major institutions have little stomach for resisting the multicultural impulse—and many seem eager to comply with whatever demands the multiculturalists make. Americans should have learned by now that policy matters. We have only to look at the failure of our welfare and crime policies to know that providing perverse incentives can change the way individuals behave—for the worse. Who is to say that if we pour enough money into dividing Americans, we won't succeed? ■

A critical point is saved for the last part of the argument.

The final point brings the essay full circle.

GUIDELINES

Writing a Position Paper

A position paper presents a thorough, extensive analysis of a noteworthy issue. This analysis, of course, stems from the writer's position, or stance, on the issue. Your goal in a position paper is to trace, as effectively as you can, your particular line of thinking on a subject. Rather than necessarily arguing for or against something, you're more interested in informing, explaining, speculating, etc. Refer to the guidelines below and the models that follow to help you develop your writing.

SEARCHING AND SELECTING

Searching ● Think of current developments in the news (decisions, laws, advancements, or controversial issues) that you feel strongly about. Also look over your current readings and course notes for ideas.

Reviewing ● If need be, review a recent issue of the *Readers' Guide to Periodical Literature* for subjects as well as other guides or indexes in the library. If you have the opportunity, you may also want to search the Internet for ideas.

GENERATING THE TEXT

Noting ● List what you already know about your subject, and state your initial position on it. Also decide what you hope to learn as you further investigate the subject.

Investigating ● Collect as many facts and details as you can to help you develop your paper. Consider primary and secondary sources of information.

Focusing ● Reassess (or state) your position after you have thoroughly researched the subject. Then determine how you will analyze (explain, defend) it, and plan accordingly.

WRITING AND REVISING

Writing ● If you can't think of a good opening, try a first line like this: "I might as well come right out with it." Then state your position and just start writing. (It worked for the writer of the second model paper. See 242-243.) Use your planning notes as a general guide to help you work in facts and details.

Revising ● Carefully review your writing. (Make sure all of your main ideas are sufficiently developed.) Revise and refine accordingly.

EVALUATING

Does the paper present an in-depth discussion of a timely subject?
Has a position been effectively analyzed (defended)?
Will readers appreciate the treatment of the subject?

Position Paper

Anna Grishchenko's position in this paper is based on speculation, on what the world may be like if corporate America controls the destiny of biogenetic engineering. The paper is an interesting blend of irreverence and reason. (It first appeared in *Merlyn's Pen: The National Magazine of Student Writing*. All rights reserved. Reprinted by permission.)

Biogenetic Engineering: a Gamble for a Bright Future

The subject of the paper is introduced in a dramatic fashion.

Commerce operates as methodically as a well-regulated clock: dutiful companies bring diverse household and business products to millions of eager customers. But industry's thirst to make people's lives easier and better may not be quenched by mere electric pencil sharpeners and automatic garage openers: soon market researchers will leave behind present-day fixation on electronic gadgetry and cleaning agents to penetrate the very fuse box of life itself—the great new world of DNA.

The day may come when an ingenious researcher will knock confidently on the company president's door and, holding up a pink test tube, announce that after isolating the gene that causes baldness, he has succeeded in simulating a new one to replace it. The president's eyes will open wide (as his pupils enlarge to almost swallow the irises, and the whites become etched with scarlet lightning bolts) and the excited executive will jump up from his chair, his face assuming the look that Dr. Frankenstein must have worn when he first heard his monster breathe.

The focus of the writer's remarks are implied in this question.

An end to baldness is just one perhaps trivial example of the future as predicted by today's budding biotechnological industry. Not many people would object to ending the nuisance of baldness, but then what about tallness, obesity, sexual preference, facial features, etc.? Such characteristics blend to create our individuality. How would we feel if these qualities were for sale? . . .

Existing research is carefully examined.

Today, bioengineering is in its latent stage; however, it will undoubtedly display far fuller foliage in the very near future. Amniocentesis, for example, allows us to "look into" the unborn baby, find out its sex, and discover whether the child has such disorders as Tay-Sachs disease or Down's syndrome. Since this process gives us no method (except abortion) of defeating the prognosis, it cannot truly be considered genetic engineering. A more recently established practice, closely related to biotechnology, is the determination of sex by the process of filtering. If a couple wants a boy, the doctor filters the male's sperm to separate the "X" cells from the "Y" cells. A "Y" sperm is joined with an egg and *voila*—a custom-ordered boy! Most couples who go through this procedure do so because of a defective gene from one of the parents that would affect offspring of only one gender. Thus, to ensure against a disorder in the child (and in future generations), the parents take the precaution of conceiving a baby of the invulnerable sex. But the reasons behind ordering a boy or a girl are not always this practical: sheer preference often plays a large role. . . .

Certain traits like tallness, slimness, and blue eyes are social favorites. If we allow people to "catalog-order" their babies, we will get an increasing number of children with "popular" genes. And more and more popular traits engineered into babies will drastically lesson individuality; in future schools we may see "herds" of children with dimpled cheeks, Shirley Temple curls, and Jimmy Carter smiles. And who knows? Perhaps such "unpopular" traits as shyness or homosexuality or obesity serve some hidden evolutionary purpose. Certain scientific studies suggest that homosexuality, for which there is a genetic inclination, may be one of nature's guards against overpopulation. What if, by mass cooperation, we eliminated a gene whose presently unrecognized purpose might have saved us from a future catastrophe?

If we probe a bit further into this hypothetical world, we become conscious of potential prejudices and injustices. If biotechnology makes elective services widely available to the public, just what sort of people would benefit? Why, anyone who has the money for such a costly extravagance. (In cases of health, all people should be equally eligible.) But in our capitalist society, many parents would be unable to afford bioengineering for their offspring.

The writer skillfully explores a hypothetical world of tomorrow.

Although it's true that the above predictions are a bit far-fetched, advances in genetic engineering could make them all possible. But what if we take a different route? Let's imagine it's the year 2150. Genetically engineered babies have been bouncing around for some time now. Satisfaction and contentment characterize most of the world's populace. Our planet is at rest: all of today's lethal bacteria and viruses have been exterminated and humans are now engineered with only "good" genes. But, during this period of global health and well-being, a mutant virus has arisen, unnoticed and unfeared. The new virus multiplies and invades the human body. The by-now vastly narrowed gene pool of human beings (everyone similarly "engineered") has no means of dealing with so sudden a threat. Perhaps one of those mysterious genes that was weeded out of the human species could have saved a few people from this plague, but

Biogenetic Engineering: a Gamble for a Bright Future
(continued)

since we are all genetically defined in the same mode, we are no longer equipped to deal with mutant viruses. . . .

This analysis brings readers back to reality.

These ideas may sound alarmist. They are only my warnings, to an overeager scientific community, to proceed slowly and think about what such a direct showdown with nature may unleash. Of course, no one is suggesting that we stop biotechnology; such a mandate would be impractical and probably impossible. Human curiosity and compassion have long led us to investigate malicious diseases and find ways to improve life. We should encourage such intervention—but only to a certain extent.

Bioengineering obviously offers heady gifts, some of which have already been put to good use. For example, insulin for diabetics, which utilizes recombinant DNA from bacteria, is a substance that has saved and improved many lives. Biogenetic research in agriculture will soon produce plants that can withstand drought and disease. Bio-technology is showing us viable ways to grow cheap and nutritious foods for today's starving masses. Toxic wastes may be eliminated. Considering such benefits, we must look to bioengineering with hope—but, again, with caution. We should not forget nature's penalty for greed and carelessness.

The writer reasserts her main concern and then offers a suggested course of action.

But greed (of one sort or another) seems ubiquitous; it motivates and propels our society. Can we really shake a warning finger at huge corporations and say, "Stop! Aren't we moving too fast?" Yes, and this is exactly what we must do before Wall Street tycoons set themselves up as the moral and ethical arbiters of biogenetic engineering. We might start by electing a body of doctors, environmentalists, philosophers and psychologists, scientists, and moderate religious leaders who, in cooperation with lawyers and government officials, will set up strict guidelines appropriate for the future bioengineering of life. My proposal would be to promote biogenetic research in strictly supervised laboratories, working with very weak strains of experimental micro-organisms, which would pose no danger to the environment in cases of escape. In addition, when we perfect the means to engineer "bad" genes out of humans and to install "good" genes in their place, we should allow such tampering only to eliminate debilitating mental and physical disease; we should not cater to mere parental vanity. These guidelines, admittedly vague, would at least start to rule out certain frightening possibilities that threaten to alter our definition of "Homo sapiens" from "thinking humankind" to "consumer goods." ■

Position Paper

In this paper, Meg Greenfield explains her position on a highly emotional issue of national (and global) importance—animal rights. As you will discover, she places herself in a philosophically vulnerable position, a position she believes many of her readers will share. (From *Newsweek,* April 17, 1989. © 1989, Newsweek, Inc. All rights reserved. Reprinted by permission.)

In Defense of the Animals

The writer immediately identifies her position.

I might as well come right out with it. Contrary to some of my most cherished prejudices, the animal-rights people have begun to get to me. I think that in some part of what they say, they are right.

I never thought it would come to this. As distinct from the old-style animal rescue, protection, and shelter organizations, the more aggressive newcomers . . . have earned a reputation in the world I live in as fanatics, and just plain kooks. And even with my own recently (relatively) raised consciousness, there remains a good deal in both their critique and their prescription for the virtuous life that I reject, being not just a practicing carnivore, a wearer of shoe leather, and so forth, but also a supportee of certain indisputably agonizing procedures visited upon innocent animals in the furtherance of human welfare, especially experiments undertaken to improve human health.

She then explores and analyzes her thesis.

So, viewed from the pure position, I am probably only marginally better than the worst of my kind, if that: I don't buy the complete "speciesist" analysis or even the fundamental language of animal "rights" and continue to find a large part of what is done in the name of that cause harmful and extreme. But I also think, patronizing as it must sound, that the zealots are required early on in any movement if it is to succeed in altering the sensibility of the leaden masses, such as me. Eventually they get your attention. And eventually you at least feel obliged to weigh their arguments and think about whether there may not be something there.

A plural first-person reference ("*our* being confronted") draws readers into the paper.

It is true that this end has often been achieved—as in my case—by means of vivid, cringe-inducing photographs, not by an appeal to reason or values so much as by an assault on squeamishness. From the famous 1970s photo of the newly skinned baby seal to the videos of animals being raised in the most dark, miserable, stunting environment as they are readied for their life's sole fulfillment as frozen patties and cutlets, these sights have had their effect. . . .

The objection to our being confronted with these dramatic, disturbing pictures is first that they tend to provoke a misplaced, uncritical, and highly emotional concern for animal life at the direct expense of a more suitable concern

In Defense of the Animals
(continued)

for human suffering. What goes into the animals' account, the reasoning goes, necessarily comes out of ours. But I think it is possible to remain stalwart in our view that the human claim comes first and in your acceptance of the use of animals for human betterment and *still* to believe that there are some human interests that should not take precedence. For we have become far too self-indulgent, hardened, careless, and cruel in the pain we routinely inflict upon these creatures for the most frivolous, unworthy purposes. And I also think that the more justifiable purposes, such as medical research, are shamelessly used as cover for other activities that are wanton.

For instance, not all of the painful and crippling experimentation that is undertaken in the lab is being conducted for the sake of medical knowledge or other purposes related to basic human well-being and health. Much of it is being conducted for the sake of super refinements in the cosmetic and other frill industries, the noble goal being to contrive yet another fragrance or hair tint or commercially competitive variation on all the daft, fizzy, multicolored "personal care" products for the medicine cabinet and dressing table, a firmer-holding hair spray, that sort of thing. . . .

This strikes me as decadent. My problem is that it also causes me to reach a position that is, on its face, philosophically vulnerable, if not absurd—the muddled, middling, inconsistent place where finally you are saying it's all right to kill them for some purposes, but not to hurt them gratuitously in doing it or to make them suffer horribly for one's own trivial whims.

I would feel more humiliated to have fetched up on this exposed rock, if I didn't suspect I had so much company. When you see pictures of people laboriously trying to clean the Exxon gunk off of sea otters even knowing that they will only be able to help out a very few, you see this same outlook in action. And I think it *can* be defended. For to me the biggest cop-out is the one that says that if you don't buy the whole absolutist, extreme position it is pointless and even hypocritical to concern yourself with lesser mercies and ameliorations. The pressure of the animal-protection groups has already had some impact in improving the way various creatures are treated by researchers, trainers, and food producers. There is much more in this vein to be done. We are talking about rejecting wanton, pointless cruelty here. The position may be philosophically absurd, but the outcome is the right one. ∎

Thinking Through an Argument

MAKING AND SUPPORTING A POINT

MAKING CLAIMS: A claim, or proposition, is the main point in argumentative writing. Claims fall into three main groups: claims of fact, claims of value, and claims of policy.

> **Claims of fact** state or claim that something is true or not true.
>> **Cigarette smoking is a leading cause of cancer.**
>
> **Claims of value** state that something has or does not have worth.
>> **The new on-campus housing plan lacks vision.**
>
> **Claims of policy** assert that something ought to be done or not done.
>> **A semester of community service ought to be a graduation requirement.**

USING QUALIFIERS: Qualifiers are terms that make a claim more flexible. Note the difference between the two claims below.

> **The policies regulating illegal immigration need reform.**
> **Some policies regulating illegal immigration need reform.**

"Some" makes a qualified claim, rather than an all-or-nothing claim. Here are some useful qualifiers:

almost	**if . . . then . . .**	**maybe**	**probably**
often	**in most cases**	**might**	**usually**

ADDING SUPPORT: Your claim or proposition needs evidence for support; the more kinds of evidence you offer, and the stronger the evidence, the more solid your argument will be. Here are some types of evidence:

Prediction:	**Opportunities in science will continue to decline.**
Observation:	**I see more and more unemployed chemists.**
Statistics:	**Washington is going to cut $30 million in research in the next budget.**
Comparison:	**The stature of science today is nowhere near what it was during the '60s and '70s.**
Expert Testimony:	**Placement Director Gillian Taylor reported, "Physics majors are finding . . ."**
Demonstration:	**At a recent seminar, the regional job market in the sciences was a leading topic of discussion.**
Analysis:	**This situation is the result of . . .**

MAKING CONCESSIONS: Concessions are "points" that you let the other side score. Making a concession often adds believability to your overall claim. Here are some expressions for making concessions:

admittedly	**granted**	**I cannot argue with**
even though	**I agree that**	**while it is true that**

USING EVIDENCE AND LOGIC

To develop an effective, convincing argument, you must think and write logically. You must draw reasonable and sensible conclusions from solid evidence. Furthermore, you must be able to recognize and avoid fallacies of thinking, or false arguments, in your work. By fallacies, we mean the habits of fuzzy or illogical thinking that may crop up in your writing if you are not careful. (They also crop up in advertisements, political appeals, and such.) Learn about the common fallacies by reading the descriptions below. Then make sure to avoid them in your own thinking and writing.

NOTE: When you develop an argument, appeal to your readers' good sense and reason, and not to their emotions.

FALLACIES OF THINKING

Appeal to Ignorance

This logical fallacy suggests that since no one has ever proved a particular claim, it must be false. Appeals to ignorance unfairly shift the burden of proof onto someone else.

Show me one study that proves cigarettes lead to heart disease.

Appeal to Pity

This fallacy may be heard in courts of law when an attorney begs for leniency because his client's mother is ill, his brother is out of work, his cat has a hair ball, and blah, blah, blah. The strong tug on the heartstrings can also be heard in the classroom.

Student: "May I have an extension on this paper? I worked on it all weekend, but it's still not done."

Bandwagon

Another way to avoid using logic in an argument is to appeal to everyone's sense of wanting to belong or be accepted. By suggesting that everyone else is doing this or wearing that or going there, you can avoid the real question—"Is this idea or claim a good one or not?"

Everyone walked out of the meeting. It was the smartest thing to do.

Broad Generalization

A broad generalization takes in everything and everyone at once, allowing no exceptions. For example, a broad generalization about voters might be, "All voters spend too little time reading and too much time being swayed by 30-second sound bites." It may be true that quite a few voters spend too little time reading about the candidates, but it is unfair to suggest that this is true of all voters. Here's another example:

College students can't manage money.

Circular Thinking

This fallacy consists of assuming, in an argument, the very point you are trying to prove. Note how circular this sort of reasoning is:

> **I hate my night class because I'm never happy when I'm there.**
> **(But what's wrong with the class?)**

Either-Or Thinking

Either-or thinking consists of reducing a solution to two possible extremes: "America: Love It or Leave It." "Put up or shut up." This fallacy of thinking eliminates every possibility in the middle.

> **Either this community provides light-rail transportation, or it will be impossible to expand in the future.**

Half-Truths

Avoid building your argument with evidence that contains part of the truth, but not the whole truth. These kinds of statements are called half-truths. They are especially misleading because they leave out "the rest of the story." They are true and dishonest at the same time.

> **The new welfare bill is good because it will get people off the public dole.**
> **(Maybe so, but it may also cause undue suffering to some truly needy individuals.)**

Oversimplification

Beware of phrases like "It all boils down to . . ." or "It's a simple question of . . ." Almost no dispute is "a simple question of" anything. Anyone who feels, for example, that capital punishment "all boils down to" a matter of protecting society ought to question a doctor, an inmate on death row, the inmate's family, a sociologist, a religious leader, etc.

> **Capital punishment is a simple question of protecting society.**

Slanted Language

By choosing words that carry strong positive or negative feelings, a person can distract the audience, leading them away from the valid arguments being made. A philosopher once illustrated the bias involved in slanted language when he compared three synonyms for the word *stubborn:* "I am *firm.* You are *obstinate.* He is *pigheaded.*"

> **No one in his right mind would ever agree to anything so ridiculous.**

Testimonial

If the testimonial or statement comes from a recognized authority in the field, great. If it comes from a person famous in another field, beware.

> **Sports hero: "I've tried every cold medicine on the market, and—believe me—nothing works like Temptrol."**

Writing
About
Literature

Personal Response

Review

Limited Literary Analysis

Extended Literary Analysis

Literary Terms

Writing About Literature

What exactly is **literature**? Is it a long, complicated novel by Dostoyevski, a series of perceptive little poems by Dickinson? Yes, of course. How about a Shaw play or some short stories by Sandra Cisneros? These, too, are literature.

Literature is fiction, drama, poetry, and much more; it is the body of high-quality, imaginative writing, well formed and rich in content. But that is only part of the story. Literature is also the interplay between you and a text. A piece of literature is mere words on paper until you interact with it and form some new understandings about it.

So why mention this? Well, don't expect to find the meaning in a literary work as if it were simply hidden somewhere, waiting to be uncovered. You create the meaning by sifting a text through your own thoughts and feelings—by reading it (more than once), by discussing it, and by writing about it.

WHAT'S AHEAD

This section provides guidelines and models for three basic types of writing about literature: personal responses, reviews, and literary analyses. Each type of writing helps you think about and react to a piece of literature in a different way. Also included in this section are ideas for writing analyses plus an extensive glossary of literary terms.

"I am a part of all that I have read." —John Kieran

Writing About Literature

Each piece of literature presents you with a slice of human experience as imagined (or perceived) by the author. When you read and study a particular selection, you're really trying to gain passage into this new world to discover how it is put together, and how it matches up with your own experience. Writing, of course, helps you to explore and clarify your ideas about a literary work. It gets you thoughtfully involved in a text, and helps make it come alive for you.

STARTING POINT: Writing about literature begins when you are asked to react to or analyze a literary work (or some other artistic endeavor, such as a live performance).

PURPOSE: Your goal is to share some new understanding gained during a reading experience. The nature of this "understanding" depends upon the particular writing task.

FORM: Personal responses can be journal entries, poems, personal reflections, and so on. Reviews are brief essays, usually somewhat loosely structured, an organic blend of information and commentary. Analyses are carefully planned academic papers, following the traditional essay form.

AUDIENCE: For the most part, you're addressing your writing peers and your instructor. Some of your reviews, however, may be intended for publication.

VOICE: Speak from both the heart and the mind in personal responses. Reviews may or may not be heartfelt; analyses seldom are.

POINT OF VIEW: Generally speaking, use first-person point of view (*I*) for personal responses and third-person (*he, she, they*) for most reviews and for analyses.

Insights into Writing

To write effectively about literature, you must be a critical reader, carefully noting your thoughts, feelings, and questions as you go along. It's good practice to read a selection once to get an overall impression of the text. Then go back a second time (and a third, if necessary), looking for answers to your questions, for connections between different characters or parts, for patterns of development.

Writing a Personal Response

A response to literature is, in effect, your reply to something that a selection says to you. A response may be a journal entry (or a series of entries) focusing on a compelling idea that the text brings to mind. It may be a poem expressing a strong feeling that you have about a selection. It may also be an essay examining your personal connection to your reading, and so on. Your goal is simply to interact with a text in a meaningful way. Use the guidelines below and the models that follow to help you with your own responses.

SEARCHING AND SELECTING

Selecting ● In most cases, you will be responding to a piece of literature that is part of your course work.

Reading ● Carefully read the text (more than once), noting your thoughts, feelings, and questions as you go along. As a matter of convenience, make your initial notations right in the text, but only if you own the book and plan on keeping it.

GENERATING THE TEXT

Collecting ● Write freely about your reading experience, starting with one of the thoughts you noted initially. (Also see 272 for possible starting points for this writing.)

Assessing ● After reviewing your notes and free writing, select one idea to develop further. (Make sure this idea meets any requirements established by your instructor.) How much planning and organizing you do depends upon the form of your response.

WRITING AND REVISING

Writing ● Develop your writing freely and naturally as thoughts come to mind—or according to any planning you may have done.

Revising ● Review your work, first checking the overall flow of your ideas, and then looking more closely at the individual parts (paragraphs, sentences, and words). Revise and refine accordingly.

NOTE: The revising notes address responses that will be shared, not *personal* journal entries.

EVALUATING

Does the writing clearly communicate a thoughtful response to a piece of literature?

Has proper attention been given to accuracy and detail?

Does the writing form a meaningful whole, moving smoothly and clearly from beginning to end?

Starting Point for Journal Responses

The following reader-response questions will help you react thoughtfully to the literature you read. This list should be used only when you need a starting point for writing. Your own thoughts are always the best source of ideas for your journal.

MAKING CONNECTIONS

1. What are your feelings after reading the opening chapter(s) of this book? After reading half the book? After finishing the book?
2. What connections are there between the book and your life?
3. In what ways are you like any of the characters? Do any of the characters remind you of other people? Explain.
4. What effect does the book have on your own beliefs?
5. What is the most important word in the book (or in a particular chapter or section)? The most important passage? The most important event? Explain.

POINTS OF INTEREST

6. What parts of this book are worth reading again and again? Why?
7. What parts (aspects, elements) detract from the book's overall effectiveness? Why?
8. What patterns have you discovered in the text (plot development, characterization)?
9. What surprised you in the book? Why?
10. What confuses you about the book, or makes you wonder?

CAREFUL REFLECTION

11. What is the significance of the title?
12. What dominant themes run throughout the text?
13. What thoughts do you have about the author?
14. What do you know now that you didn't know before?
15. What questions do you have after reading this book?

JOURNAL-WRITING tips

- **Try writing nonstop.** This is how you get the most mileage out of your writing. Your goal should be to write 10-15 minutes at a time.

- **Push an idea as far as you can.** You'll never know what thoughts you will uncover unless you explore an idea from many different angles. (Keep asking yourself "Why?" as you write.)

- **Review your entries.** Underline or star sections that seem surprising, significant, or insightful. Continue writing about these ideas in future entries or use them as starting points for more formal writing.

Personal Response

Amy Ng responds to Jack Kerouac's *On the Road* in a freely formed list poem. Her response, of course, mirrors Kerouac's writing style—surreal, spontaneous, impatient, and disturbing. (This poem first appeared in *Tiger Tales,* 1993, a high-school literary publication. It is reprinted by permission.)

Jack's Opera

The poem is fast paced, reflecting the open-road theme of Kerouac's book.

The radio reminds me
that you have left, that you have already left long ago.
I know that you lost the keys to
your fast, fast car
that night in Mexico
when you let the mosquitoes make you one of them,
the insect buzz, another layer of your skin.
In vampire tranquility
you convinced me
that our malleable fingers pressed
on the Beat.
You seduced me with your beckoning American highway.
We could smell the unharvested earth
and drink life from the lifeless.
We would exploit
for kicks
religions jumping in our blood
because atheism was said to be our murderer.

Wild imagery helps establish a disturbing, destructive tone.

Two rows of tungsten lights, our saluting watchmen,
cut through the Great Desert.
Skeletons waiting in the darkness
invite us to dance.
But you left me,
one of many scattered lovers,
bribing you with my soul.
Your one true love's riding in the front seat.
Stop whispering so close to my ear
in your low, wild, just awakened voice.
I don't want to hear anymore
when all you've left me
is your dream
and the legacy of the mosquitoes. ■

Personal Response

In this response, Elizabeth Delaney explores the effect that her personal feelings and experiences have on her interpretation of literature. Notice how effectively the writer moves between her own experiences and the two texts she compares.

Summer Undergoes a "Metamorphosis": The Function of Experience in Forgiveness

The opening remarks set the tone for an honest and thoughtful response.

At first I thought my reaction to Edith Wharton's *Summer* was too close, too personal, to ever allow me to form a coherent response with some basis in analysis. It was not until reading "The Metamorphosis" by Franz Kafka that I was able to assign some rationality to my feelings as I realized the extent to which experience shapes our understanding and appreciation of literature. In both *Summer* and "The Metamorphosis" the reader is forced to grapple with issues of fallibility and forgiveness, but in such different environments that I was initially unable to see the connection.

During my reading of *Summer*, a flood tide of half-suppressed, half-forgotten emotions washed over me, and I instinctively reached out in empathy to Charity Royall and Lucius Harney. I found that Lucius's actions were regrettable and wounding, but understandable and excusable. Others in my class saw him as cruel and wholly condemnable. I could forgive Lucius because I have forgiven someone whose relationship to me was very similar to his relationship to Charity, and while I ache with Charity over the loss, I can also understand her pride in relinquishing him.

The writer makes a link between her own life and the literature.

Because of my closeness to the situation described in *Summer*, I was angry when it was suggested that Lucius was so entirely reprehensible, particularly when Charity's "heart felt strangely light" (p. 151) during the days after sending her letter of release to him. I wanted to know, if "she did not even reproach him in her thoughts" (p. 157), then why should we? But as my classmates condemned Lucius Harney for his insensitivity, weakness, and duplicity, I began to wonder if I was the one who was blind—if I glossed over Lucius's feelings in an attempt to solace my own feelings toward my past.

Furthermore, Charity's frequent denials of her insecurities and faults forced me to reexamine my own rationales for the value of this relationship. I was in emotional turmoil over the worth of my memories and experience. One part of me debated whether or not it was out of cowardice that I did not blame Lucius, and thereby avoid blaming myself for cherishing someone in my life who had emotionally hurt me.

A connection between the two texts is made.

Reading "The Metamorphosis" gave me new insights into my response to *Summer* because a natural relationship between experience and forgiveness suddenly became clear. During class the same unsympathetic attitudes that had angered me a week earlier, crept unconsciously into my feelings toward Gregor Samsa. But just as I was able to understand Charity and Lucius, others in the class were able to understand and forgive Gregor because of their experiences with a loved one like him. The reactions of my classmates illuminated the value of Gregor's choices, revealed how pivotal it was that "he thought of his family with tenderness and love" (p. 127), and unmasked how he lost perspective on his own life in his efforts to sustain and respect them.

As I began to relate to Gregor, there appeared correlations between his behavior and Charity's. Just as Charity protectively blinded herself to her own motivations, Gregor deceived himself in judging his father's greed to be only "unexpected thrift and foresight" (p. 96). . . .

The writer reflects on her new understanding.

My view of Kafka has obviously undergone a "metamorphosis," just as my personal response to *Summer* has changed. Instead of fearing my reaction and debating its worth, I now find it easier to process my feelings and accept that my own experiences naturally play important roles in my understanding of literature. I have also learned, rather sheepishly, that I may often be too quick to judge characters with whom I do not immediately find common ground. As an acknowledgment of my own fallibility, I should not seek instant conclusions (especially when I cannot easily relate my experiences to a situation), but first look to exercise compassion and to forgive. ■

Personal Response

Heather Bachman's response to *Alice's Adventures in Wonderland* focuses on the theme of childhood imagination. She completed this writing for a class in which she was studying children's literature.

Down the Rabbit Hole

The opening paragraph establishes the focus of the writing.

Lewis Carroll's *Alice's Adventures in Wonderland* is a charming reminder of the imaginary world of children. I have always had an active imagination, and this book made me smile many times as I remembered my own fantastical excursions.

After her experiences in Wonderland, Alice begins to think "very few things were really impossible." Drinking a special liquid makes her shrink, and a nibble of sweet cake causes her to grow. Alice begins to expect the unusual; there's no limit to her dreams. I, too, have proposed some unusual ideas, and even believed (sort of) that they could come true. For an English project many years ago, I was required to make three wishes. My third wish surprised the teacher because I wanted my own planet. All the animals of the world could live on my planet, safe from oil spills and hunters. The teacher commented, "Never has a student wished for something quite so large!"

After her experiences in Wonderland, Alice begins to think "very few things were really impossible."

The writer relates aspects of her own life to Alice's imaginary world.

Alice meets many animals that chatter with her. I especially liked her discussions with the lory, dodo, crabs, and other creatures. What child hasn't imagined that animals talk? My cat, who is 17, has spent many hours by my side, and shared in all of my secrets (without ever telling a soul). Bobcat's rich purr tells me, "Everything will be okay." Whenever he enters a room, his raspy meow seems to ask, "Are you going to pet me now, or should I just hop into your lap?" Perhaps my feeling that animals talk did not fade with the end of childhood.

Alice experiences Wonderland on many levels. When she is tiny, she converses with the curious caterpillar. Tall and willowy, she has a bird's perspective. It is amazing how different the world can be from different points of view. I remember crawling around long after I learned how to walk. I saw my house in a whole new way. Table legs became mighty tree trunks. The shag carpet felt like grass. At other times I did more than change position—I became a different creature. I can remember my sister and I spending hours acting like dolphins and mermaids in our grandfather's pool. We kept out legs tight together, swimming in graceful arches. To a child, the world is never boring—with just a little help from the imagination.

One of my favorite scenes in this book is the croquet match with the Queen of Hearts. I can see Alice struggling with her flamingo/mallet only to discover the hedgehog/ball has wandered off. Kids love to give inanimate objects life. A little girl, dreaming of having a pony, rides a stick in her backyard. The garden hose coils like a python about to strike! A pencil suddenly becomes a friendly lizard, if home-work seems boring. Alice may give up the wild game of croquet, but the image is one that I won't forget.

The closing remarks include an important quotation from the text.

Alice's sister knew that the young girl "would keep, through all her riper years, the simple and loving heart of her childhood . . . the dream of Wonderland long ago . . . and find pleasure in . . . simple joys, remembering her own child-life, and the happy summer days." My childhood imagination, too, hasn't faded with time. I haven't forgotten my journeys into backyard jungles or my faithful steeds of polished wood. Creativity and imagination are precious, not to be forgotten in literature or in life. ◾

Writing a Review

Charles Dickens once said, "There are books of which the backs and covers are by far the best parts." Undoubtedly, you have equally strong opinions (both positive and negative) about many of the books you have read, or have tried to read. When you write a review, you pass judgment on a book (or some other literary or artistic endeavor), and point to various "best parts" to support your opinion. Your goal is to help readers decide about the value of the work—whether it is something they may want to read or experience themselves. Use the guidelines below and the models that follow to help you write a review.

SEARCHING AND SELECTING

Searching ● The subject of your review should be a book that you have recently read and have strong feelings about.

Selecting ● Unless you are required to review a book, you may also want to think of other worthy subjects for your writing—a play, a short story collection, a live performance, etc.

GENERATING THE TEXT

Collecting ● Gather your initial thoughts and feelings about your subject through free-writing or clustering. If, on the other hand, you would like to proceed more carefully, begin by listing your subject's strengths and its weaknesses. Continue exploring and collecting ideas as needed.

Designing ● Read through your initial gathering, making some basic decisions about the organization and design of your writing. Remember that you can't say everything. Here's a basic format to follow: In your opening remarks, offer a general impression about your subject. Follow with a brief plot summary plus a discussion of two (or more) of the text's significant features. Conclude with your overall judgment.

WRITING AND REVISING

Writing ● Develop your first draft according to your planning and organizing. Try to gain your readers' interest with a strong opening paragraph.

Revising ● Review, revise, and refine your writing until you feel it is ready for publication. (Your writing should present a lively analysis of a text.)

EVALUATING

Is the review appropriate for a specific course or for a publication?

Does the review speak with authority and make specific references to the text?

Will readers appreciate the treatment of the subject?

Book Review

In this review, writer Laura Shapiro discusses *The Hundred Secret Senses* by Amy Tan. Notice that the reviewer focuses much of her attention on the appealing story line that Tan has created in this novel. (From *Newsweek,* Nov. 6, 1995. © 1995 Newsweek, Inc. All rights reserved. Reprinted by permission.)

Ghost Story

The opening remarks provide intriguing insights into the novel.

Kwan sees ghosts, and talks to them, too. Then she reports their remarks to 6-year-old Olivia, her American half sister. Ever since Kwan came from a tiny Chinese village to live with Olivia's family in San Francisco, Olivia has been horribly embarrassed by her newfound big sister, but teenage Kwan adores the little girl whose name she renders as "Libby-ah." At night, in the room they share, Kwan spins tales and memories from an endless skein, and although Olivia can't understand Chinese, the stories seem to settle under her skin. As she grows older, she finds she has learned Chinese without meaning to; and for all her skepticism she knows very well when ghosts are bidding for her attention.

The review discusses Tan's new book in relation to the novelist's previous work.

Yes, we're back in Amy Tan country. With *The Hundred Secret Senses,* Tan has once more produced a novel wonderfully like a hologram: turn it this way and find Chinese-Americans shopping and arguing in San Francisco; turn it that way and the Chinese of Changmian village in 1864 are fleeing into the hills to hide from the rampaging Manchus. Tan ushered readers into this world of a commingled Chinese past and

"With The Hundred Secret Senses, *Tan has once more produced a novel wonderfully like a hologram."*

present with her 1989 debut, *The Joy Luck Club.* Critics and readers went wild (and a few years later, so did moviegoers). Coming up with a second book was plainly nerve-racking. *The Kitchen God's Wife* (1991) was beautifully written—Tan has yet to publish a second-rate sentence—but melodramatic. Some readers wondered if she had extracted everything she could from this territory; perhaps she should move on. But happily, Tan knew better. *The Hundred Secret Senses* doesn't simply return to a world but burrows more deeply into it, following new trails to fresh revelations.

A brief analysis of Tan's style is provided.

Tan has always specialized in storytelling and spectacle, and here she doesn't stint. But the novel is more finely nuanced than her previous two, in part because of the way

Ghost Story
(continued)

her narrator shapes its tone and direction. Olivia is a young Chinese-American who moves uneasily between history and the present. She sees her first ghost when she's 8—a little Chinese girl who demands to play with Olivia's Barbie doll. "I wasn't scared," Olivia remembers. "That was the other thing about seeing ghosts: I always felt perfectly calm, as if my whole body had been soaked in a mild tranquilizer. I politely asked this little girl in Chinese who she was." But when she grows up, she learns to apply a modern dose of cynicism to what her "hundred secret senses" are telling her. The constant clash of Olivia's mind and heart keep the plot buoyant, right up to a climax in Changmian village, where Olivia has gone in search of Kwan's childhood and her own future. With this book, Tan earns back her reputation and then some. ■

The reviewer provides just enough of the plot to pique the readers' curiosity.

Book Review

In this review, Jacqueline Williams examines a novel about the Vietnam War called *The Things They Carried* by Tim O'Brien. Williams approaches this novel (and her review) with some skepticism since there has already been so much written about this tragic time. But, as you will see, she concludes that O'Brien's book is a valuable addition to the literature about the Vietnam experience.

The Truth in Tim O'Brien's
The Things They Carried

The opening remarks establish the reviewer's connection with her subject.

Unlike the traditional college student, I come to Vietnam-era movies and novels with skepticism . . . and annoyance. Having been a college sophomore when the Vietnam conflict finally ended (or at least U.S. involvement in it), I know what Vietnam was like. My husband was in the army from 1970 to 1974, and I had several friends whose brothers served in Nam. I know it was awful. I know how kids' minds were messed up by the whole ordeal, if not their bodies. Nearly 25 years have passed since the war, and I just do not want to relive or deal with it anymore. Even the title of O'Brien's novel bothered me, *The Things They Carried,* since it obviously refers to the emotional and psychological effects of Vietnam.

Those were my feelings as I began to read this book. To my surprise, by the time I had finished O'Brien's work, I had a broader and deeper understanding of how Vietnam affected those who fought in it. Although I grimaced when reading his graphic descriptions of the horrible acts committed, I knew that the author was not embellishing the story with gore or using obscenities gratuitously. O'Brien, I think, tells these stories for therapeutic purposes—his and ours: he confronts his own personal ghosts, and he forces readers to face them as well.

A brief plot summary is provided.

The novel is actually a collection of interrelated tales about men and women who experienced Vietnam directly or indirectly. Many of the stories tell of the brutal realities of death and how soldiers meet it and deal with it. There's Ted Lavender, shot in the head after relieving himself, "zapped while zipping," as the other soldiers put it. There's Curt Lemon, blown up into a tree, remembered gruesomely by one soldier in singing the song "Lemon Tree." There's Kiowa, sucked down into a "_____ field." And there's the Vietcong soldier that the narrator himself kills. With each of these deaths, O'Brien holds back no punches—showing us the horror, tragedy, and related black humor of war.

The Truth in Tim O'Brien's
The Things They Carried
(continued)

He shows us how Vietnam changes the living. One strange story, for example, tells about Mary Anne Bell, an all-American girl smuggled into Nam by her boyfriend. In a horrifying way, she gets swallowed up by the war; in fact, this "Barbie Doll" seems to thrive on it. Another powerful change happens to Norman Bowker, who goes home eaten by guilt for Kiowa's death. All he can do, trapped in his hometown, is drive the loop around the lake over and over . . . until he kills himself. But maybe the biggest change happens to the narrator himself. Early in the novel, we see him struggle with his draft notice. He is all idealism and innocence. By the end of the novel, we see that the war has cost him both, and that they have been replaced only by personal loss, and knowledge of his own capacity for evil.

The truth O'Brien seeks is not in the events that he details, but in the emotions, attitudes, and feelings that his stories project. The stories look at courage and fear and how the imagination helps us understand and shape the truth. The novel is an illustration of how "story truth is truer than happening truth." As a fiction writer who experienced Vietnam, O'Brien wants to confront us with the imaginative truth of it all, not just the hard facts.

Tim O'Brien convinced me, even when I didn't want him to. Twenty-five years later, Vietnam is still an important daily reality for millions of Americans, and really for the whole nation. The tales in *The Things They Carried* drive home that truth. In fact, they give the reader a "truth goose," as the narrator puts it. ■

Review of a Performance

Jennifer Buckley reviews a college performance by singer Emmylou Harris in the following article. Notice how Buckley begins with an assessment of Harris and then reviews the physical aspects of the performance, the tunes Harris sings, and the vocal gifts of the performer. (Copyright 1996, The *Michigan Daily*, Ann Arbor, Michigan. Reprinted by permission.)

Emmylou Captivates Crowd with Lush Voice

The opening statement is backed up by an authoritative quotation.

No one, it seems, can hear Emmylou Harris' voice and remain unmoved. Singer/songwriter Steve Earle described his reaction to the country siren in the liner notes to his 1995 record *Train a Comin'*: "The first time I met Emmylou, she came in to sing on Guy Clark's first album . . . I wasn't the same for weeks."

Everyone who witnessed Harris' performance at the Michigan Theater Thursday night understands Earle's reaction. Onstage, Harris exuded the combination of angelic grace and earthy charm that has been drawing audiences to her work since her early '70s days as a backup vocalist for country-rock pioneer Gram Parsons.

"The first time I met Emmylou . . . I wasn't the same for weeks."

Every aspect of the concert reflected that blend of qualities: The candles glowing at the foot of the stage and the burning incense diffusing a sweet, heady scent throughout the theater created an atmosphere of otherworldly beauty brought back to reality by a big, shaggy dog wandering toward Harris. Even the singer's clothes—a long, flowing white jacket over a slim black bodysuit and black cowboy boots—seemed chosen to help create the show's distinctive mood.

Specific references to band members and changes in Harris' style indicate that the writer knows her subject.

After a set of drowsy, melodic folk-pop from Innocence Mission, the elegant, silver-haired Harris took the stage with multi-instrumentalist Buddy Miller for a lovely acoustic version of "Love Hurts," one of Parsons' most touching ballads. A tight new band, including the excellent bassist/percussionist Daryl Johnson, then joined the two for a string of songs from Harris' latest release, *Wrecking Ball*.

The Daniel Lanois-produced record marks a real shift in Harris' musical style; *Wrecking Ball* shows the singer, once a firm country traditionalist, embracing the lush, gauzy textures, booming, echoing drums, and ringing guitars that have become Lanois' trademark. It's a stunning record, and Harris' new band adapted it to live performance surprisingly well.

Emmylou Captivates Crowd with Lush Voice
(continued)

As an interpretive vocalist, Harris is simply unmatched, and the *Wrecking Ball* songs displayed her vocal gifts to perfection. She has the uncanny ability to get "inside" a song and reveal its full emotional weight. Her voice has only improved with age; still breathtakingly sweet, it's gained a slight hoarseness, and with it a new edge.

A potential weakness is cited and analyzed.

Though she's still capable of soaring highs and warm, rich lows, Harris' voice occasionally cracks on the highest notes. Though the singer seemed especially hoarse during the middle of the show, she used it to her advantage on the new songs, offering a wrenching version of Steve Earle's heartbreaking ballad "Goodbye" and a startling, throaty howl on the electrifying "Deeper Well" (a song Harris co-wrote with Lanois and Dave Olney).

Miller and Johnson's rich backup vocals complemented Harris well—especially when they were combined in spectacular three-part harmonies—and brought a new soulfulness to versions of Julie Miller's gospel-tinged "All My Tears," Gillian Welch's gorgeous "Orphan Girl," Anna McGarrigle's "Goin' Back to Harlan," and the Neil Young-penned title track.

A summary of the concert is given as well as the reviewer's personal assessment.

Though she devoted most of her set time to the songs from the Grammy-winning *Wrecking Ball,* Harris also pleased her longtime fans by pulling out plenty of "old warhorses," as she called them, from her remarkable 25-album catalogue. Highlights included the sweet country ballads "Together Again" and "Making Believe," and the rollicking "Two More Bottles of Wine," "One of These Days," and "Tulsa Queen." Overall, it was a nearly perfect concert from one of Nashville's finest performers. ■

Writing a Limited Literary Analysis

A limited literary analysis (or explication) presents your thoughtful interpretation or understanding of a literary work. The focus of your analysis depends upon the length and complexity of your subject. A short poem may be analyzed line by line for more than one element (perhaps the interplay between style and theme); whereas the analysis of a longer work should focus on a specific aspect of the plot, setting, theme, characterization, or style. Remember to limit your ideas to your own critical reading of the text. Use the guidelines below and the model that follows to help you develop your writing.

SEARCHING AND SELECTING

Searching ● In most cases, you will be provided with a list of suggested titles (or authors) to choose from. If you have any questions, consult your classmates or your instructor before you select a subject.

Reviewing ● If the assignment is open to subjects of your own choosing, look for a literary work that is personally significant to you. You might also ask your instructor if the assignment could be expanded to include movies or other artistic endeavors.

GENERATING THE TEXT

Reading ● Carry out a close reading (or rereading) to ensure that you have a good working knowledge of the text. Take careful notes as you read.

Exploring ● Think about features in the literary work that you could write about. Are you drawn to a certain character? Are you interested in one of the themes? Do you appreciate the style? (See 272 for ideas.)

Focusing ● State a possible focus for your analysis—a sentence or two expressing the main point you want to emphasize in your writing. Plan and organize your writing accordingly. (Make sure that you can support your focus with direct references to the text.)

WRITING AND REVISING

Writing ● Develop your first draft, working in ideas and details according to your planning. Make sure that your opening paragraph identifies the focus of your analysis. (See 273 for more writing tips.)

Revising ● Carefully review your first draft. Look for parts that are unclear, incomplete, or confusing. Revise and refine accordingly.

EVALUATING

Does the work present a thoughtful and thorough analysis?

Is the purpose of the analysis clearly in focus?

Are main ideas supported by direct references to the text?

Limited Literary Analysis

Qian Zhang had always wondered why the Red Guard acted so brutally during China's Cultural Revolution. As you will see in this analysis, the book *Wild Swans* answers many of her questions. Notice that Zhang's remarks stem from a very close and thorough reading of the text.

Tragic Lessons

The opening remarks establish the author's personal interest in her subject.

In November 1965, a critique of a popular play was published in Beijing, China. It went nearly unnoticed at the time by those literate members of the public at large, but it was heralded as the beginning of an era of tremendous upheaval and persecution that would last 10 years. That era is known as the Cultural Revolution. During the Cultural Revolution, Chinese society was turned upside down at the behest of a small circle of powerful despots headed by the Chairman of the Chinese Communist Party and dictator of the country, Mao Zedong. I lived through that era, and I vividly recall the terror that my family experienced during those years. My family, like thousands of others, was labeled as "black," meaning class enemies, and my house was raided by the youth brigades of the party cadre known as the Red Guard. For many years I have wondered how these young people, similar to me and my brother in so many ways, could behave so savagely. What motivated them to torture and kill people for no reason other than having independent thoughts or an "undesirable" background? What were their thoughts at the time, and what do they think now about the Cultural Revolution and their role in it? Finally, I have found some answers to these questions in the book *Wild Swans,* which was written by Jung Chang, an actual member of the Red Guard.

A thumbnail sketch of the story provides an effective starting point for the analysis.

Wild Swans is the story of three generations of women and their struggles to cope with the turmoil that swept through China in the twentieth century. Chang writes compellingly about the trials and tribulations of her grandmother, her mother, and herself. She attempts to relate their stories within the major social and political events that occurred in China from the 1920's to 1978. . . .

Each new point is clearly and thoroughly explained.

The most intriguing portion of the book, in my opinion, is that which deals with the Cultural Revolution and the Red Guard. Since it is an era I remember vividly, I wanted to see what Jung Chang offered, if anything, as an explanation for her and her generation's involvement.

The Red Guard played an important role in the Cultural Revolution, serving as Mao's frontline troops in the struggle against "class enemies." They "raided people's houses, smashed their antiques, tore up their paintings and works of calligraphy," and burned their books (Chang 284). Beatings and torture were widespread throughout the country. The victims, most often, were intellectuals such as teachers, doctors, writers, and scientists as well as the familiar old target of landlords and capitalists. Those with any traceable connection, no matter how insignificant, to the Kuomintang (Chiang Kai-Shek's Nationalists) and other lingering "right-ist" elements were also at the top of the list. Such people were systematically targeted by the Red Guard, singled out, beaten, and humiliated. Many of them faced imprisonment, forced labor, and even execution for their "crimes." Others cheated Mao and his Red Guards by committing suicide (Chang 282-285). What is such a puzzle to me is how these otherwise nice, normal, young people could bring themselves to participate in such a horrible campaign. . . .

Chang spends a good deal of her book explaining her mind-set and the mind-set of those around her during the Cultural Revolution. Her generation grew up under this campaign, and grew up under an atmosphere of total indoc-trination into what she and others have termed the "Cult of Mao." He was their idol, their god, their inspiration, and an everyday fact of life for them, morning till night, from the beginning of their lives. In Jung's words, "the purpose of (her) life had been formulated in his (Mao's) name" (Chang 366). Millions of young people throughout China were will-ing, just as she was, to die for Mao. Once he had called for the Cultural Revolution, these politically well-attuned young-sters felt it was their duty to show their unending loyalty to him in what they were told was a life-and-death struggle against enemies of the people.

Even though many Red Guards, like Jung Chang, had momentary negative feelings about the cruelty they practiced, they managed to immediately suppress them. Throughout her teenage life, Jung says, her greatest feelings of guilt came from occasionally believing she was "out of step with Mao" (Chang 258). The fact that she sometimes silently questioned the acts she and others were committing in his name upset her more than the acts themselves. She had been thoroughly conditioned. Even after her parents were vilified, beaten, and jailed, Jung Chang did not blame Mao. She suggests that she was able to retain her faith both in her parents' goodness and in Mao's leadership by convincing herself that evil counselors were misleading the Chairman (Chang 352).

In regard to this blind devotion to the Chairman, Jung relates a particularly insightful episode during which she joined a pilgrimage to Beijing to see the great Mao. During the grueling, thousands-of-miles rail journey to the capital,

The writer provides thoughtful commentary related to Chang's actions.

References from the text are weaved seamlessly into the analysis.

A "telling" experience is recalled in great detail.

Tragic Lessons
(continued)

the train was so packed with Red Guard members that literally every inch of space was occupied. Entry and exit from the train was possible only through the windows, and even the tiny toilet rooms were occupied with several students (Chang 315). When they finally arrived, they waited weeks for the chance to get a glimpse of Mao, and at the sight of him many pierced their fingers and squeezed out blood to write, "I am the happiest person in the world today. I have seen our great leader Chairman Mao!" (Chang 321). Given this fact, that so many worshipped him so fervently, I have no doubt that they were willing to do anything for him, including torturing and killing. . . .

Despite his popularity in the 1950's, Mao never stopped his purge campaigns against those who disagreed with him, and always kept up the machine-like indoctrination of the people, especially the more easily influenced young people. From the beginning of the "new" China in 1949 throughout his reign as Chairman, he engaged in one campaign after another to "suppress counter-revolutionaries" in whatever form. Millions were labeled as enemies, for whatever reason seemed convenient at the time, and ruthlessly persecuted. . . .

In closing, the writer reflects upon the significance of *Wild Swans.*

While my family and I suffered during the Cultural Revolution, I have always considered myself lucky in comparison to many others, especially those who died. Jung Chang's book *Wild Swans* has made me realize that I was lucky in another sense as well. The Red Guards were, in a sense, also victims. I had always looked on them with fear and the inability to comprehend their actions. Reading *Wild Swans* let me see the other side of the coin. The majority of the Red Guards, like Jung Chang, had been deprived since their infancy of any independent thought. Much of their adolescence was wasted in a horrible political campaign in which they were manipulated while useful, and then discarded like so much garbage. Yes, they too were victims. I hope that no country, no people, will make the same mistakes again. ■

Writing an Extended Literary Analysis

An extended analysis presents a critical understanding of a literary work (or works). This form of analysis should be based primarily on your own interpretation of your subject. But you should also refer to the viewpoints of important critics either to support your main ideas or to offer alternative interpretations. An effective extended analysis synthesizes information from multiple sources into a thoughtful, unified essay. Use the guidelines below and the model that follows to help you develop your writing.

SEARCHING AND SELECTING

Reviewing ● You will probably be provided with a list of suggested titles (or authors) to choose from. Consult with your classmates or your instructor if you have any questions about the choices.

Selecting ● Focus your attention on authors or titles that match up well with your own thoughts and interests. If you want a greater challenge, consider literary works that anger or even confuse you. (Why a particular text confuses you can be an excellent starting point for analysis.)

GENERATING THE TEXT

Collecting ● Establish a thorough understanding of your subject: carefully read (and reread) the text, generate personal responses, review class notes, consult your instructor, refer to secondary sources, and so on.

Focusing ● Decide upon a suitable focus for your essay once you have established a good critical understanding of the subject. (You might have discovered an interesting point of comparison between two texts or simply developed a new understanding about a particular work. See 272 for ideas. Also refer to 201-202.) Plan your writing accordingly.

WRITING AND REVISING

Writing ● Shape your first draft according to your planning and organizing. Develop each main point in as much detail as possible, working in direct references to the text(s) and to secondary sources when appropriate.

Revising ● Review your work for clarity, coherence, and depth of thought. Revise and refine accordingly.

EVALUATING

? Does the writing demonstrate a thorough understanding of a subject?

Is the writing focused, clear, and organized?

Are direct references/quotations properly cited?

Will readers appreciate the treatment of this subject?

Extended Literary Analysis

In this analysis, Sonya Jongsma explores a major theme in the nineteenth-century novel *Frankenstein* by Mary Shelley. Notice that the writer "extends" her analysis by citing a number of important literary critics. Also notice that she displays a thorough understanding of the text, from the plot structure to the characters' motives.

Mary Shelley's *Frankenstein:* Friendship, Alienation, and Relationship Dynamics

The opening paragraph establishes the thesis, or focus, of the analysis.

Mary Shelley's *Frankenstein* is one of the most well-known novels of the Romantic era. The story is one that has seeped into the popular imagination, albeit in a completely confused version. The novel's prophetic voice continues to be echoed today in modern science fiction, showing the impact of scientific knowledge on human life and institutions. Although the theme of scientific progress and the pride that often accompanies it is important and often understood to be the entire purpose of the novel, *Frankenstein* also focuses on the theme of isolation and the human need for friendship and relationships. This theme is central to the novel and is woven throughout the story-within-a-story structure. In this paper I will examine the theme of friendship and alienation as it plays out in Walton's letters to his sister, in Frankenstein's cautionary tale, and in the story of the monster.

Frankenstein begins with four letters from Walton to his sister Margaret. Walton is on a voyage to the North Pole. Although he looks forward to discovering "the wondrous power which attracts the needle" (Shelley 14), and he is aglow with anticipation of the completion of the journey and the resulting glory and fame which await him, he admits that he has one want which he has "never yet been able to satisfy" (Shelley 17): he has no friend. He bemoans this fact and shares with his sister his feelings about friendship. Walton sees a friend as someone who can participate in his joy when he is glowing with the enthusiasm of success, and someone

A secondary source provides authoritative support.

who can sustain him when he is feeling dejected because he has failed to accomplish his goals. He says, "I need a great enough friend who would have sense enough not to despise me as romantic, and affection enough for me to endeavor to regulate my mind" (Shelley 18).

Robert Kiely, in a collection of essays titled *The Romantic Novel in New England*, says Mary Shelley shows the Coleridgean side of herself in this novel. He says, "She sees a friend as a balancing and completing agent, one who is sufficiently alike to be able to sympathize and understand, yet sufficiently different to be able to correct and refine" (167).

This view is carried out even in the structure of the novel itself. It is written as three stories, with the monster's story at the center, surrounded by Frankenstein's personal story as told to Walton, and framed by Walton's narrative, which takes the form of a letter addressed to his sister. According to Mary Poovey, in *The Proper Lady and the Woman Writer*, focusing on a network of personal relationships enabled Shelley to write a credible story as a woman. She says, "Shelley is able to create her artistic persona through a series of relationships rather than a single act of self-assertion; and she is freed from having to take a single, definitive position on her unladylike subject" (31).

The writer examines the novel's structure in terms of its relationship to the thesis.

The stories take the form of three confessions to people with whom the speaker has unusually close ties. In the case of the monster's story, the tie is the creature/creator relationship. In Frankenstein's story, he and Walton share the common bond of wholehearted commitment to a "glorious enterprise" that each had hoped would bring himself fame and glory for his unprecedented scientific discovery. Walton and his sister share the close bond of a family relationship.

Mary Wollstonecraft, in *A Vindication of the Rights of Woman,* says, "The most holy band of society is friendship . . . this is an obvious truth" (113). Wollstonecraft continues to explain, asserting that friendship is a special, rare kind of love because it is more than just appetite or emotion. This kind of friendship is evidenced in the early relationship between Frankenstein and Elizabeth, and it is something Walton desires to have with Frankenstein.

Specific references to the text are cited throughout the analysis.

In Walton's fourth letter to his sister, he relates how he has met a stranger drawn on a sled over the ice. He writes, "I said in one of my letters, dear Margaret, that I should find no friend on the wide ocean; yet I have found a man who, before his spirit had been broken by misery, I should have been happy to have possessed as the brother of my heart" (Shelley 26).

Walton tells Frankenstein about his burning desire to reach the North Pole with this stranger. Frankenstein, in turn, sees himself mirrored in Walton's single-minded pursuit of this quest. Walton then tells him that simply achieving his goals will not make him happy, sharing his conviction that a man without a friend "could boast of little happiness" (Shelley 27).

Frankenstein agrees, and says a person isn't whole if he doesn't have someone who is "wiser, better, dearer" than himself to "lend his aid to perfectionate our weak and faulty natures" (Shelley 28). Frankenstein once had such friends, but now he has lost them and can't begin life anew. He then tells Walton his story, explaining the origins of his desire for

Mary Shelley's *Frankenstein*: Friendship, Alienation, and Relationship Dynamics
(continued)

scientific knowledge and how his passion to create a living being has had disastrous consequences.

In her book *Women in Romanticism*, Meena Alexander describes Frankenstein's act of creation as an attempt to usurp the natural relationship of mother and father to child. She says, "Victor has abandoned the monster in his helpless infancy" (28); he alienates his creation because he is repulsed by its hideousness. Frankenstein tries to create something without the structure of a family relationship, and then fails to support his creature in a relationship after it comes to life.

Kiely also sees Frankenstein's scientific experiment as unnatural because he usurps the power of women by trying to create a new species that would "bless him as its creator and source" (164). In doing such a thing, Kiely says, Frankenstein eliminates the need for woman in the creative act. He also neglects his relationship with Elizabeth during his two-year period of time-consuming, obsessive work in the laboratory.

One wonders why Frankenstein doesn't marry Elizabeth earlier and, with her cooperation, finish the job more quickly and pleasurably. After all, if the two are soul mates and have shared all things since childhood, this would be the logical step. But Frankenstein neither marries his best friend and true love, nor does he confide in her about his true purpose and plan.

Kiely says Frankenstein's actions are "the supreme symbol of egotism, the ultimate turning away from human society and into the self which must result in desolation" (167). Having moved away from family, friends, and fiancee to perform his "creative" act in isolation, Frankenstein later witnesses in horror the monster, in an exaggerated re-enactment of his own behavior, eliminate his younger brother, his dearest friend, and his beloved Elizabeth. . . .

After Frankenstein's story is told, he talks to Walton about the nature of friendship once again, and explains that he cannot ever have a close friend again. He asks Walton bitterly, "Think you that any can replace those who are gone? Can any man be to me as Clerival was; or any woman another Elizabeth?" He says friends like these "know our infantine dispositions, which, however they may be afterwards modified, are never eradicated; and they can judge of our actions with more certain conclusions as to the integrity of our motives" (Shelley 204). . . .

Frankenstein's story serves well as a cautionary tale and helps prevent Walton from making the same mistakes.

The connection between the writer's ideas and those of a critic leads to effective analysis.

A careful examination of two characters leads to interesting insights.

Unlike Frankenstein, Walton sees the possible consequences of continuing his quest, and abandons it for the greater good of those who are close to him, his crew. But Frankenstein himself has not learned from his story—he still considers his purpose one "assigned by Heaven" and asks Walton to undertake his unfinished work, to prevent the monster from living as an "instrument of mischief" (Shelley 210).

The monster returns after Frankenstein's death and in an impassioned outburst explains the agony he has gone through in carrying out the murders. He compares himself to Satan in his fall from glory, and says he accepts the fact that he will never find sympathy and is content to suffer alone, although "even that enemy of God and man had friends and associates in his desolation; I am alone" (Shelley 213).

In closing, the writer reaffirms her thesis.

Shelley is successful in showing the importance of friends and relationships for living creatures. The monster's loneliness and alienation lead to his destructive rampage, which he himself says would not have happened if he had had a companion. Frankenstein, although emphasizing the power of friends to help balance and refine a person, neglects his friendships and suffers the consequences. And Walton's newfound friendship with Frankenstein does provide the kind of guidance he needs—he learns from Frankenstein and changes his ambition, placing higher priority on his relationships, both with his sister and his crew.

Works Cited

Alexander, Meena. *Women in Romanticism: Mary Wollstonecraft, Dorothy Wordsworth and Mary Shelley.* Savage, MD: Barnes and Noble Books, 1989.

Kiely, Robert. *The Romantic Novel in England.* Cambridge, MA: Harvard University Press, 1972.

Poovey, Mary. *The Proper Lady and the Woman Writer.* Chicago: University of Chicago Press, 1984.

Shelley, Mary. *Frankenstein.* London: Penguin Books, 1992.

Wollstonecraft, Mary. *A Vindication of the Rights of Woman. The Norton Anthology of English Literature.* Ed. M. H. Abrams. New York: W. W. Norton and Company, 1993. 101-126. ■

Ideas for Literary Analyses

The ideas listed below will help you choose a specific focus for your analysis.

THEME: You can write about one of the themes presented in your selection.
- **Does the author seem to be saying something about ambition, courage, greed, jealousy, or happiness?**
- **Does the selection show you what it is like to experience racism, loneliness, etc.?**
- **Does the author say something about a specific time and place in history?**

CHARACTERIZATION AND PLOTS: You can explore aspects of character and plot development.
- **What motives determine a character's course of action?**
- **What are the most revealing aspects of one of the characters?** (Consider his or her thoughts, words, and actions.)
- **What external conflicts affect the main character?** (Consider conflicts with other characters, the setting, objects, etc.)
- **What internal conflicts make life difficult for the main character?** (Consider the thoughts, feelings, and ideas that affect him or her.)
- **How is suspense built into the story?** (Consider the important events leading up to the climax.)
- **Are there any twists or reversals in the plot?** (What do they add to the story?)
- **Does the text exhibit traits of a quest, a comedy, a tragedy, or an ironic twist on one of these patterns of development?**

SETTING: You may want to analyze the role of the setting in the story.
- **What effect does the setting have on the characters? The plot? The theme?**
- **Has the setting increased your knowledge of a specific time and place?**
- **Is the setting new and thought provoking?**

STYLE: You can give special attention to the author's style of writing.
- **What feeling or tone is created in the selection? How is it created?**
- **Is there an important symbol that adds meaning to the selection?** (How is this symbol represented in different parts?)
- **Has special attention been given to figures of speech like metaphors, similes, and personification?** (What do these devices add to the writing?)

AUTHOR: You can focus on the life and times of the author.
- **How does the text reflect aspects of the author's experience or beliefs?**
- **How does this text compare to other works by the author?**
- **How does the literary work represent the author's particular time, place, and/or culture?**

tips FOR WRITING AN ANALYSIS

WRITING THE OPENING Your opening paragraph should gain your readers' attention and identify the focus of your analysis. Use the suggestions listed below to help you get started on your opening.

1. **Summarize your subject very briefly.** Include the title, author, and the type of book (or other literary form). This can be done with a what-and-how statement.

   > Mary Shelley's *Frankenstein* is one of the most well-known novels of the Romantic era. The story is one that has seeped into the popular imagination . . .

2. **Start with a quotation from the book** and then comment upon its importance (think in terms of the focus of your analysis).

3. **Begin with an explanation of the author's purpose** and how well you think he or she achieves this purpose.

4. **Open with a few general statements** about life that relate to the focus of your analysis.

   > Chaos often rules on the fringes of society. . . .

5. **Begin with a general statement** about the type of literature you are analyzing. Then discuss your subject within this context.

   > The best science fiction always seems believable and logical within the context of the story line. This certainly is true in . . .

WRITING THE BODY Develop or support your focus in the body, or main part, of the analysis. To make sure that you effectively explain each main point in your analysis, follow these three steps:

1. **State each main point** so that it clearly relates to the focus of your analysis.

2. **Support each main point** with specific details or direct quotations from the text you are analyzing.

3. **Explain how each of these specific details** helps prove your point.

Special Note: Try to organize your writing so that each new paragraph deals with a separate main point.

WRITING THE CLOSING In the last paragraph, tie all of the important points together and make a final statement about the main focus of your analysis. (Give your readers something to think about long after they've put your analysis down.)

Literary Terms

Action is what happens in a story: the events or conflicts. If the action is well organized, it will follow a pattern, or plot.

Allegory is a story in which people, things, and actions represent an idea or a generalization about life; allegories often have a strong moral, or lesson.

Allusion is a reference in literature to a familiar person, place, or thing.

Analogy is a comparison of two or more similar objects, suggesting that if they are alike in certain respects, they will probably be alike in other ways, too.

Anecdote is a short summary of an interesting or humorous, often biographical incident or event.

Antagonist is the person or thing working against the protagonist, or hero, of the work.

Autobiography is an author's account or story of her or his own life.

Biography is the story of a person's life written by another person.

Caricature is a picture or an imitation of a person's features or mannerisms exaggerated to appear comic or absurd.

Character sketch is a short piece of writing that reveals or shows something important about a person or fictional character.

Characterization is the method an author uses to reveal or describe characters and their various personalities.

Climax is the turning point, and usually the most intense point, in a story.

Comedy is literature with a love story at its core. The basic plot often develops as follows: an old, established society tries to prevent the formation of a new one (the union of a young couple). The young couple succeed in the end. In comedy, human errors or problems may appear humorous.

Conflict is the problem or struggle in a story that triggers the action. There are five basic types of conflict:

Person vs. Person: One character in a story has a problem with one or more of the other characters.

Person vs. Society: A character has a problem with some element of society: the school, the law, the accepted way of doing things, and so on.

Person vs. Self: A character has a problem deciding what to do in a certain situation.

Person vs. Nature: A character has a problem with some natural happening: a snowstorm, an avalanche, the bitter cold, or any other element of nature.

Person vs. Fate (God): A character must battle what seems to be an uncontrollable problem. Whenever the conflict is a strange or unbelievable coincidence, it can be attributed to fate.

Context is the set of facts or circumstances surrounding an event or a situation in a piece of literature.

Convention is an established technique or device in literature or in drama. *Deus ex machina* (see below) is a common convention in Greek and Roman drama.

Denouement is the final solution or outcome of a play or story.

Deus ex machina is a person or thing that suddenly appears, providing a solution to a difficult problem. The person or thing is lowered to the stage by means of a crane in classic drama.

Dialogue is the conversation carried on by the characters in a literary work.

Diction is an author's choice of words based on their correctness, clearness, or effectiveness.

> **Archaic** words are words that are old-fashioned and no longer sound natural when used, as "I believe thee not" for "I don't believe you."

> **Colloquialism** is an expression that is usually accepted in informal situations and certain locations, as in "He really grinds my beans."

> **Jargon** (technical diction) is the specialized language used by a specific group, such as those who use computers: override, interface, download.

> **Profanity** is language that shows disrespect for someone or something regarded as holy or sacred.

> **Slang** is the language used by a particular group of people among themselves; it is also language that is used in fiction and special writing situations to lend color and feeling: awesome, chill out.

> **Trite** expressions are expressions that lack depth or originality, or are overworked or not worth mentioning in the first place.

> **Vulgarity** is language that is generally considered common, crude, gross, and, at times, offensive. It is sometimes used in fiction to add realism.

Didactic literature instructs or presents a moral or religious statement. It can also be, as in the case of Dante's *Divine Comedy* or Milton's *Paradise Lost,* a work that stands on its own as valuable literature.

Drama is the form of literature known as plays; but drama also refers to the type of serious play that is often concerned with the leading character's relationship to society.

Dramatic monologue is a literary work (or part of a literary work) in which a character is speaking about him- or herself as if another person were present. The speaker's words reveal something important about his or her character.

Elizabethan literature generally refers to the prose and poetry created during the reign of Elizabeth I (1558-1603).

Empathy is putting yourself in someone else's place and imagining how that person must feel. The phrase "What would you do if you were in my shoes?" is a request for one person to empathize with another.

Epic is a long narrative poem that tells of the deeds and adventures of a hero.

Epigram is a brief, witty poem or expression often dealing with its subject in a satirical manner.

> "There never was a good war or a bad peace."
>
> —Ben Franklin

Epitaph is a short poem or verse written in memory of someone.

Epithet is a word or phrase used in place of a person's name; it is characteristic of that person: Alexander the Great, Material Girl, Ms. Know-It-All.

Essay is a piece of prose that expresses an individual's point of view; usually, it is a series of closely related paragraphs that combine to make a complete piece of writing.

Exaggeration (hyperbole) is overstating or stretching the truth for special effect.

> "That story is as old as time."

Exposition is writing that is intended to make clear, or explain, something that might otherwise be difficult to understand; in a play or novel, it would be that portion that helps the reader to understand the background or situation in which the work is set.

Expressionism is a highly emotional form of dramatic expression exploring the ultimate nature of human experience. The expressionist playwrights focused on subconscious feelings and desires.

Fable is a short, fictional narrative that teaches a lesson. It usually includes animals that talk and act like people.

Falling action is the action of a play or story that works out the decision arrived at during the climax. It ends with the resolution.

Farce is literature based on a highly humorous and highly improbable plot.

Figurative language is language used to create a special effect or feeling. It is characterized by figures of speech or language that compares, exaggerates, or means something other than what it first appears to mean. (See "Figure of speech.")

Figure of speech is a literary device used to create a special effect or feeling by making some type of interesting or creative comparison. The most common types are *antithesis, hyperbole, metaphor, metonymy, personification, simile,* and *understatement.*

> **Antithesis** is an opposition, or contrast, of ideas.
> > "It was the best of times, it was the worst of times, it was the age of wisdom, it was the age of foolishness . . . "
> >
> > — Charles Dickens, *A Tale of Two Cities*
>
> **Hyperbole** (hi-pur´ ba-li) is an exaggeration, or overstatement.
> > "I have seen this river so wide it had only one bank."
> >
> > —Mark Twain, *Life on the Mississippi*

Metaphor is a comparison of two unlike things in which no word of comparison (*as* or *like*) is used.

Metonymy (ma-tón a-mi) is the substituting of one word for another that is closely related to it.

"The White House has decided to provide a million more public service jobs." (*White House* is substituting for *president.*)

Personification is a literary device in which the author speaks of or describes an animal, object, or idea as if it were a person.

"The rock stubbornly refused to move."

Simile is a comparison of two unlike things in which a word of comparison (*like* or *as*) is used.

"She stood in front of the altar, shaking like a freshly caught trout."
—Maya Angelou, *I Know Why the Caged Bird Sings*

Understatement is stating an idea with restraint (holding back) to emphasize what is being talked about. Mark Twain once described Tom Sawyer's Aunt Polly as being "prejudiced against snakes." Since she could not stand snakes, this way of saying so is called understatement.

Flashback is going back to an earlier time (in a story) for the purpose of making something in the present clearer.

Foreshadowing is giving hints of what is to come later in a story.

Genre refers to a category or type of literature based on its style, form, and content. The mystery novel is a literary genre.

Gothic novel is a type of fiction that is often characterized by gloomy castles, ghosts, and supernatural or sensational happenings—creating a mysterious and sometimes frightening story. Mary Shelley's *Franken-stein* is probably the best-known gothic novel still popular today.

Hubris, derived from the Greek word *hybris,* means "excessive pride." In Greek tragedy, hubris is often viewed as the flaw that leads to the downfall of the tragic hero.

Imagery is the words or phrases a writer selects to create a certain picture in the reader's mind. Imagery is usually based on sensory details.

"The sky was dark and gloomy, the air was damp and raw, the streets were wet and sloppy."
—Charles Dickens, *The Pickwick Papers*

Impressionism is the recording of events or situations as they have been impressed upon the mind as feelings, emotions, and vague thoughts; realism deals with objective facts. A writer shares his boyhood impressions of winter:

" . . . we waited to snowball the cats. Sleek and long as jaguars and horrible-whiskered, spitting and snarling, they would slink and sidle over the white back-garden walls, and the lynx-eyed hunters, Jim and I, fur-capped and moccasined trappers from Hudson Bay, off Mumbles Road, would hurl our deadly snowballs at the green of their eyes. The wise cats never appeared."
—Dylan Thomas, *A Child's Christmas in Wales*

LITERARY TERMS

Irony is using a word or phrase to mean the exact opposite of its literal or normal meaning. There are three kinds of irony:

dramatic irony, in which the reader or the audience sees a character's mistakes or misunderstandings, but the character him- or herself does not;

verbal irony, in which the writer says one thing and means another ("The best substitute for experience is being sixteen"); or

irony of **situation**, in which there is a great difference between the purpose of a particular action and the result.

Local color is the use of details that are common in a region of the country. "Mama came out and lit into me for sitting there doing nothing. Said I was no-count and shiftless and why hadn't I gathered eggs and . . ."
—Olive Ann Burns, *Cold Sassy Tree*

Malapropism is the type of pun, or play on words, that results when two words become jumbled in the speaker's mind. The term comes from a character in Sheridan's comedy, *The Rivals*. The character, Mrs. Malaprop, is constantly mixing up her words, as when she says "as headstrong as an allegory [she means alligator] on the banks of the Nile."

Melodrama is an exaggerated form of drama (as in television soap operas) characterized by heavy use of romance, suspense, and emotion.

Miracle play is an early play form, also known as a cycle play, dramatizing Christian history in episodes—from the beginning to the Last Judgement. It could also refer to any type of religious drama in the medieval period.

Mood is the feeling a piece of literature arouses in the reader: happiness, sadness, peacefulness, etc.

Moral is the particular value or lesson the author is trying to get across to the reader. The "moral of the story" is a common phrase in Aesop's fables.

Morality play is a type of allegorical drama (fifteenth century) making a moral or religious point. A morality play—*Castle of Perseverance, Everyman,* etc.—gives appreciable shape to abstract concepts.

Motif is an often-repeated idea or theme in literature. In *The Adventures of Huckleberry Finn,* Huck is constantly in conflict with the "civilized" world. This conflict becomes a motif throughout the novel.

Myth is a traditional story that attempts to explain a natural phenomenon or justify a certain practice or belief of a society.

Narration is writing that relates an event or a series of events: a story.

Narrator is the person who is telling the story.

Naturalism is an extreme form of realism in which the author tries to show the relation of a person to the environment or surroundings. Often, the author finds it necessary to show the ugly or raw side of that relationship.

Neoclassicism is the period of English literature (through the eighteenth century) influenced by classical arts and literature.

Novel is a lengthy fictional story with a plot that is revealed by the speech, action, and thoughts of the characters.

Novella is a prose work longer than the standard short story, but shorter and less complex than a full-length novel.

Oxymoron is a combination of contradictory terms, as in *jumbo shrimp, tough love,* or *cruel kindness.*

Parable is a short, descriptive story that illustrates a particular belief or moral.

Paradox is a statement that seems contrary to common sense yet may, in fact, be true: "The coach considered this a good loss."

Parody is a form of literature intended to mock a particular literary work or its style; a comic effect is intended.

Pathos is a Greek root meaning *suffering* or *passion.* It usually describes the part in a play or story that is intended to elicit pity or sorrow from the audience or reader.

Persona is the voice or personality an author assumes for a particular purpose. It is the character who speaks to the readers (and who may or may not be anything like the author).

Picaresque novel is a novel consisting of a lengthy string of loosely connected events. It usually features the adventures of a rogue, or scamp, living by his wits among the middle class. Mark Twain's *Huckleberry Finn* is a picaresque novel.

Plot is the action or sequence of events in a story. It is usually a series of related incidents that build upon one another as the story develops. There are five basic elements in a plot line.

Plot line is the graphic display of the action or events in a story: *exposition, rising action, climax, falling action,* and *resolution.*

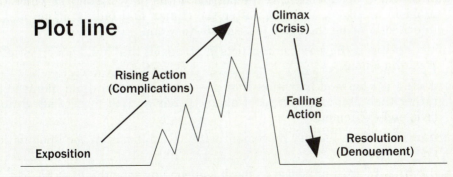

Plot line

Climax (Crisis)

Rising Action (Complications)

Falling Action

Resolution (Denouement)

Exposition

Poetic justice is a term that describes a character "getting what he deserves" in the end, especially if what he deserves is punishment. The purest form of poetic justice results when one character plots against another but ends up being caught in his or her own trap.

Poetry is an imaginative response to experience reflecting a keen awareness of language. (See 282-283 for poetry terms.)

Point of view is the vantage point from which the story is told. In the first-person point of view, the story is told by one of the characters: "I don't know what I'm doing tonight. What about you?" In the third-person point of view, the story is told by someone outside the story: The simple fact is he lacked confidence. He would rather do something he wasn't all that crazy about doing than risk looking foolish.

Protagonist is the main character or hero of the story.

Pseudonym (also known as "pen name") means "false name" and applies to the name a writer uses in place of his or her given name. George Eliot is the pseudonym of the novelist Ann Evans.

Pun is a word or phrase that is used in such a way as to suggest more than one possible meaning. Words used in a pun are words that sound the same (or nearly the same) but have different meanings.

Quest features a main character who is seeking to find something or achieve a goal. In the process, this person encounters and overcomes a series of obstacles. In the end, he or she returns, having gained knowledge and experience as a result of the adventures.

Realism is literature that attempts to represent life as it really is.

Reminiscence is writing based on the writer's memory of a particular time, place, or incident. Memoir is another term for reminiscence.

Renaissance, which means "rebirth," is the period of history following the Middle Ages. This period began late in the fourteenth century and continued through the fifteenth and sixteenth centuries. Milton (1608-1674) is often regarded as the last of the great Renaissance poets. The term now applies to any period of time in which intellectual and artistic interest is revived or reborn.

Resolution, or denouement, is the portion of the play or story in which the problem is solved. It comes after the climax and falling action and is intended to bring the story to a satisfactory end.

Rising action is the series of conflicts or struggles that build a story or play toward a climax.

Romance is a form of literature that presents life as we would like it to be rather than as it actually is. Usually, it has a great deal of adventure, love, and excitement.

Romanticism is a literary movement with an emphasis on the imagination and emotions.

Sarcasm is the use of praise to mock someone or something, as in "He's a real he-man," "She's a real winner."

Satire is a literary tone used to ridicule or make fun of human vice or weakness, often with the intent of correcting, or changing, the subject of the satiric attack.

Setting is the time and place in which the action of a literary work occurs.

Short story is a brief fictional work. It usually contains one major conflict and at least one main character.

Slapstick is a form of low comedy that makes its appeal through the use of exaggerated, sometimes violent action. The "pie in the face" routine is a classic piece of slapstick.

Slice of life is a term that describes the type of realistic or naturalistic writing that accurately reflects what life is like. This is done by giving the reader a sample, or slice, of experience.

Soliloquy is a speech delivered by a character when he or she is alone on stage.

Stereotype is a pattern or form that does not change. A character is "stereotyped" if she or he has no individuality and fits the mold of that particular kind of person.

Stream of consciousness is a style of writing in which the thoughts and feelings of the writer are recorded as they occur.

Structure is the form or organization a writer uses for her or his literary work. There are a great number of possible forms used regularly in literature: parable, fable, romance, satire, farce, slapstick, and so on.

Style is how the author uses words, phrases, and sentences to form his or her ideas. Style is also thought of as the qualities and characteristics that distinguish one writer's work from the work of others.

Symbol is a person, a place, a thing, or an event used to represent something else: the dove is a symbol of peace. Characters in literature are often symbols of good or evil.

Theme is the statement about life a particular work is trying to get across to the reader. In stories written for children, the theme is often spelled out clearly at the end. In more complex literature, the theme will not be so clearly spelled out.

Tone is the overall feeling, or effect, created by a writer's use of words. This feeling may be serious, mock-serious, humorous, satiric, and so on.

Total effect is the general impression a literary work leaves on the reader.

Tragedy is a literary work in which the hero is destroyed by some character flaw and by forces beyond his or her control.

Tragic hero is a character who experiences an inner struggle because of a character flaw. That struggle ends in the defeat of the hero.

Transcendentalism is a philosophy that requires human beings to go beyond (transcend) reason in their search for truth. An individual can arrive at the basic truths of life through spiritual insight if he or she takes the time to think seriously about them.

LITERARY TERMS

Poetry Terms

Alliteration is the repetition of initial consonant sounds in words such as "rough and ready." An example of alliteration (from "Runaway Warning" by Anne-Marie Oomen) is underlined below:

"Our gang paces the pier like an old myth . . ."

Assonance is repetition of vowel sounds without repetition of consonants.

"My words like silent rain drops fell . . ."

—Paul Simon, "Sounds of Silence"

Ballad is a poem in verse form that tells a story.

Blank verse is an unrhymed form of poetry. Each line normally consists of 10 syllables in which every other syllable, beginning with the second, is stressed. Since blank verse is often used in very long poems, it may depart from the strict pattern from time to time.

Caesura is a pause or sudden break in a line of poetry.

Canto is a main division of a long poem.

Consonance is the repetition of consonant sounds. Although it is similar to alliteration, consonance is not limited to the first letters of words:

" . . . and high school girls with clear skin smiles . . . "

—Janis Ian, "At Seventeen"

Couplet is two lines of verse the same length that usually rhyme.

End rhyme is the rhyming of words that appear at the ends of two or more lines of poetry.

Enjambment is the running over of a sentence or thought from one line to another.

Foot is the smallest repeated pattern of stressed and unstressed syllables in a poetic line. (See "Verse.")

Iambic: an unstressed followed by a stressed syllable (repeát)

Anapestic: two unstressed followed by a stressed syllable (interrúpt)

Trochaic: a stressed followed by an unstressed syllable (ólder)

Dactylic: a stressed followed by two unstressed syllables (ópenly)

Spondaic: two stressed syllables (heártbreák)

Pyrrhic: two unstressed syllables (Pyrrhic seldom appears by itself.)

Free verse is poetry that does not have a regular meter or rhyme scheme.

Heroic couplet (closed couplet) consists of two successive rhyming lines that contain a complete thought.

Internal rhyme occurs when the rhyming words appear in the same line of poetry: "You break my eyes with a look that buys sweet cake."

Lyric is a short verse that is intended to express the emotions of the author; quite often, these lyrics are set to music.

Meter is the patterned repetition of stressed and unstressed syllables in a line of poetry.

Onomatopoeia is the use of a word whose sound suggests its meaning, as in *clang, buzz,* and *twang.*

Refrain is the repetition of a line or phrase of a poem at regular intervals, especially at the end of each stanza. A song's refrain may be called the chorus.

Repetition is the repeating of a word, a phrase, or an idea for emphasis or for rhythmic effect within a poem or prose.

"His laugh, his dare, his shrug / sag ghostlike . . . "

Rhyme is the similarity or likeness of sound existing between two words. *Sat* and *cat* are perfect rhymes because the vowel and final consonant sounds are exactly the same.

Rhymed verse is verse with end rhyme; it usually has regular meter.

Rhythm is the ordered or free occurrences of sound in poetry. Ordered or regular rhythm is called meter. Free occurrence of sound is called free verse.

Sonnet is a poem consisting of 14 lines of iambic pentameter. There are two popular forms of the sonnet, the Italian (or Petrarchan) and the Shakespearean (or English).

Italian (Petrarchan) sonnet has two parts: an octave (eight lines) and a sestet (six lines), usually rhyming *abbaabba, cdecde.* Often, a question is raised in the octave and answered in the sestet.

Shakespearean (English or Elizabethan) sonnet consists of three quatrains and a final rhyming couplet. The rhyme scheme is *abab, cdcd, efef, gg.* Usually, the question or theme is set forth in the quatrains while the answer or resolution appears in the final couplet.

Stanza is a division of poetry named for the number of lines it contains:

Couplet: two-line stanza	**Sestet:** six-line stanza
Triplet: three-line stanza	**Septet:** seven-line stanza
Quatrain: four-line stanza	**Octave:** eight-line stanza
Quintet: five-line stanza	

Verse is a metric line of poetry. It is named according to the kind and number of feet composing it: iambic pentameter, anapestic tetrameter, . . . (See "Foot.")

Monometer: one foot	**Pentameter:** five feet
Dimeter: two feet	**Hexameter:** six feet
Trimeter: three feet	**Heptameter:** seven feet
Tetrameter: four feet	**Octometer:** eight feet

POETRY TERMS

The
Research
Center

Writing the Research Paper

Writing Responsibly

MLA Documentation Style

MLA Research Paper

APA Documentation Style

APA Research Paper

Searching for Information

Using Electronic Sources

Writing with a Computer

Using the Writing Center

Writing the Research Paper

One of your finest achievements as a college student will be to write a solid research paper, since doing so demands that you "put it all together": thinking, speaking, reading, and writing. More than that, the research paper challenges you to take charge of your own education. You're the leader. It's your topic, your curiosity, and your energy that make it happen. It's a big project, too, with many stages. So if you can write a good research paper, you can be trusted to manage many other complex and time-consuming tasks without losing your wits.

WHAT'S AHEAD

This section of your handbook provides you with everything you need to write a research paper, from prewriting through the final proofreading.

NOTE: **This chapter can be used with either the MLA or APA style sheet.**

- **Research Update**
- **Steps in the Process**

Research Update

Traditionally, students camped out in their libraries to find information (books, magazines, etc.) for their research papers. Today, students are also urged to gather information firsthand by using interviews, observations, questionnaires, and so on. You, as a student, are personally involved in gathering facts, finding examples, and forming ideas.

I-Search vs. Re-Search

One method of research that focuses almost entirely on a firsthand search for information is the I-Search paper. An I-Search paper begins with an individual's own natural curiosity about something. One person may wonder if he or she has what it takes to become an emergency-room nurse. Another may wonder about the risks and rewards of becoming a police officer.

Once a personal need is identified, I-Searchers set out to find information and answers they need through visits and interviews. I-Searchers use books and magazines only when they are recommended by someone during an interview or a visit. (People first, books second.) An I-Search paper is the story of an individual's own searching adventure, a story that naturally includes original thought and genuine feelings.

A Personalized Approach

Here's what we recommend for your next research paper to make it as personal and authentic as possible:

Get involved.   Start by selecting a subject that really interests you, and then carry out your research personally, using both primary and secondary sources.

Keep a journal.   Consider writing in a journal during your research. Thinking and writing about your work will help you make sense of and evaluate new information.

Personalize it.   Present the results of your searching in light of your own thoughts and decisions about what the information means. Your readers want to consider a new twist on your topic, not just look at facts they could gather themselves.

Follow the steps.   Finally, we recommend that you follow the 20 steps suggested on the following pages.

Steps in the Process

"My idea of research is to look at the thing from all sides; the person who has seen the animal, how the animal behaves, and so on." —Marianne Moore

PREWRITING

Finding a Research Topic

 SELECT AN INTERESTING SUBJECT.

Meaningful research projects start with a personal need or desire to know. *What are the best career opportunities for young people today? What are the real costs and benefits of a college education? Are we doing enough (or too much) to protect our endangered species?*

If you have a need to know, you may already have a good subject for your research paper. If you're not sure, think about it. Think about the subjects you've studied in school, the hobbies you've enjoyed, the materials you've read, the movies or television programs you've seen. Think about current controversial topics, recent stories in the news, and things that are important in your daily life. What do you need or want to know? To do good research, you need to find a subject that interests you and seems practical for the time and resources available. (See 018-019 for additional ideas for selecting a subject.)

2 THINK ABOUT YOUR SUBJECT.

Once you've selected a general subject, you need to explore it further. You can start by taking out your journal and writing down everything you know (and don't know) about your subject. You might use the basic *who, what, when, where, why,* and *how* questions:

> I already know . . .
> I want to find out *who* . . .
> I want to discover *what* . . .
> I want to learn *when* . . .
> I want to know *where* . . .
> I want to understand *why* . . .
> I want to find out *how* . . .

Also talk with other people about your subject—instructors, parents, grandparents, community leaders, local experts, whoever is available. And don't forget to do some exploratory reading. Even an encyclopedia article can offer a reliable overview of your subject and lead you to many related topics. You may also choose to review magazines, newspapers, videos, CD's, and on-line sources of information. (See 021 as you attempt to "shape" your subject.)

3 LIMIT YOUR SUBJECT.

Once you've done all your preliminary thinking, you need to take steps to find a limited subject. Let's say you've always been interested in wildlife and that recently you saw a special on television about endangered species in the United States and Canada. You were surprised to learn that many of the programs set up years ago to help preserve certain species have actually done more harm than good. And since you need a topic for your research paper, you've decided that writing a paper on some phase of this topic would be a good idea. Clearly, it's a timely, worthwhile subject, and because you also have a personal interest in it, it makes perfect sense as a research topic.

So with a general subject area in mind, you're ready to begin the process of zeroing in on a specific, limited topic, one you can adequately cover in a 5- to 10-page research paper (or whatever length you are assigned). This is how your process of limiting might go.

Wildlife

 Endangered species

  Programs to protect endangered species

   Programs to protect the gray wolf

    Programs to reintroduce the gray wolf into the lower 48 states

4 WRITE A THESIS STATEMENT.

With a limited subject in hand, you'll next want to compose a sentence to serve as the controlling idea for your research. This sentence is often called the **thesis statement**—a sentence that states what you believe your research will prove. Even though your original thesis statement may change as you do more research, it will guide you and make your research more productive. Here, and on the following page, you'll find a number of tips to help you develop a useful thesis statement.

1. Consider carefully the general information you've already gathered about your subject and decide what specifically you would like to cover in your research.

   Programs to reintroduce the gray wolf into the lower 48 states

2. Put your idea in the form of a question.

   What programs are currently in effect to reintroduce the gray wolf into the lower 48 states?

3. Now turn your question into a sentence that states exactly what you would like to say about your subject.

   The current programs to reintroduce the gray wolf into the lower 48 states are/are not achieving the desired results.

tips FOR WRITING A THESIS STATEMENT

A good thesis statement tells readers what your subject is and, more importantly, it tells them how you plan to treat your subject. It also serves as a personal guide to help you focus on your subject throughout the research project. In addition, your thesis helps you to prioritize your research time, as you decide whether to read a particular book or skim it, photocopy an article or take a few notes on it, view a video in its entirety or fast-forward to the conclusion.

THE PROCESS AT WORK

A thesis statement is usually a single sentence that contains two main elements: a limited subject plus a specific feeling or attitude toward that subject. To arrive at a final thesis, you might follow this process:

● **Select a general subject.**   Endangered species

● **Narrow your subject.**   Programs to protect the gray wolf in the U.S.

● **Select a working thesis.**   The effectiveness of programs to reintroduce the gray wolf into the lower 48 states

● **Put your thesis in the form of a question.**   How effective are the programs to reintroduce the gray wolf into the lower 48 states?

● **Compose a final thesis statement.**   The programs to reintroduce the gray wolf into the lower 48 states are/are not achieving all of the desired results.

THESIS CHECKLIST

1. Make sure your thesis statement focuses on a single, limited subject.

2. Make sure your thesis is stated in a clear, direct sentence (or sentences).

3. Make sure your thesis conveys your point of view or attitude about the topic.

4. Make sure you have access to enough good information to support your thesis statement.

5. Make sure your thesis directs you to write a paper that meets all the requirements of the assignment.

Searching for Information

5 PREPARE A PRELIMINARY BIBLIOGRAPHY.

Continue to look for information related to your thesis statement. To do this, simply head to the library or media center and dig in. (See 444-455.) As you find good sources of information, keep track of them on your computer or on 3- by 5-inch cards. Arrange the cards in alphabetical order by the authors' last names. If you don't know the name of an author, alphabetize by the first word in the title (not including *A, An,* or *The*). Either number each entry in your computer list, or number each card in the upper right-hand corner.

Begley, Sharon, with Daniel Glick. ②
  "The Return of the Native."
    Newsweek 23
    Jan. 1995: 53.

Sample Bibliography Card

Sample Note Card

Torturing of Wolves ②

  - poisoned
  - drawn and quartered
  - doused with gasoline and set on fire
  - mouths wired shut

6 READ AND TAKE NOTES.

As you begin reading the material listed in your bibliography, take notes and write down quotations related to your specific thesis.

- Keep notes on cards of the same size and style (4- by 6-inch cards are recommended).
- Write down important details and quotations, along with the page numbers where this information can be found. Also place the number of the related bibliography card in the upper right-hand corner.
- Place quotation marks around word-for-word quotations.
- Use the ellipsis (. . .) when you leave words out of a quotation. Use brackets around words you add to a quotation. (See 299.)
- Look up unfamiliar words. If you find that a particular word is important, copy its definition onto a note card.
- Give each card a descriptive heading (a word or phrase to highlight the main idea of that note card: *Torturing of Wolves*).

NOTE: As you make personal observations during the research process, write freely in a journal. This will help you clarify your thinking.

Note Taking: A Closer Look

This is a good time to develop your skimming talents. Look over the table of contents, the index, and a sample paragraph or two before deciding to read a source in its entirety.

Summarize ● To summarize, reduce what you have read to a few important points using your own words. (See 496-498.)

Paraphrase ● To paraphrase, restate what you have read using your own words. Use this method when you are trying to retrace the thinking of one of your sources. Put quotation marks around key words or phrases you borrow directly from the sources. (See 499.)

Quote Directly ● To quote someone directly, record the statement or idea word for word and put quotation marks before and after.

7 COLLECT INFORMATION FROM PRIMARY SOURCES.

If possible, collect firsthand information by conducting interviews, passing out questionnaires, or making observations. Remember to plan interview questions in advance and put your subject at ease. If you use a questionnaire, design it carefully so the results will be valid. Of course, your journal is the perfect place for recording observations.

Designing a Writing Plan

8 WRITE YOUR WORKING OUTLINE.

Organize your note cards into their most logical order and use them to construct a working outline. Your descriptive headings may be used as main points and subpoints in your outline. (See 116.)

9 CONTINUE DEVELOPING YOUR RESEARCH.

Search for any additional information that may be needed to develop your focus, or thesis. Reconsider the thesis statement you wrote in step 4 to see if your thoughts about it have changed.

10 REVISE YOUR OUTLINE.

Revise your working outline as necessary when you find new information. Your outline should serve as a blueprint for your final paper, but a blueprint that changes as improvements occurs to you.

*"The guiding question in research is 'So what?'
Answer that question in every sentence and you
will become a great scholar; answer it once a page
in a ten-page paper and you'll write a good one."*

—Donald N. McCloskey

WRITING THE FIRST DRAFT

11 WRITE THE INTRODUCTION.

The introduction should do two things. The first part should say something interesting, surprising, or personal about your subject to gain your readers' attention. (See the list below for ideas.) The second part should identify the specific focus, or thesis, of your research.

- Start out with a revealing story or quotation.
- Give important background information.
- Offer a series of interesting or surprising facts.
- Provide important definitions.
- State your reason for choosing this subject.

12 WRITE THE BODY.

The next step is to write the main part of your research paper, the part that supports or proves your thesis. There are two ways to proceed. You may write freely and openly, or you may work systematically, carefully following your notes and working outline.

WRITING FREELY AND OPENLY

One way to go about writing the body of your research paper is to put your outline and note cards aside and write as much as you can on your own. Refer to your note cards only when you need a quotation, specific facts, or figures.

After you have completed this first writing, review your outline and note cards to see if you have missed or misplaced any important points. Then continue writing, filling in or reorganizing ideas as you go along.

WRITING SYSTEMATICALLY

You may also write the body of your paper more systematically—carefully following your working outline and note cards right from the start. Begin by laying out the first section of note cards (those covering the first main point in your working outline). Then write a general statement that covers the first main point. Using the note cards you have in front of you, add supporting facts and details. Repeat this process until you have dealt with all the main points in your outline.

tips FOR RESEARCH WRITING

- **Use your own words as much as possible.** Use direct quotations only when the wording in the quotation is exactly as you want it.
- **Present your own ideas honestly and clearly.** Although you will be considering the research of others as you consult journal articles, books, newspapers, etc., be sure to analyze and compare this information. Work at offering your personal perspective on the topic.
- **Avoid fragments, abbreviations, or slang** ("you know," "no way," "forget it") in your writing. Work to achieve a formal to semiformal style.
- **Drop statements that you cannot support with facts and details.**

13 WRITE THE CONCLUSION.

The final section, or **conclusion**, of your paper should leave readers with a clear understanding of the importance of your research. Review the important points you have made and draw a final conclusion. In a more personal approach, you may discuss how your research has strengthened or changed your thinking about your subject.

"[Good] writing is concise. A sentence should contain no unnecessary words, a paragraph no unnecessary sentences, for the same reason that a drawing should have no unnecessary lines and a machine no unnecessary parts." —**William Strunk**

REVISING

14 REVISE YOUR FIRST DRAFT AT LEAST TWICE.

Revise once to make sure you have covered all of the main points and effectively supported them. Revise a second time to make sure all of your sentences are clear and smooth. (See 029-036 for help.)

15 DOCUMENT YOUR SOURCES.

Put the Works Cited section (bibliography) together, listing all of the sources you have cited in your paper. Give credit in your paper for ideas and direct quotations that you have used from different sources. Also make sure you have represented the ideas and copied the quotations accurately. (See the MLA or APA section for specific guidelines.)

"Only the hand that erases can write the true thing."

—Meister Eckhart

PREPARING THE FINAL PAPER

16 EDIT YOUR FINAL REVISION.

Check and correct punctuation, capitalization, usage, and grammar. (See 038-039 for help.)

17 PREPARE YOUR FINAL COPY.

If you use a computer, print your final copy on a good-quality printer. Do not justify your right margin. Leave a margin of one inch on all sides, except for page numbers. Double-space your entire paper, including long quotations and the Works Cited section.

Number your pages beginning with the first page of your paper and continue through the Works Cited section. Type your last name before each page number. Place the page numbers in the upper right-hand corner, one-half inch from the top and even with the right-hand margin.

18 ADD IDENTIFYING INFORMATION.

Type your name, the instructor's name, the course title, and the date in the upper left corner of the first page of the paper. (Begin one inch from the top and double-space throughout.) Center the title (double-space before and after); then type the first line of the paper. (See MLA or APA chapter.)

If your instructor requires a title page, center the title one-third of the way down from the top of the page; then center your name, the name of the instructor, and any additional information two-thirds of the way down. (See 363.)

19 TYPE YOUR FINAL OUTLINE.

If you need to submit a final outline, make sure it follows the final version of your paper. (See 363.) Double-space your outline and number its pages with small Roman numerals.

20 CHECK YOUR PAPER FROM START TO FINISH.

When you hand in your paper, it should be neat, clean, error free—and on time!

Writing Responsibly

A research paper—like any other type of meaningful writing—should be a personal process of discovering new information. Once you've collected the information, you need to go about the business of making it part of your own thinking. You should look carefully at the points on which your sources agree and disagree, and decide which ones offer the best arguments and why. You can then determine how these findings stand up to your own thinking. Research will become your own when you

- ◉ believe in the subject,
- ◉ give yourself enough time to learn about it,
- ◉ involve yourself in active, thorough research, and
- ◉ make your own voice the primary voice in your writing.

WHAT'S AHEAD

This chapter will help you understand what you can and cannot do when you use other people's words and ideas in your research paper. It's valuable information for any researcher.

- ● Writing Paraphrases
- ● Plagiarism
- ● Using Quoted Material

Writing Paraphrases

QUICK GUIDE

When you write a report or research paper, you need to support your ideas with information from other sources and give credit to those sources. (Not giving credit is a serious error called **plagiarism**.) There are two ways to share a source's information: either quote directly or paraphrase what other people have written. When you **paraphrase,** you use your own words to restate the author's ideas; when you quote directly, you include the exact words of the author and put quotation marks around them.

1 **Skim the selection first to get the overall meaning.** (Concentrate on just the main ideas, not the details.)

2 **Read the selection carefully,** paying particular attention to key words and phrases. (Check the meaning of unfamiliar words.)

3 **Try listing the main ideas on a piece of paper**—without looking at the selection.

4 **Review the selection another time** so that you have the overall meaning clearly in mind as you begin to write.

5 **Write your paraphrase,** using your own words to restate the author's ideas. Keep the following points in mind:

- Stick to the essential information.
- State each important idea as clearly and concisely as possible.
- Put quotation marks around key words or phrases taken directly from the source. (See 299.)
- Arrange the ideas into a smooth, logical order. (Your version of the author's views should be as easy to read as the original—maybe easier.)

6 **Check your final summary** by asking these questions:

- Have I kept the author's ideas and point of view clear in my paraphrase? Have I quoted where necessary?
- Have I cut enough of the original? Too much?
- Could another person get the author's main idea by simply reading my paraphrase?

Examples of Paraphrases

The passage below is taken from a book entitled *The Brain at Work* by Roger Jennings (Hillmar, 1992). Following the passage, you'll find two examples of how this passage could be paraphrased and properly credited.

> The human brain, once surrounded by myth and misconception, is no longer such a mystery. It is now understood to be the supervisory center of the nervous system that controls all voluntary (eating and thinking) and most involuntary behavior (blinking and breathing).
>
> The brain functions by receiving information from nerve cells that are located throughout the body. Recent research has provided a clear picture of exactly what happens when information first reaches the brain. It has been discovered that the cells that receive the information in the cortex of the brain are arranged in a regular pattern in columns. The columns are, in turn, arranged into a series of "hypercolumns." Each cell within each column has a specific responsibility to perceive and analyze certain kinds of incoming information. Within the columns, the analysis of this information follows a formal sequence.
>
> Eventually, the information is relayed to the higher centers of the brain where a complete picture is assembled. The brain then evaluates the information and either sends a return message or stores the information for later use. The return message travels through the body in the form of electrical and chemical signals via the billions of nerve cells (neurons). When the message reaches its destination, the muscles or glands respond with the appropriate reaction.

Basic Paraphrase

The human brain controls all voluntary and most involuntary behavior. The process begins when the brain receives information from nerve cells located throughout the body. This information is received by brain cells arranged in a series of columns with each cell having a specific responsibility to analyze certain kinds of incoming information. After the information has been analyzed, it is sent to the higher centers of the brain where a complete picture is put together. The brain then evaluates the information and either stores it for later use or sends a return message to the muscles and glands, which react appropriately (Jennings 26).

Paraphrase with Quotation

The human brain controls all voluntary and most involuntary behavior. The process begins when the brain receives information from nerve cells located throughout the body. "The cells that receive the information in the cortex of the brain are arranged in a regular pattern in columns. . . . Each cell within each column has a specific responsibility to . . . analyze certain kinds of incoming information" (Jennings 26). After the information has been analyzed, it is sent to the higher centers of the brain where a complete picture is put together. The brain then evaluates the information and either stores it for later use or sends a return message to the muscles and glands, which react appropriately.

Plagiarism

Plagiarism is the presentation of another writer's ideas or words as if they were your own, without acknowledging the source. Most students understand what plagiarism is and do their very best to avoid it. Even so, once you have researched your topic, it may be difficult to make the distinction between your own voice and the voices of those you've consulted. That's why a thorough knowledge of plagiarism is important.

The Problem with Plagiarism

Plagiarism and other forms of "intellectual currency" theft are receiving increased legal scrutiny with the advent of the Internet and other computer networks. Continuing disputes between China and the United States over copyright infringement indicate the seriousness of the subject.

While you may not think "borrowing" a phrase or two from an author for your research paper is on a par with pirating millions of dollars' worth of rock albums, the principle is the same. The author's work belongs to the author, and taking it without permission or acknowledgement is stealing. An author may feel just as strongly about his or her intellectual property as you do about your stereo. Think of how you might feel if someone passed off your work as his or her own. Below are some rules to help you avoid plagiarizing.

Guidelines for Avoiding Plagiarism

WHAT TO DO

- Indicate clearly when you use anything from another writer's work, even if only a phrase or single key word, by using quotation marks.
- When summarizing or paraphrasing, distinguish clearly where the ideas of others end and your own comments begin.
- When using a writer's idea, credit the author by name and also cite the work in which you found the idea.
- Provide a new citation when using additional information from a previously cited work.
- Err on the side of caution by giving credit whenever you suspect you are using information, other than general knowledge, from a source.

WHAT NOT TO DO

- Do not use facts, details, or ideas from a source without indicating in some way that you are doing so.
- Do not confuse your own ideas with others' ideas discovered during your research. Even if your idea resembles another writer's, you must credit that writer and the work in which the idea is shared.

Examples of Plagiarism

The brief passage below is taken from page 72 of the book *Norman Mailer* by Philip Bufithis (Ungar, 1978). Examples of how the passage might be plagiarized follow below.

> To any reader who accepts the terms of Mailer's vision, this book generates intoxicating hope, for Rojack is a pioneer of the spirit: his explorations give us a felt sense of expanding possibilities for the self. Mailer has defined character in this novel as an endless series of second chances. His hero is trying to do what the classic American heroes of James Fenimore Cooper and Herman Melville tried to do before him—get away from the enfeeblements of civilization, the crush of history.

Copying Word for Word Without Quotation Marks or Acknowledging the Author or the Source

To any reader who accepts the terms of Mailer's vision, this book generates intoxicating hope, for Rojack is a pioneer of the spirit: his explorations give us a felt sense of expanding possibilities for the self. Mailer has defined character in this novel as an endless series of second chances.

Use of Some Key Words or Phrases Without Quotation Marks or Acknowledging the Author or the Source

An American Dream may be seen as an optimistic book, for Rojack is a pioneer of the spirit. He is an example of character defined as an endless series of second chances.

NOTE: Whether many or only a few key words and phrases are copied, they should be in quotation marks, with a source and author cited.

Paraphrasing, Giving No Author or Source Credit

Rojack falls in the line of other classic American heroes created by James Fenimore Cooper and Herman Melville in his ardent individualism and his desire to escape the debilitating confines of society and accumulated weight of history.

Using an Author's Idea Without Crediting the Author or the Source

Rojack can be viewed as another Ahab or Deerslayer in his willingness to push the limits of his spiritual potential in the face of an inherently hostile universe. He struggles to redefine himself, in spite of the risk of self-destruction.

Using Quoted Material

A quotation can be a single word or an entire paragraph. You should choose quotations carefully and keep them as brief as possible. Be sure that the wording, capitalization, and punctuation of direct quotations are the same as in the original work. Clearly mark changes for your readers: (1) changes within the quotation are enclosed in brackets; (2) explanations are enclosed in parentheses at the end of the quotation before closing punctuation (like this).

SHORT QUOTATIONS: If a quotation is four typed lines or fewer, work it into the body of your paper and put quotation marks around it.

LONG QUOTATIONS: Quotations of more than four typed lines should be set off from the rest of the text by indenting each line one inch (10 spaces) and double-spacing the material. When quoting two or more paragraphs, indent the first line of each paragraph an extra quarter inch (3 spaces). Do not use quotation marks.

After the final punctuation mark of the quotation, leave two spaces and insert the appropriate parenthetical reference. Generally, a colon is used to introduce quotations set off from the text.

PARTIAL QUOTATIONS: If you want to leave out part of a quotation, use an ellipsis to show the omission. An ellipsis is three periods with a space before and after each one. (See 555.)

NOTE: Anything you take out of a quotation should not change the author's original meaning.

ADDING TO QUOTATIONS: Use brackets [like this] to signify any material you add to a quotation to help clarify its meaning.

QUOTING POETRY: When quoting up to three lines of poetry, use quotation marks and work the lines into your writing. Use a diagonal (/) to show where each line of verse ends. For verse quotations of four lines or more, indent each line one inch (10 spaces) and double-space. Do not use quotation marks.

To show that you have left out a line or more of verse, make a line of spaced periods the approximate length of a complete line of the poem.

MLA Documentation Style

Most academic disciplines have their own manuals of style for research paper documentation. The MLA style manual, for example, is widely used in the humanities (literature, history, philosophy, etc.), making it the most popular manual in high-school and college writing courses. Clearly, it's a documentation style you will want to become familiar with.

As with any research-paper style, the MLA style uses a clearly defined system for documenting sources. As a writer, it's your responsibility to understand and apply the system consistently from start to finish. (For a complete text of the MLA style manual, refer to the latest version of the *MLA Handbook for Writers of Research Papers.*)

WHAT'S AHEAD

This chapter will provide you with everything you need to know about citing sources according to the MLA style manual. Included is a special section on citing sources from the Internet and a Web site address for obtaining updated information.

301 Parenthetical References

The *MLA Handbook for Writers of Research Papers* suggests giving credit for your sources of information in the body of your research paper. To give credit, simply insert the appropriate information (usually the author and page number) in parentheses after the words or ideas taken from another source. Place them where a pause would naturally occur to avoid disrupting the flow of your writing (usually at the end of a sentence).

Model Parenthetical References

302 One Author: Citing a Complete Work

You do not need a parenthetical reference if you identify the author in your text. (See the first entry below.) However, you must give the author's last name in a parenthetical reference if it is not mentioned in the text. (See the second entry below.) A parenthetical reference could begin with an editor, a translator, a speaker, or an artist instead of the author if that is how the work is listed in the Works Cited section.

WITH AUTHOR IN TEXT (This is the preferred way of citing a complete work.)

In No Need for Hunger, Robert Spitzer recommends that the U.S. government develop a new foreign policy to help Third World countries overcome poverty and hunger.

WITHOUT AUTHOR IN TEXT

No Need for Hunger recommends that the U.S. government develop a new foreign policy to help Third World countries overcome poverty and hunger (Spitzer).

NOTE: Do not offer page numbers when citing complete works, articles in alphabetized encyclopedias, single-page articles, and unpaginated sources.

303 One Author: Citing Part of a Work

List the necessary page numbers in parentheses if you borrow words or ideas from a particular work. Leave a space between the author's last name and the page reference. No punctuation is needed.

WITH AUTHOR IN TEXT

Bullough writes that genetic engineering was dubbed "eugenics" by a cousin of Darwin's, Sir Francis Galton, in 1885 (5).

WITHOUT AUTHOR IN TEXT

Genetic engineering was dubbed "eugenics" by a cousin of Darwin's, Sir Francis Galton, in 1885 (Bullough 5).

304 Two or Three Authors

Give the last names of every author in the same order that they appear in the Works Cited section. (The correct order of the authors' names can be found on the title page of the book.)

Students learned more than a full year's Spanish in ten days using the complete supermemory method (Ostrander and Schroeder 51).

305 More Than Three Authors

Give the first author's last name as it appears in the Works Cited section followed by *et al.* (meaning *and others*).

Communication on the job is more than talking; it is "inseparable from your total behavior" (Culligan et al. 111).

NOTE: You may also choose to list all the authors' last names.

306 Anonymous Book (Work)

When there is no author listed, give the title or a shortened version of the title as it appears in the Works Cited section.

Statistics indicate that drinking water can make up 20 percent of a person's total exposure to lead (Information 572).

307 Corporate Author

If a book or other work was written by a committee or task force, it is said to have a *corporate* author. If the corporate name is long, include it in the text (rather than in parentheses) to avoid disrupting the flow of your writing. Use a shortened form of the name in the text and in references after the full name has been used at least once. For example, *Task Force* may be used for *Task Force on Education for Economic Growth* after the full name has been used at least once.

The thesis of the Task Force's report is that economic success depends on our ability to improve large-scale education and training as quickly as possible (14).

308 Indirect (or Secondary) Source

If you cite an indirect source—someone's remarks published in a second source—use the abbreviation *qtd. in* (quoted in) before the indirect source in your reference.

Paton improved the conditions in Diepkloof [a prison] by "removing all the more obvious aids to detention. The dormitories are open at night: the great barred gate is gone" (qtd. in Callan xviii).

309   Literary Works: Verse Plays and Poems

Cite verse plays and poems by division (act, scene, canto, book, part) and line, using Arabic numerals for the various divisions unless your instructor prefers Roman numerals. Use periods to separate the various numbers. If you are citing lines only, use the word *line* or *lines* in your first reference and numbers only in additional references.

> **In the first act of the play named after him, Hamlet comments, "How weary, stale, flat and unprofitable, / Seem to me all the uses of this world" (1.2.133-134).**

NOTE: A diagonal is used to show where each new line of verse begins.

Verse quotations of more than three lines should be indented one inch (10 spaces) and double-spaced. Each line of the poem or play begins a new line of the quotation; do not run the lines together.

> **Elizabeth Bishop's poem "The Fish" contains layer upon layer of specific details:**
>
> > **He was speckled with barnacles,**
> > **Five rosettes of lines**
> > **and infested**
> > **with tiny white sea-lice, . . . (16-19)**

310   Literary Works: Prose

To cite prose (novels, short stories), list more than the page number if the work is available in several editions. Give the page reference first, and then add a chapter, section, or book number in abbreviated form after a semicolon.

> **In The House of Seven Spirits, Isabel Allende describes Marcos, "dressed in mechanic's overalls, with huge racer's goggles and an explorer's helmet" (13; ch. 1).**

When you are quoting prose that takes more than four typed lines, indent each line of the quotation one inch (10 spaces) and double-space it. In this case, you put the parenthetical citation (the pages and chapter numbers) *outside* the end punctuation mark of the quotation itself.

> **Allende describes the flying machine that Marcos has assembled:**
>
> > **The contraption lay with its stomach on terra firma, heavy and sluggish and looking more like a wounded duck than like one of those newfangled airplanes they were starting to produce in the United States. There was nothing in its appearance to suggest that it could move, much less take flight across the snowy peaks. (12; ch. 1)**

Works Cited

QUICK GUIDE

The Works Cited section includes all of the sources you have cited (referred to) in your text. It does not include any sources you may have read or studied but did not refer to in your paper (that's a bibliography). Begin your list of works cited on a new page (the next page after the text), and number each page, continuing from the last page of the text. The guidelines that follow describe the form of the Works Cited section.

1 Type the page number in the upper right-hand corner, one-half inch from the top of the page, with your last name before it.

2 Center the title *Works Cited* one inch from the top; then double-space before the first entry.

3 Begin each entry flush with the left margin. If the entry runs more than one line, indent additional lines one-half inch (five spaces).

4 Double-space each entry and between entries.

5 List each entry alphabetically by the author's last name. If there is no author, use the first word of the title (disregard *A, An, The*).

6 A basic entry for a book would be as follows:

> Guillermo, Kathy Snow. Monkey Business. Washington, DC:
>
> National Press Books, 1993.

NOTE: Use single spacing between all items of a works-cited entry.

7 A basic entry for a periodical (a magazine) would be as follows:

> Murr, Andrew. "The High Cost of Defense." Newsweek 21 Mar.
>
> 1994: 70.

8 Check the following pages for specific information on other kinds of entries.

Works Cited Entries: Books

The entries that follow illustrate the information needed to cite books, sections of a book, pamphlets, and government publications.

312 ### One Author

> Angell, David. <u>The Internet Business Companion: Growing Your Business in the Electronic Age</u>. Reading, MA: Addison-Wesley, 1995.

313 ### Two or Three Authors

> Bystydzienski, Jill M., and Estelle P. Resnik. <u>Women in Cross-Cultural Transitions</u>. Bloomington, IN: Phi Delta Kappa Educational Foundation, 1994.

314 ### More Than Three Authors

> Marine, April, et al. <u>Internet: Getting Started</u>. Englewood Cliffs, NJ: PTR Prentice Hall, 1994.

NOTE: You may also choose to give all names in full in the order used on the title page.

315 ### Two or More Books by the Same Author

List the books alphabetically according to title. After the first entry, substitute three hyphens for the author's name.

> Laurence, Peter J. <u>The Peter Pyramid</u>. New York: William Morrow, 1986.
>
> - - - . <u>Why Things Go Wrong</u>. New York: William Morrow, 1985.

316 Single Work from an Anthology

> Green, Mark. "The Pro-PAC Backlash: When Money Talks, Is It
>
> > Democracy?" Points of View. Ed. Robert E. Diclerico and Allan
> >
> > S. Hammock. 3rd ed. New York: Random House, 1986. 154.

NOTE: If you cite a complete anthology, begin the entry with the editors.

> Diclerico, Robert E., and Allan S. Hammock, eds. Points of
>
> > View. 3rd ed. New York: Random House, 1986.

317 Corporate Group Author

> United States. Dept. of Labor. Bureau of Statistics.
>
> > Occupational Outlook Handbook. Washington: GPO, 1994.

318 Anonymous Book

> The World Almanac Book of the Strange. New York: New
>
> > American Library, 1977.

NOTE: The Bible is considered an anonymous book. Documentation should read exactly as it is printed on the title page.

> The Jerusalem Bible. Garden City, NY: Doubleday, 1966.

319 One Volume of a Multivolume Work

> Ziegler, Alan. The Writing Workshop. Vol. 2. New York: Teachers
>
> > and Writers, 1984.

NOTE: If you cite two or more volumes in a multivolume work, give the total number of volumes after the title. Offer specific references to volume and page numbers in the parenthetical reference in your text, like this: (8:112-114).

> Barnouw, Eric, ed. International Encyclopedia of Communications.
>
> > 9 vols. New York: Oxford University Press, 1989.

320 An Introduction, a Preface, a Foreword, or an Afterword

> Peter, Tom. Foreword. The Service Edge. By Ron Zemke. New
>
> > York: New American Library, 1989. vi-x.

321 Cross-References

To avoid unnecessary repetition when citing two or more entries from a larger collection, you may cite the collection once with complete publication information (see *Hall* below). The individual entries (see *Abbey* and *Baldwin* below) can then be cross-referenced by listing the author, title of the piece, editor of the collection, and page numbers.

> Abbey, Edward. "The Most Beautiful Place on Earth." Hall 225-41.
>
> Baldwin, James. "Notes of a Native Son." Hall 164-83.
>
> Hall, Donald, ed. The Contemporary Essay. New York: Bedford-
>
> St. Martin's, 1984.

322 Edition

An edition refers to the particular publication you are citing, as in the 3rd edition. But the term "edition" also refers to the work of one person that is prepared by another person, an editor.

> Shakespeare, William. The Merchant of Venice. Ed. Sylvan
>
> Barnet. New York: Signet-NAL, 1963.

323 Translation

> Turgenev, Ivan Sergeevich. Fathers and Sons. Trans. Michael R.
>
> Katz. New York: W. W. Norton, 1994.

324 Article in a Reference Book

It is not necessary to give full publication information for familiar reference works (encyclopedias and dictionaries). For these titles, list only the edition (if available) and the publication year. If an article is initialed, check the index of authors (in the opening section of each volume) for the author's full name.

> "Multi-tasking." Jargon: An Informal Dictionary of Computer
>
> Terms. 1993 ed.
>
> "Technical Education." Encyclopedia Americana. 1992 ed.
>
> Lum, P. Andrea. "Computerized Tomography." World Book. 1994 ed.

325 Pamphlet with No Author or Publication Information Stated

If known, list the country of publication [in brackets]. Use N.p. (no place) if the country is unknown, n.p. (no publisher) if the publisher is unknown, and n.d. if the date is unknown.

> Pedestrian Safety. [United States]: n.p., n.d.

326 **Signed Pamphlet**

Treat a pamphlet as you would a book.

> Grayson, George W. <u>The North American Free Trade Agreement.</u>
>
> New York: Foreign Policy Association, Inc., 1993.

327 **Government Publication**

State the name of the government (country, state, etc.) followed by the name of the agency.

> United States. Federal Trade Commission. <u>Shopping by Mail or</u>
>
> <u>Phone.</u> Washington: GPO, 1994.

328 **Book in a Series**

Give the series name and number (if any) before the publication information.

> Bishop, Jack. <u>Ralph Ellison.</u> Black Americans of Achievement.
>
> New York: Chelsea House, 1988.

329 **Publisher's Imprint**

The name of a publisher's imprint appears above the publisher's name on the title page. Give the imprint followed by a hyphen and the name of the publisher (Signet-NAL).

> Solzhenitsyn, Alexander. <u>One Day in the Life of Ivan Denisovich.</u>
>
> Trans. Ralph Parker. New York: Signet-NAL, 1963.

330 **Book with a Title Within a Title**

If the title contains a title normally in quotation marks, keep the quotation marks and underline the entire title.

> Harte, Bret. <u>"The Outcasts of Poker Flat" and Other Stories.</u>
>
> New York: Signet-NAL, 1961.

NOTE: If the title contains a title normally underlined, do not underline it in your entry: A Tale of Two Cities <u>as History</u>.

331 **Reference Book on CD-ROM**

If you use an encyclopedia or other reference book recorded on CD-ROM, use the form below.

> <u>The Oxford English Dictionary.</u> 2nd ed. CD-ROM. Oxford: Oxford
>
> UP, 1992.

Works Cited Entries: Periodicals

The entries that follow illustrate the information and arrangement needed to cite periodicals.

332 **Signed Article in a Magazine**

> Tully, Shawn. "The Universal Teenager." <u>Fortune</u> 4 Apr. 1994: 14-16.

333 **Unsigned Article in a Magazine**

> "Crafts Fair Showcases Women." <u>Entrepreneur</u> May 1995: 23.

334 **Article in a Scholarly Journal**

> Chu, Wujin. "Costs and Benefits of Hard-Sell." <u>Journal of</u>
>
> <u>Marketing Research</u> 32.2 (1995): 97-102.

NOTE: Journals are usually issued no more than four times a year. Number 32 refers to the volume. The issue number is not needed if the page numbers in a volume continue from one issue to the next. If the page numbers start over with each issue, then put a period and the issue number right after the volume number, with no intervening space: 32.2.

335 **Signed Newspaper Article**

> Bleakley, Fred R. "Companies' Profits Grew 48% Despite
>
> Economy." <u>Wall Street Journal</u> 1 May 1995, midwest ed.: 1.

NOTE: Cite the edition of a major daily newspaper (if given) after the date (1 May 1995, midwest ed.: 1). To cite an article in a lettered section of the newspaper, list the section and the page number. (For example, A4 would refer to page 4 in section A of the newspaper.) If the sections are numbered, however, use a comma after the year (or the edition); then indicate sec. 1, 2, 3, etc., followed by a colon and the page number.

336 Unsigned Newspaper Article

"African Roots of American Music Traced at Westchester College."

Amsterdam News [New York] 29 Jan. 1994, sec. 1: 21.

NOTE: If the unsigned article is an editorial, put *Editorial* after the title.

337 Letter to the Editor

Espy, Mike. Letter. "Abolishing the Farmer's Home Administration."

Washington Post 5 Mar. 1994: A5.

338 Review

Olsen, Jack. "Brains and Industry." Rev. of Land of Opportunity,

by Sarah Marr. New York Times 23 Apr. 1995, sec. 3: 28.

NOTE: If you cite the review of a work by an editor or a translator, use *ed.* or *trans.* instead of *by*.

339 Published Interview

O'Leary, Hazel. "Hazel O'Leary." By Linda Turbyville. Omni Apr.

1995: 75+.

NOTE: Type the word *Interview* after the interviewee's name if the interview is untitled.

340 Title or Quotation Within an Article's Title

Merrill, Susan F. "'Sunday Morning' Thoughts." English Journal

76.6 (1987): 63.

NOTE: Use single quotation marks around the shorter title if it is a title normally punctuated with quotation marks.

341 Article Reprinted in a Loose-Leaf Collection

O'Connell, Loraine. "Busy Teens Feel the Beep." Orlando

Sentinel 7 Jan. 1993: E1+. Youth. Ed. Eleanor Goldstein.

Vol. 4. Boca Raton, FL: SIRS, 1993. Art. 41.

NOTE: The entry begins with original publication information and ends with the name of the loose-leaf volume (Youth), editor, volume number, publication information including name of the *information service* (Social Issues Resources Series), and the article number.

Works Cited Entries:
Other Print and Nonprint Sources

342 Periodically Published Database on CD-ROM

Ackley, Patricia. "Jobs of the Twenty-First Century." <u>New</u>
<u>Rochelle Informer</u> 15 Apr. 1994: A4. <u>New Rochelle</u>
<u>Informer Ondisc</u>. CD-ROM. Info-Line. Oct. 1994.

NOTE: The entry begins with original publication information and ends with the title of the database (underlined), the publication medium (CD-ROM), the vendor's name (producer of the CD-ROM), and the electronic publication date.

343 Article in a Microform Collection

Davidson, Charles. "Schools in Crisis." <u>Pennsylvania Journal</u> 15
Oct. 1995: 19. <u>All-Source: Education Matters</u> 9 (1995):
fiche 2, grids B6-14.

NOTE: The entry begins with original publication information and ends with the title of the microform source (underlined), volume, year, and identification numbers.

344 Publication on Diskette

Barker, Anthony. <u>The New Earth Science</u>. Diskette. Cincinnati:
Freeman's Press, 1991.

345 Television or Radio Program

"The Ultimate Road Trip: Traveling in Cyberspace." <u>48 Hours</u>.
CBS. WBBM, Chicago. 13 Apr. 1995.

346 ## Recording

> Shocked, Michelle. Arkansas Traveler. LP. Polygram Records,
>
> 1992.

347 ## Audiocassette

> Allen, Jeffrey G. How to Turn an Interview into a Job.
>
> Audiocassette. Simon and Schuster, 1985. 52 min.

348 ## Film

> Trading Places. Dir. John Landis. Perf. Dan Akroyd, Eddie Murphy,
>
> Ralph Bellamy, and Jamie Lee Curtis. Paramount, 1983.

349 ## Filmstrip, Slide Program, Videocassette

> How to Leave Your Job and Buy a Business of Your Own.
>
> Videocassette. Self-Reliance Press, 1990. 55 min.

350 ## Letter Received by the Author (Yourself)

> Thomas, Bob. Letter to the author. 10 Jan. 1989.

351 ## Personal Interview

> Brooks, Sarah. Personal interview. 15 Oct. 1993.

352 ## Map or Chart

> Wisconsin Territory. Map. Madison: Wisconsin Trails, 1988.

353 ## Cartoon (Print)

> Trudeau, Garry. "Doonesbury." Cartoon. Chicago Tribune 23 Dec.
>
> 1988, sec. 5: 6.

354 ## Lecture, Speech, Address

> Angelou, Maya. Address. Opening General Sess. NCTE
>
> Convention. Adam's Mark Hotel, St. Louis. 18 Nov. 1988.

NOTE: If known, give the speech's title in quotation marks instead of the label *Address, Lecture,* or *Speech.*

Works Cited Entries: Computer Network Sources

355 ### Elements of On-Line Entry (No print version)

When citing on-line sources, record the necessary information in the following format. If certain items do not apply or are not available, simply skip those and go on to the next.

> **Author's surname, first name. "Title of article or document."**
>
> > **Title of journal, newsletter, conference document, or file**
> >
> > **volume number.issue number/or other identifying number**
> >
> > **(year or date of publication): number of pages or paragraphs**
> >
> > **if given/or n.pag. On-line. Name of computer network.**
> >
> > **Date of access. Available: specify electronic address**

356 ### Article in an Electronic Journal (No print version)

> **Elkhart, Wolfgang. "Planning for Resource Shortages." Earth**
> > **Care 8.3 (10 Apr. 1996): 8 pp. On-line. Internet. 6 June**
> > **1996. Available FTP: berline.cc.stanfordu.ca**

NOTE: The title of the electronic journal (underlined) is followed by a volume and issue number, date of publication, number of pages or paragraphs, the publication medium (On-line), the name of the computer network, your date of access, and the word *Available* followed by the electronic address you used to access the document.

357 ### Article in an Electronic Newsletter (No print version)

> **"Behind the Scenes at the White House." Today's Politics 2.6**
> > **(8 May 1995): n.pag. On-line. Internet. 11 May 1995.**
> > **Available FTP: newsline.bb.todays-politics.wa**

358 ## Electronic File on the World Wide Web (No print version)

Bowker, Samuel T. "Cyberspace: Debate on Research Use."

12 Sept. 1996: n.pag. On-line. Internet. 5 Oct. 1996.

Available WWW: http://www.ppc.new.edu/home/stb/com

359 ## Article from On-Line Computer Service (Also in print)

Stempel, Douglas. "Loving Our Heritage." Annapolis Reporter 3 July

1992: 12. History Index. On-line. Comptell. 13 Nov. 1995.

NOTE: The entry begins with original publication information and ends with the title of the database (underlined), the publication medium (On-line), name of the computer service, and your date of access.

360 ## Book in Electronic Text Repository (Also in print)

Austen, Jane. Sense and Sensibility. Ed. Roald Nielsen. Harmonds-

worth: Penguin, 1962. On-line. Cambridge Text Archive.

Internet. 16 Feb. 1996. Available FTP: etext.cam.ac.uk.au

NOTE: In this case, the entry ends with the publication medium (On-line), the name of the repository, the name of the computer network, your date of access, and the word *Available* followed by the address.

Important Note

Because technology is moving faster than any print source can keep up with, neither the MLA nor *Write for College* handbook is able to provide a completely current section for citing network sources. For that reason, we recommend you visit our site on the World Wide Web for updates and additional information. Our address is **thewritesource.com**.

Also, because the availability of information on computer networks can change from day to day, we recommend that you print out a copy of the material you are accessing. Then you and your readers (instructors, especially) can check the accuracy of quotations, data, and other pertinent information cited in your paper.

Finally, while the formats for all works-cited examples in this section are based on the latest edition of the *MLA Handbook,* the particulars in each case (names, dates, electronic addresses, etc.) have been created to present as clear and complete a model entry as possible.

Research Paper Abbreviations

anon.	anonymous
bk., bks.	book(s)
©	copyright
chap., ch., chs.	chapter(s)
comp.	compiler, compiled, compiled by
ed., eds.	editor(s), edition(s), edited by
e.g.	for example; *exempli gratia*
et al.	and others; *et alii*
ex.	example
f., ff.	and the following page(s)
fig., figs.	figure(s)
GPO	Government Printing Office, Washington, DC
ibid.	in the same place as quoted above; *ibidem*
i.e.	that is; *id est*
ill., illus.	illustration, illustrated by
introd.	introduction, introduced by
l., ll.	line(s)
loc. cit.	in the place cited; *loco citato*
MS, MSS	manuscript(s)
narr., narrs.	narrated by, narrator(s)
n.d.	no date given
no., nos.	number(s)
n. pag.	no pagination
n.p.	no place of publication and/or no publisher given
op. cit.	in the work cited; *opere citato*
p., pp.	page(s)
+	plus the pages that follow
pub. (or publ.), pubs.	published by, publication(s)
rev.	revised by, revision, review, reviewed by
rpt.	reprinted by, reprint
sc.	scene
sec., secs.	section(s)
sic	thus (used within brackets to indicate an error is that way in the original)
tr., trans.	translator, translation
v., vv. (or vs., vss.)	verse(s)
viz.	namely; *videlicet*
vol., vols.	volume(s): capitalize when used with Roman numerals

MLA Research Paper

Before you put your final research paper together, you may want to check your work against a student model. By examining closely the model included in this chapter, you will be able to see firsthand how the MLA guidelines are applied to a final paper.

It would be a good idea to briefly examine the entire paper first, from the title page to the Works Cited page. Try to get an overview of how the paper is constructed and how the pieces fit together. Then go back and do a close reading of the outline and opening section. Look closely at the side notes and parenthetical citations. Continue to refer to the model as necessary as you put together your own paper.

WHAT'S AHEAD

The student model that follows deals with the topic of endangered species, specifically the gray wolf. The writer uses a variety of sources, including a personal interview, federal legislation, and the Internet. The model should help you better understand how the MLA style sheet works when applied to an actual paper.

- Title Page and Outline
- Sample Research Paper

Title Page and Outline

If you are instructed to include a title page and/or an outline with your paper, use the samples below as a guide.

Cry, Wolf

Ella Berven
Professor Jennifer Jordan-Henley
Cyberspace Composition I
15 December 1995

Center the title one-third of the way down the page; center author information two-thirds of the way down.

Cry, Wolf

Introduction—How have we "pictured" wolves in the past, and are we doing the right things now to redress the slaughter that resulted?

I. Past misunderstandings about wolves
   A. Scheming killers
   B. Threat to human existence

II. Truths learned about wolves
   A. Elusive creatures
   B. Social structure like that of the human family

III. Government protection policies for wolves
   A. Endangered Species Act (1973)
   B. Department of the Interior's reintroduction program (1995)

IV. Problems with the reintroduction program
   A. Concerns of ranchers
      1. Loss of livestock
      2. Loss of grazing land
      3. High penalties for shooting wolves
   B. Exorbitant costs of program
   C. Problems for the wolves
      1. Resistance to relocation
      2. Dangers of losing "wildness"
      3. Breakdown of social structure
      4. Inhumanity of capture process

V. Misguided intentions of wildlife managers
   A. Capture and relocation not the best plan
   B. Capture and relocation another brand of human domination

Conclusion—Wolves deserve our help, but reintroduction is too controlling and disregards the wolf's essential nature.

Center the title one inch from the top of the page. Double-space throughout.

Berven 1

Ella Berven

Professor Jennifer Jordan-Henley

Cyberspace Composition I

15 December 1995

Cry, Wolf

Three little pigs dance in a circle singing, "Who's afraid of the big, bad wolf?"

Little Red Riding Hood barely escapes the cunning advances of the ravenous wolf disguised as her grandmother.

Movie audiences shriek as a gentle young man is transformed before their eyes into a bloodthirsty werewolf, a symbol for centuries of the essence of evil.

Such myths and legends have portrayed the wolf as a threat to human existence. Feared as cold-blooded killers, they were hated and persecuted. Wolves were not merely shot and killed; they were tortured as well. In what was believed to be a battle between good and evil, wolves were poisoned, drawn and quartered, doused with gasoline and set on fire, and, in some cases, left with their mouths wired shut to starve (Begley). Convinced that they were a problem to be solved, U.S. citizens gradually eradicated gray wolves from the lower 48 states over a period of years.

Today there has been a public outcry to rectify the situation created by the ignorance of our ancestors. However, in seeking to address a situation created by the human compulsion to control nature, we are again interfering with the natural order; and the very creatures we are trying to protect, we are harming.

In 1995, it is obvious that the hatred and fear that fueled the elimination of the gray wolf stemmed from a

The introduction draws in readers with references to fairy tales and stereotypes.

Examples are given of the inhumane treatment of wolves.

The final introductory paragraph ends with the paper's thesis.

Berven 2

gross misunderstanding of wolves and their behavior. Cultural myths picturing wolves as scheming, aggressive beasts plotting to pounce on innocent victims do not reflect the truth. In reality, wolves are elusive creatures who keep to themselves. The wolf's social structure is much like ours. Wolves live in family units called packs consisting of a mated pair, young pups, and older offspring. It is through the intricate relationships and interactions within the pack that offspring learn how to live as adult wolves. As the environmentalist Charles Bergman points out, "Wolves are intensely social animals, living in packs that are structured in rigid hierarchies. In the chain of power each wolf has a defined place on a ladder of dominance and submission" (31). The entire pack works together according to position to raise and nurture the pups, teaching them a highly sophisticated system of communication used "for expressing their status relative to each other" (31). Also, from parents and older siblings, young wolves learn not only how to hunt, but what to hunt as well. Wolves are trained early to go after certain prey and leave others alone. Since their prey is usually larger and stronger than they, wolves are taught specifically to hunt the weak and sick in order to avoid injury.

Information given in Friends of the Forest describes the similarity between humans and wolves. This publication states, "Like humans, some wolves stay with their families until they die; others leave the pack during adolescence in search of uninhabited territory and a mate" (1-2). Unlike humans, wolves instinctively control their population. The number in a pack rarely exceeds 12 and is determined by the availability and size of prey in their territory.

Background information is given on the wolf's social structure.

The writer quotes various experts throughout her paper.

Berven 3

Faced with the consequences of hasty actions to eliminate the wolves, as well as increased knowledge about
their behavior, the U.S. Congress passed the Endangered
Species Act in 1973, giving full protection to the gray wolf.
In Section 1531 of the act, congressional findings state
that since certain species of wildlife have been threatened
with extinction, "the United States has pledged itself as a
sovereign state in the international community to conserve
to the extent practicable the various species of fish or
wildlife and plants facing extinction" (Endangered 1, 2).

However, many believe that protection has not been
enough. In January 1995, the Department of the Interior
flew 29 wolves from Canada to Idaho's River of No Return
Wilderness Area and to Yellowstone National Park in
Wyoming. Fifteen were released directly into the Idaho
area, and the rest were put in pens in Yellowstone, sched-
uled to be released after an acclimation period of 6 to 12
weeks. This program to reintroduce the gray wolf into the
lower 48 states provides for 15 more wolves to be relo-
cated each year for the next three to five years (Begley).

Critics of the program have raised a number of
concerns. The first is the apprehension of ranchers
regarding the possible loss of livestock. Wolves have been
absent from Yellowstone for 60 years. Although some statistics claim that "less than 1 percent of the sheep and
cattle living in wolf range in Canada are killed by wolves
annually," others tell a different story. According to the
policy director of the National Wildlife Institute, "In
Canada, 41 percent of livestock found dead have been
killed by wolves" (qtd. in Richardson 30). The difference
in these statistics is alarming. Obviously, statistics can be
expressed in a variety of ways depending on what point

Background information on U.S. policy is provided.

The major points of the reintroduction program are summarized.

The first in a number of concerns is cited.

This quotation is found in a secondary source.

one is trying to prove. However, the fact remains that wolves do, at least occasionally, prey on livestock.

In addition to their concern for livestock, ranchers fear the possibility that, to help ensure the wolf's survival, wildlife managers will fence off thousands of acres now used for grazing. This could lead to the shutdown of ranches and result in the loss of hundreds of jobs.

Finally, ranchers know that they have very little recourse if the wolves prey on their livestock. They are allowed to shoot a wolf caught in the act of killing a sheep or cow if the animal belongs to them. However, it is very difficult to be in the right place at the right time to catch a wolf in the kill. It is even more unlikely that a rancher would witness the kill of his own animal. Yet the penalty for defending a neighbor's property can be as high as one year in prison and $100,000 in fines (Richardson 30).

Another problem critics point out is the exorbitant cost of implementing the reintroduction program. Estimated at $65,000 per wolf, the federal government will spend up to $13 million to helicopter-lift 200 wolves over the next five years (Richardson 28, 30). At a time when budget cuts are affecting food, housing, and medical care for the needy, it is difficult to justify this expenditure. Even certain environmentalists have questioned the advisability of capturing and relocating wolves. Recently, a lawsuit was filed by the Sierra Club Legal Defense Fund stating, "The gray wolves have been migrating steadily south from Canada for years. Some have already reached Montana, and wolf packs are expected to settle in Yellowstone in about 30 years on their own initiative" (Richardson 28). But some wildlife biologists say that 30

367

Words such as "In addition" and "Finally" provide transitions between paragraphs.

The writer includes a number of statistics to help, but not overwhelm, readers.

years is too long to wait. They want to reduce Yellowstone's overpopulated bison and elk herds now. These
biologists also want to study wolves before they settle in
naturally. However, as Richardson states, "Taxpayers
might argue that, for $65,000 per animal, the Fish and
Wildlife Service could afford to send the biologists on
weekly junkets to Alberta for wolf observation" (30).

If assurances could be made that this program would
work, perhaps the cost could be justified. However, there
are inherent problems in capturing and relocating wolves
successfully. Even biologists in favor of the program admit
that the number-one challenge is to overcome the natural
tendency of wolves to try to get home. The only solution
to this dilemma is to pen the animals up for a period of
time until they get used to their new surroundings. Unfortunately, whenever wolves are penned, there is a danger
that they will lose some of their wildness. But such measures have already been necessary in the case of one of
the wolf families in Yellowstone. Following the illegal
killing of the dominant male in one of the packs, a recent
update reports:

> The alpha female from the defunct Rose Creek
> pack remains in the Rose Creek wolf enclosure
> with her eight pups. The pups are healthy and
> have been vaccinated against about everything a
> canine can get. It is hoped that by fall (when
> they will likely be released), they will be big
> enough to fight off the coyotes. I suspect their
> winter mortality will be high, since they have
> had no opportunity to learn to hunt. (Maughan)

In an effort to help the wolves form viable packs,
biologists hope to solve the other problem that concerns

An example
helps to
make the
writer's point.

A quotation
of more than
four lines is
set off by
indenting.

No page
number is
given
because the
citation is
from an
on-line
source.

them, "the tendency of a stressed wolf to go it alone" (Carpenter). A consequence of moving wolves from their habitat is that their social structure breaks down. In an interview with Dr. Marcella Cranford, proponent of wolf reintroduction, veterinarian, and expert on wolf behavior, she explained, "Lone wolves don't make it. They survive as a family or they don't survive at all." A result of the breakdown is that "mates separate and some abandon pups in their haste to return to familiar turf" (Carpenter). Biologists believe that in order to form viable packs, they must capture wolves of different ages. The assumption is that when they calm down, the captured wolves will establish a new pack. It is evident from biologists' concerns that wolves not only are intelligent creatures, but also have ties to family and fear change, as humans do. . . .

[At this point in the paper, the writer went on to describe the "invasive and extreme" methods used to capture wolves—methods the writer believes are not merited because the gray wolf is not an endangered species.]

If the driving motivation for the reintroduction of wolves into Idaho and Yellowstone is symbolic, if its purpose is to respect and cooperate with nature, the actions of capture and relocation do not fit the symbol. Capture shows no respect for the highly developed social structure of the pack. Relocation denies the wolf's natural tendency to seek new territory when its own territory is overpopulated. The action appears to be a different kind of "dominion" rather than reciprocity between humankind and the animal kingdom.

With the best of intentions, it is all too easy for

The writer brings in a personal interview with an authority.

An assumption is drawn from experts' knowledge of wolf behavior.

Berven 7

human beings to cross the line between necessary concern and unnecessary control. The environmentalist and
author Charles Bergman makes this point in his book
Wild Echoes:

> For all the pure motives of most of our wildlife
> managers—and I honor and respect their good
> intentions—wolf control nevertheless derives
> from the same world view that has enabled
> Americans to dominate nature wherever we have
> gone. Humans are superior to nature. If we no
> longer try to conquer or eliminate wolves, we at
> least try to control them. (29)

The majestic gray wolf—skillful predator, nurturing
family member—has been misunderstood to the point of
endangerment. Fear, hatred, and the need to control the
wolf's untamable wildness created an environment in
which slaughter was not only accepted, but advocated.
There is no doubt that human beings bear responsibility
for the protection of these magnificent creatures. However,
the awe and admiration that have replaced the fear and
hatred have not removed the human need to control.
When this need to control results in tactics that are
invasive and disregardful of the wolf's own nature, the
very wildness we all seek to preserve becomes endangered.

The source is named in the text, so only the page number is cited in parentheses.

The conclusion echoes the introduction and includes a call to rethink attitudes and policies.

Berven 8

Works Cited

Askins, Renee. "Releasing Wolves from Symbolism."
Harpers April 1995: 15-17.

Begley, Sharon, with Daniel Glick. "The Return of the
Native." Newsweek 23 Jan. 1995: 53.

Bergman, Charles. Wild Echoes: Encounters with the Most
Endangered Animals in North America. New York:
McGraw-Hill, 1990.

Carpenter, Betsy. "A Precarious Return of the Wolf." U.S.
News and World Report 16 Jan. 1995: 15.

Cranford, Marcella. Personal interview. 30 Nov. 1995.

Endangered Species Act of 1973. Pub. L. 93-205. 28 Dec.
1973. Stat. 87.884. Sec. 1531.

Friends of the Forest. Ketchum, Idaho: Wolf
Education and Research Center, 1993.

Johnson, Mark. "Dual Citizenship Awarded to
Transported Wolves." International Wolf 5.2
(1995): 17.

Maughan, Ralph. "Yellowstone Wolf Update." Return to
Wolf Home Page. maugralp@cwis.isu.edu
(27 Nov. 1995).

Neimeyer, Carter. "Precapture Operation—Snaring and
Radio Collaring of 'Judas' Wolves." International
Wolf 5.2 (1995): 13.

Richardson, Valerie. "Decrying Wolves." National Review
20 Mar. 1995: 28-30.

Sources are listed in alphabetical order.

The second and third lines are indented.

An e-mail address is given for an electronic source.

APA Documentation Style

Those who write papers in the social sciences—psychology, sociology, political science, education, journalism, or public health—usually do not use the Modern Language Association (MLA) documentation style described in the previous section. Instead, they refer to the style guidelines found in the fourth edition of the *Publication Manual of the American Psychological Association* (APA). The questions and answers at topics 431 and 432 should give you the necessary guidelines for setting up your research paper. **Also ask your instructor if there are any other requirements or exceptions to the usual APA style that you should follow.**

WHAT'S AHEAD

This section provides guidelines and models for citing the sources you use in your research project, both in the text and in a list of references.

- ● **Parenthetical References**
- ● **Reference Entries: Books**
- ● **Reference Entries: Periodicals**
- ● **Reference Entries: Other Print and Nonprint Sources**
- ● **Reference Entries: Computer Network Sources**

373 Parenthetical References

In APA style, as in the MLA system, you must cite your source in parentheses in the text each time you borrow. Each of these parenthetical citations, except for personal communications such as letters, e-mail, or phone conversations, must be matched to an entry in an alphabetized list called "References" at the end of your paper. Each item in the "References" list should, in turn, be cited in the text.

374 The Form of an Entry

The APA documentation style is sometimes called the "author-date" system because both the author and the date of the publication must be mentioned in the text when you borrow from a source. Both might appear in the flow of the sentence, like this:

Six thousand children are adopted each year by people not biologically related to them, according to a 1995 article by Katherine Davis Fishman.

If either name or date does not appear in the text, it must be mentioned in parentheses at the most convenient place, like this:

According to a recent article by Katherine Davis Fishman (1995), six thousand children . . .

According to a recent article (Fishman, 1995), six thousand children . . .

Model Parenthetical References

375 One Author: Citing a Complete Work

The correct form for a parenthetical reference to a single source by a single author is *parenthesis, last name, comma, space, year of publication, parenthesis,* like this:

. . . in which the safety of waterslides has been questioned (Bonzai, 1993).

NOTE: Final punctuation should be placed outside the parentheses.

376 One Author: Citing Part of a Work

When you cite a specific part of a source, give the page number, chapter, or section, using the appropriate abbreviations (p. *or* pp., chap., *or* sec.—for other abbreviations, see 361). Always give the page number for a direct quotation.

. . . suggested that eavesdropping on cellular phones "may produce the next big public crisis in civil rights" (Tappin, 1995, p. 37).

377 One Author: More Than One Publication in the Same Year

If the same author has published two or more articles in the same year, avoid confusion by placing a small letter *a* after the first work listed in the References list, *b* after the next one, and so on. The order of such works is determined alphabetically by title.

PARENTHETICAL CITATION

Although a cure for AIDS continues to elude researchers, there is continued hope (Pennisi, 1993a, 1993b).

REFERENCES

Pennisi, E. (1993a). High-tech gene therapy to target HIV.

Science News, 144, 182.

Pennisi, E. (1993b). Take-home message: No AIDS magic bullet.

Science News, 144, 214.

378 Two to Five Authors

In APA style, all authors—up to as many as five—must be mentioned in the text citation, like this:

Perceptions of popularity can be linked to a teenager's adjustment to his or her surroundings (Reinherz, Frost, & Cohen, 1994).

NOTE: The last two authors' names are always separated by a comma and an ampersand (&) when enclosed in parentheses.

For works with more than two but less than six authors, list all the authors the first time; after that, use only the name of the first author followed by "et al." (the Latin abbreviation for *et alii,* meaning "and others"), like this:

Teenagers who feel maladjusted in some aspect of their lives are likely to think of themselves as "unpopular" (Reinherz et al., 1994).

379 Six or More Authors

If your source has six or more authors—and that sometimes happens in the social sciences—refer to the work by the first author's name followed by "et al.," both for the first reference in the text and all references after that. However, be sure to list all six or more of the authors in your References list.

380 Anonymous Book (Work)

If your source lists no author, treat the first two or three words of the title as you would an author's last name. A title of an article or chapter belongs in quotation marks, whereas the titles of books, periodicals, brochures, or reports should be underlined:

. . . the lack of trained doctors ("No Access," 1994).

381 Corporate Author

A "corporate author" is an organization, association, or agency that claims authorship of a document. Treat the name of the organization as if it were the last name of the author. If the name is long and easily abbreviated, provide the abbreviation in square brackets. Use the abbreviation without brackets in subsequent references, as follows:

First Text Citation: (National Institute of Mental Health [NIMH], 1995)

Subsequent Citations: (NIMH, 1995)

382 Indirect (or Secondary) Source

If you need to cite a source that you have found referred to in another source (i.e., a "secondary" source), mention the original source in your text. Then, in your parenthetical citation, cite the secondary source, using the words "as cited in," like this:

. . . study by Guernari (as cited in Haber, 1990).

In your References list at the end of the paper, you would write out a full citation for Haber (not Guernari).

NOTE: Citing secondary sources is taking a shortcut. You may look unscholarly if you do it often. Use primary sources when you can.

383 Two or More Works in a Parenthetical Reference

Sometimes it is necessary to lump several citations into one parenthetical reference. In that case, cite the sources as you usually would, separating the citations with semicolons. Place the citations in alphabetical order, just as they would be ordered in the References list:

The voices of today's teenagers are being heard (Atkin, 1993; Kuklin, 1993).

384 Personal Communications

If you do the kind of personal research recommended elsewhere in *Write for College,* you may have to cite personal communications that have provided you with some of your knowledge. Personal communications may be personal letters, phone calls, memos, and so forth. Since they are not published in a permanent form, they do not belong among the citations in your References list. Instead, cite them only in the text of your paper in parentheses, like this:

. . . according to M. T. Cann (personal communication, April 1, 1994).

. . . by today's standard (M. T. Cann, personal communication, April 1, 1994).

References List

QUICK GUIDE

The References section lists all of the recoverable sources you have cited in your text. It is found at the end of your research paper. Begin your list on a new page (the next page after the text) and number each page, continuing the numbering from the text. The guidelines that follow describe the form of the References list.

(1) Type the short title and page number in the upper right-hand corner, approximately one-half inch from the top of the page.

(2) Center the title, *References,* approximately one inch from the top; then double-space before the first entry.

(3) Begin each entry flush with the left margin. If the entry runs more than one line, indent additional lines approximately one-half inch (or five to seven spaces).

(4) Double-space between all lines on the References page.

(5) List each entry alphabetically by the last name of the author, or, if no author is given, by the title (disregarding *A, An,* or *The*).

(6) A basic entry for a book would be as follows:

> **Guillermo, K. S. (1993). Monkey business. Washington, DC:**
>
> **National Press Books.**

NOTE: Single-space between all items of a reference-list entry. Also note that titles are not capitalized in the usual way: only the first letter of the title (and of any subtitle) and the proper nouns are capitalized.

(7) A basic entry for a periodical (a magazine) would be as follows:

> **Murr, A. (1994, March 21). The high cost of defense.**
>
> **Newsweek, 70.**

(8) See the following pages for specific information on other kinds of entries.

Reference Entries: Books

The entries that follow illustrate the information needed to cite books, sections of a book, pamphlets, and government publications.

386 One Author

> Bode, J. (1993). <u>Death is hard to live with: Teenagers and how</u>
>
> <u>they cope with loss.</u> New York: Delacorte Press.

387 Two or More Authors

> Monroe, J. G., & Williamson, R. A. (1993). <u>First houses: Native</u>
>
> <u>American homes and sacred structures.</u> Boston: Houghton.

NOTE: Follow the first author's name with a comma; then join the two authors' names with an ampersand (&) rather than with the word "and."

388 Anonymous Book

> <u>Publication manual of the American Psychological Association</u>
>
> <u>(4th ed.).</u> (1994). Washington, DC: American Psychological
>
> Association.

NOTE: In this title, the words "American Psychological Association" are capitalized because they are a proper name. The word "manual" is not capitalized.

389 Chapter from a Book, One Author

> Rawnley, J. H. (1995). Betting on the future. In <u>Total risk: Nick</u>
>
> <u>Leeson and the fall of Barings Bank</u> (pp. 100-120). New
>
> York: HarperCollins.

390 One Volume of a Multivolume Edited Work

Sternberg, R. J. (Ed.). (1989). <u>Advances in the psychology of</u>

<u>human intelligence</u> (Vol. 5). Hillsdale, NJ: Erlbaum.

391 Single Work from an Anthology

Perkins, D. N. (1983). Why the human perceiver is a bad

machine. In J. Beck, B. Hope, & A. Rosenfeld (Eds.), <u>Human</u>

<u>and machine vision</u> (pp. 341-364). New York: Academic

Press.

NOTE: When editors' names appear in the middle of an entry, follow the usual order: initial first, surname last. Also, when inclusive page numbers are given, **do this** (pp. 341-364), not this (pp. 341-64).

392 Corporate Group Author

Amnesty International. (1989). <u>When the state kills: The death</u>

<u>penalty v. human rights.</u> New York: Author.

NOTE: The word "author" here means that the group listed as the author (i.e., "Amnesty International") is also the publisher.

393 Edited Work, One in a Series

Hunter, S., & Sundel, M. (Eds.). (1989). <u>Sage sourcebooks for the</u>

<u>human services: Vol. 7. Midlife myths: Issues, findings, and</u>

<u>practice implications.</u> Newbury Park, CA: Sage Publications.

NOTE: When a work is part of a larger series or collection, as with this example, make a two-part title of the series and the particular volume you are citing.

394 Edition Other Than the First

Bartholomae, D., & Petrosky, A. (1993). <u>Ways of reading</u> (3rd

ed.). Boston: Bedford Books.

395 Book in a Series

Detweiler, R. (1972). <u>Twayne's United States authors series: No.</u>

<u>214. John Updike.</u> Boston: Twayne.

Two or More Books by the Same Author

Wilson, I. (1987). <u>The after death experience: The physics of</u>

<u>the unphysical.</u> New York: Morrow.

Wilson, I. (1991). <u>The Columbus myth: Did men of Bristol reach</u>

<u>America before Columbus?</u> London: Simon & Schuster.

Some Rules to Follow

Here are some rules to follow when you are arranging separate entries by the same author.

- Write out the author's surname (with initials) for the first and all subsequent entries.

- When one author has written two works with different dates, the one with the earlier date is placed first.

- If two works by the same author have the same date, alphabetize the two entries by the first significant words in the titles. Place a small *a* after the date in the first entry (e.g., 1990a) and a small *b* after the date in the second entry.

- A work by a single author should be placed before an entry by the same author with one or more co-authors. If two or more entries have the same author but different co-authors, alphabetize the entries according to the last names of the second authors, etc.

- If two different authors have the same last name, alphabetize the entries according to the authors' initials.

- Use this list as a reminder:

  Simpson, B. (1989).

  Simpson, B. (1990a). <u>Cartoon trends in . . .</u>

  Simpson, B. (1990b). <u>The dysfunctional family in . . .</u>

  Simpson, B., & Groening, M. (1988).

  Simpson, B., Groening, M., & Simpson, H. (1987).

  Simpson, B., & Simpson, H. (1987).

  Simpson, H. (1990).

397 Translation

> Duby, G. (1983). The knight the lady and the priest: The making
>
> of modern marriage in medieval France. (B. Bray, Trans.).
>
> New York: Pantheon Books. (Original work published 1981)

NOTE: This reference is to a source published in English, translated from French. If you use the original French work, give the French title first, followed by the English translation of the title, not underlined, in square brackets; then cite the French publisher.

398 Article in a Reference Book, Authored

> Lynch, A. C. (1993). Russia. In Collier's encyclopedia
>
> (pp. 279-280). New York: P. F. Collier.

399 Signed Pamphlet

> Shaffer, S. M. (1986). The report card: No. 6. Gifted girls: The
>
> disappearing act [Pamphlet]. Washington, DC: The NETWORK,
>
> Mid-Atlantic Center for Sex Equity.

400 Technical or Research Report

> Comstock, G. A., & Rubinstein, E. A. (Eds.). (1971). Television
>
> and social behavior: Media content and control (Reports
>
> and Papers, Vol. 1). Rockville, MD: National Institute of
>
> Mental Health.

401 Government Publication

> National Aeronautics and Space Administration. (1989). Human
>
> spaceflight: Student activities (NASA Report No. 89-10639).
>
> Washington, DC: U.S. Government Printing Office.

402 Reprint, Different Form

> Leopold, A. (1970). A Sand County almanac, with essays on
>
> conservation from Round River. New York: Ballantine Books.
>
> (Original work published 1949 and 1953)

NOTE: This work was originally published in separate parts by Oxford University Press but was repackaged as a single work.

Reference Entries: Periodicals

The entries that follow illustrate the information and arrangement needed to cite periodicals.

403 Article in a Scholarly Journal, One Author, Consecutively Paginated

Peder, M. (1987). Rapid eye movement sleep deprivation affects

sleep similarly in castrated and noncastrated rats.

Behavioral and Neural Biology, 47, 186-196.

NOTE: Pay attention to the features of this basic reference to a scholarly journal: (1) last name and initial(s) as for a book reference, (2) year of publication, (3) title of article in lowercase, except for the first word; title not underlined or in quotations, (4) title of journal underlined, (5) volume number underlined, followed by comma, and (6) inclusive page numbers.

404 Journal Article, Paginated by Issue

Hirsch, D. (1993). Politics through action: Student services and

activism in the 90's. Change, 25 (5), 32-36.

NOTE: Following the volume number, the issue number (not underlined) is placed in parentheses only if the page numbering of the issue starts with page 1. (Some journals number pages consecutively, from issue to issue, through their whole volume year.)

405 Journal Article, Two Authors

Collins, C., & Askin, S. (1991). What about Africa?

The Progressive, 55, 39.

406 Journal Article, Three to Five Authors, Paginated by Issue

> Williard, T., Fields, D., & Cornish, E. (1991). How Americans use
>
> time. The Futurist, 35 (2), 23-27.

407 Journal Article, Six or More Authors

> Schell, B., Sherritt, H., Arthur, J., Beatty, L., Berry, L., Edmonds,
>
> L., Kaashoek, J., & Kempny, D. (1989). Development of a
>
> pornography community standard: Questionnaire results for
>
> two Canadian cities. Canadian Journal of Criminology, 29,
>
> 133-152.

NOTE: In the text, abbreviate the parenthetical citation as follows:
(Schell et al., 1989).

408 Abstract of a Scholarly Article from a Secondary Source

> Anspaugh, L., Catlin, R., & Goldman, M. (1988). The
>
> global impact of the Chernobyl reactor incident. Science,
>
> 242, 1513-1518. (From Abstracts in Anthropology, 1989,
>
> 19, Abstract No. 3082)

NOTE: When the dates of the article and the secondary-source
abstract differ, the reference in your text would cite both dates, the
original first, separated by a slash (1988/1989).

409 Review

> Mandel, H. (1994, April). Jazz communions [Review of the film
>
> The complete blue note: 1964-66 Jackie McLean sessions].
>
> Downbeat: Jazz, Blues, & Beyond, 44-45.

NOTE: If a journal or magazine does not use volume numbers, include
the month, month and day, or season designation with the year.

410 Signed Article in a Magazine

> Fishman, K. D. (1992). Problem adoptions. The Atlantic, 270
>
> (3), 37-69.

411 Unsigned Article in a Magazine

Saving the elephant, nature's great masterpiece: Banning the ivory trade is the wrong way to save Africa's vanishing elephants. (1989, July 1). <u>Economist</u> (London), 15-17.

412 Signed Newspaper Article

Trost, C. (1989, July 18). Born to lose: Babies of crack users crowd hospitals, break everybody's heart. <u>The Wall Street Journal</u>, p. 1.

NOTE: For newspapers, use "p." or "pp." before the page numbers.

413 Unsigned Newspaper Article

Angry pilot quits airliner on field as passenger suggests he is drunk. (1990, April 22). <u>The New York Times</u>, p. 20.

414 Letter to the Editor

Burnside, P. (1990, April 17). Against styrofoam packaging [Letter to the editor]. <u>The Milwaukee Journal</u>, p. 9A.

NOTE: The "A" indicates that the letter appears in the A section of the newspaper.

415 Title or Quotation Within an Article's Title

Prince, S. (1988). Dread, taboo, and "The Thing": Toward a social theory of the horror film. <u>Wide Angle, 10</u> (3), 19-29.

Reference Entries: Other Print and Nonprint Sources

416 Computer Software

Microsoft word: Version 3.0 for the Apple Macintosh [Computer word processing program]. (1987). Redmond, WA: Microsoft Corporation.

NOTE: Treat software as an unauthored work unless an individual has property rights to it.

417 Abstract of Journal Article on CD-ROM

Seyler, T. (1994). College-level studies: New memory techniques [CD-ROM]. New Century Learners, 30, 814-822. Abstract from: Platinum File: EduPLUS Item: 40-18421

418 Television or Radio Program (Episode in a Series)

Clark, K. (Narrator). (1971). The worship of nature. In M. Gill & P. Montagnon (Producers), Civilisation [Television series]. London: British Broadcasting Corporation.

419 Audiocassette

Dobson, J. C. (Speaker). (1989). Love must be tough [Audiocassette]. Waco, TX: Word Books.

420   Recording

Moon, M. (Compiler). (1980). <u>Movement soul: Sounds of the</u>

<u>freedom movement in the South 1963-1964</u> [Record].

New York: Folkways Records.

NOTE: Give the name and function of the originators or primary contributors (in this case, Moon, who is the compiler). Indicate the recording medium, in brackets, immediately following the title: compact disk, record, cassette, etc.

421   Film

John, A. (Director). (1973). <u>Solar flares burn for you</u> [Film].

London: British Film Institute.

422   Filmstrip, Slide Program, Videotape

Chaplin, C. (Director). (1978). <u>Modern times</u> [Videotape].

Farmington Hills, MI: Magnetic Video Corporation. (Original

film produced 1936)

NOTE: In text, use the parenthetical citation (Chaplin, 1936/1978). For any other medium, including audiotapes, slides, maps, charts, or artwork, follow this same order: name the principal contributor(s) or creator(s); follow with the contributor's role in parentheses; following the title, identify the medium in brackets.

423   Published Interview, Titled, No Author

Dialogue on film: Steven Spielberg [Interview with Steven

Spielberg]. (1988, June). <u>American Film, 13,</u> 12-16.

424   Published Interview, Titled, Single Author

Goodman, S. (1993, November). Experiences of a teenage

HIV-positive hemophiliac [Interview with Darren Sacks].

<u>Current Health, 20</u> (3), 8-9.

Reference Entries:
Computer Network Sources

As of January 1997, a standard for referencing information obtained on the Internet and other computer networks had not been established. APA style prefers a reference to the print form of a source, even if it is available on the "Net."

However, when you must cite the electronic form, follow the same general format for the author, date, and title elements of print sources (if you can't find the "publication" date, give the exact date of your search instead); then substitute an "availability statement" for the location and publisher information, naming the *protocol* (Internet, Telnet, FTP, etc.), the *directory,* and the *file.*

425 Elements of On-Line Journal Reference

Author, I. (year, month day). Title of article [no. of paragraphs].

Name of Periodical [On-line serial], vol. no. (issue no.).

Available: specify path

426 Article in On-Line Journal

Carter, D. L. (1995, April). A nation embraces capitalism

[11 paragraphs]. Economic Perspectives [On-line serial], 6

(18). Available FTP: 342.323.342.1 Directory: pub/baccon/

EconomicPerspectives/1995.6 File: economic

perspectives.95.6.18.capitalism.14.carter<.txt

NOTE: The title of the article is followed by the number of paragraphs [in brackets], the name of the periodical (underlined), the publication medium [On-line serial], and the volume (underlined) and issue numbers (in parentheses). The entry ends with the availability statement, omitting end punctuation.

427 On-Line Abstract of Journal Article

> Stark, M. A., & Lang, D. (1994). Brain function in comatose
>
> patients [On-line]. Biochemistry Quarterly, 12, 576-585.
>
> Abstract from: INFORM File: MedTOPS Item: 90-23561

NOTE: In this case, the publication medium [On-line] follows the title of the abstract, not the name of the journal. This means that only the abstract is found at this electronic address. The journal's name, volume no., and page numbers can be used to find the print form of the article, if necessary.

428 Electronic File on the World Wide Web

> Bowker, S. T. (12 September 1996). Cyberspace: Debate on
>
> research use [On-line]. Available WWW: http://
>
> www.ppc.new.edu/home/stb/com

429 Information Service

> Lathrop, M. (1992). Welfare reform within caring parameters.
>
> (NewsBank Document Reproduction Service N. EV 25: F15).

Important Note

Because technology is moving faster than any print source can keep up with, neither the APA nor *Write for College* handbook is able to provide a completely current section for citing network sources. For that reason, we recommend you visit our site on the World Wide Web for updates and additional information. Our address is **thewritesource.com**.

Also, because the availability of information on computer networks can change from day to day, we recommend that you print out a copy of the material you are accessing. This will enable you and your readers (instructors, especially) to check the accuracy of quotations, data, and other pertinent information cited in your paper.

Finally, while the formats for all reference examples in this section are based on the latest edition of APA's *Publication Manual* or on Li and Crane's *Electronic Style*, the particulars in each case (names, dates, electronic addresses, etc.) have been created to present as clear and complete a model entry as possible.

APA Research Paper

As with any important writing project, you may want to check your research paper against a student model. Examining the model paper included in this chapter, will give you a firsthand look at how the APA guidelines work in actual practice.

You can begin by looking over the entire paper, from the abstract to the references page to the final graph. Try to get an overview of how the paper is constructed and how the pieces fit together. Then go back and do a close reading of the abstract and opening page or two. Examine the side notes and parenthetical references. Finally, continue to refer to the model as you put your own paper together.

WHAT'S AHEAD

The chapter begins with a few commonly asked questions (and answers) related to the APA style sheet. The student model reports the results of original research conducted on the topic of social loafing. It should help you better understand how the APA style sheet works when applied to an actual paper.

- ● Questions and Answers
- ● Abstract
- ● Sample Research Paper

APA Research Paper Guidelines

Questions & Answers

Is a separate title page required?

Yes. Include your paper's title, your name, and your instructor (or school if requested) on three separate lines, double-spaced, centered, and beginning approximately one-third of the way down from the top of the page. Place your short title and page number 1 in the top right corner. (See "What about paging?" on the next page.)

What is an abstract and where does it go?

An abstract is a 100- to 150-word paragraph summarizing your research paper. (See 434 and 500.) Place your abstract on a new page and label it "Abstract" (centered); type your short title and page number 2 flush right a half inch from the top.

Are references placed in the text?

Yes. Include the author and year; for quotations, add page number.

Do you need a bibliography of sources used in the paper?

Yes. Full citations for all sources used (books, periodicals, etc.) are placed in an alphabetized list labeled "References" at the end of the paper.

Do you need an appendix?

Maybe. Ask your instructor. In student papers, charts, tables, and graphs may sometimes be incorporated at appropriate points in the text, making appendixes unnecessary.

Is the research paper double-spaced?

Yes. Do not single-space anywhere, unless your instructor allows you to do so in a table or some other circumstance for the sake of readability.

What about longer quotations?	Type quotations of 40 or more words block style (all lines flush left) five spaces in from the left-hand margin. Do indent the first lines of any additional paragraphs in the long quotation five spaces in from the quotation margin.
What about margins?	Leave a margin of at least 1 inch on all four sides (if you are binding your paper somehow, leave 1$\frac{1}{2}$" at left margin); computer users may use a justified right margin, and end-of-line hyphens are acceptable.
What about paging?	Page numbers appear at the top right margin, above the first line of text. Instead of your name, place the short title (first two or three words) either above, or five spaces to left of, each page number.
What about headings?	Headings, like an outline, show the organization of your paper and the importance of each topic. All topics of equal importance should have headings of the same level, or style. Below are the various levels of headings used in APA papers. (In most research papers, only levels 1, 3, and 4 are used. See 437.)

LEVEL 1:   Centered Uppercase and Lowercase Heading

LEVEL 2:   Centered, Underlined, Uppercase and Lowercase Heading

LEVEL 3:   Flush Left, Underlined, Uppercase and Lowercase Side Heading

LEVEL 4:   Indented, underlined, lowercase paragraph heading ending with a period.

Any other special instructions?	Always inquire whether your school or department has special requirements that may take precedence over these.

Running head: SOCIAL LOAFING

Social Loafing:

Individual vs. Group Performance

Merrick Gulker and Libby Kragt

Dordt College

Put 5 spaces between running head and number.

Running head (abbreviated title in uppercase letters) typed flush left

Title, authors, and school name typed in uppercase and lowercase letters

The abstract summarizes the problem studied, participants, methods used, results, and conclusions.

Abstract

This study examined the effects of social loafing, the tendency for individuals to expend less effort when working with others than when working alone. By testing participants' work individually and in groups, the study tried to determine changes in productivity from one setting to the other. Participants (27 college students aged 17-20; 13 men, 14 women) completed a word-construction task in both an individual and group situation. Each participant's success at forming words out of the letters of a given word was measured twice: (1) while working alone and (2) while working in a group. Results showed significant evidence of social loafing. In addition, males were found to have a higher tendency toward social loafing than females. These results indicate that business managers and teachers should (1) think hard about whether to assign a task to an individual or to a group and (2) take measures to combat social loafing.

Center the title one inch from the top. Double-space throughout.

Social Loafing:

Individual vs. Group Performance

The writers open with a question that introduces the topic.

In what ways do individuals perform differently when working alone and when working in a group? Psychologists have long been interested in this question, and one answer they have found is the social loafing theory. This study tests the workings of this theory.

"Social loafing" is defined and examples of past research are cited.

Social loafing, the tendency for individuals to expend less effort when working with others than when working alone, has been studied because of its practical importance for daily life (Karau & Williams, 1993). For example, employers and managers need to know if it is better to assign projects to teams or to individuals: understanding group dynamics and social loafing could help them make these decisions. Educators also could benefit from insights into social loafing because they also make decisions about assigning group versus individual work.

What, then, has the research about social loafing shown? Basically, in a group setting, social loafing decreases individuals' productivity (Meyers, 1993). Much of the research has tried to get at the reasons for this drop. In one of the earliest studies done on individual versus group problem solving, G. B. Watson tested subjects individually and in a group setting on a word-construction task. In analyzing the results, he concluded that one group member took leadership and did most of the work (as cited in Shaw, 1976).

One cause of social loafing is identified.

A more recent study added fear and reliance to the list of possible causes. According to Paulus and Dzindolet (1993), subject apprehension decreases productivity. Because group members worry about how their ideas will be received, they withhold those ideas. In addition, these researchers argue, individuals may free-ride in interactive groups—counting on other group members to pick up the slack. Paulus and Dzindolet came to these conclusions by setting up an experiment in which participants were

Cause number 2

Cause number 3

instructed to brainstorm in a group or individually. The number and level of contributions were compared between the two environments.

Cause number 4

Another cause of decreased productivity in a group setting can be found in motivation (or lack of it). By combining some of the results from different studies in social loafing, Karau and Williams (1993) claimed that motivation is an underlying factor in individual and group performance. In other words, what an individual thinks of the process, himself, and other group members affects the individual's motivation to work at the task.

Researchers have tried to uncover not only the causes behind decreased productivity but also the best ways to study social loafing. For example, Harkins and Szymanski (1989) worked to identify ways of measuring the social loafing effect. As an example, they had subjects (both individually and in a group) identify as many uses for objects as possible. They claim that to evaluate the loafing effect, the experimenters must get two pieces of information: some measure of output (e.g., how many uses a person generated) and a standard against which this output can be compared (e.g., the number of uses generated by others in the group). In other words, the number of uses generated by others serves as an example of a social standard.

The writers give examples of how researchers test for social loafing and what is part of an effective test.

The writers summarize their study and anticipate the outcome.

In our study, then, we shall evaluate the loafing effect by gathering and analyzing data related to subject output in an individual and group setting. Taking into account the various factors affecting social loafing, we are led to predict that individuals will put forth less effort in a group situation than if they were working on their own. More specifically, we propose that the participants in our study will generate more words working alone than in a group because of decreased motivation, free-riding, apprehension, or the dynamics of leading and following.

Method

Participants

The participants in this study were 27 students (13 males and 14 females) from an introductory psychology class who received course credit for their participation. Their ages ranged from 17 to 20 years. Seven additional students, also receiving course credit, were used as secretaries but were not measured on the key variable. The selection process was based on students' voluntary sign-up.

Measures/Instruments

Participants were required to form as many words as possible using the letters in a word that had been given to them (such as the word "painters"). The words formed had to be at least three letters in length and could not be proper nouns. The participants had 3 minutes to complete the task. They were first tested individually and then in groups of 3. The number of words generated by the subjects in the individual setting was compared to the number of words they each generated in the group. A different word was used for each testing round.

Procedure

Testing took place over 2 days, and each day's testing fell into two parts—an individual stage and a group stage.

Individual stage. We had 15 participants and 5 secretaries come in on the first day of testing. During the first part of the experiment, secretaries sat on the side of the room and watched as each participant was assigned a subject number and then given a sheet of paper (face down) that contained a word. Then the participants were given a brief introduction and were read a set of instructions explaining what they should do with the word. At this point, participants were told to turn their papers over and work individually for the next 3 minutes to find and write

---

Headings and subheadings show the paper's organization.

The experiment's method is carefully and accurately described.

Using subheadings, transitions, and numbers, the writers break down the experiment into stages and steps.

down as many words as possible using the letters in the word on their page. After 3 minutes elapsed, we collected the papers and set them aside for later tabulation of the data.

    Group stage. The second part of the procedure followed these steps:

1. We divided the 15 participants randomly into 5 groups of 3. (No effort was made to control the gender mix of the groups.)
2. One secretary was randomly assigned to each group.
3. We gave a new word on a sheet of paper (face down) to each group's secretary.
4. When signaled, the secretaries turned the sheet over so that all group members could see the word.
5. For 3 minutes, group members collaborated to make words out of the letters in the word provided. As they called out words, the secretaries recorded them.
6. After 3 minutes expired, the secretaries were instructed to write an individual's subject number next to each word the individual produced.
7. This group process was repeated a second time with a new word.
8. All papers were then collected and the participants were debriefed on what had just occurred.

    On the second day, the 12 participants who had not tested on the first day completed the same procedures as the group of 15. For purposes of counterbalancing, however, we reversed the order of the test, doing part two and then part one.

    After the data was tabulated and the group scores were averaged, we made comparisons between the number of words that each individual generated while working alone with the number this person generated while working in a group.

Attention is shown to control features.

The writers follow APA guidelines for using numbers and numerals.

The writers summarize their data and statistical analysis, using two paragraphs to describe their two main conclusions.

Results

Test results lead us to conclude that social loafing strongly influences individual performance within groups. Comparing the individual mean (29.04 words generated and a Standard Deviation of 9.06) and the group mean (13.3 words generated and a Standard Deviation of 5.5) produces a t-value of 14.56 and a significance level less than .001.

Interestingly, gender also was an influential factor in individual and group performance. On an individual basis, the female mean was significantly higher than the male mean, 32.43 words generated to 25.39 words generated, respectively. These numbers, in turn, create a t-value of 2.16 and a .041 significance level. In addition, within their groups, individual females were more productive. The average mean of females within the group setting was 15.61 words generated, whereas the male average mean within groups was 10.81 words generated, producing a t-value of 2.48 and a significance level of .02. (See Figure 1.)

"See Figure 1" indicates that a figure (graph, photograph, chart, or drawing) is contained in the paper.

Discussion

In our experiment, we tried to learn the effect that social loafing has on an individual's word-production performance within a group. The experiment results support our hypothesis. When the mean score for all 27 individuals working in groups is multiplied by 3, the output result for three people is approximately 39.9 words generated. However, when the mean score for the 27 individuals working alone is multiplied by 3, the output for three people is approximately 87 words generated. These numbers show that the productivity of individuals working alone is approximately 29 words in 3 minutes (87 divided by 3), but the number drops to approximately 13 words in 3 minutes (39.9 divided by 3) when they work together.

The writers present and interpret statistical findings.

Social loafing's effect, as shown in these numbers, is

**Implications
of the
study are
suggested.**

important for people working in business and education.
Both managers and teachers would benefit from discovering ways of counteracting social loafing and maintaining
the individual's performance level within a group setting.

In an attempt to minimize social loafing, Supervisory
Management, a publication of the American Management
Association, gave suggestions for limiting social loafing's
effect on work performance. Things such as setting clear
assignments with due dates, inviting members of management to attend team sessions, alerting the team that you
will be reporting on team progress on a regular basis, and
meeting with each team member to discuss his/her performance—all make group work more productive ("How to
Prevent," 1995).

**The writers
qualify the
second
conclusion of
their study.**

The second major result of our study—gender differences—may be explained by the nature of the experiment.
The significant difference in means between females and
males may have resulted from the test's focus on verbal
skills, an area in which females have been known to excel
(Maccoby & Jacklin, 1974). Although we managed to find
a significant difference in the performance of men versus
women, previous studies have not provided evidence for
this difference (e.g., Herschel, 1994). This area, however,
deserves further research.

**The writers
address
possible
problem
areas in the
experiment's
design and
recommend
directions for
further
research.**

Finally, future research would have to address potential design problems, especially the measuring methods
used in the group setting: (1) using a fallible secretary to
record and give credit for words, and (2) equating individual productivity with words said out loud. In order to
measure how the individual productivity variable is
affected in the group setting, a better method of recording
and measuring individual work in the group would have to
be designed.

References

Harkins, S. G., & Szymanski, K. (1989). Social loafing and group evaluation. Journal of Personality and Social Psychology, 56, 834-841.

Herschel, R. (1994). The impact of varying gender composition on group brainstorming performance in a GSS environment. In Computers-in-Human-Behavior [ERIC].

How to prevent social loafing on teams. (1995, Sept.). Supervisory Management, 40, 1.

Karau, S. J., & Williams, K. D. (1993). Social loafing: A meta-analytical review and theoretical integration. Journal of Personality and Social Psychology, 65, 681-706.

Maccoby, E., & Jacklin, C. (1974). The psychology of sex differences. Stanford, CA: Stanford University Press.

Meyers, D. G. (1993). Social psychology (4th ed.). New York: McGraw-Hill.

Paulus, P. B., & Dzindolet, M. T. (1993). Social influence processes in group brainstorming. Journal of Personality and Social Psychology, 64, 575-586.

Shaw, M. E. (1976). Group dynamics: The psychology of small group behavior (2nd ed.). New York: McGraw-Hill.

All works referred to in the paper appear on the reference page, listed alphabetically.

Figure Caption

Figure 1. Social loafing: a comparison of male vs. female
participation showing group vs. individual averages.
Note. From "How to Prevent Social Loafing on Teams,"
1995, Supervisory Management, 40, p. 1.

Figures or any illustrations (graphs, photographs, drawings) other than tables are numbered consecutively in the order that they are first mentioned in the text.

PLACEMENT OF FIGURES

Be certain to check with your instructor about specific requirements concerning the placement of figures. They are sometimes
placed at the end of the paper (as shown here) or at the appropriate
places in the text. For instance, in this paper, the "Social Loafing"
graph would appear on a separate page immediately following page 7,
where it was first mentioned. The figure caption would be typed
beneath the graph.

PLACEMENT OF TABLES

Tables (none shown) are displays of numbers and data arranged
in columns and rows. You should number tables consecutively
throughout the text and insert them either in the text or in the appendix. Introduce a table by typing "Table" plus its number flush left
(example: Table 1). Skip two lines and insert the table. (Tables are not
listed on the Figure Caption page.)

A graph, referred to as "Figure 1" on page 7, includes a clear title and "graphic" information.

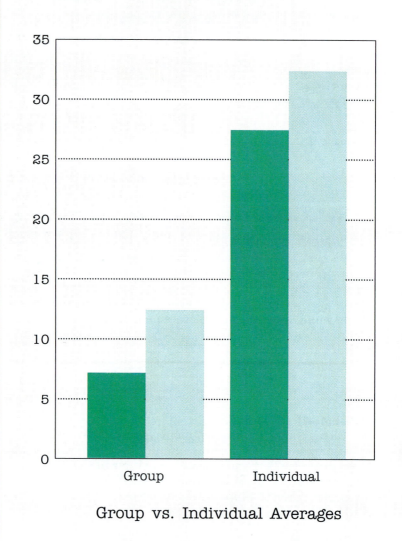

Social Loafing

Male vs. Female Participation

Group vs. Individual Averages

■ Males   ▢ Females

The running head and the figure number (Social Loafing/ Figure 1) is printed on the **back side**—not on the graph itself.

Searching for Information

Have you ever waited until the last minute to write a paper or finish an important project? Then, late Sunday afternoon, it's off to the library or into an encyclopedia or computer program to find some quick, ready-made information. At least that's the plan. It worked last time. But what if you can't find the information you're looking for? What if the library yields no sources, the encyclopedia article is too short, and your computer isn't able to access the files you need? Then what?

Maybe a better approach would be to take some time now—with no deadlines staring you in the face—to learn where and how to find the right information quickly and efficiently.

WHAT'S AHEAD

This section of your handbook will help you understand better how to locate and evaluate information, assuring you of a more successful result the next time you're faced with an important long-term project.

- Using the Library
- Locating Books and References
- Finding Articles in Periodicals
- Evaluating Information

SEARCHING **tips**

1. **Give yourself enough time.** Other people may check out the books you need, or you may need to get them through an interlibrary loan. Computer networks shut down or get backed up, and Web pages can take longer to download than you'd like—especially if you don't have a fast modem.

2. **Narrow your search to a few key questions.** Be realistic about how much ground you can cover.

3. **Don't get sidetracked.** When you're studying the fall of the Russian czars, for example, don't get sidetracked by a description of Rasputin and delve into a study of hypnosis.

4. **Be aware of the limits of your resources.** Information in books may be out-of-date. On-line information may be more current, but it may lack the historical perspective you need.

5. **Use the resources you find to discover more resources.** One source will often point the way to another source of equal or greater value. Pay attention to books, articles, and the names of experts that you find mentioned in a reliable source.

6. **Learn what the technology can and cannot do.** Working on-line or with a CD-ROM takes a certain amount of expertise. Be patient; get past the frustration point. Take the time to learn how to make technology work for you.

7. **Get to know the right people.** Information specialists are everywhere—in the library, the computer lab, the classroom, and on the Internet. Look for the experts who can help, make them your allies, and work with them respectfully.

8. **Develop lists of often-used phone numbers and e-mail addresses.** If you've collected them on little scraps of paper, transfer them to one central location or book.

9. **"Bookmark" useful Web sites.** Include reference works and academic resources related to your major.

10. **Organize your sources for maximum efficiency.** Have some key resources in your dorm room—dictionary, thesaurus, writing handbook, paper files, and electronic file folders if you own a computer.

Using the Library

Libraries are information centers that not only store information in a multitude of forms but provide a variety of research services and access to information sources around the globe.

The Basic Components

Libraries are changing every day. However, a college library is made up of some basic components that remain the same.

Librarians: Librarians are information experts who manage the library's materials, guide you to resources, and help you perform on-line, CD-ROM, and database searches.

Catalogs: Catalogs are databases that guide you to the materials you need. Most library catalogs are computerized databases, although manual card catalogs still exist alone or alongside computerized catalogs in some places. In addition, most large college and university libraries catalog materials according to the Library of Congress classification system, whereas most public high schools and local libraries use the Dewey decimal system.

Collections: A library's collection is all the materials it contains. It varies greatly from one library to the next, but the collection usually includes the following:

- **books**—fiction and nonfiction

- **periodicals**—magazines, journals, newspapers, microfilm, CD-ROM's

- **reference materials**—directories, indexes, handbooks, encyclopedias, abstracts, and almanacs

- **audiovisual and multimedia materials**—videotapes, CD's, audiotapes, microfilm, laser discs

- **special collections**—government and historical documents, local history, artwork, rare books, artifacts, archive materials

- **computer resources**—the catalog itself, connections to the campuswide network and to interlibrary loan, on-line databases, Internet access, and links with document delivery services

Using Information Services

Learning to use your campus information network—from computer labs to libraries—will make your course work and research more productive. Here are some suggestions for getting the most from the information services at your school.

USE YOUR LIBRARIAN'S EXPERTISE

Ask the librarians for maps and guides to library resources. Most libraries provide tours to acquaint new users with what they have available. Take the tour. Become familiar with everything the library offers.

- **Become an expert user of the computerized catalog.** The library may have a new system or one that you are not familiar with. The librarians can save you hours of time by showing you how to search for items efficiently.
- **Learn what special services are available.** Locate library terminals and work-stations. Find out about on-line help and tutorials. Learn how you can access the campus's network. (Most colleges have a computer network. Make sure you know exactly what you can access and how to do it.)
- **Ask for help with library resources.** A librarian can assist you in finding an article on a specific subject, working the microfilm machine, doing a key-word search, etc.
- **Put books that you need on reserve** or ask for an interlibrary loan. If you need to do a database search, make an appointment with a librarian.
- **Call the library.** If you are working on a project and need a simple fact, call the reference desk for the answer.

 Check out your college's home page on the Internet. You'll be surprised at all the information it contains, as well as all the additional information it can lead you to.

CHECK OUT AN INDEX AND THE CD-ROM COLLECTION

Learn to use indexes and the CD-ROM collection to find articles you would not otherwise have available to you.

- **Explore the computerized index.** Which print indexes have been collected in this index? What years do they cover? What information do the citations give you?
- **Explore a general index** such as one of the following: the *Readers' Guide to Periodical Literature* (general-interest magazines), *Business Periodicals Index* (or another index specific to your discipline), the *New York Times Index* (or another specific newspaper index).
- **Browse through the library's CD-ROM collection.** Become familiar with general reference CD-ROM's, but also learn which specialized CD-ROM's are useful for doing research in your major.

The Computerized Catalog

A computerized catalog makes searching for books, videos, and other material quick and easy. Here is a sample citation.

Author: Farr, Michael J. **1**
Title: **2** America's top technical and trade
              jobs/ 2nd ed.
Published: Indianapolis, IN: JIST, c 1994. **3**
Description: 1v.: ill.; 28 cm. **4**
Subjects: **5** Labor market--United States.
              Employment forecasting--United
              States.
              Occupations--United States.
              Vocational guidance--United States.
              Job hunting--United States.
Status: **6** Due on 3/27/97
Call number: 331.702 AME **7**
Location: General collection **8**

1 Author's name
2 Title heading
3 Publisher and copyright date
4 Descriptive information
5 Subject heading(s)
6 Library status
7 Call number
8 Location information

Classification Systems

In the Library of Congress classification system used in most colleges, the call number begins with a letter rather than a number. The letters used in this system represent the 20 subject classes; each is listed below. The corresponding Dewey decimal number is listed in a separate column.

THE LIBRARY OF CONGRESS AND DEWEY DECIMAL SYSTEMS

LC Category		Dewey Decimal	LC Category		Dewey Decimal
A	General Works	000-099	K	Law	340-349
B	Philosophy	100-199	L	Education	370-379
	Psychology	150-159	M	Music	780-789
	Religion	200-299	N	Fine Arts	700-799
C	History:		P	Language and	400-499
	Auxiliary Sciences	910-929		Literature	800-899
D	History: General and		Q	Science	500-599
	Old World	930-999	R	Medicine	610-619
E-F	History: American	970-979	S	Agriculture	630-639
G	Geography	910-919	T	Technology	600-699
	Anthropology	571-573	U	Military Science	355-359, 623
	Recreation	700-799	V	Naval Science	359, 623
H	Social Sciences	300-399	Z	Bibliography and	010-019
J	Political Science	320-329		Library Science	020-029

Keyword Searching

Because an on-line catalog is a computerized database, it offers you tremendous power to find material through a technique called *keyword searching.* How does it work?

◉ By following commands or choosing items from menus, you can search a catalog's entries to see which ones have a particular word—an author's name, a word in a title, or a word that describes its subject matter.

◉ In a few seconds, the computer will tell you how many entries contain that keyword. You can then look at each entry to see how useful the material might be and to get the call number.

For example, if you want information on the fish industry, you could type "fisheries" for your keyword and get a list of 15 books that are either about fisheries or have the word in the title.

Broadening or Narrowing a Search

To further control your search, combine keywords using commands such as *or, and,* and *not.*

BROADENING A SEARCH

To broaden a search, use "or." For example, for works on modern fish farming and on traditional fisheries, you might type "fisheries **or** aquaculture" and get 25 entries with either keyword in them.

NARROWING A SEARCH

To narrow a search, use "and" or "not" to limit your options. Sometimes too many possibilities make your research difficult. For example, typing "fisheries **and** oil spills" would give you only entries that contain both keywords—and far fewer entries than if you had typed "or." Similarly, if you typed "oil spills **not** *Exxon Valdez*," you would get entries on oil spills, but not entries including the *Exxon Valdez* spill.

So, how do you choose your keywords? You may refer to the on-line catalog instructions, ask a librarian, or look at the Library of Congress subject headings listed in a book on the same subject.

Boolean Characters for Broadening or Narrowing a Search

AND:	find records that contain more than one term / **bats and radar**
OR:	find records that contain either term / **teen or adolescent**
NOT:	exclude records that contain a term / **oil spills not Exxon Valdez**
SAME:	specifies that the related terms be in the same field (title, subject) / **browning same elizabeth**
WITH:	helps you find terms near each other / **blues with guitar**

NOTE: Each search cataloging system may vary in exactly how it uses these Boolean characters. Some search systems simply use ordinary phrases.

Locating Books and References

To locate a book, a video, or other reference item, you need to find where it is shelved. To do that, you'll need its call number. The call number refers to the classification scheme used to organize materials in the library's collection.

Using the Library of Congress Classification System

This system, used by most colleges and universities, combines letters and numbers to specify a book's broad subject area, topic, and authorship or title. To find a book or a video, or other items, use both alphabetical and numerical order. Here is a sample call number for *Arctic Refuge: A Vanishing Wilderness?*, a video produced by the Audubon Society, Turner Broadcasting, and PBS:

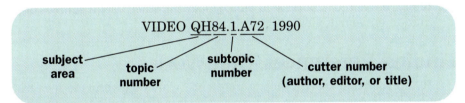

VIDEO QH84.1.A72 1990

subject area — topic number — subtopic number — cutter number (author, editor, or title)

To find this video in the library, first note the tag VIDEO. This word, though not part of the actual call number, is a locator telling you to find this item in the library's video collection. Once you've located the videos, follow the core elements of the call number one at a time:

1. Find the section on natural history, the "QH" designation.

2. Once you've located "QH" items, follow the numbers until you reach "84."

3. Then, within the "84" items, find those with the subtopic "1."

4. Use the cutter "A72" to locate the book alphabetically with "A" and numerically with "72."

NOTE: In the Library of Congress system, pay careful attention to subject-area letters, topic numbers, and subtopic numbers: Q98 comes before QH84; QH84 before QH8245; QH84.A72 before QH84.1.A72.

SOUND advice Take time to explore those areas of the classification scheme that are related to your major. Becoming familiar with how these materials are organized will improve your ability to do research.

Finding the Right Book

When you locate a book you think might be helpful, give it a quick scan before spending any real time reading it.

1. Check out the information in the front. The original publication date can tell you if the information is current. Library of Congress subject headings can tell you if the book will be useful to you or not. The preface will also give you a good overview.

2. Scan the book. Examine the table of contents for the specific topics you need. Look for headings and subheadings within chapters and read introductory paragraphs and summaries.

3. Search the index for the topics you need. Determine whether there are plenty of pages on your topic or just a few.

4. Look through the appendix and glossary at the back of the book for important information—statistics, tables, graphs, definitions.

5. Check the author's notes and bibliography for other useful sources of information on your topic.

Finding References That Work

Whatever your specific needs, reference works can provide a myriad of details about many subjects. The key is learning how to get the most out of these materials without spending too much time in the process.

1. Learn to locate them. Find the reference section in your college library, and check out those works related to your major. Buy reference works that you will use regularly, and know how to locate useful reference tools on the Internet.

2. Use the handiest form of the reference work. A specific reference tool often comes in many forms—book, CD-ROM, on-line, etc. Use the form that is effective and efficient for your purposes.

3. Discover the work's structure. To find the information you want, look at the structure of the reference. Check how items are organized, look for instructions at the beginning, and use the index.

4. Understand what the work covers. Each reference work contains a limited amount of information. Check those limits by looking for these at the beginning:

- the date the reference work was published
- the time frame covered (July 1995 to June 1996)
- specific information details (For example, the *Dictionary of American Negro Biography* contains summaries of the lives of prominent African-Americans who are no longer living.)

Using Yearbooks, Almanacs, Atlases, . . .

Ready to do some number crunching? Some globe-trotting (with your fingers doing the trotting)? Some name-dropping? First practice up on reading charts, tables, and graphs; then turn to books or on-line databases like these:

Yearbooks cover major developments on specific topics during the previous year.

> *Statistical Abstract of the United States: The National Data Book* provides statistical information about the U.S., from population figures to data on geography, social trends, politics, employment, and business.

Almanacs are regular (usually annual) publications filled with diverse facts and statistics. Originally, almanacs were used as community calendars and information books. Today they're broader in scope but function the same way.

> *The World Almanac and Book of Facts* presents information on many topics: business, politics, history, religion, social programs, sports, education, and the year's major events.

Atlases are just a bunch of maps, right? Well, they include maps, but they also contain data on countries, transportation, climate, and more.

> *The Rand McNally Commercial Atlas and Marketing Guide* includes maps of the U.S. and its major cities as well as information on transportation and communication, economics, and population.

> *Street Atlas USA on CD-ROM* allows you to call up street maps for any place in the United States. Are you heading for Helena, Montana? Hannibal, Missouri? Call it up and print out a map of the city.

Directories are lists of people and groups. (Directories are now widely used on the Internet.)

> *The National Directory of Addresses and Telephone Numbers* provides nationwide coverage of companies, associations, schools, etc.

Guides and Handbooks offer guidelines and models for exploring a topic, a program, an area of knowledge, or a profession.

> *Occupational Outlook Handbook,* published by the Department of Labor, explores the job market—where jobs are and might be and how to prepare for the workplace.

Indexes contain an alphabetical listing of topics and their location in the book.

> The *Readers' Guide to Periodical Literature* lists articles (published on specific topics during specific time periods) and explains where to find them.

Finding Articles in Periodicals

The best tools for locating articles in periodicals (magazines and journals) are the journal indexes that can be found in the reference or periodical section of the library. The most widely used journal index is the *Readers' Guide to Periodical Literature*. Some libraries also carry a CD-ROM version of this index. Other libraries carry a similar computer index called the *General Periodicals Index*.

Readers' Guide to Periodical Literature

If you are looking for information on a current topic, the *Readers' Guide* will direct you to specific magazine articles. It will also help you find magazine articles from years ago.

LOCATING ARTICLES

Because there are thousands of periodicals, finding one article sounds difficult. But you can do it if you follow these steps:

Discover what article you want by using an index:
- a hard-copy version of the *Readers' Guide to Periodical Literature* or an index that lists periodicals on one specific subject
- an on-line catalog version of the hard-copy *Readers' Guide* or several indexes combined in one database
- a CD-ROM or on-line database that gives you either whole articles or lists of articles to look up

Check the library's current list of periodicals.

Look especially at the dates of the issues contained in the library and note the form of the periodical (hard copy or microfilm).

Locate and get the article.

You might have to give your librarian a call slip listing the periodical's title, date, and volume so that he or she can get it for you. Or you might have to get the periodical yourself by checking in the periodical collection.

A CLOSER LOOK AT THE *READERS' GUIDE*

- Articles are arranged alphabetically by subject and author; the title of the article is listed under each of these two entries.
- Each subject entry is divided into subtopics whenever there are several articles on the same subject listed together.
- The *Readers' Guide* is cross-referenced, giving other subject headings where you may find additional articles on related topics.

Sample *Readers' Guide* Page

"SEE ALSO" REFERENCE

PAGE NUMBER(S)

VOLUME

NAME OF MAGAZINE

NAME OF AUTHOR

SUBTOPIC

DATE

"SEE" CROSS-REFERENCE

TITLE OF ARTICLE

SUBJECT ENTRY

AUTHOR ENTRY

ENVIRONMENTAL MOVEMENT
See also
Conservation of resources
Environmental associations
Industry and the environment
Minorities and the environment
Field observations [interview with W. Berry] J. Fisher-Smith. il por *Orion* v12 p50-9 Aut '93
Pacific Northwest
Reconciling rural communities and resource conservation [Pacific Northwest; with editorial comment by Timothy O'Riordan] K. Johnson. bibl f il *Environment* v35 p inside cover, 16-20+ N '93
Vancouver Island (B.C.)
Brazil of the North? [battle over logging in Vancouver Island's Clayoquot Sound area] C. A. White. il *Canada and the World* v59 p8-9 S '93

ENVIRONMENTAL POLICY
See also
Air pollution—Laws and regulations
Genetic research—Environmental aspects
Industry and the environment
The compensation game [taking cases] F. Williams. il por *Wilderness* v57 p28-33 Fall '93
Images of home [population and the environment] C. A. Douglas. il *Wilderness* v57 p10-22 Fall '93
Unfunded federal environmental mandates. P. H. Abelson. *Science* v262 p1191 N 19 '93
International aspects
The best environment of 1993. il *Time* v143 p74 Ja 3 '94
Public opinion
Of global concern: results of the Health of the planet survey [cover story] R. E. Dunlap and others. bibl f il *Environment* v35 p6-15+ N '93
United States
See Environmental policy

ENVIRONMENTAL RACISM *See* Minorities and the environment

ENVIRONMENTAL REGULATIONS *See* Environmental policy

ENVIRONMENTAL SYSTEMS PRODUCTS INC.
Playing favorites [L. Weicker fires L. Goldberg over Connecticut state contract for auto emissions testing] C. Byron. il pors *New York* v27 p12-13 Ja 10 '94

ENVIROTEST SYSTEMS CORPORATION
Playing favorites [L. Weicker fires L. Goldberg over Connecticut state contract for auto emissions testing] C. Byron. il pors *New York* v27 p12-13 Ja 10 '94

EPHRON, NORA
about
Sleepless in Seattle's Nora Ephron [interview] C. Krupp. il por *Glamour* v91 p147-8 Ag '93

EPIDEMICS
See also
AIDS (Disease)

Evaluating Information

Once you've found what you think is the right information for your particular needs, put it to the test. On the surface, all information looks the same. It all seems to be valid and trustworthy. But not all information is created or recorded equally. It's your responsibility to sort it out before presenting it to your readers. The questions below should help you evaluate all information, no matter who or where it comes from.

Quality Control

1. Is the information current? A book on computers written five years ago may be ancient history by now. But a book on Abraham Lincoln could be 40 years old and still be the best source on the market.

   NOTE: If your information comes from a Web site, when was it created and when was it last updated? Are the hyperlinks in the site current?

2. Is the information complete? Try to see the whole picture. If you're given data from an experimental group, you should be given results from a control group for comparison. If your source shows you highlights, ask to see the "lowlights," too.

3. Is the information accurate? Mistakes can result from bad research design, misinterpreting results, poor reporting, computer goofs, or even problems in fax transmission. (Unfortunately, mistakes don't come with little red flags that say "Oops." You've got to detect them the old-fashioned way: by thinking about them.)

4. Is the source an expert? An expert is someone who has mastered a whole subject area, someone that everyone regards as an authority. Be careful. When experts go outside their fields of expertise, they may not have much more authority than the fire extinguisher. Be especially cautious in evaluating information on the Internet. While there is an incredible amount of information available, there's also a ton of misinformation, and many documents are prepared by people whose only expertise is knowing how to create a Web page.

5. Is your source biased? A "bias" means, literally, a tilt toward one side. Biased sources—such as political "spin doctors," TV infomercials, or corporate spokespersons—have everything to gain by slanting facts and emotions their way. Keep your eyes open for obviously beneficial connections between authors, financial backers, and the points of view shared. Put two and two together.

Slanted language or distorted statistics reveal many sorts of biases to watch out for: bias toward (or against) a region of the country, a political party, males or females, a certain race or ethnic group, a certain religion.

Using Electronic Sources

"Get informed. Be informed. Stay informed." This refrain rings through much of life these days—including college life. We find ourselves in an information age dominated by an information explosion fueled by new technologies. To do well in college, you'll need to understand how these technologies work—how you can find them, access them, and put them to use in your day-to-day tasks.

As a student, you already use a computer to put together your papers and reports. And some of you may already use your computer to network with other sources to gather information for projects. But there's more to it than just grabbing the first piece of information you find out there. You need to find the best possible information, the latest information, the most reliable information.

WHAT'S AHEAD

This section of your handbook will help you become "technology literate." You'll get the latest information on using computer networks, on-line services, the Internet, and CD-ROM's, so that you can tap into the best possible sources of information for each task you face.

- ● Computer Networks
- ● Traveling on the Information Superhighway
- ● Using CD-ROM's

Computer Networks

You already know that computers can be a valuable source of information. Most schools and businesses these days could hardly operate without them. And, if you've ever used a computer network, you were probably hooked on it immediately. So much interesting and useful information is made immediately available to you. The material that follows should help get you up to speed on how you can use a PC to connect to computers and databases in your community and around the globe.

Networking from Your PC

Now that personal computers are finding their way into more schools, offices, and homes than ever before, nearly everyone has access to a computer network of one kind or another. PC's open up a world of news, databases, conversation, and more. Imagine using your personal computer to do the following:

◉ Gather information on upcoming concerts, exhibits, and events of personal interest or educational value.

◉ Send out a piece of writing and get reactions from instructors and students from around the world.

◉ Explore the collections of thousands of schools, agencies, and companies, and copy selected documents to your PC for viewing or to print out.

Think of computer networking as just another program on your PC, only this one doesn't process words or crunch numbers. Instead, it calls other computers and exchanges data with them.

The Internet

The Internet allows millions of computer networks to share information with each other. When you arrive at college, you'll be given an account on your school's computer network connecting you to the campus library, an on-line student directory, and other local resources. You will also have access to the Internet and be able to turn your desktop PC into a global library.

First, however, you'll need to understand how the system works and what tools you'll need to "surf the Net." On the following two pages, you'll find summaries and guidelines to help you move successfully through the Internet and its various components.

Before using the Internet as a serious research tool, consult 355-360 and 425-429 for information about citing electronic sources. You will want to carefully document where you found your information in order to prepare your bibliographic references.

Electronic Mail (E-Mail): E-mail gives network users a channel for sending messages to electronic mailboxes. Your account should come with instructions on using e-mail to communicate with people on your local network and/or over the Internet.

- An Internet e-mail address consists of the name (or initials) of the person you are mailing to, followed by the @ ("at") symbol, followed by the name of the computer they're on (**Example:** president@whitehouse.gov).
- You must enter an e-mail address exactly as it is given to you, otherwise your e-mail will "bounce" (return to sender), or be sent to the wrong location.

NOTE: Keep paper and pencil handy so that you can jot down e-mail addresses. Some search tools or on-line services have "white pages" for searching out names and addresses. Usually, however, the best way to find out someone's e-mail address is to ask them for it.

World Wide Web (WWW): One of the most exciting and popular uses of the Internet is to display words, pictures, sounds, and video by a complex technology called the World Wide Web, also known as the "Web."

- Millions of Web "pages" are available for browsing. They are called pages because Web technology lets pictures and text be arranged in a way that resembles pages from a book.
- The Web also uses "hypertext links" that connect WWW pages to one another. You might be reading a Web page about travel in Africa, and by selecting the word "Zaire" be instantly switched to a full-color map of that African nation.
- There are special WWW pages that allow you to search the entire Internet according to keywords you type in. You can then go to any of the Web pages that come up as a result of your search.

File Transfer Protocol (FTP): You can use the Internet's FTP tool to transfer whole files, such as computer programs or informational documents, anywhere in the world.

- Many files are available for anonymous FTP. You log in to another computer over the Internet, using "anonymous" as your log-in name and typing in your e-mail address instead of a password. Anonymous FTP was set up to allow a free exchange of information between all persons with Internet access.
- Transferring files over the Internet can be done easily through most WWW home pages. Instead of typing in a WWW location, type the FTP location.
- Using the search tools available on the WWW allows you to search the entire Internet for files available for FTP. Like a computerized card catalog, it uses keywords you type in to locate specific files.

Usenet News: Electronic libraries are great to have, but what if you need a librarian? That's why there's Usenet News, a collection of thousands of electronic bulletin boards on topics ranging from astronomy to motorcycles to personal finance to Zoroastrianism. Millions of people read Usenet "newsgroups," as these bulletin boards are called, every week.

- It's best to get acquainted with a newsgroup before posting any new messages to it. Look around for a frequently asked questions file (FAQ) for the newsgroup—most have one. FAQ's are often chock-full of useful information, and if you're interested enough in the subject, they are worth downloading to your PC.

- Remember that messages on Usenet are like having a conversation with a friend—not like reading an encyclopedia. Check things you read in newsgroups against other sources to make sure the information you're getting is accurate.

On-Line Services: If you're new to computer networking, you might want to start by subscribing to an on-line service such as Prodigy, Compuserve, or America Online. Such on-line services offer their members numerous informational sources:

- Reference materials, such as electronic encyclopedias, popular magazines and newspapers, and business and financial references

- Forums where you can discuss subjects you're interested in and receive comments and answers from other members (Most on-line services have hundreds of these forums, divided into specific subject areas and staffed by knowledgeable experts.)

- Electronic mail from other members on the service, or from anyone on the Internet

Netiquette

Use the Internet properly by observing network etiquette (called Netiquette):

1. When sending electronic mail, check it for grammar and spelling as you would a written letter or a term paper. Use paragraphs often to reduce eyestrain for your readers.

2. Read the newsgroup FAQ (news.newusers.questions) to acquaint yourself with the proper use of Usenet.

3. Use the Internet efficiently by downloading files from nearby machines and by doing lengthy downloads outside of peak-use hours (they'll go much faster, too).

4. Respect other people's copyright and license agreements for files and programs you download.

tips FOR TRAVELING ON THE INFORMATION SUPERHIGHWAY

Before you strike out in search of productive information, you might want to consider the following advice.

1. Be patient.

Sometimes a search can get complicated. Computer networks often experience traffic jams, and Internet locations occasionally shut down without warning. Be patient, detour to another destination, and try again later.

2. Work intelligently.

An electronic search is high-tech intelligence work, so use your smarts:

- Think of keywords that will narrow your search (Example: *prison reform* is better than *justice).*
- Each search is like exploring the branches of a large tree, so don't forget to look at all the branches.
- Learn to "cut your losses"—start over from scratch if your current search is going nowhere.

3. Realize that the technology you use to find information is just a tool, not magic.

Like a hammer or a saw, an information tool—from a book to a CD-ROM—becomes useful to you only with practice. Learn what each technology can and cannot do. Don't hammer with a saw.

4. Get to know the right people.

Information specialists are everywhere—beside you in the workplace, in libraries, in companies, in government, over the Internet. Make them your allies.

5. Arrange information around you for efficiency.

Information resources that you use often should be close at hand. Keep a list of your favorite computer shortcuts next to your PC. Learn to use the bookmark feature of your Web browser.

CD-ROM

QUICK GUIDE

Many libraries are switching from print versions to CD-ROM versions of their most popular reference tools. Users can search CD-ROM databases much more quickly than books, and CD-ROM's are much more compact sources of information. Here are some types of CD-ROM's commonly kept by libraries:

- national and international telephone directories
- encyclopedias and atlases
- lists of books in print
- government statistics and health information
- various guides to magazines and newspapers

Using CD-ROM's

The great thing about CD-ROM's is that they're easy to use; but even so, they take some practice. The following may help:

1 Make sure you have the right CD-ROM, because the contents of CD-ROM's are not displayed as obviously as those for books.

2 Remember that each database has a different set of rules for searching. Be sure you understand how to conduct a search, or ask for help. Become adept at keyword searching. (See 449.) Identify the word and the synonyms that most clearly pinpoint your subject. Combine these words with AND, OR, or NOT to find the exact information you need.

3 Understand the limits of your CD-ROM. Its database "back files" may not go back far enough to meet your needs. If you are searching for a magazine article from three years ago, and your CD-ROM's back file is one year, you won't find what you need.

4 Find out how recently the CD-ROM has been updated. Most CD's are updated monthly, but the librarians may not have had a chance to load the latest version.

5 Rely on other sources, not CD-ROM's, if you need to be absolutely sure that you have the latest information on a subject. You may need to find the latest print materials or conduct an on-line computer search. (See 457 for more.)

Writing with a Computer

If you have written much at all, you know that rewriting is the key to good writing. But revising a first draft that you've written in longhand can be a tedious process—crossed-out lines, squeezed-in words, arrows going down the side of the paper; it's a mess. By contrast, revising with a word-processing program is a breeze. You can easily add, delete, and rearrange copy as well as print out versions from time to time to see how the whole thing looks in hard copy.

In addition to revising and editing your own papers, computers make it possible to work collaboratively with your classmates or receive feedback from your instructors without leaving home. Learning to use a computer effectively will pay big dividends in the classroom and beyond.

WHAT'S AHEAD

In this chapter you'll learn about the advantages of a computer at all stages of the writing process as well as solutions to some of its drawbacks. Even if you are already technologically proficient, you may pick up a tip or two that will improve your computer-aided writing process or save you grief.

- The Writing Process in Action
- Computer and Internet Terms

The Writing Process in Action

Prewriting

THE UPSIDE

- Prewriting can be a breeze on a computer. For example, think about free writing. You can fill the screen and keep going, without so much as having to flip over a sheet of paper. Also, if you type quickly, you can get ideas down faster by keyboarding than by writing.
- If you prewrite messily in longhand, using the computer can free you from worry about handwriting you (or your teacher) can't read later.
- Some people are more inventive in front of a screen. If you are one of these people, using a computer may relax your thought process and help you get words on paper.

THE DOWNSIDE

- Some writers do less prewriting and planning when they are using a computer, partly because they aren't able to use certain prewriting techniques, like clustering.
- The monitor is too tempting for some writers; they constantly stop to read what they have written. Solution: Turn the resolution of the monitor down to stop yourself from deleting or editing.

Best Advice: Try it out! Find out whether prewriting on paper or prewriting on a screen is better for you. It's your choice.

Writing the First Draft

THE UPSIDE

- Using a computer helps a writer stay with a piece of writing longer and develop it more thoroughly.
- Computers allow you to concentrate on ideas rather than on the finished copy.
- Drafting on a computer can make it easier for you to share ideas. You can simply print out a hard copy for others to read. By sharing, you also become more aware of a real audience.

THE DOWNSIDE

- Deleting sections of copy on a computer is very tempting for some writers. Most experts agree that it is important to save all of your ideas in early drafts. Solution: Don't push that "delete" key!

Best Advice: Do your drafting on a computer and print out and share copies of what you've written.

Revising

THE UPSIDE

- A big plus for computer writing is the time and toil it saves you when producing revision after revision, especially on longer essays and research papers.
- A computer makes revising easier because you can move, delete, and add large chunks of information by using a few simple commands. As a result, you no longer have to be afraid to try new things during revision.
- Group revision is also made easier with quick, clean printouts for everyone to read and react to.

THE DOWNSIDE

- Some people find it difficult to carefully reread and evaluate writing on a screen. Solution: Simply print out the document, make the changes on paper, and then input them.

Best Advice: Use your computer for revising. Take advantage of the speed and ease of using a computer, but do slow down long enough to reflect on and rethink what you've written. (If you print out a copy of your work first, and then revise on-screen, you can easily undo any hasty revising later.)

Editing and Proofreading

THE UPSIDE

- Because making changes is so easy, you can easily produce a clean final copy.
- Programs are available to help you prepare your writing for publication. The spell checkers and search-and-replace capabilities in some word-processing programs are especially helpful.
- Some programs make it simple to create the bibliography, table of contents, and index for a research paper.

THE DOWNSIDE

- You may not see errors such as missing words, misplaced commas, or misspelled words as easily on a screen as on paper. You may also come to rely too much on your spell and grammar checkers. Solution: Watch as the computer does its work; then do a final read yourself.

Best Advice: Do your editing and proofreading on a computer. Clearly, the computer serves best in this final step of preparing a paper for publication.

Computer and Internet Terms

Access is to open and look into a computer file.

Applications software is a computer program designed for a specific purpose, such as word processing, desktop publishing, accounting, etc.

ASCII (American Standard Code for Information Exchange) is a file that contains only "text" characters—numbers, letters, and standard punctuation.

Backup is a duplicate copy of a program or file made to protect the original copy in case it is lost, stolen, or destroyed.

Binary is the number system commonly used by computers because the values 0 and 1 can easily be represented electronically in the computer.

Bit (binary digit) is the basic unit of computer memory; one binary digit.

Boot is to start up a computer system by loading a program into the memory.

Browser is a computer program for reading information on the World Wide Web.

Bug is an error in a computer program.

Bulletin board is a service that permits users to leave, store, or receive messages by computer modem.

Byte is eight bits of information acting as a single piece of data.

CD-ROM is a compact disk that can hold large amounts of information, including moving video images.

Character is a letter or number used to display information on a computer screen or printer.

Chip is a small piece of silicon containing thousands of electrical elements. Also known as an integrated circuit.

Clear is to erase stored or displayed data.

Command is an instruction to a computer to perform a special task like "print."

Computer program is a piece of software containing statements and commands that tell the computer to perform a function or task.

Configuration is a computer and all devices connected to it.

Control character is a character that is entered by holding down the control key while hitting another key.

CPU (Central Processing Unit) is the "brain" of the computer that controls all of its functions.

Crash is to have a computer or program stop working.

CRT (Cathode Ray Tube) is the computer screen; the electronic vacuum tube found in a TV.

Cursor is a pointer on the computer screen that shows you where the next character typed from the keyboard will appear.

Data is information given to or produced by a computer.

Database is a program or collection of information that is organized in such a way that a computer can sort it quickly.

Debug is to remove errors from a computer program.

Desktop publishing is using a computer, software, and a laser printer to produce professional-looking documents.

Device driver is software that sometimes must be used to tell the computer how to work with the device (e.g., a "printer driver").

Directory is the table of contents for all files on a disk.

Disk is a magnetic storage device used to record computer information. Each disk appears flat and square on the outside; inside, the disk is circular and rotates so that information can be stored on its many circular tracks.

Disk drive is the device that writes onto and reads information from the disk.

Documentation is writing and graphics that explain how to use and maintain a piece of hardware or software.

Download is to transfer programs or files to your computer from another computer, usually over a modem connection.

Drag is to move the cursor across the screen by sliding the mouse while pressing down on the mouse button. It's useful for moving objects like "windows" around the computer screen.

Edit is to change an original document or program by adding, deleting, or replacing certain parts.

E-mail (electronic mail) is a system that uses telecommunications to send messages from one computer to another.

Error message is a message, displayed or printed, that tells you what error or problem is present in a program.

Execute is to run a computer program.

Exit is to leave or quit a program.

Fax (facsimile) is a device used to scan and transmit printed pages over the phone lines from one location to another.

File is a collection of computer information stored under a single name.

Floppy disk is a storage device made of a thin, magnetically coated plastic.

Font is the style or kind of type a printer uses; most printers have several fonts or typestyles to choose from.

Footprint is the space on a desk or table taken up by a computer.

Format is to prepare a blank disk for use (also initialize).

FTP (File Transfer Protocol) is a method of downloading files over the Internet.

GB (Gigabyte) is 1,000 megabytes, or 1 million kilobytes.

Global search is a computer search throughout an entire document for words or characters that need to be located or changed.

Gopher is an information retrieval system created by the University of Minnesota.

Graphics is information that is displayed as pictures or images.

Hacker is a skilled programmer or someone who spends a lot of time working with computers. Also used to describe people who use computers for criminal activities or mischief.

Hard copy is a printed copy.

Hard disk is the device that stores software and documents on the computer for later use. Also known as "hard drive."

Hardware is the electronic and mechanical parts of a computer system. A floppy disk is hardware; the program stored on it is software.

Header is information or graphics automatically printed at the top of each page.

Hypertext is computer text that is linked to text located elsewhere. By selecting a piece of hypertext, you are linked to the related text automatically.

Icon is a small picture or graphic used to identify computer folders or files.

Inkjet printer is a medium-resolution printer that prints with tiny bubbles of ink.

Input is information placed into a computer from a disk drive, keyboard, or other device.

Interactive means that the computer user can make selections on a computer or other electronic device and the device responds accordingly.

Interface is the hardware and software that are used to link one computer or computer device to another.

Internet is the worldwide collection of networks, also called the Net. (See 457.)

IRC (Internet Relay Chat) is a method that allows several people at one time to communicate with each other over the Internet by typing short messages from a shared "chat room." Method's shortened name is "chat."

K (Kilobyte) is a term used when describing the capacity of a computer memory or storage device. For example, 16K equals 16 x 1,024 or 16,384 bits of memory.

Keyboard is an input device used to enter information on a computer using keys labeled much like those on a typewriter.

Laser printer is a high-resolution printer. The more dots per inch (DPI) a laser printer has, the better the printout.

List is a display or printout of a computer program or file.

Listserver is a computer program that distributes mailing lists, usually over the Internet.

Load is to take information from an external storage device and place or load it into a computer's memory.

LOGO is a language that combines pictures and words to teach children programming.

Loop is a series of instructions that is repeated, usually with different data on each pass.

Mailing list is a way to send the same piece of e-mail to many people at one time. There are thousands of mailing lists on the Internet for discussing topics or sharing information.

Mainframe is a large computer much more powerful than the personal computer. Many university computer centers use mainframe to perform complex tasks.

MB (Megabyte) is 1,000 kilobytes.

Memory (See RAM.)

Menu is a detailed list of choices presented in a program from which a user can select.

Merge is to combine data from two or more different sources.

Modem (modulator demodulator) is a device that allows computers to communicate over telephone lines.

Monitor is a video screen on which information from a computer can be displayed.

Mouse is a small manual device that controls the pointer on the screen.

Multimedia is a combination of text, video, graphics, voice, music, and animation.

Network is a series of computers (or other devices) connected together.

Output is information that a computer sends out to a monitor, printer, or modem.

Peripheral is a device connected to a computer such as a storage device or printer.

Program is a piece of software or set of instructions that tells the computer what to do.

Programmer is a person involved in the writing, editing, and production of a computer program.

Programming language is the language used when writing a computer program.

Prompt is a question appearing on the screen that asks the user to put information into the computer.

RAM (Random Access Memory) is the part of the computer's memory where data, instructions, and results can be recorded and stored. Some complex computer programs require a lot of RAM to work.

Resolution is the quality of the "picture" on a computer screen.

Save is to preserve a program or document on the computer's hard disk or other storage device, either for later use or as a backup.

Scanner is a device used to "read," or scan, an image or text and send it into a computer.

Server is a central computer located on a network that interacts with other computers. A server often acts as a librarian, storing files that can be downloaded by users on other computers over the network.

Shareware is a method of software distribution in which software is freely distributed and the shareware author is paid after a user decides to keep it.

Software is the program that tells a computer how to perform a certain task.

Spreadsheet is a program used to organize numbers and figures into a worksheet form so they are easier to read.

Storage is the main memory or external devices where information or programs can be stored.

Surfing is exploring the Internet with no particular goal in mind.

System is the collection of hardware and software that work together to form a working computer.

Telecommunications is receiving and sending information from one computer to another over phone lines, satellites, etc.

Telnet is a computer program for using your computer as a terminal to connect to a server over the Internet.

Terminal is a keyboard and a monitor that look like a computer but have very limited capabilities. Instead, terminals connect with servers over the Internet or another network, and use the servers to perform tasks.

Text is the words, letters, and numbers that can be read by an individual.

Track is a fraction of the recording surface on a disk. (A track can be compared to the space used by each song on an album.) The number of tracks on a disk varies.

URL (Uniform Resource Locator) is the accepted format for locating a document on the Internet.

Usenet newsgroups are like bulletin boards, but exist only on the Internet.

User is a person using a computer.

Virus is a bug deliberately but secretly hidden in a computer system in order to wipe out stored information.

WAIS (Wide Area Information Services) is a set of full-text databases of information on hundreds of topics.

Web page is a document containing text, pictures, and other multimedia items that can be read over the World Wide Web.

Word processor is a program (or computer) that helps a user to write letters, memos, and other kinds of text.

World Wide Web is a popular method of using the Internet. (See 457-458.)

Write-protect is to fix a floppy disk so that new information cannot be written onto the disk.

Using the Writing Center

A college writing center, also known as a writing lab, is a place set aside for students to develop and strengthen their writing. It is a place where students can consult with trained advisers concerning their works in progress.

In most colleges, the writing center serves the whole student body, not just the English department. Often, the center provides other resources, such as writing models, handbooks, reference works, and exercises. Some lucky students go to colleges that provide all the "bells and whistles": private carrels, testing services, computer word processing, Internet connections, on-line writing laboratories (known as OWL's), computer "chat rooms," reference librarians, reading specialists, and more.

Plain or fancy, the heart of the writing center remains the one-on-one, face-to-face interaction between a trained adviser and a student with a draft of his or her writing in hand.

WHAT'S AHEAD

This chapter is designed to help you understand how writing labs work and how you can take maximum advantage of your local lab.

How Does a Writing Center Work?

Ssh! We're eavesdropping on Terri and Stu. Terri is a trained peer adviser in her college's writing center. Stu is a freshman in a composition course. He's just finished reading the rough draft of his personal essay to Terri.

TERRI: Thanks for reading it aloud. Did you notice how your voice changed when you hit the rough patches?

STU: Yeh. Reading really helped. Some of those mistakes were just silly.

TERRI: Mistakes are inevitable. Was it your decision to bring this to the writing center?

STU: Sort of. Our instructor suggested we come in if we felt insecure about writing, so I thought I'd give it a try.

TERRI: Great. We're here to help. What exactly was the assignment?

STU: Well, I've got the assignment sheet here. But the professor said we should write a personal essay, reflecting on the importance of a past experience.

TERRI: Did the past experience have to happen a long time ago?

STU: I'm not sure. I think so.

TERRI: Well, you wrote about an early experience. So that seems good. You know, we could start with the things that grab attention first, like misspellings, comma splices, and stuff. But I'd like to get to that last. I'd rather put major time into major matters. Okay?

STU: Sure. But what do you mean, "major"?

TERRI: The major things are purpose and development of content. Do you have good, well-focused material? And is there a payoff, a "so what?"

STU: Well, I'm kind of worried about that.

TERRI: Then why don't we back up? How about if you turn your paper over and just tell me what you want a reader like me to get out of your essay?

Time-out. Yes, this is a fabricated exchange—relaxed, efficient, and productive. But what should you notice about it?

- First, Terri is not an instructor but a fellow student. Stu can safely feel that she is an ally who can empathize with his situation.
- Second, Terri has a method. She gets important points established while making Stu feel at home.
- Third, Stu doesn't ask Terri just to "fix" his paper, and she doesn't offer. Terri is concerned about the entire thinking/writing process, and is willing to help Stu back up to the beginning and rethink the whole paper if necessary.

A Closer Look . . .

If you're like most students, you may be a little reluctant to visit your writing lab. After all, isn't that where students who are having trouble go? And if you're not having trouble, why should you bother? Good question. And here's a good answer . . . and some more good questions, and more good answers.

Is the writing center just for "remedial" writers?

No. All students are welcome in most writing centers. At least twice as many freshmen as upperclass students are likely to use the center regularly. But the mark of a healthy writing environment on campus is widespread use of the writing center: all majors, all class levels, all levels of ability. Some of the most successful students are the quickest to seek an adviser.

When should I take my paper to the writing center?

You don't even have to have a draft yet. You can come in and brainstorm with an adviser about writing ideas, or try out your thesis and talk about ways to research it. The mistake many students make is waiting until it's too late. They come in breathless, 10 minutes before closing time the night before the paper is due, and say, "Can you fix this?" When you need advice about a draft, give yourself at least several days lead time before the due date.

Is it fair to ask the adviser to fix the paper?

No. A writing center is not a free editing and proofreading service. A well-trained adviser will decline to correct all spelling errors, typos, etc. That's your job. However, she or he will probably try to point out any systematic type of error and teach you the principles involved in correcting it. The adviser may also show you how to find answers for yourself in standard reference works.

What if the adviser tells me the paper is fine, and I don't think it is?

Advisers aren't perfect, and most papers aren't either. Don't settle for that answer. Ask the adviser to spell out the strengths of the paper. Then think together about different possible approaches. Ask how you can get from good to excellent, or from excellent to dynamite!

What's the difference between a peer adviser and an instructor?

A peer adviser is a collaborator and doesn't "grade" papers for a living. He or she sits in the same classes you do, does the same assignments, and sees the world from your perspective. A peer adviser probably won't lecture you and has a better overview of writing "across the campus" than most instructors have time to obtain.

How do most students view the writing center?

At first, many students feel embarrassed or uncertain about going to the center. They think that getting help is a kind of punishment or confession of failure. But afterward, many students are relieved and grateful. Some even come away inspired. And many return again and again.

tips FOR GETTING THE MOST OUT OF THE WRITING CENTER

- Visit the center at least several days before a paper's due date.
- Bring your assignment sheet with you to each advising session.
- Read your work aloud, slowly.
- Expect to rethink your writing from scratch.
- Do not defend your wording—if it needs defense, it needs revision.
- Ask questions (no question is "too dumb").
- Request clarification of anything you don't understand.
- Ask for examples or illustrations of important points.
- Write down all practical suggestions.
- Ask the adviser to summarize his or her remarks.
- Rewrite as soon as possible after, or even during, the advising session.
- Return to the writing center for a response to your revisions.

A Healthy Collaboration

When you visit your campus's writing center, there are certain things you can expect the adviser to do. There are other things that only you can do. Here's a chart of the differences for quick reference:

ADVISER'S JOB	YOUR JOB
Make you feel at home	Be respectful
Find out about your assignment	Be open to suggestions
Help choose a topic	Decide on a topic
Discuss your purpose and audience	Know your purpose and audience
Help you generate ideas	Embrace the best ideas
Help you develop your logic	Consider other points of view; stretch your own
Help you research your material	Do the research
Read your draft	Share your writing
Identify problems in organization, logic, expression, and format	Recognize and fix problems
Teach ways to correct weaknesses	Learn important principles
Help with grammar, usage, diction, vocabulary, and mechanics	Correct all errors

The On-Line Writing Lab (OWL)

As helpful as a human, face-to-face encounter can be, there are some things a computer can do that a person cannot. If you have access to the Internet, a world of help is at your fingertips.

The Writing Connection

Get on an academically oriented browser such as *Alta Vista*. In the "query" line, write "on-line writing labs." With a little "surfin' " you'll soon find yourself at, say, Purdue University's on-line writing lab, or theUniversity of Michigan's, or Carnegie Mellon University's, or any one of a host of others that are now on-line. Be sure to make a "bookmark" when you've found an especially good Web site.

Here are some of the things you can get from an OWL:

- **Writing samples of all kinds**
- **Exercises in points of grammar**
- **Strunk and White's *Elements of Style***
- **Electronic dictionaries and thesauruses**
- **Interactive tutoring**
- **Real-time tutoring sessions**
- **Chat rooms about writing problems**
- **Links to electronic research engines**

SOUND advice If you haven't learned to navigate on the information superhighway yet, take some "driving lessons" soon. (See 457-460.) It's a challenge, but it can bring a new level of excitement to your writing endeavors.

The
Tools
of Learning

Reading to Learn

Critical Listening and Note Taking

Writing to Learn

Taking Tests

Building a College-Sized Vocabulary

Speaking Effectively

Succeeding in College

Reading to Learn

You've just been given a typical reading assignment: the first 360 lines of John Milton's *Paradise Lost, Book 1*. After heaving a big sigh and a small groan, do you (A) raid the fridge; (B) find a comfortable chair, preferably a recliner; (C) put on your favorite CD; or (D) all of the above?

WRONG! None of the above. Any of those choices will almost surely become a ticket to a nice nap with dreams of spring break, and your acquaintance with *Paradise Lost* will never happen.

So what's wrong with this picture? First of all, realize that *Paradise Lost* is not *Sports Illustrated* or *Rolling Stone*. For most of us, the missing component is interest. This is probably not a work you'd choose on your own, even though it's one of the more memorable you'll ever read. What you need to do is prepare for this type of assignment, much as you would for any other challenging task: You need to get serious!

WHAT'S AHEAD

This chapter offers helpful advice on preparing for challenging reading assignments, as well as for reading novels and poetry.

- Reading to Learn
- Study-Reading: PQ4R
- Reading a Novel
- Reading a Poem

Reading to Learn

Whenever you are asked to read a complex assignment, you should do three things before you begin:

- ◉ **create an appropriate environment,**
- ◉ **gather the necessary tools, and**
- ◉ **allow sufficient time to accomplish the work.**

Preparing to Read

Consider the environment. Your goal is to be comfortable—but not too comfortable. So cancel the easy chair. Slide yourself up to a well-lighted desk or table where you can read and write efficiently. (Have paper, pen, dictionary, and other reference books handy as well.)

It's okay to have a cold drink, coffee, or tea at hand; but nix the music (an exception might be instrumental music to help block out any annoying background noise). Make sure the room temperature is relatively cool, since warm rooms are notoriously sleep inducing. The point is, you need all your powers of concentration focused on the task at hand. Never begin a major reading session when you are overly hungry or tired, either.

Also, and this may seem too obvious, be sure that you know exactly what the assignment is and when it is due. Finally, have all your class materials close at hand (notebook, assignment sheet, handouts, etc.).

STUDY–READING tips

- ● **Read in half-hour to 45-minute spurts, followed by short breaks.**
- ● **Sit up straight in your chair (you don't want to get too comfortable).**
- ● **Create an outline or cluster as you go along.**
- ● **Draw helpful pictures or diagrams in your notes.**
- ● **Write out possible test questions.**
- ● **Predict what will come next.**
- ● **Read especially difficult parts out loud.**
- ● **Use your senses—try to visualize your subject.**
- ● **Underline, highlight, star, circle—whatever—but only if the book belongs to you.**
- ● **Stop and write.**
- ● **Take turns reading out loud with a partner.**

Study-Reading: PQ4R

There are a number of study-reading techniques with strange titles—KWL, SQ3R, and PQRST, to mention a few. Well, here's one more: PQ4R. It stands for *preview, question, read, recite, review,* and *review again.* All of these techniques are designed to make you an "active" rather than a "passive" reader and learner.

PREVIEW

The first step in the PQ4R process is previewing. Previewing actually begins when you first get a textbook. By reading the preface, table of contents, and whatever other introductory material is offered, you will get a good overview of the entire text.

When you preview a reading assignment, you are attempting to get a general picture of what the assignment is about. Look briefly at each page, paying special attention to the headings, chapter titles, illustrations, charts, graphs, etc. It's also a good idea to skim the first and last paragraphs on each page.

Previewing gives you a chance to familiarize yourself with main ideas that can become reference points during the actual reading. Think about how you will use this material in the future, and how you will be tested on it. You may want to do a brief outline of the assignment, jotting down section titles and paragraph headings as the major and minor points. As you do a more thorough reading, you can fill in your outline with the necessary details.

TAKE
note

Previewing serves two important purposes: (1) it gives you the big picture, and (2) it gets you into the assignment. Sometimes getting started is the hardest part. So go ahead, preview everything you read. You'll notice the difference almost immediately.

QUESTION

Are you the kind of person who asks a lot of questions, especially about class work? No? Well, now would be a good time to change your habits. Asking questions may be the most important step in the study-reading process. You should begin asking before you even pick up your assignment, and not stop until you sit down to take your final exam. Start with questions about what you hope to find out (or need to know) from the reading material.

One quick way to do this is to turn the headings and subheadings in the text into questions. For example, if you're reading a biology text and run across the subtitle "The Metabolism of the Red Cedar," you might be prompted to ask, "A tree has a metabolism?" Or, if you think more as a scientist does, you might ask, "Is a tree's metabolism similar to a human's? Does the metabolism of a tree vary depending upon its species? Its age? Its location? Its health?" Actually, any questions about metabolism or red cedars will do.

Another way to generate questions is to imagine a specific test question for each of the major points. In fact, once you get to know your instructor, this becomes a very natural way to approach a reading assignment. You may also create questions by carrying on an imaginary dialogue with the author. Ask him or her anything. Question everything. Ask how, who, what, when, where, and why, why, why.

"Question everything. Ask how, who, what, when, where, and why, why, why."

READ

Read the assignment carefully from start to finish. But, before you begin, you need to clear your mind. (If you've got a lot of other issues brewing, try making a list of things to do later.) You also need to eliminate distractions. Notify your friends and family that you are not to be disturbed—and, yes, that includes phone calls.

Once you get into the actual reading, you need to do two things: (1) continue asking questions, and (2) take notes.

First, you need to ask yourself, "What does this mean? What is the author saying? How does this connect to the previous material? What will probably come next?" These questions force you to think about what you're reading—the more you think about it, the better your understanding will be.

Second, you need to write a few things down in a well-organized way— an outline, a mind map, whatever. Certainly, you need to write down any questions you have about what you're reading. Then, after you've completed the first reading, you can go back and try to find the answers.

NOTE: If it feels like you're stretching beyond your limit of understanding, don't panic. Challenging reading assignments are designed to make you a better thinker. Simply raise any still unanswered questions in the next class discussion. You'll soon see that other people have similar questions.

RECITE

One of the often overlooked steps in the study-reading process is the reciting step. Reciting is just what it sounds like—repeating, out loud, what you have just learned from your reading. (You may want to whisper quietly to yourself if you are in a public place.)

One way to approach the reciting step is to stop at the end of each page, section, or chapter and answer the *who, what, when, where, why,* and *how* questions. As you recite the answers, you are in effect testing yourself on what you have just read. It will be clear what you do and do not understand, and what you may want to go back and reread. Repeating ideas out loud not only tests what you are able to recall immediately, but also provides audio reinforcement, which helps you remember the material.

Reciting works well in a group study session as well. Let each group member recite what he or she remembers about a certain section of the assignment. This would also be a good time to share successful methods for reading and remembering.

REVIEW

Before you pack things up, you need to review or summarize what you have just read. If you have questions to answer or a short paper to write, do it now. If not, consider putting together an outline, flash cards, illustrations, a graphic organizer, etc., to use as study tools in the future.

If you can't review your reading immediately, try very hard to do so within a day. Research shows that reviewing within 24 hours goes a long way in moving information from your short-term to your long-term memory. When you do take time to review reading material, consider the special memory techniques listed below:

MEMORY TECHNIQUES

- Relate the material to your life.
- Recite ideas and facts out loud.
- Try to relax; you'll remember more.
- Draw diagrams, illustrations, clusters.
- Put the material in your own words.
- Write about it.
- Study with someone or teach it to someone.
- Visualize it.
- Study your most difficult material during daylight hours.
- Use acronyms, rhymes, raps, and flash cards.
- Ask others about the memory techniques they use.

REVIEW AGAIN

If the material you've read is something you will be tested on weeks later, you need to continue to review on a regular basis—maybe once a week. These follow-up reviews can be very short (4-5 minutes) and can take place nearly anywhere—while you're waiting for the bus, riding in a car, or finishing your lunch. You can review anywhere you're able to pull out a notebook or a few note cards without causing too big a distraction.

You can also review with classmates whenever time permits. Agree to show up for class a few minutes early each day and ask each other practice test questions. E-mail your classmates with questions or observations when you've got a few extra minutes; they can return a message at their convenience. Just remember that nothing is too hokey or corny. If it works, do it.

Reading a Novel

Reading a novel as a class assignment is different from reading a novel for your own enjoyment. This doesn't mean you won't enjoy your reading. In fact, you may find that you get more out of the experience because you are putting more into it. With practice, you will find that you can apply the same kind of concentration to everything you read. These suggestions should help:

- **Be certain you understand the reading "schedule";** if your instructor sets certain "due dates" for portions of the reading, write them down.

- **Make your own "due dates" for assignments.** If your instructor has assigned a novel with the statement "This is due in three weeks," just use common sense: read one-third of the novel each week.

- **Find a good place to read:** somewhere that's quiet and away from distractions. But don't get too comfortable! Choose a straight-backed chair (not an easy chair), preferably at a desk or table, with a good light. Keep a notebook and pen at hand so that you can take notes as you read.

- **Look over your questions.** If your instructor has provided you with a list of questions to consider as you read, look them over before you begin your assignment. This will give you an idea of the things you should be looking for as you read. Then read! Go straight through the assignment without stopping to look anything up or write down any answers.

- **Think about what you've read** after you've finished a fair portion, and ask yourself if you could summarize what you've understood so far. If you can, great! If you can't, you've read too far without concentrating sufficiently. Pause for a moment to refresh your brain (not too long!) and continue reading. If you find yourself becoming more and more confused, put a light pencil question mark next to whatever you don't understand. You can always go back later and work on it. Your first priority should be to get to the end of the assignment.

  NOTE: If the assignment seems too long to read in one sitting, divide it into manageable chunks and deal with them one at a time.

- **Take a break.** Once you've made it to the end of the assignment, get away for a few minutes. Then go back to your chair, sit down, and read (or skim) the material again. Now is the time to look up words you don't know, work out the answers to any questions you may have had in the initial reading, and make connections between characters, plot developments, etc. (If you have assigned questions, take time to answer them.)

- **Ask yourself questions.** As you do your final reading, keep your mind alert by asking yourself questions like these: "What's going on here?" "Who are these characters?" "Why are they behaving this way?" Keeping a reading log or journal is a good way to keep track of your questions. The whole point is to maintain your concentration and get involved with your reading.

Reading a Poem

The poet Archibald MacLeish once said that "a poem should not *mean,* but *be.*" That may sound a bit odd at first, but if you think about it, it just might point you in the right direction when it comes to reading a poem. Maybe thinking about what a poem "is" and what it "does" might be a better way to approach a poem than regarding it as a puzzle or riddle to be solved for some concealed meaning.

It might also help to remember that poems don't jump fully formed into a poet's mind. Poems (at least most of them) are created gradually. You shouldn't expect to grasp everything a poem has to offer in one reading, especially if the poem is lengthy or complex. Below are some strategies to help you get started in the process.

FIRST READING

- **Read the poem all the way through at your normal reading speed.**
- **Try to gain an overall impression of the poem.** Don't stop to analyze individual lines or sections.
- **Respond by jotting down your immediate reaction to the entire poem.** Basically, this reaction will be your first thoughts or feelings.

SECOND READING

- **Read the poem again**—out loud, if possible. Pay attention to the "sound effects" of the poem—both of the individual words and of the overall impact.
- **Read slowly and carefully**—word by word, syllable by syllable—observing the punctuation, spacing, and special treatment of words and syllables.
- **Note examples of sound devices in the poem**—alliteration, assonance, rhyme, etc. This will help you understand the proper phrasing and rhythm of the poem.
- **Think about what the poem is saying** or where the poem is going.

THIRD READING

- **Try to identify the type of poem you're reading.** Does this poem follow the usual pattern of that particular type? If not, why not?
- **Determine the literal sense of the poem.** What is the poem about? What does the poem seem to say about its subject?
- **Look carefully for figurative devices in the poem.** How do these devices—metaphors, similes, personification, symbols, etc.—support the literal level of the poem?

PUTTING IT ALL TOGETHER

- **Give the poem as many additional readings as necessary.**
- **Do a 10-minute free writing.** Write down everything you can about the poem. Relate what you've read to what you know or have experienced.

Critical Listening and Note Taking

Experts have long told us that people remember only about half of what they hear—even if they're tested immediately after hearing it. A couple of months later, that percentage drops to 25 percent. That may be no big deal if you're listening to *All My Children,* but if you only remember 25 percent of what you heard in your Humanities I class, you may be in big trouble.

Listening is a skill, and like all other skills, it can be improved with time and practice. The same is true for note taking. In fact, the two skills work hand in hand: You will be a better listener if you take good notes, and you will take better notes if you listen carefully.

WHAT'S AHEAD

This section of your handbook introduces guidelines and strategies designed to improve both your listening and note-taking skills. And, if you read carefully, you may just pick up a bonus or two along the way.

- ● Improving Critical Listening Skills
- ● Taking Lecture Notes
- ● Using a Note-Taking Guide
- ● Electronic Note Taking

Improving Critical Listening Skills

Listening is much more than sitting up straight, looking in the direction of the person speaking, and following the gist of what is being said. Training in what you should think about and do during the listening process can help you improve your ability to truly listen.

Lots of things can interfere with listening. Some distractions, like outside noise or the temperature of a classroom, may be out of your control. But other things, like staying up too late, overeating before a class, or daydreaming, are within your power to control. What you need is a positive attitude and some suggestions to follow. Here are the suggestions:

1 **Prepare to listen and keep a goal in mind.**

Think ahead about what you may hear and keep an open mind about the speaker and the topic. Take time to figure out why you are listening (to gather information for tests, to learn how to . . . , etc.).

2 **Listen carefully.**

Listen not only to what the speaker is actually saying but also to what the speaker is implying (saying between the lines). The speaker's voice, facial expression, and gestures can tell you what's really important.

3 **Listen for the facts.**

Listen to find out the *who, when, where, what, why,* and *how* of something. This will teach you to pull important facts out of what you hear and arrange them in a way that will help you remember them.

4 **Separate fact from opinion.**

Listen for bias or opinion disguised as fact. (See 245-246.)

5 **Listen for signals.**

Your instructor will often tell you exactly what is important. He or she may not use a megaphone to say, "Now hear this!" but it may be almost as obvious.

Examples: And don't forget to _____ .

Remember, the best way to _____ is _____ .

The two reasons are _____ .

Four characteristics are _____ .

This all means that _____ .

The bottom line is _____ .

Listen for patterns of organization.

Textbooks and lectures often follow five "patterns of organization." If you can discover how a speaker has organized information and where she or he is going with the material, you have important clues to follow. Discovering a speaker's pattern of organization is a listening skill that will go far to improve your ability to learn by listening.

Five Basic Patterns of Organization

Listing ● In this pattern, the speaker introduces a list of items to be discussed. For example, a biology instructor might say, "There are four types of simple cells." The listing pattern can be visualized by a column of lines and letters (or numerals).

Time Sequence ● In this pattern, events are presented in time order. How-to presentations are always in time sequence. Time sequence is also important in discussions of history and current events, in explanations of processes in science and math, and in the study of literature. Visualize this pattern as steps that build upon one another.

General Statement Plus Examples ● In this pattern, the speaker begins with a general statement such as, "Children, even the very young, can easily show their understanding of spatial relationships." Examples are then given to support this general statement. You can visualize this pattern as a table top (generalization) being supported by table legs (examples).

Cause and Effect ● This pattern can be worked in two directions. A speaker can present a cause that led to a specific result, or effect. Or, a speaker can present a result or an effect that came about because of an event or a cause. In either case, the speaker is stressing a relationship; one thing happens because something else happened. You can visualize this pattern as a slanted line being pushed from either side.

Comparison and Contrast ● In this pattern, the speaker explains something by telling how it is similar to (comparison) or different from (contrast) another thing. Visualize this pattern as two lines going in the same direction for comparison and two lines going in different directions for contrast.

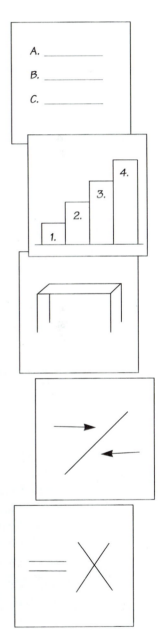

7 **Listen for details.**

Don't be satisfied with understanding the general drift of a story or a lecture. Pay full attention to what a speaker is saying. If you allow the details to slip through the cracks, you are less likely to remember what is being said. Details, examples, and anecdotes help a lecture come alive, and they also provide "hooks" for your memory.

8 **Listen to directions.**

How often have you sat down, ready to begin an assignment, only to be confused because you could not remember exactly what an instructor asked you to do? Your ability to listen to directions is basic. You may be able to e-mail your instructor later to ask for the directions again, but he or she may not be too impressed.

9 **Think about what is being said.**

How does this material relate to you? What can you relate it to in your personal life to help you remember? How might you use the information in the future?

10 **Put the lecture into your own words.**

Put the speaker's statements into your own words. Identify each main point and draw conclusions about the importance of each. In this way you begin to "own" the material.

When the Lecturer Talks Fast

- **Use a system of shorthand.** (See 490.)

- **Prepare well before class.** In a class where the instructor is whizzing through material you haven't previewed, you'll be totally lost.

- **Try to attend another section of the class.** Your instructor may teach several sections of the same class. Drop in on another section and see if listening twice improves your understanding.

- **Use a tape recorder.** (See 492.)

- **Talk to the instructor.** Ask questions before, during, and after class about points that you don't understand. Also, don't be afraid to simply ask him or her (very politely) to slow down.

- **Meet with other students from the class;** compare and exchange notes.

Taking Lecture Notes

Note taking is a skill—an important skill. It is an active approach to learning, one that gets you personally involved in the learning process and helps you focus on the most important information. However, if your note-taking skills aren't all that great, don't worry: they can be improved. The most important thing to understand about note taking is that it's not simply hearing and writing; it's listening, thinking, reacting, questioning, summarizing, organizing, listing, labeling, illustrating—and writing. The following tips will get you headed in the right direction.

BEFORE THE LECTURE

1. **Write your name and phone number in each of your notebooks.** Then, if you leave a notebook behind, you've got a better-than-even chance that some good Samaritan will call you to return it.

2. **Use a three-ring binder.** That way you can punch holes in handouts and add them to your notes in the appropriate places.

3. **Label and date your notes at the beginning of each class period.** If you are using loose-leaf paper, number and date each page.

4. **Insert the course outline or overview in the front of your notebook.** At a glance you'll be able to see where you are, where you've been, and where you're going.

5. **Start learning the common words and jargon of the course.** Begin a card file of these words, write accurate definitions, and learn them.

6. **Choose a seat that will help you accomplish the business at hand.** Position yourself so that you have no trouble paying attention to the lecturer, viewing the board or overhead screen, participating in discussions, etc.

7. **Get enough sleep before the lecture and dress in layers** so that you can take off your jacket and/or sweater if the room is warm. Sit up straight and rivet your attention on the instructor, even if this isn't your favorite class. You'll learn more.

8. **Do the assigned reading before you come to class** so that you can follow the lecture and don't have to look at the floor every time the instructor asks a question.

SOUND
advice
If your instructor writes anything on the board—a word, a formula, a definition—copy it accurately word for word. It will probably show up on an exam.

DURING THE LECTURE

1. Use one side of your paper only. This will make it possible later on to line up sheets of notes and see the flow of ideas. (If the thought of all that half-used paper makes you feel ecologically irresponsible, fill up the back side with textbook notes, comments, or questions about the lecture.)

2. Write all assignments, instructions, and test dates in one place in your notebook. You'll be glad you did.

3. Use a note-taking guide. Choose the guide that best fits your needs, or create a variation of your own. (See 487-489.)

4. Leave wide margins or skip a line or two between main ideas. Don't cram a lot of words on a page. When you're reviewing later, you'll have room to add study notes.

5. Condense information. Use phrases and lists rather than recording complete sentences.

6. Write legibly and in ink. If you have a laptop or notebook computer, try using it to take notes. (See 491.)

7. Use stars, underlining, and arrows to flag the most important points. Instructors often signal exactly what it is they want you to remember. Don't rely on your memory. Mark it right away.

8. Use abbreviations and speed-writing symbols for common words. See the chart on 490 for tips on how to build your own system.

9. Draw simple illustrations, charts, or diagrams whenever you can. You will remember the point better if you add visuals to words.

AFTER THE LECTURE

1. Read over your notes as soon as possible after the lecture to review the main points. Then, if something is unclear or doesn't make sense, you can make a point of asking a question to get the idea cleared up in your mind as soon as possible.

2. Jot down key words in the left-hand column. These labels will help you to pinpoint what is important.

3. Cover your notes and try to restate what was said about each key word. An early review of your notes will help to "fix" them in your mind.

4. Relate new information to things you already know or to experiences you've had. Associating what you've learned with what you already know will help you retain the new information.

5. Review your notes periodically. In most classes, knowledge is cumulative. Remembering what you learned at the beginning of the semester will help you understand concepts introduced later on.

6. Make note cards of the most important points in your notes. They can be used as flash cards and are particularly useful for any class in which you must memorize a lot of material.

Using a Note-Taking Guide

Note taking helps you listen in class, organize your instructor's ideas, and remember what was said. But there are pitfalls. You can take so many notes that you are overwhelmed when it comes to reviewing them. Or you can take notes in such a haphazard fashion that it's impossible to follow them. That's when a note-taking guide comes into play. By using the right guide for each situation, you can optimize your efforts. A note-taking guide can help you coordinate your textbook, lecture, and review notes into an efficient system.

Keeping Text and Lecture Notes Together

If the lecturer follows the textbook pretty closely, try using your reading-assignment notes as a classroom note-taking guide. As you follow your reading notes, you will be prepared to answer any questions your teacher may ask and take additional notes as well. Simply follow along and jot down anything that helps to clarify or adds to your understanding of the material. By combining your reading and classroom notes in this way, you should end up with one set of well-organized study notes.

NOTE: Use the left two-thirds of your paper for reading notes; use the right one-third for class notes.

Use this format when a lecturer follows the text closely.

Topic	Date
Textbook Reading Notes ← 5" →	**Lecture Notes** ← 3" →

Adding a Review Column

If you want to keep all your notes together, you can add a third column at the left of your page. Leave this review column blank during class; but after class, read through your notes and add key words and phrases that summarize what is in each section of your notes. This will help you review and remember your notes.

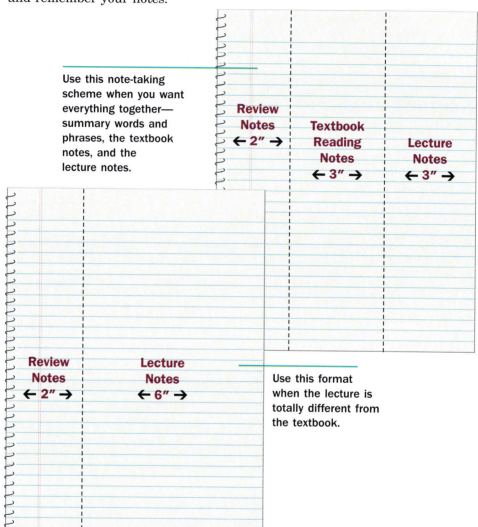

Use this note-taking scheme when you want everything together—summary words and phrases, the textbook notes, and the lecture notes.

Review Notes ← 2" →

Textbook Reading Notes ← 3" →

Lecture Notes ← 3" →

Review Notes ← 2" →

Lecture Notes ← 6" →

Use this format when the lecture is totally different from the textbook.

Keeping Lecture and Text Notes Separate

If your instructor does not base his or her lecture on the class text, you may want to keep your class and textbook notes separate. In that case your class notes will have only two columns—a wide right column for lecture notes and a narrow left column where you can add review notes.

Creating a Mind Map

A mind map helps you organize material in a creative, nonlinear way. You can create a mind map during a lecture and use it as a review tool later on. You start with a central concept or key idea at the center, such as "Stamp Act" or "Aerodynamics," and then you keep adding branches that relate to each other and to the central word.

Mind maps work well because they use both sides of your brain—the logical left side and the creative right side. They also force you to be more than a passive recorder of information. And, when you're finished, you can see at a glance how all the parts relate to each other.

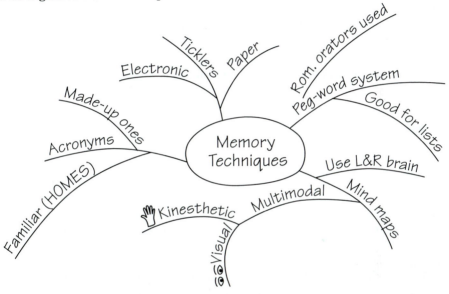

tips FOR DRAWING MIND MAPS

- Write your topic in the center of the paper. Draw a circle or box around it.

- Draw lines out from the center topic for your subtopics. Write above each line and try to condense your thoughts into no more than three or four words per line. Further subdivisions and examples should branch off from the subtopics.

- Add graphics, arrows, question marks, stick figures, silly drawings, and anything else that will help fix an idea in your mind.

- Use markers when you have finished to color-code or emphasize important concepts.

Creating a Shorthand System

QUICK GUIDE

You will be taking a lot of notes during your college career. Start now to develop your own personal shorthand system. Here are some guidelines:

1 Omit all articles *(a, an, the)*.

2 Use abbreviations without the periods.

    lbs   st   pres   Jan

3 Use common mathematical and technical symbols.

    + - = % # < > ÷ x

4 Eliminate vowels from words.

    mdl for *middle*   *psbl* for *possible*

5 Use word beginnings.

    intro for *introduction*   *psych* for *psychology*

NOTE: Use your abbreviations consistently. Otherwise, you will end up wondering if *psych* means *psychology, psychiatry,* or *psychic.*

6 Create abbreviations for the most commonly used words in a particular course. (Review your notes to find these words.) You can probably forget them once the course is over. Write these words and their abbreviations at the front of your notebook.

    PNS for *parasympathetic nervous system*
    QE for *quadratic equation*

7 Keep adding to your personal shorthand system. Here are some examples to get you started:

w/	*with*		*w/o*	*without*
e.g.	*for example*		*b/c*	*because*
b4	*before*		*SB*	*should be*
SNB	*should not be*		*2*	*two, to, too*

Electronic Note Taking

Even though you may never want to rely totally on electronic methods of note taking (computer or tape recorder), they can prove extremely useful in certain situations. Read the suggestions that follow.

Using a Computer

With laptop (notebook, subnotebook) computers becoming lighter and cheaper every year, more and more students are packing them off to class and taking notes electronically instead of in longhand.

THE UPSIDE

- **Usually, you can record more information than you can in longhand.**
- **You can search your notes electronically for key words.**
- **After class you can reorganize your notes quickly in any way you choose.**
- **Many word-processing programs allow you to compose notes in outline form, making them easier to review.**

THE DOWNSIDE

- **Despite the advances, nothing is as light, portable, or dependable as plain old paper and pencil.**
- **It's easy to get behind if you don't have an efficient technique.**
- **Your battery may run out at some crucial moment.**
- **Finally, your computer can crash, leaving you with no notes at all. Disaster!**

tips FOR TAKING NOTES ON A LAPTOP

- Read your laptop computer manual for tips on battery conservation. Turning down your backlighting will save battery power, as will using certain word-processing programs over others.
- Use lots of paragraphs. Otherwise your notes will be one long, formidable block of words. Keep hitting the "return" button.
- Print out a copy of your notes at the end of each lecture.
- Make a full backup of your hard disk at least once a week, and make sure you back up the folder containing all your notes.
- The ultimate backup is still paper and pen. Don't leave home without them.

Using a Tape Recorder

THE UPSIDE

One way to improve your note-taking skills is to tape-record lectures. That way, if you miss a point or two, or don't understand an important concept, you can hear it again. Consider taping a lecture in any of the following situations:

- **The class material is technical or very unfamiliar to you.** Hearing it a second time may help you understand the material.

- **You have to be absent from class.** Just make sure the friend who is taping for you is familiar with all the features on your tape recorder and knows exactly what to do. (Backup batteries and tapes are a good idea.)

- **You want a backup to your notes.** Then, if you come across something puzzling in your notes, you can fast-forward to that part and listen to it a second time.

- **You need to maximize time.** Listening to tapes can be a fruitful pastime for people who drive, run, or do a lot of walking. Instead of popping in your favorite music tape, listen to a lecture tape from one of your classes.

As a courtesy, ask your instructor's permission before you tape the first time. Usually, taping is not a problem; but in rare instances, the instructor may not want to have the class taped, or will ask you to turn off the recorder when class discussion occurs.

THE DOWNSIDE

Taping a lecture may seem like a surefire way to get every last word an instructor utters; but before you throw all your notebooks away, consider the following:

- **Taping encourages daydreaming or half-listening.** Knowing that you have the lecture on tape can encourage you to zone out. To keep this from happening, take notes as usual.

- **Listening to a taped lecture takes time**—a lot of time. Reviewing a good set of notes can be a much more efficient use of your time.

- **Tape recorders are machines,** and the cardinal rule with machines is that if they can malfunction, they will. Always double-check the obvious:

  ✔ Are the batteries fresh?
  ✔ Is the record button on?
  ✔ Is the volume adequate?
  ✔ Is the recorder close enough to clearly pick up the speaker?

Writing to Learn

Writing to learn is writing that helps you understand a subject or an experience. By writing about something or summarizing its essence, you are forced to begin making sense out of the random thoughts floating around in your brain. Writing helps you clarify your thinking and gain mastery over a subject.

Writing summaries, paraphrases, and learning-log entries will sharpen your ability to distill the meaning from someone else's writing, and will often reveal what you do not understand. Writing to learn forces you to think hard and use all your evaluating skills.

WHAT'S AHEAD

The following pages give you a number of opportunities to examine writing to learn—how to keep a learning log, how to write a summary, how to paraphrase an original text, and how to condense an entire paper into a one-paragraph abstract.

- Writing in Learning Logs
- Writing a Summary
- Writing a Paraphrase
- Writing an Abstract

Writing in Learning Logs

Writing about a particular topic so you can understand and remember it better—that's what writing to learn is all about. It's really that simple. When you write to learn, you are *not* trying to show how well you can write or how much you already know about a topic; you are writing to learn more. Writing to learn should be free and natural.

And that's exactly what learning logs are all about—writing that is free, natural, and intended to help you learn more. Keeping a learning log may be the best way to truly learn anything. What follows is an explanation of how best to keep a log, along with several samples that should allow you to try out learning logs for yourself in the weeks and months ahead.

Guidelines for Keeping a Learning Log

A learning log gets you actively involved in your course work and gives you the opportunity to explore important ideas freely and naturally. This free flow of ideas and questions promotes true learning.

- **Write about class activities**—anything from a class discussion to an important exam. Consider what was valuable, confusing, interesting, humorous, worth remembering, etc.

- **Personalize new ideas and concepts.** Consider how this new information relates to what you already know.

- **Evaluate your progress in a particular class.** Consider your strengths, your weaknesses, your relationship with members of the class.

- **Discuss your course work with a particular audience:** a young child, a foreign exchange student, an object, an alien from another planet.

- **Question what you are learning.** Dig deeply into the importance of the concepts presented. (One way to do this is to write a dialogue.)

- **Confront ideas that confuse you.** Back them into a corner and quiz them until you finally understand the problem.

- **Develop a mock essay test.** Answer one or more of the questions yourself.

- **Keep a record of your thoughts and feelings.** This can be especially helpful during an extended lab or research assignment.

- **Start a glossary** of important and interesting vocabulary words. Use these words in your log entries.

- **Argue for or against a topic.** The topic can be anything that comes up in a discussion, in your reading, or in a lecture.

Sample Learning Logs

The sample learning-log entries below were written in response to a newspaper article (company merger), a literary work *(Canterbury Tales),* and a class discussion (traffic psychology). Notice how each entry is personalized.

Response to a Newspaper Article

I just read an article by Ellen Goodman. It's interesting how cautiously she responds to the news of a gigantic merger between a phone company and a cable TV company that are forming an electronic superhighway. She recalls how the concrete highway system of the 1950's brought unintended consequences such as smog, traffic jams, and drive-by shootings. Similarly, the electronic superhighway system may deliver more data than meaning, more commerce than education, and more isolation than community. It's an interesting thought.

Response to Chaucer's *Canterbury Tales*

I think the order in which characters appear in the *Prologue* helps readers compare and contrast the different characters. If the Miller did not follow the Knight, then the parody would have been much more difficult to see, and if the Reeve did not follow the Miller, then his tale would have lost most of its revenge themes. Even the Franklin's tale is connected to the previous tale told by the Squire. Order is very important in connecting the themes in the *Canterbury Tales*. I guess that's true in all things, from commercials to baseball lineups to lunch menus. By organizing things in a certain order, different components can be compared more easily and special connections become more apparent.

On-line Log for Traffic Psychology Class

I'd have to say that we spend at least three-fourths of the class time letting out our frustrations and talking about problems we've encountered on the computer. It seems like we're just discussing the same driving behaviors over and over again, like we're going in circles and we're not getting anywhere. We're not fulfilling the "traffic psychology" part of this course; we're putting more emphasis on the computer stuff instead of on driving behavior. This is actually a computer class, in my opinion. When I signed up for this class, I expected to learn about driving behavior, not about creating computer files and commands! It seems like we have to do double the work!

Writing a Summary

A summary is a condensed version of someone else's work. A good summary concentrates on the factual information contained in the original document and does not contain personal opinions or evaluations. During college you will often need to write summaries of books, book chapters, lectures, and, as a useful study technique, portions of your class notes. Summarizing forces you to think carefully about the ideas and concepts in any body of information. When you write summaries, you call on your ability to comprehend, analyze, synthesize, and evaluate information—all important thinking skills. Developing your summarizing skills will prime you for success in college and beyond.

Guidelines for Writing a Summary

- **Skim the selection. Then read it carefully, paying particular attention to key words and phrases.**

- **Jot down a few of the key words and phrases and put the selection aside.**

- **Write your summary without looking at the selection.** This will help you to avoid plagiarizing—using someone's exact words without giving due credit. (See 297-298.)

- **Refer to the original source to verify the accuracy of the information in your summary.** Make any necessary corrections.

- **When you write your summary, make sure that you do the following:**

  1. State the source you are summarizing and its main idea in your opening sentence.

  2. Include essential information—names, dates, times, and places.

  3. Leave out examples and descriptive details.

  4. Write each important idea in one clear sentence.

  5. Arrange your ideas in the most logical order.

  6. Conclude with a sentence that ties all your points together and brings the summary to an effective end.

  7. Read your summary to a friend. Does he or she understand the main idea of the selection? If so, you've succeeded.

INSIDE info

If you're asked to write a *précis* (a form of summary), keep the following in mind:
- Keep the same voice and perspective as the original.
- Use paraphrases instead of direct quotations.
- Aim for brevity—your précis should be no longer than one-third of the original.

Student Models

Suppose you were asked to summarize chapter 7, "How Can X Be Summarized?" from *Twenty Questions for the Writer* by Jacqueline Berke. One student wrote this summary.

ORIGINAL SUMMARY

> According to Jacqueline Berke, one of the greatest challenges to the intellect is to digest complex written communications and to boil them down to manageable size. The author says she will treat summary as a significant and recurring question. The chapter goes on to offer examples of summaries, showing the different styles in which they can be written and the different purposes they can serve. In all summaries, however, the key to success is repeated rereading and accurate critical thinking. Under the first main heading, "Summarizing Ideas," Berke offers a long, hard paragraph by John Stuart Mill. . . .

The preceding summary includes more information than is necessary. Using too many ideas and details from a piece may result in a paraphrase instead of a summary. (For information on paraphrasing, see 499.)

In the student's second attempt, she simply highlights the main points and purpose of the chapter, freely rearranging ideas for the sake of greater clarity. In fact, before the student wrote her summary, she jotted down a few notes on paper—not an outline, but a scattering of key words and phrases that would capture the gist of Berke's chapter.

IMPROVED SUMMARY

> Summary, according to Jacqueline Berke in chapter 7 of *Twenty Questions for the Writer,* is a process of distilling "the heart of the matter" from any detailed piece of written prose. In all three types of summaries for which she offers examples—summaries of ideas, of plots (also called a synopsis), and of events—Berke stresses that summary is a demanding process of analysis and careful and sustained critical thinking. The quality of a summary, she says, is not determined by its length; a summary by nature must be a condensation of the original, but depending on one's purpose in writing it, whether subjective and evaluative or objective and descriptive, a summary may be fairly involved, or it may be extremely brief. The chapter concludes with a section of in-class and out-of-class assignments.

The beauty of this summary is that it gets to the "heart of the matter" quickly, just as Berke recommends. In addition, this summary doesn't waste any time on illustrations, examples, and other minor points. It refers to the entire content of the chapter while focusing only on its essence.

Personal Summaries

Many of the summaries that you write will have an objective, academic tone. A personal summary, on the other hand, is an excellent way to learn about a subject by relating it to your own life. The differences between the two types of summaries are apparent in the examples that follow.

TEXTBOOK SUMMARY

When humans or other vertebrates are in a dangerous or stressful situation, a chain reaction is set in motion. First, the central nervous system stimulates the adrenal medulla to release the hormones epinephrine and norepinephrine into the bloodstream. The whole sympathetic nervous system is activated, in fact, and even more norepinephrine is released. These two hormones—epinephrine and norepinephrine—make the heart pump faster and faster. At the same time the pressure inside the blood vessels increases. This causes the blood to circulate more rapidly throughout the whole body. Another organ, the liver, releases extra glucose or blood sugar into the bloodstream. The blood vessels in the muscles dilate in response to the increased blood supply. The muscles are supplied with extra oxygen and glucose and are prepared to either fight or run away. Because the body does not have time to eat, digest, or eliminate food, the supply of blood to the kidneys, stomach, and intestines is greatly reduced.

PERSONAL SUMMARY

I remember our biology instructor talking about the "fight or flight" syndrome. I always wondered what causes this whole chain of events to kick in. Why does it happen? What happens? All I have to do is remember the last time I walked into a class unprepared and the instructor said the dreaded words— pop quiz. Believe me, I could feel those hormones kicking in. My heart started thumping, my muscles tightened, and if somebody had offered me my favorite snack, I would not have responded. My body was psyched to either fight the demon or run from it. Instead, I was trapped in an overheated classroom with nothing but a pen and regrets for not having studied. Sometimes I think our ancestors had it easier. They could take physical advantage of all that activity within the sympathetic nervous system. I wonder if the increased heart rate and blood pressure improve thinking and remembering in any way.

INSIDE info

Another way to get the most out of a learning opportunity is to do a summary "on the run." It's called a *stop 'n' write* and can be done during a reading assignment or class discussion. By stopping to write, you're forced to evaluate your understanding of the topic and reflect on what you've just read or heard.

Writing a Paraphrase

A paraphrase is a type of summary that is written in your own words. It is particularly good for clarifying the meaning of a difficult or symbolic piece of writing (poems, proverbs, documents). Because it often includes your interpretation, it is sometimes longer than the original.

Guidelines for Writing a Paraphrase

- Skim the passage or selection quickly.
- Then read the passage carefully, noting key words and ideas.
- Look up any unfamiliar words.
- Summarize each idea in the passage in a clear statement.
- Expand or amplify the text to make it clearer, but be sure to maintain the meaning and tone of the original text.

ORIGINAL PASSAGE

Each man has his own vocation. The talent is the call. There is one direction in which all space is open to him. He has faculties silently inviting him thither to endless exertion. He is like a ship in a river; he runs against obstructions on every side but one; on that side all obstruction is taken away, and he sweeps serenely over a deepening channel into an infinite sea.
—Ralph Waldo Emerson, "Spiritual Laws"

Notice that the paraphrase that follows "translates" some of the archaic language *(faculties, thither)* by putting the passage into words that make sense to modern readers. Notice, too, how the paraphrase changes the problematic male pronouns in the original to gender-inclusive plurals, while still retaining Emerson's meaning.

PARAPHRASE

Everyone has a calling in life. Our abilities and talents and energies silently call us to work at developing them further. People who respond to their calling are like ships in a river flowing toward the sea. There are banks on both sides, and only one direction in which to move with ease. These people will only run into obstacles if they try to change directions. And, like ships moving surely through a channel to the sea, people following their true calling will move with great peace of mind toward the open water of unlimited possibilities.

Writing an Abstract

The abstract is a summary that presents an overview of an article or a report. Many journals publish abstracts of all the articles in an issue. If you are looking for information on a particular subject, an abstract can help you determine whether the article is worth reading in its entirety. In addition, many collections of abstracts are available in databases that you can search using keywords. When you are asked to write an abstract of a paper or project, follow the guidelines below.

Guidelines for Writing an Abstract

- **Using a copy of the paper, highlight key information.**
- **Begin with the thesis statement (article's purpose).**
- **Summarize key points in the order they appear in the paper.**
- **Include only essential information, methods, and results.**
- **Limit the length of your abstract to one paragraph of 100-150 words.**
- **Avoid technical terminology, specific quotations, and interpretations.**

The following abstract is taken from the model APA research paper, "Social Loafing: Individual vs. Group Performances." In 146 words, it explains the scope and purpose of the paper. The abstract summarizes the problem being studied, including participants in the study, research methods, results, and conclusions. To better understand how to write a clear, concise abstract, compare the model below to the research paper itself. (See 434-443.)

ABSTRACT

This study examined the effects of social loafing, the tendency for individuals to expend less effort when working with others than when working alone. By testing participants' work individually and in groups, the study tried to determine changes in productivity from one setting to the other. Participants (27 college students aged 17-20; 13 men, 14 women) completed a word-construction task in both an individual and group situation. Each participant's success at forming words out of the letters of a given word was measured twice: (1) while working alone and (2) while working in a group. Results showed significant evidence of social loafing. In addition, males were found to have a higher tendency toward social loafing than females. These results indicate that business managers and teachers should (1) think hard about whether to assign a task to an individual or to a group and (2) take measures to combat social loafing.

Taking Tests

There is nothing more disheartening than sitting down to take a test you're not prepared to take. The results are pretty predictable—and they're not pretty. Once in a while you can luck out or fake your way through an essay question, but usually you're in for a long session. On the other hand, there is nothing more exhilarating than walking out of a classroom after nailing a test. The feeling can carry you for hours, days, weeks. This is especially true in a college setting where tests count for so much and second chances and extra credit are so rare.

WHAT'S AHEAD

So if you prefer exhilaration to frustration, you may want to take a close look at the chapter that follows. Like most chapters in your hand-book, it is filled with good advice and helpful hints, including some especially useful tips on reviewing for tests on a daily, weekly, and monthly basis. There's even a special section on dealing with test anxiety and another one on how to get the most out of a study group.

- Reviewing for Tests
- Taking the Essay Test
- Taking an Objective Test

Reviewing for Tests

Do you consider yourself a "bad" test taker? Do you know the material yet somehow do poorly on the test? Do you feel overwhelmed by all the information you have to cover when studying for a test? Does even the thought of studying so much material make you nervous? What you need is a positive mental attitude—and good, good study habits. Together they can make the difference between "spacing" during a test, and "acing" it.

Daily Reviews

WHY DAILY? Begin your reviews the first day of class; and if you miss a day or two (and you will), just dust yourself off and start over again. Daily reviews are especially good because you tend to forget new information rapidly. Reviewing while the material is fresh helps to move it from your short-term memory into your long-term memory. (See the tips below.)

HOW MUCH TIME? Even 5-10 minutes before or after each class will pay big dividends. Depending on the day's class, you may read through (or talk through) your notes, look over the headings in a reading assignment, or skim any summaries you have.

WHAT TO DO
- Put "Daily review of . . . " on your "To Do" list, calendar, or date book.
- Use the buddy system. Make a pact with a classmate and review together.
- Put your subconscious to work by reviewing material before you go to sleep.

tips TO IMPROVE YOUR MEMORY

● **Intend to remember.** Scientists say that our brains never forget anything. It's our recall that is at fault. Who forgets that they have tickets to a rock concert? Most of us remember the things that are important to us.

● **Link new information to things you already know.** Make connections. Stimulate those brain synapses and they'll come through in the crunch.

● **Organize the material in a way that makes sense to you.** Don't try to memorize isolated facts. Understand the big picture and then divide the information you need to know into smaller, more manageable categories.

● **Review new material as soon as possible.** The newest additions to your brain are the ones you have the most trouble recalling. After a while your forgetting "levels off."

● **Create and use memory aids whenever possible.** (See 504.)

Weekly Reviews

WHY WEEKLY? More than anything else, repetition helps anchor memory. You can cram a lot of data into your brain the night before an exam, but a day or two later you won't remember much of anything. And when final exam time comes, you'll have to learn it all over again.

HOW MUCH TIME? Plan to spend about an hour a week for each class. (This can either be alone or with a study group.) Remember that repetition is the single most important factor in learning anything.

WHAT TO DO
- Make mind maps (see 489) and flash cards of important information.
- Practice answering review questions out loud and by writing out short answers.
- Organize a study group.

Forming a Study Group

A study group can do wonders for keeping you interested in a subject, forcing you to keep up, and increasing your retention. Energy in the group is apt to be contagious, and you will hear other points of view and other ways of approaching a subject that you may never have thought of on your own. To get started, follow these guidelines.

1. Find five to six people.
- Consider people who seem highly motivated.
- Ask your instructor for help in identifying interested students.

2. Arrange a meeting time and place.
- Plan only one meeting to begin, in case it becomes obvious that your group won't work out.
- Agree on a time limit for the initial meeting.
- Agree to divide any costs for snacks, photocopying notes, etc.
- Choose somebody in the group to keep everyone on task, and agree to accept any prodding and nudging in good humor.

3. Set realistic goals and decide on a "plan of action."
- Discuss what the group needs to accomplish.
- Decide what part of the course work you will review (lectures? labs? texts? test questions?).

4. At the end of the first meeting, reevaluate.
- Honestly and tactfully discuss any problems that arose.
- Ask who wants to continue.
- Decide on a meeting time and place.
- Determine an agenda for the next meeting.
- Exchange phone numbers.

Mnemonics and Other Memory Aids

QUICK GUIDE

Mnemonics is the art of improving memory by using formulas or other aids, which create "file tabs" in your brain that help you pull out hard-to-remember information.

ACRONYMS: Use the first letter in each word to form a new word. Everyone learns a few of these during their school years, but feel free to make up your own.

> HOMES (the Great Lakes—Huron, Ontario, Michigan, Erie, Superior)

ACROSTICS: Form a phrase or silly sentence in which the first letter of each word helps you remember the items in a series.

> Zoe Cooks Chowder In Pink Pots In Miami. (essential minerals—zinc, calcium, chromium, iron, potassium, phosphorus, iodine, magnesium)

CATEGORIES: Organize your information into categories for easier recall.

> Types of joints in body (immovable, slightly movable, freely movable)

MOVEMENT: Move around and use your acting ability to make another connection with the material you are trying to remember.

> Reenact a dialogue between Custer and Sitting Bull.

PEG WORDS: Create a chain of associations with objects in a room, a familiar sequence of events, or a pattern that you are familiar with (such as the positions on a baseball diamond).

> To remember a sequence of Civil War battles, you might "peg" them to the positions on a baseball field: e.g., Shiloh to home plate (think of the "high" and "low" balls); the Battle of Bull Run to the pitcher's mound (think of the pitcher's battle for no runs); etc.

RHYMES: Make up rhymes or puns.

> Brown v. Board of Education / ended public-school segregation.

TAPE RECORDINGS: Make a tape recording of vocabulary, class notes, foreign language lessons, etc.

> Listen to tapes when you're walking to class, exercising, or waiting in line. Using the sense of hearing helps reinforce memory.

VISUALIZATIONS: Transform an abstract idea into a mental image that is as personal and specific as possible.

> Whether you're learning about the life and times of Charles Dickens or of Isabel Allende, picture the scene. In fact, use as many of your senses as possible to reinforce your memory.

Taking the Essay Test

One of the most significant differences between high school and college involves your instructors' expectations concerning essay-test answers. Not only do college teachers expect you to include all the right information, they also expect you to organize it in a clear, well-thought-out way. They expect you to evaluate, synthesize, predict, analyze, and generally go beyond the obvious.

Understanding the Question

The obvious starting point with any essay test is the question itself. Before you can write a worthwhile answer, you must understand—fully understand—the question. Read the question several times, paying special attention to the key words. The key words will tell you how to present all of the information you've accumulated.

Key Words

Here is a list of key terms, along with a definition and an example of how each is used. Studying these terms carefully is the first step to improving your essay-test scores.

Analyze: To **analyze** is to break down a problem or situation into separate parts or relationships.

> **Analyze the imagery in Amy Lowell's poem "Patterns."**

Classify: To **classify** is to place persons or things (especially animals and plants) together in a group because they are alike or similar. Science uses a special classification or group order: *phylum* (or *division*), *class, order, family, genus, species,* and *variety.*

Compare: To **compare** is to use examples to show how things are similar and different, with the greater emphasis on similarities.

> **Compare popular Taoism and esoteric, or mystical, Taoism.**

Contrast: To **contrast** is to use examples to show how things are different in one or more important ways.

> **Contrast the views of Robert Oppenheimer and Robert Teller in the development of the atomic bomb.**

Define: To **define** is to give a clear, concise definition or meaning for a term. Generally, to define consists of identifying the class to which a term belongs and telling how it differs from other things in that class.

> **Define what is meant by the term "primogeniture."**

Describe: To **describe** is to give a detailed sketch or impression of the topic.

> **Describe the opening scene in Josephina Niggli's play *The Ring of General Macias.***

Diagram: To **diagram** is to explain with lines or pictures—a flowchart, a map, or some other graphic device. Generally, a good diagram will label the important points or parts.

Diagram the parts of a cell.

Discuss: To **discuss** is to talk about an issue from all sides. A discussion answer must be carefully organized to stay on track.

Discuss the impact of the Kinsey Report on American social thought.

Evaluate: To **evaluate** is to make a value judgment, to give the pluses and minuses along with supporting evidence. (See 216.)

Evaluate Elizabeth Barrett Browning's attitude toward love in Sonnet 43.

Explain: To **explain** is to bring out into the open, to make clear, to analyze. This term is similar to *discuss* but places more emphasis on cause-effect relationships or step-by-step sequences. (See 207.)

Explain the immediate effects of a regressive tax.

Illustrate: To **illustrate** is to show by means of a picture, a diagram, or some other graphic aid. At times, however, specific examples or instances can be used to illustrate a law, rule, or principle.

Illustrate the relationship of Brownian motion to proof of the existence of atoms.

Justify: To **justify** is to tell why a position or point of view is good or right. A justification should be mostly positive, meaning the advantages are stressed over the disadvantages.

Justify the U.S. involvement in the Persian Gulf War.

Outline: To **outline** is to organize a set of facts or ideas by listing main points and subpoints. A good outline shows at a glance how topics or ideas fit together or relate to one another. (See "Outlining," 116.)

Outline the events in the first chapter of *The Illiad*.

Prove: To **prove** is to bring out the truth by giving evidence and facts to back up a point.

Prove that dialysis is cost-effective.

Review: To **review** is to reexamine or to summarize the key characteristics or major points of the topic. Generally speaking, a review presents material in the order in which it happened or in decreasing order of importance.

Review the political achievements of Indira Gandhi.

State: To **state** is to present a brief, concise statement of a position, fact, or point of view.

State your reasons for supporting affirmative action.

Summarize: To **summarize** is to present the main points of an issue in a shortened form. Details, illustrations, and examples are usually not given.

Summarize the primary responsibilities of the CIA.

Trace: To **trace** is to present—in step-by-step sequence—a series of facts that are somehow related. Usually, the facts are presented in time order.

Trace the events leading up to the French Revolution.

Planning and Writing the Essay-Test Answer

In addition to a basic understanding of the key words, you must also understand the process of writing the essay answer.

1. Read the question several times. (Pay special attention to any key words used in the question.)

2. Rephrase the question into a topic sentence (thesis statement) with a clear point. It often works well to drop the question's key word from your thesis statement.

Question:
Describe the working conditions at the Lowell Mills in the 1840's.

Thesis statement:
The working conditions at the Lowell Mills in the 1840's worsened with time and led to massive strikes.

3. Outline the main points you plan to cover in your answer. Time will probably not allow you to include all supporting details in your outline.

4. Write your essay (or paragraph). Begin with your thesis statement (or topic sentence). Add whatever background information may be needed, and then follow your outline, writing as clearly as possible.

Sample Essay Answer

ONE-PARAGRAPH ANSWER

If you feel that only one paragraph is needed to answer the question, use the main points of your outline as supporting details for your thesis statement. (Your thesis statement now serves as the topic sentence of your single-paragraph answer.)

Question: Describe the working conditions at the Lowell Mills in the 1840's.

> The working conditions at the Lowell Mills in the 1840's worsened with time and led to massive strikes. Eighty percent of the workers in the Lowell Mills were young women from rural areas. At first, the Lowell Mills seemed like good places to work—wages were good, and the company built decent housing for the women at its own expense. The women seemed happy to achieve some amount of social and economic independence. But things began to slip. By today's standards, the Lowell Mills were soon horrible places to work. They were deafeningly loud, hot, and—because the cotton needed it—humid to a very unhealthy level. Girls as young as 10 years old worked 14 hours a day, with a half hour off for breakfast and dinner. When the country went into a recession in the mid-1840's, the workers' wages were cut. When they protested, they were replaced by new immigrants. Due to these conditions and because the foremen would sometimes speed up the production line, the women finally "turned out," or went on strike. Conditions at the Lowell Mills had gone from very bad to unbearable.

MULTIPARAGRAPH ANSWER

If the question is too complex to be handled in one paragraph, your opening paragraph should include your thesis statement and any essential background information. Begin your second paragraph by rephrasing one of the main points from your outline into a suitable topic sentence. Support this topic sentence with examples, reasons, or other appropriate details. Additional paragraphs should be handled in the same manner. If time permits, add a summary or concluding paragraph to bring all of your thoughts to a logical close.

Question: Discuss the characteristics of Creon in <u>Antigone</u> that make him a tragic figure.

Outline
I. Creon is a classic case of the tragic hero.
II. Creon possesses excessive pride.
III. Creon evokes pity from the reader.
IV. Creon's traditional values begin to break down.
V. Creon's people question his judgment.
VI. Creon falls.

The essay question is rephrased into a topic sentence.

Each paragraph follows a point in the outline.

A close look at the life of Creon in <u>Antigone</u> reveals a classic case of the tragic hero in action. Creon is a generally balanced individual, neither exceptionally good nor exceptionally bad. He does, however, have several tragic flaws.

The worst of Creon's flaws is his excessive pride, or hubris. His pride immediately sets him apart from his subjects, who perceive him as stubborn and aloof. But he is their king, so he also appears heroic. It is this combination of characteristics that sets Creon up for his inevitable fall.

During the course of the play, Creon evokes pity from the reader, another characteristic of the tragic hero. The reader is moved when Creon can't fix his mistakes and is left surrounded by death. "Let death come quickly, and be kind to me," Creon says at the end of the play. His ultimate failure is hastened by the external forces of war and fate, and Creon's eventual situation prompts the reader to ask, Why do good men suffer? Why can't things work out after an individual repents? But this is not what happens to a tragic hero. He must deal with the harsh consequences of his hubris.

Creon also experiences the breakdown of traditional values throughout the play. He has to deal with the turmoil in the city, stemming from the war between his nephews. In addition, Creon places himself at odds with the gods by forbidding the burial of Polynices. Then Antigone (Creon's daughter) breaks the law and threatens his authority. He responds by banishing her.

Creon's world continues to crumble when his son defies him, and he is told that his people are questioning his judgment. Tiresias, the blind prophet, is not afraid to tell Creon what the people have quietly thought all along: that Creon's actions have undeniably been wrong. Creon realizes this when the choragas (leader of the dramatic chorus) agrees with Tiresias, but it is too late to repair the damage that his foolish pride has already done. Antigone is dead, as are his son and his wife. Just as Tiresias warned him, he has paid for his actions, "corpse for corpse, flesh of [his] own flesh."

After all these terrible things occur, Creon begins to realize the extent of his mistakes and cries out in despair, "I have killed my son and my wife!" He wants to die, but realizes that he can't. He must live with his guilt, a fallen hero, a classic tragic figure. ■

Specific examples are used to support each point.

Each new paragraph adds strength to the writer's case.

The conclusion pulls everything together.

Taking the Essay Test

QUICK GUIDE

1 **Make sure you are ready for the test both mentally and physically.**

2 **Listen to or carefully read the instructions.**

- How much time do you have to complete the test?
- Do all the essay questions count equally?
- May you use any aids such as a dictionary or handbook?
- Are there any corrections, changes, or additions to the test?

3 **Begin the test immediately and watch the time.** Don't spend so much time answering one question that you run out of time before answering the others.

4 **Read all the essay questions carefully, paying special attention to the key words.** (See 505-506.)

5 **Ask the instructor to clarify any question (or key word) you may not understand.**

6 **Rephrase each question into a controlling idea for your essay answer.** (This becomes your thesis statement.)

7 **Think before you write.** Jot down all the important information and work it into a brief outline. Do this on the back of the test sheet or on a piece of scrap paper.

8 **Use a logical pattern of organization and a strong topic sentence for each paragraph.** Tie your points together with clear, logical transitions.

9 **Write concisely without using abbreviations or nonstandard language.**

10 **Write about those areas of the subject you are most sure of first; then work on the remaining areas as time permits.**

11 **Keep your test paper neat with reasonable margins.** Neatness is always important, and readability is a must, especially on an essay exam.

12 **Revise and proofread as carefully and completely as time permits.**

Taking an Objective Test

Even though objective tests are pretty straightforward and clear, there are some tips that can help you avoid making any foolish mistakes.

TRUE/FALSE TEST

- **Read the entire question before answering.** Often the first half of a statement will be true or false, while the second half is just the opposite. For an answer to be true, the entire statement must be true.

- **Read each word and number.** Pay special attention to names, dates, and numbers that are similar and could easily be confused.

- **Beware of true/false statements that contain words like *all, every, always, never,* etc.** Very often these statements will be false.

- **Watch for statements that contain more than one negative word.** *Remember:* Two negatives make a positive. (Example: It is unlikely ice will not melt when the temperature rises above 32 degrees F.)

MATCHING TEST

- **Read through both lists quickly before you begin answering.** Note any descriptions that are similar and pay special attention to the differences.

- **When matching word to word, determine the part of speech of each word.** If the word is a verb, for example, match it with another verb.

- **When matching word to phrase, read the phrase first and look for the word it describes.**

- **Cross out each answer as you find it**—unless you are told that the answer can be used more than once.

- **Use capital letters rather than lowercase letters** since they are less likely to be misread by the person correcting the test.

MULTIPLE-CHOICE TEST

- **Read the directions to determine whether you are looking for the correct answer or the best answer.** Also check to see if some questions can have two (or more) correct answers.

- **Read the first part of the question, looking for negative words like *not, never, except, unless,* etc.**

- **Try to answer the question in your mind before looking at the choices.**

- **Read all the choices before selecting your answer.** This is especially important on tests in which you must select the best answer, or on tests where one of your choices is a combination of two or more answers. (Example: **d.** Both a and b **e.** All of the above **f.** None of the above)

tips FOR COPING WITH TEST ANXIETY

- **Get a good night's sleep and eat a healthful, light meal** (donuts and coffee are not a healthful, light meal).

- **Get some exercise.** Aerobic exercise (running, swimming, walking, aerobics, etc.) is a great way to relieve stress, but it has also been proven to actually help you think quicker and more clearly.

- **Hit the showers.** Hot water is relaxing, cold water is stimulating, warm water is soothing. Take your pick, or start with hot and end with a cold splash.

- **Give yourself enough time to get to class early** . . . but not too early! Hurrying increases anxiety, but so does waiting.

- **Pick a seat from which you can see the clock** and where you are as isolated as possible from friends (who may freak you out by working while you are pausing to think, or by turning in their papers early).

- **Relax.** Take a few deep breaths, close your eyes, and think positive thoughts. The more relaxed you are, the better your memory will serve you.

- **Glance through the test, plan your time, and pace yourself.** You don't want to discover with only 5 minutes of class time left that the last question is an essay that counts for 50 percent of your grade.

- **Begin by filling in all the answers you know.** This relieves anxiety and helps to trigger answers for other questions that you may not know immediately. Also jot down important facts and formulas you know you will need later on.

- **Don't panic if you can't remember an answer.** Take a deep breath, exhale completely, and go on to another question.

- **Don't panic if other people start handing in their papers** long before you are finished. They may have given up or rushed through the exam. Often, the best students finish last.

Building a College-Sized Vocabulary

Everyone knows that reading—lots of reading—is the best way to build a bigger vocabulary, and that having a bigger vocabulary pays off. The problem is that building vocabulary through an intensive reading program is a long and gradual process. What can you do if you have an immediate need to improve your vocabulary? How can you supplement a reading program and start building a better vocabulary today?

WHAT'S AHEAD

This chapter will help you expand your vocabulary and, in doing so, broaden both what you understand and how you communicate in college and beyond. Recognizing context clues, making good use of a thesaurus, figuring out difficult words by learning prefixes, suffixes, and roots—all these will help. So will a daily commitment to building your vocabulary. We offer you a number of practical, painless suggestions.

- Using Context Clues
- Using a Thesaurus
- Using Word Parts: Prefixes, Suffixes, Roots

Building Your Vocabulary

QUICK GUIDE

Many experts say that the single most important thing that you can do to improve your grades is to build a bigger vocabulary. Here are some ways to do that:

1 **Use context clues:** Begin by studying the various kinds of context clues. (See 515-516.) Then look for clues as you encounter new words in your reading. You'll be amazed at how many definitions you can figure out on your own.

2 **Learn common word roots, prefixes, and suffixes.** With a knowledge of these, you can often infer the meaning of a word. (See 518-528.)

3 **Keep a vocabulary notebook.** Include the definition, pronunciation, and the part of speech for each word. If you've found the new word in your reading, copy the sentence it came from into your notebook. Words learned in context are more likely to be remembered than words learned in isolation.

4 **Use flash cards.** Print the new word on the front of an index card with the definition on the back. Carry the cards with you and flip through them when you're waiting in line with nothing to do.

5 **Use your dictionary.** Every time you look up a word, put a dot next to it in your dictionary. If a word has two or more dots, include it in your flash cards.

6 **Learn the origins of words.** Pay attention to the etymologies (origins of words) in the dictionary. Many of these are interesting enough to help you remember a word.

7 **Make a tape.** Make a tape in which you record new words along with their definitions. Instead of listening to your latest music tape when you're going somewhere, pop in your vocabulary tape. (Nobody will ever know.)

8 **Use a thesaurus.** Use a thesaurus to find all the synonyms for a common word, such as *stupid.* For starters, there's *imbecilic, obtuse, insipid,* and *vacuous;* but these words are not interchangeable. Learn the subtle differences and connotations for each word.

9 **Use foreign languages.** Use your knowledge of foreign languages, however limited, to decode and remember new words. For example, if you remember that "amigo" means "friend" in Spanish, you might guess the meaning of the word "amity" (peaceful relations or friendship).

Using Context Clues

When you come across a word you don't know, do you stop to look it up? Usually that's a good idea, but it's not always necessary. Sometimes you can figure out the meaning of a word through its context—the words surrounding it. You already do this naturally, but becoming conscious of various "context clues" will improve this skill enormously. The following chart lists eight types of context clues. Become familiar with each of these and learn to use them when you come across unfamiliar words in your reading.

Types of Context Clues

Definitions or Descriptions: This is the most obvious type of clue. The sentence itself tells you what something is. The tip-off for this type of clue is some form of the verb "be" *(am, is, are, was, were).*

> A **zealot** is someone who is enthusiastic about a cause or an activity in a way that goes far beyond ordinary interest.

Synonyms: A second, easier word defines the first.

> Sometimes individuals display **altruistic,** selfless behavior toward complete strangers who are in great need.

Comparisons: A comparison is made that helps you define the word. Comparisons are often signaled by words such as *like* and *as.*

> After a war, the wrath of the population often falls on those people who have **collaborated** with the enemy, like the people who supported the Vichy government in France during World War II.

Contrasts: A contrast helps you define the word. Contrasts are often signaled by words such as *although, but, on the other hand,* or *on the contrary.*

> Although modern medicine has proven very effective in dealing with acute conditions and traumas, it has not been as successful in treating **chronic** conditions for which surgery or medication are problematic.

Restatements: A term is restated in other words. Demonstrative pronouns such as *this, that,* and *those* may indicate restatements; so do appositives, which are signaled by commas, parentheses, and dashes.

> Thousands of otherwise healthy adults suffer from **agoraphobia.** This fear of open spaces has been successfully treated by a variety of methods from medication to behavioral therapy.
>
> (A demonstrative pronoun signals the restatement.)
>
> In an age of computers, typewriters have become almost an **anachronism,** a thing of the past.
>
> (An appositive signals the restatement.)

Items in a Series: Even if you don't recognize all the items in a series, you can assume that they are all part of the same family.

> **Cantatas, concertos, oratorios, sonatas, and suites—all of these were part of the enormous output of Baroque composer Johann Sebastian Bach.**

Tone and Setting: Picturing, or getting a sense of a particular scene, will often provide helpful clues to a word's meaning.

> **During the long and tedious trial, the jury was kept sequestered day and night from the public, in quarters where there were no televisions, radios, or daily newspapers.**

Cause and Effect: From a cause-and-effect sequence in a sentence, you can often deduce the meaning of a word.

> **Because genetic mutations can be caused by the effects of chemicals, radiation, or even ordinary heat on DNA, reliable genetic research requires constant vigilance.**

 INSIDE info Context clues do not always appear immediately before or after the word you are studying. In a lengthy piece of writing, the clues might appear several paragraphs later (or earlier). Be aware of all clues—whenever they appear.

Now You Try It

See how well you can apply context clues. Look carefully at the boldfaced words in the passage below taken from Jack London's *Call of the Wild*. Then look for direct and indirect context clues to help you understand the meaning of those words. In addition to the clues available in this single paragraph, any reader of this novel would have the advantage of having read a number of pages already. Taken together, there is a good chance the reader could figure out the meaning of most of the boldfaced words. See how your defining efficiency improves, now that you understand more about context clues.

> They made Sixty Miles, which is a fifty-mile run, on the first day; and the second day saw them booming up the Yukon well on their way to Pelly. But such splendid running was achieved not without great trouble and **vexation** on the part of Francois. The **insidious** revolt led by Buck had destroyed the **solidarity** of the team. It no longer was as one dog leaping in the traces. The encouragement Buck gave the rebels led them into all kinds of petty **misdemeanors**. No more was Spitz a leader greatly to be feared. The old awe departed, and they grew equal to challenging his authority. Pike robbed him of half a fish one night and gulped it down under the protection of Buck. Another night Dub and Joe fought Spitz and made him forego the punishment they deserved. And even Billee, the good-natured, was less good-natured, and whined not half so **placatingly** as in former days. Buck never came near Spitz without snarling and bristling **menacingly**. In fact, his conduct approached that of a bully, and he was given to swaggering up and down before Spitz's very nose. ■

Using a Thesaurus

A thesaurus is, in a sense, the opposite of a dictionary. You go to a dictionary when you know the word but need the definition. You go to a thesaurus when you know the definition but need the word. As a reference tool, a thesaurus is a treasure chest of *synonyms*—words with similar meanings.

Locating Word Lists

Go to a thesaurus when you have a word in mind, but it doesn't fit the bill exactly. For example, let's say you're writing an essay on Hamlet and need a word for *fear* (a certain kind of fear) to complete the following sentence:

Hamlet delays his revenge in part out of _____ that the ghost may be an evil spirit sent to deceive him.

If you have a thesaurus in dictionary form, simply look up *fear* alphabetically. If, however, you have a traditional thesaurus, you must first look up your word in the alphabetical index at the back of the book. Using guide numbers, the index will point you to entries in the body of the thesaurus. There, you might find a list of synonyms for *fear: timidity, fearfulness, diffidence, apprehensiveness, solicitude, anxiety, misgiving, mistrust, suspicion, qualm.* You choose a word and complete the sentence:

Hamlet delays his revenge in part out of <u>suspicion</u> that the ghost may be an evil spirit sent to deceive him.

Choosing Synonyms

The key to getting the most out of a thesaurus is learning to choose synonyms correctly: the word must fit the situation.

- **Review the entire list of synonyms in an entry before making a decision.**
- **Choose the best word by considering the following factors:**
  1. Which word feels like it fits best in the context of your sentence?
  2. What are the connotations of these various words?
  3. What are the fine distinctions in meaning and emphasis between these words?
  4. What level of diction do these words belong to, and what level is appropriate for the piece of writing you are working on?

 **TAKE note**

The word-processing program you use may have a built-in thesaurus. If so, learn how to use this tool, and do so during the drafting and revising steps of your writing projects.

Using Word Parts

Another extremely useful tool for building your reading vocabulary is the ability to chop unfamiliar words into pieces, so that you can examine each part—namely, the *prefix, suffix,* and *root.* For this technique to work, you need to know the meanings of commonly used word parts, and how they work together. Notice the samples below.

PREFIXES ● A **prefix** is a word part added to the beginning of a base word:

Prefix	Base Word	New Word
a (not)	**typical**	**atypical**
di (two)	**oxide**	**dioxide**
meta (beyond)	**physical**	**metaphysical**

The prefix *a* means "not." Knowing this meaning will help you understand and remember that *atypical* means "not typical."

SUFFIXES ● A **suffix** is a word part added to the ending of a base word:

Base Word	Suffix	New Word
duck	**ling** (small)	**duckling**
assist	**ant** (one who)	**assistant**

The suffix *ant* means "the performer or agent of a task." Knowing this meaning will help you remember that *assistant* means "someone who assists."

ROOTS ● A **root** is a base upon which a word is built:

Root	Meaning	Word
biblio	(book)	**bibliophile**
phile	(love)	

Knowing that the root *biblio* means "book" and *phile* means "love" will help you to remember that *bibliophile* means "someone who loves books."

A Study Plan

You already know and use many common prefixes, suffixes, and roots every day. To increase your speaking and writing vocabulary, study the meanings of those prefixes, suffixes, and roots that are not familiar to you. The following pages contain nearly 500 of them! Scan a page until you come to a word part that is "new." Learn its meanings and at least one of the sample words listed. Then apply your knowledge as you encounter new words in your textbooks, your favorite magazines, and even as you surf the Net. You'll see a payoff almost immediately.

Prefixes

Prefixes are those "word parts" that come before the root word (*pre* = "before"). Depending upon its meaning, a prefix changes the intent, or sense, of the base word. As a skilled reader, you will want to know the meanings of the most common prefixes and then watch for them when you read.

a, an [not, without] amoral (without a sense of moral responsibility), atypical, atom (not cutable), apathy (without feeling), anesthesia (without sensation)

ab, abs, a [from, away] abnormal, abduct, absent, avert (turn away)

acro [high] acropolis (high city), acrobat, acronym, acrophobia (fear of height)

ambi, amb [both, around] ambidextrous (skilled with both hands), ambiguous, amble, ambient (on all sides)

amphi [both] amphibious (living on both land and water), amphitheater

ante [before] antedate, anteroom, antebellum, antecedent (happening before)

anti, ant [against] anticommunist, antidote, anticlimax, antacid

be [on, away] bedeck, belabor, bequest, bestow, beloved

bene, bon [well] benefit, benefactor, benevolent, benediction, bonanza, bonus

bi, bis, bin [both, double, twice] bicycle, biweekly, bilateral, biscuit, binoculars

by [side, close, near] bypass, bystander, by-product, bylaw, byline

cata [down, against] catalog, catastrophe, catapult, cataclysm

cerebro [brain] cerebrospinal, cerebellum, cerebrum, cerebral

circ, circum [around] circular, circumspect, circumference, circumnavigate

co, con, col, com [together, with] co-pilot, conspire, collect, compose

contra, counter [against] controversy, contradict, counterpart, contraindicate

de [from, down] demote, depress, degrade, deject, deprive, devoid, deviate

deca [ten] decade, decathlon, decapod (ten feet), decagon, decagram

di [two, twice] divide, dilemma, dilute, ditto, dioxide, dipole, digraph, diplopia (vision disorder, seeing two images)

dia [through, between] diameter, diagonal, diagram, dialogue (speech between people)

dis, dif [apart, away, reverse] distinguish, dismiss, distort, diffuse

dys [badly, ill] dyspepsia (digesting badly), dystrophy, dysentery, dysfunction

em, en [in, into] embrace, enslave

epi [upon] epidermis (upon the skin, outer layer of skin), epitaph, epithet

eu [well] eulogize (speak well of, praise), euphony, eugenics, euphoria

ex, e, ec, ef [out] ex-mayor, expel (drive out), exorcism, eject, eccentric (out of the center position), efflux

extra, extro [beyond, outside] extraordinary (beyond the ordinary), extrovert, extracurricular, extraneous

for [away, off] forswear (to renounce an oath), forgo, forlorn

fore [before in time] forecast, foretell (to tell beforehand), foreshadow

hemi, demi, semi [half] hemisphere, demitasse, semicircle (half of a circle)

hex [six] hexameter, hexagon

homo [man] Homo sapiens, homicide (killing man)

hyper [over, above] hypersensitive (overly sensitive), hyperactive

hypo [under] hypodermic (under the skin), hypothesis

il, ir, in, im [not] illegal, illegible, irregular, incorrect, immoral

in, il, im [into] inject, inside, illuminate, illustrate, impose, implant, imprison

infra [beneath] infrared, infrastructure

inter [between] intercollegiate, interfere, intervene, interrupt (break between)

intra [within] intramural, intravenous (within the veins), intracellular

intro [into, inward] introduce, introvert (turn inward), introspection

macro [large, excessive] macrodent (having large teeth), macrocosm

mal [badly, poorly] malady, maladjusted, malnutrition, malfunction

meta [beyond, after, with] metaphor, metamorphosis, metaphysical

mis [incorrect, bad] misuse, misprint

miso [hate] misanthrope, misogynist

mono [one] monoplane, monotone, monochrome, monocle

multi [many] multiply, multiform

neo [new] neopaganism, neoclassic, neologism, neophyte

non [not] nontaxable (not taxed), nontoxic, nonexistent, nonsense

ob, of, op, oc [toward, against] obstruct, offend, oppose, occur

oct [eight] octagon, octave, octopus, octane, octameter

paleo [ancient] paleoanthropology (pertaining to ancient man), paleontology (study of ancient life-forms)

para [beside, almost] parasite (one who eats beside or at the table of another), paraphrase, paramedic, parallel, parody

penta [five] pentagon (figure or building having five angles or sides), pentameter, pentathlon

per [throughout, completely] pervert (completely turn wrong, corrupt), perfect, perceive, permanent, persuade

peri [around] perimeter (measurement around an area), periphery, periscope, pericardium, period

poly [many] polygon (figure having many angles or sides), polygamy, polyglot, polychrome

post [after] postpone, postwar, postscript, posterity

pre [before] prewar, preview, precede, prevent, premonition

pro [forward, in favor of] project (throw forward), progress, promote, prohibition

pseudo [false] pseudonym (false or assumed name), pseudoscientific, pseudopodia

quad [four] quadruple (four times as much), quadriplegic, quadratic, quadrant

quint [five] quintuplet, quintuple, quintet, quintile

re [back, again] reclaim, revive, revoke, rejuvenate, retard, reject, return

retro [backward] retrospective (looking backward), retroactive, retrorocket

se [aside] seduce (lead aside), secede, secrete, segregate

self [by oneself] self-determination, self-employed, self-service, selfish

sesqui [one and a half] sesquicentennial (one and one-half centuries)

sex, sest [six] sexagenarian (sixty years old), sexennial, sextant, sextuplet, sestet

sub [under] submerge (put under), submarine, subhuman, substitute, subsoil

suf, sug, sup, sus [from under] suffer, sufficient, suggest, support, suspect, suspend

super, supr [above, over, more] supervise, superman, supernatural, supreme

syn, sym, sys, syl [with, together] synthesis, synchronize (time together), synonym, sympathy, symphony, system, syllable

trans, tra [across, beyond] transoceanic, transmit (send across), transfusion, tradition, transform

tri [three] tricycle, triangle, tripod, tristate

ultra [beyond, exceedingly] ultramodern, ultraviolet, ultraconservative

un [not, release] unfair, unnatural, unbutton

under [beneath] underground, underlying

uni [one] unicycle, uniform, unify, universe, unique (one of a kind)

vice [in place of] vice president, vice admiral, viceroy

Numerical Prefixes

Prefix	Symbol	Multiples and Submultiples	Equivalent	Prefix	Symbol	Multiples and Submultiples	Equivalent
tera	T	10^{12}	trillionfold	centi	c	10^{-2}	hundredth part
giga	G	10^{9}	billionfold	milli	m	10^{-3}	thousandth part
mega	M	10^{6}	millionfold	micro	u	10^{-6}	millionth part
kilo	k	10^{3}	thousandfold	nano	n	10^{-9}	billionth part
hecto	h	10^{2}	hundredfold	pico	p	10^{-12}	trillionth part
deka	da	10	tenfold	femto	f	10^{-15}	quadrillionth part
deci	d	10^{-1}	tenth part	atto	a	10^{-18}	quintillionth part

Suffixes

Suffixes come at the end of a word. Very often a suffix will tell you what kind of word it is part of (noun, adverb, adjective, etc.). For example, words ending in -*dom* are usually nouns, words ending in -*ly* are usually adverbs, and words ending in -*able* are usually adjectives.

able, ible [able, can do] capable, agreeable, edible, visible (can be seen)

ade [result of action] blockade (the result of a blocking action), lemonade

age [act of, state of, collection of] salvage (act of saving), storage, forage

al [relating to] sensual, gradual, manual, natural (relating to nature)

algia [pain] neuralgia (nerve pain)

an, ian [native of, relating to] African, Canadian

ance, ancy [action, process, state] assistance, allowance, defiance, truancy

ant [agent, one who] assistant, servant

ary, ery, ory [relating to, quality, place where] dictionary, bravery, dormitory

ate [cause, make] liquidate, segregate

cian [having a certain skill or art] musician, beautician, magician, physician

cule, ling [very small] molecule, ridicule, duckling, sapling

cy [action, function] hesitancy, prophecy, normalcy (function in a normal way)

dom [quality, realm, office] freedom, kingdom, wisdom (quality of being wise)

ee [one who receives the action] employee, nominee (one who is nominated), refugee

en [made of, make] silken, frozen, oaken (made of oak), wooden, lighten

ence, ency [action, state of, quality] difference, conference, urgency

er, or [one who, that which] baker, miller, teacher, racer, amplifier, doctor

escent [in the process of] adolescent (in the process of becoming an adult), obsolescent

ese [a native of, the language of] Japanese, Vietnamese

esis, osis [action, process, condition] genesis, hypnosis, neurosis, osmosis

ess [female] actress, goddess, lioness

et, ette [a small one, group] midget, octet, baronet, majorette

fic [making, causing] scientific, specific

ful [full of] frightful, careful, helpful

fy [make] fortify, simplify, amplify

hood [order, condition, quality] womanhood, manhood, brotherhood

ic [nature of, like] metallic, heroic, poetic

ice [condition, state, quality] justice, malice

id, ide [a thing connected with or belonging to] fluid, fluoride

ile [relating to, suited for, capable of] juvenile, senile (related to being old), missile

ine [nature of] feminine, genuine, medicine

ion, sion, tion [act of, state of, result of] contagion, aversion, infection

ish [origin, nature, resembling] foolish, Irish, clownish (resembling a clown)

ism [system, manner, condition, characteristic] alcoholism, heroism, Communism

ist [one who, that which] violinist, artist, dentist

ite [nature of, quality of, mineral product] Israelite, dynamite, graphite, sulfite

ity, ty [state of, quality] captivity, clarity

ive [causing, making] abusive, exhaustive

ize [make] emphasize, publicize, idolize

less [without] baseless, careless (without care), artless, fearless, helpless

ly [like, manner of] carelessly, fearlessly, hopelessly, shamelessly

ment [act of, state of, result] contentment, amendment (state of amending)

ness [state of] carelessness, restlessness

oid [resembling] asteroid, spheroid, tabloid

ology [study, science, theory] biology, anthropology, geology, neurology

ous [full of, having] gracious, nervous, spacious, vivacious (full of life)

ship [office, state, quality, skill] friendship, authorship, dictatorship

some [like, apt, tending to] lonesome, threesome, gruesome

tude [state of, condition of] gratitude, aptitude, multitude (condition of being many)

ure [state of, act, process, rank] culture, literature, rupture (state of being broken)

ward [in the direction of] eastward, forward, backward

y [inclined to, tend to] cheery, crafty, faulty

Roots

Knowing the root of a difficult word can go a long way toward helping you figure out its meaning—even without a dictionary. Because improving your vocabulary is so important to success in all your classes (and beyond school), learning the following roots will be very valuable.

acer, acid, acri [bitter, sour, sharp] acerbic, acidity (sourness), acrid, acrimony

acu [sharp] acute, acupuncture

ag, agi, ig, act [do, move, go] agent (doer), agenda (things to do), agitate, navigate (move by sea), ambiguous (going both ways), action

ali, allo, alter [other] alias (a person's other name), alibi, alien (from another place), alloy, alter (change to another form)

altus [high, deep] altimeter (a device for measuring heights), altitude

am, amor [love, liking] amiable, amorous, enamored

anni, annu, enni [year] anniversary, annually (yearly), centennial (occurring once in 100 years)

anthrop [man] anthropology (study of mankind), misanthrope (hater of mankind), philanthropy (love of mankind)

antico [old] antique, antiquated, antiquity

arch [chief, first, rule] archangel (chief angel), architect (chief worker), archaic (first; very early), monarchy (rule by one person), matriarchy (rule by the mother)

aster, astr [star] aster (star flower), asterisk, asteroid, astronomy (star law), astronaut (star traveler; space traveler)

aud, aus [hear, listen] audible (can be heard), auditorium, audio, audition, auditory, audience, ausculate

aug, auc [increase] augur, augment (add to; increase), auction

auto, aut [self] automobile (self-moving vehicle), autograph (self-writing), automatic (self-acting), autobiography, author

belli [war] rebellion, belligerent (warlike or hostile), bellicose

biblio [book] Bible, bibliography (writing, list of books), bibliomania (craze for books), bibliophile (book lover)

bio [life] biology (study of life), biopsy (cutting living tissue for examination), biography

brev [short] abbreviate, brevity, brief

cad, cas [to fall] cadaver, cadence, caducous (falling off), cascade

calor [heat] calorie (a unit of heat), calorify (to make hot), caloric

cap, cip, cept [take] capable, capacity, capture, reciprocate, accept, except, forceps

capit, capt [head] decapitate (to remove the head from), capital, captain, caption

carn [flesh] carnivorous (flesh-eating), incarnate, reincarnation

caus, caut [burn, heat] caustic, cauldron, cauterize (to make hot; burn)

cause, cuse, cus [cause, motive] because, excuse (to attempt to remove the blame or cause), accusation

ced, ceed, cede, cess [move, yield, go, surrender] procedure, proceed (move forward), cede (yield), concede, intercede, precede, recede, secede (move aside from), success

centri [center] concentric, centrifugal, centripetal, eccentric (out of center)

chrom [color] chrome, chromosome (color body in genetics), Kodachrome, monochrome (one color), polychrome

chron [time] chronological (in order of time), chronometer (time-measured), chronicle (record of events in time), synchronize (make time with, set time together)

cide, cise [cut down, kill] suicide (self-killer), homicide (man, human killer), pesticide (pest killer), germicide (germ killer), insecticide, decide (cut off uncertainty), precise (cut exactly right), incision, scissors

cit [to call, start] incite, citation, cite

civ [citizen] civic (relating to a citizen), civil, civilian, civilization

clam, claim [cry out] exclamation, clamor, proclamation, reclamation, acclaim

clud, clus, claus [shut] include (to take in), conclude, recluse (one who shuts himself away from others), claustrophobia (abnormal fear of being shut up, confined)

cognosc, gnosi [know] recognize (to know again), incognito (not known), prognosis (forward knowing), diagnosis

cord, cor, cardi [heart] cordial (hearty, heartfelt), concord, discord, courage, encourage (put heart into), discourage (take heart out of), core, coronary, cardiac

corp [body] corporation (a legal body), corpse, corpulent

cosm [universe, world] cosmos (the universe), cosmic, cosmonaut, microcosm, cosmopolitan (world citizen), macrocosm

crat, cracy [rule, strength] democratic, autocracy

crea [create] creature (anything created), recreation, creation, creator

cred [believe] creed (statement of beliefs), credo (a creed), credence (belief), credit (belief, trust), credulous (believing too readily, easily deceived), incredible

cresc, cret, crease, cru [rise, grow] crescendo (growing in loudness or intensity), concrete (grown together, solidified), increase, decrease, accrue (to grow)

crit [separate, choose] critical, criterion (that which is used in choosing), hypocrite

cur, curs [run] current (running or flowing), concurrent, concur (run together, agree), incur (run into), recur, occur, courier, precursor (forerunner), cursive

cura [care] curator, curative, manicure (caring for the hands)

cycl, cyclo [wheel, circular] Cyclops (a mythical giant with one eye in the middle of his forehead), unicycle, bicycle, cyclone (a wind blowing circularly; a tornado)

deca [ten] decade, decalogue, decathlon

dem [people] democracy (people-rule), demography (vital statistics of the people: deaths, births, etc.), epidemic (on or among the people)

dent, dont [tooth] dental (relating to teeth), denture, dentifrice, orthodontist

derm [skin] hypodermic (injected under the skin), dermatology (skin study), epidermis (outer layer of skin), taxidermy (arranging skin; mounting animals)

dict [say, speak] diction (how one speaks, what one says), dictionary, dictate, dictator, dictaphone, dictatorial, edict, predict, verdict, contradict, benediction

doc [teach] indoctrinate, document, doctrine

domin [master] dominate, dominion, predominant, domain

don [give] donate, condone

dorm [sleep] dormant, dormitory

dox [opinion, praise] doxy (belief, creed, or opinion), paradox (contradictory), orthodox (having the correct, commonly accepted opinion), heterodox (differing opinion)

drome [run, step] syndrome (run together; symptoms), hippodrome (a place where horses run)

duc, duct [lead] induce (lead into, persuade), seduce (lead aside), produce, reduce, aquaduct (water leader or channel), viaduct, conduct, conduit, subdue, duke

dura [hard, lasting] durable, duration, endurance

dynam [power] dynamo (power producer), dynamic, dynamite, hydrodynamics

endo [within] endoral (within the mouth), endocardial (within the heart), endoskeletal

equi [equal] equinox, equilibrium

erg [work] energy, erg (unit of work), allergy, ergophobia (morbid fear of work), ergometer, ergograph

fac, fact, fic, fect [do, make] factory (place where workmen make goods of various kinds), fact (a thing done), manufacture, amplification, confection

fall, fals [deceive] fallacy, falsify

fer [bear, carry] ferry (carry by water), coniferous (bearing cones, as a pine tree), fertile (bearing richly), defer, infer, refer

fid, fide, feder [faith, trust] confidante, Fido, fidelity, confident, infidelity, infidel, federal, confederacy

fila, fili [thread] filament (a threadlike conductor heated by electrical current), filter, filet, filibuster, filigree

fin [end, ended, finished] final, finite, finish, confine, fine, refine, define, finale

fix [fix] fix, fixation (the state of being attached), fixture, affix, prefix, suffix

flex, flect [bend] flex (bend), reflex (bending back), flexible, flexor (muscle for bending), inflexibility, reflect, deflect

flu, fluc, fluv [flowing] influence (to flow in), fluid, flue, flush, fluently, fluctuate (to wave in an unsteady motion)

form [form, shape] form, uniform, conform, deform, reform, perform, formative, formation, formal, formula

fort, forc [strong] fort, fortress (a strong point), fortify (make strong), forte (one's strong point), fortitude

fract, frag [break] fracture (a break), infraction, fragile (easy to break), fraction (result of breaking a whole into equal parts), refract (to break or bend)

gam [marriage] bigamy (two marriages), monogamy, polygamy (many spouses or marriages)

gastr(o) [stomach] gastric, gastronomic, gastritis (inflammation of the stomach)

gen [birth, race, produce] genesis (birth, beginning), genetics (study of heredity), eugenics (well-born), genealogy (lineage by race, stock), generate, genetic

geo [earth] geometry (earth measurement), geography (earth-writing), geocentric (earth-centered), geology

germ [vital part] germination (to grow), germ (seed; living substance, as the germ of an idea), germane

gest [carry, bear] gestation, congestive (causing clogging), congest (bear together, clog)

gloss, glot [tongue] glossary, polyglot (many tongues), epiglottis

glu, glo [lump, bond, glue] glue, agglutinate (make to hold in a bond), conglomerate (bond together)

grad, gress [step, go] grade (step, degree), gradual (step-by-step), graduate (make all the steps, finish a course), graduated (in steps or degrees), progress

graph, gram [write, written] graph, graphic (written; vivid), autograph (self-writing; signature), photography (light-writing), graphite (carbon used for writing), phonograph (sound-writing), bibliography, telegram, diagram

grat [pleasing] congratulate (express pleasure over success), gratuity (mark of favor, a tip), grateful, ingrate (not thankful)

grav [heavy, weighty] grave, gravity, aggravate, gravitate

greg [herd, group, crowd] gregarian (belonging to a herd), congregation (a group functioning together), segregate (tending to group aside or apart)

helio [sun] heliograph (an instrument for using the sun's rays to send signals), heliotrope (a plant that turns to the sun)

hema, hemo [blood] hemorrhage (an outpouring or flowing of blood), hemoglobin, hemophilia

here, hes [stick] adhere, cohere, cohesion

hetero [different] heterogeneous (different in birth), heterosexual (with interest in the opposite sex)

homo [same] homogeneous (of same birth or kind), homonyn (word with same name or pronunciation as another), homogenize

hum, human [earth, ground, man] humus, exhume (to take out of the ground), humane (compassion for other humans)

hydr, hydra, hydro [water] dehydrate (take water out of; dry), hydrant (water faucet), hydraulic, hydraulics, hydrogen, hydrophobia (fear of water)

hypn [sleep] hypnosis, Hypnos (god of sleep), hypnotherapy

ignis [fire] ignite, igneous, ignition

ject [throw] deject, inject, project (throw forward), eject, object

join, junct [join] adjoining, enjoin (to lay an order upon; to command), juncture, conjunction, injunction, conjunction

juven [young] juvenile, rejuvenate (to make young again)

lau, lav, lot, lut [wash] launder, lavatory, lotion, ablution (a washing away), dilute (to make a liquid thinner and weaker)

leg [law] legal (lawful; according to law), legislate (to enact a law), legislature, legitimize (make legal)

levi [light] alleviate (lighten a load), levitate, levity (light conversation; humor)

liber, liver [free] liberty (freedom), liberal, liberalize (to make more free), deliverance

liter [letters] literary (concerned with books and writing), literature, literal, alliteration, obliterate

loc, loco [place] locality, locale, location, allocate (to assign; to place), relocate (to put back into place), locomotion (act of moving from place to place)

log, logo, ology [word, study, speech] catalog, prologue, dialogue, logogram (a symbol representing a word), zoology (animal study), psychology (mind study)

loqu, locut [talk, speak] eloquent (speaking well and forcefully), loquacious (talkative), colloquial (talking together; conversational or informal), soliloquy, locution

luc, lum, lus, lun [light] translucent (letting light come through), lumen (a unit of light), luminary (a heavenly body; someone who shines in his profession), luster (sparkle; shine), Luna (the moon goddess)

magn [great] magnify (make great, enlarge), magnificent, magnanimous (great of mind or spirit), magnate, magnitude, magnum

man [hand] manual, manage, manufacture, manacle, manicure, manifest, maneuver, emancipate

mand [command] mandatory (commanded), remand (order back), mandate

mania [madness] mania (insanity; craze), monomania (mania on one idea), kleptomania, pyromania (insane tendency to set fires), maniac

mar, mari, mer [sea, pool] marine (a sailor serving on shipboard), marsh (wetland, swamp), maritime (relating to the sea and navigation), mermaid (fabled marine creature, half fish)

matri [mother] matrimony (state of wedlock), matriarchate (rulership of women), maternal (relating to the mother), matron

medi [half, middle, between, halfway] mediate (come between, intervene), medieval (pertaining to the Middle Ages), mediterranean (lying between lands), mediocre, medium

mega [great] megaphone (great sound), megalopolis (great city; an extensive urban area including a number of cities), megacycle (a million cycles), megaton

mem [remember] memo (a reminder; a note), commemoration (the act of remembering by a memorial or ceremony), memento, memoir, memorable

meter [measure] meter (a metric measure), voltameter (instrument to measure volts), barometer, thermometer

micro [small] microscope, microfilm, microcard, microwave, micrometer (device for measuring small distances), omicron, micron (a millionth of a meter), microbe (small living thing)

migra [wander] migrate (to wander), emigrant (one who leaves a country), immigrate (to come into the land to settle)

mit, miss [send] emit (send out, give off), remit (send back, as money due), submit, admit, commit, permit, transmit (send across), omit, intermittent (sending between, at intervals), mission, missile

mob, mot, mov [move] mobile (capable of moving), motionless (without motion), motor, emotional (moved strongly by feelings), motivate, promotion, movement, demote

mon [warn, remind] monitor, monument (a reminder or memorial of a person or event), premonition (forewarning), admonish (warn)

mor, mort [mortal, death] mortal (causing death or destined for death), immortal (not subject to death), mortality (rate of death), mortician (one who prepares the dead for burial), mortuary (place for the dead, a morgue)

morph [form] amorphous (with no form, shapeless), metamorphosis (a change of form, as a caterpillar into a butterfly), morphology

multi [many, much] multifold (folded many times), multilinguist (one who speaks many languages), multiped (an organism with many feet), multiply

nat, nasc [to be born, to spring forth] innate (inborn), natal, native, nativity, renascence (a rebirth; a revival)

neur [nerve] neuritis (inflammation of a nerve), neuropathic (having a nerve disease), neurologist (one who practices neurology), neural, neurosis, neurotic

nom [law, order] autonomy (self-law, self-government), astronomy, gastronomy (stomach law; art of good eating), economy

nomen, nomin [name] nomenclature, nominate (name someone for an office)

nov [new] novel (new; strange; not formerly known), renovate (to make like new again), novice, nova, innovate

nox, noc [night] nocturnal, equinox (equal nights), noctilucent (shining by night)

numer [number] numeral (a figure expressing a number), numeration (act of counting), enumerate (count out, one by one), innumerable

omni [all, every] omnipotent (all-powerful), omniscient (all-knowing), omnipresent (present everywhere), omnivorous

onym [name] anonymous (without name), pseudonym (false name), antonym (against name; word of opposite meaning), synonym

oper [work] operate (to labor; function), cooperate (work together), opus (a musical composition or work)

ortho [straight, correct] orthodox (of the correct or accepted opinion), orthodontist (tooth straightener), orthopedic (originally pertaining to straightening a child), unorthodox

pac [peace] pacifist (one for peace only; opposed to war), pacify (make peace, quiet), Pacific Ocean (peaceful ocean)

pan [all] Pan-American, panacea (cure-all), pandemonium (place of all the demons; wild disorder), pantheon (place of all the gods in mythology)

pater, patr [father] paternity (fatherhood, responsibility, etc.), patriarch (head of the tribe or family), patriot, patron (a wealthy person who supports as would a father)

path, pathy [feeling, suffering] pathos (feeling of pity, sorrow), sympathy, antipathy (against feeling), apathy (without feeling), empathy (feeling or identifying with another), telepathy (far feeling; thought transference)

ped, pod [foot] pedal (lever for a foot), impede (get the feet in a trap, hinder), pedestal (foot or base of a statue), pedestrian (foot traveler), centipede, tripod (three-footed support), podiatry (care of the feet), antipodes (opposite feet)

pedo [child] orthopedic, pedagogue (child leader; teacher), pediatrics (medical care of children)

pel, puls [drive, urge] compel, dispel, expel, repel, propel, pulse, impulse, pulsate, compulsory, expulsion, repulsive

pend, pens, pond [hang, weigh] pendant (a hanging object), pendulum, suspend, appendage, pensive (weighing thought)

phil [love] philosophy (love of wisdom), philanthropy, philharmonic, bibliophile, Philadelphia (city of brotherly love)

phobia [fear] claustrophobia (fear of closed spaces), acrophobia (fear of high places), aquaphobia (fear of water)

phon [sound] phonograph, phonetic (pertaining to sound), symphony (sounds with or together)

photo [light] photograph (light-writing), photoelectric, photogenic (artistically suitable for being photographed), photosynthesis (action of light on chlorophyll to make carbohydrates)

plac, plais [please] placid (calm, peaceful), placebo, placate, complacent (pleased)

plu, plur, plus [more] plural (more than one), pluralist (a person who holds more than one office), plus (indicating that something more is to be added)

pneuma, pneumon [breath] pneumatic (pertaining to air, wind, or other gases), pneumonia (disease of the lungs)

pod (see *ped*)

poli [city] metropolis (mother city; main city), police, politics, Indianapolis, megalopolis, Acropolis (high city, upper part of Athens)

pon, pos, pound [place, put] postpone (put afterward), component, opponent (one put against), proponent, expose, impose, deposit, posture (how one places oneself), position, expound, impound

pop [people] population (the number of people in an area), populous (full of people), popular

port [carry] porter (one who carries), portable, transport (carry across), report, export, import, support, transportation

portion [part, share] portion (a part; a share, as a portion of pie), proportion (the relation of one share to others)

prehend [seize] apprehend (seize a criminal), comprehend (seize with the mind), comprehensive (seizing much, extensive)

prim, prime [first] primacy (state of being first in rank), prima donna (the first lady of opera), primitive (from the earliest or first time), primary, primal, primeval

proto [first] prototype (the first model made), protocol, protagonist, protozoan

psych [mind, soul] psyche (soul, mind), psychiatry (healing of the mind), psychology, psychosis (serious mental disorder), psychotherapy (mind treatment), psychic

punct [point, dot] punctual (being exactly on time), punctuation, puncture, acupuncture

reg, recti [straighten] regiment, regular, rectify (make straight), correct, direct, rectangle

ri, ridi, risi [laughter] deride (mock; jeer at), ridicule (laughter at the expense of another; mockery), ridiculous, derision

rog, roga [ask] prerogative (privilege; asking before), interrogation (questioning; the act of questioning), derogatory

rupt [break] rupture (break), interrupt (break into), abrupt (broken off), disrupt (break apart), erupt (break out), incorruptible (unable to be broken down)

sacr, sanc, secr [sacred] sacred, sacrosanct, sanction, consecrate, desecrate

salv, salu [safe, healthy] salvation (act of being saved), salvage, salutation

sat, satis [enough] satient (giving pleasure, satisfying), saturate, satisfy (to give pleasure to; to give as much as is needed)

sci [know] science (knowledge), conscious (knowing, aware), omniscient (knowing everything)

scope [see, watch] telescope, microscope, kaleidoscope (instrument for seeing forms), periscope, stethoscope

scrib, script [write] scribe (a writer), scribble, inscribe, describe, subscribe, prescribe, manuscript (written by hand)

sed, sess, sid [sit] sediment (that which sits or settles out of a liquid), session (a sitting), obsession (an idea that sits stubbornly in the mind), possess, preside (sit before), president, reside, subside

sen [old] senior, senator, senile (old; showing the weakness of old age)

sent, sens [feel] sentiment (feeling), consent, resent, dissent, sentimental (having strong feeling or emotion), sense, sensation, sensitive, sensory, dissension

sequ, secu, sue [follow] sequence (following of one thing after another), sequel, consequence, subsequent, prosecute, consecutive (following in order), second (following first), ensue, pursue

serv [save, serve] servant, subservient, servitude, preserve, conserve, reservation, service, conservation, observe, deserve

sign, signi [sign, mark, seal] signal (a gesture or sign to call attention), signature (the mark of a person written in his own handwriting), design, insignia (distinguishing marks), significant

simil, simul [like, resembling] similar (resembling in many respects), assimilate (to make similar to), simile, simulate (pretend; put on an act to make a certain impression)

sist, sta, stit [stand] assist (to stand by with help), persist (stand firmly; unyielding; continue), circumstance, stamina (power to withstand, to endure), status (standing), state, static, stable, stationary, substitute (to stand in for another)

solus [alone] solo, soliloquy, solitaire, solitude

solv, solu [loosen] solvent (a loosener, a dissolver), solve, absolve (loosen from, free from), resolve, soluble, solution, resolution, resolute, dissolute (loosened morally)

somnus [sleep] insomnia (not being able to sleep), somnambulist (a sleepwalker)

soph [wise] sophomore (wise fool), philosophy (love of wisdom), sophisticated (world wise)

spec, spect, spic [look] specimen (an example to look at, study), specific, spectator (one who looks), spectacle, aspect, speculate, inspect, respect, prospect, retrospective (looking backward), introspective, expect, conspicuous

sphere [ball, sphere] sphere (a planet; a ball), stratosphere (the upper portion of the atmosphere), hemisphere (half of the earth), spheroid

spir [breath] spirit (breath), conspire (breathe together; plot), inspire (breathe into), aspire (breathe toward), expire (breathe out; die), perspire, respiration

string, strict [draw tight] stringent (drawn tight; rigid), strict, restrict, constrict (draw tightly together), boa constrictor (snake that constricts its prey)

stru, struct [build] construe (build in the mind, interpret), structure, construct, instruct, obstruct, destruction, destroy

sume, sump [take, use, waste] consume (to use up), assume (to take; to use), sump pump (a pump that takes up water), presumption (to take or use before knowing all the facts)

tact, tang, tag, tig, ting [touch] tactile, contact (touch), intact (untouched, uninjured), intangible (not able to be touched), tangible, contagious (able to transmit disease by touching), contiguous, contingency

tele [far] telephone (far sound), telegraph (far writing), telegram, telescope (far look), television (far seeing), telephoto (far photography), telecast, telepathy (far feeling)

tempo [time] tempo (rate of speed), temporary, extemporaneously, contemporary (those who live at the same time), pro tem (for the time being)

ten, tin, tain [hold] tenacious (holding fast), tenant, tenure, untenable, detention, retentive, content, pertinent, continent, obstinate, contain, abstain, pertain, detain

tend, tent, tens [stretch, strain] tendency (a stretching; leaning), extend, intend, contend, pretend, superintend, tender, extent, tension (a stretching, strain), pretense

terra [earth] terrain, terrarium, territory, terrestrial

test [to bear witness] testament (a will; bearing witness to someone's wishes), detest, attest (bear witness to), testimony

the, theo [God, a god] monotheism (belief in one god), polytheism (belief in many gods), atheism, theology

therm [heat] thermometer, therm (heat unit), thermal, thermos bottle, thermostat, hypothermia (subnormal temperature)

thesis, thet [place, put] antithesis (place against), hypothesis (place under), synthesis (put together), epithet

tom [cut] atom (not cutable; smallest particle of matter), appendectomy (cutting out an appendix), tonsillectomy, dichotomy (cutting in two; a division), anatomy (cutting, dissecting to study structure)

tort, tors [twist] torture (twisting to inflict pain), retort (twist back, reply sharply), extort (twist out), distort (twist out of shape), contort, torsion (act of twisting, as a torsion bar)

tox [poison] toxic (poisonous), intoxicate, antitoxin

tract, tra [draw, pull] tractor, attract, subtract, tractable (can be handled), abstract (to draw away), subtrahend (the number to be drawn away from another)

trib [pay, bestow] tribute (to pay honor to), contribute (to give money to a cause), attribute, retribution, tributary

turbo [disturb] turbulent, disturb, turbid, turmoil

typ [print] type, prototype (first print; model), typical, typography, typewriter, typology (study of types, symbols), typify

ultima [last] ultimate, ultimatum (the final or last offer that can be made)

uni [one] unicorn (a legendary creature with one horn), unify (make into one), university, unanimous, universal

vac [empty] vacate (to make empty), vacuum (a space entirely devoid of matter), evacuate (to remove troops or people), vacation, vacant

vale, vali, valu [strength, worth] equivalent (of equal worth), valiant, validity (truth; legal strength), evaluate (find out the value), value, valor (value; worth)

ven, vent [come] convene (come together, assemble), intervene (come between), venue, convenient, avenue, circumvent (come or go around), invent, convent, venture, event, advent, prevent

ver, veri [true] very, aver (say to be true, affirm), verdict, verity (truth), verify (show to be true), verisimilitude

vert, vers [turn] avert (turn away), divert (turn aside, amuse), invert (turn over), introvert (turn inward), convertible, reverse (turn back), controversy (a turning against; a dispute), versatile (turning easily from one skill to another)

vic, vicis [change, substitute] vicarious, vicar, vicissitude

vict, vinc [conquer] victor (conqueror, winner), evict (conquer out, expel), convict (prove guilty), convince (conquer mentally, persuade), invincible (not able to be conquered)

vid, vis [see] video (television), evident, provide, providence, visible, revise, supervise (oversee), vista, visit, vision

viv, vita, vivi [alive, life] revive (make live again), survive (live beyond, outlive), vivid, vivacious (full of life), vitality, vivisection (surgery on a living animal)

voc [call] vocation (a calling), avocation (occupation not one's calling), convocation (a calling together), invocation (calling in), evoke, provoke, revoke, advocate, provocative, vocal

vol [will] malevolent, benevolent (one of goodwill), volunteer, volition

volcan, vulcan [fire] volcano (a mountain erupting fiery lava), vulcanize (to undergo volcanic heat), Vulcan (Roman god of fire)

volu [turn about, roll] voluble (easily turned about or around), voluminous (winding), convolution (a twisting or coiling)

vor [eat greedily] voracious, carnivorous (flesh-eating), herbivorous (plant-eating), omnivorous (eating everything), devour (eat greedily)

zo [animal] zoo (short for zoological garden), zoology (study of animal life), zoomorphism (attributing animal form to God), zodiac (circle of animal constellations), protozoa (one-celled animals)

bottom LINE

By learning two or three new word parts a day (and a word that each is used in), you will soon become a word expert. For example, by learning that *hydro* means "water," you have a good start at adding dozens of words to your vocabulary: *hydrogen, hydrofoil, hydroid, hydrolysis, hydrometer, hydrazide, hydrophobia, hydrochloride, hydrosphere, hydrokinetic, hydroponics,* etc.

Speaking Effectively

In college, you will use your speaking skills every day—occasionally to give a traditional formal speech, and more often to accomplish one of the following activities:

- ◎ Talking one-on-one with students or instructors, inside and outside the classroom
- ◎ Interviewing people to get information and ideas about a topic you're researching; or being interviewed for an internship, assistantship, or job
- ◎ Giving oral reports on research projects or class work

WHAT'S AHEAD

This chapter provides guidelines for handling any of the above-mentioned speaking activities, including a special section on adding "style" to your formal speeches.

- ● Preparing to Give a Speech
- ● Writing the Speech
- ● Rehearsing and Delivering the Speech
- ● A Closer Look at Style
- ● Conducting Interviews

Preparing to Give a Speech

A speech is a rare opportunity for both learning and teaching. The success of this opportunity depends on how well you pay attention to the occasion, audience, and purpose. How does your speech relate to the other activities in the class (the occasion)? How does it relate to your listeners— your instructor and fellow students (the audience)? How does it relate to the assignment (the purpose)? The guidelines that follow should help.

Choosing the Topic

When you may choose any topic, select one that falls within the guidelines of the assignment and helps the class learn something new and interesting.

- Address the topic from a new direction—one that you and your audience will find informative and interesting.
- Develop the topic by consulting current, reliable sources of information.

Choosing the Form and Style

Students and teachers are in the classroom to explore and learn together. Make the experience worthwhile by following these guidelines:

- Speak only as long as you must in order to make your point.
- Organize the speech so clearly that listeners get the point immediately.
- Use humor (when appropriate), insightful quotations, clarifying examples, interesting anecdotes.
- Speak frankly and openly.
- Show that you care about your audience by discussing real issues, finding strong support, and presenting an effective speech.

Choosing the Method of Delivery

Use the method of delivery that is appropriate for the occasion, audience, purpose, topic, and the time you have to prepare the speech.

- **IMPROMPTU:** Use this method when you have little time to prepare, or you want to be informal (effective for introductions and other brief presentations when you're thoroughly familiar with the topic).

- **OUTLINE:** Use this method when you have more time and want to shape the speech carefully (effective for reports or speeches when you want to pick up and respond to audience feedback).

- **MANUSCRIPT:** Use this method when you want the most precision and formality (effective for reports containing complex arguments or technical information). See 536-538 for a model manuscript speech.

Writing the Speech

The way you gather information, organize your ideas, and write them down depends primarily on the kind of speech you're giving and your method of delivery. For example, if you're giving a 5-minute impromptu speech during a meeting of students in the Amnesty International Club, you probably have no time to gather information, and only a few minutes to outline your thoughts. On the other hand, if you're giving an oral report on a research project in history class, you will have days or even weeks to search for information, to write out your speech in manuscript form, and to rehearse your delivery.

The important step in writing any speech is searching for information. For help on how and where to find information, look in the index under "Information." After collecting the information and working with it to develop your thinking, organize your ideas into a speech with an introduction, a body, and a conclusion.

INTRODUCTION

The introduction sets the tone and direction of your speech by

◉ getting your audience's attention and introducing the topic,

◉ stating your central idea or purpose,

◉ briefly identifying the main points, and

◉ making your audience interested in what you have to say.

NOTE: An introduction that clearly sets out a speech's framework is particularly important in reports or presentations where your audience needs help to follow complex arguments and understand detailed, technical information.

To get and keep the audience's attention throughout your speech, use one or more of the following:

◉ an interesting quotation,

◉ an amazing fact or a startling statement,

◉ a funny story or personal anecdote,

◉ an illustration or a colorful visual aid,

◉ a series of questions,

◉ a short history of the topic, or

◉ a strong statement demonstrating the topic's relevance by showing how it relates to important political, social, or scientific issues.

NOTE: In a project or research report, consider "hooking" your audience in the introduction by showing how the information that you will present connects to the subject your class is studying, or to projects other students are doing.

BODY

The body of your speech contains the main message, including the primary arguments and supporting evidence. As a result, the way you organize information is very important because the audience must understand it after hearing it only once! There are seven common ways of organizing information in the body of your speech.

1. **ORDER OF IMPORTANCE:** Arrange information according to its importance: least to greatest, or greatest to least.

   A speech in Communication 101 outlining the choices college students must make in order to graduate in four years

2. **CHRONOLOGICAL ORDER:** Arrange information according to time—the order in which events take place.

   A report on a two-week environmental-studies project during which you spent an hour a day at a nature preserve observing migrating geese

3. **COMPARISON/CONTRAST:** Give information about subjects by comparing them (showing similarities) and contrasting them (showing differences).

   A report to a political science class comparing and contrasting Proposition 209 (the California civil rights initiative) with the current California civil rights laws

4. **CAUSE AND EFFECT:** Give information about an event, a phenomenon, or a problem by showing (1) the situation's causes and (2) its effects.

   A lab report explaining your chemistry project and its results

5. **SPATIAL:** Arrange information about subjects according to where things are in relation to each other.

   A guide's presentation to prospective freshmen on a walking tour of the campus

6. **TOPICAL:** Arrange your ideas in related groups according to themes or topics in your speech.

   A speech in Art 101 in which you role-play a famous artist, showing slides of "your" paintings and discussing recurring themes

7. **PROBLEM/SOLUTION:** Describe a problem and then present a solution to solve it.

   A report in an education class on how students with comprehension problems improve their reading by learning three techniques for building background concepts

CONCLUSION

A good conclusion completes the argument or thesis while it also helps your audience understand

- what they have heard,
- why it's important, and
- what they should do about it.

Rehearsing and Delivering the Speech

Good speakers understand that preparing your script for delivery, revising it as necessary, and rehearsing repeatedly are necessary steps in the speaking process. Just how you prepare the script for delivery depends on your speech. The following information should help get you started.

For an **impromptu speech**, think about your purpose and write an abbreviated outline that includes the following:

● Your opening sentence

● Two or three phrases, each of which summarizes one main point

● Your closing sentence

> I. Opening Sentence
> II. Phrase #1
>   Phrase #2
>   Phrase #3
> III. Closing Sentence

For an **outline speech**, one that you have time to research and rehearse, think about your purpose, topic, and audience. Then outline your speech as follows:

● Opening statement in sentence form

● All main points in sentence form

● Quotations written in full

● All supporting numbers, technical details, and sources listed

● Closing statement in sentence form

● Notes indicating visual aids you plan to use

> I. Introduction
>   A. Point with support
>   B. Point (purpose or thesis)
> II. Body (with 3-5 main points)
>   A. Main point with details
>   B. Main point with details
>   C. Main point with details
> III. Conclusion
>   A. Point (restatement of thesis)
>   B. Point (possibly a call to action)

For a **manuscript speech**, use the guidelines below and write out the speech exactly as you plan to give it (for a model, see 536-538):

● Pages double-spaced

● Pages or cards numbered

● Abbreviations used only when you plan to say them (*FBI, YMCA,* but not *w/o*)

● Each sentence complete on a page—not running from one page to another

● All difficult words marked for pronunciation

● Script marked for interpretation (see symbols on the next page)

Rehearsing the Speech

Rehearse your speech until you're comfortable with it. Ask a classmate or friend to listen and offer feedback, or use a tape recorder or video recorder so you can hear and see yourself. Practice these techniques:

- Stand, walk to the lectern or front of the room, and face the audience with your head up and back straight.
- Speak loudly and clearly.
- Don't rush. Take your time and look at your notes (or your script) when you need to.
- Think about what you're saying so your audience hears the feeling in your voice.
- Use the symbols for interpretation (illustrated below).
- Talk with your hands—use gestures that help you communicate.
- Talk with your eyes and facial expressions by looking at the audience as you speak.
- If you plan to use audiovisual equipment, displays, or props during your speech, rehearse with them.
- Conclude the speech by picking up your materials and walking to your seat. Or, if your speech is a report on a research project, be prepared to stay in front of the room to answer questions regarding your research techniques, sources, and special problems encountered during the project.

Marking for Interpretation

As you decide what changes you need to make in your speech, note them on your copy. Do the same for changes in delivery. Putting notes about delivery techniques on your paper is called "marking your copy" and involves using a set of symbols to represent voice patterns. These symbols will remind you to pause in key places during your speech or to emphasize a certain word or phrase. Here is a list of copy-marking symbols.

Inflection *(arrows)* .... for a rise in pitch, for a drop in pitch.

Emphasis *(underlining or boldface)*........................ for additional <u>drive</u> or **force.**

Color *(wavy line or italic)* .... for additional feeling or *emotion*.

Pause *(dash, diagonal, ellipsis)* .... for a pause—or / break . . . in the flow.

Directions *(brackets)* .... for movement [*walk to chart*] or use of visual aids [*hold up chart*].

Using Visual Aids

While writing (or outlining) your speech, think about visual aids that would get the audience's attention and help them understand the message. For example, in her speech on corporal punishment, student writer Emily Buys used three overheads that helped her audience listen to the speech and follow her logic: (1) arguments for corporal punishment, (2) arguments against corporal punishment, and (3) two statements that influenced her decision about the topic. To see how Ms. Buys used the overheads, read the notes beside the text of her speech. (See 536-538.)

MODEL OVERHEADS

ARGUMENTS FOR CORPORAL PUNISHMENT

1. It's effective and consistent when thoughtfully administered.
2. It's unpleasant and prompts changed behavior.
3. It's brief and doesn't promote long-term anger.

ARGUMENTS AGAINST CORPORAL PUNISHMENT

1. It's ineffective when thoughtlessly administered.
2. It teaches violent behavior.
3. It undermines self-esteem by fostering anger, mistrust, and loss of self-respect.

FOOD FOR THOUGHT

"There is no psychological research to support the notion that physical punishment is an effective disciplinary method; indeed, study after study reveals that the opposite is true."

"Children tend to follow the guidance of those who inspire affection and admiration, not loathing and fear."
— Julius & Zelda Segal
"Does Spanking Work?"

Model Speech

"To Spank or Not to Spank—That Is the Question" is a speech by student writer Emily Buys who argues against using corporal punishment. Watch how she "hooks" her audience by (1) beginning with a question and a personal anecdote and (2) stating her own position only after presenting all other arguments. The model below would be appropriate as a persuasive speech in a communication class, or as a report in a psychology or sociology class.

NOTE: In the speech text, the speaker includes no page numbers for sources; however, in case an audience member requests the information, she keeps the information in her outline (not shown here).

Speaker introduces the topic and states the focus of the speech.

She uses a question and a personal anecdote to "hook" her audience.

She repeats the topic and tells the audience what's ahead.

Speaker turns on the projector and follows the three points on the overhead.

To Spank or Not to Spank— That Is the Question

To spank, or not to spank?—that's the question I plan to ask and answer during this speech. I won't argue whether it's nobler in the eyes of children to receive a scolding rather than a swat on the butt; however, I shall ask whether it's wiser in the minds of parents to discipline with methods other than spanking.

Why is this question important? It's important to me for two reasons. First, when I was growing up, my parents used corporal punishment, or spanking, as one way to discipline my siblings and me. While their choice taught us good things, and caused no long-term damage, I still wonder if it was the best choice.

Second, this question is important because I want children of my own someday, and I want to be the best parent that I can be. Some of you may also want that. However, in order to be the best, we need to answer questions like, "When my child dumps chocolate syrup on the kitchen floor—for the second time in three days—what do I decide: To spank—or not to spank?"

As I see it, there are three arguments for corporal punishment, and three against.

First, when administered carefully, corporal punishment is effective because it's consistent.

Edward L. Vockell from Purdue University makes this point in "Corporal Punishment: the Pros and Cons" when he says that if parents lay out specific rules about what type of physical action will be taken, corporal punishment can be effective. Children want to know—and need to know—what to expect.

Speaker cites an authority.

Ms. Buys summarizes pro arguments; introduces con arguments.

She sets up second overhead and makes her first point.

As speaker says "SWAT!" she claps her hands to create the sound.

Speaker quotes a local authority she has interviewed.

Second, corporal punishment is effective because it's unpleasant.

In other words, the purpose of punishment is to change a child's behavior, and because a spanking is unpleasant, it's an effective method for getting the child to change.

Third, corporal punishment is brief.

Vockell also makes this point by saying that corporal punishment allows parent-child relations to return to normal more quickly than many other methods. For example, if a child's punishment is loss of TV privileges for two weeks, he may be angry for two weeks. On the other hand, the anger following physical punishment may last only two days, or two hours.

Those who argue for physical punishment say it's good discipline because it can be effective, unpleasant, and brief. But that's only one side of the argument. Here's the other side.

First, corporal punishment is often administered thoughtlessly.

One example of this thoughtlessness is the parent who disciplines by imitation—he spanks his child only because he was spanked by his own parents. This parent disciplines by imitation rather than by thought.

Another example is the parent whose physical punishment is merely a reflex. When a child misbehaves, regardless of the time or crime—SWAT! It's a one-size-fits-all approach to discipline. As Nancy Samalin and Patricia McCormick explain in "What's Wrong with Spanking," this parent thinks too little about making the punishment fit the crime . . . or the child.

A third example is cited by Edward L. Vockell. Often, the parent chooses physical punishment to vent his or her own emotions. The child misbehaves, the parent gets upset, and SLAP!

These examples—discipline by imitation, reflex, and emotion—all illustrate parents who punish without thinking about whether their method of punishing is effective.

Second, corporal punishment teaches children to use violence.

Ms. Joyce Meer, director of the local Bird's Nest Childcare, made this point when I interviewed her: "If a child sees his parent use force," she said, "the child may think it's okay to hit when he has a problem." Most research supports Ms. Meer's observation.

Third, corporal punishment may cause a child to feel *anger* rather than *remorse, fear* rather than *trust,* and *loss of self-respect* rather than *development of self-esteem.*

Nancy Samalin and Patricia McCormick make this point in their book, Human Behavior, when noting that a child's anger about physical punishment may replace any remorse for misbehaving. Brian G. Gilmartin says in "The Case Against Spanking" that some children lose trust in authority figures who use corporal punishment, and the children react with fear instead.

John Martin Rich in "The Use of Corporal Punishment" notes that most victims of corporal punishment say it was humiliating and shameful. These emotions, he says, harm a child's self-respect.

So what is a parent to do? Now that you've heard all the arguments, how would you advise me to respond when my child dumps the chocolate syrup? Should I spank or not?

My answer is this: When my child needs to be punished, I want enough self-discipline to find alternatives to spanking. While corporal punishment can be effective, unpleasant, and brief, other methods also can be effective—without the negative side effects.

While the arguments we've just heard obviously influenced my decision, the following two statements by psychologists Julius and Zelda Segal influenced me most. They forced me to ask what kind of parent I want to be—and that helped me decide whether to use spanking with my children.

In their article, "Does Spanking Work?" the Segals say, "There is no psychological research to support the notion that physical punishment is an effective disciplinary method; indeed, study after study reveals that the opposite is true." I want to be an informed parent who uses research to decide how to treat my children.

Listen again to the Segals: "Children tend to follow the guidance of those who inspire affection and admiration, not loathing and fear." I want to be a parent who disciplines more by inspiration than by fear of punishment.

Like all of you, I want to be the best parent that I can be. I want to be *informed* and *inspiring.* I want my children to trust me, not fear me. I want them to respect me, and, more importantly, respect themselves. For me, the answer is finding an alternative to spanking. What about you? ■

She introduces the conclusion by citing an illustration used earlier.

She states her position, rejecting three pro arguments.

Speaker sets up third overhead and points to the first quotation.

Speaker emphasizes words in italics while restating her thesis.

A Closer Look at Style

More than any other president of recent times, John F. Kennedy is remembered for the appealing style and tone of his speeches. By looking at sample portions of his speeches, you should get a better feel for how style and tone can help strengthen the spoken word. By using special stylistic devices (allusion, analogy, anecdote, etc.), you can improve the style and impact of your speech.

By using special appeals (democratic principle, common sense, pride, etc.), you can control the tone or feeling of what you have to say. (The type of appeal used is listed above each Kennedy speech excerpt.)

Allusion is a reference to a familiar person, place, or thing.

Appeal to the Democratic Principle

One hundred years of delay have passed since President Lincoln freed the slaves, yet their heirs, their grandsons, are not fully free (Radio and Television Address, 1963).

Analogy is a comparison of an unfamiliar idea to a simple, familiar one. The comparison is usually quite lengthy, suggesting several points of similarity. An analogy is especially useful when attempting to explain a difficult or complex idea.

Appeal to Common Sense

In our opinion the German people wish to have one united country. If the Soviet Union had lost the war, the Soviet people themselves would object to a line being drawn through Moscow and the entire country defeated in war. We wouldn't like to have a line drawn down the Mississippi River . . . (Interview, November 25, 1961).

Anecdote is a short story told to illustrate a point.

Appeal to Pride, Commitment

Frank O'Connor, the Irish writer, tells in one of his books how as a boy, he and his friends would make their way across the countryside and when they came to an orchard wall that seemed too high and too doubtful to try and too difficult to permit their voyage to continue, they took off their hats and tossed them over the wall—and then they had no choice but to follow them. This nation has tossed its cap over the wall of space, and we have no choice but to follow it. Whatever the difficulties, they will be overcome (San Antonio Address, November 21, 1963).

Antithesis is balancing or contrasting one word or idea against another, usually in the same sentence.

Appeal to Common Sense, Commitment

Mankind must put an end to war, or war will put an end to mankind (Address to the U.N., 1961).

Irony is using a word or phrase to mean the exact opposite of its literal meaning, or to show a result that is the opposite of what would be expected or appropriate, an odd coincidence.

Appeal to Common Sense

They see no harm in paying those to whom they entrust the minds of their children a smaller wage than is paid to those to whom they entrust the care of their plumbing (Vanderbilt University, 1961).

Negative definition is describing something by telling what it is *not* rather than, or in addition to, what it *is*.

Appeal for Commitment

. . . members of this organization are committed by the Charter to promote and respect human rights. Those rights are not respected when a Buddhist priest is driven from his pagoda, when a synagogue is shut down, when a Protestant church cannot open a mission, when a cardinal is forced into hiding, or when a crowded church service is bombed (United Nations, September 20, 1963).

Parallel structuring is the repeating of phrases or sentences that are similar (parallel) in meaning and structure; **repetition** is the repeating of the same word or phrase to create a sense of rhythm and emphasis.

Appeal for Commitment

Let every nation know, whether it wishes us well or ill, that we shall pay any price, bear any burden, meet any hardship, support any friend, oppose any foe, in order to assure the survival and the success of liberty (Inaugural Address, 1961).

Quotations, especially of well-known individuals, can be effective in nearly any speech.

Appeal for Emulation or Affiliation

At the inauguration, Robert Frost read a poem which began "the land was ours before we were the land's"—meaning, in part, that this new land of ours sustained us before we were a nation. And although we are now the land's—a nation of people matched to a continent—we still draw our strength and sustenance . . . from the earth (Dedication Speech, 1961).

Rhetorical question is a question posed for emphasis of a point, not for the purpose of getting an answer.

Appeal to Common Sense, Democratic Principle

"When a man's ways please the Lord," the Scriptures tell us, "he maketh even his enemies to be at peace with him." And is not peace, in the last analysis, basically a matter of human rights—the right to live out our lives without fear of devastation—the right to breathe air as nature provided it—the right of future generations to a healthy existence (Commencement Address, 1963)?

Conducting Interviews

The idea of the interview is simple: You talk with someone who has expert knowledge or has had important experiences with your topic. For example, for a botany paper, you might discuss the benefits of forest fires with a forest ranger or botanist. An interview can be as informal as a phone call to ask a single question, or as complex as a videotaped interview on location.

PREPARING FOR AN INTERVIEW

1. Know the person and the subject that you will discuss. Come to the interview informed so that you can build on what you know.

2. When you arrange the interview, be thoughtful. Set it up at the interviewee's convenience. Explain who you are, what your purpose is, the topics you'd like to cover, and how long it may take.

3. Write out some questions ahead of time. This will give the interview some structure and help you cover the necessary topics.

- Review the types of questions that you can ask—the 5 W's and H: who, what, when, where, why, and how.

- Think about the specific topics you want to cover in the interview and draft related questions for each topic.

- Organize your questions in a logical order so that the interview moves smoothly from one subject to the next.

- Understand open and closed questions. Closed questions ask for simple answers; open questions ask for an explanation.

  Closed: **How did you vote on the recent budget proposal?**

  Open: **Can you describe the process the Congress went through to arrive at the current budget?**

- Avoid slanted or loaded questions that suggest you want a specific answer.

  Slanted: **Don't you agree that liberal politicians are spending our country into bankruptcy? Won't conservative politicians' approach to slashing social programs hurt the family?**

  Better: **What are some key differences between liberal and conservative political positions on spending?**

4. Write the questions on the left side of the page. Leave room for quotations, information, and impressions on the right side.

5. Be prepared. Take pens and paper. If you plan on taping the interview, get permission ahead of time. Take along a tape recorder or camcorder with blank tapes and extra batteries.

DOING THE INTERVIEW

1. Begin by reminding the person why you've come. Provide whatever background information is necessary to help him or her feel comfortable and ready to focus on the specific topic.

2. If the person gives permission, tape the interview. However, make sure the recording equipment doesn't interfere. If you are videotaping the interview, set your camcorder on a tripod at a comfortable distance from the interviewee—if possible. If you are using a tape recorder, place it off to the side so that its presence isn't a distraction. Try to use a tape recorder with a counter. Then, when the interviewee makes an interesting or important point, jot down the number. Later, you'll be able to find these points quickly.

3. Write down key information. Even if you are using a recorder, note descriptive words for the voice, actions, and expressions of the interviewee.

4. Listen actively. Use body language—from nods to smiles—to show you're listening. Pay attention not only to what the person says but how he or she says it—the word choice, connotations, syntax, and context. If you don't understand something, ask politely for clarification.

5. Be flexible. If the person looks puzzled by a question, rephrase it or ask another. If the discussion gets off track, gently redirect it. Based on the interviewee's responses, ask follow-up questions that occur to you at that moment in order to dig deeper. (Don't be handcuffed by the questions you wrote out before the interview.)

6. Be tactful. If the person avoids a difficult question, politely rephrase it or ask for clarification.

 Anticipate that important points may come up late in the interview as the person develops a trust in you.

FOLLOWING THE INTERVIEW

1. As soon as possible, review all your notes and fill in responses you remember but couldn't record at the time. If you recorded the interview, replay it and listen carefully for key quotations.

2. Thank the person with a note or phone call. At the same time, check to make sure the information and quotations are accurate.

3. Let the person see the outcome of the interview. That might be a videotape of the interview, the report you hand in, or a copy of the speech you present or article you publish.

Succeeding in College

When college was attended by a select few, the professors closely guided and monitored small groups of students throughout their four years of study. And they constantly engaged in discussions and debates. It was a very active and communal enterprise. Colleges today are very busy places, sometimes good-sized communities unto themselves. As a result, it is pretty much up to each student to monitor his or her own progress, especially the everyday, commonsense side of college life.

WHAT'S AHEAD

This section of your handbook introduces you to some of the basic principles involved in understanding and dealing with the day-to-day aspects of campus living. It also contains a glossary of terms commonly used on college campuses. We hope you find it all helpful.

- The Keys to Success
- Managing Your Time
- If Only I Had Known . . .
- Glossary of College Terms

The Keys to Success

DETERMINATION

College is designed to help you grow beyond whatever point you've reached. Did you get straight A's in high school? Well, the things that brought A's in high school—doing the work, mastering the material, getting it in on time—will simply be assumed now. It will be the extra effort, the unusual originality, or the uncommon discipline that will cause you to excel in college.

In other words, the rewards are harder to come by. The bar is raised. Even the very brightest college students must work diligently. But the rewards are worth it. So be determined to persevere—determined to stick to your work—even when college life seems to offer a world of distractions and challenges.

1

CURIOSITY

More than high school, college taps the whole range of learning resources—the larger world of knowledge, information, and argument. Despite all you already know, you must humbly adopt the attitude that you have much more to learn. Learn how to poke around, letting questions become your best friends. Search for a new and sounder perspective and always remain open-minded. In short, be intellectually hungry and curious about what others think.

2

3

SELF-RELIANCE

College isn't elementary school. Teachers won't watch over you on a daily basis. The way you keep notes is your business. Same with studying for tests, thinking up topics for most of your papers, and choosing a major. You'll also have to make more decisions for yourself than you've ever made before: how to get places, how to earn money, how to live, who to trust, whether or not to go to class. When you no longer have "Mom" or "Dad" right there to guide your decision making, you will have to be the one with the answers—the one who makes it happen.

Managing Your Time

One of the biggest obstacles to succeeding is failing to plan. Managing your time requires planning. Almost everyone has failed to plan at one time or another and suffered the consequences. You may find the following suggestions helpful:

Making Progress

1. **Turn big jobs into smaller ones.** Successful people will tell you that they often divide up their big jobs into smaller, more manageable steps. Spreading a project over a reasonable period of time will reduce the pressure that comes from letting everything go until the last minute. Tackle your tasks as they need to be done, and develop a process for working through the big jobs. Then follow your plan.

2. **Keep a weekly schedule.** If you haven't started a personal calendar to keep track of appointments and assignments, what are you waiting for? You'll have your day at a glance and be twice as likely to keep the appointments you write down. Design your planner to meet your needs; the more personalized you make it, the more likely you'll be to use it.

   NOTE: Planners and calendars can be purchased at a reasonable cost if that seems easier than making your own. Also, most word-processing programs have built-in notepads and calendars.

3. **Make lists.** Making a daily list of things to do may strike you as overdoing it at first, but you'll soon change your mind. You'll also rest easier at night, knowing that you've got the next day covered.

4. **Plan your study time.** Good advice, but most of us seldom take it. Good planning means having everything you need where you need it. Schedule your study time as early in the day as you can, take short breaks, keep snacks to a minimum, interact with the page by asking questions (out loud, if no one objects), and summarize what you've learned before you put the books away.

5. **Stay flexible.** Plans do change and new things can pop up daily. Be realistic, willing to change those events that can be changed and exercising patience for those that cannot. You'll save yourself lots of wear and tear if you remain flexible and upbeat.

 **TAKE note**

If you are having trouble getting started on your assignments, try doing them at the same time and place each day. This will help you control the urge to wait until you are "in the mood" before starting.

If Only I Had Known . . .

Here's a list of 20 things you should think about now, so that later you won't have to say, "If only I had known . . . ."

1. **Basic computer skills, such as using word processing or e-mail, or even "surfing the net," are becoming essential in college.** Although not every college is boogie-boarding on the wave of high technology, many are. And many will want you to boogie, too. But don't worry; if you're not an expert yet, most schools have computer labs with helpful assistance and 24-hour access.

2. **Classes fill up in a hurry.** Be sure to register for classes as soon as possible—like yesterday.

3. **Bookstores can run short on books.** The solution is to buy your books as soon as you've completed registration. Don't wait until the day before classes begin. Bookstores often understock, and you may end up sharing a textbook with the kid down the hall—not a happy thought.

4. **It's essential to memorize your social security number.** To some, it will be far more important than your name.

5. **It's not essential to decide on a major immediately.** You don't need to declare a major during your first two years of college. Most freshman courses fill some requirement or other, but you should also try to fit in a course or two in areas that interest you. By the time you're a junior, your own searching plus the advice of your family and faculty advisor will help you make a wise choice.

6. **Poor class attendance is the major cause of student suffering.** Enough said.

7. **You'll be in class for far fewer hours than when you were in high school;** but the time needed for reading and studying will be much greater.

8. **There is no—repeat—no substitute for daily study and review.** Cramming for exams is about as good for learning as cramming chocolate bars is good for health. Take advantage of how your brain works, and use repeated study to deepen those mental grooves.

9. **The library is a great place to study!** Plan to use it. Then, even if your roommate is Godzilla's second cousin, you'll have a better chance at harmony in that most important of places, your room.

10. **It's essential to lock your room if you're leaving for only a few minutes.** That's a lesson you'd rather not learn by experience.

11. **If you have a roommate, you should agree on a set of guidelines for living together.** Negotiate a reasonable lights-and-stereos-off time; talk about when visiting is okay, and discuss what you can and can't borrow from one another.

12. **You have to clean up after yourself**—even when you have the flu, your roommate is unsympathetic, you have a term paper due, and you're auditioning for a play.

13. **You should never wash white clothing with other colors** (especially red) even when you're low on quarters—unless you really like pink and gray.

14. **Time management is the king of all subjects.** Many schools have a freshman or new-student seminar that can help you learn time-management skills, as well as test-taking skills and effective use of campus and support services.

15. **Gaining 10-15 pounds in your freshman year is quite normal.** (It's called the "freshman fifteen.") Don't panic, don't get depressed, and don't crash diet. Above all, don't let peer pressure ease you into an eating disorder. Eat well and stay active—walk, jog, swim, play racquetball, take the stairs instead of the elevator, etc.

16. **Keeping a folder with all your college records, financial aid papers, and grade reports is essential.** This will save time when you need them for any reason.

17. **It's important to try new things inside and outside the classroom.** College is a banquet of experiences, but you'll miss it if you spend all your time in the library, the dorm, and the local bars.

18. **Getting to know people who are different from you is part of a good education.** This includes people of different races and classes; people who have different religious affiliations; people who are disabled in some way; people who have different talents than you have; upperclassmen; and, yes, even professors.

19. **Dating is fine, but make wise choices.** If you're a female, don't single-date or bring back to the dorm anyone you don't know well. And don't let alcohol or drugs cloud your judgment. This is serious. Stories about date rapes are true, but the reports you'll hear about on the news are only the tip of the iceberg. Group dates provide good, relaxed, safe, fun ways to get to know people.

20. **It's smart to stick to your values and beliefs.** Consider new ideas and points of view, but don't be swayed easily. In short, be true to yourself.

Glossary of College Terms

Academic Advisor: An academic advisor is a faculty member or counselor who helps you choose your courses each term and can help you choose a major. Advisors make sure that you meet the school's graduation requirements, but they are also there to answer nonacademic questions and concerns.

Academic Freedom: Academic freedom is the right of faculty members, with no threat of being fired, to present any issue or body of information, regardless of its controversial or unpopular nature. This freedom applies, however, only as long as the students' health and civil rights are not threatened.

Academic Probation: Probation is a formal warning that your grades do not meet your school's academic standards. With the warning comes a request that students do what is necessary (and ethical) to raise their grade point averages. Failure to do so can eventually mean dismissal from the college—without a degree.

Admissions: This office processes the applications to a college or university. Forms must be filled out carefully and returned to meet any deadlines. Acceptance to the school does not necessarily guarantee acceptance into all of its programs.

Alumnus: An alumnus is a graduate of a college or university. Alumni offices keep graduates posted on their school's progress, and may also ask for support on occasion.

Associate Degree: An associate degree is a two-year degree. Such degrees are often earned at community colleges or technical schools, but some large universities also offer this shorter route. *Remember:* While some state schools accept associate-degree credits toward a bachelor's degree, others do not.

Athletic Director: This person heads up the athletic department at your school and coordinates all the athletic programs.

Attrition: Attrition refers to the number or percentage of students who drop out of a course, a program of study, or a school.

Bachelor's Degree: You earn a bachelor's degree after completing your undergraduate studies. The two most common undergraduate degrees are the bachelor of arts (B.A.) and the bachelor of science (B.S.), which are generally received after a four- or five-year course of full-time study.

Carrel: A carrel is either a small room or a desk and chair arrangement used for quiet study and located in the college library (or other designated area). Sometimes these are assigned to students and must be requested from the librarian.

Chancellor: The chancellor is the person in charge of a college or university. In a statewide university, there will usually be a president over the entire system and a chancellor over each campus.

Coed (Coeducational): This term refers to a school that accepts both women and men. Today, most colleges and universities are coeducational.

Commons: The commons is an open square or area of land on campus where students can gather to talk, read, eat, etc.

Core Curriculum: The core curriculum is a set of basic requirements—courses in English, math, science, and history—that must be completed before going on to the upper-level courses needed to obtain a bachelor's degree. These basic courses are generally completed during a student's freshman and sophomore years.

Course Outline: In most classes, you will receive this outline, or syllabus, on the first day of class. It will give you an overview of what the instructor will be teaching and will probably also explain your responsibilities—papers due, reading assignments, test schedules, etc.

Credit: When you complete a course successfully, you receive credit for it. The number of credits assigned to a course is related to the number of class-time hours required each week. (See *quarter hour* and *semester hour*.)

Dean: An academic dean is the person in charge of one of the divisions, or schools, within a college. One dean heads up the school of education, another the school of arts and sciences, and so on. Some universities also hire a dean of student affairs and a dean of business affairs.

Dean's List: Much like being on the honor roll during high school, getting on the dean's list at the end of the term is an academic honor bestowed on those students who maintain a certain grade point average.

Department: Each major academic division, or school, within a university is further divided into departments. For example, the school of arts and sciences may be divided into the art department, the biology department, the chemistry department, and so on.

Drop/Add: During a specified number of weeks at the beginning of each term, and following a set procedure, students may drop courses that they find unsatisfactory and add others.

Elective: An elective is a course taken in addition to those needed to satisfy students' core curriculum, major, and minor requirements. A certain number of electives are actually required, offering you the chance to pursue other interests and thereby broaden your education.

Fraternity: A fraternity is a men's student organization with a Greek-letter name, formed mostly for social purposes.

Freshman Fifteen: The "freshman fifteen" refers to the weight you may gain during your first year at college. It is speculated that your teenage growth-spurt eating habits, an easy access to junk food and/or starchy all-you-can-eat meals, plus the lack of aerobic exercise all contribute to this phenomenon. You *can do* something about all three factors.

GPA (Grade Point Average): This is a cumulative average of your college grades, often figured on a 4-point scale (A=4, B=3, C=2, D=1, F=0). You can compute your GPA for a semester in this way: **Multiply** the number of points for each final grade you receive times the number of credits assigned to each course. **Add** up the points earned for all your courses. Finally, **divide** this point total by the number of credits you handled for the semester. The result is your GPA.

Grad Student: A grad student is someone who already has a B.A. or a B.S. degree and is working toward a master's degree or a doctorate, or is enrolled in some other advanced program such as medical school or law school.

Greeks: This term is used to refer to students who belong to fraternities or sororities.

Health Services: This is your "doctor's office" away from home. Students with minor injuries and illnesses can go to health services for professional treatment.

Honor Fraternities/Sororities: These are Greek-letter organizations formed not for social reasons, but to honor students for scholastic achievement in specific academic programs—social work, forensics, biology, music, etc.

Honors: Your school will have various ways of honoring outstanding academic achievement—the dean's list is one example. Superior students may also graduate *cum laude* (with distinction or honor), *magna cum laude* (with great distinction), or *summa cum laude* (with highest distinction).

Hours: "Hours" is another way of saying "credits." If a student is handling 15 credits, he or she is said to be "taking 15 hours."

Incomplete: Receiving an incomplete (I) for a final grade means you did not finish a portion of the required course work.

Independent Study: This term is most often used to mean a course for which you complete the necessary work on your own time, in a nonclassroom setting, and usually under the direction of a professor.

Instructor: An instructor is a college teacher, but not necessarily a professor. The teaching staff ranks (from the top) as follows: professor, lecturer, instructor, teaching assistant.

Inter-Fraternity Council: This is a board of representatives from all campus fraternities. Together they set policies governing the various frats' activities.

Internship: An internship, which is a work experience form of study, is required in fields like nursing and medicine. While students work, they receive college credit toward their degrees. Classroom prerequisites and an application process precede most internships.

Lecture Hall: This is a very large room for addressing many students at once.

Lecturer: A lecturer is a college teacher, but not necessarily a professor. (See *instructor.*)

Lower Division: "Lower division" refers to the courses students usually take during their freshman and sophomore years. These courses prepare you for the more advanced study required later on.

Major: A major refers to the subject area you choose to concentrate on for your degree. Usually students take a third to a half of their courses in their major.

Master's Degree: This is the graduate degree (M.A. or M.S.) you can work toward after having received your B.A. or B.S. Admission requirements for graduate study should be obtained from your school's graduate studies office. In general, a master's program will help you to further develop your capabilities in your chosen discipline.

Mid-Terms: Mid-terms are tests given halfway through the semester or quarter that tell both you and your instructors how well you are mastering the course work. Keeping up with daily work will make mid-terms far more manageable.

Minor: In colleges that require it, this is a subject area, usually related in some way to your major, in which you must take a pre-scribed number of credits before you can graduate.

Orals: Orals are tests during which you answer, aloud, questions posed by one or more professors. This type of test is gener-ally reserved for graduate students.

Orientation: An extremely useful activity, during which many schools set aside a day or more to introduce new students and their parents to the campus facilities, services, and academic programs. Usually, you may also ask for class-scheduling advice and preregister for classes.

Panhellenic Council: This is a board of representatives from all campus sororities and/or fraternities. Together they set policies governing their planned activities throughout the year.

Pass/Fail: Some colleges allow students to take certain courses (usually the electives) in this fashion (also called **pass/no pass** or **satisfactory/unsatisfactory**). Either *pass* or *fail* appears on your transcript, so no points can be assigned to these credits. They apply toward your degree but cannot be figured into your GPA.

Plagiarism: This serious offense, usually most tempting when writing term papers, entails using someone else's ideas or actual words as your own—in other words, failing to give credit where credit is due. If discov-ered, this act can put you on probation or get you dismissed from school.

Pledge: A pledge is a person who has been newly accepted into a fraternity or sorority.

Practicum: Much like an internship, this is a type of work-and-study learning experi-ence for which you usually earn credit. Practicums generally cover a limited amount of material in depth, whereas the internship is broader in its scope.

Preregistration: At some midpoint in the academic term, many colleges ask students to preregister for the following term. When you select the courses you want to take and the professors you want to study under, schools can better plan their programs. You also have a better chance of getting the courses and sections that you want.

Prerequisite: A prerequisite usually refers to a course or courses that you must com-plete satisfactorily before you can take the more advanced course. Sometimes a pre-requisite for a course involves a certain class standing or GPA.

Probation: See *academic probation*.

Professional Societies: These are groups composed of students who are working toward degrees in specific areas of study—art, advertising, marketing, geology, and music, to name just a few. Sometimes these groups have Greek-letter designations.

Professor: Professors have the highest ranking among the teachers on campus, and they are also ranked themselves: assis-tant professor, associate professor, and full professor (or professor). Often, professors have their doctoral degrees, but this is not always the case.

Quarter: When a college operates on the quarter system, there are four quarters of study per year—fall, winter, spring, and summer. However, you do not have to take the summer quarter in order to finish a four-year degree—this can be done by going to school three quarters per year for four years.

Quarter Hour: The quarter hour is the credit unit given at a school that uses quar-ter terms, which last approximately 10 weeks. (See *credit* and *hours*.)

Registrar: This is the person in charge of directing the registration process at a col-lege. He or she also oversees the correct posting of final grades to the students' transcripts.

Residence Hall: In plain language, this is a dormitory—student housing provided by your college.

Residence Hall Staff: Usually, there will be a resident manager (also known as a hall director) to whom you may take concerns about your room, such as broken furniture, missing items that are sup-posed to be part of the deal, showers that don't work, etc. Also, a responsible upper-classman will be appointed residential assistant, or counselor, over 20 to 25 stu-dents. This person has been trained to help students adjust to dorm life. He or she can answer your questions; organize activities, discussions, and meetings; mediate room-mate disagreements; and much more.

Room and Board: This is a term referring to the cost of staying in a residence hall and partaking in a meal plan established by the college. Even if you stay off campus, you can take advantage of a meal plan—in this case, your room and board would be the cost of your rent and the meal plan combined.

Semester: Operating on a semester system, a college will offer three terms of study each year—the fall semester, spring semester, and summer school. It is possible to attend eight semesters, skipping summer school, and obtain a degree in four years.

Semester Hour: A semester hour is the credit unit earned at a school that uses the semester system. (See *credit* and *hours*.)

Seminar: A seminar is a class with far fewer students than a lecture course has. The smaller size allows for teacher-led discussions in which all students can participate. Usually, it is the graduate classes that are run in this fashion, although you may find a few seminar courses at the undergraduate level.

Social Probation: Regulations to govern student conduct vary from school to school; when these are violated on a regular basis, a student may be put on social probation. Depending upon the school and upon the student's response to the warning, dismissal can result.

Sorority: A sorority is a women's student organization with a Greek-letter name, formed mostly for social purposes.

Student Center: The student center is often referred to as the student union. It is a building where you can meet with other students for leisure activities—seeing a movie, playing cards, eating and conversing, etc.

Student Government Association: This is the equivalent of your high-school student council, and your most important channel of communication with your school's administration. A student senate may be very involved in the governing of the institution it serves, making recommendations regarding student life and services as well as sitting with faculty members on departmental and administrative committees. Usually, the student body has the opportunity each term to elect eligible students to serve as senators.

Student Housing Department: This is the department in charge of the residence halls on your campus. The individual resident directors, or managers, report to this office. Often, the student housing department can also help you find suitable off-campus housing by publishing lists of available apartments.

Syllabus: See *course outline*.

Teaching Assistant (TA): A teaching assistant, often a graduate student, is hired by the college to teach certain sections or portions of a course—perhaps a lab section or discussion hour.

Term Paper: This kind of paper is generally an important part of your grade, and your teacher will probably tell you about it in the course outline. Generally, you have the entire term to complete this paper. Know which style manual your teacher prefers.

Thesis: A thesis is a longer, more involved research paper than the term paper. It is usually required of graduate students before they can receive their master's degrees, but some schools also assign senior theses as a graduation requirement.

Transcript: Your transcript, updated each term by the registrar's office, is your official college "report card." On this form, you and any future employers can see the grades you earned in all your course work, your GPA, and graduation information.

Transfer Credit: When you choose to transfer to another college or university, the number of courses that your new school is willing to accept toward your degree are your transfer credits.

Trimester: Some schools divide the academic year into three terms.

Tuition: Separate from room and board, books, and other supply costs, tuition is the money charged for your college courses. Usually, tuition costs are given per semester or term. In a state university system, residents of the state pay considerably less tuition than do out-of-state students.

Union: See *student center*.

Upper Division: This term refers to the courses you will take in your junior and senior years at college. These courses usually cover your chosen field of study in a more in-depth fashion than do the lower-division courses you took previously.

Work-Study Program: This is a program in which students are offered campus jobs to earn money toward the cost of their education. Students with financial need are considered first for these positions.

Proofreader's Guide

Marking Punctuation

Checking Mechanics

Using the Right Word

Understanding Our Language

Using the Language

"It is not wise to violate the rules until you know how to observe them." —T. S. Eliot

Marking Punctuation

PERIOD

552 A **period** is used to end a sentence that makes a statement or that gives a command that is not an exclamation.

> (Statement)
> **The best way to keep the wolf from the door is with a sheepskin.** —Laurence J. Peter

> (Mild command) **If it sounds like writing, rewrite it.**

> (Request) **Please read the instructions carefully.**

NOTE: It is not necessary to place a period after a statement that has parentheses around it and is part of another sentence.

> **Think about joining a club (the student government office should have a list of campus organizations) for fun and for leadership experience.**

553 A period should be placed after an initial or an abbreviation.

Mr.	**B.C.**	**Ph.D.**	**Edna St. V. Millay**
Jr.	**D.D.S.**	**U.S.**	**Booker T. Washington**
Prof.	**p.m.**	**B.A.**	**F. Scott Fitzgerald**

NOTE: When an abbreviation is the last word in a sentence, use only one period at the end of the sentence.

> **Don't be afraid to use the many resources available at most colleges: academic advisors, teaching assistants, writing labs, health services, etc.**

554 A period is used as a decimal point.

> **The government spends approximately $15.5 million each year just to process student loan forms.**

Using the Ellipsis

An **ellipsis** (three periods) is used to show that one or more words have been omitted in a quotation. (When typing, leave one space before and after each period.)

(Original)

We the people of the United States, in order to form a more perfect Union, establish justice, insure domestic tranquility, provide for the common defense, promote the general welfare, and secure the blessings of liberty to ourselves and our posterity, do ordain and establish this Constitution for the United States of America. —Preamble, U.S. Constitution

(Quotation)

"We the people . . . in order to form a more perfect Union . . . establish this Constitution for the United States of America."

If words from a quotation are omitted at the end of a sentence, the ellipsis is placed after the period or other end punctuation.

"Five score years ago, a great American, in whose symbolic shadow we stand, signed the Emancipation Proclamation. . . . But one hundred years later, we must face the tragic fact that the Negro is still not free."

—Martin Luther King, Jr., "I Have a Dream"

NOTE: If the quoted material is a complete sentence (even if it was not in the original), use a period, then an ellipsis.

(Original)

I am tired; my heart is sick and sad. From where the sun now stands I will fight no more forever.

—Chief Joseph of the Nez Percé

(Quotations)

"I am tired. . . . From where the sun now stands I will fight no more forever."

or

"I am tired. . . . I will fight no more forever."

An ellipsis may be used to indicate a pause.

I can't figure out . . . this number doesn't . . . just how do I apply the equation in this case? —Student in a quandary

COMMA

556 A **comma** may be used between two independent clauses that are joined by coordinating conjunctions such as these: *but, or, nor, and, for, yet, so*.

> **Most colleges require students to stay in a dorm their first year, and some even require students to use the college food services.**

> **Your dorm will become your home away from home, but you shouldn't count on it for serious study sessions.**

NOTE: Do not confuse a sentence with a compound verb for a compound sentence.

> **Many students living in dorms are distracted by friends and activities and cannot concentrate on their studies.**

557 Commas are used to separate individual words, phrases, or clauses in a series. (A series contains at least three items.)

> **College students have to do their own laundry, get their own meals, and take care of themselves when they get the flu.**

NOTE: Do not use commas when the items in a series are connected with *or, nor,* or *and*.

> **College students have to do their own laundry and get their own meals and take care of themselves when they get the flu.**

558 Commas are used to separate adjectives that *equally* modify the same noun. (Notice in the examples below that no comma separates the last adjective from the noun.)

> **It's very important for college students to exercise regularly and follow a sensible, healthful diet.**

> **A good diet is one that includes lots of high-protein, low-fat foods.**

---

on|ine   To determine whether the adjectives in a sentence modify *equally*, use these two tests.

(1) Shift the order of the adjectives; if the sentence is clear, the adjectives modify equally. (If *high-protein* and *low-fat* as well as sensible and healthful were shifted in the examples above, the sentences would still be clear; therefore, use a comma.)

(2) Insert *and* between the adjectives; if the sentence reads well, use a comma. (If *and* were inserted in the sentences above, they would still read well.)

559 Commas are used to enclose an explanatory word or phrase.

> **Time management, an important skill for all students, is taught in workshops at many colleges.**

560 A specific kind of explanatory word or phrase called an **appositive** identifies or renames a preceding noun or pronoun. (Do not use commas with *restrictive appositives*. A restrictive appositive is essential to the basic meaning of the sentence. See 563.)

> **A syllabus, the professor's plan of action for the class, is usually handed out during the first week of class.**
>
> **This syllabus, which is really a course outline, can help you manage your time from the very first day.**

561 Commas are used to separate contrasted elements within a sentence.

> **We work to become, not to acquire.**
>
> —Eugene Delacroix
>
> **Where all think alike, no one thinks very much.**
>
> —Walter Lippmann

562 A comma should separate an adverb clause or a long modifying phrase from the independent clause that follows it.

> **When it comes to college roommates, not all the baggage arrives in a suitcase.**

NOTE: A comma is usually omitted if the phrase or adverb clause follows the independent clause.

> **Not all the baggage arrives in a suitcase when it comes to college roommates.**

563 Commas are used to enclose **nonrestrictive phrases** and clauses. Nonrestrictive phrases or clauses are those that are not essential or necessary to the basic meaning of the sentence. **Restrictive phrases** or clauses—phrases or clauses that are needed in the sentence because they restrict or limit the meaning of the sentence—are not set off with commas.

> **An academic advisor, *who is usually a faculty member,* can help you select your courses.** (nonrestrictive)
>
> **The federal work-study program, *which provides jobs right on campus,* is available to all students needing financial aid.** (nonrestrictive)

NOTE: The two italicized clauses in the examples above are merely additional information; they are nonrestrictive (not required). If the clauses were left out of the sentences, the meaning of the sentences would remain clear. Clauses are restrictive if they are necessary to the sense of the sentence.

> **At many universities, the academic advisors *who help the premed students plan their course loads* are faculty members in the life-sciences department.** (restrictive)
>
> **The federal program *that provides jobs right on campus* is available to all students needing financial aid.** (restrictive)

---

on|ine Remember that restrictive phrases are *required* in a sentence; nonrestrictive phrases are *not required*. Compare the following restrictive and nonrestrictive phrases:

> **The famous mathematician and physicist *Albert Einstein* developed the theory of relativity.** (restrictive)
>
> **Albert Einstein, *the famous mathematician and physicist,* developed the theory of relativity.** (nonrestrictive)

---

564 Commas are used to set off items in an address and items in a date.

> **Send your letter to 1600 Pennsylvania Avenue NW, Washington, DC 20006, before January 1, 1999, or send e-mail to president@whitehouse.gov.**

NOTE: No comma is placed between the state and ZIP code. Also, no comma separates the items if only the month and year are given: January 1999, but January 1, 1999.

565 Commas are used to set off the exact words of the speaker from the rest of the sentence.

> **"Never be afraid to ask for help," advised Ms. Kane.**

566 Commas are used to separate a **vocative** from the rest of the sentence. (A vocative is the noun that names the person or persons spoken to.)

> **Jamie, would you please stop whistling while I'm trying to work?**

567 A comma is used to separate an interjection or a weak exclamation from the rest of the sentence.

> **Okay, so now what do I do?**

568 Commas are used to set off a word, phrase, or clause that interrupts the movement of a sentence. Such expressions usually can be identified through the following tests: (1) They may be omitted without changing the meaning of a sentence. (2) They may be placed nearly anywhere in the sentence without changing its meaning.

> **For me, *well,* it was just a good job gone!**
> —Langston Hughes, "A Good Job Gone"
>
> ***As a general rule,* always come to class ready for a pop quiz on the day's assignment.**

569 Commas are used to separate a series of numbers in order to distinguish hundreds, thousands, millions, etc.

> **Do you know how to write the amount $2,025 on a check?**
> **25,000   973,240   18,620,197**

570 Commas are used to enclose a title or initials and names that follow a surname.

> **Until Martin, Sr., was fifteen, he never had more than three months of schooling in any one year.**
> —Ed Clayton, *Martin Luther King: The Peaceful Warrior*
>
> **Sanders, Gregg T., and Sanders, Greg P., are forever getting confused on these class lists.**

571 A comma may be used for clarity or for emphasis. There will be times when none of the traditional comma rules call for a comma, but one will be needed to prevent confusion or to emphasize an important idea. Use a comma in either case.

> **What she does, does matter to us.**
>
> **It may be those who do most, dream most.**
> —Stephen Leacock

---

on**l**ine **Do not use a comma** that could cause confusion. There should be no comma between the subject and its verb or the verb and its object. Also, use no comma before an indirect quotation. (The commas circled below should not be used.)

> **My roommate said⊙ that she doesn't understand the negative effects of DDT use.** (misuse of a comma before an indirect quotation)
>
> **For starters, I think she should read⊙ *Silent Spring* by Rachel Carson.** (misuse of a comma between a verb and its object)

SEMICOLON

572 A **semicolon** is used to join two or more independent clauses that are not connected with a coordinating conjunction. (In other words, each of the clauses could stand alone as a separate sentence.)

> **I was thrown out of college for cheating on the metaphysics exam; I looked into the soul of the boy next to me.**
>
> —Woody Allen

NOTE: The exception to this rule occurs when the two clauses are closely related, short, or conversational in tone. Then a comma may be used.

> **Genius has limits, stupidity does not.**

573 A semicolon is used before a conjunctive adverb when the word connects two independent clauses in a compound sentence. A comma should follow the adverb in this case. (Common conjunctive adverbs are these: *also, besides, for example, however, in addition, instead, meanwhile, then,* and *therefore.*)

> **College freshmen often put on extra weight; however, a good diet and regular exercise can prevent things from getting out of hand.**

574 A semicolon is used to separate independent clauses that are long or contain commas.

> **Make sure your stereo, computer, bike, and other valuables are covered by a homeowner's insurance policy; and be sure to use the locks on your dorm door, bike, and storage area.**

575 A semicolon is used to separate groups of words that already contain commas.

> **My favorite foods are liver and onions; peanut butter and banana sandwiches; pizza with cheese, pepperoni, onions, and mushrooms; and diet ginger ale. Is that a problem?**

COLON

576 A **colon** may be used after the salutation of a business letter.

Dear Mr. Spielberg: **Dear Professor Higgins:**

577 A colon is used between the parts of a number indicating time.

8:30 p.m.   **9:45 a.m.**   **10:10 p.m.**

578 A colon may be used to emphasize a word, phrase, clause, or sentence that explains or adds impact to the main clause.

I have one goal for myself: to become the first person in my family to graduate from college.

Don't ever slam a door: you might want to go back.

—Don Herold

579 A colon is used to introduce a list.

Besides basic skills, a college student needs two things: determination and a positive attitude.

---

on|ine A colon should not separate a verb from its object or complement, and it should not separate a preposition from its object.

Incorrect:	**Dave likes: comfortable space and time to think.**
Correct:	**Dave likes two things: comfortable space and time to think.**
Incorrect:	**There was a show on the radio this morning about: stress and laughter.**
Correct:	**This morning there was a show on the radio about an interesting subject: stress and laughter.**

---

580 A colon is used to distinguish between title and subtitle, volume and page, and chapter and verse in literature.

Writers INC: School to Work

Encyclopedia Americana IV: 211

Psalm 23:1-6

581 A colon may be used to formally introduce a sentence, a question, or a quotation.

John Locke is credited with this prescription for a good life: "A sound mind in a sound body."

Lou Gottlieb, however, offered this version: "A sound mind or a sound body—take your pick."

HYPHEN

582 A **hyphen** is used to make a compound word.

> **great-great-grandfather**   **mother-in-law**   **three-year-old**
>
> **And they pried pieces of baked-too-fast sunshine cake from the roofs of their mouths and looked once more into the boy's eyes.**
> > —Toni Morrison, *Song of Solomon*

583 A hyphen is used to join a capital letter to a noun or participle.

> **T-shirt**   **U-turn**   **V-shaped**

584 A hyphen is used to join the words in compound numbers from twenty-one to ninety-nine when it is necessary to write them out. (See 655.)

> **On this day in 1955, a forty-two-year-old woman was on her way home from work.**
> > —Robert Fulghum, *It Was on Fire When I Lay Down on It*

585 A hyphen is used between the elements of a fraction, but not between the numerator and denominator when one or both of them are already hyphenated.

> **four-tenths**   **five-sixteenths**   **(7/32) seven thirty-seconds**

586 Use hyphens when two or more words have a common element that is omitted in all but the last term.

> **We have cedar posts in four-, six-, and eight-inch widths.**

587 A hyphen is usually used to form new words beginning with the prefixes *self, ex, all, great,* and *half.* It is also used to join any prefix to a proper noun, a proper adjective, or the official name of an office. A hyphen is used with the suffix *elect.*

> **half-eaten**   **great-grandson**   **ex-mayor**   **self-taught**
>
> **post-Depression**   **governor-elect**   **mid-May**
>
> **America is the best half-educated country in the world.**
> > —Nicholas Murray Butler

NOTE: Use a hyphen with other prefixes or suffixes to avoid confusion or awkward spelling.

> **re-cover** (not *recover*) **the sofa**
> **shell-like** (not *shelllike*) **shape**

588 A hyphen is used to join numbers indicating a span of time, scores, amounts, etc.

> **The average college student needs to study 30-40 hours a week to be successful.**

589 A hyphen is used to divide a word at the end of a line of print. A word may be divided only between syllables, and the hyphen is always placed after the syllable at the end of the line—never before a syllable at the beginning of the following line.

Guidelines for Word Division

1. Always leave enough of the word at the end of the line so that the word can be identified.

2. Never divide a one-syllable word: *rained, skills, through.*

3. Avoid dividing a word of five letters or less: *paper, study, July.*

4. Never divide a one-letter syllable from the rest of the word: *omit-ted,* not *o-mitted.*

5. Always divide a compound word between its basic units: *sister-in-law,* not *sis-ter-in-law.*

6. Never divide abbreviations or contractions: *shouldn't,* not *should-n't.*

7. When a vowel is a syllable by itself, divide the word after the vowel: *epi-sode,* not *ep-isode.*

8. Avoid dividing a number written as a figure: *1,000,000;* not *1,000,-000.* (If a figure must be broken, divide it after one of the commas.)

9. Avoid dividing the last word in a paragraph.

10. Never divide the last word in more than two lines in a row.

---

590 Use a hyphen to join two or more words that serve as a single adjective (a single-thought adjective) before a noun.

In real life I am a large, big-boned woman with rough, man-working hands.

—Alice Walker, "Everyday Use"

NOTE: When words forming the adjective come after the noun, do not hyphenate them.

In real life, I am large and big boned.

NOTE: When the first of these words is an adverb ending in *ly*, do not use a hyphen; also, do not use a hyphen when a number or letter is the final element in a one-thought adjective.

freshly painted **barn** (adverb ending in *ly*)

grade A **milk** (letter is the final element)

DASH

591 The **dash** is used to indicate a sudden break or change in a sentence.

> **Near the semester's end—and this is not always due to poor planning—some students may find themselves in academic trouble.**

NOTE: A dash is indicated by two hyphens--without spacing before or after--in all handwritten material. Don't use a single hyphen when a dash (two hyphens) is required.

592 A dash is used to set off an introductory series from the clause that explains the series.

> **Freedom of inquiry, freedom of discussion, and freedom of teaching—without these a university cannot exist.**
>
> —Barrows Dunham

593 A dash may also be used to show that words or letters are missing.

> **Mr.—won't let us marry.**
>
> —Alice Walker, *The Color Purple*

594 A dash is used to show interrupted or faltering speech in dialogue.

> **Well, I—ah—had this terrible case of the flu, and—then—ah—the library closed because of that flash flood, and—the high humidity jammed my printer.**
>
> —Excuse No. 101

595 A dash may be used to emphasize a word, series, phrase, or clause.

> **Life is like a grindstone—whether it grinds you down or polishes you up depends on what you're made of.**
> **This is how the world moves—not like an arrow, but a boomerang.**
>
> —Ralph Ellison

> **College is more than books and term papers—get involved in campus life.**

QUESTION MARK

596 A **question mark** is used at the end of a direct question.

> **What can I know? What ought I to do? What may I hope?**
> > **—Immanuel Kant**
>
> **Since when do you have to agree with people to defend them from injustice?**
> > **—Lillian Hellman**

597 No question mark is used after an indirect question.

> **After listening to Edgar sing, Mr. Noteworthy asked him if he had ever had formal voice training.**

598 When two clauses within a sentence both ask questions, one question mark is used.

> **Do you often ask yourself, "What should I be?"**

599 The question mark is placed within parentheses to show uncertainty.

> **This August will be the 25th (?) anniversary of the first moon walk.**

600 A short question within parentheses—or a question set off by dashes—is punctuated with a question mark.

> **You must consult your handbook (what choice do you have?) when you need to know a punctuation rule.**
>
> **Maybe somewhere in the pasts of these humbled people, there were cases of bad mothering or absent fathering or emotional neglect—what family surviving the '50s was exempt?—but I couldn't believe these human errors brought the physical changes in Frank.**
> > **—Mary Kay Blakely, *Wake Me When It's Over***

EXCLAMATION POINT

601 An **exclamation point** is used to express strong feeling. It may be placed after a word, a phrase, or a sentence. (The exclamation point should be used sparingly.)

> **"That's not the point," said Wangero. "These are all pieces of dresses Grandma used to wear. She did all this stitching by hand. Imagine!"**
> > **—Alice Walker, "Everyday Use"**
>
> **Su-su-something's crawling up the back of my neck!**
> > **—Mark Twain, *Roughing It***
>
> **She was on tiptoe, stretching for an orange, when they heard, "HEY YOU!"**
> > **—Beverly Naidoo, *Journey to Jo'burg***

QUOTATION MARKS

602 **Quotation marks** are used to punctuate titles of songs, poems, short stories, lectures, episodes of radio or television programs, chapters of books, unpublished works, and articles found in magazines, newspapers, or encyclopedias. (For punctuation of other titles, see 608.)

> **"Bookends"** (song)
>
> **"Two Friends"** (short story)
>
> **"Multiculturalism and the Language Battle"** (lecture title)
>
> **"The New Admissions Game"** (magazine article)
>
> **"Reflections on Advertising"** (chapter in a book)
>
> **"Force of Nature"** (television episode from *Star Trek*)

NOTE: In titles, capitalize the first word, the last word, and every word in between except articles, short prepositions, and coordinating conjunctions.

603 Quotation marks also may be used (1) to distinguish a word that is being discussed, (2) to indicate that a word is slang, or (3) to point out that a word is being used in a special way.

(1) **A commentary on the times is that the word "honesty" is now preceded by "old-fashioned."**

—Larry Wolters

(2) **I drank a Dixie and ate bar peanuts and asked the bartender where I could hear "chanky-chank," as Cajuns call their music.**

—William Least Heat-Moon, *Blue Highways*

(3) **In order to be popular, he works very hard at being "cute."**

NOTE: Italics (underlining) may be used in place of quotation marks for each of these three functions.

604 Periods and commas are always placed inside quotation marks.

> **"Dr. Slaughter wants you to have liquids, Will," Mama said anxiously. "He said not to give you any solid food tonight."**
>
> —Olive Ann Burns, *Cold Sassy Tree*

605 An exclamation point or a question mark is placed inside quotation marks when it punctuates the quotation; it is placed outside when it punctuates the main sentence.

> **I almost croaked when he asked, "That won't be a problem, will it?"**
>
> **Did he really say, "Finish this by tomorrow"?**

606 Semicolons or colons are always placed outside quotation marks.

> **I just read "Computers and Creativity"; I now have some different ideas about the role of computers in the arts.**

Marking Quoted Material

QUICK GUIDE

■ Quotation marks are placed before and after direct quotations. Only the exact words quoted are placed within the quotation marks.

> **Sitting in my one-room apartment, I remembered Ms. Ricchio saying, "Apply early for first-choice housing." I hadn't.**

■ Quotation marks are placed before and after a quoted passage. Any word or punctuation mark that is not part of the original quotation must be placed inside brackets.

> (Original) **First of all, it must accept responsibility for providing shelter for the homeless.**

> (Quotation) **"First of all, it [the federal government] must accept responsibility for providing shelter for the homeless."**
> —Amy Douma, "Helping the Homeless"

NOTE: If you quote only part of the original passage, be sure to construct a sentence that is both accurate and grammatically correct.

> **The report goes on to say that the federal government "must accept responsibility for providing shelter for the homeless."**

■ If more than one paragraph is quoted, quotation marks are placed before each paragraph and at the end of the last paragraph (Example A). Quotations that are more than four lines on a page are usually set off from the text by indenting 10 spaces from the left margin (block form). Quotation marks are placed neither before nor after the quoted material unless they appear in the original (Example B).

Example A

Example B

■ Single quotation marks are used to punctuate a quotation within a quotation.

> **"Read 'Compiling a Working Bibliography' for tomorrow," said Mr. Feldsher.**

ITALICS (UNDERLINING)

608 **Italics** is a printer's term for a style of type that is slightly slanted. In this sentence the word *happiness* is printed in italics. In material that is handwritten or typed on a machine that cannot print in italics, each word or letter that should be in italics is underlined.

> In <u>The Road to Memphis</u>, racism is a contagious disease. (typed)

> Mildred Taylor's *The Road to Memphis* exposes racism. (printed)

609 Italics are used to indicate the titles of magazines, newspapers, books, pamphlets, plays, films, radio and television programs, book-length poems, ballets, operas, lengthy musical compositions, record albums, CD's, legal cases, and the names of ships and aircraft. (Also see 602.)

> <u>Newsweek</u> (magazine)
>
> <u>Sister Carrie</u> (book)
>
> <u>Babe</u> (film)
>
> <u>Nightline</u> (television program)
>
> <u>Othello</u> (play)
>
> <u>Off to College</u> (pamphlet)
>
> <u>New York Times</u> or New York <u>Times</u> (newspaper)

610 When one title appears within another title, punctuate as follows:

> "The <u>Fresh Prince of Bel-Air</u> Rings True"
> (title of TV program in an article title)

611 Italics are used to indicate a foreign word that has not been adopted into the English language; they also denote scientific names.

> Say <u>arrivederci</u> to your fears and try new activities.

PARENTHESES

612   **Parentheses** are used to enclose explanatory or supplementary material that interrupts the normal sentence structure.

> **If you are living on campus, your RA (resident advisor) may turn out to be your best college resource.**

613   Punctuation is placed within parentheses when it is intended to mark the material within the parenthetical. Please note, however, that words enclosed by parentheses do not have to begin with a capital letter—even if they create a complete sentence (See the second example below.)

> **But Mom doesn't say boo to Dad; she's always sweet to him. (Actually she's sort of sweet to everybody.)**
> —Norma Fox Mazer, *Up on Fong Mountain*
>
> **And, since your friend won't have the assignment (he was just thinking about calling you), you'll have to make a couple more calls to actually get it.**
> —Ken Taylor, "The Art and Practice of Avoiding Homework"

NOTE: For unavoidable parentheses within parentheses (. . . [. . .] . . .), use brackets. Avoid overuse of parentheses by using commas instead.

BRACKETS

614   **Brackets** are used before and after material that a writer adds when quoting another writer.

> **"Sometimes I think it [my writing] sounds like I walked out of the room and left the typewriter running."**
> —Gene Fowler

NOTE: The brackets indicate that the words *my writing* are not part of the quotation but were added for clarification.

615   Place brackets around material that has been added by someone other than the author or speaker.

> **"And in conclusion, <u>docendo discimus</u>. Let the school year begin!" [huh?]**

616   Place brackets around an editorial correction.

> **"Brooklyn alone has eight percent of the lead poisoning [victims] nationwide," said Marjorie Moore.**
> —Donna Actie, student writer

617   Brackets should be placed around the letters *sic* (Latin for "as such"); the letters indicate that an error appearing in the quoted material was made by the original speaker or writer.

> **"There is a higher principal [sic] at stake here: Is the school administration trustworthy?"**

APOSTROPHE

618 An **apostrophe** is used to show that one or more letters have been left out of a word to form a contraction.

> **don't — *o* is left out**   **she'd — *woul* is left out**   **it's — *i* is left out**

NOTE: An apostrophe is also used to show that one or more letters or numbers have been left out of numerals or words that are spelled as they are actually spoken.

> **class of '85 — *19* is left out**   **good mornin' — *g* is left out**

619 An apostrophe and *s* are used to form the plural of a letter, a number, a sign, or a word discussed as a word.

> **A — A's   8 — 8's   You use too many *and*'s in your writing.**

NOTE: When two apostrophes are called for in the same word, simply omit the second one.

> **Follow closely the do's and don'ts (not *don't's*) on the checklist.**

620 The possessive form of singular nouns is usually made by adding an apostrophe and an *s*.

> **Spock's ears   my computer's memory**

NOTE: When a singular noun ends with an *s* or a *z* sound, the possessive may be formed by adding just an apostrophe. When the singular noun is a one-syllable word, however, the possessive is usually formed by adding both an apostrophe and an *s*.

> **Dallas' sports teams** (or) **Dallas's sports teams**
>
> **Kiss's last concert   my boss's generosity** (one-syllable word)

621 The possessive form of plural nouns ending in *s* is usually made by adding just an apostrophe.

> **Joneses' great-grandfather   bosses' office**

---

on|ine You will punctuate possessives correctly if you remember that the word immediately before the apostrophe is the owner.

> **girl's guitar** (*girl* is the owner)
> **girls' guitar** (*girls* are the owners)
> **boss's office** (*boss* is the owner)
> **bosses' office** (*bosses* are the owners)

---

622 When possession is shared by more than one noun, use the possessive form for the last noun in the series.

> **Jason, Kamil, and Elana's sound system** (All own one system.)
> **Jason's, Kamil's, and Elana's sound systems** (Each owns a system.)

623 The possessive of a compound noun is formed by placing the possessive ending after the last word.

> his mother-in-law's (singular) **career**
> the secretary of state's (singular) **spouse**
>
> their mothers-in-law's (plural) **careers**
> the secretaries of state's (plural) **spouses**

624 The possessive of an indefinite pronoun is formed by placing an apostrophe and an *s* on the last word. (See 774 and 777.)

> **everybody's   one another's   somebody else's**

625 An apostrophe is used with an adjective that is part of an expression indicating time or amount.

> **yesterday's news   a day's wage   a month's pay**

DIAGONAL

626 A **diagonal** (also called a slash) is used to form a fraction. Also place a diagonal between and/or to indicate that either is acceptable (avoid this use of the diagonal in formal writing).

> **My shoe size is 5 1/2 unless I'm wearing running shoes; then it's 6 1/2.**
>
> **A large radio/tape player is a boombox or a stereo or a box or a large metallic ham sandwich with speakers. It is not a "ghetto blaster."**
> —Amoja Three Rivers, "Cultural Etiquette: A Guide"

627 When quoting more than one line of poetry, use a diagonal to show where each line ends.

> **A dryness is upon the house / My father loved and tended. / Beyond his firm and sculptured door / His light and lease have ended.**
> —Gwendolyn Brooks, "In Honor of David Anderson Brooks, My Father"

628

Punctuation Marks

´	Accent, acute	,	Comma	( )	Parentheses
`	Accent, grave	†	Dagger	.	Period
'	Apostrophe	—	Dash	?	Question mark
*	Asterisk	/	Diagonal/Slash	" "	Quotation marks
{ }	Brace	¨ (ü)	Dieresis	§	Section
[ ]	Brackets	. . .	Ellipsis	;	Semicolon
∧	Caret	!	Exclamation point	~	Tilde
॒ (ç)	Cedilla	-	Hyphen	_____	Underscore
ˆ	Circumflex	...	Leaders		
:	Colon	¶	Paragraph		

"Write as freely and as rapidly as possible and throw the whole thing on paper. Never correct or rewrite until the whole thing is down." —John Steinbeck

Checking Mechanics

CAPITALIZATION

629 **Capitalize** all proper nouns and all proper adjectives (adjectives derived from proper nouns). The chart below provides a quick overview of capitalization rules. The pages following explain specific or special uses of capitalization.

Capitalization at a Glance

Days of the week	**Sunday, Monday, Tuesday**
Months	**June, July, August**
Holidays, holy days	**Thanksgiving, Easter, Hanukkah**
Periods, events in history	**Middle Ages, World War I**
Special events	**the Battle of Bunker Hill**
Political parties	**Republican Party, Socialist Party**
Official documents	**the Declaration of Independence**
Trade names	**Oscar Mayer hot dogs, Pontiac Sunbird**
Formal epithets	**Alexander the Great**
Official titles	**Mayor John Spitzer, Senator Feinstein**
Official state nicknames	**the Badger State, the Aloha State**
Geographical names	
Planets, heavenly bodies	**Earth, Jupiter, the Milky Way**
Continents	**Australia, South America**
Countries	**Ireland, Grenada, Sri Lanka**
States, provinces	**Ohio, Utah, Nova Scotia**
Cities, towns, villages	**El Paso, Burlington, Wonewoc**
Streets, roads, highways	**Park Avenue, Route 66, Interstate 90**
Sections of the U.S. and the world	**the Southwest, the Far East**
Landforms	**the Rocky Mountains, the Sahara Desert**
Bodies of water	**Nile and Ural Rivers, Lake Superior, Bee Creek**
Public areas	**Yosemite, Yellowstone National Park**

630 Capitalize the first word in every sentence and the first word in a full-sentence direct quotation.

> **Attending** the orientation for new students is a good idea.
>
> **Max suggested, "Let's take the self-guided tour of the campus first."**

631 Capitalize the first word in each sentence that is enclosed in parentheses if that sentence comes before or after another complete sentence.

> **Educational computer software is available at the university bookstore. (Now all I need is the computer.)**

NOTE: Do *not* capitalize a sentence that is enclosed in parentheses and is located in the middle of another sentence.

> **Your college will probably offer everything (it will supply general access to a computer) that you'll need for a successful school year.**

632 Capitalize a complete sentence that follows a colon only if that sentence is a formal statement or a quotation. You may also capitalize the sentence following a colon if you want to emphasize that sentence.

> **Sydney Harris had this to say about computers: "The real danger is not that computers will begin to think like people, but that people will begin to think like computers."**

633 Words that indicate sections of the country are proper nouns and should be capitalized; words that simply indicate direction are not proper nouns.

> **Many businesses are moving to the sunny South.**
> (section of the country)
>
> **They move south to cut fuel costs and other expenses.** (direction)

634 Capitalize races, nationalities, languages, and religions.

> **African-American   Navajo   French   Latino   Spanish   Muslim**

635 Capitalize the first word of a title, the last word, and every word in between except articles (*a, an, the*), short prepositions, and coordinating conjunctions. Follow this rule for titles of books, newspapers, magazines, poems, plays, songs, articles, films, works of art, pictures, and stories.

> *Going to Meet the Man*   *Chicago Tribune*
> **"Nothing Gold Can Stay"   "Job Hunting in the '90s"**
> *A Midsummer Night's Dream*

636 Capitalize the name of an organization, or a team and its members.

> **American Indian Movement   Republican Party**
>
> **Tampa Bay Buccaneers   Tucson High School Drama Club**

637 Capitalize abbreviations of titles and organizations. Some other abbreviations are also capitalized. (See 656-658.)

> **U.S.A.   NAACP   M.D.   Ph.D.   A.D.   B.C.   R.R.   No.**

638 Capitalize the letters used to indicate form or shape.

> **U-turn   I-beam   S-curve   U-shaped   T-shirt**

639 Capitalize words like *father, mother, uncle, senator,* and *professor* when they are parts of titles that include a personal name, or when they are substituted for proper nouns (especially in direct address).

> Hello, **Senator** Feingold. (*Senator* is part of the name.)
> Our **senator** is an environmentalist.
> Who was your chemistry **professor** last quarter?
> I had **Professor** Williams for Chemistry 101.

NOTE: To test whether a word is being substituted for a proper noun, simply read the sentence with a proper noun in place of the word. If the proper noun fits in the sentence, the word being tested should be capitalized. (*Further note:* Usually the word is not capitalized if it follows a possessive—*my, his, our,* etc.)

> Did **Dad** (**Brad**) pack the stereo in the trailer? (*Brad* works here.)
> Did your **dad** (**Brad**) pack the stereo in the trailer? (*Brad* does not work here; the word *dad* follows the possessive *your.*)

640 Words such as *technology, history,* and *science* are proper nouns when they are included in the titles of specific courses; they are common nouns when they name a field of study.

> Who teaches **Art History 202?** (title of a specific course)
> Professor Bunker loves teaching **history.** (a field of study)

NOTE: The words *freshman, sophomore, junior,* and *senior* are not capitalized unless they are part of an official title.

> The **seniors** who maintained high GPA's are honored at the Mount Mary **Senior** Honors Banquet.

641 Nouns that refer to the Supreme Being are capitalized. So are the word *Bible,* the books of the Bible, and the names of other holy books.

> **God**   **Jehovah**   **the Savior**   **Book of Psalms**
> **Allah**   **the Lord**   **the Koran**   **Ecclesiastes**

642 Do *not* capitalize any of the following: (1) a prefix attached to a proper noun, (2) seasons of the year, (3) words used to indicate direction or position, or (4) common nouns that appear to be part of a proper noun.

CAPITALIZE	DO NOT CAPITALIZE
American . . . . *un-American*
January, February . . . . *winter, spring*
The South is quite conservative. . . . . . . *Turn south at the stop sign.*
Duluth Central High School . . . . *a Duluth high school*
Chancellor John Bohm . . . . *John Bohm, our chancellor*

PLURALS

643 The **plurals** of most nouns are formed by adding an *s* to the singular.

   academic—**academics**   credit—**credits**   midterm—**midterms**

644 The plurals of nouns ending in *sh, ch, x, s,* and *z* are made by adding *es* to the singular.

   lunch—**lunches**   wish—**wishes**   class—**classes**

NOTE: Some nouns remain unchanged when used as plurals: *deer, sheep, salmon,* etc.

645 The plurals of common nouns that end in *y*—preceded by a consonant—are formed by changing the *y* to *i* and adding *es.*

   dormitory—**dormitories**   sorority—**sororities**

646 The plurals of nouns that end in *y*—preceded by a vowel—are formed by adding only an *s.*

   attorney—**attorneys**   money—**moneys**

NOTE: The plurals of proper nouns ending in *y* are formed by adding an *s.*

647 The plurals of words ending in *o* (preceded by a vowel) are formed by adding an *s.*

   radio—**radios**   cameo—**cameos**   studio—**studios**

648 Most nouns ending in *o* (preceded by a consonant) are formed by adding *es.*

   echo—**echoes**   hero—**heroes**   tomato—**tomatoes**

Exception: Musical terms always form plurals by adding an *s;* consult your dictionary for other words of this type.

   alto—**altos**   banjo—**banjos**   solo—**solos**   piano—**pianos**

649 The plurals of nouns that end in *f* or *fe* are formed in one of two ways: If the final *f* sound is still heard in the plural form of the word, simply add *s;* if the final sound is a *v* sound, change the *f* to *ve* and add an *s.*

   Plural ends with *f* sound: roof—**roofs**; chief—**chiefs**
   Plural ends with *v* sound: wife—**wives**; loaf—**loaves**
   Plural ends with either sound: hoof—**hoofs, hooves**

650 Many foreign words (as well as some of English origin) form a plural by taking on an irregular spelling; others are now acceptable with the commonly used *s* or *es* ending.

   alumnus—**alumni**
   syllabus—**syllabi, syllabuses**
   radius—**radii, radiuses**

651   The plurals of symbols, letters, figures, and words discussed as words are formed by adding an apostrophe and an *s*.

> **Many colleges have now added A/B's and B/C's as standard grades.**

NOTE: Some writers omit the apostrophe when the omission does not cause confusion.

> **1990's** *or* **1990s**   **YMCA's** *or* **YMCAs**   **CD's** *or* **CDs**

652   The plurals of nouns that end with *ful* are formed by adding an *s* at the end of the word.

> **three pailfuls   two tankfuls**

NOTE: Do not confuse these examples with three *pails full* (when you are referring to three separate pails full of something) or two *tanks full*.

653   The plurals of compound nouns are usually formed by adding an *s* or *es* to the important word in the compound.

> **brothers-in-law   maids of honor   secretaries of state**

654   Pronouns referring to a collective noun may be singular or plural. A pronoun is singular when the group (noun) is considered a unit. A pronoun is plural when the group (noun) is considered in terms of its individual components.

> **The class brainstormed with its professor.** (group as a unit)
> **The class brainstormed with their professor.** (group as individuals)

Numbers

QUICK GUIDE

■ Numbers from one to nine are usually written as words; all numbers 10 and over are usually written as numerals.

two   seven   nine   10   25   106   1,079

Exception: If numbers are used infrequently in a piece of writing, you may spell out those that can be written in no more than two words.

ten   twenty-five   two hundred   fifty thousand

NOTE: Numbers being compared or contrasted should be kept in the same style.

8 to 11 years old *or* eight to eleven years old

■ Use numerals to express numbers in the following forms: money, decimal, percentage, chapter, page, address, telephone, ZIP code, time, dates, identification numbers, and statistics.

$2.39	**26.2**	**8 percent**	**chapter 7**
A.D. 79	**July 6, 1945**	**44 B.C.**	**pages 287-289**
4:30 p.m.	**Highway 36**	**24 mph**	**a vote of 23 to 4**

Exception: If numbers are used infrequently in a piece of writing, you may spell out amounts of money and percentages when you can do so in two or three words.

nine cents   one hundred dollars   thirty-five percent

NOTE: Always use numerals with abbreviations and symbols.

5'4"   8%   10 in.   3 tbsp.   6 lbs. 8 oz.   90° F

■ Use words to express numbers that begin a sentence.

Fourteen students "forgot" their assignments.

NOTE: Change the sentence structure if this rule creates a clumsy construction.

Clumsy: *Six hundred thirty-nine* students are new to the campus this fall.

Better: This fall, 639 students are new to the campus.

■ Use words for numbers that precede a compound modifier that includes another number.

She sold twenty 35-millimeter cameras in one day.

NOTE: You may use a combination of words and numerals for very large numbers.

1.5 million   3 billion to 3.2 billion   6 billion

ABBREVIATIONS

656 An **abbreviation** is the shortened form of a word or phrase. The following abbreviations are always acceptable in both formal and informal writing:

Mr.   Mrs.   Miss   Ms.   Dr.   a.m. (A.M.)   p.m. (P.M.)

In formal writing, **do not abbreviate** the names of states, countries, months, days, units of measure, or courses of study. Do not abbreviate the words *Street, Road, Avenue, Company,* and similar words when they are part of a proper name. Also do not use signs or symbols (%, &, #, @) in place of words. The dollar sign is, however, appropriate when numerals are used to express an amount of money ($325).

657

Address Abbreviations

State Abbreviations

	Standard	Postal
Alabama	Ala.	AL
Alaska	Alaska	AK
Arizona	Ariz.	AZ
Arkansas	Ark.	AR
California	Calif.	CA
Colorado	Colo.	CO
Connecticut	Conn.	CT
Delaware	Del.	DE
District of Columbia	D.C.	DC
Florida	Fla.	FL
Georgia	Ga.	GA
Guam	Guam	GU
Hawaii	Hawaii	HI
Idaho	Idaho	ID
Illinois	Ill.	IL
Indiana	Ind.	IN
Iowa	Iowa	IA
Kansas	Kan.	KS
Kentucky	Ky.	KY
Louisiana	La.	LA
Maine	Maine	ME
Maryland	Md.	MD
Massachusetts	Mass.	MA
Michigan	Mich.	MI
Minnesota	Minn.	MN
Mississippi	Miss.	MS
Missouri	Mo.	MO
Montana	Mont.	MT
Nebraska	Neb.	NE
Nevada	Nev.	NV
New Hampshire	N.H.	NH
New Jersey	N.J.	NJ
New Mexico	N.M.	NM
New York	N.Y.	NY
North Carolina	N.C.	NC
North Dakota	N.D.	ND
Ohio	Ohio	OH
Oklahoma	Okla.	OK
Oregon	Ore.	OR
Pennsylvania	Pa.	PA
Puerto Rico	P.R.	PR
Rhode Island	R.I.	RI
South Carolina	S.C.	SC
South Dakota	S.D.	SD
Tennessee	Tenn.	TN
Texas	Texas	TX
Utah	Utah	UT
Vermont	Vt.	VT
Virginia	Va.	VA
Virgin Islands	V.I.	VI
Washington	Wash.	WA
West Virginia	W.Va.	WV
Wisconsin	Wis.	WI
Wyoming	Wyo.	WY

Canadian Provinces

	Standard	Postal
Alberta	Alta.	AB
British Columbia	B.C.	BC
Labrador	Lab.	LB
Manitoba	Man.	MB
New Brunswick	N.B.	NB
Newfoundland	N.F.	NF
Northwest Territories	N.W.T.	NT
Nova Scotia	N.S.	NS
Ontario	Ont.	ON
Prince Edward Island	P.E.I.	PE
Quebec	Que.	PQ
Saskatchewan	Sask.	SK
Yukon Territory	Y.T.	YT

Address Abbreviations

	Standard	Postal
Apartment	Apt.	APT
Avenue	Ave.	AVE
Boulevard	Blvd.	BLVD
Circle	Cir.	CIR
Court	Ct.	CT
Drive	Dr.	DR
East	E.	E
Expressway	Expy.	EXPY
Freeway	Fwy.	FWY
Heights	Hts.	HTS
Highway	Hwy.	HWY
Hospital	Hosp.	HOSP
Junction	Junc.	JCT
Lake	L.	LK
Lakes	Ls.	LKS
Lane	Ln.	LN
Meadows	Mdws.	MDWS
North	N.	N
Palms	Palms	PLMS
Park	Pk.	PK
Parkway	Pky.	PKY
Place	Pl.	PL
Plaza	Plaza	PLZ
Post Office Box	P.O. Box	PO BOX
Ridge	Rdg.	RDG
River	R.	RV
Road	Rd.	RD
Room	Rm.	RM
Rural	R.	R
Rural Route	R.R.	RR
Shore	Sh.	SH
South	S.	S
Square	Sq.	SQ
Station	Sta.	STA
Street	St.	ST
Suite	Ste.	STE
Terrace	Ter.	TER
Turnpike	Tpke.	TPKE
Union	Un.	UN
View	View	VW
Village	Vil.	VLG
West	W.	W

Common Abbreviations

abr. abridge; abridgment
AC, ac alternating current
ack. acknowledgement
A.D. in the year of the Lord (Latin *anno Domini*)
AM amplitude modulation
A.M., a.m. before noon (Latin *ante meridiem*)
AP advanced placement
ASAP as soon as possible
avg., av. average
B.A. bachelor of arts degree
BBB Better Business Bureau
B.C. 1. before Christ **2.** British Columbia
bibliog. bibliographer; bibliography
biog. biographer; biographical; biography
B.S. bachelor of science degree
C 1. Celsius **2.** centigrade **3.** coulomb
c. 1. circa (about) **2.** cup
cc. chapters
cc 1. cubic centimeter **2.** carbon copy **3.** community college
CDT, C.D.T. central daylight time
CEEB College Entrance Examination Board
cm centimeter
c.o., c/o care of
COD, C.O.D 1. cash on delivery **2.** collect on delivery
co-op cooperative
CST, C.S.T. central standard time
cu 1. cubic **2.** cumulative
D.A. district attorney
d.b.a. doing business as
DC, dc direct current
dec. deceased
dept. department
disc. discount
DST, D.S.T. daylight saving time
dup. duplicate
ed. edition; editor
e.g. for example (Latin *exempli gratia*)
EST, E.S.T. eastern standard time
etc. and so forth (Latin *et cetera*)
F Fahrenheit
FM frequency modulation
F.O.B., f.o.b. free on board
g 1. gravity **2.** gram
gal. gallon
gds. goods
gloss. glossary
GNP gross national product
GPA grade point average

hdqrs. headquarters
HIV human immunodeficiency virus
hp horsepower
Hz hertz
id. the same (Latin *idem*)
i.e. that is (Latin *id est*)
illus. illustration
inc. incorporated
IQ, I.Q. intelligence quotient
IRS Internal Revenue Service
ISBN International Standard Book Number
JP, J.P. justice of the peace
K 1. kelvin (temperature unit) **2.** Kelvin (temperature scale)
kc kilocycle
kg kilogram
km kilometer
kn knot
kw kilowatt
l liter
lat. latitude
l.c. lowercase
lit. literary; literature
log logarithm
long. longitude
Ltd., ltd. limited
m meter
M.A. master of arts degree
man. manual
Mc, mc megacycle
M.C., m.c. master of ceremonies
M.D. doctor of medicine (Latin *medicinae doctor*)
mdse. merchandise
mfg. manufacture; manufactured
mg milligram
mi. 1. mile **2.** mill (monetary unit)
misc. miscellaneous
ml milliliter
mm millimeter
mpg, m.p.g. miles per gallon
M.S. master of science degree
mph, m.p.h. miles per hour
MS 1. manuscript **2.** Mississippi **3.** multiple sclerosis
Ms. title of courtesy for a woman
MST, M.S.T. mountain standard time
NE northeast
neg. negative
N.S.F., n.s.f. not sufficient funds
NW northwest
oz, oz. ounce
PA public-address system
pct. percent
pd. paid
PDT, P.D.T. Pacific daylight time

Pfc, Pfc. private first class
pg., p. page
Ph.D. doctor of philosophy
P.M., p.m. after noon (Latin *post meridiem*)
POW, P.O.W. prisoner of war
pp. pages
ppd. 1. postpaid **2.** prepaid
PR, P.R. 1. public relations **2.** Puerto Rico
PSAT Preliminary Scholastic Aptitude Test
psi, p.s.i. pounds per square inch
PST, P.S.T. Pacific standard time
PTA, P.T.A. Parent-Teacher Association
R.A. residence assistant
RF radio frequency
R.P.M., rpm revolutions per minute
R.S.V.P., r.s.v.p. please reply (French *répondez s'il vous plaît*)
SE southeast
SAT Scholastic Aptitude Test
SOS 1. international distress signal **2.** any call for help
Sr. 1. senior (after surname) **2.** sister (religious)
SRO, S.R.O. standing room only
std. standard
SW southwest
syn. synonymous; synonym
T.A. teaching assistant
tbs., tbsp. tablespoon
TM trademark
UHF, uhf ultrahigh frequency
V 1. *Physics:* velocity **2.** *Electricity:* volt **3.** volume
VA, V.A. 1. Veterans Administration **2.** Virginia
VHF, vhf very high frequency
VIP *Informal:* very important person
vol. 1. volume **2.** volunteer
vs. versus
W 1. *Electricity:* watt **2.** *Physics:* (also **w**) work **3.** west
whse., whs. warehouse
whsle. wholesale
wkly. weekly
w/o without
wt. weight

ACRONYMS AND INITIALISMS

659 An **acronym** is a word formed from the first (or first few) letters of words in a set phrase. Even though acronyms are a form of abbreviation, they are not followed by a period(s).

radar	**radio detecting and ranging**
CARE	**Cooperative for American Relief to Everywhere**
NASA	**National Aeronautics and Space Administration**
VISTA	**Volunteers in Service to America**
UNICEF	**United Nations International Children's Emergency Fund**

660 An **initialism** is similar to an acronym except that the initials used to form this abbreviation cannot be pronounced as a word.

CIA	**Central Intelligence Agency**
FBI	**Federal Bureau of Investigation**
FHA	**Federal Housing Administration**

661

Common Acronyms and Initialisms

AIDS	acquired immunodeficiency syndrome	**ORV**	off-road vehicle	
APR	annual percentage rate	**OSHA**	Occupational Safety and Health Administration	
CAD	computer-aided design	**PAC**	political action committee	
CAM	computer-aided manufacturing	**PIN**	personal identification number	
CETA	comprehensive Employment and Training Act	**POP**	point of purchase	
FAA	Federal Aviation Administration	**PSA**	public service announcement	
FCC	Federal Communications Commission	**REA**	Rural Electrification Administration	
FDA	Food and Drug Administration	**RICO**	Racketeer Influenced and Corrupt Organizations (Act)	
FDIC	Federal Deposit Insurance Corporation	**ROTC**	Reserve Officers' Training Corps	
FEMA	Federal Emergency Management Agency	**SADD**	Students Against Drunk Driving	
FmHA	Farmers Home Administration	**SASE**	self-addressed stamped envelope	
FTC	Federal Trade Commission	**SPOT**	satellite positioning and tracking	
IRS	Internal Revenue Service			
MADD	Mothers Against Drunk Driving	**SSA**	Social Security Administration	
NAFTA	North American Free Trade Agreement	**SWAT**	Special Weapons and Tactics	
NATO	North Atlantic Treaty Organization	**TDD**	telecommunications device for the deaf	
NYC	Neighborhood Youth Corps	**TMJ**	temporomandibular joint	
OEO	Office of Economic Opportunity	**TVA**	Tennessee Valley Authority	
OEP	Office of Emergency Preparedness	**VA**	Veterans Administration	
		WHO	World Health Organization	

Spelling Rules

RULE 1: Write *i* before *e* except after *c*, or when sounded like *a* as in *neighbor* and *weigh*.

Examples: **receive   perceive   relief**

<u>Exceptions:</u> This sentence contains eight exceptions: **Neither sheik dared leisurely seize either weird species of financiers.**

RULE 2: When a one-syllable word (*bat*) ends in a consonant (*t*) preceded by one vowel (*a*), double the final consonant before adding a suffix that begins with a vowel (*batting*).

sum — summary   god — goddess

When a multisyllable word (*control*) ends in a consonant (*l*) preceded by one vowel (*o*), the accent is on the last syllable (*con trol´*), and the suffix begins with a vowel (*ing*)—the same rule holds true: double the final consonant (*controlling*).

prefer — preferred   begin — beginning
forget — forgettable   admit — admittance

RULE 3: If a word ends with a silent *e*, drop the *e* before adding a suffix that begins with a vowel. You do not drop the *e* when the suffix begins with a consonant.

state — stating — statement   like — liking — likeness
use — using — useful   nine — ninety — nineteen

<u>Exceptions:</u> *judgment, truly, argument, ninth*

RULE 4: When *y* is the last letter in a word and the *y* is preceded by a consonant, change the *y* to *i* before adding any suffix except those beginning with *i*.

fry — fries   hurry — hurried   lady — ladies
ply — pliable   happy — happiness   beauty — beautiful

When forming the plural of a word that ends with a *y* that is preceded by a vowel, add *s*.

toy — toys   play — plays   monkey — monkeys

NOTE: Never trust your spelling to even the best spell checker. Carefully proofread. Use a dictionary for questionable words your spell checker does not cover.

COMMONLY MISSPELLED WORDS

A

ab-bre-vi-ate
a-brupt
ab-scess
ab-sence
ab-so-lute (-ly)
ab-sorb-ent
ab-surd
a-bun-dance
ac-a-dem-ic
ac-cede
ac-cel-er-ate
ac-cept (-ance)
ac-ces-si-ble
ac-ces-so-ry
ac-ci-den-tal-ly
ac-com-mo-date
ac-com-pa-ny
ac-com-plice
ac-com-plish
ac-cor-dance
ac-cord-ing
ac-count
ac-crued
ac-cu-mu-late
ac-cu-rate
ac-cus-tom (ed)
ache
a-chieve (-ment)
ac-knowl-edge
ac-quaint-ance
ac-qui-esce
ac-quired
ac-tu-al
a-dapt
ad-di-tion (-al)
ad-dress
ad-e-quate
ad-journed
ad-just-ment
ad-mi-ra-ble
ad-mis-si-ble
ad-mit-tance
ad-van-ta-geous
ad-ver-tise-ment
ad-ver-tis-ing
ad-vice (n.)

ad-vis-able
ad-vise (v.)
ad-vis-er
ae-ri-al
af-fect
af-fi-da-vit
a-gainst
ag-gra-vate
ag-gres-sion
a-gree-able
a-gree-ment
aisle
al-co-hol
a-lign-ment
al-ley
al-lot-ted
al-low-ance
all right
al-most
al-ready
al-though
al-to-geth-er
a-lu-mi-num
al-um-nus
al-ways
am-a-teur
a-mend-ment
a-mong
a-mount
a-nal-y-sis
an-a-lyze
an-cient
an-ec-dote
an-es-thet-ic
an-gle
an-ni-hi-late
an-ni-ver-sa-ry
an-nounce
an-noy-ance
an-nu-al
a-noint
a-non-y-mous
an-swer
ant-arc-tic
an-tic-i-pate
anx-i-ety
anx-ious
a-part-ment
a-pol-o-gize

ap-pa-ra-tus
ap-par-ent (-ly)
ap-peal
ap-pear-ance
ap-pe-tite
ap-pli-ance
ap-pli-ca-ble
ap-pli-ca-tion
ap-point-ment
ap-prais-al
ap-pre-ci-ate
ap-proach
ap-pro-pri-ate
ap-prov-al
ap-prox-i-mate-ly
ap-ti-tude
ar-chi-tect
arc-tic
ar-gu-ment
a-rith-me-tic
a-rouse
ar-range-ment
ar-riv-al
ar-ti-cle
ar-ti-fi-cial
as-cend
as-cer-tain
as-i-nine
as-sas-sin
as-sess (-ment)
as-sign-ment
as-sist-ance
as-so-ci-ate
as-so-ci-a-tion
as-sume
as-sur-ance
as-ter-isk
ath-lete
ath-let-ic
at-tach
at-tack (ed)
at-tempt
at-tend-ance
at-ten-tion
at-ti-tude
at-tor-ney
at-trac-tive
au-di-ble
au-di-ence

au-dit
au-thor-i-ty
au-to-mo-bile
au-tumn
aux-il-ia-ry
a-vail-a-ble
av-er-age
aw-ful
aw-ful-ly
awk-ward

B

bac-ca-lau-re-ate
bach-e-lor
bag-gage
bal-ance
bal-loon
bal-lot
ba-nan-a
ban-dage
bank-rupt
bar-gain
bar-rel
base-ment
ba-sis
bat-tery
beau-ti-ful
beau-ty
be-com-ing
beg-gar
be-gin-ning
be-hav-ior
be-ing
be-lief
be-lieve
ben-e-fi-cial
ben-e-fit (-ed)
be-tween
bi-cy-cle
bis-cuit
bliz-zard
book-keep-er
bought
bouil-lon
bound-a-ry
break-fast
breath (n.)
breathe (v.)

brief
bril-liant
Brit-ain
bro-chure
brought
bruise
bud-get
bul-le-tin
buoy-ant
bu-reau
bur-glar
bury
busi-ness
busy

C

caf-e-te-ria
caf-feine
cal-en-dar
cam-paign
can-celed
can-di-date
can-is-ter
ca-noe
ca-pac-i-ty
cap-i-tal
cap-i-tol
cap-tain
car-bu-ret-or
ca-reer
car-i-ca-ture
car-riage
cash-ier
cas-se-role
cas-u-al-ty
cat-a-log
ca-tas-tro-phe
caught
cav-al-ry
cel-e-bra-tion
cem-e-ter-y
cen-sus
cen-tu-ry
cer-tain
cer-tif-i-cate
ces-sa-tion
chal-lenge

chan-cel-lor
change-a-ble
char-ac-ter (-is-tic)
chauf-feur
chief
chim-ney
choc-o-late
choice
choose
Chris-tian
cir-cuit
cir-cu-lar
cir-cum-stance
civ-i-li-za-tion
cli-en-tele
cli-mate
climb
clothes
coach
co-coa
co-er-cion
col-lar
col-lat-er-al
col-lege
col-le-giate
col-lo-qui-al
colo-nel
col-or
co-los-sal
col-umn
com-e-dy
com-ing
com-mence
com-mer-cial
com-mis-sion
com-mit
com-mit-ment
com-mit-ted
com-mit-tee
com-mu-ni-cate
com-mu-ni-ty
com-par-a-tive
com-par-i-son
com-pel
com-pe-tent
com-pe-ti-tion
com-pet-i-tive-ly
com-plain
com-ple-ment
com-plete-ly
com-plex-ion

com-pli-ment
com-pro-mise
con-cede
con-ceive
con-cern-ing
con-cert
con-ces-sion
con-clude
con-crete
con-curred
con-cur-rence
con-demn
con-de-scend
con-di-tion
con-fer-ence
con-ferred
con-fi-dence
con-fi-den-tial
con-grat-u-late
con-science
con-sci-en-tious
con-scious
con-sen-sus
con-se-quence
con-ser-va-tive
con-sid-er-ably
con-sign-ment
con-sis-tent
con-sti-tu-tion
con-tempt-ible
con-tin-u-al-ly
con-tin-ue
con-tin-u-ous
con-trol
con-tro-ver-sy
con-ven-ience
con-vince
cool-ly
co-op-er-ate
cor-dial
cor-po-ra-tion
cor-re-late
cor-re-spond
cor-re-spond-ence
cor-rob-o-rate
cough
coun-cil
coun-sel
coun-ter-feit
coun-try
cour-age

cou-ra-geous
cour-te-ous
cour-te-sy
cous-in
cov-er-age
cred-i-tor
cri-sis
crit-i-cism
crit-i-cize
cru-el
cu-ri-os-i-ty
cu-ri-ous
cur-rent
cur-ric-u-lum
cus-tom
cus-tom-ary
cus-tom-er
cyl-in-der

D

dai-ly
dair-y
dealt
debt-or
de-ceased
de-ceit-ful
de-ceive
de-cid-ed
de-ci-sion
dec-la-ra-tion
dec-o-rate
de-duct-i-ble
de-fend-ant
de-fense
de-ferred
def-i-cit
def-i-nite (-ly)
def-i-ni-tion
del-e-gate
de-li-cious
de-pend-ent
de-pos-i-tor
de-pot
de-scend
de-scribe
de-scrip-tion
de-sert
de-serve
de-sign
de-sir-able

de-sir-ous
de-spair
des-per-ate
de-spise
des-sert
de-te-ri-o-rate
de-ter-mine
de-vel-op
de-vel-op-ment
de-vice
de-vise
di-a-mond
di-a-phragm
di-ar-rhe-a
dic-tio-nary
dif-fer-ence
dif-fer-ent
dif-fi-cul-ty
di-lap-i-dat-ed
di-lem-ma
din-ing
di-plo-ma
di-rec-tor
dis-agree-able
dis-ap-pear
dis-ap-point
dis-ap-prove
dis-as-trous
dis-ci-pline
dis-cov-er
dis-crep-an-cy
dis-cuss
dis-cus-sion
dis-ease
dis-sat-is-fied
dis-si-pate
dis-tin-guish
dis-trib-ute
di-vide
di-vis-i-ble
di-vi-sion
doc-tor
doesn't
dom-i-nant
dor-mi-to-ry
doubt
drudg-ery
du-al
du-pli-cate
dye-ing
dy-ing

E

ea-ger-ly
ear-nest
eco-nom-i-cal
econ-o-my
ec-sta-sy
e-di-tion
ef-fer-ves-cent
ef-fi-ca-cy
ef-fi-cien-cy
eighth
ei-ther
e-lab-o-rate
e-lec-tric-i-ty
el-e-phant
el-i-gi-ble
e-lim-i-nate
el-lipse
em-bar-rass
e-mer-gen-cy
em-i-nent
em-pha-size
em-ploy-ee
em-ploy-ment
e-mul-sion
en-close
en-cour-age
en-deav-or
en-dorse-ment
en-gi-neer
En-glish
e-nor-mous
e-nough
en-ter-prise
en-ter-tain
en-thu-si-as-tic
en-tire-ly
en-trance
en-vel-op (v.)
en-ve-lope (n.)
en-vi-ron-ment
equip-ment
equipped
e-quiv-a-lent
es-pe-cial-ly
es-sen-tial
es-tab-lish
es-teemed
et-i-quette
ev-i-dence

ex-ag-ger-ate
ex-ceed
ex-cel-lent
ex-cept
ex-cep-tion-al-ly
ex-ces-sive
ex-cite
ex-ec-u-tive
ex-er-cise
ex-haust (-ed)
ex-hi-bi-tion
ex-hil-a-ra-tion
ex-is-tence
ex-or-bi-tant
ex-pect
ex-pe-di-tion
ex-pend-i-ture
ex-pen-sive
ex-pe-ri-ence
ex-plain
ex-pla-na-tion
ex-pres-sion
ex-qui-site
ex-ten-sion
ex-tinct
ex-traor-di-nar-y
ex-treme-ly

F

fa-cil-i-ties
fal-la-cy
fa-mil-iar
fa-mous
fas-ci-nate
fash-ion
fa-tigue (d)
fau-cet
fa-vor-ite
fea-si-ble
fea-ture
Feb-ru-ar-y
fed-er-al
fem-i-nine
fer-tile
fic-ti-tious
field
fierce
fi-ery
fi-nal-ly
fi-nan-cial-ly

fo-li-age
for-ci-ble
for-eign
for-feit
for-go
for-mal-ly
for-mer-ly
for-tu-nate
for-ty
for-ward
foun-tain
fourth
frag-ile
fran-ti-cal-ly
freight
friend
ful-fill
fun-da-men-tal
fur-ther-more
fu-tile

G

gad-get
gan-grene
ga-rage
gas-o-line
gauge
ge-ne-al-o-gy
gen-er-al-ly
gen-er-ous
ge-nius
gen-u-ine
ge-og-ra-phy
ghet-to
ghost
glo-ri-ous
gnaw
go-ril-la
gov-ern-ment
gov-er-nor
gra-cious
grad-u-a-tion
gram-mar
grate-ful
grat-i-tude
grease
grief
griev-ous
gro-cery
grudge

grue-some
guar-an-tee
guard
guard-i-an
guer-ril-la
guess
guid-ance
guide
guilty
gym-na-si-um
gyp-sy
gy-ro-scope

H

hab-i-tat
ham-mer
hand-ker-chief
han-dle (d)
hand-some
hap-haz-ard
hap-pen
hap-pi-ness
ha-rass
har-bor
hast-i-ly
hav-ing
haz-ard-ous
height
hem-or-rhage
hes-i-tate
hin-drance
his-to-ry
hoarse
hol-i-day
hon-or
hop-ing
hop-ping
horde
hor-ri-ble
hos-pi-tal
hu-mor-ous
hur-ried-ly
hy-drau-lic
hy-giene
hymn
hy-poc-ri-sy

I

i-am-bic
i-ci-cle
i-den-ti-cal
id-io-syn-cra-sy
il-leg-i-ble
il-lit-er-ate
il-lus-trate
im-ag-i-nary
im-ag-i-na-tive
im-ag-ine
im-i-ta-tion
im-me-di-ate-ly
im-mense
im-mi-grant
im-mor-tal
im-pa-tient
im-per-a-tive
im-por-tance
im-pos-si-ble
im-promp-tu
im-prove-ment
in-al-ien-able
in-ci-den-tal-ly
in-con-ve-nience
in-cred-i-ble
in-curred
in-def-i-nite-ly
in-del-ible
in-de-pend-ence
in-de-pend-ent
in-dict-ment
in-dis-pens-able
in-di-vid-u-al
in-duce-ment
in-dus-tri-al
in-dus-tri-ous
in-ev-i-ta-ble
in-fe-ri-or
in-ferred
in-fi-nite
in-flam-ma-ble
in-flu-en-tial
in-ge-nious
in-gen-u-ous
in-im-i-ta-ble
in-i-tial
ini-ti-a-tion
in-no-cence
in-no-cent

in-oc-u-la-tion
in-quir-y
in-stal-la-tion
in-stance
in-stead
in-sti-tute
in-struc-tor
in-sur-ance
in-tel-lec-tu-al
in-tel-li-gence
in-ten-tion
in-ter-cede
in-ter-est-ing
in-ter-fere
in-ter-mit-tent
in-ter-pret (-ed)
in-ter-rupt
in-ter-view
in-ti-mate
in-va-lid
in-ves-ti-gate
in-ves-tor
in-vi-ta-tion
ir-i-des-cent
ir-rel-e-vant
ir-re-sis-ti-ble
ir-rev-er-ent
ir-ri-gate
is-land
is-sue
i-tem-ized
i-tin-er-ar-y

J

jan-i-tor
jeal-ous (-y)
jeop-ar-dize
jew-el-ry
jour-nal
jour-ney
judg-ment
jus-tice
jus-ti-fi-able

K

kitch-en
knowl-edge
knuck-le

L

la-bel
lab-o-ra-to-ry
lac-quer
lan-guage
laugh
laun-dry
law-yer
league
lec-ture
le-gal
leg-i-ble
leg-is-la-ture
le-git-i-mate
lei-sure
length
let-ter-head
li-a-bil-i-ty
li-a-ble
li-ai-son
lib-er-al
li-brar-y
li-cense
lieu-ten-ant
light-ning
lik-able
like-ly
lin-eage
liq-ue-fy
liq-uid
lis-ten
lit-er-ary
lit-er-a-ture
live-li-hood
log-a-rithm
lone-li-ness
loose
lose
los-ing
lov-able
love-ly
lun-cheon
lux-u-ry

M

ma-chine
mag-a-zine
mag-nif-i-cent
main-tain

main-te-nance
ma-jor-i-ty
mak-ing
man-age-ment
ma-neu-ver
man-u-al
man-u-fac-ture
man-u-script
mar-riage
mar-shal
ma-te-ri-al
math-e-mat-ics
max-i-mum
may-or
mean-ness
meant
mea-sure
med-i-cine
me-di-eval
me-di-o-cre
me-di-um
mem-o-ran-dum
men-us
mer-chan-dise
mer-it
mes-sage
mile-age
mil-lion-aire
min-i-ature
min-i-mum
min-ute
mir-ror
mis-cel-la-neous
mis-chief
mis-chie-vous
mis-er-a-ble
mis-ery
mis-sile
mis-sion-ary
mis-spell
mois-ture
mol-e-cule
mo-men-tous
mo-not-o-nous
mon-u-ment
mort-gage
mu-nic-i-pal
mus-cle
mu-si-cian
mus-tache
mys-te-ri-ous

N

na-ive
nat-u-ral-ly
nec-es-sary
ne-ces-si-ty
neg-li-gi-ble
ne-go-ti-ate
neigh-bor-hood
nev-er-the-less
nick-el
niece
nine-teenth
nine-ty
no-tice-able
no-to-ri-ety
nu-cle-ar
nui-sance

O

o-be-di-ence
o-bey
o-blige
ob-sta-cle
oc-ca-sion
oc-ca-sion-al-ly
oc-cu-pant
oc-cur
oc-curred
oc-cur-rence
of-fense
of-fi-cial
of-ten
o-mis-sion
o-mit-ted
op-er-ate
o-pin-ion
op-po-nent
op-por-tu-ni-ty
op-po-site
op-ti-mism
or-di-nance
or-di-nar-i-ly
orig-i-nal
out-ra-geous

P

pag-eant
pam-phlet
par-a-dise
para-graph
par-al-lel
par-a-lyze
pa-ren-the-ses
pa-ren-the-sis
par-lia-ment
par-tial
par-tic-i-pant
par-tic-i-pate
par-tic-u-lar-ly
pas-time
pa-tience
pa-tron-age
pe-cu-liar
per-ceive
per-haps
per-il
per-ma-nent
per-mis-si-ble
per-pen-dic-u-lar
per-se-ver-ance
per-sis-tent
per-son-al (-ly)
per-son-nel
per-spi-ra-tion
per-suade
phase
phe-nom-e-non
phi-los-o-phy
phy-si-cian
piece
planned
pla-teau
plau-si-ble
play-wright
pleas-ant
plea-sure
pneu-mo-nia
pol-i-ti-cian
pos-sess
pos-ses-sion
pos-si-ble
prac-ti-cal-ly
prai-rie
pre-cede
pre-ce-dence

pre-ced-ing
pre-cious
pre-cise-ly
pre-ci-sion
pre-de-ces-sor
pref-er-a-ble
pref-er-ence
pre-ferred
prej-u-dice
pre-lim-i-nar-y
pre-mi-um
prep-a-ra-tion
pres-ence
prev-a-lent
pre-vi-ous
prim-i-tive
prin-ci-pal
prin-ci-ple
pri-or-i-ty
pris-on-er
priv-i-lege
prob-a-bly
pro-ce-dure
pro-ceed
pro-fes-sor
prom-i-nent
pro-nounce
pro-nun-ci-a-tion
pro-pa-gan-da
pros-e-cute
pro-tein
psy-chol-o-gy
pub-lic-ly
pump-kin
pur-chase
pur-sue
pur-su-ing
pur-suit

Q

qual-i-fied
qual-i-ty
quan-ti-ty
quar-ter
ques-tion-naire
qui-et
quite
quo-tient

R

raise
rap-port
re-al-ize
re-al-ly
re-cede
re-ceipt
re-ceive
re-ceived
rec-i-pe
re-cip-i-ent
rec-og-ni-tion
rec-og-nize
rec-om-mend
re-cur-rence
ref-er-ence
re-ferred
reg-is-tra-tion
re-hearse
reign
re-im-burse
rel-e-vant
re-lieve
re-li-gious
re-mem-ber
re-mem-brance
rem-i-nisce
ren-dez-vous
re-new-al
rep-e-ti-tion
rep-re-sen-ta-tive
req-ui-si-tion
res-er-voir
re-sis-tance
re-spect-a-bly
re-spect-ful-ly
re-spec-tive-ly
re-spon-si-bil-i-ty
res-tau-rant
rheu-ma-tism
rhyme
rhythm
ri-dic-u-lous
route

S

sac-ri-le-gious
safe-ty
sal-a-ry

sand-wich
sat-is-fac-to-ry
Sat-ur-day
scarce-ly
scene
scen-er-y
sched-ule
schol-ar-ship
sci-ence
scis-sors
sec-re-tary
seize
sen-si-ble
sen-tence
sen-ti-nel
sep-a-rate
ser-geant
sev-er-al
se-vere-ly
shep-herd
sher-iff
shin-ing
siege
sig-nif-i-cance
sim-i-lar
si-mul-ta-ne-ous
since
sin-cere-ly
ski-ing
sol-dier
sol-emn
so-phis-ti-cat-ed
soph-o-more
so-ror-i-ty
source
sou-ve-nir
spa-ghet-ti
spe-cif-ic
spec-i-men
speech
sphere
spon-sor
spon-ta-ne-ous
sta-tion-ary
sta-tion-ery
sta-tis-tic
stat-ue
stat-ure
stat-ute
stom-ach
stopped

straight
strat-e-gy
strength
stretched
study-ing
sub-si-dize
sub-stan-tial
sub-sti-tute
sub-tle
suc-ceed
suc-cess
suf-fi-cient
sum-ma-rize
su-per-fi-cial
su-per-in-tend-ent
su-pe-ri-or-i-ty
su-per-sede
sup-ple-ment
sup-pose
sure-ly
sur-prise
sur-veil-lance
sur-vey
sus-cep-ti-ble
sus-pi-cious
sus-te-nance
syl-la-ble
sym-met-ri-cal
sym-pa-thy
sym-pho-ny
symp-tom
syn-chro-nous

T

tar-iff
tech-nique
tele-gram
tem-per-a-ment
tem-per-a-ture
tem-po-rary
ten-den-cy
ten-ta-tive
ter-res-tri-al
ter-ri-ble
ter-ri-to-ry
the-ater
their
there-fore
thief
thor-ough (-ly)

though
through-out
tired
to-bac-co
to-geth-er
to-mor-row
tongue
to-night
touch
tour-na-ment
tour-ni-quet
to-ward
trag-e-dy
trai-tor
tran-quil-iz-er
trans-ferred
trea-sur-er
tru-ly
Tues-day
tu-i-tion
typ-i-cal
typ-ing

U

unan-i-mous
un-con-scious
un-doubt-ed-ly
un-for-tu-nate-ly
unique
u-ni-son
uni-ver-si-ty
un-nec-es-sary
un-prec-e-dent-ed
un-til
up-per
ur-gent
us-able
use-ful
using
usu-al-ly
u-ten-sil
u-til-ize

V

va-can-cies
va-ca-tion
vac-u-um
vague
valu-able

va-ri-ety
var-i-ous
veg-e-ta-ble
ve-hi-cle
veil
ve-loc-i-ty
ven-geance
vi-cin-i-ty
view
vig-i-lance
vil-lain
vi-o-lence
vis-i-bil-i-ty
vis-i-ble
vis-i-tor
voice
vol-ume
vol-un-tary
vol-un-teer

W

wan-der
war-rant
weath-er
Wednes-day
weird
wel-come
wel-fare
where
wheth-er
which
whole
whol-ly
whose
width
wom-en
worth-while
wor-thy
wreck-age
wres-tler
writ-ing
writ-ten
wrought

Y

yel-low
yes-ter-day
yield

Steps to Becoming a

Better Speller

(1) Be patient. Learning to become a good speller takes time.

(2) Check the correct pronunciation of each word you are attempting to spell. Knowing the correct pronunciation of each word is important to remembering its spelling.

(3) Note the meaning and history of each word as you are checking the dictionary for pronunciation. Knowing the meaning and history of a word can provide you with a better notion of how and when the word will probably be used. This fuller understanding will help you remember the spelling of a particular word.

(4) Before you close the dictionary, practice spelling the word. You can do this by looking away from the page and trying to "see" the word in your "mind's eye." Write the word on a piece of paper. Check the spelling in the dictionary and repeat the process until you are able to spell the word correctly.

(5) Learn some spelling rules. The four rules in this handbook (662) are four of the most useful, although there are others.

(6) Make a list of the words that you misspell. Select the first 10 and practice spelling them.

STEP A: Read each word carefully; then write it on a piece of paper. Look at the written word to see that it's spelled correctly. Repeat the process for those words that you misspelled.

STEP B: When you have finished your first 10 words, ask someone to read the words to you so you can write them again. Again, check for misspellings. If you find none, congratulations! Repeat both steps with your next 10 words.

(7) Write often. As noted educator Frank Smith said,

"There is little point in learning to spell if you have little intention of writing."

"The difference between the right word and the nearly right word is the same as that between lightning and the lightning bug." —Mark Twain

Using the Right Word

669 **a lot, alot** *Alot* should not be one word; *a lot* (two words) is a vague descriptive phrase that should probably not be used too often, especially in formal writing.

670 **accept, except** The verb *accept* means "to receive or believe"; the preposition *except* means "other than."

> The instructor accepted the student's story about being late, but she asked why no one except him forgot to reset his clock for daylight savings time.

671 **adapt, adopt** *Adapt* means "to adjust or change to fit"; *adopt* means "to choose and treat as your own" (a child, an idea).

> After much thought and deliberation, we agreed to adopt the black Lab from the shelter; now we have to agree on how to adapt our lifestyle to fit our new roommate.

672 **adverse, averse** *Adverse* means "hostile, unfavorable, or harmful." *Averse* means "to have a definite feeling of distaste—disinclined."

> Groans and other adverse reactions were noted as the new students, averse to strenuous exercise, were ushered past the X-5000 pump-and-crunch machine.

673 **advice, advise** *Advice* is a noun meaning "information or recommendation"; *advise* is a verb meaning "to recommend."

> Successful people will often give you sound advice, so I advise you to listen.

674 **affect, effect** *Affect* means "to influence"; the noun *effect* means "the result."

> The employment growth in a field will affect your chances of getting a job. The effect may be a new career choice.

675 **aid, aide** As a verb, *aid* means "to help"; as a noun, *aid* means "the help given." *Aide* is a person who acts as an assistant.

676 **allusion, illusion** *Allusion* is an indirect reference to something; *illusion* is a false picture or idea.

> **The man who makes allusions to his abilities is usually trying to reinforce the illusion that he's exceptionally talented.**

677 **already, all ready** *Already* is an adverb meaning "before this time" or "by this time." *All ready* is an adjective meaning "fully prepared."

> **By the time you're a senior, you should have already taken your SAT's. That way, you will be all ready to apply early to the college of your choice.**

678 **all right, alright** *Alright* is the incorrect form of *all right*. (Please note, the following are spelled correctly: *always, altogether, already, almost*.)

679 **altogether, all together** *Altogether* means "entirely." The phrase *all together* means "in a group" or "all at once."

> **All together there are 35,000 job titles to choose from. That's altogether too many to even think about.**

680 **among, between** *Among* is usually used when emphasizing distribution throughout a body or group; *between* is used when emphasizing distribution to individuals.

> **There was discontent among the servants after learning that their employer had divided her entire fortune between a canary, a dog, and a favorite waitress at the local cafe.**

681 **amoral, immoral** *Amoral* means "neither moral (right) nor immoral (wrong)"; *immoral* means "wrong, or in conflict with traditional values."

> **Carnivores are amoral in their hunt; poachers are immoral in theirs.**

682 **amount, number** *Amount* is used for bulk measurement. *Number* is used to count separate units. (See also **fewer, less**.)

> **The number of new instructors hired next year will depend upon the amount of revenue raised by the new sales tax.**

683 **annual, biannual, semiannual, biennial, perennial** An *annual* event happens once every year. A *biannual* event happens twice a year (*semiannual* is the same as *biannual*). A *biennial* event happens every two years. A *perennial* event is active throughout the year and continues to happen every year.

684 **beside, besides** *Beside* is an adverb meaning "nearby." *Besides* is a preposition meaning "other than or in addition to."

> **Besides the two suitcases you've already loaded into the trunk, remember the smaller one beside the van.**

685 **bring, take** *Bring* suggests the action is directed toward the speaker; *take* suggests the action is directed away from the speaker.

> **Mom says that she brings home the bacon, so I have to take out the garbage.**

686 **can, may** In formal contexts, *can* is used to mean "being able to do"; *may* is used to mean "having permission to do."

> **I can start working on my research paper tomorrow if I may borrow your in-line skates to get to the library.**

687 **capital, capitol** The noun *capital* refers to a city or to money. The adjective *capital* means "major or important." *Capitol* refers to a building.

> **The capitol building is in the capital city for a capital reason. The city government contributed capital for the building expense.**

688 **cent, sent, scent** *Cent* is a coin; *sent* is the past tense of the verb "send"; *scent* is an odor or a smell.

> **For 32 cents, I sent my girlfriend a mushy love poem in a perfumed envelope. She adored the scent but hated the poem.**

689 **chord, cord** *Chord* may mean "an emotion or feeling," but it also may mean "the combination of two or more tones sounded at the same time," as with a guitar chord. A *cord* is a string or rope.

690 **chose, choose** *Chose* (choz) is the past tense of the verb *choose* (chooz).

> **For generations, people chose their careers based on their parents' careers; in the future, people will choose their careers based on the job market.**

691 **climactic, climatic** *Climactic* refers to the climax, or high point, of an event; *climatic* refers to the climate, or weather conditions.

> **If we use the open-air amphitheater, climatic conditions in these foothills will just about guarantee the wind gusts we need for the climactic third act.**

692 **coarse, course** *Coarse* means "of inferior quality, rough, or crude"; *course* means "a direction or path taken." *Course* also means "a class or series of studies."

> **The instructor of your freshman writing course may require all coarse writers to sign up for extra credit.**

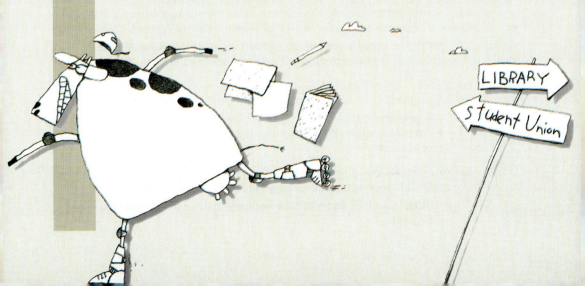

LIBRARY

Student Union

693 compare with, compare to Things of the same class are *compared with* each other; things of different classes are *compared to* each other.

694 complement, compliment *Complement* means "to complete or go well with." *Compliment* means "to offer an expression of admiration or praise."

> We really wanted to compliment Zach on his decorating efforts, but the bright yellow walls just didn't complement the purple carpet.

695 continual, continuous Although these word are synonyms, *continual* often implies that something is happening often, recurring; *continuous* usually implies that something keeps happening, uninterrupted.

> The continuous loud music during the night gave the building manager not only a headache, but also continual phone calls.

696 counsel, council As a noun, *counsel* means "advice"; when used as a verb, *counsel* means "to advise." *Council* refers to a group that advises.

> The city council was asked to counsel our student council on running an efficient meeting. Their counsel was very helpful.

697 desert, dessert *Desert* is barren wilderness. *Dessert* is food served at the end of a meal. The verb *desert* means "to abandon."

698 different from, different than Use *different from* in formal writing; use either form in informal or colloquial settings.

699 disinterested, uninterested Both words mean "not interested." However, *disinterested* is also used to mean "unbiased or impartial."

> A good referee must be disinterested in the outcome of the game, but never uninterested in the sport.

700 elicit, illicit *Elicit* is a verb meaning "to bring out." *Illicit* is an adjective meaning "unlawful."

> It took two quick hand signals from the lookout at the corner to elicit the illicit exchange of cash for drugs.

701 eminent, imminent *Eminent* means "prominent, conspicuous, or famous"; *imminent* means "ready or threatening to happen."

> With the island's government about to collapse, assassination attempts on several eminent officials seemed imminent.

702 explicit, implicit *Explicit* means "expressed directly or clearly defined"; *implicit* means "implied or unstated."

> The professor explicitly asked that the experiment be wrapped up on Monday, implicitly demanding that her lab assistants work on the weekend.

703 farther, further *Farther* refers to a physical distance; *further* refers to additional time, quantity, or degree.

> Further research showed that walking farther would improve his health.

704   **fewer, less** *Fewer* refers to the number of separate units; *less* refers to bulk quantity.

> **Because of spell checkers, students can produce papers containing fewer errors in less time.**

705   **figuratively, literally** *Figuratively* means "in a metaphorical or analogous way—describing something by comparing it to something else"; *literally* means "actually or virtually."

> **The lab was literally filled with sulfurous gases—figuratively speaking, dragon's breath.**

706   **fiscal, physical** *Fiscal* means "related to financial matters"; *physical* means "related to material things."

> **The school's fiscal work is handled by its accounting staff.**
> **The physical work is handled by its maintenance staff.**

707   **for, fore, four** *For* is a conjunction meaning "because," or a preposition used to indicate the object or recipient of something; *fore* means "earlier" or "the front"; *four* is the number 4.

708   **good, well** *Good* is an adjective; *well* is nearly always an adverb. (When used to indicate state of health, *well* is an adjective.)

> **A good job offers opportunities for advancement, especially for those who do their jobs well.**

709   **healthful, healthy** *Healthful* means "causing or improving health"; *healthy* means "possessing health."

> **Healthful foods and regular exercise build healthy bodies.**

710   **hear, here** You *hear* with your ears. *Here* means "the area close by."

711   **immigrate, emigrate** *Immigrate* means "to come into a new country or environment." *Emigrate* means "to go out of one country to live in another."

> **Immigrating to a new country is a challenging experience.**
> **People emigrating from their homelands need to consider this.**

712   **imply, infer** *Imply* means "to suggest or express indirectly"; *infer* means "to draw a conclusion from facts." (A writer or speaker *implies;* a reader or listener *infers.*)

> **Dad implied I should study more and drive around less; I inferred he meant my grades had to improve, or my car would disappear.**

713   **ingenious, ingenuous** *Ingenious* means "intelligent, discerning, clever"; *ingenuous* means "unassuming, natural, showing childlike innocence and candidness."

> **Many thought it an ingenious plan to put the boy-king in charge of diplomatic affairs; his ingenuous comments could sooth the sorest egos.**

714   **interstate, intrastate** *Interstate* means "existing between two or more states"; *intrastate* means "existing within a state."

715   **it's, its** *It's* is the contraction of "it is." *Its* is the possessive form of "it."

> It's not hard to see why my roommate feeds that alley cat; its pitiful limp and mournful mewing would melt any heart.

716   **later, latter** *Later* means "after a period of time." *Latter* refers to the second of two things mentioned.

717   **lay, lie** *Lay* means "to place." *Lay* is a transitive verb. (See 785.)

> If you lay another book on my table, I won't have room for anything else. Yesterday, you laid two books on the table. Over the last few days, you must have laid at least 20 books there.

Lie means "to recline." *Lie* is an intransitive verb. (See 788.)

> The cat likes to lie down anywhere.
> It lay down yesterday on my homework.
> It has lain down many times on the kitchen table.

718   **learn, teach** *Learn* means "to acquire information"; *teach* means "to give information."

> Sometimes it's easier to teach someone else a lesson than it is to learn one yourself.

719   **leave, let** *Leave* means "to allow something to remain behind." *Let* means "to permit."

> Please let me help you carry that chair; otherwise, leave it for the movers to pick up.

720   **lend, borrow** *Lend* means "to give for temporary use"; *borrow* means "to receive for temporary use."

> I told Mom I needed to borrow $15 for a CD, but she said her lending service was for school supplies only.

721   **liable, libel** *Liable* is an adjective meaning "responsible" or "exposed to an adverse action"; *libel* (noun) is a written defamatory statement about someone, and the verb *libel* means "to publish or make such a statement."

> Supermarket tabloids, liable for ruining many a reputation, make a practice of libelling the rich and the famous.

722   **liable, likely** *Liable* means "responsible according to the law" or "exposed to an adverse action"; *likely* means "in all probability."

> The "flat tire on the freeway in rush-hour traffic" seems a likely story; but I still think you're liable to be in deep trouble for missing your final exam.

723   **like, as** *Like* is a preposition meaning "similar to"; *as* is a conjunction with several meanings. *Like* usually introduces a phrase; *as* usually introduces a clause.

> Like the others in my study group, I do my work as any serious student would—carefully and thoroughly.

724   **loose, lose, loss** *Loose* (loos) means "free, untied, unrestricted"; *lose* (looz) means "to misplace or fail to find or control"; *loss* (los) means "something that is misplaced and cannot be found."

725   **miner, minor** A *miner* digs in the ground for ore. A *minor* is a person who is not legally an adult. A *minor* problem is one of no great importance.

> **The use of minors as miners is no minor problem.**

726   **oral, verbal** *Oral* means "uttered with the mouth"; *verbal* means "relating to or consisting of words and the comprehension of words."

> **The actor's oral abilities were outstanding, her pronunciation and intonation impeccable, but I doubted the playwright's verbal skills after trying to decipher the play's meaning.**

727   **past, passed** *Passed* is a verb. *Past* can be used as a noun, as an adjective, or as a preposition.

> **That Escort passed my 'Vette. (verb)**
>
> **Many senior citizens hold dearly to the past. (noun)**
>
> **I'm sorry, but my past life is not your business. (adjective)**
>
> **Old Rosebud walked past us and never smelled the apples. (preposition)**

728   **peace, piece** *Peace* means "tranquility or freedom from war." *Piece* is a part or fragment.

> **Someone once observed that peace is not a condition, but a process—a process of building goodwill one piece, or one step, at a time.**

729   **people, person** Use *people* to refer to human populations, races, or groups; use *person* to refer to an individual or the physical body.

> **What the American people need is a good insect repellent. The forest ranger recommends that we check our persons for wood ticks when we leave the woods.**

730   **percent, percentage** A *percent* is only one part in a hundred; a *percentage* is a portion of the whole, that portion being expressed as an amount of something or as a certain number of percents (25 percent, 50 percent, etc.).

> **Each person's percentage of the reward amounted to $125—25 percent of the $500 offered by Crimestoppers.**

NOTE: In everyday usage, you will often see the word "percent" being used in place of the word "percentage."

> **What percent (instead of percentage) of your paycheck do you save?**

731 **personal, personnel** *Personal* means "private." *Personnel* are people working at a particular job.

> **Although choosing a major is a personal decision, it can be helpful to consult with guidance personnel.**

732 **pore, pour, poor** A *pore* is an opening in the skin. *Pour* means "a constant flow or stream." *Poor* means "needy or pitiable."

> **Tough exams on late spring days make my poor pores pour.**

733 **precede, proceed** To *precede* means "to go or come before," while *proceed* means "to move on or go ahead."

> **Our zany biology instructor often preceded his lecture with these words: "All alert sponges, proceed to soak up more fascinating facts!"**

734 **principal, principle** As an adjective, *principal* means "primary." As a noun, it can mean "a school administrator" or "a sum of money." A *principle* is an idea or a doctrine.

> **His principal gripe is lack of freedom. (adjective)**
> **The principal expressed his concern about open campus. (noun)**
> **After 20 years, the amount of interest was higher than the principal. (noun)**
> **The principle of *caveat emptor* is "Let the buyer beware."**

735 **quiet, quit, quite** *Quiet* is the opposite of noisy. *Quit* means "to stop." *Quite* means "completely or to a considerable extent."

> **The library remained quite quiet until the librarian quit watching us.**

736 **quote, quotation** *Quote* is a verb; *quotation* is a noun.

> **The quotation I used was from Woody Allen. You may quote me on that.**

737 **real, very, really** Do not use *real* in place of the adverbs *very* or *really*.

> **My mother's cake is usually very (not real) fresh. But this cake is really stale—I mean, it's just about fossilized.**

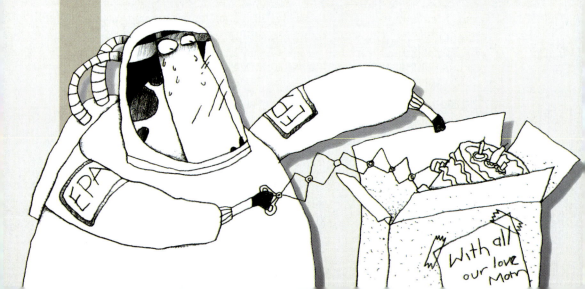

738 **right, write, wright, rite** *Right* means "correct or proper"; it also refers to that which a person has a legal claim to, as in *copyright*. *Write* means "to inscribe or record." A *wright* is a person who makes or builds something. *Rite* is a ritual or ceremonial act.

> **Did you write that it is the right of the shipwright to perform the rite of christening—breaking a bottle of champagne on the stern of the ship?**

739 **scene, seen** *Scene* refers to the location where something happens; it also may mean "sight or spectacle." *Seen* is the past participle of the verb "see."

> **An exhibitionist likes to be seen making a scene.**

740 **set, sit** *Set* means "to place." *Sit* means "to put the body in a seated position." *Set* is a transitive verb; *sit* is an intransitive verb.

> **How can you just sit there and watch as I set all these chairs in place?**

741 **sight, cite, site** *Sight* means "the act of seeing" or "something that is seen." *Cite* means "to quote" or "to summon to court." *Site* means "location or position."

> **After sighting the faulty wiring and the overloaded I-beam, the inspector cited the building contractor for breaking two city codes at a downtown work site.**

742 **some, sum** *Some* refers to an unknown thing, a number, or a part. *Sum* is a certain amount of money, or the result of adding numbers together.

> **Some of the students answered too quickly, without thinking, and came up with the wrong sum.**

743 **stationary, stationery** *Stationary* means "not movable"; *stationery* refers to the paper and envelopes used to write letters.

744 **than, then** *Than* is used in a comparison; *then* tells when.

> **Just remember to study more than you party. Then you will probably be satisfied with your grades.**

745 **their, there, they're** *Their* is the possessive personal pronoun. *There* is an adverb used to point out location. *They're* is the contraction for "they are."

> **If there is a comfortable place for students to study for their exams, they're more likely to do a good job.**

746 **threw, through** *Threw* is the past tense of "throw." *Through* means "passing from one side of something to the other."

747 **to, too, two** *To* is a preposition that can mean "in the direction of." *To* is also used to form an infinitive. *Too* means "also" or "very." *Two* is the number 2.

> **Two causes of visual problems among students are lights that fail to illuminate properly and computer screens with too much glare.**

748 **vain, vane, vein** *Vain* means "valueless or fruitless"; it may also mean "holding a high regard for one's self." *Vane* is a flat piece of material set up to show which way the wind blows. *Vein* refers to a blood vessel or a mineral deposit.

> **The weather vane indicates the direction of the wind; the blood vein determines the direction of flowing blood; the vain mind moves in no particular direction and is content to think only about itself.**

749 **vary, very** *Vary* means "to change"; *very* means "to a high degree."

> **To ensure the very best employee relations, the workloads should not vary greatly from worker to worker.**

750 **waist, waste** *Waist* is the part of the body just above the hips. The verb *waste* means "to lose through inaction" or "to wear away, decay"; the noun *waste* refers to material that is unused or useless.

> **Her waist is small because she wastes no opportunity to exercise.**

751 **wait, weight** *Wait* means "to stay somewhere expecting something." *Weight* refers to a degree or unit of heaviness.

752 **ware, wear, where** *Ware* refers to a product that is sold; *wear* means "to have on or to carry on one's body"; *where* asks the question "In what place?" or "In what situation?"

> **The designer boasted, "Where can one wear my ware? Anywhere."**

753 **weather, whether** *Weather* refers to the condition of the atmosphere. *Whether* refers to a possibility.

> **Weather conditions affect nearly all of us, whether we are farmers, pilots, or plumbers.**

754 **who, which, that** *Who* refers to people. *Which* refers to nonliving objects or to animals. (*Which* should never refer to people.) *That* may refer to animals, people, or nonliving objects.

755 **who, whom** *Who* is used as the subject of a verb; *whom* is used as the object of a preposition or as a direct object. (*Who* is used in place of *whom* for most everyday communication.)

756 **who's, whose** *Who's* is the contraction for "who is." *Whose* is the possessive pronoun.

> **Whose car are we using, and who's going to pay for the gas?**

757 **your, you're** *Your* is a possessive pronoun. *You're* is the contraction for "you are."

> **If you're like most Americans, you will have held hold eight jobs by your 40th birthday.**

"If you scoff at language study . . . how will you scoff?" —Mario Pei

Understanding Our Language

Parts of Speech

758 **Parts of speech** are the eight different ways words are used in our language—as *nouns, pronouns, verbs, adjectives, adverbs, prepositions, conjunctions,* or *interjections.*

NOUN

759 A **noun** is a word that names something: a person, a place, a thing, or an idea.

> **Larry Vanderhoef**/chancellor   ***Lone Star***/film   **Renaissance**/era
> **UC-Davis**/university   **A Congress of Wonders**/book

Classes of Nouns

760 The classes of nouns are *proper, common, concrete, abstract,* and *collective.*

■ A **proper noun** names a particular person, place, thing, or idea. Proper nouns are always capitalized.

> **Rembrandt, Bertrand Russell** (people); **Stratford-on-Avon, Tower of London** (places); **"The Night Watch," Rosetta Stone** (things); **Rousseauism, Populism** (ideas)

■ A **common noun** is any noun that does not name a particular person, place, thing, or idea. Common nouns are not capitalized.

> **campus**   **instructor**   **biology**   **exam**   **transcript**

■ A **concrete noun** names a thing that is tangible (can be seen, touched, heard, smelled, or tasted).

> **dormitory**   **roommate**   **microwave**   **Pearl Jam**   **pizza**

■ An **abstract noun** names an idea, a condition, or a feeling—in other words, something that cannot be touched, seen, or heard.

> **Freudian psychology**   **anxiety**   **ergophobia**   **theory**

■ A **collective noun** names a group or unit.

> **Georgetown University**   **team**   **crowd**   **sorority**

Forms of Nouns

761 Nouns are grouped according to their *number, gender,* and *case.*

NUMBER OF A NOUN

762 **Number** indicates whether a noun is singular or plural.

A **singular noun** refers to one person, place, thing, or idea.

> college student class note grade result

A **plural noun** refers to more than one person, place, thing, or idea.

> colleges students classes notes grades results

GENDER OF A NOUN

763 **Gender** indicates whether a noun is masculine, feminine, neuter, or indefinite.

> **Masculine:** father king brother men bull rooster
> **Feminine:** mother queen sister women cow hen
> **Neuter:** book disc car stapler (without sex)
> **Indefinite:** professor chancellor dean (masculine or feminine)

CASE OF A NOUN

764 **Case** tells how nouns are related to other words used with them. There are three cases: *nominative, possessive,* and *objective.*

■ **Nominative case** describes a noun used as the subject of a clause.

> The **chancellor** is in charge of running a college or university.

A noun is also in the nominative case when it is used as a predicate noun (or predicate nominative). A predicate noun follows a form of the *be* verb *(is, are, was, were, been)* and repeats or renames the subject.

> Either the president or the chancellor is the **person** to talk to about the university's goals.

■ **Possessive case** describes a noun that shows possession or ownership.

> Our **chancellor's** willingness to discuss concerns with students has boosted campus morale.

■ **Objective case** describes a noun used as a direct object, an indirect object, or an object of the preposition.

> Recent budget cuts have given university **students** and **staff** **plenty** to talk about. (*Plenty* is the direct object of *have given; students* and *staff* are indirect objects.)
>
> To survive, institutions of higher **learning** must serve the **communities** that support them. (*Learning* is the object of the preposition *of; communities* is the direct object of *must serve.*)

PRONOUN

765 A **pronoun** is a word used in place of a noun.

> **I, you, she, it, which, that, themselves, whoever, me, he, they, whatever, my, mine, ours**

766 All pronouns have **antecedents**. An antecedent is the noun that the pronoun refers to or replaces.

> **As the wellness counselor checked *her* chart, students *who* were next in line stuffed candy wrappers in *their* pockets. (*Counselor* is the antecedent of *her*; students is the antecedent of *who* and *their*.)**

NOTE: Each pronoun must agree with its antecedent in number, person, and gender. (See 849-851.)

Pronouns are distinguished according to their *type, class, number, gender, person,* and *case*. There are three **types**.

> **Simple:**   **I, you, he, she, it, we, they, who, what**
>
> **Compound:**   **myself, yourself, himself, herself, ourselves, itself**
>
> **Phrasal:**   **one another, each other**

NOTE: There are five **classes** of pronouns: *personal, relative, indefinite, interrogative,* and *demonstrative*.

Forms of Personal Pronouns

767 The **form** of a personal pronoun indicates its *number* (singular or plural), its *person* (first, second, or third), its *case* (nominative, possessive, or objective), and its *gender* (masculine, feminine, or neuter).

NUMBER OF A PRONOUN

768 A personal pronoun is either singular *(I, you, he, she, it)* or plural *(we, you, they)* in number.

> **You** (singular) **need to have a budget and stick to it** (singular).
>
> **We** (plural) **can help new students learn about budgeting.**

PERSON OF A PRONOUN

769 The **person** of a pronoun indicates whether that pronoun is speaking, is spoken to, or is spoken about.

■ **First person** is used in place of the name of the speaker.

> **I know I need to handle my stress in a healthful way, especially during exam week; my usual chips-and-donuts binge isn't helping.**
> **We all decided to bike to the tennis court.**

■ **Second person** is used to name the person or thing spoken to.

> **Maria, you (singular) grab the rackets, okay?**
> **John and Tanya, can you (plural) find the water bottles?**

■ **Third person** is used to name the person or thing spoken about.

> **Today's students are interested in wellness issues. They are concerned about their health, fitness, and nutrition.**
> **Maria practices hatha yoga and feels she is calmer for her choice.**
> **John likes to be more active, so he is always riding his bike.**

CASE OF A PRONOUN

770 The **case** of each pronoun tells how it is related to the other words used with it. There are three cases: *nominative, possessive,* and *objective.*

■ **Nominative case** describes a pronoun used as the subject of a clause. The following are nominative forms: *I, you, he, she, it, we, they.*

> **He likes himself when things go well.**
> **You must live life in order to love life.**

NOTE: A pronoun is also in the nominative case when it is used as a predicate nominative. A predicate nominative follows a form of the *be* verb *(am, is, are, was, were, been),* and it repeats the subject.

> **We have met the enemy, and they are we.**

■ **Possessive case** describes a pronoun that shows possession or ownership. An apostrophe, however, is not used with a personal pronoun to show possession.

> **my   mine   our   ours   his   her   hers   their   theirs   its   your   yours**

■ **Objective case** describes a pronoun used as the direct object, indirect object, or object of a preposition.

> **Professor Adler hired her.** (*Her* is the direct object of the verb *hired.*)
> **He showed her the language lab.** (*Her* is the indirect object of the verb *showed.*)
> **He introduced her to two other assistants and said she'd be training with them.** (*Them* is the object of the preposition *with.*)

771 ## Number, Person, and Case of Personal Pronouns

	Nominative Case	Possessive Case	Objective Case
First Person Singular	I	my, mine	me
Second Person Singular	you	your, yours	you
Third Person Singular	he	his	him
	she	her, hers	her
	it	its	it

	Nominative Case	Possessive Case	Objective Case
First Person Plural	we	our, ours	us
Second Person Plural	you	your, yours	you
Third Person Plural	they	their, theirs	them

SPECIAL PERSONAL PRONOUNS

772 A **reflexive pronoun** is formed by adding *-self* or *-selves* to a personal pronoun. A reflexive pronoun can act as a direct object or an indirect object of a verb, an object of a preposition, or a predicate nominative.

> He loves **himself**. (direct object of *loves*)
> He gives **himself** A's for fashion sense. (indirect object of *gives*)
> He smiles at **himself** in store windows. (object of preposition *at*)
> He can be **himself** anywhere. (predicate nominative)

NOTE: A reflexive pronoun is called an **intensive pronoun** when it intensifies, or emphasizes, the noun or pronoun it refers to.

> Leo **himself** taught his children to invest their lives in others.
> The lesson was sometimes painful—but they learned it **themselves**.

Other Kinds of Pronouns

773 A **relative pronoun** relates one part of a sentence to a word in another part of the sentence. Specifically, a relative pronoun relates an adjective clause to the noun or pronoun it modifies. (The noun is underlined in each example below; the relative pronoun is in boldface.)

> Freshmen **who** believe they have a lot to learn are absolutely right.
> Just knowing where you are on campus, **which** is important for obvious reasons, can be challenging.

774 An **indefinite pronoun** refers to unnamed or unknown people or things.

> **Nothing is more unnerving than rushing last minute into the wrong room for the wrong class.** (The antecedent of *nothing* is unknown.)

775 An **interrogative pronoun** asks a question.

> **So which will it be—highlighting and attaching a campus map to the inside of your backpack (or cap), or being lost and late for the first two weeks?**

776 A **demonstrative pronoun** points out specific people, places, or things.

> **We advise this: attach as many maps and schedules as you need, in as many places as you need to. And remember to smile . . . that always helps.**

777

Classes of Pronouns

PERSONAL

I, me, my, mine / we, us, our, ours
you, your, yours / they, them, their, theirs
he, him, his, she, her, hers, it, its
myself, himself, herself, itself, yourself, themselves, ourselves

RELATIVE

who, whose, whom, which, what, that

INDEFINITE

all	both	everything	nobody	several
another	each	few	none	some
any	each one	many	no one	somebody
anybody	either	most	nothing	someone
anyone	everybody	much	one	something
anything	everyone	neither	other	such

INTERROGATIVE

who, whose, whom, which, what

DEMONSTRATIVE

this, that, these, those

VERB

Forms of Verbs

778 A **verb** is a word that expresses action or state of being. A verb's form differs depending on its number (singular, plural); person (first, second, third); voice (active, passive); tense (present, past, future, present perfect, past perfect, future perfect); and mood (indicative, imperative, subjunctive).

NUMBER OF A VERB

779 **Number** indicates whether a verb is singular or plural. The verb and its subject both must be singular, or they both must be plural.

> My **college enrolls** high schoolers in summer programs. (singular)
>
> Many **colleges enroll** high schoolers in semester courses. (plural)

PERSON OF A VERB

780 **Person** indicates whether the subject of the verb is *first, second,* or *third person* and whether the subject is singular or plural. Verbs usually have a different form only in third person singular of the present tense.

	Singular	Plural
First Person	I think	we think
Second Person	you think	you think
Third Person	he/she/it thinks	they think

VOICE OF A VERB

781 **Voice** indicates whether the subject is acting or being acted upon.

■ **Active voice** indicates that the subject of the verb is doing something.

> You **should update** your parents on a regular basis.

■ **Passive voice** indicates that the subject of the verb is being acted upon. A passive verb combines a *be* verb with a past participle.

> Your parents **should be updated** on a regular basis.

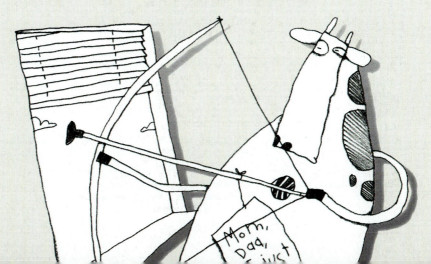

TENSE OF A VERB

Tense indicates time. Each verb has three principal parts: the *present, past,* and *past participle.* All six of the tenses are formed from these principal parts. The past and past participle of regular verbs are formed by adding *ed* to the present form. The past and past participle of irregular verbs are usually different words. (See 790 for examples.)

■ **Present tense** expresses action that is happening at the present time, or action that happens continually, regularly.
More than 75 percent of today's U.S. workers work in service industries.

■ **Past tense** expresses action that was completed at a time in the past.
A hundred years ago, more than 75 percent worked in agriculture.

■ **Future tense** expresses action that will take place in the future.
By the year 2000, service jobs will make up 80 percent of all jobs.

■ **Present perfect tense** expresses action that began in the past but continues in the present or is completed at the present.
Our economy has seen great changes over the years.

■ **Past perfect tense** expresses action that began in the past and was completed in the past.
We had expected our lives to be different from our parents'.

■ **Future perfect tense** expresses action that will begin in the future and be completed by a specific time in the future.
During our lifetimes, we will have seen more changes than any other generation in history.

TENSE	Active Voice		Passive Voice	
	Singular	Plural	Singular	Plural
PRESENT	I see	we see	I am seen	we are seen
	you see	you see	you are seen	you are seen
	he/she/it sees	they see	he/she/it is seen	they are seen
PAST	I saw	we saw	I was seen	we were seen
	you saw	you saw	you were seen	you were seen
	he saw	they saw	he was seen	they were seen
FUTURE	I will see	we will see	I will be seen	we will be seen
	you will see	you will see	you will be seen	you will be seen
	he will see	they will see	he will be seen	they will be seen
PRESENT PERFECT	I have seen	we have seen	I have been seen	we have been seen
	you have seen	you have seen	you have been seen	you have been seen
	he has seen	they have seen	he has been seen	they have been seen
PAST PERFECT	I had seen	we had seen	I had been seen	we had been seen
	you had seen	you had seen	you had been seen	you had been seen
	he had seen	they had seen	he had been seen	they had been seen
FUTURE PERFECT	I will have seen	we will have seen	I will have been seen	we will have been seen
	you will have seen	you will have seen	you will have been seen	you will have been seen
	he will have seen	they will have seen	he will have been seen	they will have been seen

MOOD OF A VERB

783 The **mood** of the verb indicates the tone or attitude with which a statement is made.

■ **Indicative mood** is used to state a fact or to ask a question.

Can any theme capture the essence of the complex 1960's U.S. culture? President John F. Kennedy's directive (stated below) represents one ideal popular during that decade.

■ **Imperative mood** is used to give a command.

Ask not what your country can do for you. Ask what you can do for your country. —John F. Kennedy

■ **Subjunctive mood** is no longer commonly used; however, it continues to be used by careful writers to express the exact manner in which their statements are meant.

(1) Use the subjunctive *were* to express a condition that is contrary to fact.

If each of your brain cells were one person, there would be enough people to populate 25 planets.

(2) Use the subjunctive *were* after *as though* or *as if* to express doubt or uncertainty in the past.

Experts have sometimes talked as though the human brain were nothing more than a complex computer.

(3) Use the subjunctive *be* in "that clauses" to express necessity, parliamentary motions, or legal decisions.

I propose that the following truth be embraced: "grayware" (brain power) is more powerful than software (computer power).

Classes of Verbs

AUXILIARY VERBS

784 **Auxiliary verbs,** or helping verbs, help to form some of the *tenses* (782), the *mood* (783), and the *voice* (781) of the main verb. In the following examples, the auxiliary verbs are in boldface, and the main verbs are in italics.

I *believe*, I have always *believed*, and I will always *believe* in private enterprise as the backbone of economic well-being in America.
—Franklin D. Roosevelt

Common Auxiliary Verbs

is	are	was	were	am	been	shall	will	would
did	must	can	may	have	had	has	do	should

TRANSITIVE VERBS

785 A **transitive** verb communicates action and is always followed by an object that receives the action and completes the meaning of the verb.

> The health care industry **employs** more than 7 million *workers* in the U.S.

■ **Active voice**: A transitive verb in the active voice directs the action from the subject to the object.

> All students in this broad field **take** biology *courses.*

■ **Passive voice**: If a transitive verb is in the passive voice, the subject of the sentence receives the action. (In the example below, the subject *degree* receives the action of the verb *is required.*)

> A one- or two-year degree **is required** for some health care positions.

786 A **direct object** receives the action of a transitive verb directly from the subject.

> On the other hand, getting a degree in pharmacy takes five **years.** (*Years* is the direct object.)

787 An **indirect object** receives the action of a transitive verb, but indirectly. An indirect object names the person (or thing) to whom (or to what) or for whom (or for what) something is done.

> A degree in clinical laboratory science offers a **student** several career options. (*Student* is the indirect object.)

NOTE: When the word naming the indirect receiver of the action is contained in a prepositional phrase, it is no longer considered an indirect object.

> The health science advisor can offer advice to **you** about these choices. (*You* is the object of the preposition *to.*)

INTRANSITIVE VERBS

788 An **intransitive verb** refers to an action that is complete in itself. It does not need an object to receive the action.

> The best college advisors **encourage** and **direct.**

NOTE: Some verbs can be either *transitive* or *intransitive.*

> My advisor **teaches** *physiology* and *microbiology.* (transitive)
> She **teaches** well. (intransitive)

789 A **linking verb** is a special type of intransitive verb that links the subject to a noun or an adjective in the predicate.

> A good *teacher* **is** a *gift.*

Common Linking Verbs

is	are	was	were	be	been	am	smell	look
seem	grow	become	appear	sound	taste	feel	remain	stand

790 Common Irregular Verbs and Their Principal Parts

Present Tense	Past Tense	Past Participle	Present Tense	Past Tense	Past Participle	Present Tense	Past Tense	Past Participle
am, be	was, were	been	freeze	froze	frozen	show	showed	shown
begin	began	begun	give	gave	given	shrink	shrank	shrunk
bite	bit	bitten	go	went	gone	sing	sang	sung
blow	blew	blown	grow	grew	grown	sink	sank, sunk	sunk
break	broke	broken	hang (execute)	hanged	hanged	sit	sat	sat
bring	brought	brought	hang (suspend)	hung	hung	speak	spoke	spoken
burst	burst	burst	hide	hid	hidden	spring	sprang,	
catch	caught	caught	know	knew	known		sprung	sprung
choose	chose	chosen	lay	laid	laid	steal	stole	stolen
come	came	come	lead	led	led	strive	strove	striven
dive	dived	dived	lie (recline)	lay	lain	swear	swore	sworn
do	did	done	lie (deceive)	lied	lied	swim	swam	swum
drag	dragged	dragged	raise	raised	raised	swing	swung	swung
draw	drew	drawn	ride	rode	ridden	take	took	taken
drink	drank	drunk	ring	rang	rung	tear	tore	torn
drive	drove	driven	rise	rose	risen	throw	threw	thrown
eat	ate	eaten	run	ran	run	wake	woke,	woken,
fall	fell	fallen	see	saw	seen		waked	waked
fight	fought	fought	set	set	set	wear	wore	worn
flee	fled	fled	shake	shook	shaken	weave	wove	woven
flow	flowed	flowed	shine (light)	shone	shone	wring	wrung	wrung
fly	flew	flown	shine (polish)	shined	shined	write	wrote	written

SPECIAL VERB FORMS

791 A **verbal** is a word that is derived from a verb, has the power of a verb, but acts as another part of speech. Like a verb, a verbal may take an object, a modifier (adjective, adverb), and sometimes a subject; but unlike a verb, a verbal functions as a noun, an adjective, or an adverb. Three types of verbals are *gerunds, infinitives,* and *participles.*

792 A **gerund** is a verb form that ends in *ing* and is used as a noun.

> **Getting up** each morning is the first challenge. (subject)
> I start **moving** at about seven o'clock. (direct object)
> I work at **jump-starting** my weary system. (object of the preposition)
> Like Woody Allen once said, "Eighty percent of life is **showing up**."
> (predicate noun)

793 An **infinitive** is a verb form that is usually introduced by *to;* the infinitive may be used as a noun, as an adjective, or as an adverb.

> **To succeed** is not easy. (noun subject)
> That is the most important thing **to remember.** (adjective)
> Students are wise **to work** hard. (adverb)

794 A **participle** is a verb form usually ending in *ing* or *ed*. A participle functions as a verb because it can take an object; a participle functions as an adjective because it can modify a noun or pronoun.

> The students **reading** those study-skill handouts are definitely **interested**. The prospect of **aced** tests and assignments must be **appealing**. (All of these participles function as adjectives: *reading* students, *interested* students, *aced* tests and assignments, and *appealing* prospect. *Reading* also functions as a verb with a direct object, *handouts*.)

ADJECTIVE

795 An **adjective** describes or modifies a noun or pronoun. Articles *a, an,* and *the* are adjectives.

> Advertising is **a big** and **powerful** industry.
> (*A, big,* and *powerful* modify *industry*.)

■ Adjectives can be common or proper. **Proper adjectives** are created from proper nouns and are capitalized.

> **English** (proper noun) **has been influenced by advertising slogans.**

> The **English** (proper adjective) **language is subject to constant change.**

NOTE: Some words can be either adjectives or pronouns (*that, these, many, some,* etc.). These words are adjectives if they come before a noun and modify that noun; they are pronouns if they stand alone.

> **Some advertisements are less than truthful.**
> (*Some* modifies advertisements; it is an adjective.)

> **Many cause us to chuckle at their outrageous claims.**
> (*Many* stands alone; it is a pronoun.)

■ A **predicate adjective** follows a form of the *be* verb (or other linking verb) and describes the subject.

> **At its best, advertising is useful; at its worst, deceptive.**
> (*Useful* and *deceptive* modify *advertising*.)

Forms of Adjectives

796 Adjectives have three forms: *positive, comparative,* and *superlative.*

■ The **positive form** describes a noun or pronoun without comparing it to anyone or anything else.

> **Pathfinder walking shoes are sturdy and comfortable.**

■ The **comparative form** (*er* or *more*) compares two persons, places, things, or ideas.

> **Air soles make Mile Eaters sturdier and more comfortable than Pathfinders.**

■ The **superlative form** (*est* or *most*) compares three or more persons, places, things, or ideas.

> **Really. I believe my old Canvas Wonders are the sturdiest, most comfortable walking shoes of all!**

ADVERB

797 An **adverb** modifies a verb, an adjective, or another adverb. An adverb tells *how, when, where, why, how often,* or *how much.*

> **Sales fell sharply.** (***Sharply*** modifies the verb ***fell.***)
> **Sales were quite low.** (***Quite*** modifies the adjective ***low.***)
> **Sales dropped very quickly.** (***Very*** modifies the adverb ***quickly.***)

■ Adverbs can be grouped in four ways: *time, place, manner,* and *degree.*

Time (These adverbs tell *when, how often,* and *how long.*)
> **today, yesterday   daily, weekly   briefly, eternally**

Place (These adverbs tell *where, to where,* and *from where.*)
> **here, there   nearby, yonder   backward, forward**

Manner (These adverbs tell *how* something is done.)
> **precisely   regularly   regally   smoothly   well**

Degree (These adverbs tell *how much* or *how little.*)
> **substantially   greatly   entirely   partly   too**

NOTE: Some adverbs can be written with or without the *ly* ending. When in doubt, use the *ly* form.
> **slow, slowly   loud, loudly   fair, fairly   tight, tightly   quick, quickly**

Forms of Adverbs

798 Adverbs have three forms: *positive, comparative,* and *superlative.*

■ The **positive form** describes a verb, an adjective, or another adverb without comparing it to anyone or anything else.
> **With Pathfinder shoes, you'll walk fast. They support your feet well.**

■ The **comparative form** (*er* or *more*) compares two persons, places, things, or ideas.
> **Wear Mile Eaters instead of Pathfinders, and you'll walk faster.**
> **Mile Eaters' special soles support your feet better.**

■ The **superlative form** (*est* or *most*) compares three or more persons, places, things, or ideas.
> **Really. I walk fastest wearing my old Canvas Wonders. They seem to support my feet, my knees, and my pocketbook best of all.**

POSITIVE	COMPARATIVE	SUPERLATIVE
well	better	best
badly	worse	worst
fast	faster	fastest
effectively	more effectively	most effectively

PREPOSITION

799　A **preposition** is a word (or group of words) that introduces a phrase, which in turn modifies some other word in the sentence. The first noun or pronoun following the preposition is its object.

> **Regarding your reasons for going to college,** do they all hinge **on getting a good job after graduation,** or does earning a college degree offer more **than that?** (In this sentence, *reasons, going, college, getting, graduation,* and *that* are objects of their preceding prepositions *regarding, for, to, on, after,* and *than.*)

NOTE: There are three kinds of prepositions: *simple* (at, in, of, on, with), *compound* (within, outside, underneath), and *phrasal* (on account of, on top of, in addition to).

■ A **prepositional phrase** includes the preposition, the object of the preposition, and the modifiers of the object. A prepositional phrase may function as an adverb or as an adjective.

> A broader knowledge **of the world** is one benefit **of higher education.** (The phrases function as adjectives modifying the nouns *knowledge* and *benefit* respectively.)

> The opportunity to do new things and meet new people is appreciated **by most students.** (The phrase functions as an adverb modifying the verb *is appreciated.*)

800

List of Prepositions

aboard	back of	except for	near to	round
about	because of	excepting	notwithstanding	save
above	before	for	of	since
according to	behind	from	off	subsequent to
across	below	from among	on	together with
across from	beneath	from between	on account of	through
after	beside	from under	on behalf of	throughout
against	besides	in	onto	till
along	between	in addition to	on top of	to
alongside	beyond	in behalf of	opposite	toward
alongside of	but	in front of	out	under
along with	by	in place of	out of	underneath
amid	by means of	in regard to	outside	until
among	concerning	inside	outside of	unto
apart from	considering	inside of	over	up
around	despite	in spite of	over to	upon
as far as	down	instead of	owing to	up to
aside from	down from	into	past	with
at	during	like	prior to	within
away from	except	near	regarding	without

CONJUNCTION

801 A **conjunction** connects individual words or groups of words.

> **When we came back to Paris, it was clear and cold and lovely.**
> (The conjunction *and* connects equal adjectives.)
> —Ernest Hemingway

■ **Coordinating conjunctions** connect a word to a word, a phrase to a phrase, or a clause to a clause. The words, phrases, or clauses joined by a coordinating conjunction must be equal or of the same type.

> **Civilization is a race between education and catastrophe.**
> (The conjunction *and* joins the two objects of the preposition *between*.)
> —H. G. Wells

■ **Correlative conjunctions** are conjunctions used in pairs (*either, or; neither, nor; not only, but also; both, and; whether, or; as, so*).

> **There are two inadvisable ways to think: either believe everything or doubt everything.**

■ **Subordinating conjunctions** are words that connect, and show the relationship between, two clauses that are not equally important. A subordinating conjunction connects a dependent clause to an independent clause in order to complete the meaning of the dependent clause.

> **Experience is the worst teacher; it gives the test before it presents the lesson.** (The clause *before it presents the lesson* is dependent. It depends on the rest of the sentence to complete its meaning.)

Kinds of Conjunctions

Coordinating: and, but, or, nor, for, yet, so

Correlative: either, or; neither, nor; not only, but also; both, and; whether, or; as, so

Subordinating: after, although, as, as if, as long as, as though, because, before, if, in order that, provided that, since, so, so that, that, though, till, unless, until, when, where, whereas, while

NOTE: Relative pronouns (773) and conjunctive adverbs (573) can also connect clauses.

INTERJECTION

802 An **interjection** is included in a sentence in order to communicate strong emotion or surprise. Punctuation (often a comma or an exclamation point) is used to set off an interjection from the rest of the sentence.

> **Help! Ouch! I'm stuck! Well, I guess no one hears me.**

Parts of Speech

QUICK GUIDE

1 A **noun** is a word that names something: a person, a place, a thing, or an idea.

> **Larry Vanderhoef**/chancellor   ***Lone Star***/film
> **UC-Davis**/university
> **A Congress of Wonders**/book   **Renaissance**/era

2 A **pronoun** is a word used in place of a noun.

> | I | me | that | she | which | mine | whatever |
> |---|----|------|-----|-------|------|----------|
> | it | my | ours | you | whoever | they | themselves |

3 A **verb** is a word that expresses action or state of being.

> | is | was | sit | fly | see | drag | break |
> |----|-----|-----|-----|-----|------|-------|
> | are | run | eat | bite | tear | were | catch |

4 An **adjective** describes or modifies a noun or pronoun. (The articles *a, an,* and *the* are adjectives.)

> **Advertising is a big** and **powerful** industry.
> (**A, big,** and ***powerful*** modify ***industry.***)

5 An **adverb** modifies a verb, an adjective, or another adverb. An adverb tells *how, when, where, why, how often,* or *how much.*

> | here | there | today | slowly | precisely | regularly |
> |------|-------|-------|--------|-----------|-----------|
> | slow | quick | partly | greatly | quickly | yesterday |

6 A **preposition** is a word (or group of words) that introduces a phrase, which in turn modifies some other word in the sentence. The first noun or pronoun following the preposition is its object.

> | on | to | of | off | out | over | above | across |
> |----|----|----|-----|-----|------|-------|--------|
> | by | up | in | for | with | from | until | through |

7 A **conjunction** connects individual words or groups of words.

> and but or nor for yet so because

8 An **interjection** is included in a sentence in order to communicate strong emotion or surprise. Punctuation (often a comma or an exclamation point) is used to set an interjection off from the rest of the sentence.

> Help! Ouch! Good grief, I'm stuck again!

"The limits of my language stand for the limits of my world." —Ludwig Wittgenstein

Using the Language

Constructing Sentences

804 A **sentence** is made up of one or more words that express a complete thought.

NOTE: A sentence begins with a capital letter; it ends with a period, a question mark, or an exclamation point.

> **Computers deliver the universe in a box.**

805 A sentence must have a **subject** and a **predicate** that express a complete thought. The subject is the element of the sentence about which something is said. The predicate is the element of the sentence that says something about the subject. (The primary part of a predicate is the word or words that function as a verb.)

> **Technology fascinates many people.**

NOTE: In the sentence above, *technology* is the subject—the sentence talks about technology. *Fascinates,* a verb, is the primary part of the predicate—it says something about the subject.

806 Either the subject or the predicate or both may be "missing" from a sentence, but both must be clearly **understood.**

> **"What's the big deal?"** (*What* is the subject; the predicate is expressed by the contraction: *'s* for *is.*)

> **"Information."** (*Information* is the subject; the predicate *is* is understood.)

> **"Get on-line."** (The subject *you* is understood; *get* is the predicate.)

NOTE: In sentences that begin with *There is, It is, There was,* or *It was,* the subject follows the verb.

> **There were 70,000 fans in the stadium.** (The subject is *fans; were* is the predicate. *There* or *It* used in this way are *expletives,* empty words used with a form of the verb *be.*)

THE SUBJECT

807 The **subject** is always a noun, or a word or phrase that functions as a noun, such as a pronoun, an infinitive, a gerund, or a noun clause.

> **Technology makes it impossible for a business to work without some kind of gizmo.** (noun)
>
> **In most businesses you will find a computer and a fax.** (pronoun)
>
> **To survive without technology is difficult.** (infinitive phrase)
>
> **Downloading information from a computer is easy.** (gerund phrase)
>
> **That the information age would arrive was inevitable.** (noun clause)

■ A **simple subject** is the subject without the words that modify it.

> **Thirty years ago, reasonably well-trained mechanics could fix any car on the road.**

■ A **complete subject** is the simple subject and the words that modify it.

> **Thirty years ago, reasonably well-trained mechanics could fix any car on the road.**

■ A **compound subject** is composed of two or more simple subjects.

> **Today, mechanics and technicians would need to master a half million manual pages to fix every car on the road.**

THE PREDICATE (VERB)

808 A **predicate** is the sentence part that says something about the subject.

> **All students need technical skills as well as basic academic skills.**

■ A **simple predicate** is the predicate without the words that describe or modify it.

> **Today's workplace requires employees to have a broad range of skills.**

■ A **complete predicate** is the simple predicate and all the words that modify or explain it.

> **Today's workplace requires employees to have a broad range of skills.**

■ A **compound predicate** is composed of two or more simple predicates.

> **Workers analyze, reason, calculate, and troubleshoot.**

■ A **compound subject** and a **compound predicate** sometimes appear in the same sentence.

> **Both high-school students and their college counterparts need strong organizational skills and must make studying a priority.**

■ A **direct object** receives the action of the predicate. (See 786.)

> **Before choosing a college, Marcos requested about a dozen catalogs.**

■ The **direct object** may be **compound**.

> **The catalogs explained the academic programs and the application process.**

Using Phrases

809 A **phrase** is a group of related words that lacks either a subject or a predicate or both.

> **amazing triumphs of technology** (The subject lacks a predicate.)
>
> **can be found** (The predicate lacks a subject.)
>
> **in ancient civilizations** (The phrase lacks a subject and a predicate.)
>
> Amazing triumphs of technology can be found in ancient civilizations.
> (Together, these three phrases present a complete thought.)

TYPES OF PHRASES

Phrases appear in several types: *noun, verb, prepositional, appositive, absolute,* and *verbal.*

810 A **noun phrase** consists of a noun and its modifiers; the whole phrase functions as a simple noun would.

> **My early-morning class schedule** allows plenty of time for working, studying, and recreation. (subject)
>
> The campus library has **many quiet, comfortable study carrels.**
> (direct object)

811 A **verb phrase** consists of a verb and its modifiers.

> Students, some of them panic-stricken, **practically camp out at the library during exam weeks.**

812 A **prepositional phrase** consists of a preposition, its object, and the object's modifiers.

> Denying the existence **of exam week** hasn't worked **for anyone yet.** (adjective modifying *existence;* adverb modifying *has worked*)
>
> Test days still dawn, and GPA's still plummet **for the unprepared.**
> (adverb modifying *dawn* and *plummet*)

813 An **appositive phrase,** which stands beside another noun and renames it, consists of a noun and its modifiers. An appositive adds new information about the noun it follows.

> An olympic-size pool, **the prized addition to the physical education building,** gets plenty of use. (The appositive phrase renames *pool*.)

814 An **absolute phrase** consists of a noun and a participle (plus the object of the participle and any modifiers). Because it has a subject and a verbal, an absolute phrase resembles a clause; however, the verbal does not show tense and number the way the main verb of a clause does.

> **Their enthusiasm often waning,** the landlubbing students who cannot swim are required to take lessons. (*Enthusiasm,* the noun, is modified by the present participle, *waning.*)

815 A **verbal phrase** is a phrase based on one of the three types of verbals: *gerund, infinitive,* or *participle.* (See 791-794.)

816 A **gerund phrase** is based on a gerund and functions as a noun.

> **Becoming a marine biologist** is Katie's dream. (subject)
>
> She has acquainted herself with the various methods for **collecting sea-life samples.** (object of preposition)

817 An **infinitive phrase** is based on an infinitive and functions as a noun, an adjective, or an adverb.

> **To dream** is the first step in any endeavor. (subject)
>
> You can keep dreaming, too; but remember **to make a plan to realize your dream.** (*To make a plan* is a direct object; *to realize your dream* is an adjective modifying *plan.*)
>
> Finally, apply all of your talents and skills **to achieve your goals.** (adverb modifying the verb *apply*)

818 A **participial phrase** consists of a past or present participle and its modifiers; the whole phrase functions as an adjective.

> **Doing poorly in calculus by midterm,** Scott wisely made an appointment with his professor and signed up for a tutor. (adjective modifying *Scott*)
>
> Some students, **frustrated by difficult course work,** neglect to pursue the avenues of help open to them. (adjective modifying *students*)

---

on|ine Phrases can add valuable information to sentences. However, beware of expressions that add nothing but "fat" to your writing. For a list of phrases to avoid, see 059.

Using Clauses

819 A **clause** is a group of related words that has both a subject and a predicate. (A phrase never has both.)

■ An **independent clause** presents a complete thought and can stand alone as a sentence.

> **Airplanes are twentieth-century inventions, but people throughout history have dreamed of flying.**

NOTE: The above sentence has two independent clauses joined by the conjunction *but*. Each independent clause can also be written as a sentence.

> **Airplanes are twentieth-century inventions.**
>
> **People throughout history have dreamed of flying.**

■ A **dependent clause** (sometimes called a subordinate clause) cannot stand alone as a sentence. It can, however, add interesting and important detail to a sentence.

> **Because the U.S. Weather Bureau had recommended it** (dependent clause)**, Wilbur and Orville Wright selected a deserted beach in Kitty Hawk, South Carolina, to test their new flying machine.**

TYPES OF CLAUSES

There are three basic types of dependent or subordinate clauses: *adverb, adjective,* and *noun.*

820 An **adverb clause** is used like an adverb to modify or place some condition upon a verb.

> **Although the Wright brothers suffered many failures, they were finally successful.** (modifies *were*)

NOTE: Adverb clauses begin with a subordinating conjunction. (See 801.)

821 An **adjective clause** is used like an adjective to modify a noun or pronoun. The clause answers the questions *what kind?* or *which one?*

> **The men who invented the first airplane were brothers, Orville and Wilbur Wright.** (Answers *which men.*)
>
> **Orville and Wilbur Wright first performed 700 successful glider flights, which were not powered by an engine.** (Answers *what kind.*)

822 A **noun clause** is used in place of a noun. Noun clauses can appear as subjects, as direct or indirect objects, as predicate nominatives, or as objects of prepositions.

> **What made later aviation possible was the determination of people who kept dreaming and believing that people would one day soar like the birds.** (subject)

Using Sentence Variety

823 A **sentence** may be classified according to the type of statement it makes, the way it is constructed, and its arrangement of words.

KINDS OF SENTENCES

Sentences can make five different kinds of statements depending upon the mood of their main verbs: *declarative, interrogative, imperative, exclamatory,* or *conditional.*

824 **Declarative sentences** make statements. They tell us something about a person, a place, a thing, or an idea.

> **In 1955, Rosa Parks refused to follow segregation rules on a bus in Montgomery, Alabama.**

825 **Interrogative sentences** ask questions.

> **Do you think Ms. Parks envisioned a dawn of new freedoms, and only then decided to remain seated?**

826 **Imperative sentences** give commands. They often contain an understood subject *(you).*

> **Read chapters 6-10 for tomorrow and be prepared to discuss question sheets A & B.**

827 **Exclamatory sentences** communicate strong emotion or surprise.

> **I simply can't keep up with these ridiculously long reading assignments!**

828 **Conditional sentences** express wishes ("if . . . then" statements) or conditions contrary to fact.

> **If you practice a few study-reading techniques and learn how to adjust your reading rate according to the level of difficulty, college reading loads will be manageable.**

STRUCTURE OF A SENTENCE

A sentence may be *simple, compound, complex,* or *compound-complex* in structure, depending on the relationship between the independent and dependent clauses in it.

829 A **simple sentence** may have a single subject or a compound subject. It may have a single predicate or a compound predicate. But a simple sentence has only one independent clause, and it has no dependent clauses. A simple sentence may, however, contain one or more phrases.

> **My back aches.** (single subject; single predicate)
>
> **My teeth and my eyes hurt.** (compound subject; single predicate)
>
> **My memory and my logic come and go.** (compound subject; compound predicate)
>
> **I must be getting over-the-hill.** (single subject: *I;* single predicate: *must be getting;* phrase: *over-the-hill*)

830 A **compound sentence** consists of two independent clauses. The clauses must be joined by a coordinating conjunction, by punctuation, or by both.

> **Energy is part of youth, so why am I so exhausted?**
>
> **It couldn't be my fault; I take good care of myself.**

831 A **complex sentence** contains one independent clause (in boldface) and one or more dependent clauses (in lighter type).

> When I can, **I get eight hours of sleep.** (dependent clause; independent clause)
>
> When I get up on time, and if my brother hasn't used up all the milk, **I eat breakfast.** (two dependent clauses; independent clause)

832 A **compound-complex sentence** contains two or more independent clauses (in boldface) and one or more dependent clauses (in lighter type).

> If I'm not in a hurry, **I take long, leisurely walks, and I stop to smell the roses.** (dependent clause; two independent clauses)

ARRANGEMENT OF A SENTENCE

Depending on the arrangement of the words and the placement of emphasis, a sentence may also be classified as *loose, balanced, periodic,* or *cumulative.*

833 A **loose sentence** expresses the main thought near the beginning and adds explanatory material as needed.

> **A prime mover is what makes a machine run,** though there are a great number of things that fit into the category of prime mover.

834 A **balanced sentence** is arranged so that it emphasizes a similarity or contrast between two or more of its parts (words, phrases, or clauses).

> Everything from **dogsleds** to **windmills** to **jackhammers** requires a prime mover. (All three boldfaced nouns have a similar function in the sentence.)

835 A **periodic sentence** is one that postpones the crucial or most surprising idea until the end.

> Though gasoline and diesel engines are the prime movers for many kinds of machines, **the simplest prime mover is human muscle power.**

836 A **cumulative sentence** places the general idea in the main clause and gives it greater precision with modifying words, phrases, or clauses placed before it, after it, or in the middle of it.

> Straining with all their might, **the team of workhorses slowly pulled their heavy load forward** as the owner shouted words of encouragement from the sidelines.

Getting Sentence Parts to Agree

837 Agreement of Subject and Verb

The subject and verb of any clause must agree in both **person** and **number**. There are **three persons: first person** *(I)*, **second person** *(you)*, and **third person** *(he, she, it)*. Checking sentences for agreement in **person** is simply a matter of reading carefully. (See 769 and 780.) Checking sentences for agreement in **number** (singular or plural) requires a much closer look. Read the following guidelines.

AGREEMENT IN NUMBER

838 A verb must agree in number (singular or plural) with its subject.

> The **student was** proud of her semester grades. (Both the subject **student** and the verb **was** are singular; they agree in number.)

NOTE: Do not be confused by phrases that come between the subject and verb. Such phrases may begin with the words *in addition to, as well as, accompanied by,* or *together with.*

> The **pilot, as well as the flight attendants, is** required to display courtesy. (Pilot, not **flight attendants,** is the subject.)

ALSO NOTE: When the subject of the sentence is a title or a word (or phrase) being used as a word (or phrase), the verb should be singular.

> *Lyrical Ballads* **was** published in 1798 by two of England's greatest poets, Wordsworth and Coleridge. (Even though the title of the book, *Lyrical Ballads,* is plural in form, it is still a single title being used as the subject, correctly taking the singular verb **was.**)

> **"Over-the-counter drugs" is** a phrase that makes some doctors shudder. (Even though the phrase is plural in form, it is still a single phrase being used as the subject, correctly taking the singular verb **is.**)

839 **Delayed subjects** occur when the verb comes *before* the subject in a sentence. In these inverted sentences, the true (delayed) subject must be made to agree with the verb.

> There **are** many hardworking **students** in our schools.
> Here **is** the **syllabus** you need.
> (**Students** and **syllabus** are the true subjects of these sentences, not **there** and **here.**)

NOTE: Using an inverted sentence, on occasion, will lend variety to your writing style. Simply remember to make the delayed subjects agree with the verbs.

> Not surprisingly, at the bottom of Megin's to-do list **were "clean dorm room"** and **"do laundry."** (Since the true subject here is plural—two items connected by *and*—the plural verb **were** is correct.)

> However, included among the list's topmost items **was "revise research paper."** (Since the true subject here is singular—one item in a list—the singular verb **was** is correct.)

840   **Compound subjects** connected with *and* usually require a plural verb.

> **Strength and balance are necessary for good posture.**

If a compound subject joined by *and* is thought of as a unit, use a singular verb.

> **Macaroni and cheese** is **always available in the cafeteria.**

841   **Singular subjects** joined by *or* or *nor* take a singular verb.

> **Neither Bev nor Connie is going to the Friday night game.**

NOTE: When one of the subjects joined by *or* or *nor* is singular and one is plural, the verb is made to agree with the subject nearer the verb.

> **Neither Mr. Kemper nor his students are able to find the activity passes.** (The plural subject **students** is nearer the verb; therefore, the plural verb **are** is used to agree with **students.**)

842   The **indefinite pronouns** *each, either, neither, one, no one, another, anybody, everyone, everybody, everything, nobody, somebody,* and *someone* are singular; they require a singular verb.

> **Everybody is invited to the cafeteria for the group interview.**
>
> **Everyone was told to leave the cameras at home, however.**

NOTE: Do not be confused by words or phrases that come between the indefinite pronoun and the verb.

> **Each of the candidates is (not are) required to bring a list of references to the interview.**

843   The **indefinite pronouns** *both, few, many,* and *several* are plural; they require a plural verb.

> **Few are ready to tackle the most difficult issues.**
>
> **Several promise to make entertaining speeches.**

844   The **indefinite pronouns** *all, any, half, most, none,* and *some* may be either singular or plural when they are used as subjects. These pronouns are singular if the number of the noun in the prepositional phrase is singular; they are plural if the noun is plural.

> **Half of the cookies were missing.**
> (**Cookies,** the noun in the prepositional phrase, is plural; therefore, the pronoun **half** is considered plural, and the plural verb **were** is used to agree with it.)
>
> **Half of the lecture was over by the time we arrived.**
> (Because **lecture** is singular, **half** is also singular, requiring the singular verb **was.**)
>
> **Most of the football field was littered with confetti.** (Since **field** is singular, **most** requires the singular verb **was.**)
>
> **Most of the players were exhausted.** (Since **players** is plural, **most** requires the plural verb **were.**)

845   **Collective nouns** (*faculty, pair, crew, assembly, congress, species, crowd, army, team, committee,* etc.) take a singular verb when they refer to a group as a unit; collective nouns take a plural verb when they refer to the individuals within the group.

> **My lab team does a lot of extra-credit experiments.**
> (**Team** refers to a group as a unit; it requires a singular verb, **does.**)
>
> **The team assume separate responsibilities for each study they undertake.** (In this example, **team** refers to the individuals within the group. Substituting the word **individuals** for **team** makes it clear that the plural verb **assume** is needed in this sentence.)

846   Some nouns that are **plural in form but singular in meaning** take a singular verb: *mumps, measles, news, mathematics, economics,* etc.

> **Economics is sometimes called "the dismal science."**

> Exceptions: *scissors, trousers, tidings, robotics*
>
> **The scissors are missing again.**

NOTE: Mathematical phrases and phrases that name a period of time, a unit of measurement, or an amount of money take a singular verb.

> **Three and three is six. Ten miles is a long way to walk.**
> **Sixteen years is a common life span for a house cat.**

847   When a **relative pronoun** *(who, which, that)* is used as the subject of a clause, the number of the verb is determined by the antecedent of the pronoun. (The antecedent is the word to which the pronoun refers.)

> **This is one of the books that are required for English class.**
> (The relative pronoun **that** requires the plural verb *are* because its antecedent **books** is plural. To test this type of sentence for agreement, read the *of* phrase first: **Of the books that are . . .**)

NOTE: Always look carefully for the true antecedent of the relative pronoun, especially in sentences containing phrases that begin with "one of" or "the only one of."

> **Dr. Martin wondered why Mr. Sing was the only one of her patients who was not responding to treatment.** (In this case, the addition of the modifiers "the only" changes the sense of the sentence. The antecedent of **who** is **one,** not **patients.** Only one patient was not responding.)

848   When a sentence contains a form of the *be* verb, and the subject has a *predicate noun* complement, the verb must agree with the subject even if the *predicate noun* is different in number.

> **The cause of his problem was the car's bad brakes. The car's bad brakes were the cause of his problem.** (**Cause** requires a singular verb, even though the subject's complement, **brakes,** is plural. **Brakes** requires a plural verb, even though the subject's complement, **cause,** is singular.)

Agreement of a Pronoun and Its Antecedent

849   A pronoun must agree in number, person, and gender (sex) with its *antecedent*. (The antecedent is the word to which the pronoun refers.)

> **Bill brought his laptop computer to school.**
> (The pronoun *his* refers to the antecedent *Bill.* Both the pronoun and its antecedent are singular, third person, and masculine; therefore, the pronoun is said to agree with its antecedent.)

850   Use a singular pronoun to refer to such antecedents as *each, either, neither, one, anyone, everyone, everybody, somebody, another, nobody,* and *a person.*

> **Each of the dormitories has its (not their) doors locked at night.**

NOTE: When *a person* or *everyone* is used to refer to both sexes or either sex, you will have to choose whether to offer optional pronouns or avoid the "problem" by rewriting the sentence.

> **A person must learn to wait his or her turn.** (optional pronouns)
> **People must learn to wait their turn.** (rewritten in plural form)

851   Two or more antecedents joined by *and* are considered plural; two or more singular antecedents joined by *or* or *nor* are referred to by a singular pronoun.

> **Tom and Bob are finishing their assignments.**
> **Either Connie or Sue left her headset in the library.**

NOTE: If one of the antecedents is masculine and one feminine, the pronouns should likewise be masculine and feminine.

> **Is either Dave or Phyllis bringing his or her laptop computer?**

NOTE: If one of the antecedents joined by *or* or *nor* is singular and one is plural, the pronoun is made to agree with the nearer antecedent.

> **Neither Hugo nor his roomies will be spending their spring break on campus!**

Almanac

Tables and Lists

World Maps

U.S. Constitution

Tables and Lists

Holidays

LEGAL FEDERAL HOLIDAYS

New Year's Day:	January 1
Martin Luther King Day:	Third Monday in January
Presidents' Day:	Third Monday in February
Memorial Day:	Last Monday in May
Independence Day:	July 4
Labor Day:	First Monday in September
Columbus Day:	Second Monday in October
Veterans Day:	November 11
Thanksgiving Day:	Fourth Thursday in November
Christmas Day:	December 25

SPECIAL DAYS

Valentine's Day:	February 14	**Mother's Day:**	Second Sunday in May
St. Patrick's Day:	March 17	**Father's Day:**	Third Sunday in June
May Day:	May 1	**Halloween:**	October 31
Cinco de Mayo:	May 5	**Kwanza:**	December 26

NOTE: Religious holidays such as Easter, Hanukkah, First Day of Ramadan, and Yom Kippur fall on different calendar dates each year.

Weights and Measures

Linear Measure

1 inch	=	2.54 centimeters
1 foot	=	12 inches
		0.3048 meter
1 yard	=	3 feet
		0.9144 meter
1 rod (or pole or perch)	=	5 1/2 yards or 16 1/2 feet
		5.029 meters
1 furlong	=	40 rods
		201.17 meters
1 (statute) mile	=	8 furlongs
		1,760 yards
		5,280 feet
		1,609.3 meters
1 (land) league	=	3 miles
		4.83 kilometers

Square Measure

1 square inch	=	6.452 sq. centimeters
1 square foot	=	144 square inches
		929 square centimeters
1 square yard	=	9 square feet
		0.8361 square meter
1 square rod	=	30 1/4 square yards
		25.29 square meters
1 acre	=	160 square rods
		4,840 square yards
		43,560 square feet
		0.4047 hectare
1 square mile	=	640 acres
		259 hectares
		2.59 square kilometers

Cubic Measure

1 cubic inch	=	16.387 cubic centimeters
1 cubic foot	=	1,728 cubic inches
		0.0283 cubic meter
1 cubic yard	=	27 cubic feet
		0.7646 cubic meter
1 cord foot	=	16 cubic feet
1 cord	=	8 cord feet
		3.625 cubic meters

Chain Measure
(Gunter's or surveyor's chain)

1 link	=	7.92 inches
		20.12 centimeters
1 chain	=	100 links or 66 feet
		20.12 meters
1 furlong	=	10 chains
		201.17 meters
1 mile	=	80 chains
		1,609.3 meters

(Engineer's chain)

1 link	=	1 foot
		0.3048 meter
1 chain	=	100 feet
		30.48 meters
1 mile	=	52.8 chains
		1,609.3 meters

Surveyor's (Square) Measure

1 square pole	=	625 square links
		25.29 square meters
1 square chain	=	16 square poles
		404.7 square meters
1 acre	=	10 square chains
		0.4047 hectare
1 square mile or 1 section	=	640 acres
		259 hectares
		2.59 square kilometers
1 township	=	36 square miles
		9,324 hectares
		93.24 square kilometers

Nautical Measure

1 fathom	=	6 feet
		1.829 meters
1 cable's length (ordinary)	=	100 fathoms

(In the U.S. Navy 120 fathoms or 720 feet = 1 cable's length; in the British Navy 608 feet = 1 cable's length.)

1 nautical mile	=	6,076.10333 feet; *by international agreement in 1954*
		10 cables' length
		1.852 kilometers
		1.1508 statute miles; *length of a minute of longitude at the equator*
1 marine league	=	3.45 statute miles
		3 nautical miles
		5.56 kilometers
1 degree of a great circle of the earth	=	60 nautical miles

Dry Measure

1 pint	=	33.60 cubic inches
		0.5505 liter
1 quart	=	2 pints
		67.20 cubic inches
		1.1012 liters
1 peck	=	8 quarts
		537.61 cubic inches
		8.8096 liters
1 bushel	=	4 pecks
		2,150.42 cubic inches
		35.2383 liters

Liquid Measure

4 fluid ounces (see next table)	=	1 gill
		7.219 cubic inches
		0.1183 liter
1 pint	=	4 gills
		28.875 cubic inches
		0.4732 liter
1 quart	=	2 pints
		57.75 cubic inches
		0.9463 liter
1 gallon	=	4 quarts
		231 cubic inches
		3.7853 liters

Apothecaries' Fluid Measure

1 minim . . . . = 0.0038 cubic inch
0.0616 milliliter

1 fluid dram . . . . = 60 minims
0.2256 cubic inch
3.6966 milliliters

1 fluid ounce. . . . . = 8 fluid drams
1.8047 cubic inches
0.0296 liter

1 pint . . . . = 16 fluid ounces
28.875 cubic inches
0.4732 liter

Circular (or Angular) Measure

1 minute ('). . . . . = 60 seconds (")
1 degree (°) . . . . = 60 minutes
1 quadrant or 1 right angle . = 90 degrees
1 circle . . . . = 4 quadrants
360 degrees

Avoirdupois Weight

(The grain, equal to 0.0648 gram,
is the same in all three tables of weight.)

1 dram or 27.34 grains . . . . = 1.772 grams

1 ounce . . . . = 16 drams
437.5 grains
28.3495 grams

1 pound . . . . = 16 ounces
7,000 grains
453.59 grams

1 hundredweight . . . . = 100 pounds
45.36 kilograms

1 ton . . . . = 2,000 pounds
907.18 kilograms

Troy Weight

(The grain, equal to 0.0648 gram,
is the same in all three tables of weight.)

1 carat . . . . = 3.086 grains
200 milligrams

1 pennyweight . . . . = 24 grains
1.5552 grams

1 ounce . . . . = 20 pennyweights
480 grains
31.1035 grams

1 pound . . . . = 12 ounces
5,760 grains
373.24 grams

Apothecaries' Weight

(The grain, equal to 0.0648 gram,
is the same in all three tables of weight.)

1 scruple. . . . . = 20 grains
1.296 grams

1 dram . . . . = 3 scruples
3.888 grams

1 ounce . . . . = 8 drams
480 grains
31.1035 grams

1 pound . . . . = 12 ounces
5,760 grains
373.24 grams

Miscellaneous

1 palm . . . . = 3 inches
1 hand . . . . = 4 inches
1 span . . . . = 6 inches
1 cubit . . . . = 18 inches
1 Bible cubit . . . . = 21.8 inches
1 military pace . . . . = 2 $\frac{1}{2}$ feet

ADDITIONAL UNITS OF MEASURE

Astronomical Unit (A.U.): 93,000,000 miles, the average distance of the earth from the sun. Used in astronomy.

Board Foot (bd. ft.): 144 cubic inches (12 in. x 12 in. x 1 in.). Used for lumber.

Bolt: 40 yards. Used for measuring cloth.

Btu: British thermal unit. Amount of heat needed to increase the temperature of one pound of water by one degree Fahrenheit.

Gross: 12 dozen or 144.

Knot: Not a distance, but a speed of one nautical mile per hour.

Light, Speed of: 186,281.7 miles per second.

Light-Year: 5,880,000,000,000 miles, the distance light travels in a year at the rate of 186,281.7 miles per second.

Pi (π): 3.14159265+. The ratio of the circumference of a circle to its diameter. For all practical purposes: 3.1416.

Roentgen: Dosage unit of radiation exposure produced by X rays.

Sound, Speed of: 1,088 ft. per second at 32° F at sea level.

The Metric System

In 1975, the United States signed the Metric Conversion Act, declaring a national policy of encouraging voluntary use of the metric system. Today, the metric system exists side by side with the U.S. customary system. The debate on whether the United States should adopt the metric system has been going on for nearly 200 years, leaving the United States the only country in the world not totally committed to adopting the system.

The metric system is considered a simpler form of measurement. It is based on the decimal system (units of 10) and eliminates the need to deal with fractions as we currently use them.

Linear Measure

1 centimeter	=	10 millimeters
		0.3937 inch
1 decimeter	=	10 centimeters
		3.937 inches
1 meter	=	10 decimeters
		39.37 inches
		3.28 feet
1 decameter	=	10 meters
		393.7 inches
1 hectometer	=	10 decameters
		328 feet 1 inch
1 kilometer	=	10 hectometers
		0.621 mile
1 myriameter	=	10 kilometers
		6.21 miles

Volume Measure

1 cubic centimeter	=	1,000 cubic millimeters
		.06102 cubic inch
1 cubic decimeter	=	1,000 cubic centimeters
		61.02 cubic inches
1 cubic meter	=	1,000 cubic decimeters
		35.314 cubic feet

Capacity Measure

1 centiliter	=	10 milliliters
		.338 fluid ounce
1 deciliter	=	10 centiliters
		3.38 fluid ounces
1 liter	=	10 deciliters
		1.0567 liquid quarts
		0.9081 dry quart
1 decaliter	=	10 liters
		2.64 gallons
		0.284 bushel
1 hectoliter	=	10 decaliters
		26.418 gallons
		2.838 bushels
1 kiloliter	=	10 hectoliters
		264.18 gallons
		35.315 cubic feet

Square Measure

1 square centimeter	=	100 square millimeters
		0.15499 square inch
1 square decimeter	=	100 square centimeters
		15.499 square inches
1 square meter	=	100 square decimeters
		1,549.9 square inches
		1.196 square yards
1 square decameter	=	100 square meters
		119.6 square yards
1 square hectometer	=	100 square decameters
		2.471 acres
1 square kilometer	=	100 square hectometers
		0.386 square mile

Land Measure

1 centare	=	1 square meter
		1,549.9 square inches
1 are	=	100 centares
		119.6 square yards
1 hectare	=	100 ares
		2.471 acres
1 square kilometer	=	100 hectares
		0.386 square mile

Weights

1 centigram	=	10 milligrams
		0.1543 grain
1 decigram	=	10 centigrams
		1.5432 grains
1 gram	=	10 decigrams
		15.432 grains
1 decagram	=	10 grams
		0.3527 ounce
1 hectogram	=	10 decagrams
		3.5274 ounces
1 kilogram	=	10 hectograms
		2.2046 pounds
1 myriagram	=	10 kilograms
		22.046 pounds
1 quintal	=	10 myriagrams
		220.46 pounds
1 metric ton	=	10 quintals
		2,204.6 pounds

HANDY CONVERSION FACTORS

TO CHANGE	TO	MULTIPLY BY
acres	hectares	.4047
acres	square feet	43,560
acres	square miles	.001562
Celsius	Fahrenheit	*1.8
		*(then add 32)
centimeters	inches	.3937
centimeters	feet	.03281
cubic meters	cubic feet	35.3145
cubic meters	cubic yards	1.3079
cubic yards	cubic meters	.7646
degrees	radians	.01745
Fahrenheit	Celsius	*.556
		* (after subtracting 32)
feet	meters	.3048
feet	miles (nautical)	.0001645
feet	miles (statute)	.0001894
feet/sec.	miles/hr.	.6818
furlongs	feet	660.0
furlongs	miles	.125
gallons (U.S.)	liters	3.7853
grains	grams	.0648
grams	grains	15.4324
grams	ounces avdp.	.0353
grams	pounds	.002205
hectares	acres	2.4710
horsepower	watts	745.7
hours	days	.04167
inches	millimeters	25.4000
inches	centimeters	2.5400
kilograms	pounds avdp.	2.2046
kilometers	miles	.6214
kilowatts	horsepower	1.341
knots	nautical miles/hr.	1.0
knots	statute miles/hr.	1.151
liters	gallons (U.S.)	.2642
liters	pecks	.1135
liters	pints (dry)	1.8162
liters	pints (liquid)	2.1134
liters	quarts (dry)	.9081

TO CHANGE	TO	MULTIPLY BY
liters	quarts (liquid)	1.0567
meters	feet	3.2808
meters	miles	.0006214
meters	yards	1.0936
metric tons	tons (long)	.9842
metric tons	tons (short)	1.1023
miles	kilometers	1.6093
miles	feet	5,280
miles (nautical)	miles (statute)	1.1516
miles (statute)	miles (nautical)	.8684
miles/hr.	feet/min.	88
millimeters	inches	.0394
ounces avdp.	grams	28.3495
ounces	pounds	.0625
ounces (troy)	ounces (avdp.)	1.09714
pecks	liters	8.8096
pints (dry)	liters	.5506
pints (liquid)	liters	1.4732
pounds ap. or t.	kilograms	.3732
pounds avdp.	kilograms	.4536
pounds	ounces	16
quarts (dry)	liters	1.1012
quarts (liquid)	liters	.9463
rods	meters	5.029
rods	feet	16.5
square feet	square meters	.0929
square kilometers	square miles	.3861
square meters	square feet	10.7639
square meters	square yards	1.1960
square miles	square kilometers	2.5900
square yards	square meters	.8361
tons (long)	metric tons	1.1060
tons (short)	metric tons	.9072
tons (long)	pounds	2,240
tons (short)	pounds	2,000
watts	Btu/hr.	3.4129
watts	horsepower	.001341
yards	meters	.9144
yards	miles	.0005682

ten ways to
measure when you don't have a ruler

1. Many floor tiles are 12-inch squares (30.48-cm squares).
2. Paper money is 6-1/8 inches by 2-5/8 inches (15.56 cms x 6.67 cms).
3. A quarter is approximately 1 inch wide (2.54 cms).
4. A penny is approximately 3/4 of an inch wide (1.9 cms).
5. Typing paper is 8-1/2 inches by 11 inches (21.59 cms x 27.94 cms).

Each of the following items can be used as a measuring device by multiplying its length by the number of times it is used to measure an area in question.

6. A shoelace   7. A tie   8. A belt
9. Your feet—placing one in front of the other to measure an area
10. Your outstretched arms from fingertip to fingertip

6-Year Calendar

1997

JANUARY

S	M	T	W	T	F	S
			1	2	3	4
5	6	7	8	9	10	11
12	13	14	15	16	17	18
19	20	21	22	23	24	25
26	27	28	29	30	31	

FEBRUARY

S	M	T	W	T	F	S
						1
2	3	4	5	6	7	8
9	10	11	12	13	14	15
16	17	18	19	20	21	22
23	24	25	26	27	28	

MARCH

S	M	T	W	T	F	S
						1
2	3	4	5	6	7	8
9	10	11	12	13	14	15
16	17	18	19	20	21	22
23	24	25	26	27	28	29
30	31					

APRIL

S	M	T	W	T	F	S
		1	2	3	4	5
6	7	8	9	10	11	12
13	14	15	16	17	18	19
20	21	22	23	24	25	26
27	28	29	30			

MAY

S	M	T	W	T	F	S
				1	2	3
4	5	6	7	8	9	10
11	12	13	14	15	16	17
18	19	20	21	22	23	24
25	26	27	28	29	30	31

JUNE

S	M	T	W	T	F	S
1	2	3	4	5	6	7
8	9	10	11	12	13	14
15	16	17	18	19	20	21
22	23	24	25	26	27	28
29	30					

JULY

S	M	T	W	T	F	S
		1	2	3	4	5
6	7	8	9	10	11	12
13	14	15	16	17	18	19
20	21	22	23	24	25	26
27	28	29	30	31		

AUGUST

S	M	T	W	T	F	S
					1	2
3	4	5	6	7	8	9
10	11	12	13	14	15	16
17	18	19	20	21	22	23
24	25	26	27	28	29	30
31						

SEPTEMBER

S	M	T	W	T	F	S
	1	2	3	4	5	6
7	8	9	10	11	12	13
14	15	16	17	18	19	20
21	22	23	24	25	26	27
28	29	30				

OCTOBER

S	M	T	W	T	F	S
			1	2	3	4
5	6	7	8	9	10	11
12	13	14	15	16	17	18
19	20	21	22	23	24	25
26	27	28	29	30	31	

NOVEMBER

S	M	T	W	T	F	S
						1
2	3	4	5	6	7	8
9	10	11	12	13	14	15
16	17	18	19	20	21	22
23	24	25	26	27	28	29
30						

DECEMBER

S	M	T	W	T	F	S
	1	2	3	4	5	6
7	8	9	10	11	12	13
14	15	16	17	18	19	20
21	22	23	24	25	26	27
28	29	30	31			

1998

JANUARY

S	M	T	W	T	F	S
				1	2	3
4	5	6	7	8	9	10
11	12	13	14	15	16	17
18	19	20	21	22	23	24
25	26	27	28	29	30	31

FEBRUARY

S	M	T	W	T	F	S
1	2	3	4	5	6	7
8	9	10	11	12	13	14
15	16	17	18	19	20	21
22	23	24	25	26	27	28

MARCH

S	M	T	W	T	F	S
1	2	3	4	5	6	7
8	9	10	11	12	13	14
15	16	17	18	19	20	21
22	23	24	25	26	27	28
29	30	31				

APRIL

S	M	T	W	T	F	S
			1	2	3	4
5	6	7	8	9	10	11
12	13	14	15	16	17	18
19	20	21	22	23	24	25
26	27	28	29	30		

MAY

S	M	T	W	T	F	S
					1	2
3	4	5	6	7	8	9
10	11	12	13	14	15	16
17	18	19	20	21	22	23
24	25	26	27	28	29	30
31						

JUNE

S	M	T	W	T	F	S
	1	2	3	4	5	6
7	8	9	10	11	12	13
14	15	16	17	18	19	20
21	22	23	24	25	26	27
28	29	30				

JULY

S	M	T	W	T	F	S
			1	2	3	4
5	6	7	8	9	10	11
12	13	14	15	16	17	18
19	20	21	22	23	24	25
26	27	28	29	30	31	

AUGUST

S	M	T	W	T	F	S
						1
2	3	4	5	6	7	8
9	10	11	12	13	14	15
16	17	18	19	20	21	22
23	24	25	26	27	28	29
30	31					

SEPTEMBER

S	M	T	W	T	F	S
		1	2	3	4	5
6	7	8	9	10	11	12
13	14	15	16	17	18	19
20	21	22	23	24	25	26
27	28	29	30			

OCTOBER

S	M	T	W	T	F	S
				1	2	3
4	5	6	7	8	9	10
11	12	13	14	15	16	17
18	19	20	21	22	23	24
25	26	27	28	29	30	31

NOVEMBER

S	M	T	W	T	F	S
1	2	3	4	5	6	7
8	9	10	11	12	13	14
15	16	17	18	19	20	21
22	23	24	25	26	27	28
29	30					

DECEMBER

S	M	T	W	T	F	S
		1	2	3	4	5
6	7	8	9	10	11	12
13	14	15	16	17	18	19
20	21	22	23	24	25	26
27	28	29	30	31		

1999

JANUARY

S	M	T	W	T	F	S
					1	2
3	4	5	6	7	8	9
10	11	12	13	14	15	16
17	18	19	20	21	22	23
24	25	26	27	28	29	30
31						

FEBRUARY

S	M	T	W	T	F	S
	1	2	3	4	5	6
7	8	9	10	11	12	13
14	15	16	17	18	19	20
21	22	23	24	25	26	27
28						

MARCH

S	M	T	W	T	F	S
	1	2	3	4	5	6
7	8	9	10	11	12	13
14	15	16	17	18	19	20
21	22	23	24	25	26	27
28	29	30	31			

APRIL

S	M	T	W	T	F	S
				1	2	3
4	5	6	7	8	9	10
11	12	13	14	15	16	17
18	19	20	21	22	23	24
25	26	27	28	29	30	

MAY

S	M	T	W	T	F	S
						1
2	3	4	5	6	7	8
9	10	11	12	13	14	15
16	17	18	19	20	21	22
23	24	25	26	27	28	29
30	31					

JUNE

S	M	T	W	T	F	S
		1	2	3	4	5
6	7	8	9	10	11	12
13	14	15	16	17	18	19
20	21	22	23	24	25	26
27	28	29	30			

JULY

S	M	T	W	T	F	S
				1	2	3
4	5	6	7	8	9	10
11	12	13	14	15	16	17
18	19	20	21	22	23	24
25	26	27	28	29	30	31

AUGUST

S	M	T	W	T	F	S
1	2	3	4	5	6	7
8	9	10	11	12	13	14
15	16	17	18	19	20	21
22	23	24	25	26	27	28
29	30	31				

SEPTEMBER

S	M	T	W	T	F	S
			1	2	3	4
5	6	7	8	9	10	11
12	13	14	15	16	17	18
19	20	21	22	23	24	25
26	27	28	29	30		

OCTOBER

S	M	T	W	T	F	S
					1	2
3	4	5	6	7	8	9
10	11	12	13	14	15	16
17	18	19	20	21	22	23
24	25	26	27	28	29	30
31						

NOVEMBER

S	M	T	W	T	F	S
	1	2	3	4	5	6
7	8	9	10	11	12	13
14	15	16	17	18	19	20
21	22	23	24	25	26	27
28	29	30				

DECEMBER

S	M	T	W	T	F	S
			1	2	3	4
5	6	7	8	9	10	11
12	13	14	15	16	17	18
19	20	21	22	23	24	25
26	27	28	29	30	31	

2000

JANUARY

S	M	T	W	T	F	S
						1
2	3	4	5	6	7	8
9	10	11	12	13	14	15
16	17	18	19	20	21	22
23	24	25	26	27	28	29
30	31					

FEBRUARY

S	M	T	W	T	F	S
		1	2	3	4	5
6	7	8	9	10	11	12
13	14	15	16	17	18	19
20	21	22	23	24	25	26
27	28	29				

MARCH

S	M	T	W	T	F	S
			1	2	3	4
5	6	7	8	9	10	11
12	13	14	15	16	17	18
19	20	21	22	23	24	25
26	27	28	29	30	31	

APRIL

S	M	T	W	T	F	S
						1
2	3	4	5	6	7	8
9	10	11	12	13	14	15
16	17	18	19	20	21	22
23	24	25	26	27	28	29
30						

MAY

S	M	T	W	T	F	S
	1	2	3	4	5	6
7	8	9	10	11	12	13
14	15	16	17	18	19	20
21	22	23	24	25	26	27
28	29	30	31			

JUNE

S	M	T	W	T	F	S
				1	2	3
4	5	6	7	8	9	10
11	12	13	14	15	16	17
18	19	20	21	22	23	24
25	26	27	28	29	30	

JULY

S	M	T	W	T	F	S
						1
2	3	4	5	6	7	8
9	10	11	12	13	14	15
16	17	18	19	20	21	22
23	24	25	26	27	28	29
30	31					

AUGUST

S	M	T	W	T	F	S
		1	2	3	4	5
6	7	8	9	10	11	12
13	14	15	16	17	18	19
20	21	22	23	24	25	26
27	28	29	30	31		

SEPTEMBER

S	M	T	W	T	F	S
					1	2
3	4	5	6	7	8	9
10	11	12	13	14	15	16
17	18	19	20	21	22	23
24	25	26	27	28	29	30

OCTOBER

S	M	T	W	T	F	S
1	2	3	4	5	6	7
8	9	10	11	12	13	14
15	16	17	18	19	20	21
22	23	24	25	26	27	28
29	30	31				

NOVEMBER

S	M	T	W	T	F	S
			1	2	3	4
5	6	7	8	9	10	11
12	13	14	15	16	17	18
19	20	21	22	23	24	25
26	27	28	29	30		

DECEMBER

S	M	T	W	T	F	S
					1	2
3	4	5	6	7	8	9
10	11	12	13	14	15	16
17	18	19	20	21	22	23
24	25	26	27	28	29	30
31						

2001

JANUARY

S	M	T	W	T	F	S
	1	2	3	4	5	6
7	8	9	10	11	12	13
14	15	16	17	18	19	20
21	22	23	24	25	26	27
28	29	30	31			

FEBRUARY

S	M	T	W	T	F	S
				1	2	3
4	5	6	7	8	9	10
11	12	13	14	15	16	17
18	19	20	21	22	23	24
25	26	27	28			

MARCH

S	M	T	W	T	F	S
				1	2	3
4	5	6	7	8	9	10
11	12	13	14	15	16	17
18	19	20	21	22	23	24
25	26	27	28	29	30	31

APRIL

S	M	T	W	T	F	S
1	2	3	4	5	6	7
8	9	10	11	12	13	14
15	16	17	18	19	20	21
22	23	24	25	26	27	28
29	30					

MAY

S	M	T	W	T	F	S
		1	2	3	4	5
6	7	8	9	10	11	12
13	14	15	16	17	18	19
20	21	22	23	24	25	26
27	28	29	30	31		

JUNE

S	M	T	W	T	F	S
					1	2
3	4	5	6	7	8	9
10	11	12	13	14	15	16
17	18	19	20	21	22	23
24	25	26	27	28	29	30

JULY

S	M	T	W	T	F	S
1	2	3	4	5	6	7
8	9	10	11	12	13	14
15	16	17	18	19	20	21
22	23	24	25	26	27	28
29	30	31				

AUGUST

S	M	T	W	T	F	S
			1	2	3	4
5	6	7	8	9	10	11
12	13	14	15	16	17	18
19	20	21	22	23	24	25
26	27	28	29	30	31	

SEPTEMBER

S	M	T	W	T	F	S
						1
2	3	4	5	6	7	8
9	10	11	12	13	14	15
16	17	18	19	20	21	22
23	24	25	26	27	28	29
30						

OCTOBER

S	M	T	W	T	F	S
	1	2	3	4	5	6
7	8	9	10	11	12	13
14	15	16	17	18	19	20
21	22	23	24	25	26	27
28	29	30	31			

NOVEMBER

S	M	T	W	T	F	S
				1	2	3
4	5	6	7	8	9	10
11	12	13	14	15	16	17
18	19	20	21	22	23	24
25	26	27	28	29	30	

DECEMBER

S	M	T	W	T	F	S
						1
2	3	4	5	6	7	8
9	10	11	12	13	14	15
16	17	18	19	20	21	22
23	24	25	26	27	28	29
30	31					

2002

JANUARY

S	M	T	W	T	F	S
		1	2	3	4	5
6	7	8	9	10	11	12
13	14	15	16	17	18	19
20	21	22	23	24	25	26
27	28	29	30	31		

FEBRUARY

S	M	T	W	T	F	S
					1	2
3	4	5	6	7	8	9
10	11	12	13	14	15	16
17	18	19	20	21	22	23
24	25	26	27	28		

MARCH

S	M	T	W	T	F	S
					1	2
3	4	5	6	7	8	9
10	11	12	13	14	15	16
17	18	19	20	21	22	23
24	25	26	27	28	29	30
31						

APRIL

S	M	T	W	T	F	S
	1	2	3	4	5	6
7	8	9	10	11	12	13
14	15	16	17	18	19	20
21	22	23	24	25	26	27
28	29	30				

MAY

S	M	T	W	T	F	S
			1	2	3	4
5	6	7	8	9	10	11
12	13	14	15	16	17	18
19	20	21	22	23	24	25
26	27	28	29	30	31	

JUNE

S	M	T	W	T	F	S
						1
2	3	4	5	6	7	8
9	10	11	12	13	14	15
16	17	18	19	20	21	22
23	24	25	26	27	28	29
30						

JULY

S	M	T	W	T	F	S
	1	2	3	4	5	6
7	8	9	10	11	12	13
14	15	16	17	18	19	20
21	22	23	24	25	26	27
28	29	30	31			

AUGUST

S	M	T	W	T	F	S
				1	2	3
4	5	6	7	8	9	10
11	12	13	14	15	16	17
18	19	20	21	22	23	24
25	26	27	28	29	30	31

SEPTEMBER

S	M	T	W	T	F	S
1	2	3	4	5	6	7
8	9	10	11	12	13	14
15	16	17	18	19	20	21
22	23	24	25	26	27	28
29	30					

OCTOBER

S	M	T	W	T	F	S
		1	2	3	4	5
6	7	8	9	10	11	12
13	14	15	16	17	18	19
20	21	22	23	24	25	26
27	28	29	30	31		

NOVEMBER

S	M	T	W	T	F	S
					1	2
3	4	5	6	7	8	9
10	11	12	13	14	15	16
17	18	19	20	21	22	23
24	25	26	27	28	29	30

DECEMBER

S	M	T	W	T	F	S
1	2	3	4	5	6	7
8	9	10	11	12	13	14
15	16	17	18	19	20	21
22	23	24	25	26	27	28
29	30	31				

Common Parliamentary Procedures

Motion	Purpose	Needs Second	Debatable	Amend-able	Vote	May Interrupt Speaker	Subsidiary Motion Applied
I. ORIGINAL OR PRINCIPAL MOTION							
1. Main Motion (general) Main Motions (specific)	To introduce business	Yes	Yes	Yes	Majority	No	Yes
a. To reconsider	To reconsider previous motion	Yes	When original motion is	No	Majority	Yes	No
b. To rescind	To nullify or wipe out previous action	Yes	Yes	Yes	Majority or two-thirds	No	No
c. To take from the table	To consider tabled motion	Yes	No	No	Majority	No	No
II. SUBSIDIARY MOTIONS							
2. To lay on the table	To defer action	Yes	No	No	Majority	No	No
3. To call for previous question	To close debate and force vote	Yes	No	No	Two-thirds	No	Yes
4. To limit or extend limits of debate	To control time of debate	Yes	No	Yes	Two-thirds	No	Yes
5. To postpone to a certain time	To defer action	Yes	Yes	Yes	Majority	No	Yes
6. To refer to a committee	To provide for special study	Yes	Yes	Yes	Majority	No	Yes
7. To amend	To modify a motion	Yes	When original motion is	Yes (once only)	Majority	No	Yes
8. To postpone indefinitely	To suppress action	Yes	Yes	No	Majority	No	Yes
III. INCIDENTAL MOTIONS							
9. To raise a point of order	To correct error in procedure	No	No	No	Decision of chair	Yes	No
10. To appeal for decision of chair	To change decision on procedure	Yes	If motion does not relate to indecorum	No	Majority or tie	Yes	No
11. To suspend rules	To alter existing rules and order of business	Yes	No	No	Two-thirds	No	No
12. To object to consideration	To suppress action	No	No	No	Two-thirds	Yes	No
13. To call for division of house	To secure a countable vote	No	No	No	Majority if chair desires	Yes	Yes
14. To close nominations	To stop nomination of officers	Yes	No	Yes	Two-thirds	No	Yes
15. To reopen nominations	To permit additional nominations	Yes	No	Yes	Majority	No	Yes
16. To withdraw a motion	To remove a motion	No	No	No	Majority	No	No
17. To divide motion	To modify motion	No	No	Yes	Majority	No	Yes
IV. PRIVILEGED MOTIONS							
18. To fix time of next meeting	To set time of next meeting	Yes	No, if made when another question is before the assembly	Yes	Majority	No	Yes
19. To adjourn	To dismiss meeting	Yes	No	Yes	Majority	No	No
20. To take a recess	To dismiss meeting for specific time	Yes	No, if made when another question is before the assembly	Yes	Majority	No	Yes
21. To raise question of privilege	To make a request concerning rights of assembly	No	No	No	Decision of chair	Yes	No
22. To call for orders of the day	To keep assembly to order of business	No	No	No	None unless objection	Yes	No
23. To make a special order	To ensure consideration at specified time	Yes	Yes	Yes	Two-thirds	No	Yes

Periodic Table of the Elements

Key (example):

Atomic Number	2
Symbol	He
	Helium
Atomic Weight (or Mass Number of most stable isotope if in parentheses)	4.00260

Legend:
- Alkali metals
- Alkaline earth metals
- Transition metals
- Lanthanide series
- Actinide series
- Other metals
- Nonmetals
- Noble gases

1a	2a	3b	4b	5b	6b	7b		8		1b	2b	3a	4a	5a	6a	7a	0
1 **H** Hydrogen 1.00797																	2 **He** Helium 4.00260
3 **Li** Lithium 6.941	4 **Be** Beryllium 9.0128											5 **B** Boron 10.811	6 **C** Carbon 12.01115	7 **N** Nitrogen 14.0067	8 **O** Oxygen 15.9994	9 **F** Fluorine 18.9984	10 **Ne** Neon 20.179
11 **Na** Sodium 22.9898	12 **Mg** Magnesium 24.305											13 **Al** Aluminum 26.9815	14 **Si** Silicon 28.0855	15 **P** Phosphorus 30.9738	16 **S** Sulfur 32.064	17 **Cl** Chlorine 35.453	18 **Ar** Argon 39.948
19 **K** Potassium 39.0983	20 **Ca** Calcium 40.08	21 **Sc** Scandium 44.9559	22 **Ti** Titanium 47.88	23 **V** Vanadium 50.94	24 **Cr** Chromium 51.996	25 **Mn** Manganese 54.9380	26 **Fe** Iron 55.847	27 **Co** Cobalt 58.9332	28 **Ni** Nickel 58.69	29 **Cu** Copper 63.546	30 **Zn** Zinc 65.39	31 **Ga** Gallium 69.72	32 **Ge** Germanium 72.59	33 **As** Arsenic 74.9216	34 **Se** Selenium 78.96	35 **Br** Bromine 79.904	36 **Kr** Krypton 83.80
37 **Rb** Rubidium 85.4678	38 **Sr** Strontium 87.62	39 **Y** Yttrium 88.905	40 **Zr** Zirconium 91.224	41 **Nb** Niobium 92.906	42 **Mo** Molybdenum 95.94	43 **Tc** Technetium (98)	44 **Ru** Ruthenium 101.07	45 **Rh** Rhodium 102.906	46 **Pd** Palladium 106.42	47 **Ag** Silver 107.868	48 **Cd** Cadmium 112.41	49 **In** Indium 114.82	50 **Sn** Tin 118.71	51 **Sb** Antimony 121.75	52 **Te** Tellurium 127.60	53 **I** Iodine 126.905	54 **Xe** Xenon 131.29
55 **Cs** Cesium 132.905	56 **Ba** Barium 137.33	57-71* Lanthanides	72 **Hf** Hafnium 178.49	73 **Ta** Tantalum 180.948	74 **W** Tungsten 183.85	75 **Re** Rhenium 186.207	76 **Os** Osmium 190.2	77 **Ir** Iridium 192.22	78 **Pt** Platinum 195.08	79 **Au** Gold 196.967	80 **Hg** Mercury 200.59	81 **Tl** Thallium 204.383	82 **Pb** Lead 207.19	83 **Bi** Bismuth 208.980	84 **Po** Polonium (209)	85 **At** Astatine (210)	86 **Rn** Radon (222)
87 **Fr** Francium (223)	88 **Ra** Radium 226.025	89-103** Actinides (227)	104 **Db** Dubnium (261)	105 **Jl** Joliotium (262)	106 **Rf** Rutherfordium (263)	107 **Bh** Bohrium (262)	108 **Hn** Hahnium (265)	109 **Mt** Meitnerium (266)	110 (269)	111 (272)							

*Lanthanides	57 **La** Lanthanum 138.906	58 **Ce** Cerium 140.12	59 **Pr** Praseodymium 140.908	60 **Nd** Neodymium 144.24	61 **Pm** Promethium (145)	62 **Sm** Samarium 150.36	63 **Eu** Europium 151.96	64 **Gd** Gadolinium 157.25	65 **Tb** Terbium 158.925	66 **Dy** Dysprosium 162.50	67 **Ho** Holmium 164.930	68 **Er** Erbium 167.26	69 **Tm** Thulium 168.934	70 **Yb** Ytterbium 173.04	71 **Lu** Lutetium 174.967
**Actinides	89 **Ac** Actinium 227.028	90 **Th** Thorium 232.038	91 **Pa** Protactinium 231.036	92 **U** Uranium 238.029	93 **Np** Neptunium 237.048	94 **Pu** Plutonium (244)	95 **Am** Americium (243)	96 **Cm** Curium (247)	97 **Bk** Berkelium (247)	98 **Cf** Californium (251)	99 **Es** Einsteinium (252)	100 **Fm** Fermium (257)	101 **Md** Mendelevium (258)	102 **No** Nobelium (259)	103 **Lr** Lawrencium (260)

(Names of elements 104-109 subject to approval by International Union of Pure & Applied Chemistry.)

Index to World Maps

Country	Latitude		Longitude		Country	Latitude		Longitude	
Afghanistan	33°	N	65°	E	China	35°	N	105°	E
Albania	41°	N	20°	E	Colombia	4°	N	72°	W
Algeria	28°	N	3°	E	Comoros	12°	S	44°	E
Andorra	42°	N	1°	E	Congo	1°	S	15°	E
Angola	12°	S	18°	E	Costa Rica	10°	N	84°	W
Antigua and Barbuda	17°	N	61°	W	Croatia	45°	N	16°	E
Argentina	34°	S	64°	W	Cuba	21°	N	80°	W
Armenia	41°	N	45°	E	Cyprus	35°	N	33°	E
Australia	25°	S	135°	E	Czech Republic	50°	N	15°	E
Austria	47°	N	13°	E	Denmark	56°	N	10°	E
Azerbaijan	41°	N	47°	E	Djibouti	11°	N	43°	E
Bahamas	24°	N	76°	W	Dominica	15°	N	61°	W
Bahrain	26°	N	50°	E	Dominican Republic	19°	N	70°	W
Bangladesh	24°	N	90°	E	Ecuador	2°	S	77°	W
Barbados	13°	N	59°	W	Egypt	27°	N	30°	E
Belarus	54°	N	25°	E	El Salvador	14°	N	89°	W
Belgium	50°	N	4°	E	Equatorial Guinea	2°	N	9°	E
Belize	17°	N	88°	W	Eritrea	17°	N	38°	E
Benin	9°	N	2°	E	Estonia	59°	N	26°	E
Bhutan	27°	N	90°	E	Ethiopia	8°	N	38°	E
Bolivia	17°	S	65°	W	Fiji	19°	S	174°	E
Bosnia-Herzegovina	44°	N	18°	E	Finland	64°	N	26°	E
Botswana	22°	S	24°	E	France	46°	N	2°	E
Brazil	10°	S	55°	W	Gabon	1°	S	11°	E
Brunei	4°	N	114°	E	The Gambia	13°	N	16°	W
Bulgaria	43°	N	25°	E	Georgia	43°	N	45°	E
Burkina Faso	13°	N	2°	W	Germany	51°	N	10°	E
Burundi	3°	S	30°	E	Ghana	8°	N	2°	W
Cambodia	13°	N	105°	E	Greece	39°	N	22°	E
Cameroon	6°	N	12°	E	Greenland	70°	N	40°	W
Canada	60°	N	95°	W	Grenada	12°	N	61°	W
Cape Verde	16°	N	24°	W	Guatemala	15°	N	90°	W
Central African Republic	7°	N	21°	E	Guinea	11°	N	10°	W
Chad	15°	N	19°	E	Guinea-Bissau	12°	N	15°	W
Chile	30°	S	71°	W	Guyana	5°	N	59°	W

Country	Latitude	Longitude
Haiti	19° N	72° W
Honduras	15° N	86° W
Hungary	47° N	20° E
Iceland	65° N	18° W
India	20° N	77° E
Indonesia	5° S	120° E
Iran	32° N	53° E
Iraq	33° N	44° E
Ireland	53° N	8° W
Israel	31° N	35° E
Italy	42° N	12° E
Ivory Coast	8° N	5° W
Jamaica	18° N	77° W
Japan	36° N	138° E
Jordan	31° N	36° E
Kazakhstan	45° N	70° E
Kenya	1° N	38° E
Kiribati	0° N	175° E
North Korea	40° N	127° E
South Korea	36° N	128° E
Kuwait	29° N	47° E
Kyrgyzstan	42° N	75° E
Laos	18° N	105° E
Latvia	57° N	25° E
Lebanon	34° N	36° E
Lesotho	29° S	28° E
Liberia	6° N	10° W
Libya	27° N	17° E
Liechtenstein	47° N	9° E
Lithuania	56° N	24° E
Luxembourg	49° N	6° E
Macedonia	43° N	22° E
Madagascar	19° S	46° E
Malawi	13° S	34° E
Malaysia	2° N	112° E
Maldives	2° N	70° E
Mali	17° N	4° W
Malta	36° N	14° E
Mauritania	20° N	12° W
Mauritius	20° S	57° E
Mexico	23° N	102° W
Moldova	47° N	28° E
Monaco	43° N	7° E
Mongolia	46° N	105° E
Montenegro	43° N	19° E
Morocco	32° N	5° W
Mozambique	18° S	35° E
Myanmar	25° N	95° E
Namibia	22° S	17° E
Nauru	1° S	166° E
Nepal	28° N	84° E
Netherlands	52° N	5° E
New Zealand	41° S	174° E
Nicaragua	13° N	85° W
Niger	16° N	8° E
Nigeria	10° N	8° E
Northern Ireland	55° N	7° W
Norway	62° N	10° E
Oman	22° N	58° E
Pakistan	30° N	70° E
Panama	9° N	80° W
Papua New Guinea	6° S	147° E
Paraguay	23° S	58° W

Country	Latitude	Longitude
Peru	10° S	76° W
Philippines	13° N	122° E
Poland	52° N	19° E
Portugal	39° N	8° W
Qatar	25° N	51° E
Romania	46° N	25° E
Russia	60° N	80° E
Rwanda	2° S	30° E
St. Kitts & Nevis	17° N	62° W
Saint Lucia	14° N	61° W
Saint Vincent and the Grenadines	13° N	61° W
San Marino	44° N	12° E
Sao Tome and Principe	1° N	7° E
Saudi Arabia	25° N	45° E
Scotland	57° N	5° W
Senegal	14° N	14° W
Serbia	45° N	21° E
Seychelles	5° S	55° E
Sierra Leone	8° N	11° W
Singapore	1° N	103° E
Slovakia	49° N	19° E
Slovenia	46° N	15° E
Solomon Islands	8° S	159° E
Somalia	10° N	49° E
South Africa	30° S	26° E
Spain	40° N	4° W
Sri Lanka	7° N	81° E
Sudan	15° N	30° E
Suriname	4° N	56° W
Swaziland	26° S	31° E
Sweden	62° N	15° E
Switzerland	47° N	8° E
Syria	35° N	38° E
Taiwan	23° N	121° E
Tajikistan	39° N	71° E
Tanzania	6° S	35° E
Thailand	15° N	100° E
Togo	8° N	1° E
Tonga	20° S	173° W
Trinidad/Tobago	11° N	61° W
Tunisia	34° N	9° E
Turkey	39° N	35° E
Turkmenistan	40° N	55° E
Tuvalu	8° S	179° E
Uganda	1° N	32° E
Ukraine	50° N	30° E
United Arab Emirates	24° N	54° E
United Kingdom	54° N	2° W
United States	38° N	97° W
Uruguay	33° S	56° W
Uzbekistan	40° N	68° E
Vanuatu	17° S	170° E
Venezuela	8° N	66° W
Vietnam	17° N	106° E
Wales	53° N	3° W
Western Samoa	10° S	173° W
Yemen	15° N	44° E
Yugoslavia	44° N	19° E
Zaire	4° S	25° E
Zambia	15° S	30° E
Zimbabwe	20° S	30° E

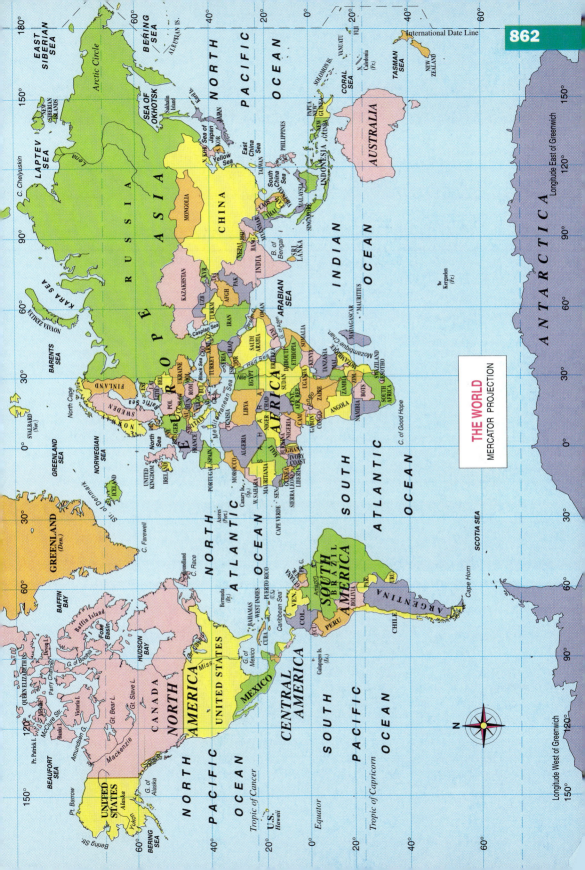

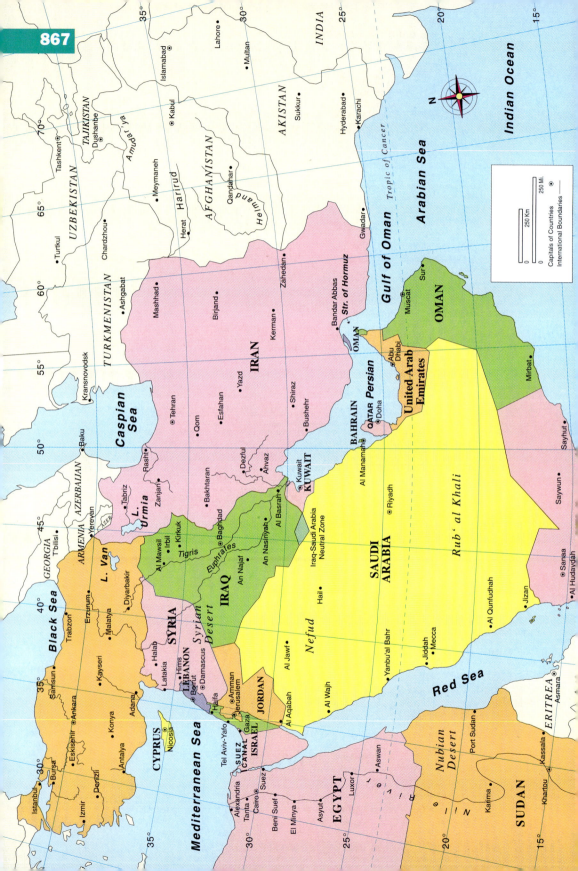

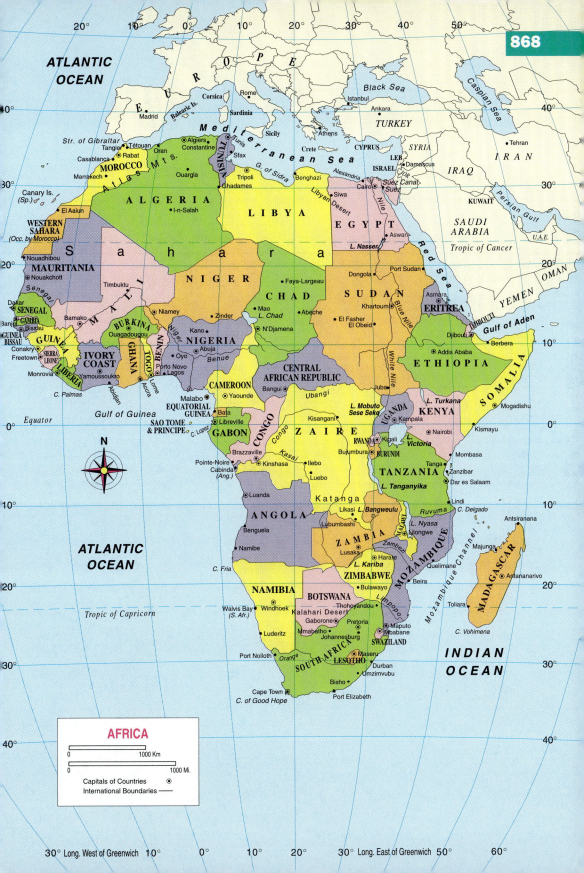

U.S. Constitution

NOTE: *The original text of the Constitution has been edited to conform to contemporary American usage. The bracketed words have been added to help you locate information more quickly; they are not part of the Constitution.*

[Preamble]

We the people of the United States, in order to form a more perfect Union, establish justice, insure domestic tranquility, provide for the common defense, promote the general welfare, and secure the blessings of liberty to ourselves and our posterity, do ordain and establish this Constitution for the United States of America.

ARTICLE I
Section 1

[Legislative powers vested in Congress] All legislative powers herein granted shall be vested in a Congress of the United States, which shall consist of a Senate and House of Representatives.

Section 2

1. **[Makeup of the House of Representatives]** The House of Representatives shall be composed of members chosen every second year by the people of the several States, and the electors in each State shall have the qualifications requisite for electors of the most numerous branch of the State Legislature.

2. **[Qualifications of Representatives]** No person shall be a Representative who shall not have attained to the age of twenty-five years, and been seven years a citizen of the United States, and who shall not, when elected, be an inhabitant of that State in which he shall be chosen.

3. **[Apportionment of Representatives and direct taxes—census]** (Representatives and direct taxes shall be apportioned among the several States which may be included within this Union, according to their respective numbers, which shall be determined by adding to the whole number of free persons, including those bound to service for a term of years, and excluding Indians not taxed, three-fifths of all other persons.—*Amended by the 14th Amendment, section 2.)* The actual enumeration shall be made within three years after the first meeting of the Congress of the United States, and within every subsequent term of ten years, in such manner as they shall by law direct. The number of Representatives shall not exceed one for every thirty thousand, but each State shall have at least one Representative; and until such enumeration shall be made, the State of New Hampshire shall be entitled to choose three; Massachusetts, eight; Rhode Island and Providence Plantations, one; Connecticut, five; New York, six; New Jersey, four; Pennsylvania, eight; Delaware, one; Maryland, six; Virginia, ten; North Carolina, five; South Carolina, five; and Georgia, three.

4. **[Filling of vacancies in representation]** When vacancies happen in the representation from any State, the Executive Authority thereof shall issue writs of election to fill such vacancies.

5. **[Selection of officers; power of impeachment]** The House of Representatives shall choose their Speaker and other officers; and shall have the sole power of impeachment.

Section 3

1. **[The Senate]** (The Senate of the United States shall be composed of two Senators from each State, chosen by the Legislature thereof, for six years; and each Senator shall have one vote.—*Amended by the 17th Amendment, section 1.*)

2. **[Classification of Senators; filling of vacancies]** Immediately after they shall be assembled in consequence of the first election, they shall be divided as equally as may be into three classes. The seats of the Senators of the first class shall be vacated at the expiration of the second year, of the second class at the expiration of the fourth year, and of the third class at the expiration of the sixth year, so that one-third may be chosen every second year; and if vacancies happen by resignation, or otherwise (during the recess of the Legislature of any State), the Executive thereof may make temporary appointments (until the next meeting of the Legislature, which shall then fill such vacancies.—*Amended by the 17th Amendment.*)

3. **[Qualification of Senators]** No person shall be a Senator who shall not have attained to the age of thirty years, and been nine years a citizen of the United States, and who shall not, when elected, be an inhabitant of that State for which he shall be chosen.

4. **[Vice President to be President of Senate]** The Vice President of the United States shall be President of the Senate, but shall have no vote, unless they be equally divided.

5. **[Selection of Senate officers; President pro tempore]** The Senate shall choose their other officers, and also a President pro tempore, in the absence of the Vice President, or when he shall exercise the office of President of the United States.

6. **[Senate to try impeachments]** The Senate shall have the sole power to try all impeachments. When sitting for that purpose, they shall be on oath or affirmation. When the President of the United States is tried, the Chief Justice shall preside: and no person shall be convicted without the concurrence of two-thirds of the members present.

7. **[Judgment in cases of impeachment]** Judgment in cases of impeachment shall not extend further than to removal from office, and disqualification to hold and enjoy any office of honor, trust, or profit under the United States; but the party convicted shall nevertheless be liable and subject to indictment, trial, judgment, and punishment, according to Law.

Section 4

1. **[Control of congressional elections]** The times, places, and manner of holding elections for Senators and Representatives shall be prescribed in each State by the Legislature thereof; but the Congress may at any time by law make or alter such regulations, except as to the places of choosing Senators.

2. **[Time for assembling of Congress]** The Congress shall assemble at least once in every year, (and such meeting shall be on the first Monday in December, unless they shall by law appoint a different day.—*Amended by the 20th Amendment, section 2.*)

Section 5

1. **[Each House to be the judge of the election and qualifications of its members; regulations as to quorum]** Each House shall be the judge of the elections, returns, and qualifications of its own members, and a majority of each shall constitute a quorum to do business; but a smaller number may adjourn from day to day, and may be authorized to compel the attendance of absent members, in such manner, and under such penalties as each House may provide.

2. **[Each House to determine its own rules]** Each House may determine the rules of its proceedings, punish its members for disorderly behavior, and, with the concurrence of two-thirds, expel a member.

3. **[Journals and yeas and nays]** Each House shall keep a journal of its proceedings, and from time to time publish the same, excepting such parts as may in their judgment require secrecy; and the yeas and nays of the members of either House on any question shall, at the desire of one-fifth of those present, be entered on the journal.

4. **[Adjournment]** Neither House, during the session of Congress, shall, without the consent of the other, adjourn for more than three days, nor to any other place than that in which the two Houses shall be sitting.

Section 6

1. **[Compensation and privileges of members of Congress]** The Senators and Representatives shall receive a compensation for their services, to be ascertained by law, and paid out of the Treasury of the United States. They shall in all cases, except treason, felony, and breach of the peace, be privileged from arrest during their attendance at the session of their respective Houses, and in going to and returning from the same; and for any speech or debate in either House, they shall not be questioned in any other place.

2. **[Incompatible offices; exclusions]** No Senator or Representative shall, during the time for which he was elected, be appointed to any civil office under the authority of the United States, which shall have been created, or the emoluments whereof shall have been increased during such time; and no person holding any office under the United States shall be a member of either House during his continuance in office.

Section 7

1. **[Revenue bills to originate in House]** All bills for raising revenue shall originate in the House of Representatives; but the Senate may propose or concur with amendments as on other bills.

2. **[Manner of passing bills; veto power of President]** Every bill which shall have passed the House of Representatives and the Senate, shall, before it becomes a law, be presented to the President of the United States; if he approve, he shall sign it, but if not he shall return it, with his objections to that House in which it shall have originated, who shall enter the objections at large on their journal, and proceed to reconsider it. If after such reconsideration two-thirds of that House shall agree to pass the bill, it shall be sent, together with the objections, to the other House, by which it shall likewise be reconsidered, and if approved by two-thirds of that House, it shall become a law. But in all such cases the votes of both Houses shall be determined by yeas and nays, and the names of the persons voting for and against the bill shall be entered on the journal of each House, respectively. If any bill shall not be returned by the President within ten days (Sundays excepted) after it shall have been presented to him, the same shall be a law, in like manner as if he had signed it, unless the Congress by their adjournment prevent its return, in which case it shall not be a law.

3. **[Concurrent orders or resolutions to be passed by President]** Every order, resolution, or vote to which the concurrence of the Senate and House of Representatives may be necessary (except on a question of adjournment) shall be presented to the President of the United States; and before the same shall take effect, shall be approved by him, or being disapproved by him, shall be repassed by two-thirds of the Senate and House of Representatives, according to the rules and limitations prescribed in the case of a bill.

Section 8

[General powers of Congress] The Congress shall have the power:

1. **[Taxes, duties, imposts, and excises]** To lay and collect taxes, duties, imposts, and excises, to pay the debts and provide for the common defense and general welfare of the United States; but all duties, imposts, and excises shall be uniform throughout the United States; *(See the 16th Amendment.)*

2. **[Borrowing of money]** To borrow money on the credit of the United States;

3. **[Regulation of commerce]** To regulate commerce with foreign nations, and among the several States, and with the Indian tribes;

4. **[Naturalization and bankruptcy]** To establish a uniform rule of naturalization, and uniform laws on the subject of bankruptcies throughout the United States;

5. **[Money, weights, and measures]** To coin money, regulate the value thereof, and of foreign coin, and fix the standard of weights and measures;

6. **[Counterfeiting]** To provide for the punishment of counterfeiting the securities and current coin of the United States;

7. **[Post offices]** To establish post offices and post roads;

8. **[Patents and copyrights]** To promote the progress of science and useful arts, by securing for limited times to authors and inventors the exclusive right to their respective writings and discoveries;

9. **[Inferior courts]** To constitute tribunals inferior to the Supreme Court;

10. **[Piracies and felonies]** To define and punish piracies and felonies committed on the high seas, and offenses against the law of nations.

11. **[War; marque and reprisal]** To declare war, grant letters of marque and reprisal, and make rules concerning captures on land and water;

12. **[Armies]** To raise and support armies, but no appropriation of money to that use shall be for a longer term than two years;

13. **[Navy]** To provide and maintain a navy;

14. **[Land and naval forces]** To make rules for the government and regulation of the land and naval forces;

15. **[Calling out militia]** To provide for calling forth the militia to execute the laws of the Union, suppress insurrections, and repel invasions.

16. **[Organizing, arming, and disciplining militia]** To provide for organizing, arming, and disciplining the militia, and for governing such part of them as may be employed in the service of the United States, reserving to the States, respectively, the appointment of the officers, and the authority of training the militia according to the discipline prescribed by Congress;

17. **[Exclusive legislation over District of Columbia]** To exercise exclusive legislation in all cases whatsoever, over such district (not exceeding ten miles square) as may, by cession of particular States, and the acceptance of Congress, become the seat of the Government of the United States, and to exercise like authority over all places purchased by the consent of the Legislature of the State in which the same shall be, for the erection of forts, magazines, arsenals, dockyards, and other needful buildings;—And

18. **[To enact laws necessary to enforce Constitution]** To make all laws which shall be necessary and proper for carrying into execution the foregoing powers, and all other powers vested by this Constitution in the Government of the United States, or in any department or officer thereof.

Section 9

1. **[Migration or importation of certain persons not to be prohibited before 1808]** The migration or importation of such persons as any of the States now existing shall think proper to admit, shall not be prohibited by the Congress prior to the year one thousand eight hundred and eight, but a tax or duty may be imposed on such importation, not exceeding ten dollars for each person.

2. **[Writ of habeas corpus not to be suspended; exception]** The privilege of the writ of habeas corpus shall not be suspended, unless when in cases of rebellion or invasion the public safety may require it.

3. **[Bills of attainder and ex post facto laws prohibited]** No bill of attainder or ex post facto law shall be passed.

4. **[Capitation and other direct taxes]** No capitation, or other direct, tax shall be laid, unless in proportion to the census or enumeration herein before directed to be taken. *(See the 16th Amendment.)*

5. **[Exports not to be taxed]** No tax or duty shall be laid on articles exported from any State.

6. **[No preference to be given to ports of any State; interstate shipping]** No preference shall be given by any regulation of commerce or revenue to the ports of one State over those of another: nor shall vessels bound to, or from, one State, be obliged to enter, clear, or pay duties in another.

7. **[Money, how drawn from treasury; financial statements to be published]** No money shall be drawn from the Treasury, but in consequence of appropriations made by law; and a regular statement and account of the receipts and expenditures of all public money shall be published from time to time.

8. **[Titles of nobility not to be granted; acceptance by government officers of favors from foreign powers]** No title of nobility shall be granted by the United States; and no person holding any office of profit or trust under them, shall, without the consent of the Congress, accept of any present, emolument, office, or title, of any kind whatever, from any king, prince, or foreign state.

Section 10

1. **[Limitations of the powers of the several States]** No state shall enter into any treaty, alliance, or confederation; grant letters of marque and reprisal; coin money; emit bills of credit; make anything but gold and silver coin a tender in payment of debts; pass any bill of attainder, ex post facto law, or law impairing the obligation of contracts, or grant any title of nobility.

2. **[State imposts and duties]** No State shall, without the consent of the Congress, lay any imposts or duties on imports or exports, except what may be absolutely necessary for executing its inspection laws: and the net produce of all duties and imposts, laid by any State on imports or exports, shall be for the use of the Treasury of the United States; and all such laws shall be subject to the revision and control of the Congress.

3. **[Further restrictions on powers of States]** No State shall, without the consent of Congress, lay any duty of tonnage, keep troops, or ships of war in time of peace, enter into any agreement or compact with another state, or with a foreign power, or engage in war, unless actually invaded, or in such imminent danger as will not admit of delay.

ARTICLE II
Section 1

1. **[The President; the executive power]** The executive power shall be vested in a President of the United States of America. He shall hold his office during the term of four years, and together with the Vice President, chosen for the same term, be elected, as follows:

2. **[Appointment and qualifications of presidential electors]** Each State shall appoint, in such manner as the Legislature thereof may direct, a number of electors, equal to the whole number of Senators and Representatives to which the State may be entitled in the Congress: but no Senator or Representative, or person holding an office of trust or profit under the United States, shall be appointed an elector.

3. **[Original method of electing the President and Vice President]** (The electors shall meet in their respective States, and vote by ballot for two persons, of whom one at least shall not be an inhabitant of the same State with themselves. And they shall make a list of all the persons voted for, and of the number of votes for each; which list they shall sign and certify, and transmit sealed to the seat of the Government of the United States, directed to the President of the Senate. The President of the Senate shall, in the presence of the Senate and House of Representatives, open all the certificates, and the votes shall then be counted. The person having the greatest number of votes shall be the President, if such number be a majority of the whole number of electors appointed; and if there be more than one who have such majority, and have an equal number of votes, then the House of Representatives shall immediately choose by ballot one of them for President; and if no person have a majority, then from the five highest on the list the said House shall in like manner choose the President. But in choosing the President, the votes shall be taken by States, the representation from each State having one vote; a quorum for this purpose shall consist of a member or

members from two-thirds of the States, and a majority of all the states shall be necessary to a choice. In every case, after the choice of the President, the person having the greatest number of votes of the electors shall be the Vice President. But if there should remain two or more who have equal votes, the Senate should choose from them by ballot the Vice President.—*Replaced by the 12th Amendment.*)

4. **[Congress may determine time of choosing electors and day for casting their votes]** The Congress may determine the time of choosing the electors, and the day on which they shall give their votes; which day shall be the same throughout the United States.

5. **[Qualifications for the office of President]** No person except a natural born citizen, or a citizen of the United States, at the time of the adoption of this Constitution, shall be eligible to the office of President; neither shall any person be eligible to that office who shall not have attained to the age of thirty-five years, and been fourteen years a resident within the United States. *(For qualifications of the Vice President, see the 12th Amendment.)*

6. **[Filling vacancy in the office of President]** (In case of the removal of the President from office, or of his death, resignation, or inability to discharge the powers and duties of the said office, the same shall devolve on the Vice President, and the Congress may by law provide for the case of removal, death, resignation or inability, both of the President and Vice President, declaring what officer shall then act as President, and such officer shall act accordingly, until the disability be removed, or a President shall be elected.—*Amended by the 20th and 25th Amendments.*)

7. **[Compensation of the President]** The President shall, at stated times, receive for his services, a compensation, which shall neither be increased nor diminished during the period for which he shall have been elected, and he shall not receive within that period any other emolument from the United States, or any of them.

8. **[Oath to be taken by the President]** Before he enter on the execution of his office, he shall take the following oath or affirmation:—"I do solemnly swear (or affirm) that I will faithfully execute the office of President of the United States, and will to the best of my ability, preserve, protect, and defend the Constitution of the United States."

Section 2

1. **[President to be Commander-in-Chief of army and navy and head of executive departments; may grant reprieves and pardons]** The President shall be Commander-in-Chief of the Army and Navy of the United States, and of the militia of the several States, when called into the actual service of the United States;

he may require the opinion, in writing, of the principal officer in each of the executive departments, upon any subject relating to the duties of their respective offices, and he shall have power to grant reprieves and pardons for offenses against the United States, except in cases of impeachment.

2. **[President may, with concurrence of Senate, make treaties, appoint ambassadors, etc.; appointment of inferior officers, authority of Congress over]** He shall have power, by and with the advice and consent of the Senate, to make treaties, provided two-thirds of the Senators present concur; and he shall nominate, and by and with the advice and consent of the Senate, shall appoint ambassadors, other public ministers and consuls, judges of the Supreme Court, and all other officers of the United States, whose appointments are not herein otherwise provided for, and which shall be established by law: but the Congress may by law vest the appointment of such inferior officers, as they think proper, in the President alone, in the courts of law, or in the heads of departments.

3. **[President may fill vacancies in office during recess of Senate]** The President shall have power to fill up all vacancies that may happen during the recess of the Senate, by granting commissions which shall expire at the end of their session.

Section 3

[President to give advice to Congress; may convene or adjourn it on certain occasions; to receive ambassadors, etc.; have laws executed and commission all officers] He shall from time to time give to the Congress information of the state of the Union, and recommend to their consideration such measures as he shall judge necessary and expedient; he may, on extraordinary occasions, convene both Houses, or either of them, and in case of disagreement between them, with respect to the time of adjournment, he may adjourn them to such time as he shall think proper; he shall receive ambassadors and other public ministers: he shall take care that the laws be faithfully executed, and shall commission all the officers of the United States.

Section 4

[All civil officers removable by impeachment] The President, Vice President, and all civil officers of the United States shall be removed from office on impeachment for, and conviction of, treason, bribery, or other high crimes and misdemeanors.

ARTICLE III
Section 1

[Judicial powers; how vested; term of office and compensation of judges] The judicial power of the United States, shall be vested in one Supreme Court, and in such inferior courts as the Congress may from time to time ordain and establish. The judges, both of the supreme and inferior courts, shall hold their offices during good behavior, and shall, at stated times, receive for their services, a compensation, which shall not be diminished during their continuance in office.

Section 2

1. **[Jurisdiction of Federal courts]** (The judicial power shall extend to all cases, in law and equity, arising under this Constitution, the laws of the United States, and treaties made, or which shall be made, under their authority; to all cases affecting ambassadors, other public ministers and consuls; to all cases of admiralty and maritime jurisdiction; to controversies to which the United States, shall be a party; to controversies between two or more States; between a State and citizens of another State; between citizens of different States, between citizens of the same State claiming lands under grants of different states, and between a State, or the citizens thereof, and foreign states, citizens, or subjects.— *Amended by the 11th Amendment.*)

2. **[Original and appellate jurisdiction of Supreme Court]** In all cases affecting ambassadors, other public ministers and consuls, and those in which a State shall be party, the Supreme Court shall have original jurisdiction. In all the other cases before mentioned, the Supreme Court shall have appellate jurisdiction, both as to law and fact, with such exceptions, and under such regulations, as the Congress shall make.

3. **[Trial of all crimes, except impeachment, to be by jury]** The trial of all crimes, except in cases of impeachment, shall be by jury; and such trial shall be held in the State where the said crimes shall have been committed; but when not committed within any State, the trial shall be at such place or places as the Congress may by law have directed.

Section 3

1. **[Treason defined; conviction of]** Treason against the United States, shall consist only in levying war against them, or, in adhering to their enemies, giving them aid and comfort. No person shall be convicted of treason unless on the testimony of two witnesses to the same overt act, or on confession in open court.

2. **[Congress to declare punishment for treason; proviso]** The Congress shall have power to declare the punishment of treason, but no attainder of treason shall work corruption of blood, or forfeiture except during the life of the person attainted.

ARTICLE IV
Section 1
[Each State to give full faith and credit

to the public acts and records of other States] Full faith and credit shall be given in each State to the public acts, records, and judicial proceedings of every other State. And the Congress may by general laws prescribe the manner in which such acts, records, and proceedings shall be proved, and the effect thereof.

Section 2

1. **[Privileges of citizens]** The citizens of each State shall be entitled to all privileges and immunities of citizens in the several States.

2. **[Extradition between the several States]** A person charged in any State with treason, felony, or other crime, who shall flee from justice, and be found in another State, shall on demand of the Executive authority of the State from which he fled, be delivered up, to be removed to the State having jurisdiction of the crime.

3. **[Persons held to labor or service in one State, fleeing to another, to be returned]** (No person held to service or labor in one State, under the laws thereof, escaping into another, shall, in consequence of any law or regulation therein, be discharged from such service or labor, but shall be delivered up on claim of the party to whom such service or labor may be due.— *Eliminated by the 13th Amendment.*)

Section 3

1. **[New States]** New States may be admitted by the Congress into this Union; but no new State shall be formed or erected within the jurisdiction of any other State; nor any State be formed by the junction of two or more States, or parts of States, without the consent of the Legislatures of the States concerned as well as of the Congress.

2. **[Regulations concerning territory]** The Congress shall have power to dispose of and make all needful rules and regulations respecting the territory or other property belonging to the United States; and nothing in this Constitution shall be so construed as to prejudice any claims of the United States, or of any particular State.

Section 4

[Republican form of government and protection guaranteed the several States] The United States shall guarantee to every State in this Union a Republican form of government, and shall protect each of them against invasion; and on application of the Legislature, or of the Executive (when the Legislature cannot be convened) against domestic violence.

ARTICLE V

[Ways in which the Constitution can be amended] The Congress, whenever two-thirds of both Houses shall deem it necessary, shall propose amendments to this Constitution, or, on the application of the Legislatures of two-thirds of the several States shall call a convention for proposing amendments, which, in either case, shall be valid to all intents and purposes, as part of this Constitution, when ratified by the Legislatures of three-fourths of the several States, or by conventions in three-fourths thereof, as the one or the other mode of ratification may be proposed by the Congress; provided that no amendment which may be made prior to the year one thousand eight hundred and eight shall in any manner affect the first and fourth clauses in the ninth Section of the first Article; and that no State, without its consent, shall be deprived of its equal suffrage in the Senate.

ARTICLE VI

1. **[Debts contracted under the confederation secured]** All debts contracted and engagements entered into, before the adoption of this Constitution, shall be as valid against the United States under this Constitution, as under the Confederation.

2. **[Constitution, laws, and treaties of the United States to be supreme]** This Constitution, and the laws of the United States which shall be made in pursuance thereof; and all treaties made, or which shall be made, under the authority of the United States, shall be the supreme law of the land; and the judges in every State shall be bound thereby, anything in the Constitution or laws of any State to the contrary notwithstanding.

3. **[Who shall take constitutional oath; no religious test as to official qualification]** The Senators and Representatives before mentioned, and the members of the several State Legislatures, and all executive and judicial officers, both of the United States and of the several States, shall be bound by oath or affirmation, to support this Constitution; but no religious test shall ever be required as a qualification to any office or public trust under the United States.

ARTICLE VII

[Constitution to be considered adopted when ratified by nine States] The ratification of the conventions of nine States shall be sufficient for the establishment of this Constitution between the States so ratifying the same.

Amendments to the
Constitution of the United States

AMENDMENT 1

[Freedom of religion, speech, of the press, and right of petition] Congress shall make no law respecting an establishment of religion, or prohibiting the free exercise thereof; or abridging the freedom of speech, or of the press; or the right of the people peaceably to assemble, and to petition the Government for a redress of grievances.

AMENDMENT 2

[Right of people to bear arms not to be infringed] A well-regulated militia, being necessary to the security of a free State, the right of the people to keep and bear arms, shall not be infringed.

AMENDMENT 3

[Quartering of troops] No soldier shall, in time of peace be quartered in any house, without the consent of the owner, nor in time of war, but in a manner to be prescribed by law.

AMENDMENT 4

[Persons and houses to be secure from unreasonable searches and seizures] The right of the people to be secure in their persons, houses, papers, and effects, against unreasonable searches and seizures, shall not be violated, and no warrants shall issue, but upon probable cause, supported by oath or affirmation, and particularly describing the place to be searched, and the persons or things to be seized.

AMENDMENT 5

[Trials for crimes; just compensation for private property taken for public use] No person shall be held to answer for a capital, or otherwise infamous crime, unless on a presentment or indictment of a Grand Jury, except in cases arising in the land or naval forces, or in the militia, when in actual service in time of war or public danger; nor shall any person be subject for the same offense to be twice put in jeopardy of life or limb; nor shall be compelled in any criminal case to be a witness, against himself, nor be deprived of life, liberty, or property, without due process of law; nor shall private property be taken for public use, without just compensation.

AMENDMENT 6

[Right to speedy trial, witnesses, counsel] In all criminal prosecutions, the accused shall enjoy the right to a speedy and public trial, by an impartial jury of the State and district wherein the crime shall have been committed, which district shall have been previously ascertained by law, and to be informed of the nature and cause of the accusation; to be confronted with the witnesses against him; to have compulsory process for obtaining witnesses in his favor, and to have the assistance of counsel for his defense.

AMENDMENT 7
[Right of trial by jury] In suits at common law, where the value in controversy shall exceed twenty dollars, the right of trial by jury shall be preserved, and no fact tried by a jury, shall be otherwise re-examined in any court of the United States, than according to the rules of the common law.

AMENDMENT 8
[Excessive bail, fines, and punishments prohibited] Excessive bail shall not be required, nor excessive fines imposed, nor cruel and unusual punishments inflicted.

AMENDMENT 9
[Reserved rights of people] The enumeration in the Constitution, of certain rights, shall not be construed to deny or disparage others retained by the people.

AMENDMENT 10
[Rights of States under Constitution] The powers not delegated to the United States by the Constitution, nor prohibited by it to the States, are reserved to the States, respectively, or to the people.

AMENDMENT 11
(The proposed amendment was sent to the states March 5, 1794, by the Third Congress. It was ratified Feb. 7, 1795. It changes Article III, Sect. 2, Para. 1.)

[Judicial power of United States not to extend to suits against a State] The judicial power of the United States shall not be construed to extend to any suit in law or equity, commenced or prosecuted against one of the United States by citizens of another State, or by citizens or subjects of any foreign state.

AMENDMENT 12
(The proposed amendment was sent to the states Dec. 12, 1803, by the Eighth Congress. It was ratified July 27, 1804. It replaces Article II, Sect. 1, Para. 3.)

[Manner of electing President and Vice President by electors] (The electors shall meet in their respective states, and vote by ballot for President and Vice President, one of whom, at least, shall not be an inhabitant of the same state with themselves; they shall name in their ballots the person voted for as President, and in distinct ballots the person voted for as Vice President, and they shall make distinct lists of all persons voted for as President, and of all persons voted for as Vice President, and of the number of votes for each, which lists they shall sign and certify, and transmit

sealed to the seat of the government of the United States, directed to the President of the Senate; the President of the Senate shall, in the presence of the Senate and House of Representatives, open all the certificates and the votes shall then be counted; the person having the greatest number of votes for President, shall be the President, if such number be a majority of the whole number of electors appointed; and if no person have such majority, then from the persons having the highest numbers not exceeding three on the list of those voted for as President, the House of Representatives shall choose immediately, by ballot, the President. But in choosing the President, the votes shall be taken by states, the representation from each State having one vote; a quorum for this purpose shall consist of a member or members from two-thirds of the states, and a majority of all the states shall be necessary to a choice. And if the House of Representatives shall not choose a President whenever the right of choice shall devolve upon them, before the fourth day of March next following, then the Vice President shall act as President, as in the case of the death or other constitutional disability of the President. The person having the greatest number of votes as Vice President, shall be the Vice President, if such number be a majority of the whole number of electors appointed, and if no person have a majority, then from the two highest numbers on the list, the Senate shall choose the Vice President; a quorum for the purpose shall consist of two-thirds of the whole number of Senators, and a majority of the whole number shall be necessary to a choice. But no person constitutionally ineligible to the office of President shall be eligible to that of Vice President of the United States.— *Amended by the 20th Amendment, sections 3 and 4.)*

AMENDMENT 13
(The proposed amendment was sent to the states Feb. 1, 1865, by the Thirty-eighth Congress. It was ratified Dec. 6, 1865. It eliminates Article IV, Sect. 2, Para. 3.)

Section 1
[Slavery prohibited] Neither slavery nor involuntary servitude, except as a punishment for crime whereof the party shall have been duly convicted, shall exist within the United States, or any place subject to their jurisdiction.

Section 2
[Congress given power to enforce this article] Congress shall have power to enforce this article by appropriate legislation.

AMENDMENT 14
(The proposed amendment was sent to the states June 16, 1866, by the Thirty-ninth Congress. It was ratified July 9, 1868. It changes Article 1, Sect. 2, Para. 3.)

Section 1

[Citizenship defined; privileges of citizens] All persons born or naturalized in the United States, and subject to the jurisdiction thereof, are citizens of the United States and of the State wherein they reside. No State shall make or enforce any law which shall abridge the privileges or immunities of citizens of the United States; nor shall any State deprive any person of life, liberty, or property, without due process of law; nor deny to any person within its jurisdiction the equal protection of the laws.

Section 2

[Apportionment of Representatives] Representatives shall be apportioned among the several States according to their respective numbers, counting the whole number of persons in each State, excluding Indians not taxed. But when the right to vote at any election for the choice of electors for President and Vice President of the United States, Representatives in Congress, the executive and judicial officers of a State, or the members of the Legislature thereof, is denied to any of the male inhabitants of such State, being twenty-one years of age, and citizens of the United States, or in any way abridged, except for participation in rebellion, or other crime, the basis of representation therein shall be reduced in the proportion which the number of such male citizens shall bear to the whole number of male citizens twenty-one years of age in such State.

Section 3

[Disqualification for office; removal of disability] No person shall be a Senator or Representative in Congress, or elector of President and Vice President, or hold any office, civil or military, under the United States, or under any State, who, having previously taken an oath, as a member of Congress, or as an officer of the United States, or as a member of any State Legislature, or as an executive or judicial officer of any State, to support the Constitution of the United States, shall have engaged in insurrection or rebellion against the same, or given aid or comfort to the enemies thereof. But Congress may by a vote of two-thirds of each House, remove such disability.

Section 4

[Public debt not to be questioned; payment of debts and claims incurred in aid of rebellion forbidden] The validity of the public debt of the United States, authorized by law, including debts incurred for payment of pensions and bounties for services in suppressing insurrection or rebellion, shall not be questioned. But neither the United States nor any State shall assume or pay any debt or obligation incurred in aid of insurrection or rebellion against the United States, or any claim for the loss or emancipation of any slave; but all such debts, obligations, and claims shall be held illegal and void.

Section 5

[Congress given power to enforce this article] The Congress shall have power to enforce, by appropriate legislation, the provisions of this article.

AMENDMENT 15

(The proposed amendment was sent to the states Feb. 27, 1869, by the Fortieth Congress. It was ratified Feb. 3, 1870.)

Section 1

[Right of certain citizens to vote established] The right of citizens of the United States to vote shall not be denied or abridged by the United States or by any State on account of race, color, or previous condition of servitude.

Section 2

[Congress given power to enforce this article] The Congress shall have power to enforce this article by appropriate legislation.

AMENDMENT 16

(The proposed amendment was sent to the states July 12, 1909, by the Sixty-first Congress. It was ratified Feb. 3, 1913.)

[Income taxes authorized] The Congress shall have power to lay and collect taxes on incomes, from whatever source derived, without apportionment among the several States, and without regard to any census or enumeration.

AMENDMENT 17

(The proposed amendment was sent to the states May 16, 1912, by the Sixty-second Congress. It was ratified April 8, 1913. It changes Article 1, Sect. 3, Para. 1 and 2.)

[Election of United States Senators; filling of vacancies; qualifications of electors] The Senate of the United States shall be composed of two Senators from each State, elected by the people thereof, for six years; and each Senator shall have one vote. The electors in each State shall have the qualifications requisite for electors of the most numerous branch of the State Legislatures.

When vacancies happen in the representation of any State in the Senate, the executive authority of such State shall issue writs of election to fill such vacancies: Provided, that the legislature of any State may empower the executive thereof to make temporary appointment until the people fill the vacancies by election as the legislature may direct.

This amendment shall not be so construed as to affect the election or term of any Senator chosen before it becomes valid as part of the Constitution.

AMENDMENT 18

(The proposed amendment was sent to the states Dec. 18, 1917, by the Sixty-fifth Congress. It

was ratified by three-quarters of the states by Jan. 16, 1919, and became effective Jan. 16, 1920. It was repealed by the 21st Amendment.)

Section 1

[Manufacture, sale, or transportation of intoxicating liquors, for beverage purposes, prohibited] After one year from the ratification of this article the manufacture, sale, or transportation of intoxicating liquors within, the importation thereof into, or the exportation thereof from the United States and all territory subject to the jurisdiction thereof for beverage purposes is hereby prohibited.

Section 2

[Congress and the several States given concurrent power to pass appropriate legislation to enforce this article] The Congress and the several States shall have concurrent power to enforce this article by appropriate legislation.

Section 3

[Provisions of article to become effective, when adopted by three-fourths of the States] This article shall be inoperative unless it shall have been ratified as an amendment to the Constitution by the legislatures of the several States, as provided in the Constitution, within seven years from the date of the submission hereof to the States by Congress.

AMENDMENT 19

(The proposed amendment was sent to the states June 4, 1919, by the Sixty-sixth Congress. It was ratified Aug 18, 1920.)

[The right of citizens to vote shall not be denied because of sex] The right of citizens of the United States to vote shall not be denied or abridged by the United States or by any State on account of sex.

[Congress given power to enforce this article] Congress shall have power to enforce this article by appropriate legislation.

AMENDMENT 20

(The proposed amendment, sometimes called the "Lame Duck Amendment," was sent to the states March 3, 1932, by the Seventy-second Congress. It was ratified Jan. 23, 1933; but, in accordance with Section 5, Sections 1 and 2 did not go into effect until Oct. 15, 1933. It changes Article 1, Sect. 4, Para. 2 and the 12th Amendment.)

Section 1

[Terms of President, Vice President, Senators, and Representatives] The terms of the President and Vice President shall end at noon on the twentieth day of January, and the terms of Senators and Representatives at noon on the third day of January, of the years in which such terms would have ended if this article had not been ratified; and the terms of their successors shall then begin.

Section 2

[Time of assembling Congress] The Congress shall assemble at least once in every year, and such meeting shall begin at noon on the third day of January, unless they shall by law appoint a different day.

Section 3

[Filling vacancy in office of President] If, at the time fixed for the beginning of the term of the President, the President-elect shall have died, the Vice President-elect shall become President. If a President shall not have been chosen before the time fixed for the beginning of his term, or if the President-elect shall have failed to qualify, then the Vice President shall have qualified; and the Congress may by law provide for the case wherein neither a President-elect nor a Vice President-elect shall have qualified, declaring who shall then act as President, or the manner in which one who is to act shall be selected, and such person shall act accordingly until a President or Vice President shall have qualified.

Section 4

[Power of Congress in Presidential succession] The Congress may by law provide for the case of the death of any of the persons from whom the House of Representatives may choose a President whenever the right of choice shall have devolved upon them, and for the case of the death of any of the persons from whom the Senate may choose a Vice President whenever the right of choice shall have devolved upon them.

Section 5

[Time of taking effect] Sections 1 and 2 shall take effect on the 15th day of October following the ratification of this article.

Section 6

[Ratification] This article shall be inoperative unless it shall have been ratified as an amendment to the Constitution by the legislatures of three-fourths of the several States within seven years from the date of its submission.

AMENDMENT 21

(The proposed amendment was sent to the states Feb. 20, 1933, by the Seventy-second Congress. It was ratified Dec. 5, 1933. It repeals the 18th Amendment.)

Section 1

[Repeal of Prohibition Amendment] The eighteenth article of amendment to the Constitution of the United States is hereby repealed.

Section 2

[Transportation of intoxicating liquors] The transportation or importation into any State, territory, or possession of the United States for delivery or use therein of intoxicating liquors, in violation of the laws thereof, is hereby prohibited.

Section 3

[Ratification] This article shall be inoperative unless it shall have been ratified as an amendment to the Constitution by convention in the several States, as provided in the Constitution, within seven years from the date of the submission thereof to the States by the Congress.

AMENDMENT 22

(The proposed amendment was sent to the states March 21, 1947, by the Eightieth Congress. It was ratified Feb. 27, 1951.)

Section 1

[Limit to number of terms a President may serve] No person shall be elected to the office of the President more than twice, and no person who has held the office of President, or acted as President for more than two years of a term to which some other person was elected President shall be elected to the office of the President more than once. But this article shall not apply to any person holding the office of President when this article was proposed by the Congress, and shall not prevent any person who may be holding the office of President, or acting as President, during the term within which this article becomes operative from holding the office of President or acting as President during the remainder of such term.

Section 2

[Ratification] This article shall be inoperative unless it shall have been ratified as an amendment to the Constitution by the legislatures of three-fourths of the several States within seven years from the date of its submission to the States by the Congress.

AMENDMENT 23

(The proposed amendment was sent to the states June 16, 1960, by the Eighty-sixth Congress. It was ratified March 29, 1961.)

Section 1

[Electors for the District of Columbia] The District constituting the seat of Government of the United States shall appoint in such manner as the Congress may direct:

A number of electors of President and Vice President equal to the whole number of Senators and Representatives in Congress to which the District would be entitled if it were a State, but in no event more than the least populous State; they shall be in addition to those appointed by the States, but they shall be considered, for the purposes of the election of President and Vice President, to be electors appointed by a State; and they shall meet in the District and perform such duties as provided by the twelfth article of amendment.

Section 2

[Congress given power to enforce this article] The Congress shall have the power to enforce this article by appropriate legislation.

AMENDMENT 24

(The proposed amendment was sent to the states Aug. 27, 1962, by the Eighty-seventh Congress. It was ratified Jan. 23, 1964.)

Section 1

[Payment of poll tax or other taxes barred in federal elections] The right of citizens of the United States to vote in any primary or other election for President or Vice President, for electors for President or Vice President, or for Senator or Representative in Congress, shall not be denied or abridged by the United States or any State by reasons of failure to pay any poll tax or other tax.

Section 2

[Congress given power to enforce this article] The Congress shall have the power to enforce this article by appropriate legislation.

AMENDMENT 25

(The proposed amendment was sent to the states July 6, 1965, by the Eighty-ninth Congress. It was ratified Feb. 10, 1967.)

Section 1

[Succession of Vice President to Presidency] In case of the removal of the President from office or of his death or resignation, the Vice President shall become President.

Section 2

[Vacancy in office of Vice President] Whenever there is a vacancy in the office of the Vice President, the President shall nominate a Vice President who shall take office upon confirmation by a majority vote of both Houses of Congress.

Section 3

[Vice President as Acting President] Whenever the President transmits to the President pro tempore of the Senate and the Speaker of the House of Representatives his written declaration that he is unable to discharge the powers and duties of his office, and until he transmits to them a written declaration to the contrary, such powers and duties shall be discharged by the Vice President as Acting President.

Section 4

[Vice President as Acting President]
Whenever the Vice President and a majority of either the principal officers of the executive departments or of such other body as Congress may by law provide, transmit to the President pro tempore of the Senate and the Speaker of the House of Representatives their written declaration that the President is unable to discharge the powers and duties of his office, the Vice President shall immediately assume the powers and duties of the office as Acting President.

Thereafter, when the President transmits to the President pro tempore of the Senate and the Speaker of the House of Representatives his written declaration that no inability exists, he shall resume the powers and duties of his office unless the Vice President and a majority of either the principal officers of the executive department or of such other body as Congress may by law provide, transmit within four days to the President pro tempore of the Senate and the Speaker of the House of Representatives their written declaration that the President is unable to discharge the powers and duties of his office. There upon Congress shall decide the issue, assembling within forty-eight hours for that purpose if not in session. If the Congress, within twenty-one days after receipt of the latter written declaration, or, if Congress is not in session, within twenty-one days after Congress is required to assemble, determines by two-thirds vote of both Houses that the President is unable to discharge the powers and duties of his office, the Vice President shall continue to discharge the same as Acting President; otherwise, the President shall resume the powers and duties of his office.

AMENDMENT 26

(The proposed amendment was sent to the states March 23, 1971, by the Ninety-second Congress. It was ratified July 1, 1971.)

Section 1

[Voting for 18-year-olds] The right of citizens of the United States, who are 18 years of age or older, to vote shall not be denied or abridged by the United States or by any state on account of age.

Section 2

[Congress given power to enforce this article] The Congress shall have power to enforce this article by appropriate legislation.

AMENDMENT 27

(The proposed amendment was sent to the states September 25, 1789, by the First Congress. It was ratified May 7, 1992.)

No law, varying the compensation for the services of the Senators and Representatives, shall take effect, until an election of Representatives shall have intervened.

Order of Presidential Succession

1. Vice president
2. Speaker of the House
3. President pro tempore of the Senate
4. Secretary of state
5. Secretary of the treasury
6. Secretary of defense
7. Attorney general
8. Secretary of the interior
9. Secretary of agriculture
10. Secretary of commerce
11. Secretary of labor
12. Secretary of health and human services
13. Secretary of housing and urban development
14. Secretary of transportation
15. Secretary of energy
16. Secretary of education
17. Secretary of veterans affairs

A

A lot / alot, 669
Abbreviations, 656-658
    Common, 658
    Punctuation of, 553
    Research paper, 361
    State, 657
Absolute phrase, 814
Abstract, APA, 431, 434
    Writing an, 500
Abstract noun, 760
Academic writing, 145-273
    Basic essay, 110-127
Accent,
    Acute, 628
    Grave, 628
Accept / except, 670
Acronym, 504, 659, 661
Acrostics, 504
Action, 274
Active voice, 058, 778, 781,
    782, 784, 785
Adapt / adopt, 671
Address,
    Abbreviations, 657
    Punctuation of, 564
Adjective, 558, 795-796, 803
    Clause, 773, 821
    Infinitive phrase, acting as,
        817
    Participial phrase, acting as,
        818
    Prepositional phrase, acting
        as, 799
    For time or amount, 625
Adverb, 797-798, 799, 803
    Clause, 820
    Conjunctive, 573, 801
    Infinitive phrase, acting as,
        817
Adverse / averse, 672
Advice / advise, 673
Affect / effect, 674
Agreement, 837-851
    Antecedent/pronoun, 849-851
    Subject/verb, 837-848
Aid / aide, 675
Allegory, 274
Alliteration, 282
All right / alright, 678
Allusion, 274, 539
Allusion / illusion, 676
Almanac, 852-883
Already / all ready, 677
Alright / all right, 678
Alternative style, 057
Altogether / all together, 679
Ambiguous wording, 078

Amendments,
    Constitutional, 878-883
    Parliamentary motions, 857
Among / between, 680
Amoral / immoral, 681
Amount / number, 682
Analogy, 274, 539
Analysis, 042, 187-221, 505
    Graphic organizers, 220-221
    Literary, 263-273
    Process, 189-192
Anapestic foot, 282
Anecdote, 055, 274, 539
Annual / biannual / semiannual /
    biennial / perennial, 683
Antagonist, 274
Antecedent, 766, 847, 849-851
Antithesis, 276, 539
APA,
    Abstract, 434
    Documentation style,
        372-429
    Guidelines, 431-432
    Research paper, 433-443
Apostrophe, 618-625, 628
Appeals, 245
Application, letter of, 137
    Essay, 139-140
Appositive,
    Phrase, 813
    Punctuation, 560
    Restrictive, 560
    In sentence combining, 093
Archaic words. *See* Diction.
Argumentation, 042
    Essay of, 232-237
    Logical, thinking, 244-246
Arrangement, 042
    Within the sentence, 069-095,
        829-836
    In speeches, 531-532
    In writing, 101-107
Articles, 635, 795
As / like, 723
Assessment,
    Essay, 122, 125
Assignments,
    Handling, 545
    Understanding, 112
Assonance, 282
Asterisk, 628
Audience, 042
Autobiography, 274
Auxiliary verbs, 784
Averse / adverse, 672

B

Balance, 042, 056
Balanced sentence, 056, 834
Ballad, 282
Bandwagon, 245
Beside / besides, 684
Between / among, 680
Biannual / semiannual /
    biennial / annual /
    perennial, 683
Bibliography, 289
    APA references, 372-429
    MLA citations, 300-360
Biography, 274
Blank verse, 282
Book,
    Punctuation of titles, 602,
        609
Book review, writing a, 256-260
Boolean characters, 449
Borrow / lend, 720
Brace, 628
Brackets, 614-617, 628
Brainstorming, 042
Bring / take, 685
Business letters, 130-134
Business writing, 128-144
    Addressing envelope, 134
    Cover letter, 137
    E-mail, 143-144
    Folding the letter, 134
    Follow-up letter, 142
    Format guidelines, 130
    Forms of address, 134
    Letter of application, 137
    Letter of complaint, 133
    Letter of request, 138
    Memo, 143-144
    Résumé, 135-136

C

Caesura, 282
Calendar, 6-year, 857
Call number, 450
Can / may, 686
Canto, 282
Capital / capitol, 687
Capitalization, 629-642, 804
Captions, APA, 442
Card catalog, 446, 450
    On-line, 448-450
Caret, 628
Caricature, 274
Case,
    Nouns, 764
    Pronouns, 766, 767, 770-771
Case study, 042

Essay Directory

The following chart directs you to guidelines and models for specific types of essays included in *Write for College*. (Also see "Mastering the College Essay," 110-127, for additional information.)